BricsCAD V24 Basics Tutorial

Tutorial Books

Contents

Introduction to BricsCAD V24

In this chapter, you will learn about:

- **BricsCAD user interface**
- **Customizing user interface**

System requirements

The following are system requirements for running BricsCAD smoothly on your system.

- Microsoft Windows 11 or Windows 10 (64 - bit only).

- Intel Core i5, or AMD® Ryzen 5 processor (Intel® Core™ i7, AMD Ryzen™ 7 or higher version recommended)

- 8 GB RAM (16 GB or more recommended)

- 3 GB available hard disk space

- 1920 x 1080 screen resolution (3840 x 2160 (4K) recommended)

Starting BricsCAD V24

To start **BricsCAD V24**, double-click the **BricsCAD V24 (x64) en_US** icon on your Desktop (or) click **Start > All apps > B > Bricsys > BricsCAD V24 (x64) en_US**.

BricsCAD user interface

When you double-click the **BricsCAD V24 (x64) en_US** icon on the desktop, the **BricsCAD Launcher** window will appear. On this window, click the **2D Drafting** button, and the **Welcome** screen will appear with many default templates to create a new drawing. Click on any of the default templates, or click the **New Drawing** button to open a new drawing file. The drawing file consists of a graphics window, ribbon, toolbars, command line, and other screen components.

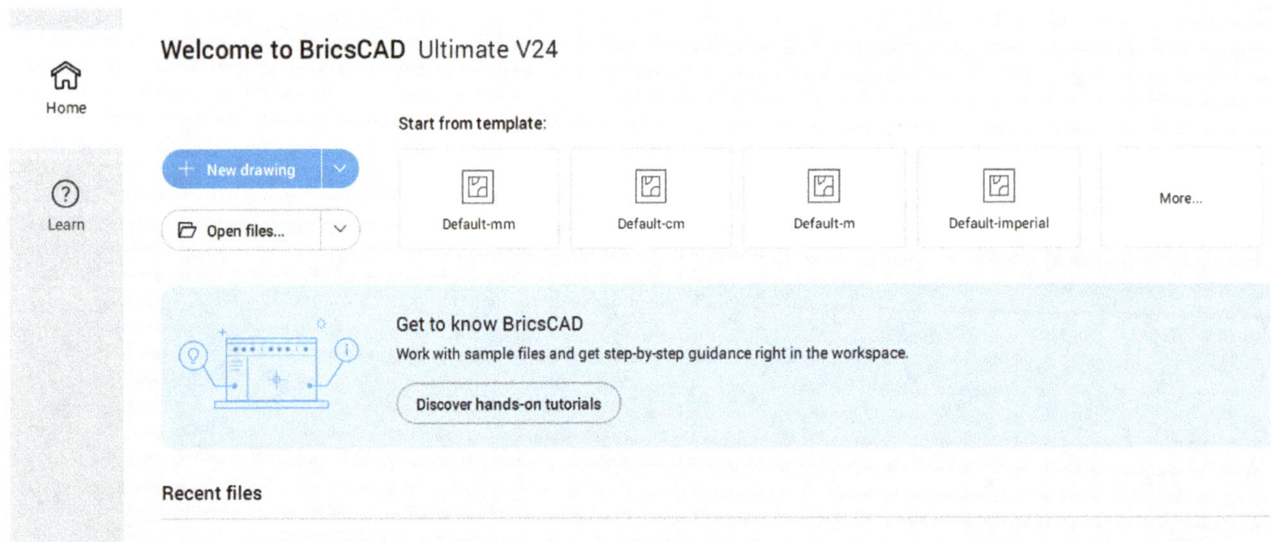

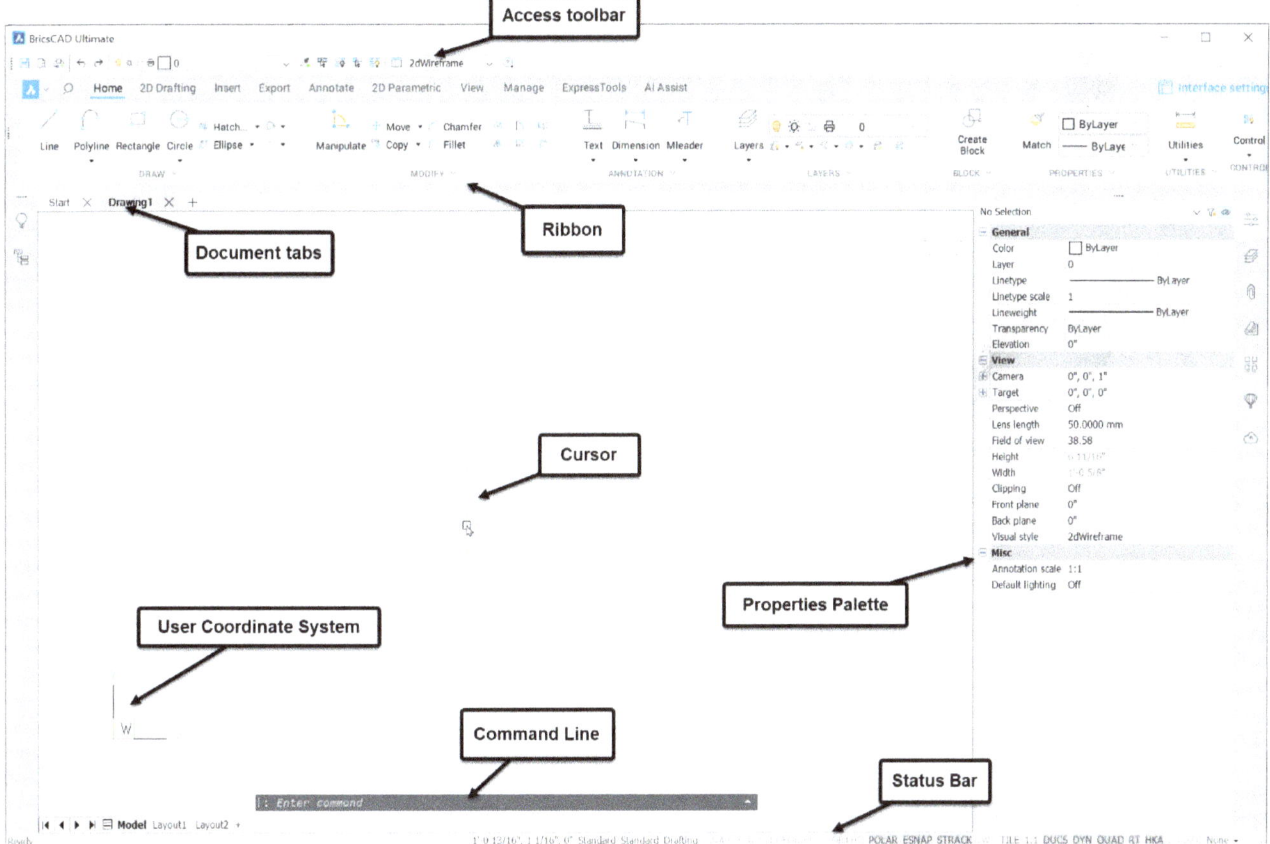

Changing the Color theme

BricsCAD V24 is available in two different color themes: **Dark** and **Light**. You can change the color theme by using the **Options** dialog. Click the right mouse button on the ribbon, and then select the **Dark Interface** option.

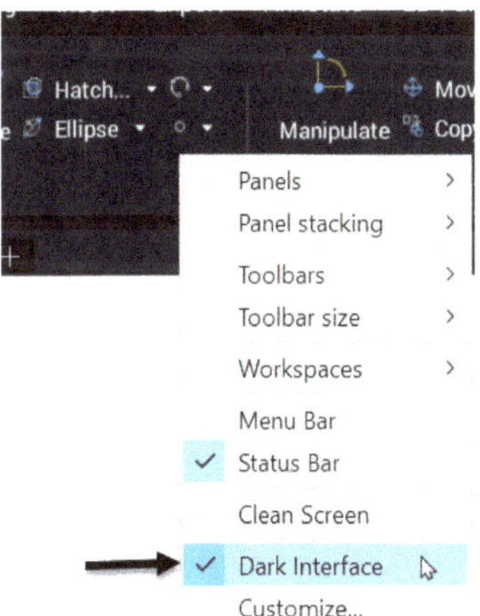

Workspaces in BricsCAD

There are four workspaces available in BricsCAD: **Drafting**, **Modeling**, **BIM**, **Mechanical**, **Civil**, and **Complete**. The **Drafting** workspace is used to create 2D drawings. To enable this, right click on the ribbon, and select **Workspaces > Drafting**.

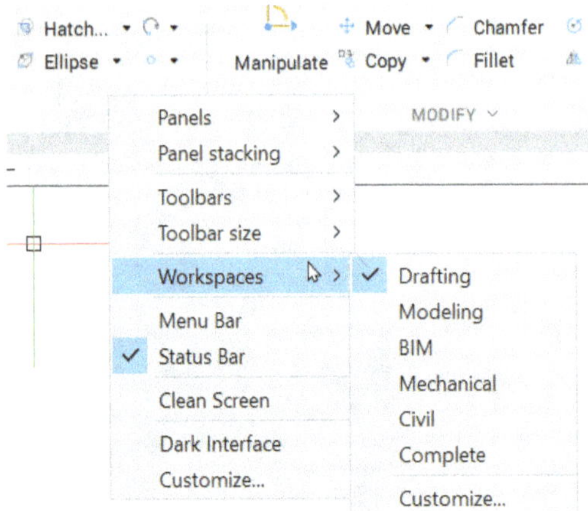

Drafting Workspace

This workspace has all the tools to create a 2D drawing. It has a ribbon located at the top of the screen. The ribbon is arranged in a hierarchy of tabs, panels, and tools. Panels such as **Draw**, **Modify**, and **Layers** consist of tools that are grouped based on their usage. Panels, in turn, are grouped into various tabs. For example, the panels, such as **Draw**, **Modify**, and **Layers**, are located in the **Home** tab.

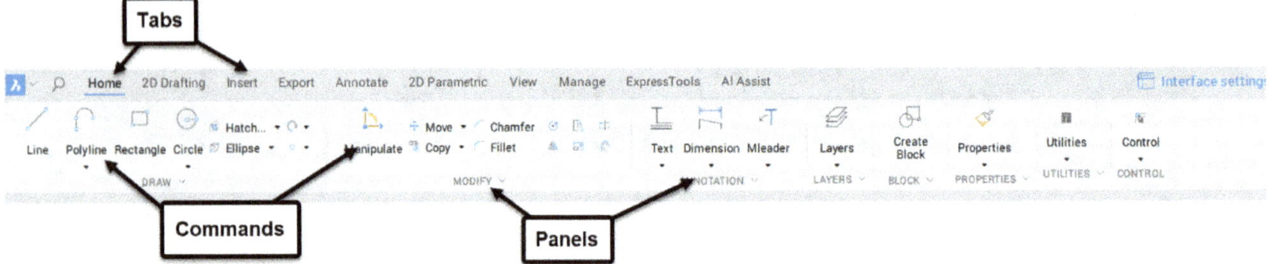

Modeling Workspace

This workspace are used to create 3D models. It includes all the tools required for creating 3D models. By default, the **Home** tab is activated in the ribbon. From this tab, you can access the tools for creating and editing solids and meshes, modifying the model display, working with coordinate systems, and sectioning 3D models.

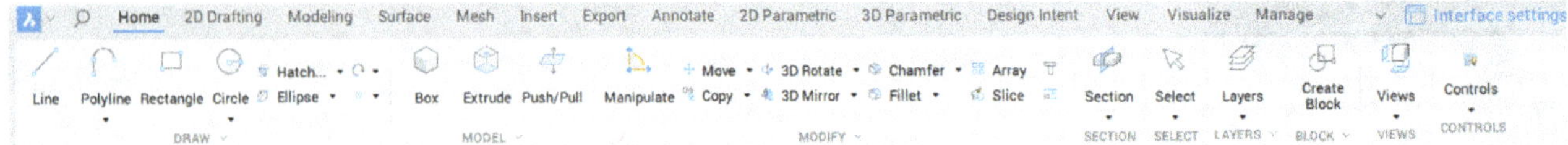

Application Menu

The **Application Menu** appears when you click on the icon located at the top left corner of the window. The **Application Menu** consists of a list of options such as **New**, **Open**, **Save**, and **Print**.

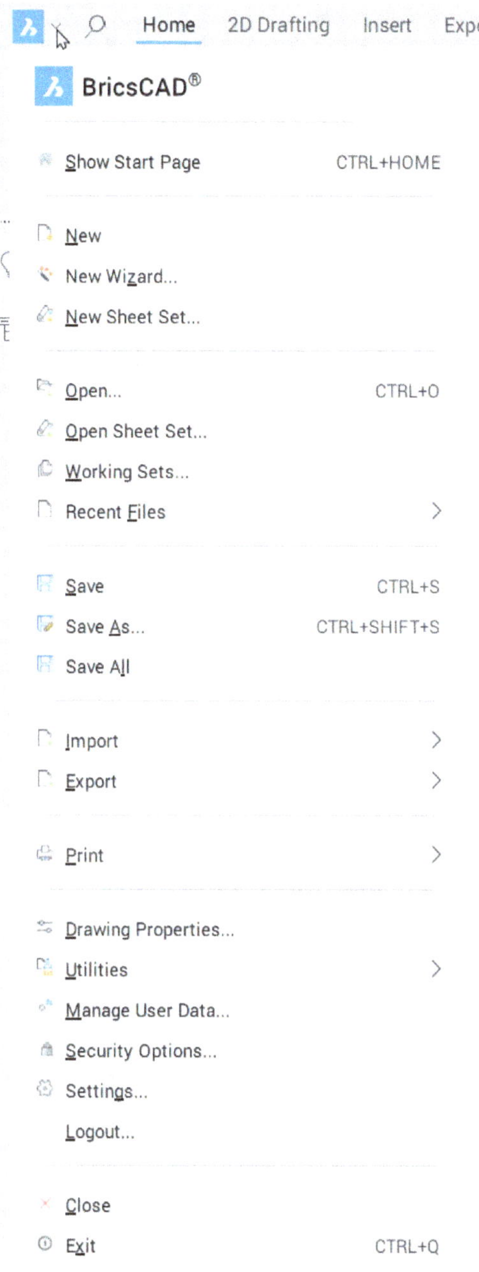

Access Toolbar

The Access Toolbar is located at the top left corner of the window and helps you to access commands quickly. It consists of commonly used commands such as **Save**, **Plot Preview**, **Publish**, **Undo** and **Redo**,

Document tabs

The Document tabs are located below the ribbon. You can switch between different drawing files by using the Document tabs. Also, you can open a new file by using the + button, easily.

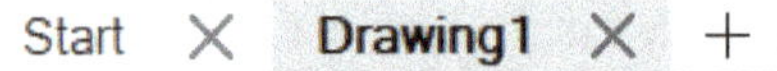

Graphics Window

The Graphics window is the blank space located below the file tabs. You can draw objects and create 3D graphics in the graphics window.

Look From Widget

The Look From Widget located at the top-right corner of the graphics window. The Look From Widget allows you to switch between the standard and isometric views. Using the Look From Widget, you can set the orientation of the model. For example, if you want to change the orientation of the model to top view, then place the cursor in the middle of the Look From Widget; the Top message appears. Click to change the view orientation. Likewise, if you want to change the orientation to Top Front Left, then place the pointer on the bottom left segment of the ring; the Top Front Left message appears. Click to change the view orientation to Top Front Left.

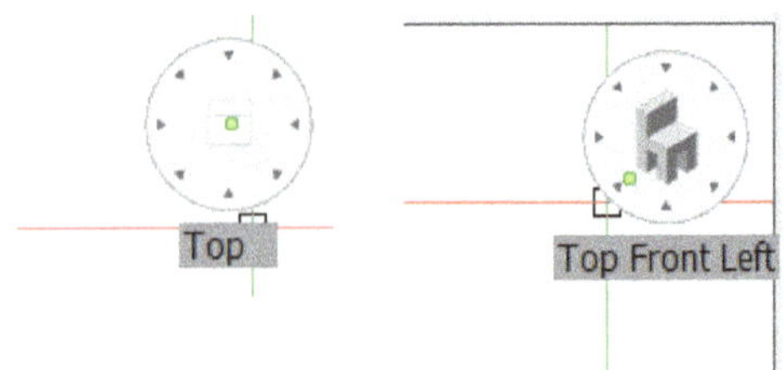

Likewise, you can click on the different sectors of the two rings to switch to the respective views, as shown.

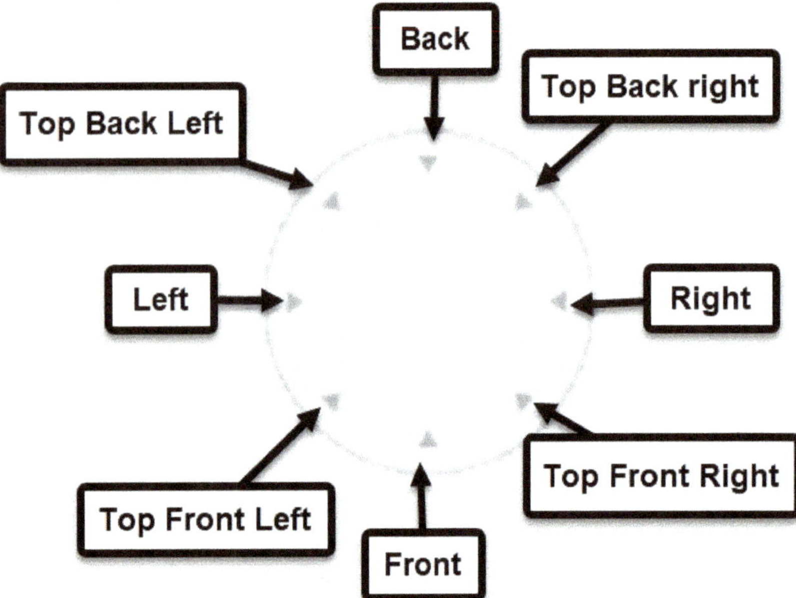

Command Line

The command line is located below the graphics window. It is effortless to execute a command using the command line. You can just type the first letter of a command, and it lists all the commands starting with that letter. It helps you to activate commands very quickly and increases your productivity.

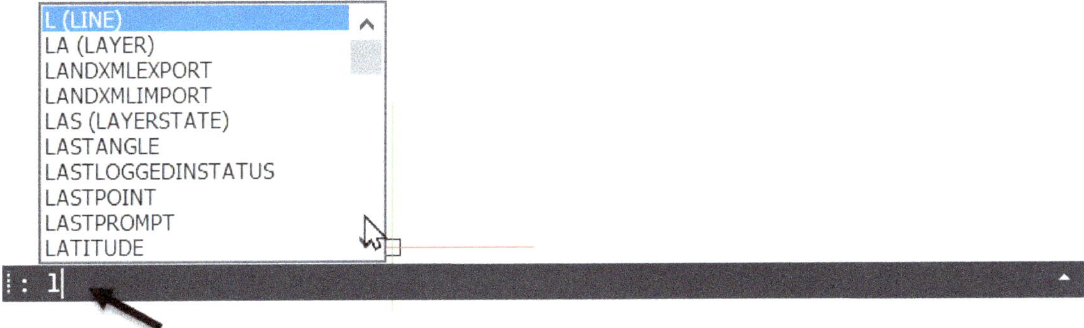

Also, the command line shows the current state of the drawing. It shows various prompts while working with any command. These prompts are a series of steps needed to execute a command successfully. For example, when you activate the LINE command, the command line displays a prompt, "Start of line." You need to click in the graphics window to specify the start point of the line. After defining the start t point, the prompt, "Set end point or [Angle/Length/Follow/Undo]:" appears. Now, you need to determine the next end of the line. It is recommended that you should always have a look at the command line to know the next step while executing a command.

Status Bar

Status Bar is located at the bottom of the BricsCAD window. It contains many buttons which help you to create a drawing very easily. You can turn ON or OFF these buttons just by clicking on them. The buttons available on the status bar are briefly discussed in the following section.

9 3/8", 5/8", 0" Standard Standard Drafting SNAP GRID HIDEOBJECTS ORTHO **POLAR ESNAP STRACK** LWT TILE 1:1 **DUCS DYN QUAD RT HKA** LOCKUI None ▾

Button	Description
(280.368,235.809,0) **Cursor Coordinate Values**	It displays the drawing coordinates when you move the cursor in the graphics window.
Snap	The Snap button aligns the pointer only with the Grid points. When you turn ON this button, the pointer will be able to select only the Grid points.
Grid	It turns the Grid display ON or OFF. You can set the spacing between the grid lines by right-clicking on the **Grid** button and selecting the **Settings** option. Next, specify the **X** and **Y** values under the **Grid Unit** section on the **Settings** dialog. Next, close the **Settings** dialog.

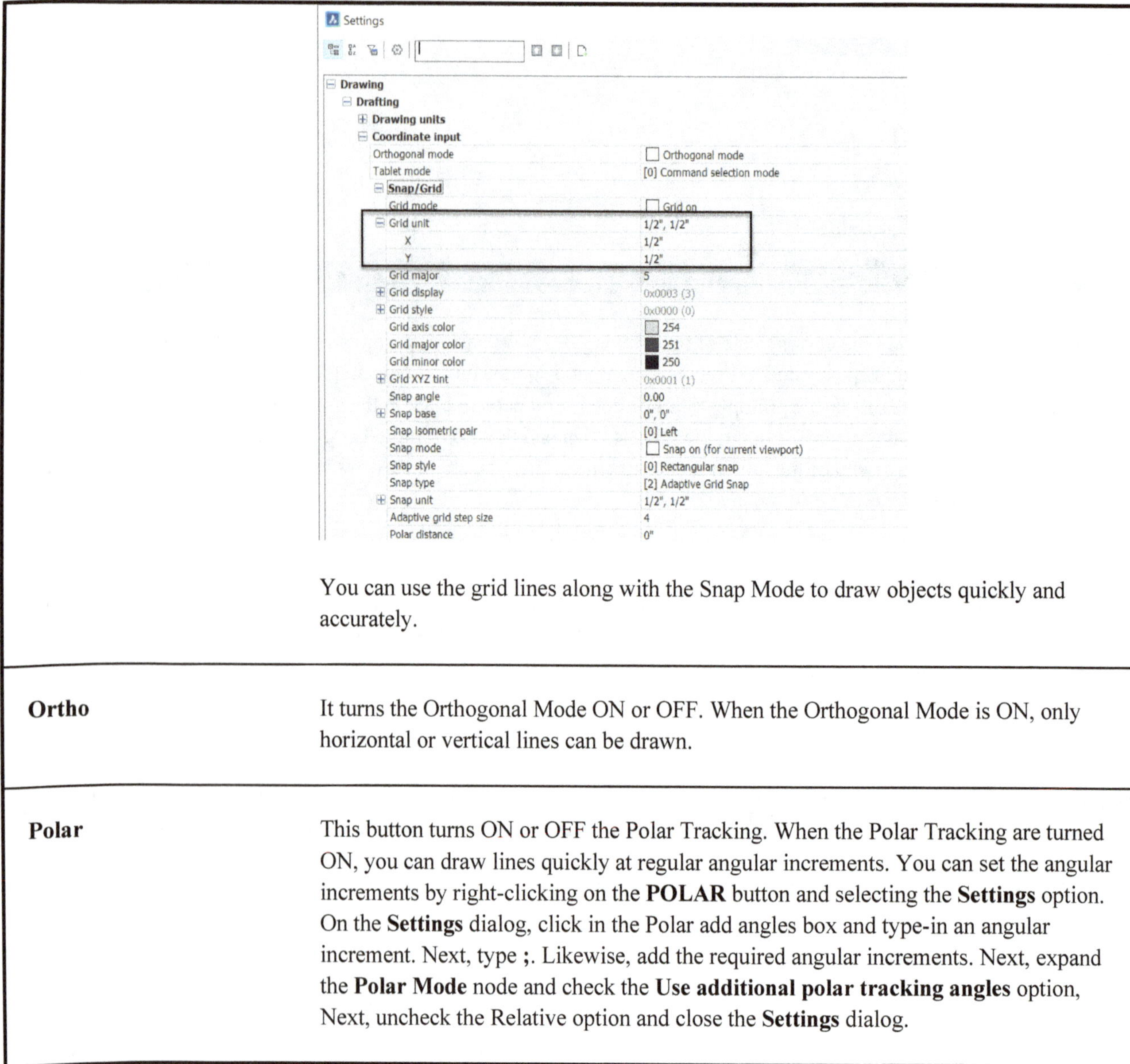

You can use the grid lines along with the Snap Mode to draw objects quickly and accurately.

| **Ortho** | It turns the Orthogonal Mode ON or OFF. When the Orthogonal Mode is ON, only horizontal or vertical lines can be drawn. |
| **Polar** | This button turns ON or OFF the Polar Tracking. When the Polar Tracking are turned ON, you can draw lines quickly at regular angular increments. You can set the angular increments by right-clicking on the **POLAR** button and selecting the **Settings** option. On the **Settings** dialog, click in the Polar add angles box and type-in an angular increment. Next, type **;**. Likewise, add the required angular increments. Next, expand the **Polar Mode** node and check the **Use additional polar tracking angles** option, Next, uncheck the Relative option and close the **Settings** dialog. |

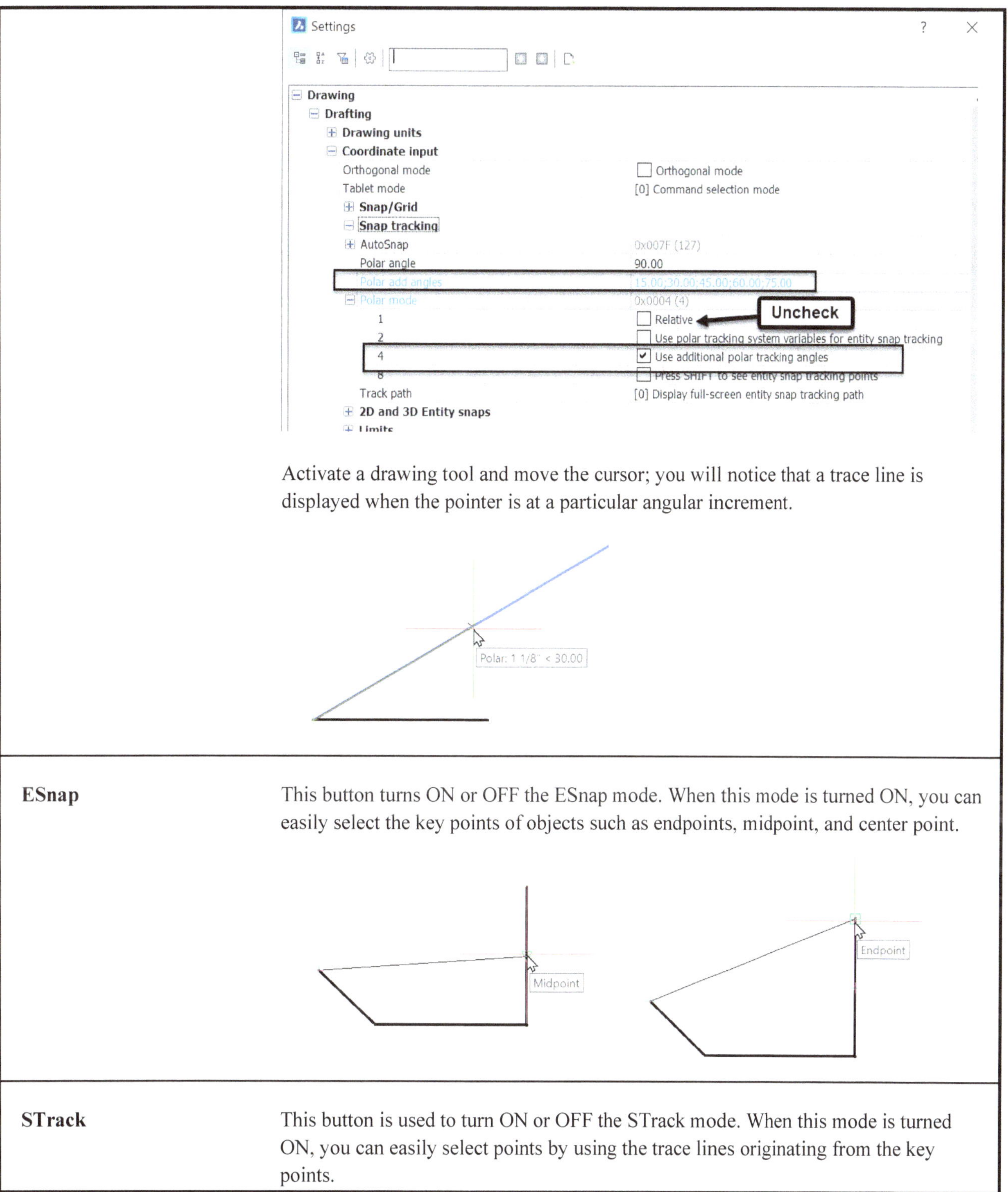

Activate a drawing tool and move the cursor; you will notice that a trace line is displayed when the pointer is at a particular angular increment.

ESnap	This button turns ON or OFF the ESnap mode. When this mode is turned ON, you can easily select the key points of objects such as endpoints, midpoint, and center point.
STrack	This button is used to turn ON or OFF the STrack mode. When this mode is turned ON, you can easily select points by using the trace lines originating from the key points.

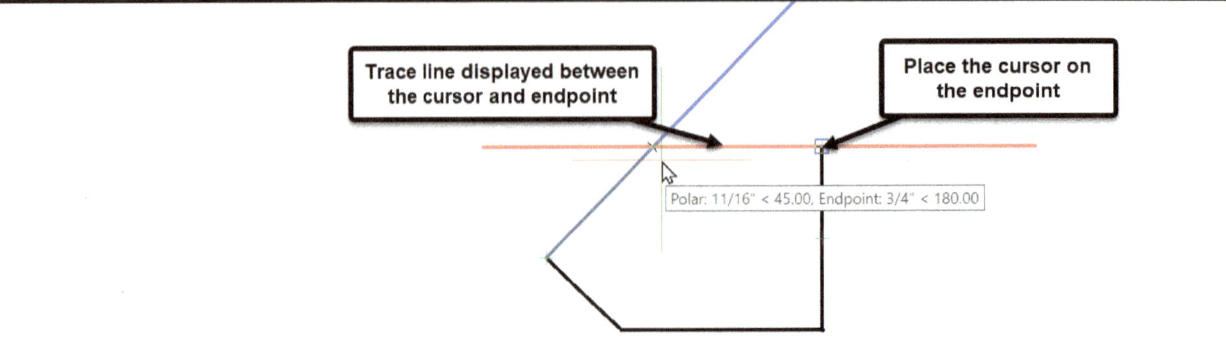

Dynamic User Coordinate System	This button turns ON/OFF the Dynamic UCS. When the DUCS is turned ON, you can draw and create objects on any face of a 3D Model, dynamically. 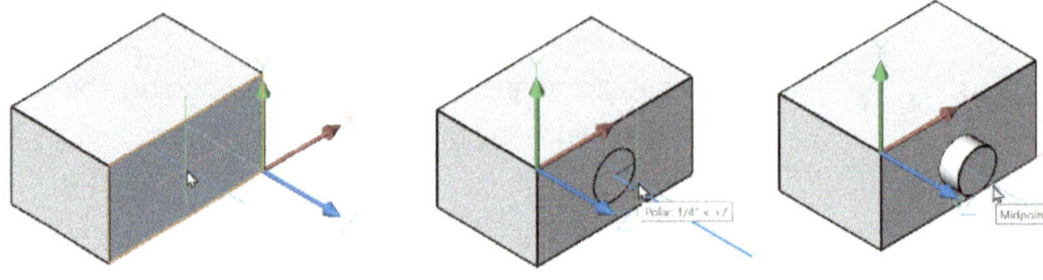
DYN	This button turns ON or OFF the Dynamic Input mode. When this mode is turned ON, a dynamic input box is attached to the pointer along with a prompt. You can directly enter a value in the dynamic input box. You can use Dynamic Input in place of the command line. 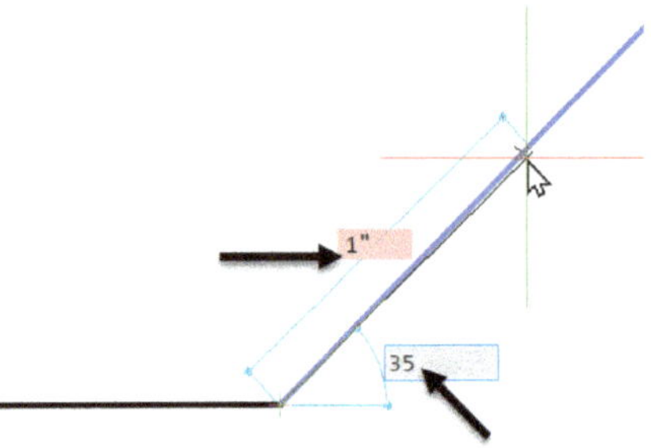
LWT	This button turns ON or OFF the lineweight. Line weight is the thickness of objects. You can set the thickness of objects by specifying the lineweight. If the Lineweight is turned OFF, the objects are displayed with the default thickness. 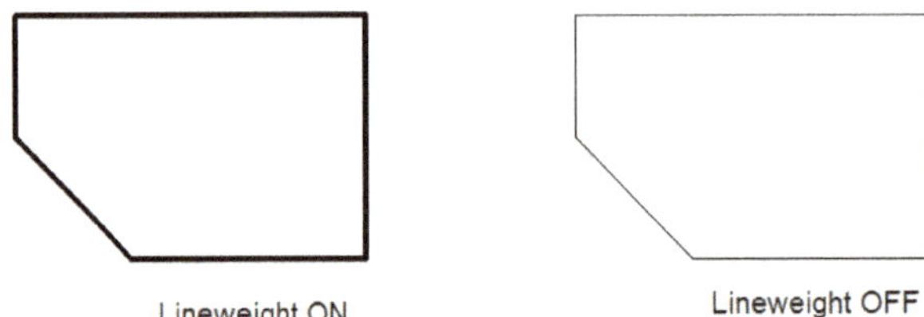

RT	This button when turned ON displays the properties of an entity when you place the cursor on it. 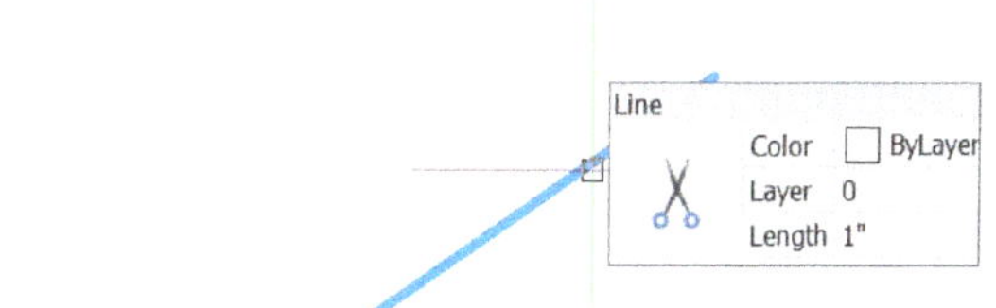
ANNOMON	This button turns the Annotation Monitor ON or OFF. The Annotation Monitor checks whether the annotations are attached to their respective objects. When an annotation is not connected to any object, it displays an error message. 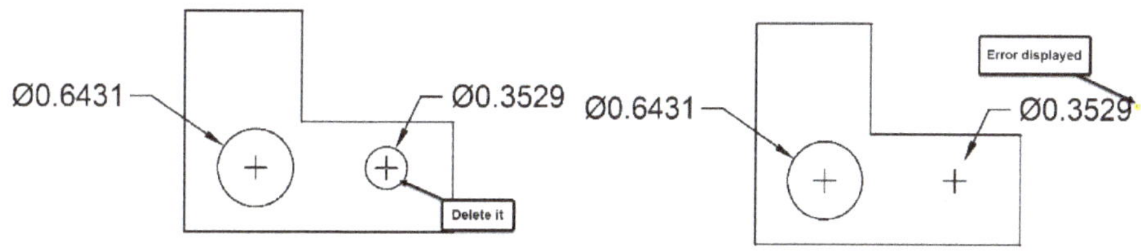
Annotation Scale	This option adjusts the size of annotative objects. Annotative objects are dimensions, texts, notes, and other objects which can be sized as per the drawing scale. 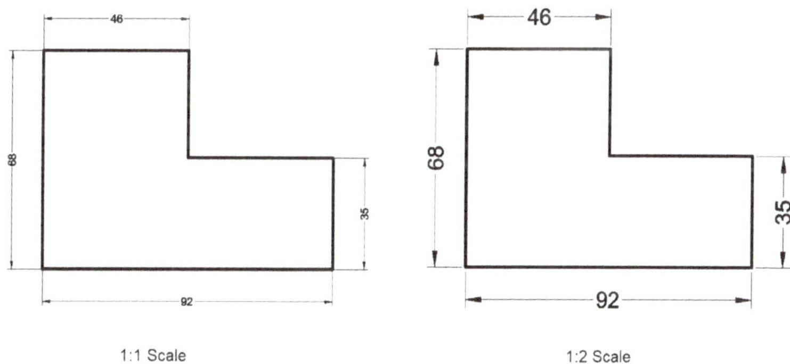
QUAD	When activated, this button displays the Quad when you hover the cursor over an object. Hovering over the Quad will reveal commands related to the selected entity. There are few categories of commands on the Quad. Hover over these categories to view the specific commands within them.

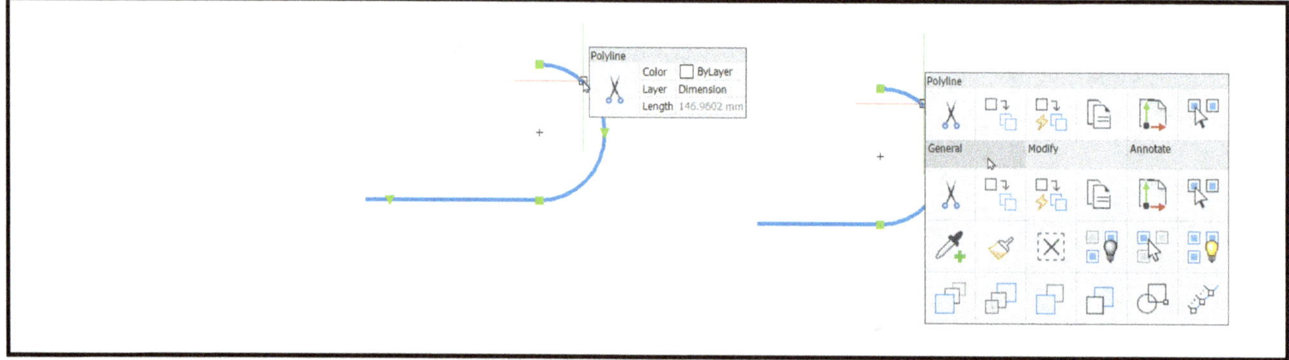

Ribbon

The Ribbon is not displayed by default. To display the ribbon, click the right mouse button on the ribbon and select the Ribbon option; the Ribbon appears at the top of the window just below the title bar. It contains various menus such as File, Edit, View, Insert, Settings, Tools, Draw, Dimensions, Modify, and so on. Clicking on any of the words on the Ribbon displays a menu. The menu contains various tools and options. There are also sub-options available on the list. These sub-options are displayed if you click on an option with an arrow.

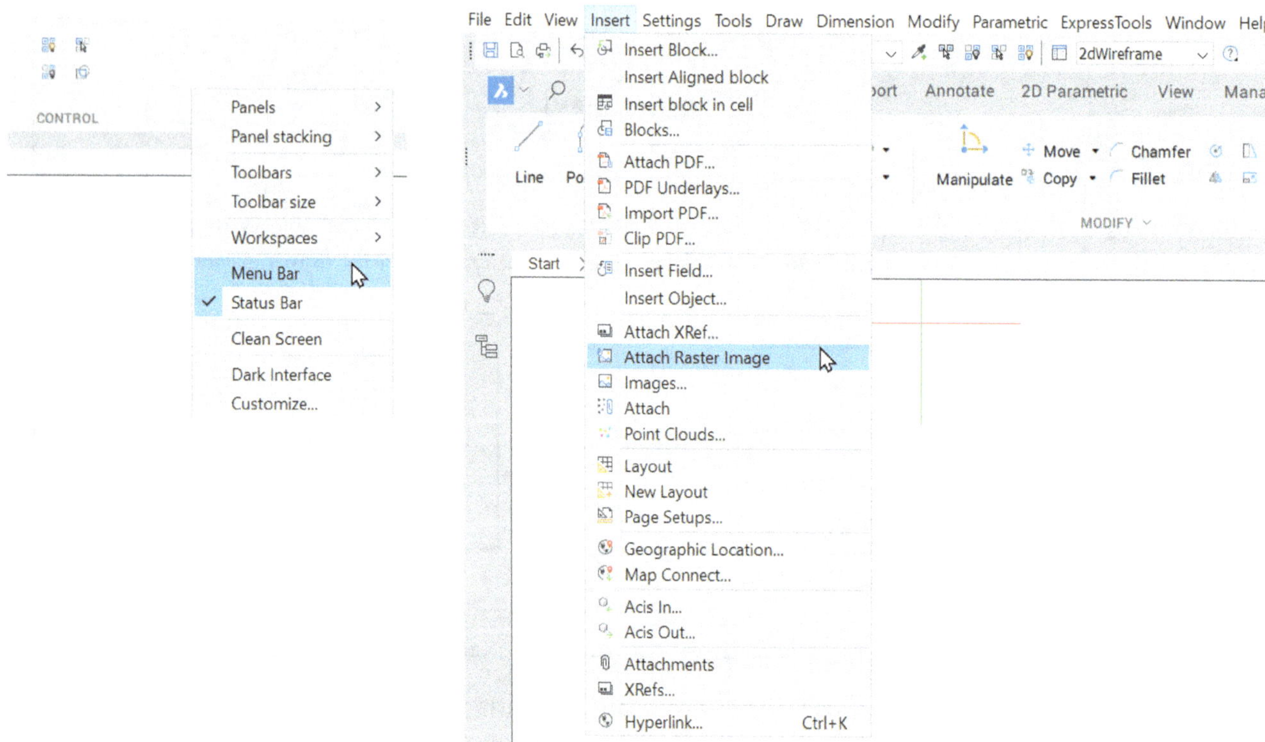

Dialogs and Palettes

Dialogs and Palettes are part of the BricsCAD user interface. Using a dialog or a palette, you can easily specify many settings and options at a time. Examples of dialogs and palettes are as shown below.

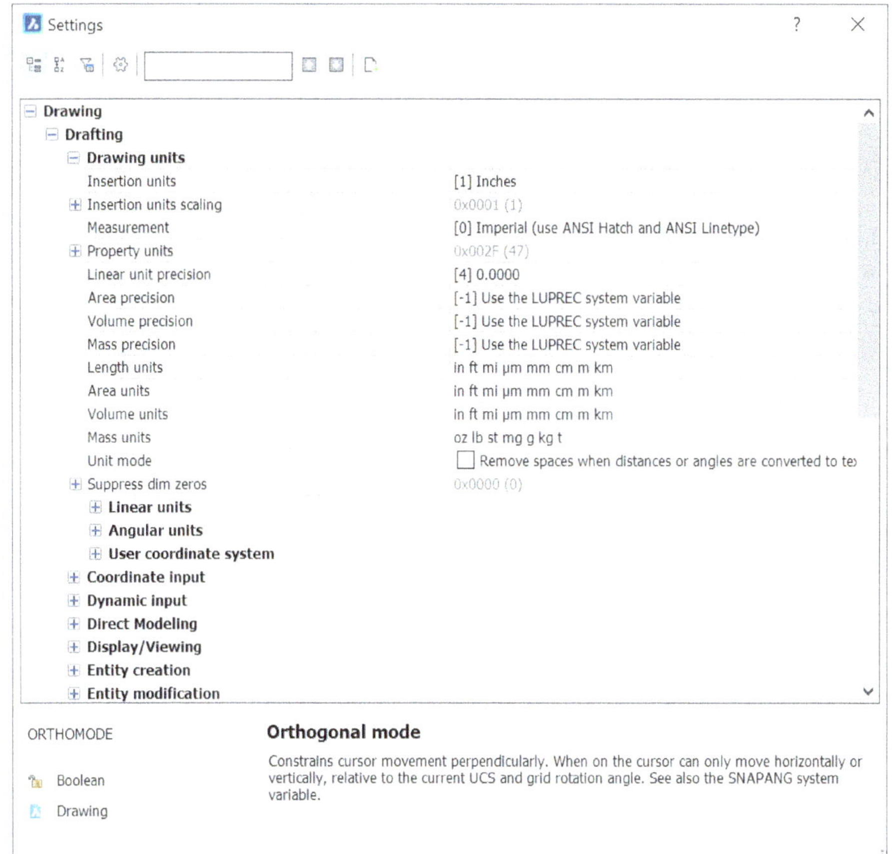
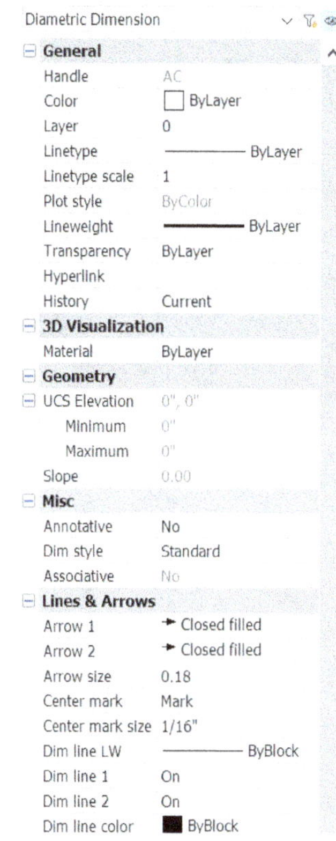

Shortcut Menus

Shortcut Menus appear when you right-click in the graphics window and drag. BricsCAD provides various shortcut menus to help you access tools and options very easily and quickly. There are multiple types of shortcut menus available in BricsCAD. Some of them are discussed next.

Right-click Menu

This shortcut menu appears whenever you right-click in the graphics window and drag without activating any command or selecting an object.

Select and Right-click menu

This shortcut menu appears when you select an object from the graphics window and right-click. It consists of editing and selection options.

Shift+Right-click shortcut menu

This shortcut menu appears when you press and hold the SHIFT key and right-click in the graphic window. The options on this shortcut menu allow you to specify the running object snaps.

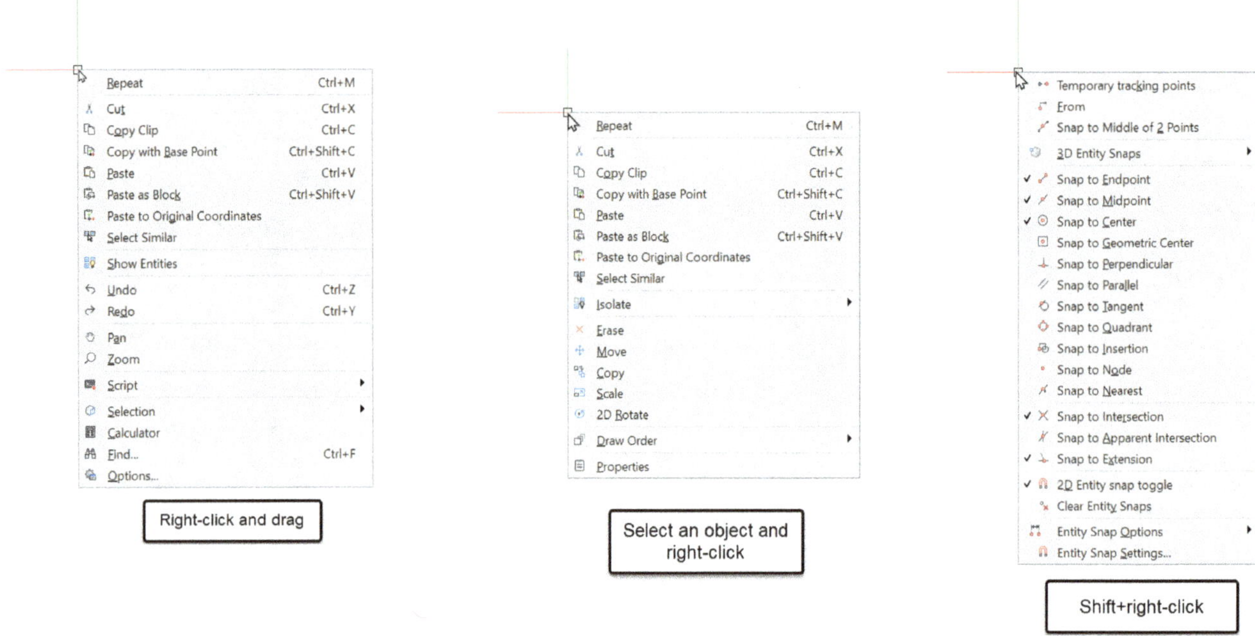

Selection Window

A selection window is used to select multiple elements of a drawing. You can select various elements by using two types of selection windows. The first type is a rectangular selection window. You can create this type of selection window by defining its two diagonal corners. When you set the first corner of the selection window on the left and second corner on the right side, the elements which fall entirely under the selection window will be selected.

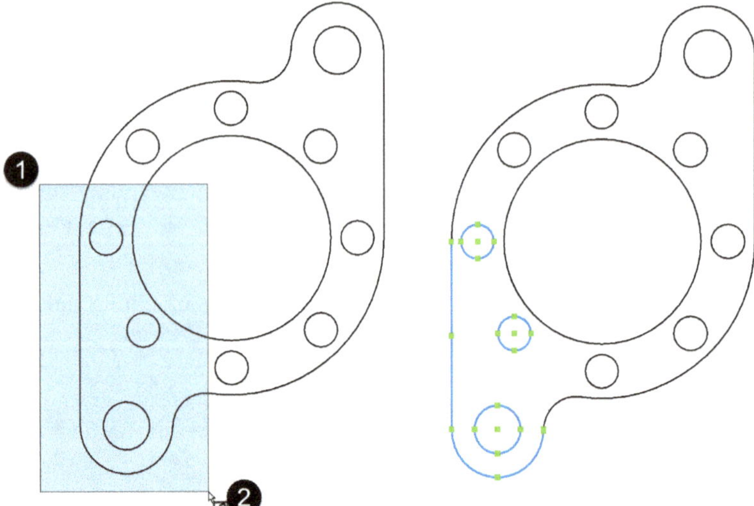

However, if you define the first corner on the right side and the second corner on the left side, the elements, which fall entirely or partially under the selection window, will be selected.

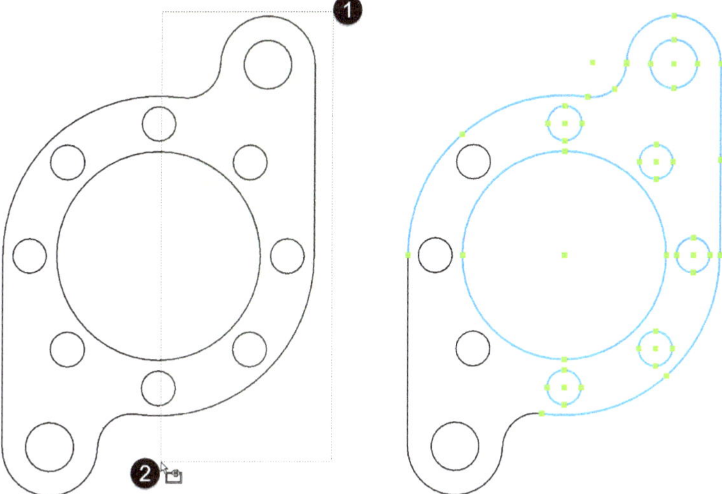

The second type of selection window is Lasso. Lasso is an irregular shape created by holding the left mouse button and dragging the pointer across the elements to select. If you drag the pointer from left to right, the elements falling entirely under the lasso will be selected.

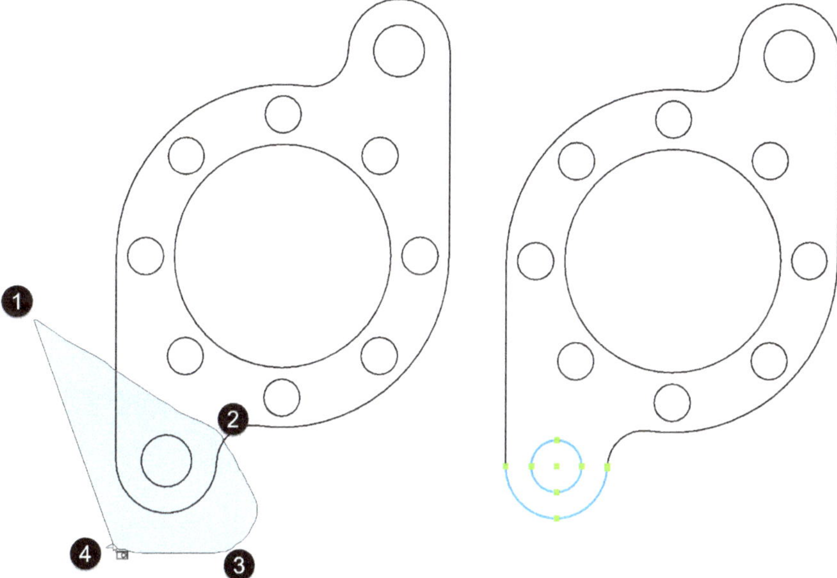

If you drag the pointer from right to left, the elements which fall wholly or partially under the lasso will be selected.

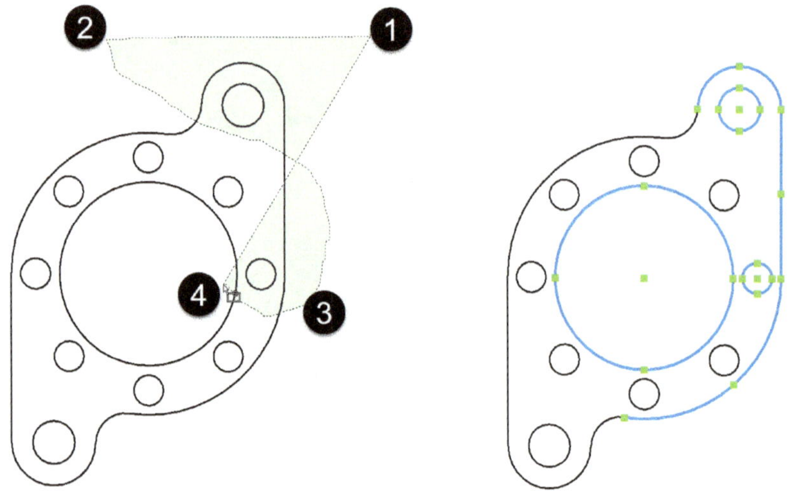

Help

Click the **Help** icon located on the Access toolbar.

Tutorial 1: Creating the Floor Plan

In this example, you will learn to create an architectural drawing.

Creating Outer Walls

- Double-click on the **BricsCAD V24(x64) en_US** icon on your desktop.

- Click the **Start** button in the **2D Drafting** section on the **BricsCAD Launcher** pop up window.

- Click **Start from Template > Default-Imperial**; a new document is created.

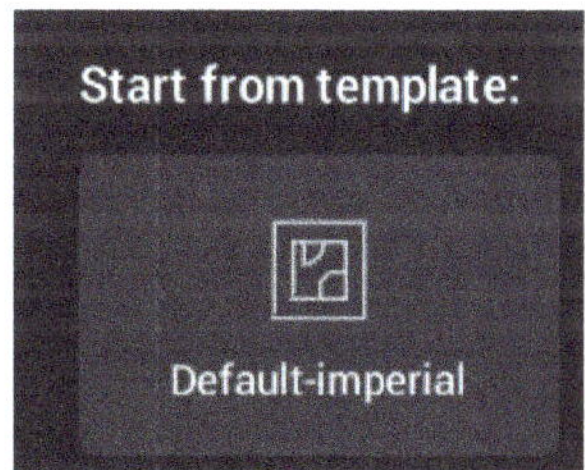

- Right-click on the ribbon and deselect the **Dark Interface** option.

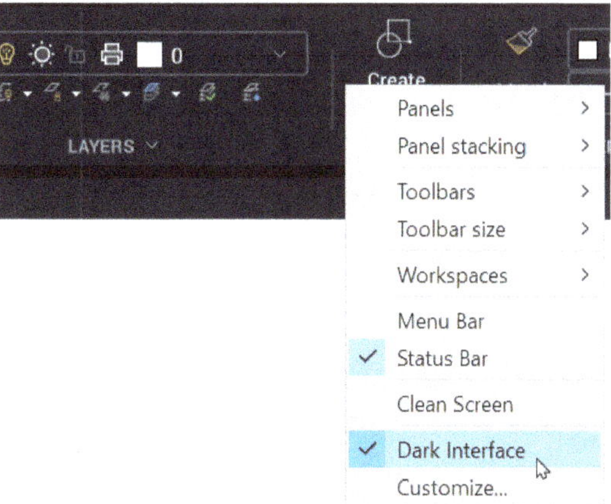

- Click **Manage > Customization > Settings** on the ribbon.

- On the **Settings** dialog, expand the **Program options > Display** branch.

- Change the **Background color** to **White**.

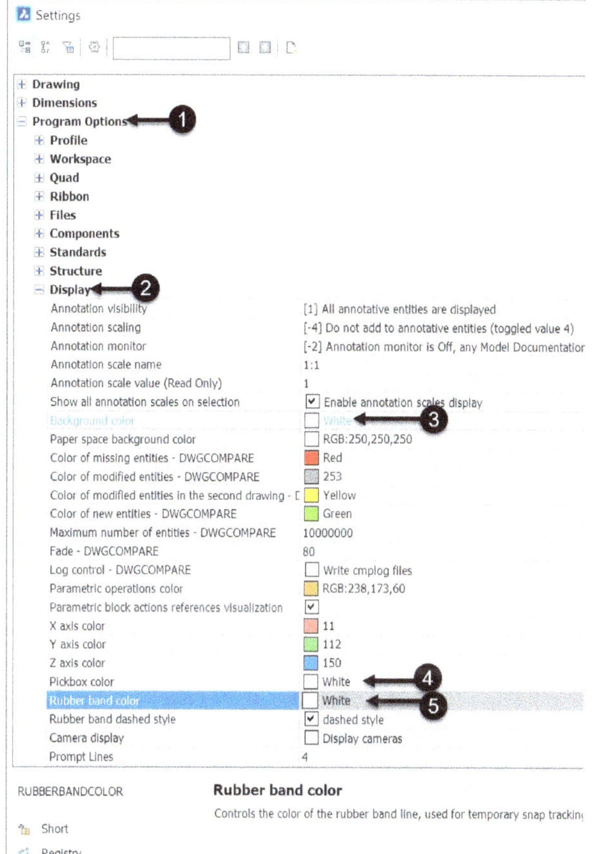

- Type LIMITS in the command line and press Enter.

- Press Enter to accept 0, 0 as the lower limit.

- Type **100', 80'** in the command line, and press Enter. The program sets the upper limit of the drawing.

- Click **View > Zoom > Zoom Extents** on the ribbon.

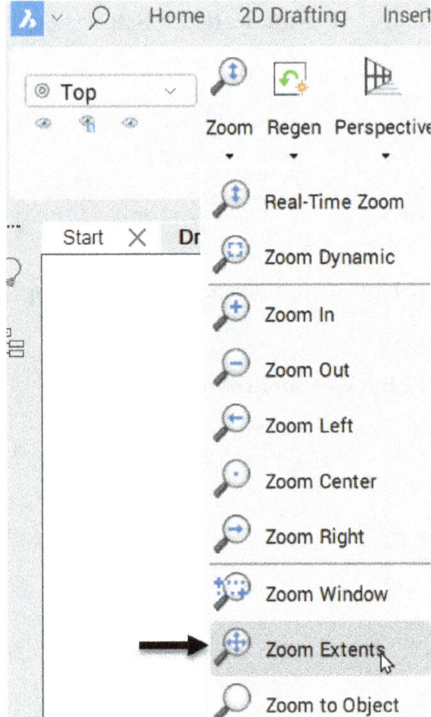

- Make sure that the **Grid** icon is turned OFF on the status bar.

- On the Status bar, turn ON the **Ortho** icon.

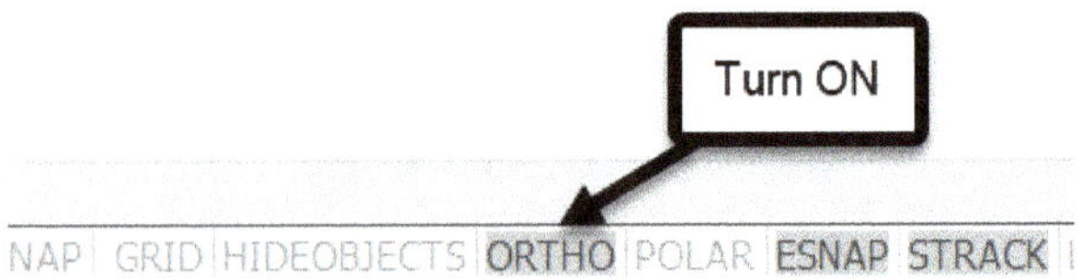

- On the ribbon, click **Home > Draw > Line**.

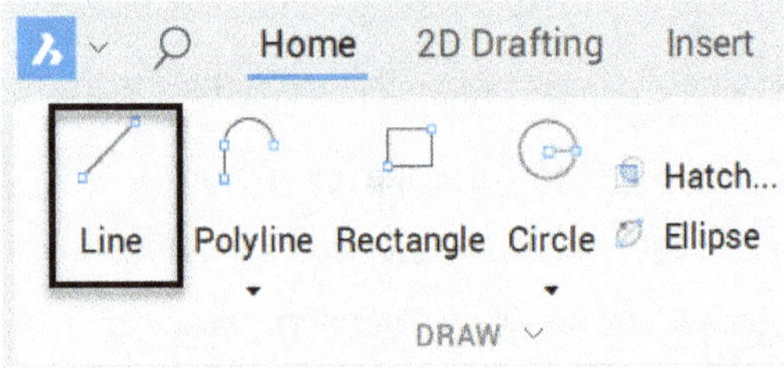

- Select an arbitrary point. It defines the start point of the line.
- Move the pointer toward right horizontally and type **412** in the Dynamic Input box — press Enter.

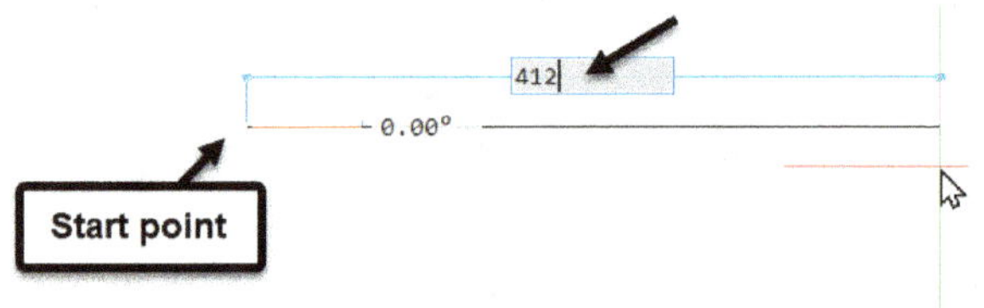

- Move the pointer upward, type **338** in the Dynamic Input box – press Enter.

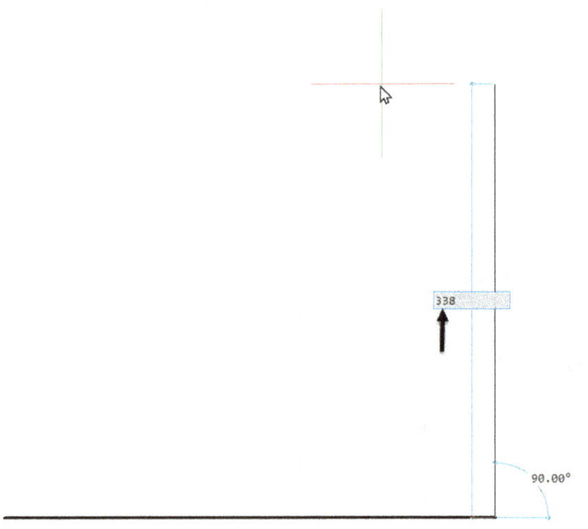

- Move the pointer onto the starting point of the drawing, and then move it upwards. You will notice that a trace line appears.

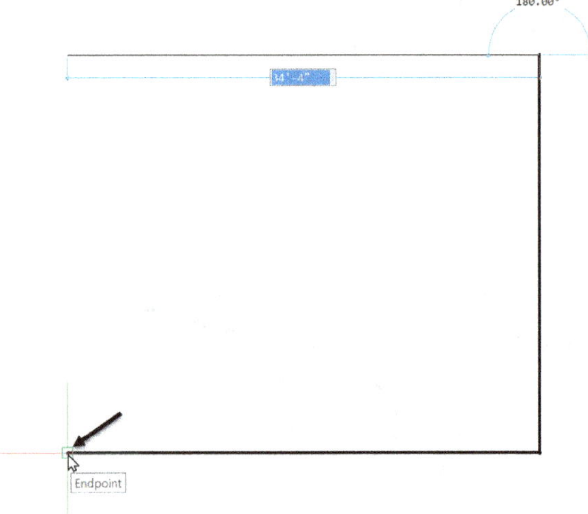

- Click to create a horizontal line. You will notice that the two horizontal lines are of the same length.
- Type C in the command line to select the **Close** option.

- On the ribbon, click **Home > Modify > Offset**. Next, type-in **6** in the command line and press Enter.

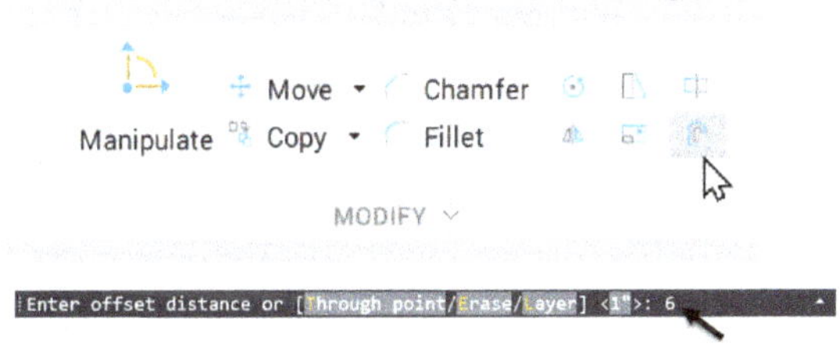

- Select the left vertical line of the drawing.

- Move the pointer inside the drawing and click to create an offset line.

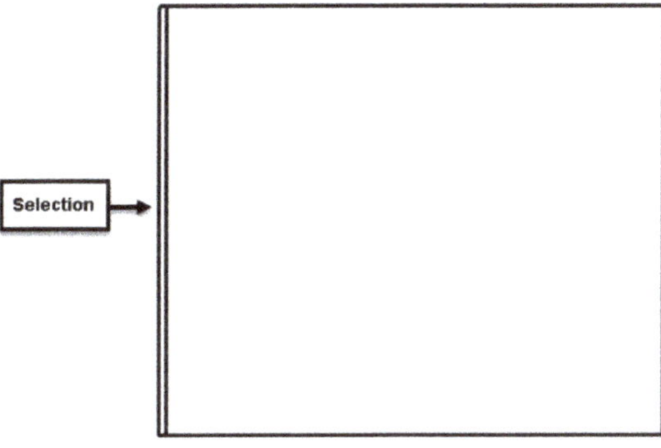

- Likewise, offset the other lines, as shown below.

- On the ribbon, click **View > Zoom > Zoom Window**.

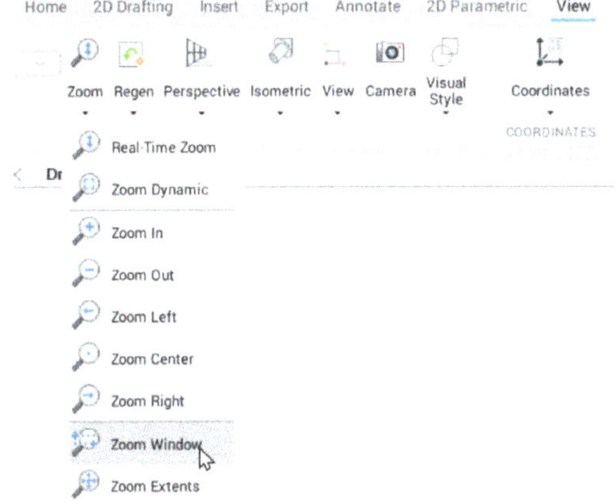

- Create a window on the top left corner of the drawing. The corner portion will be zoomed in.

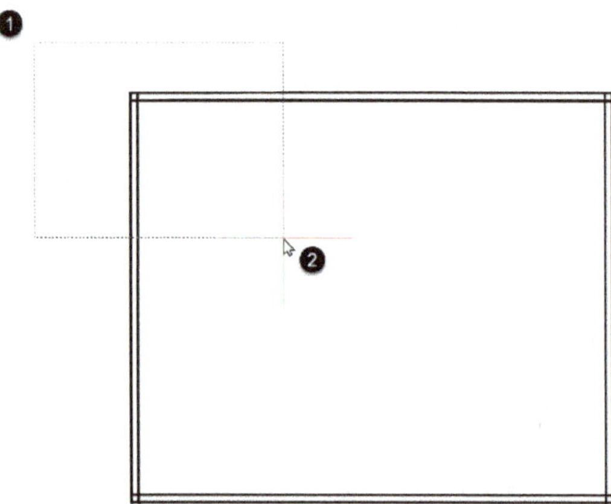

- On the ribbon, click **Home > Modify > Fillet**.

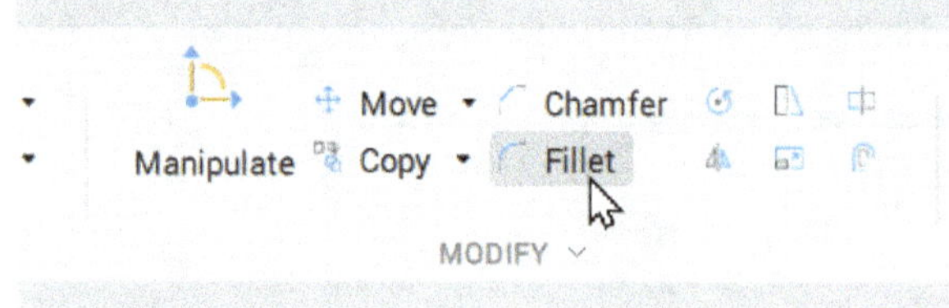

- Type **R** in the command line and press ENTER.
- Type **0** in the command line and press ENTER to define the radius.
- Select the inner offset lines, as shown below. Next, press ESC.

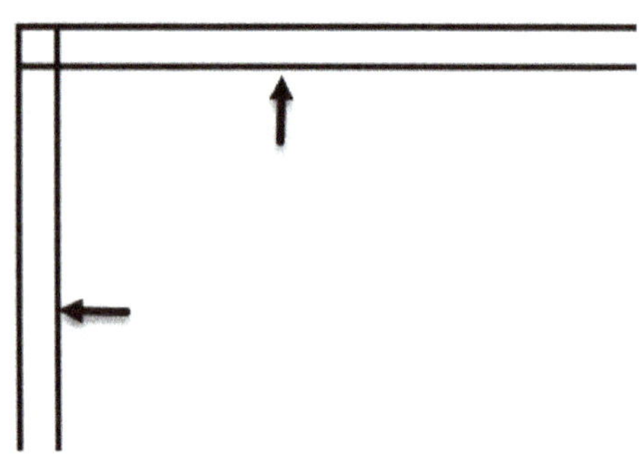

- On the **View** tab > **Zoom** > **Zoom Extents** on the ribbon.

- On the ribbon, click **Home > Modify > Fillet**. Select the inner offset lines, as shown below.

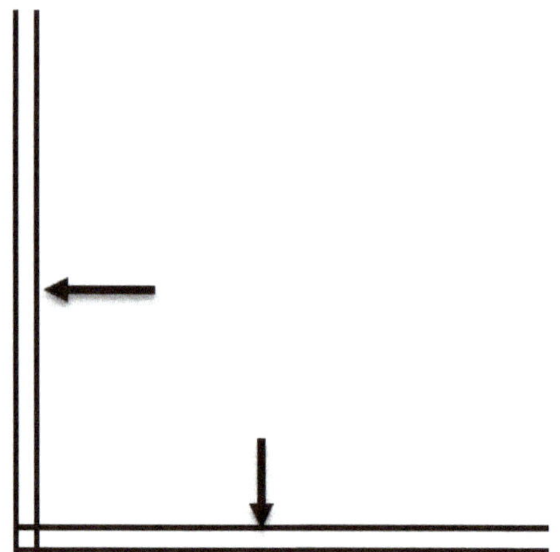

- Likewise, fillet the other inner corners, as shown.

- Click **Save** on the **Access** toolbar. Next, type **Tutorial_1** in the **File name** box and click **Save**.
- Make sure that you save the drawing after each section.

Creating Inner Walls

- On the ribbon, click **Home > Modify > Offset**. Next, type **130** in the command line and press Enter.
- Select the inner line of the right sidewall. Next, move the pointer toward the left and click.

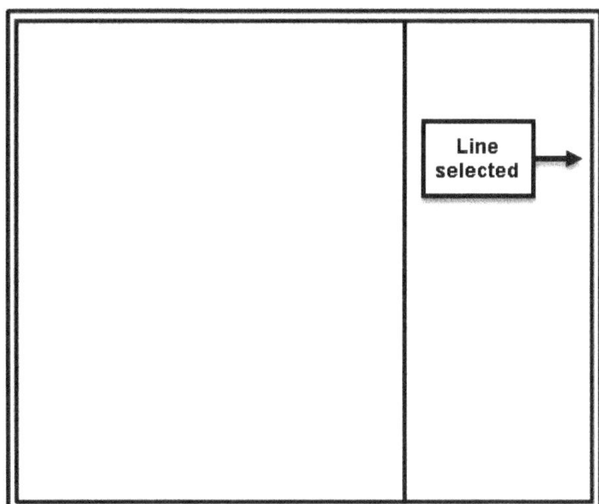

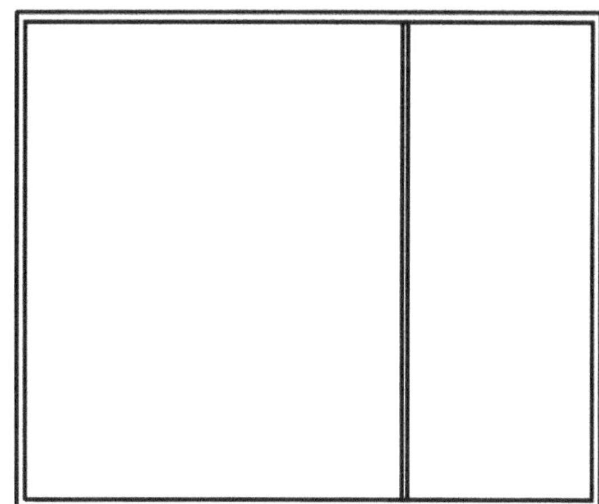

- Press ENTER in the Command line.
- Activate the **Offset** command. Next, type **4** in the Command line and press Enter.
- Select the new offset line and move the pointer toward the left. Next, click to create another offset line and press **Esc**.

- Activate the **Offset** command and type **118**. Press Enter.
- Select the line, as shown in the figure. Next, move the pointer towards left and click to create the offset line.

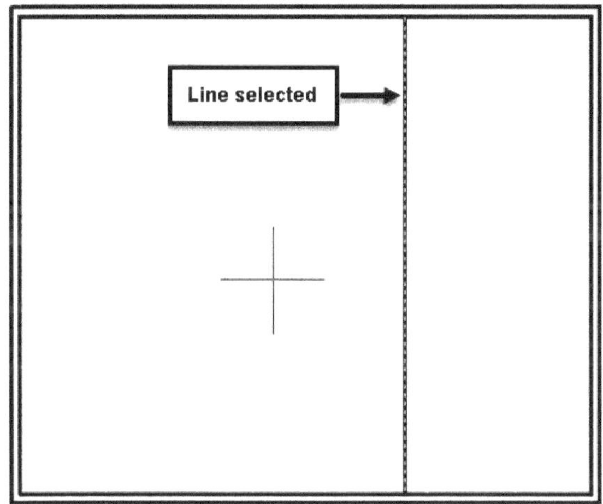

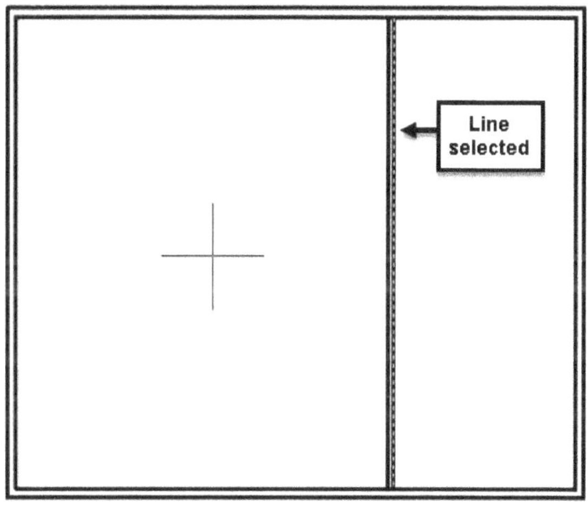

- Likewise, create another offset line with offset distance **122**, as shown below.

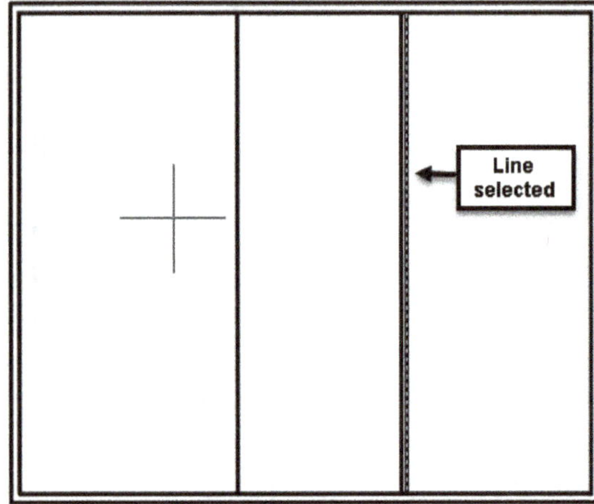

- Likewise, create horizontal offset lines, as shown below.

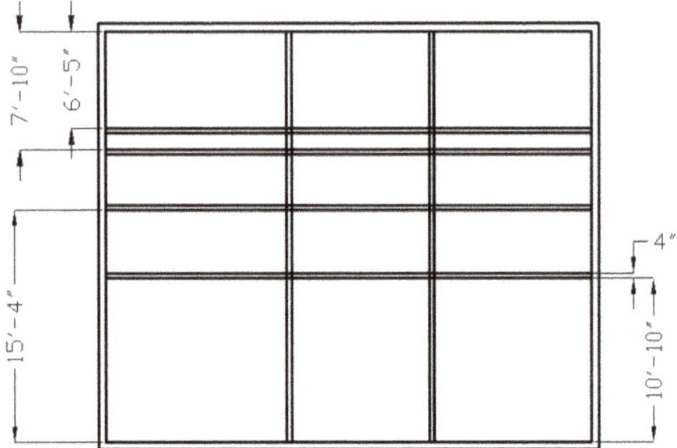

- On the ribbon, click **Home** > **Modify** > **Trim** .
- Press Enter to select all the elements of the drawing.
- Type C in the command line and press ENTER to select the **Crossing** option.

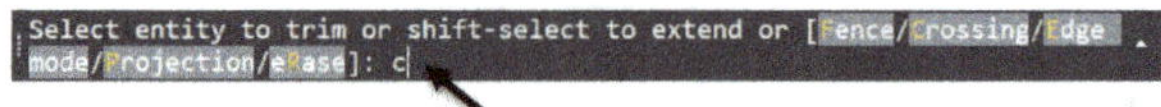

- Press and hold the left mouse button and drag a selection box across the horizontal lines, as shown below.

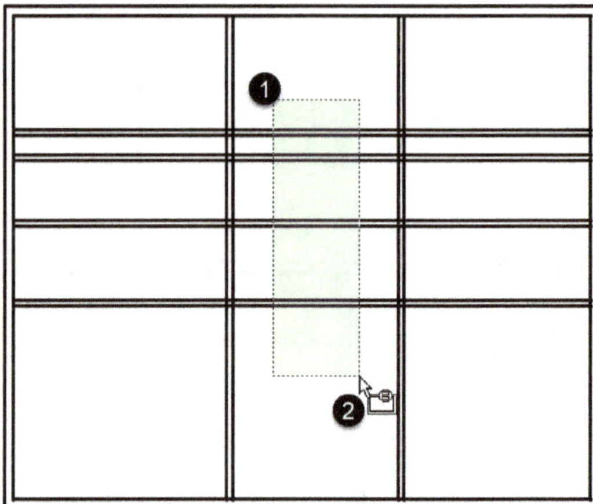

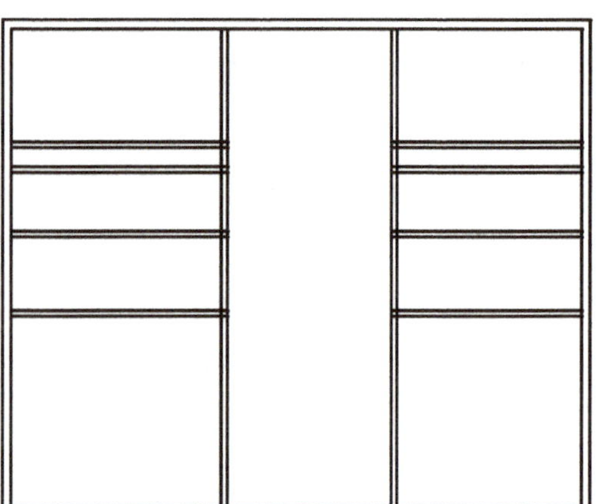

- Likewise, trim other entities using the **Crossing** option in the command line, as shown below.

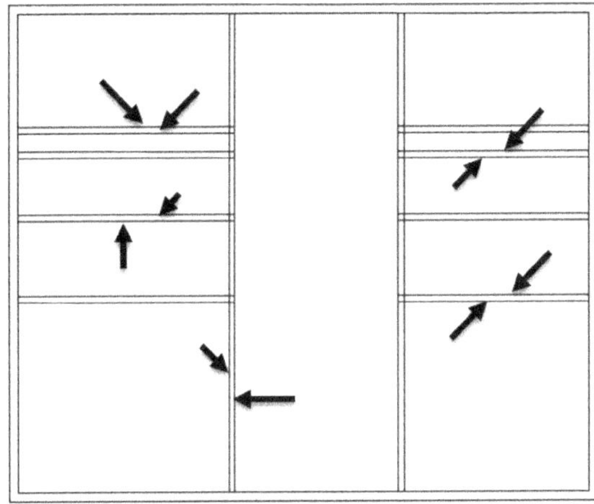

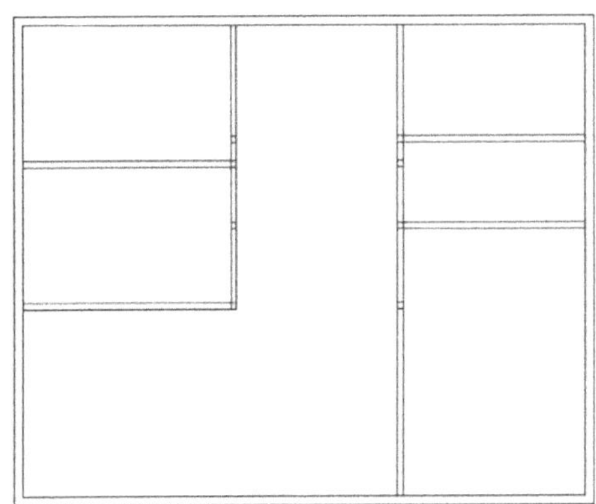

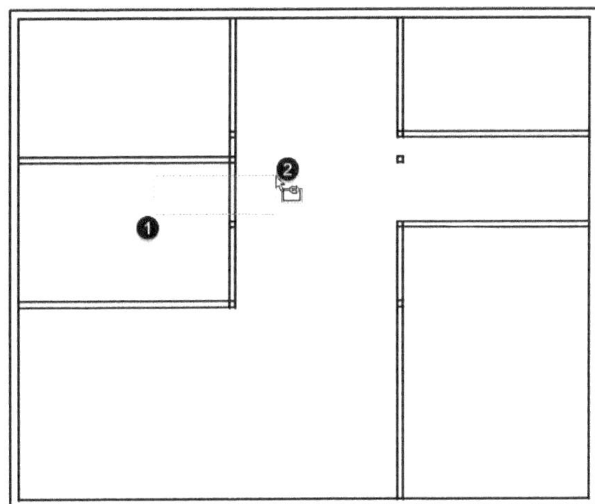

- Make sure that the **Trim** command is active.
- Click and drag selection windows across the elements, as shown. Next, press **Esc** to exit the command.

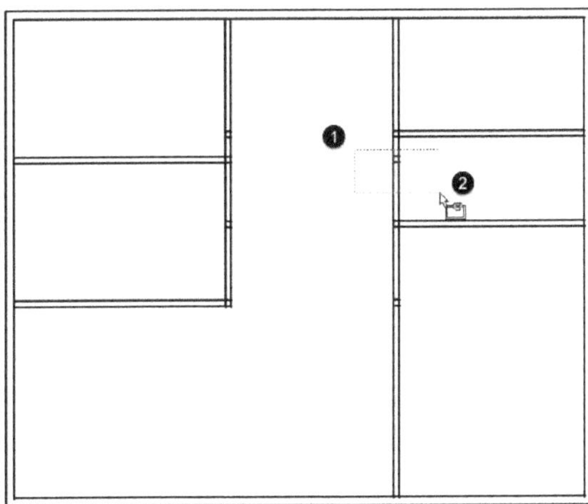

- Zoom to the top portion of the drawing by placing the pointer in the top portion and rotating the mouse scroll in the forward direction.
- On the ribbon, click **Home** > **Modify** > **Trim**. Next, press ENTER to select all the elements as cutting edges.
- Select the portion of the horizontal line that lies between the lines of the inner walls by using the selection box.

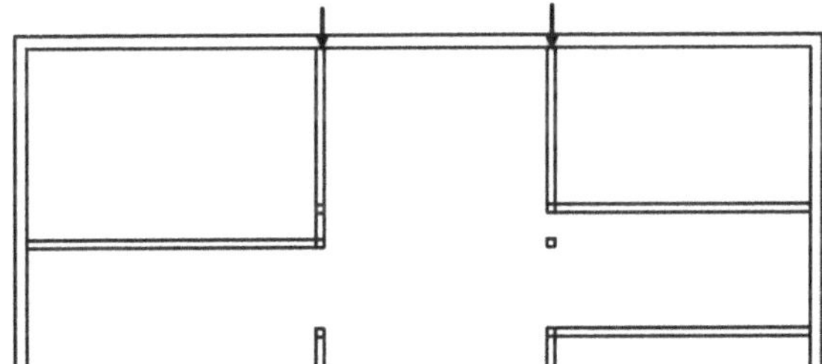

The selected portions will be trimmed.

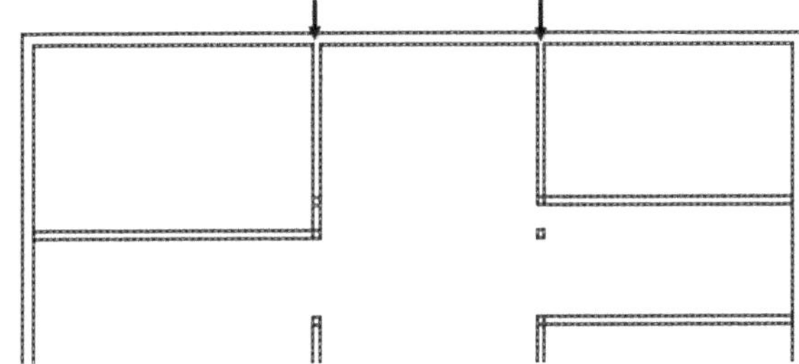

- Press and hold the mouse scroll wheel and drag downwards until the lower portion of the drawing is visible.
- Trim the unwanted portion, as shown below.

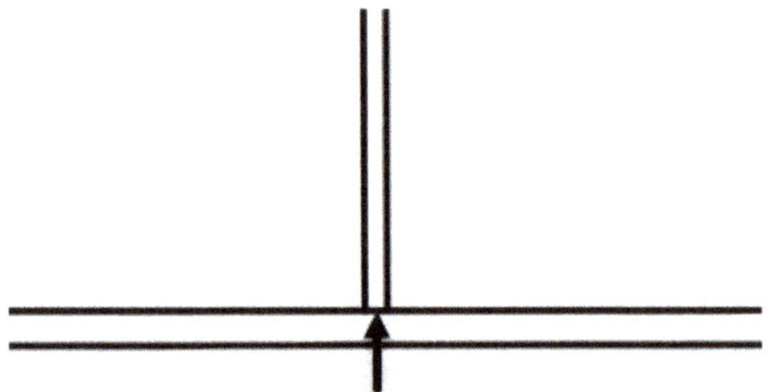

- Trim the unwanted portions, as shown below. Also, trim the unwanted portions at the corners.

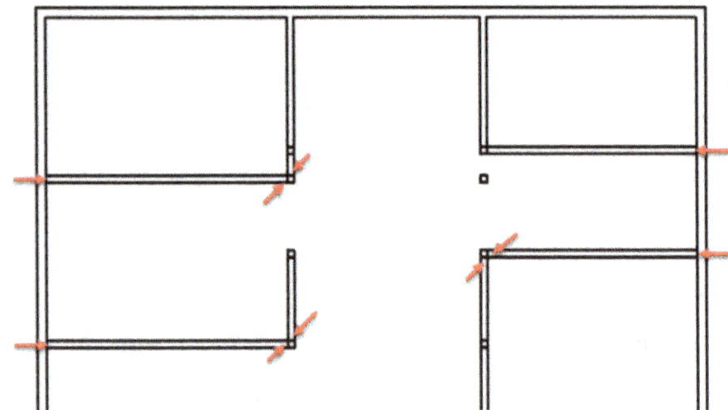

- Make sure that the **Trim** command is active. Next, type R in the command line and press ENTER to select the **eRase** option from the Command line.
- Select the unwanted elements, as shown. Next, press ENTER.

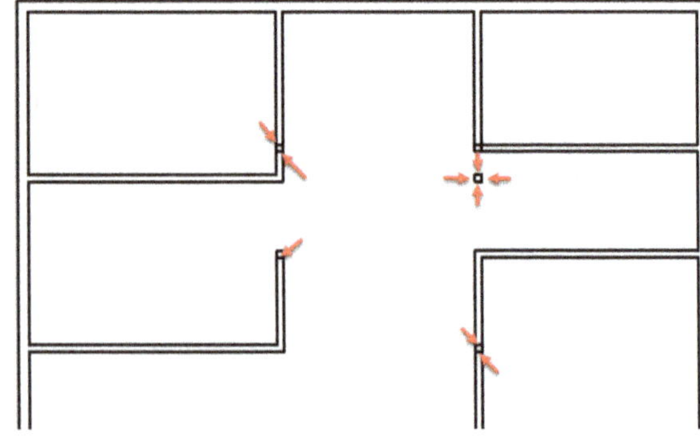

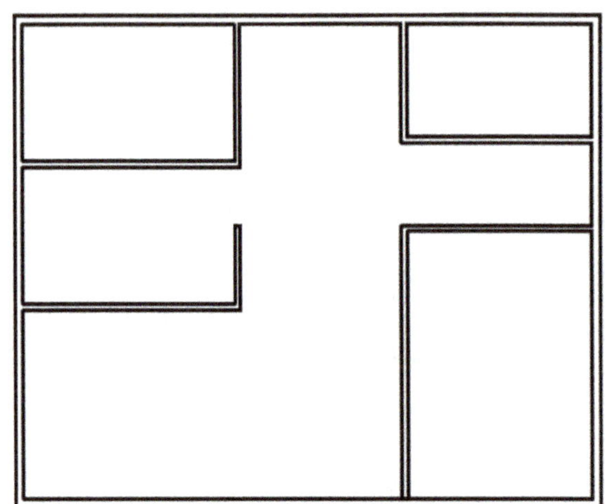

Creating Openings and Doors

- Activate the **Line** command and select the corner of the inner wall, as shown below.
- Move the pointer downward and select the other corner point.

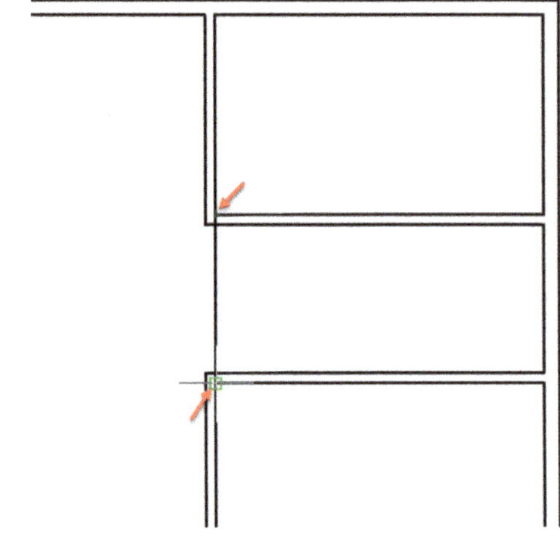

- Press **Esc** and select the new line.
- Select the middle point of the new line and move the pointer toward the right.

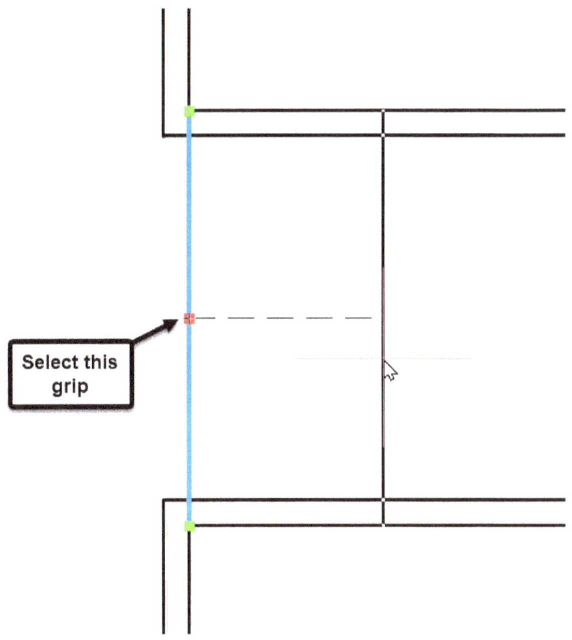

- Type-in **6** and press Enter.

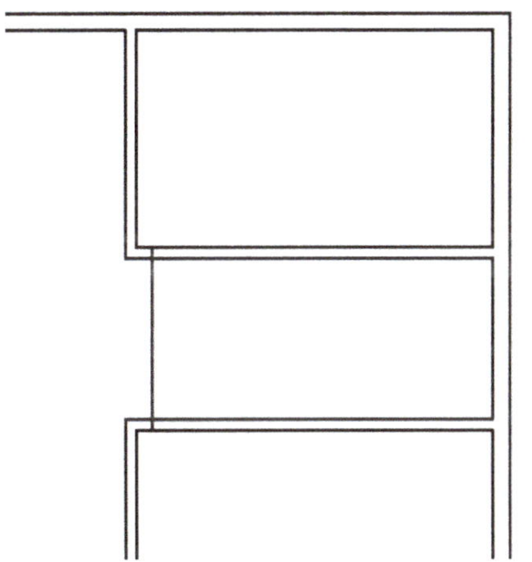

- On the ribbon, click **Home > Modify > Offset** command. Type **32** as the offset distance, and then press ENTER.
- Select the new line and move the pointer towards right, and then click.

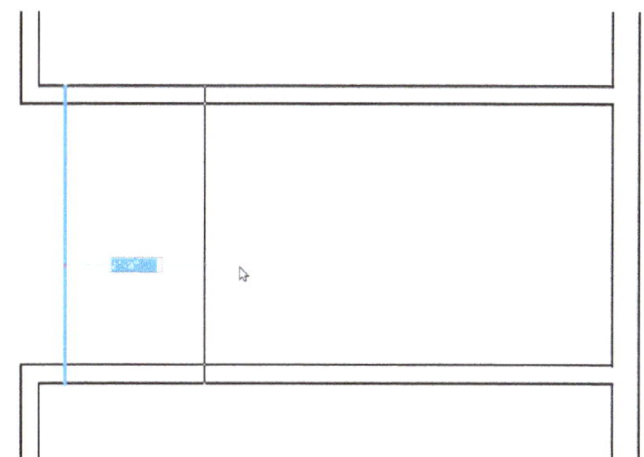

- Right-click to exit the command.
- On the ribbon, click Home > **Modify >Trim**.
- Press Enter to select all the elements as the boundary edges.
- Click and drag a selection box across the unwanted portions, as shown below.

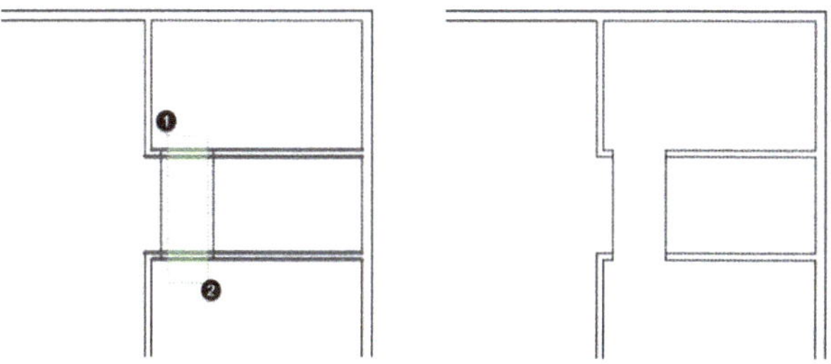

- Make sure that the **Trim Vectors** command is active. Next, click the **Crossing** option on the Command line.
- Click and drag a selection box across the unwanted portions, as shown below.

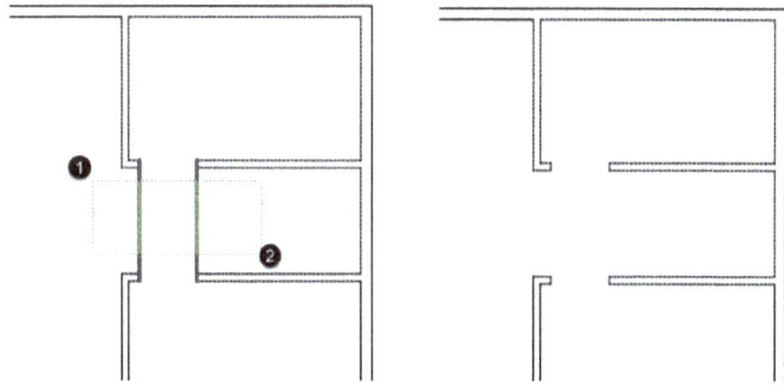

- Activate the **Line** command and create the lines, as shown below.
- Offset the newly created lines. The offset distances are given in the figure below.

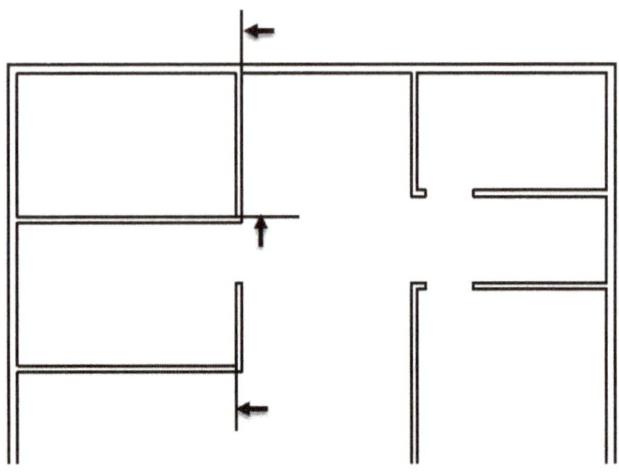

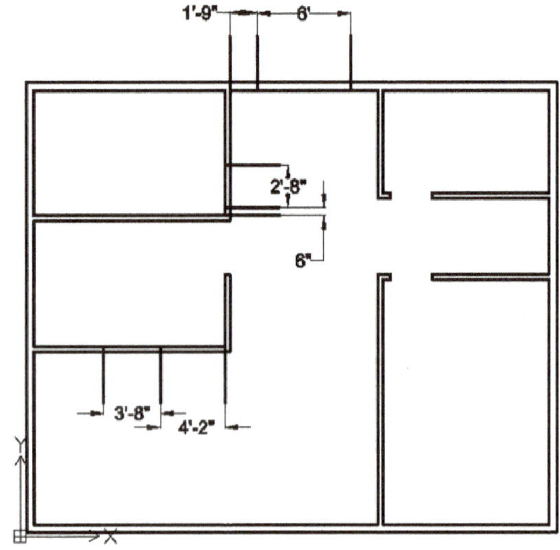

- On the ribbon, click **Home > Modify > Trim** to trim the unwanted portions.
- Press Enter to select all the elements as the boundary edges.
- Create a selection window across the horizontal line, as shown. The horizontal lines are trimmed.

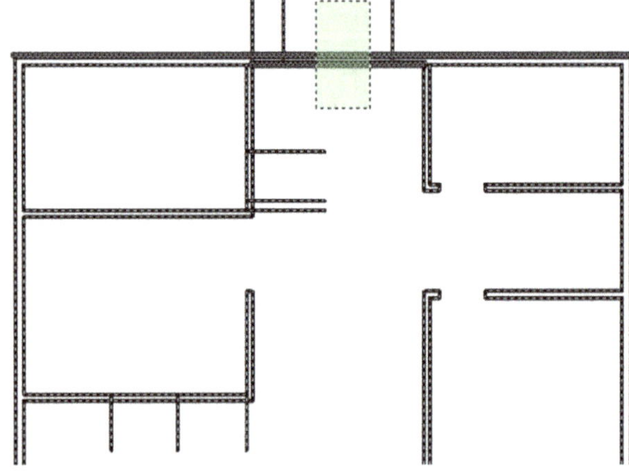

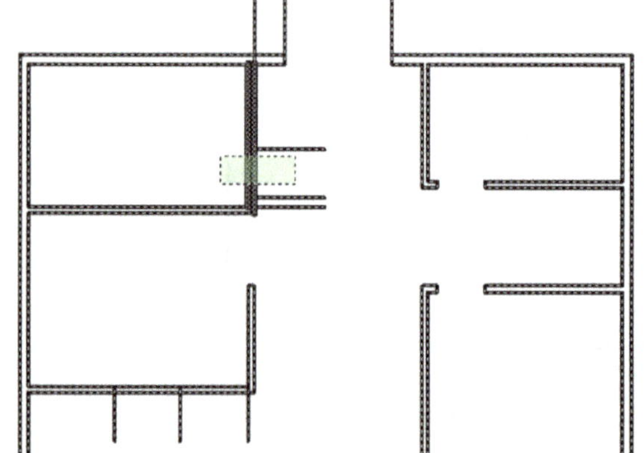

- Likewise, draw a selection box for the rest of lines, as shown.

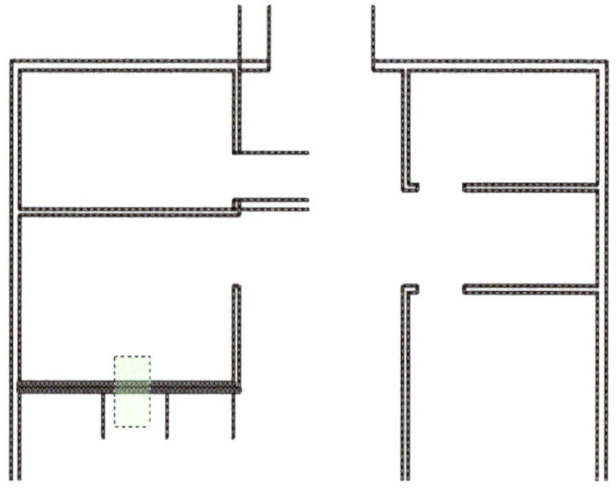

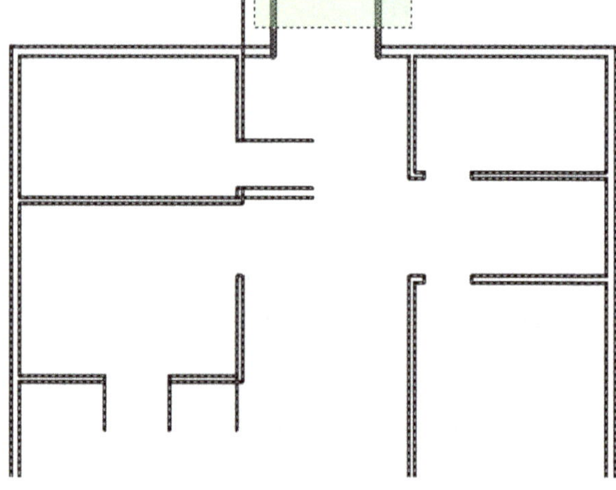

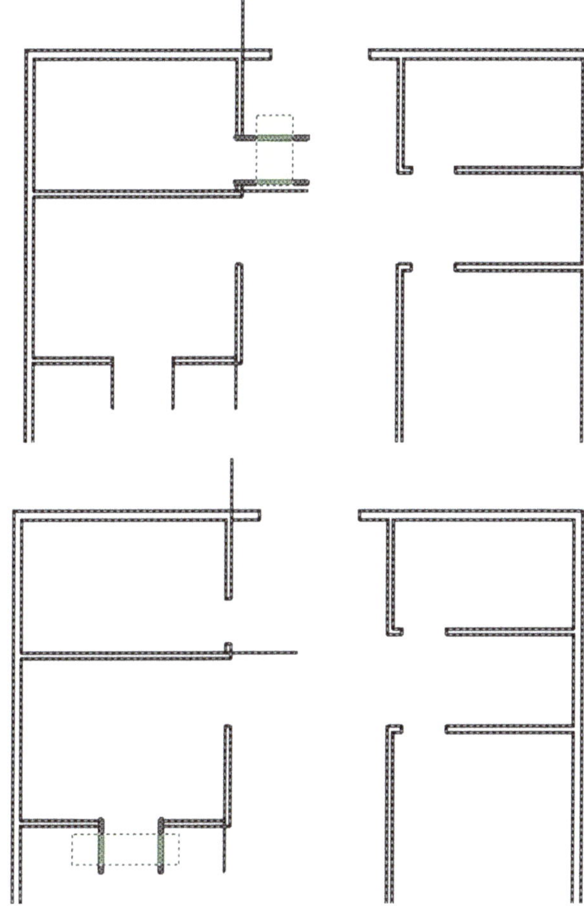

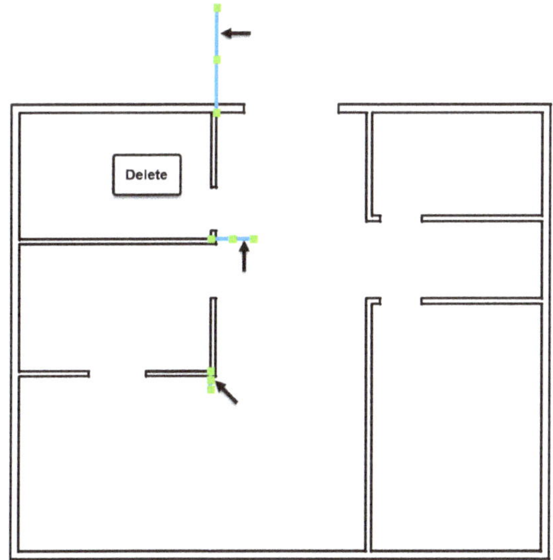

- Press **Esc** on the Keyboard.
- Select the remaining unwanted lines and press DELETE.

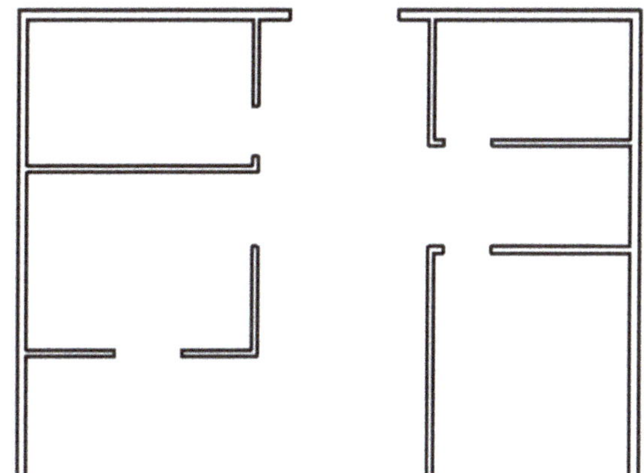

- On the ribbon, click **Home** > **Draw** > **Rectangle**. Next, select the endpoint of the opening, as shown below.

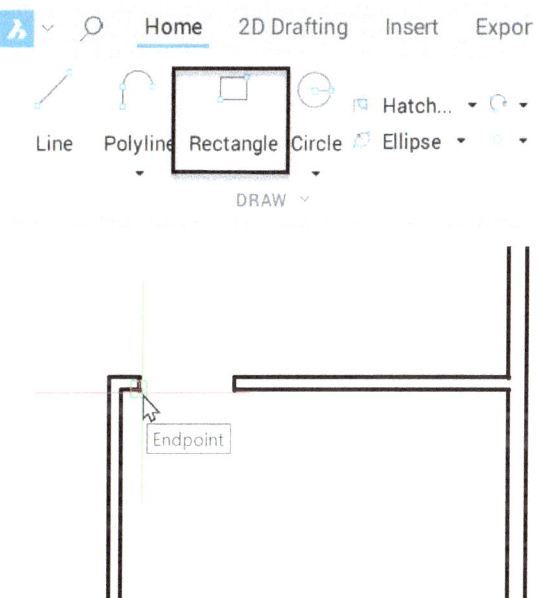

- Move the pointer downward.
- Type-in **1** and press TAB. It defines the length of the rectangle.
- Type-in **32** and press Enter. It defines the width of the rectangle.

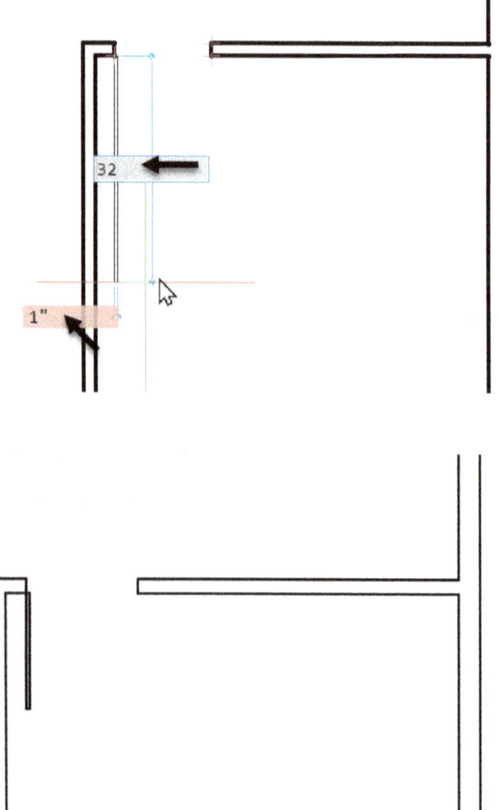

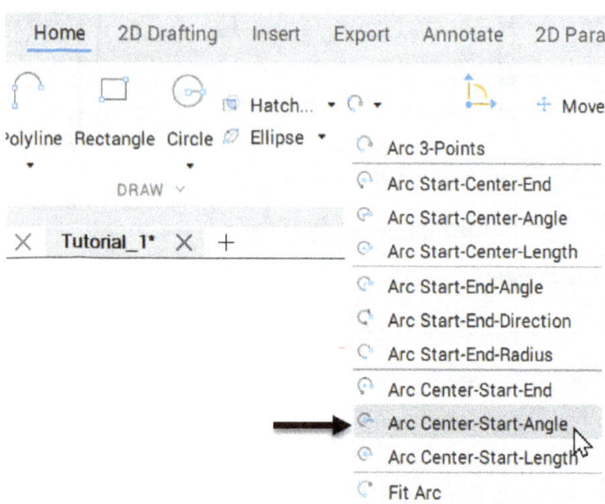

Now, you need to create the door swing.

* On the ribbon, click **Home** > **Draw** > **Arc drop-down** > **Arc Center-Start-Angle**.

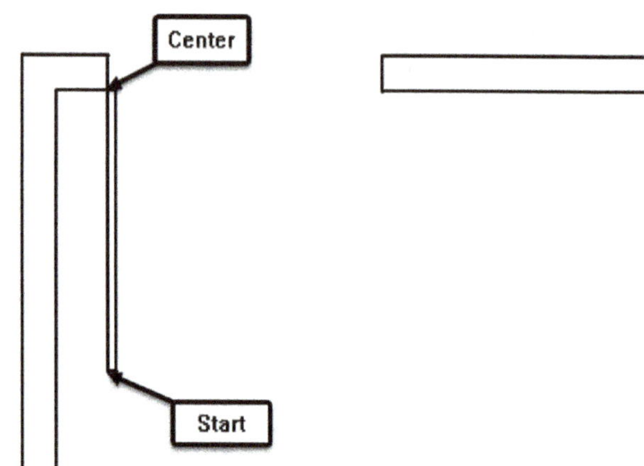

* Type 90, and press ENTER.

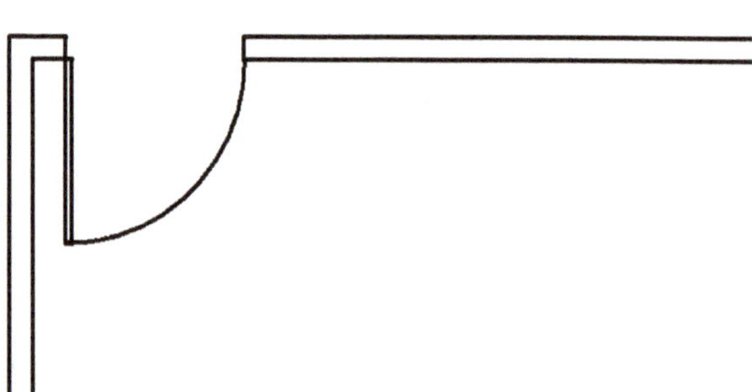

* Select the door and door swing.

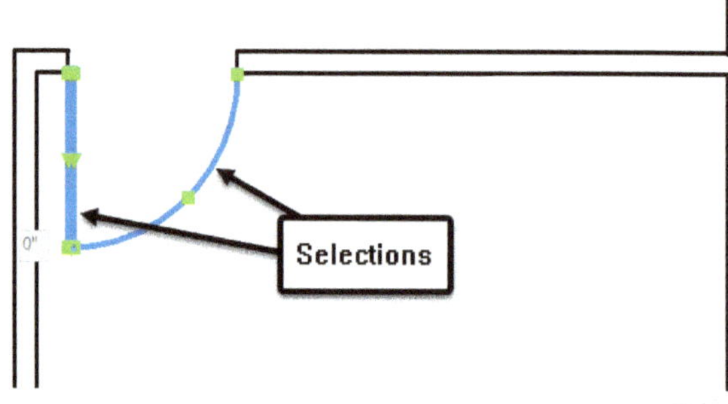

* On the ribbon, click **Home > Modify > Copy**.

* Select the corner point of the rectangle as the base point.

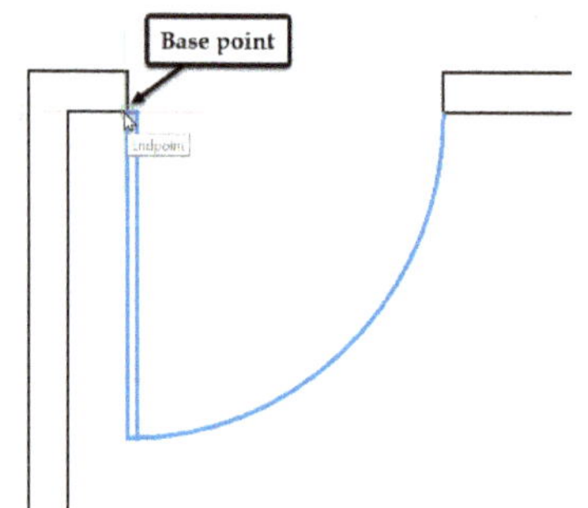

* Select the corner points of openings, as shown below.

Arc 3-Points
Arc Start-Center-End
Arc Start-Center-Angle
Arc Start-Center-Length
Arc Start-End-Angle
Arc Start-End-Direction
Arc Start-End-Radius
Arc Center-Start-End
Arc Center-Start-Angle
Arc Center-Start-Length
Fit Arc

* Select the top left corner of the rectangle to define the center of the arc.
* Select the bottom left corner of the rectangle to define the starting point of the arc.

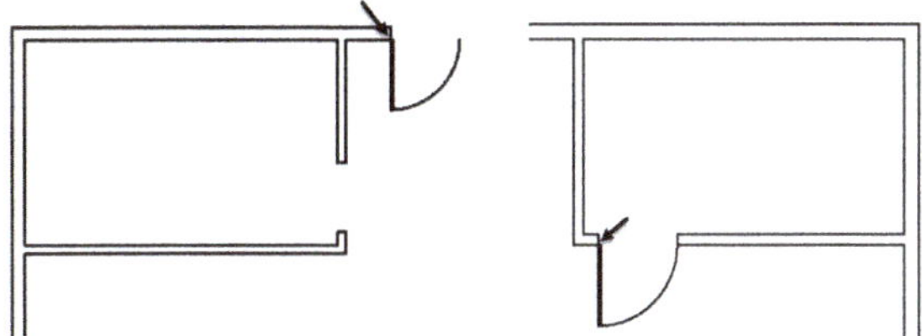

- Press Esc to deactivate the **Copy** command.

- Click the right mouse button on the **ESNAP** icon on the status bar.

- Select the **Midpoint** option from the menu.

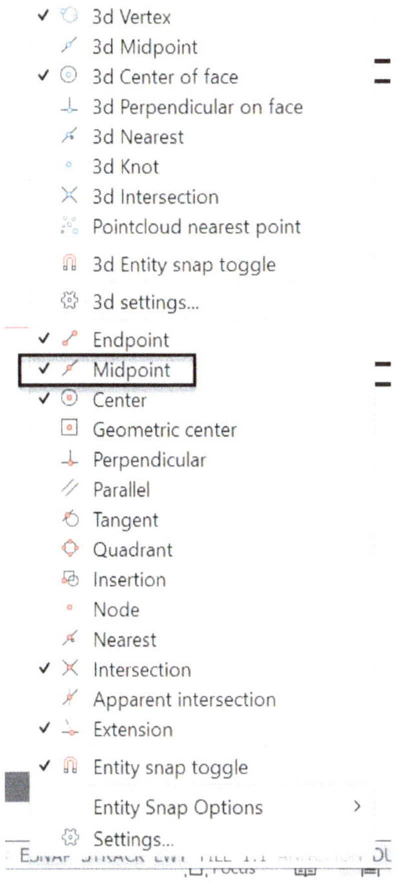

- On the ribbon, click **Home > Modify > 2D Mirror**.

- Select the door and swing of the bathroom, as shown. Press Enter to accept the selection.

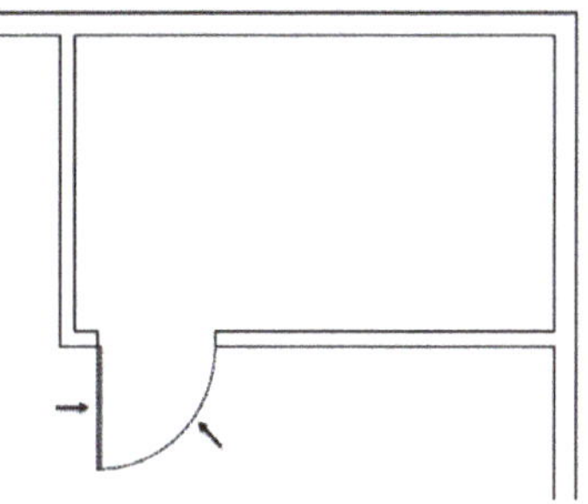

- Define the mirror line by selecting the points, as shown below.

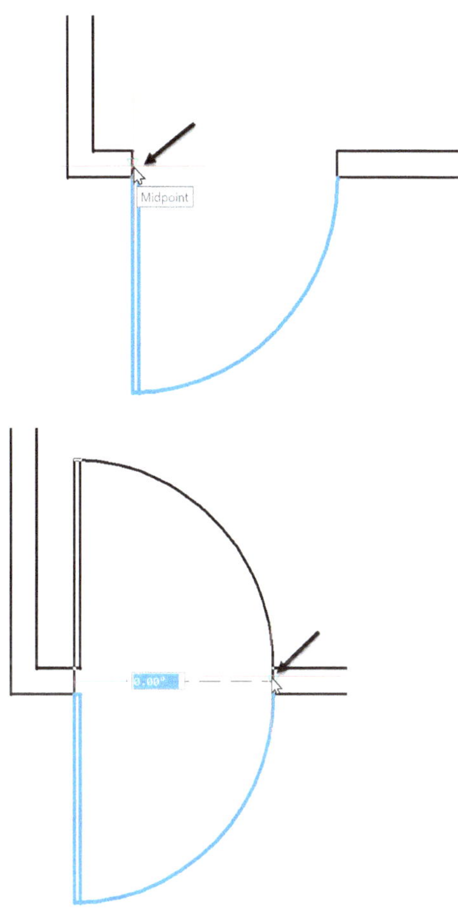

- Select **Yes – delete entities** to delete the original object.

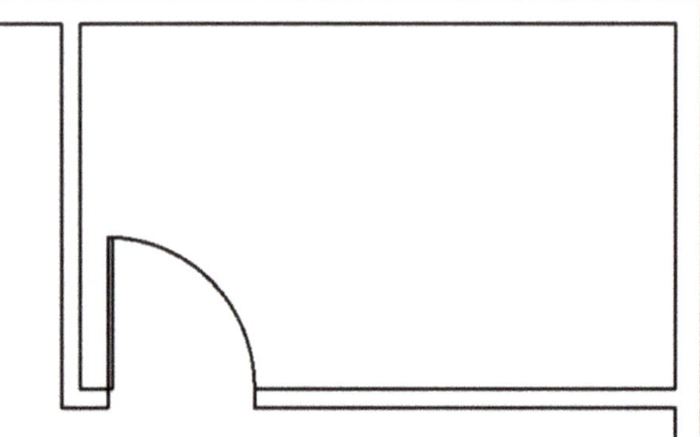

- On the ribbon, click **Home > Modify > Scale** .

- Select the door & swing at the main entrance — press Enter.

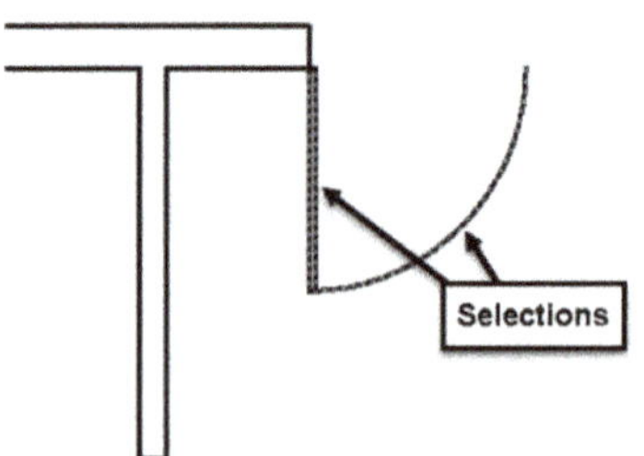

- Select the base point, as shown below.

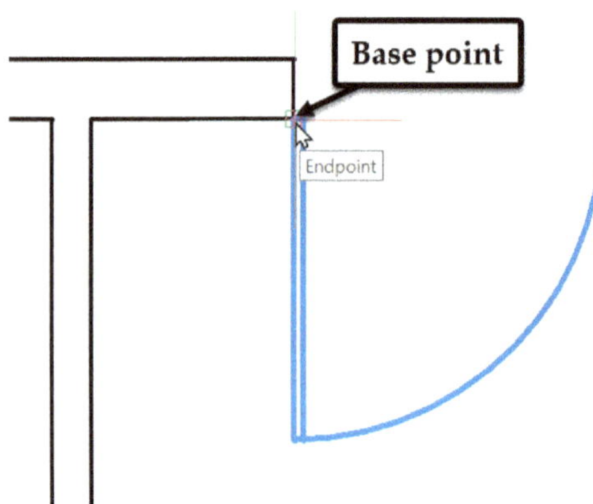

- Select the **Reference Length** option from the command line.

- Select the two endpoints, as shown below. It defines the reference length of the objects. Now, you need to define the length up to which you want to scale the objects.

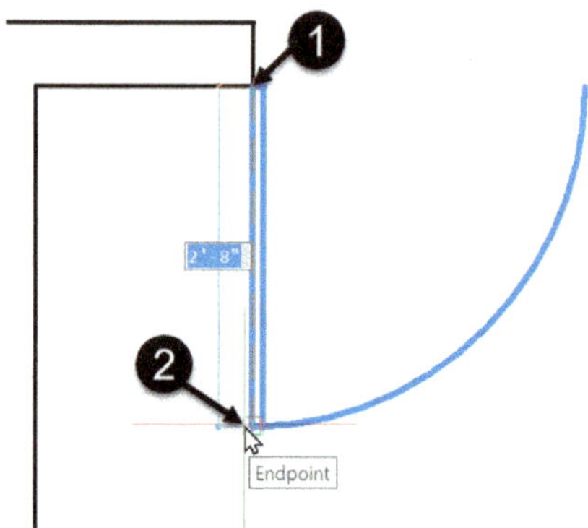

- Type-in **36** and press Enter. The objects will be scaled.

- Select the door & swing at the entrance.

- Place the cursor on the Quad displayed next to the cursor; the Quad is expanded.

- Place the cursor on the Modify category of the Quad.

- Select the **2D Mirror** tool from the expanded **Modify** category.

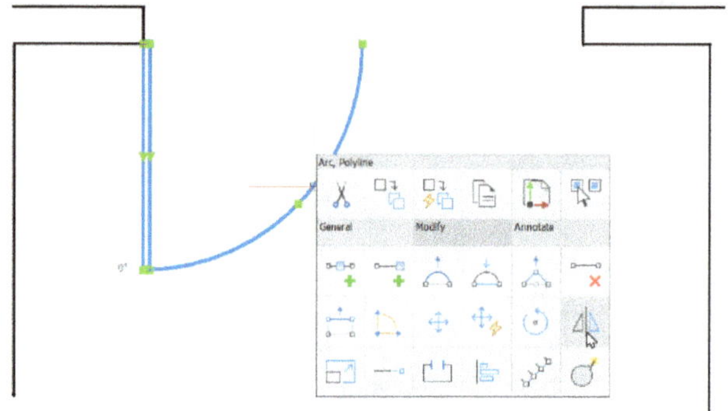

- Define the mirror line by selecting the points, as shown below.

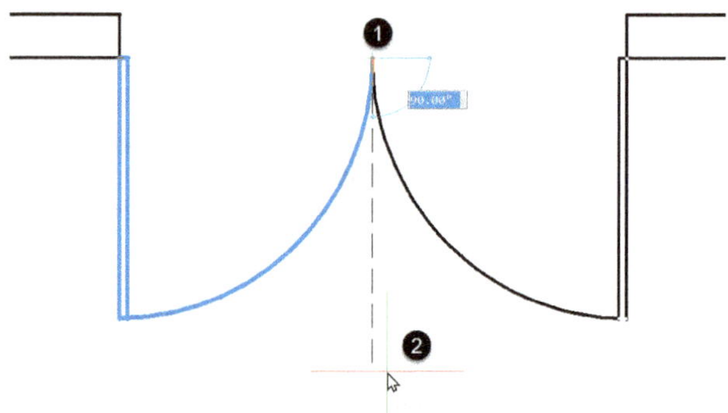

- Select **No – keep entities** to keep the original object.

- Copy the door & swing of the bathroom and place it at the opening, as shown below.

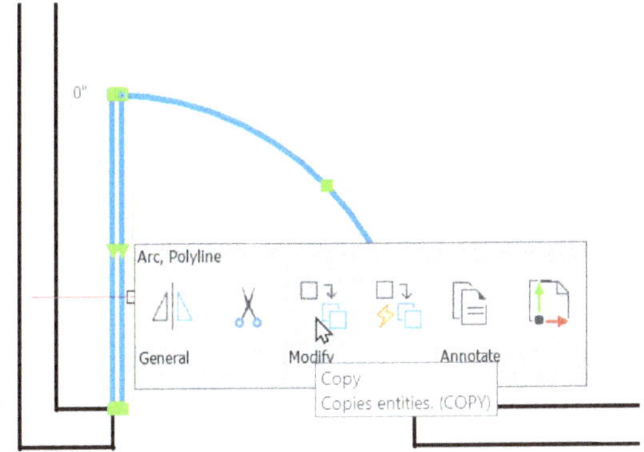

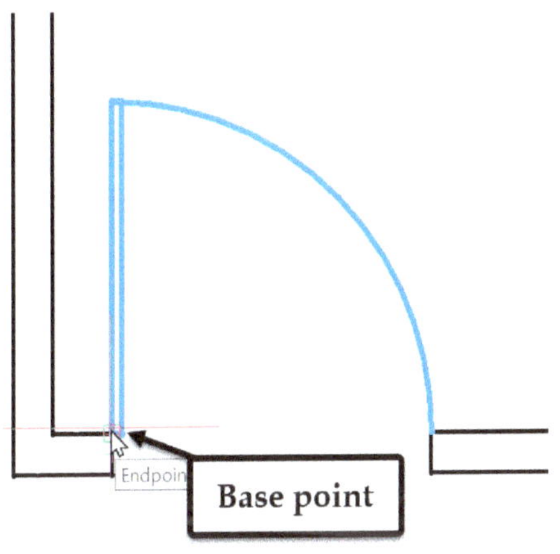

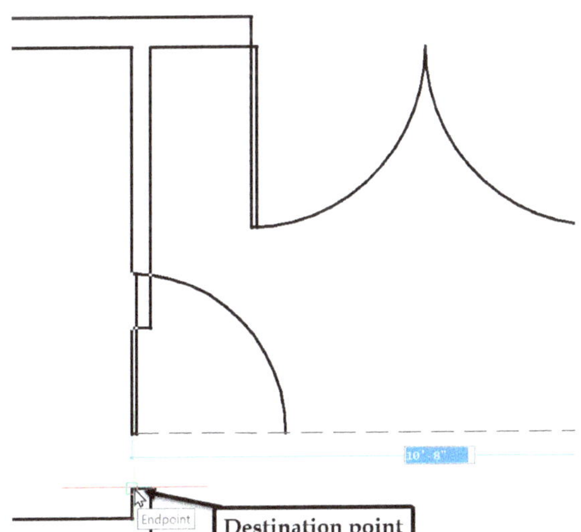

- Press Esc.
- On the ribbon, click **Home > Modify > 2D Rotate**

  , and then select the copied object. Next, press Enter.

- Select the base point, as shown.

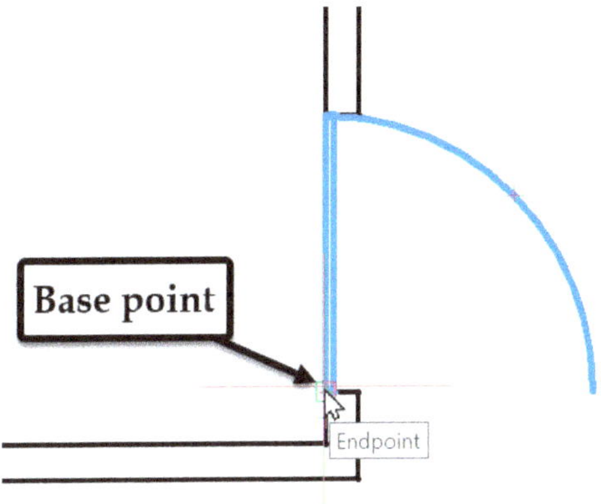

- Move the pointer vertically upward, and then click.

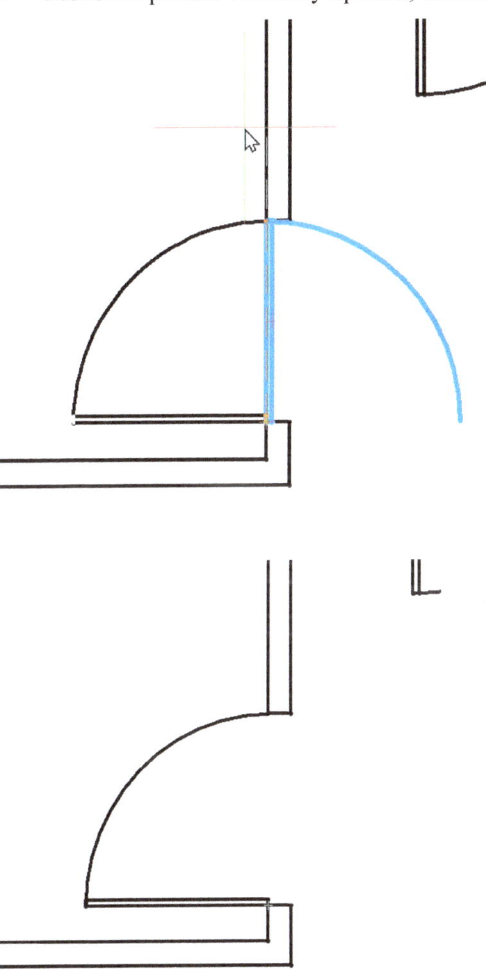

- Create an opening on the rear side of the plan, as shown below.

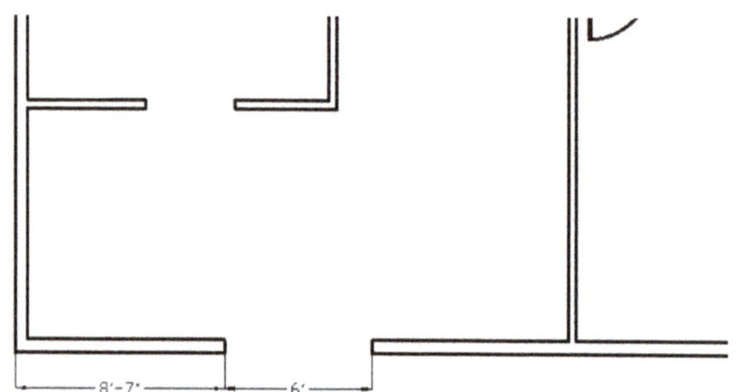

Now, you will create a sliding door in the opening.

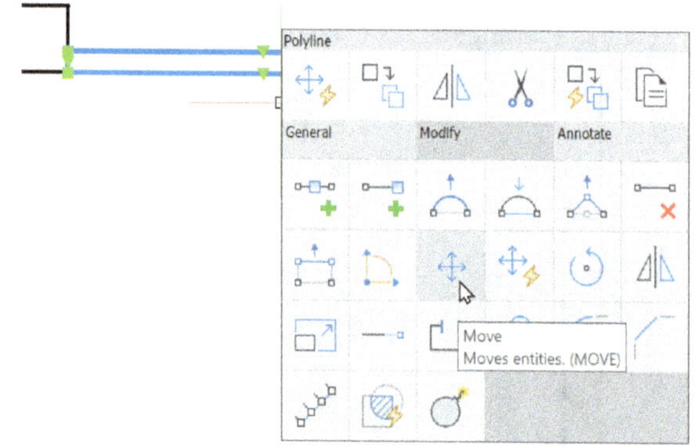

- Activate the **Rectangle by Two Points** command.

- Select the **Dimensions** option from the command line.

- Type 37 and press ENTER to define the length.

- Type 2 and press ENTER to define the width of the rectangle.

- Select the corner point of the opening, as shown below.

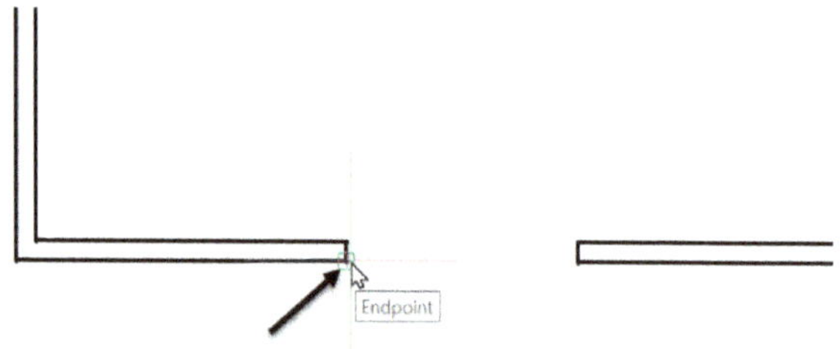

- Move the pointer upward and click to create the rectangle.

- Select the rectangle, and then place the cursor on the Quad to expand it.

- Expand the **Modify** category on the **Quad** and select the **Move** tool.

- Select its lower-left corner point to define the base point. Move the pointer upward and type-in 1 in the command line, and then press Enter.

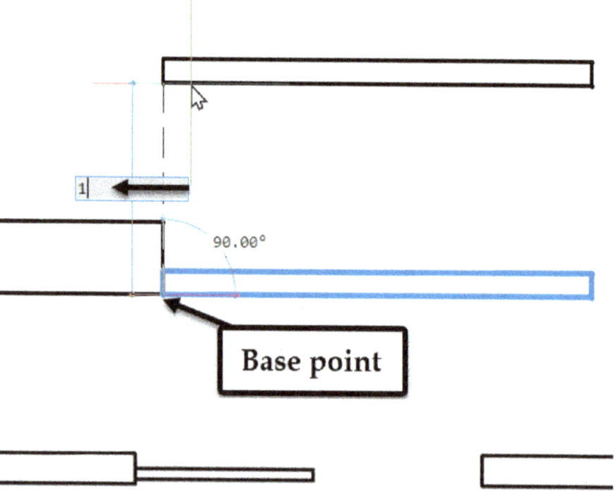

- On the ribbon, click **Draw > Modify > Explode**, and select the rectangle. Press Enter to explode the rectangle.

- Activate the **Offset** command and specify 2 as the offset distance.

- Offset the left and right vertical lines of the rectangle. Press **Esc** to deactivate the **Offset** command.

- Activate the **Line** command and select the midpoints of the offset lines. It creates a line connecting the offset lines. It creates one part of the sliding door.

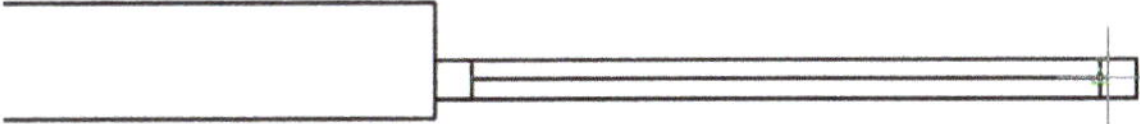

- Press **Esc** to deactivate the **Line** command.
- Type-in **CO** and press Enter. Next, drag a selection window covering all the elements of the sliding door. Press Enter.

- Select the lower-left corner of the sliding door as the base point.
- Move the pointer and select the endpoint of the offset line, as shown.

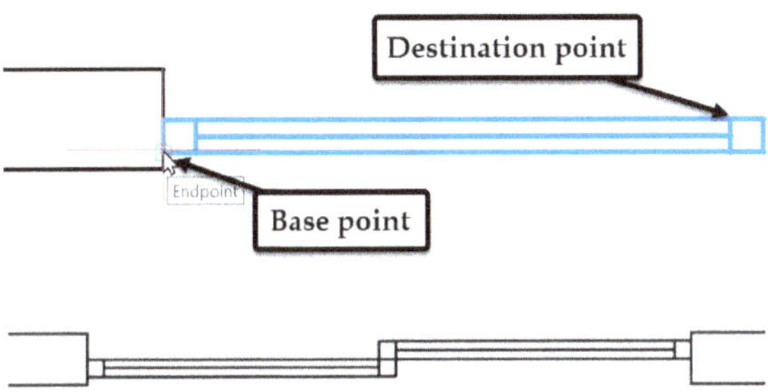

- Press **Esc** to deactivate the **Copy** command.

Now, you need to draw thresholds on the door openings.

- Zoom to the front door area using the **Zoom Window** tool.

- On the ribbon, click **Home > Draw > Rectangle**.
- Select the left corner point of the door opening.
- Move the pointer toward right.

- Type 72 in length box and press the TAB key.
- Type 2 and press ENTER to create the rectangle.

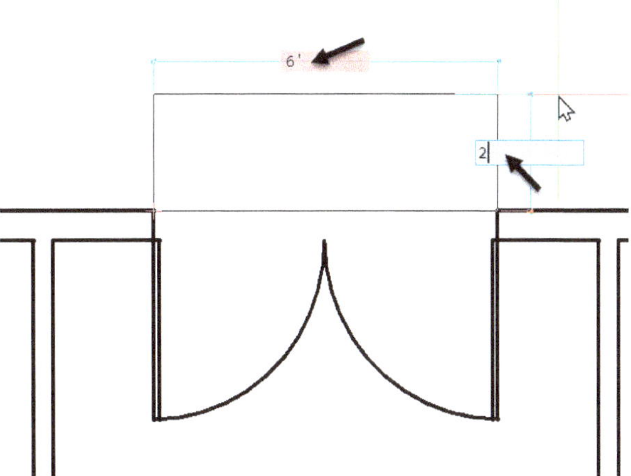

- Select the select newly created rectangle.
- Select the Midpoint grip of the left vertical edge of the rectangle and move the pointer toward left.

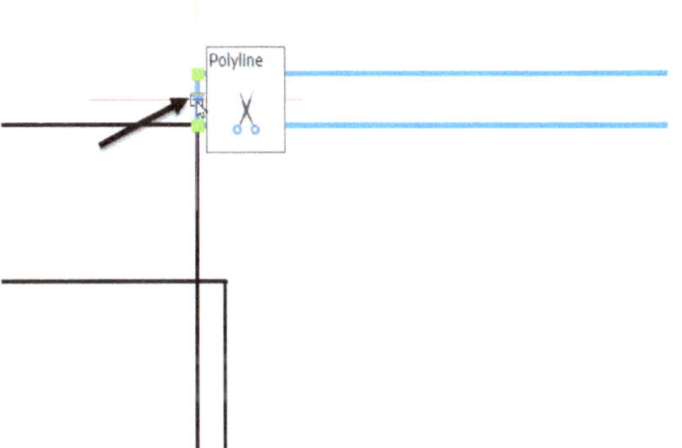

- Type 3 and press ENTER.

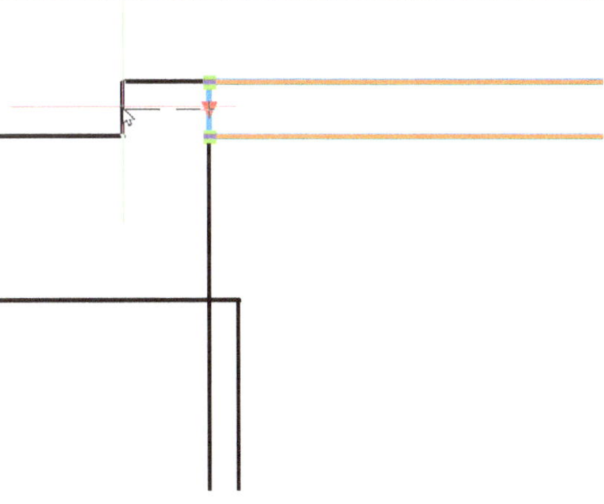

- Select the Midpoint grip of the right vertical edge of the rectangle and move the pointer toward right.

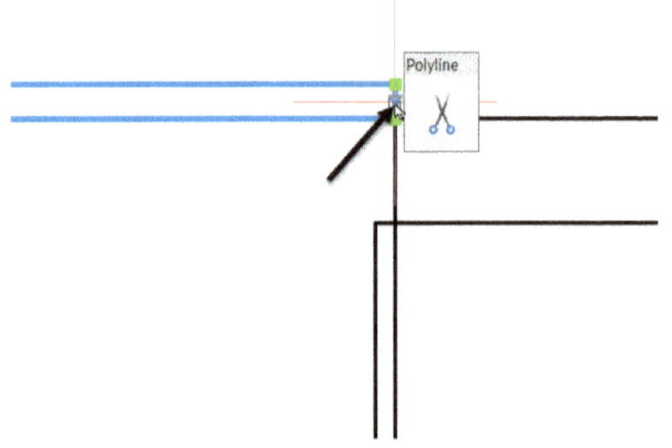

- Type 3 and press ENTER.

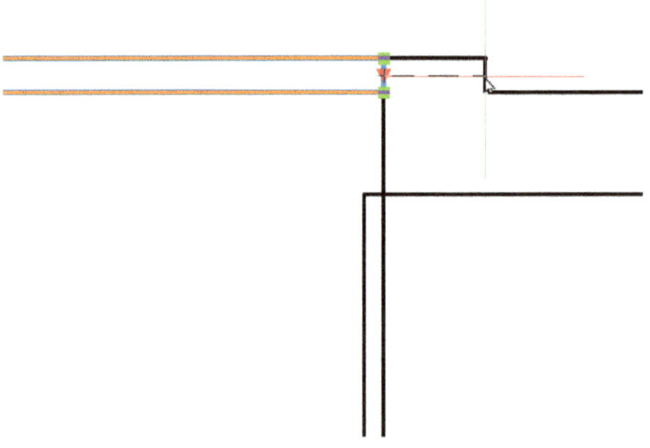

- Likewise, create a threshold on the sliding glass door.

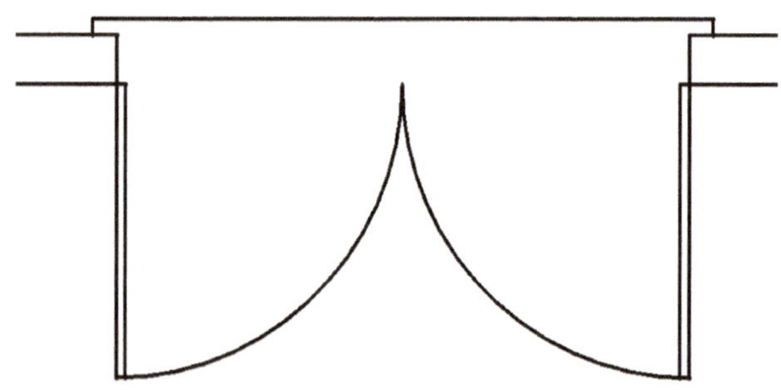

- Select the rectangle and click **Modify > Explode** on the Quad.

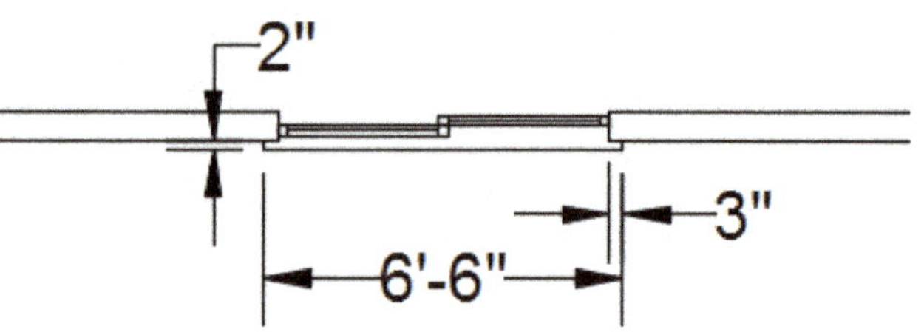

Creating Kitchen Fixtures

- Zoom to the kitchen area by using the **Zoom Window** tool.

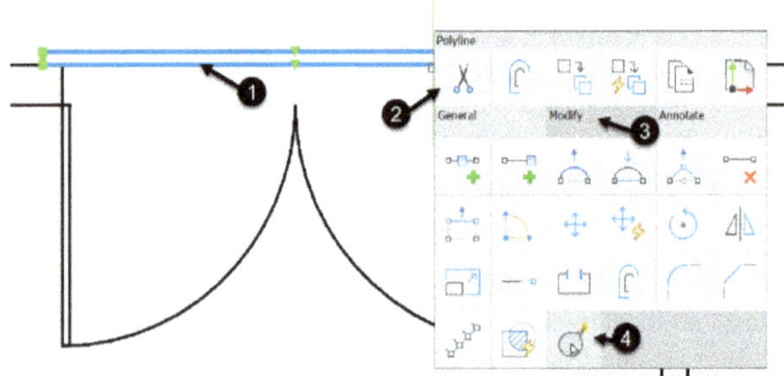

- Select the bottom horizontal line of the rectangle and press DELETE.

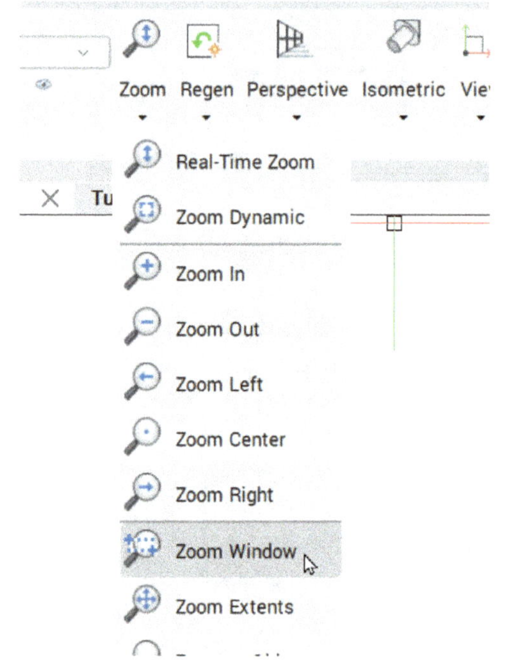

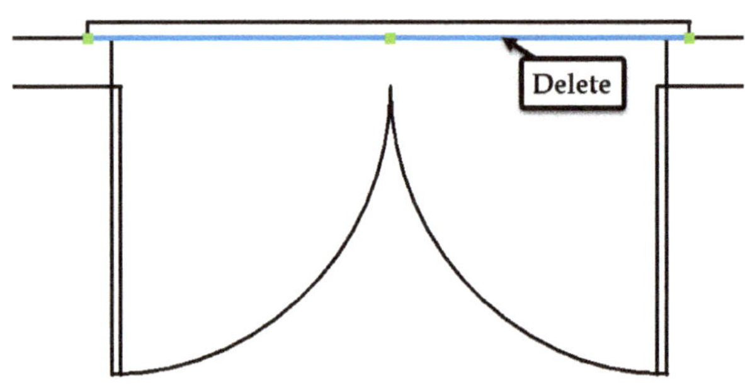

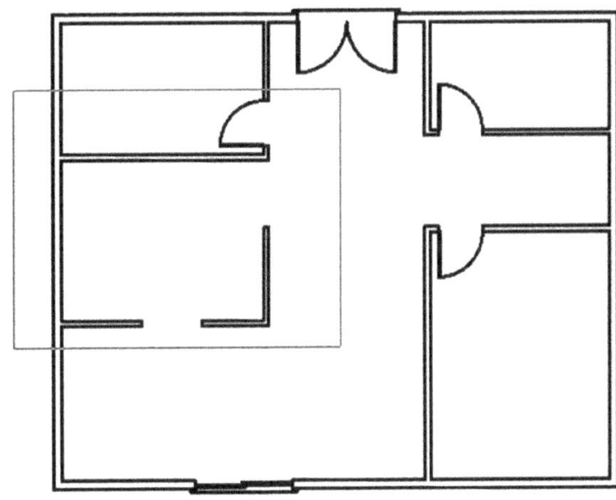

- Activate the **Offset** command and specify **26** as the offset distance. Next, offset the lines shown below.

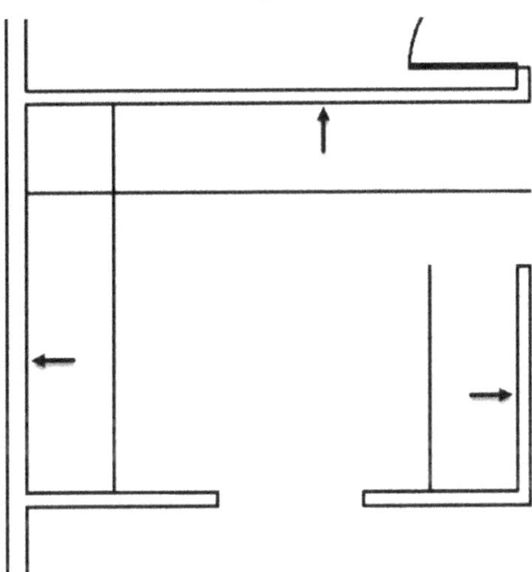

- On the ribbon, click **Home > Modify** > **Trim**. Next, press ENTER to select all the elements.
- Select the unwanted portions, as shown.

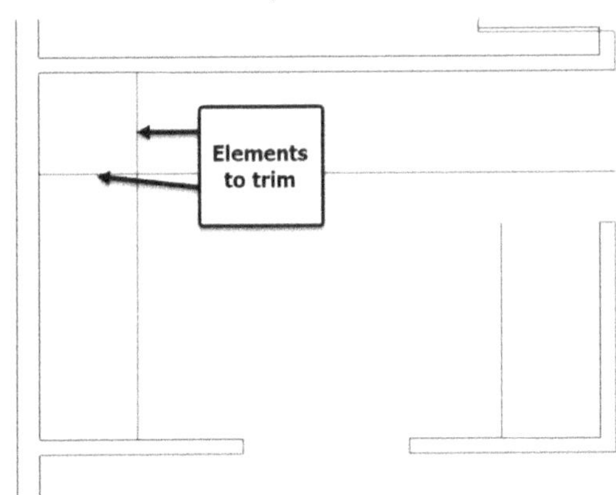

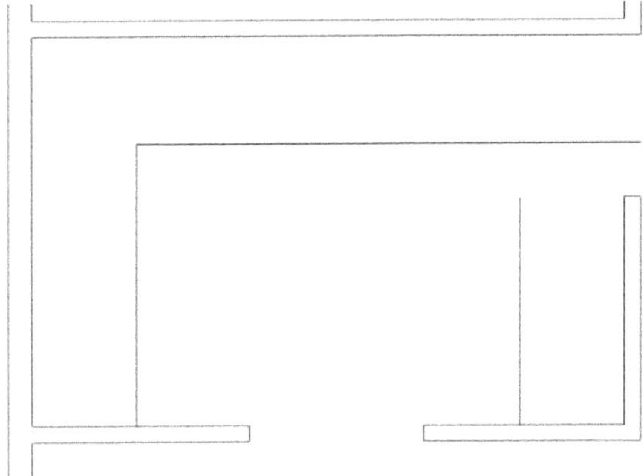

- Create another offset line at **54** distance, and then trim the unwanted elements.

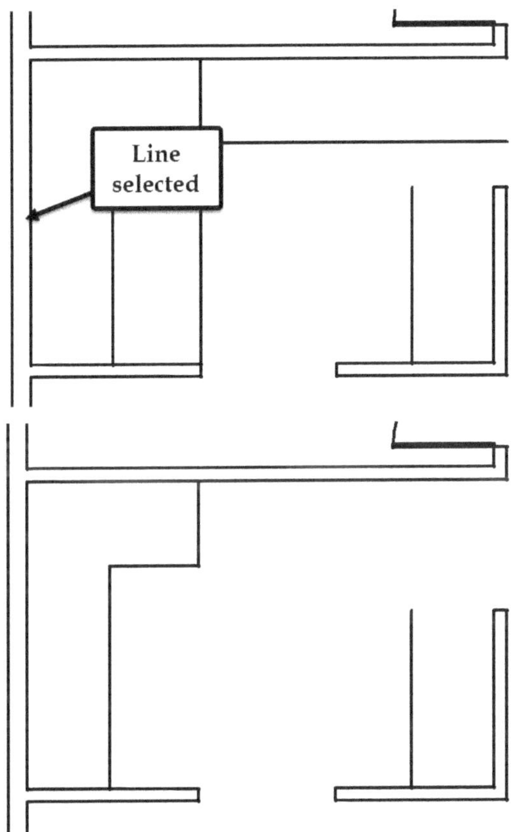

- Create another line, as shown below.

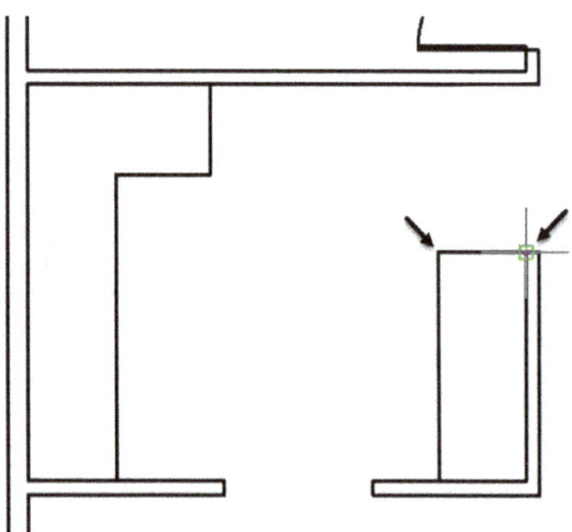

Now, you have finished drawing the counters. You need to draw a refrigerator, stove and sink.

- On the ribbon, click **Home > Draw > Rectangle**.
- Select the **Dimensions** option from the command line.
- Type **28** and press ENTER to define the horizontal dimension.
- Type **28** and press ENTER to define the vertical dimension.
- Select the corner point of the counter.
- Move the pointer towards right and click to create the rectangle.

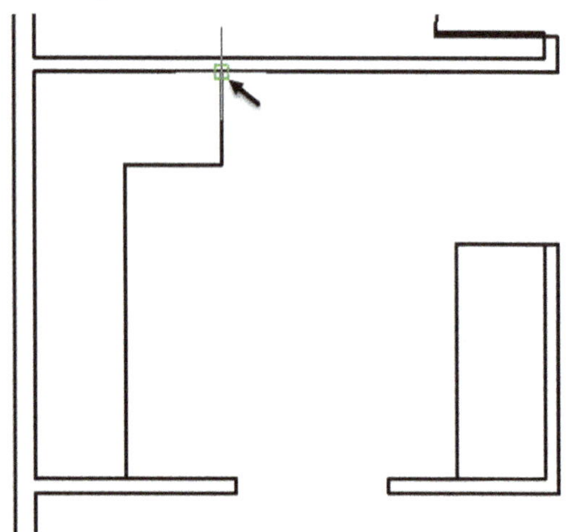

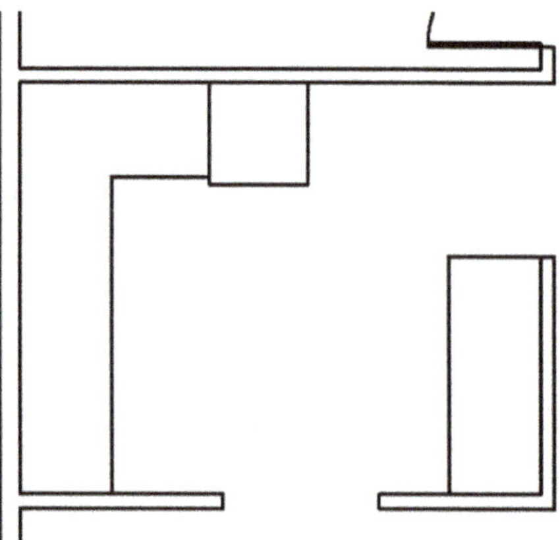

- Select the rectangle and click **Modify > Move** on the Quad.

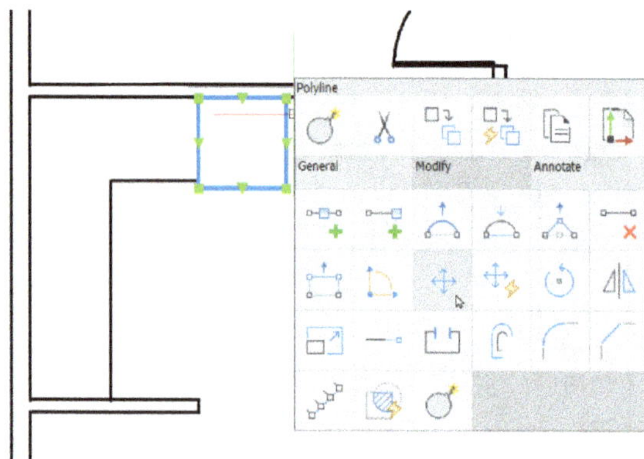

- Select the top left corner of the rectangle. Next, move the pointer toward right and type **2**. Press ENTER to move the rectangle.

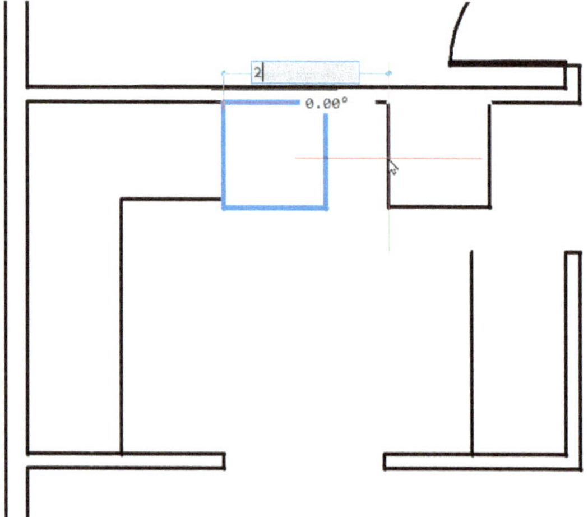

- Likewise, move the rectangle **2** inches and downwards.

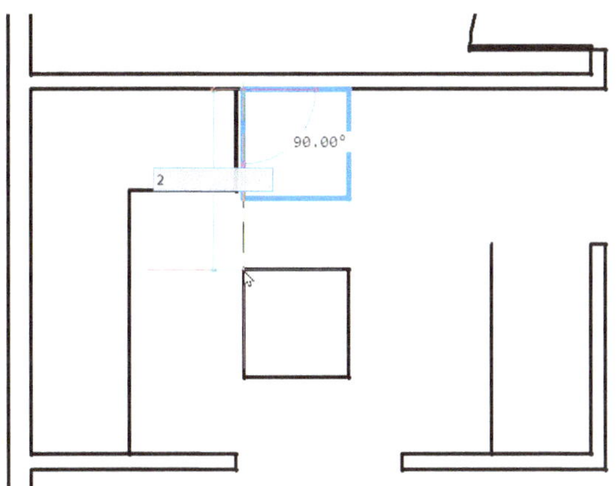

- Create the outline of the stove using the **Offset** and **Trim** commands.

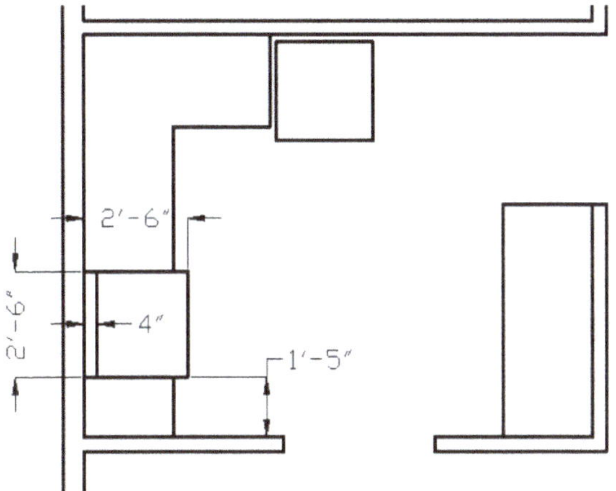

Now, you need to create the sink.

- Use the **Offset** command and create offset lines, as shown below.

- Trim the unwanted elements, as shown below.

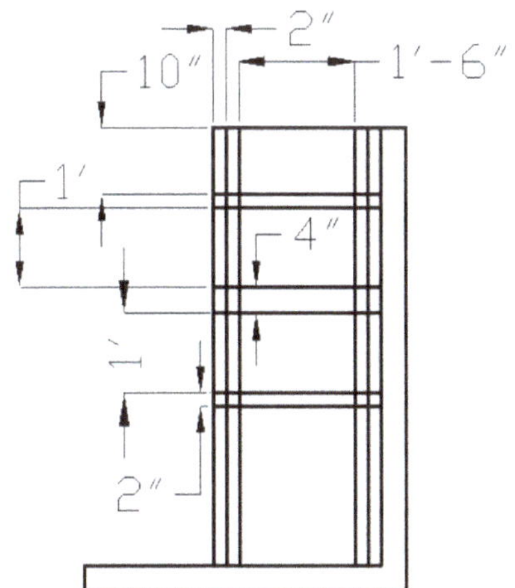

- On the ribbon, click **Home** > **Modify** > **Fillet**.

- Select the **Radius** option from the command line.

- Type **2** in the radius box and click **OK**. Next, select the horizontal and vertical lines forming a corner, as shown.

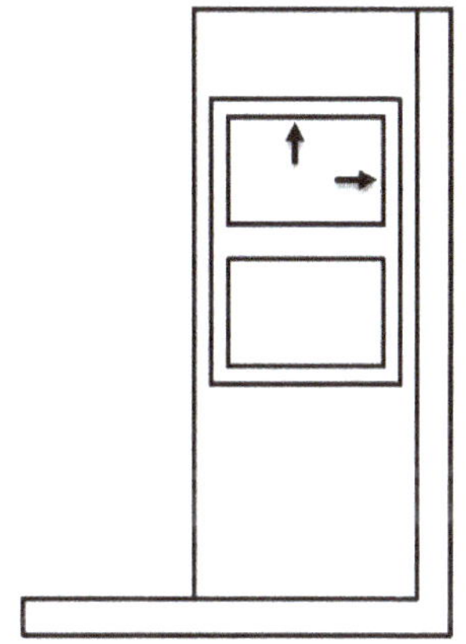

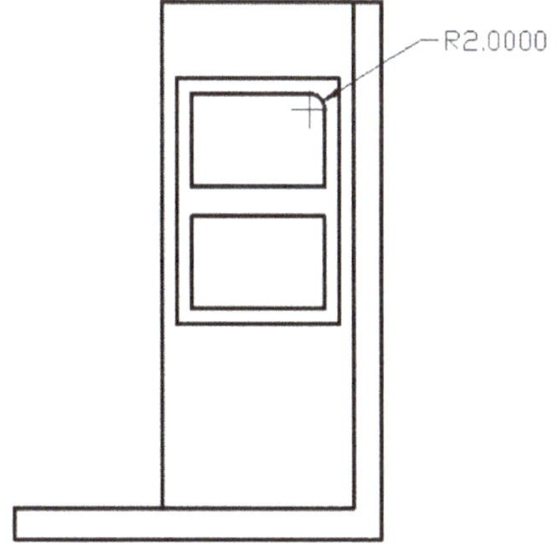

- Likewise, fillet the remaining corners with a fillet radius of 2 and 4, respectively.

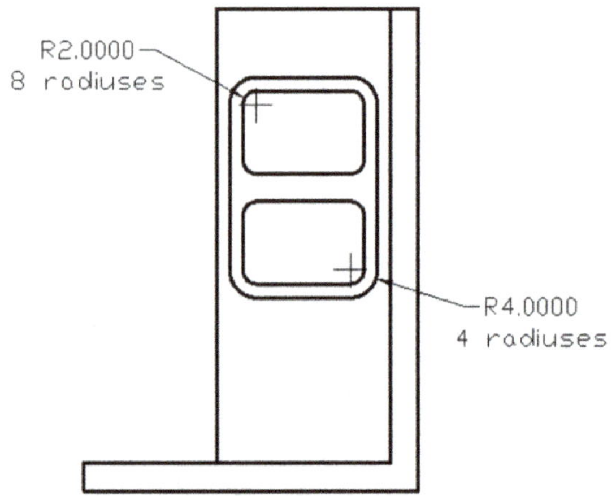

- On the ribbon, click **Home** > **Draw** > **Infinite Line**.

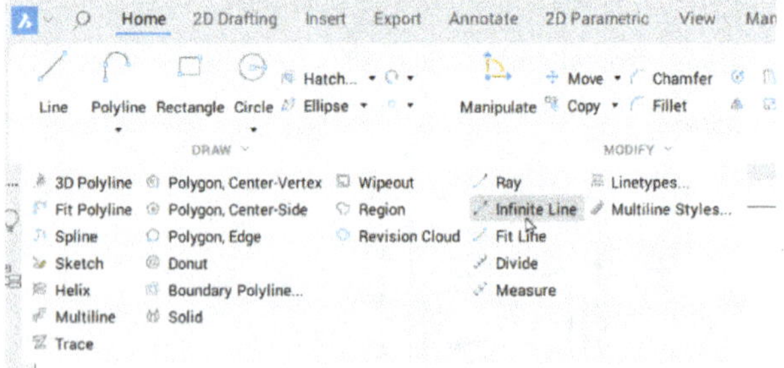

- Select the **Horizontal** option from the command line.

- Select the midpoint of the vertical line, as shown.

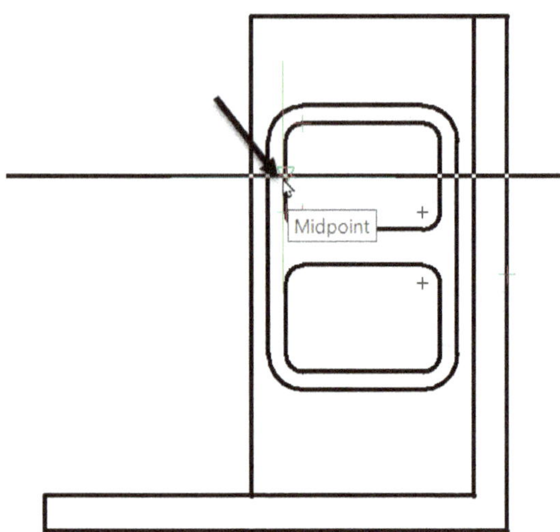

- Likewise, create another horizontal construction line by selecting the midpoint of the vertical line, as shown.

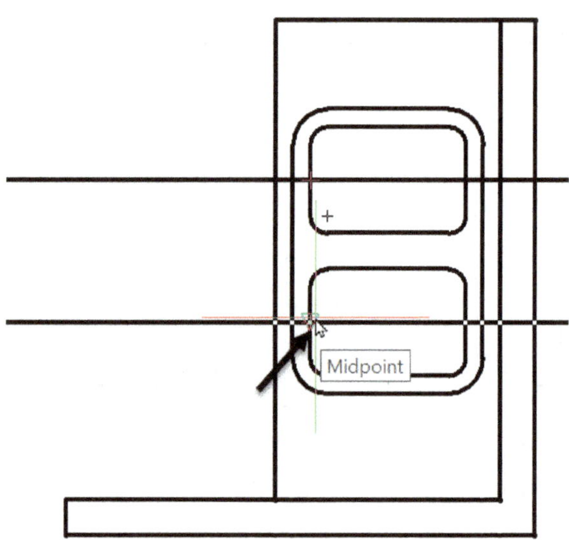

- Press ENTER twice to deactivate the **Infinite Line** command and then activate it again.

- Select the **Vertical** option from the command line.

- Select the midpoint of the horizontal line, as shown.

- Press **Esc** to deactivate the **Infinite Line** command.

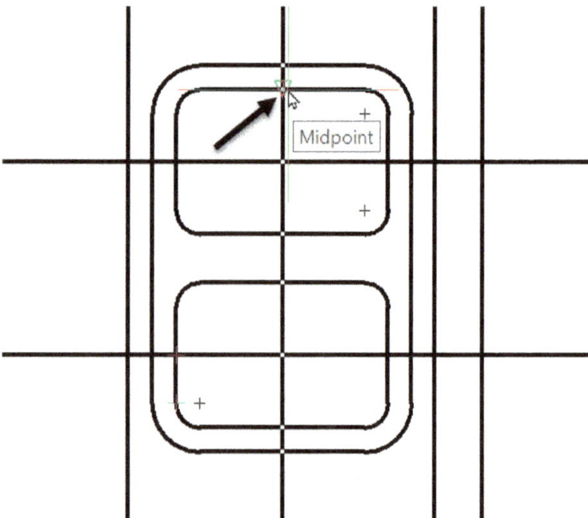

- On the ribbon, click **Home** > **Draw** > **Circle** drop-down > **Circle Center-Diameter**.

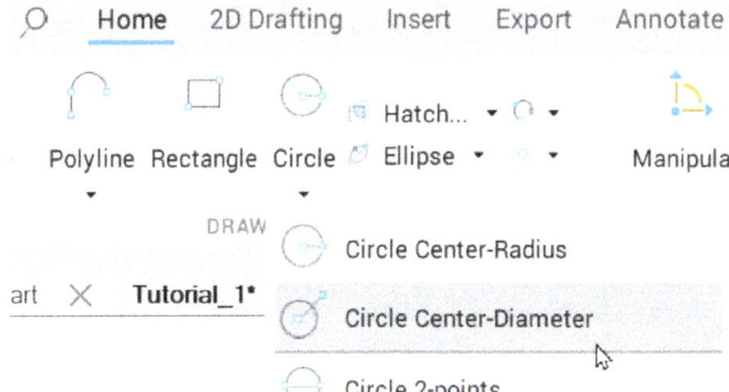

- Select the intersection point of the two infinite lines, as shown.

- Move the pointer outward, and then type **4**. Next, press ENTER.

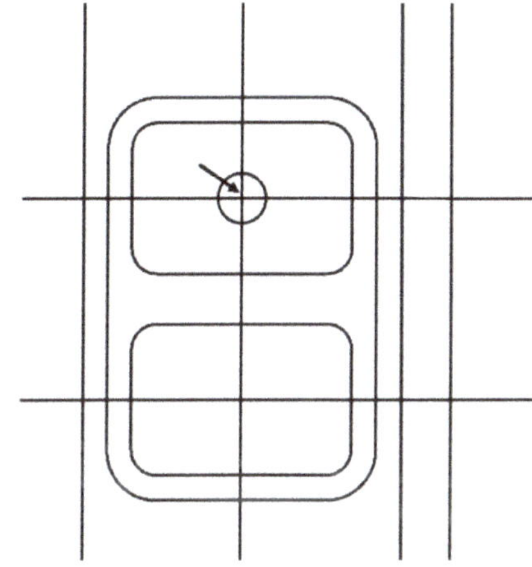

- Press ENTER and select the intersection point of the infinite lines.

- Select the **Diameter** option from the command line.

- Move the pointer outward, type **6**, and press ENTER.

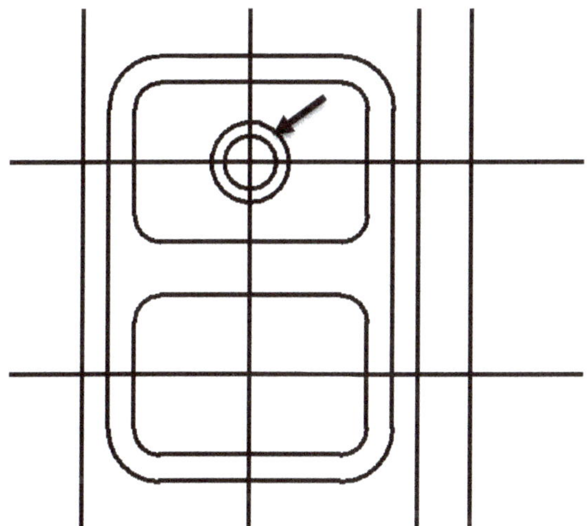

- Likewise, create two more circles, as shown. Next, delete the infinite lines.

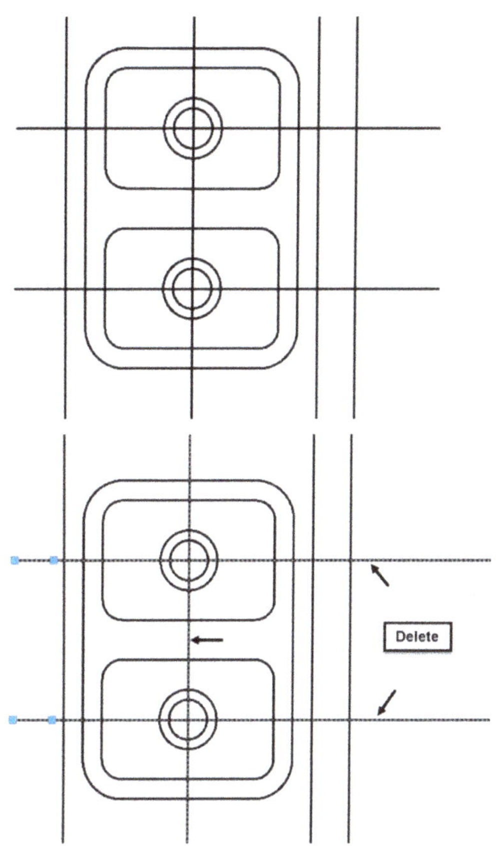

Creating Bathroom Fixtures

- Zoom into the bathroom area and create offset lines, as shown below.

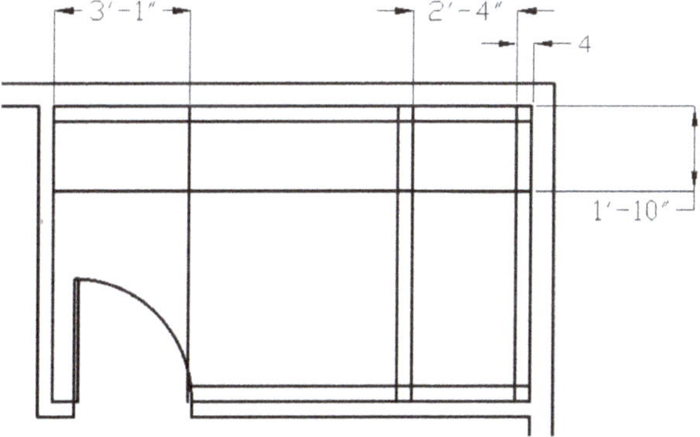

- Trim the unwanted elements, as shown below.

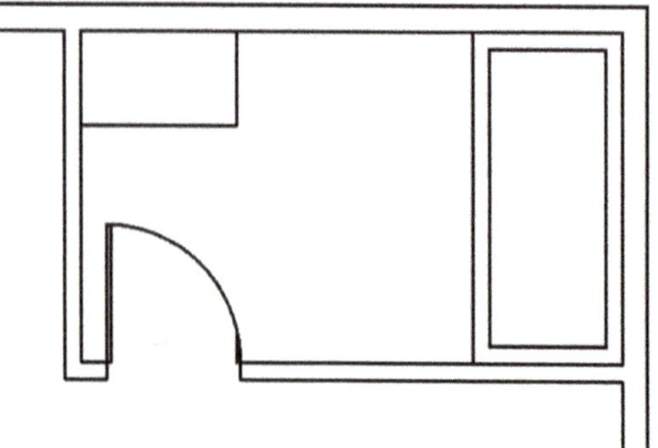

- Fillet the corners, as shown below. The fillet radius is **4**.

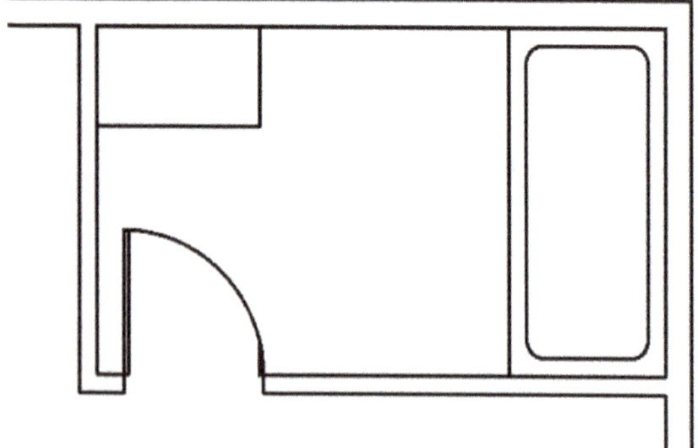

- Create two infinite lines, as shown.

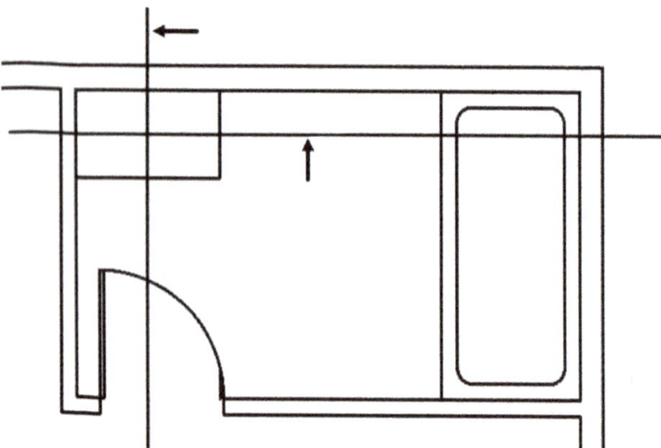

- On the ribbon, click Home > **Draw** > **Ellipse** drop-down > **Ellipse Center-Axes**.

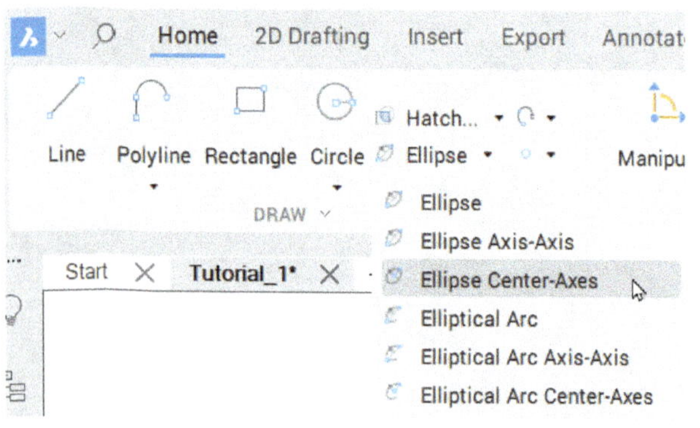

- Select the intersection point of the construction lines, as shown.

- Move the pointer toward the right and type in **10**, and then press Enter. It defines the major radius of the ellipse.

- Move the pointer downward and type in **5**, and then press Enter. It defines the minor radius of the ellipse.

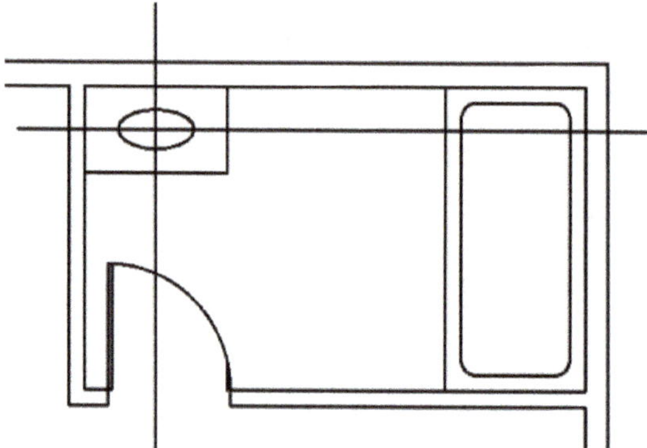

- Likewise, create another ellipse of **11** major radius and **7** minor radius.

- Delete the construction lines.

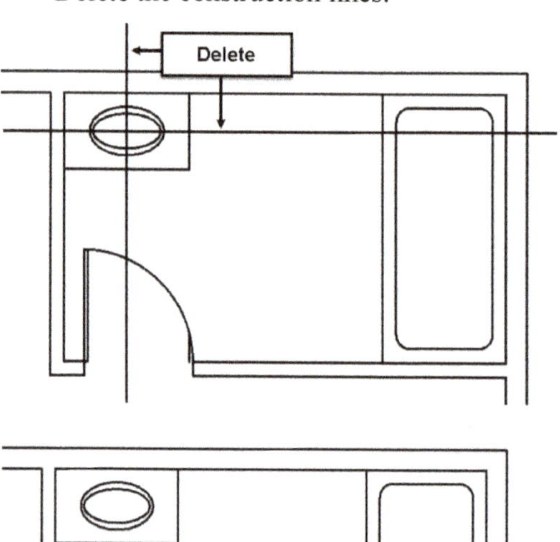

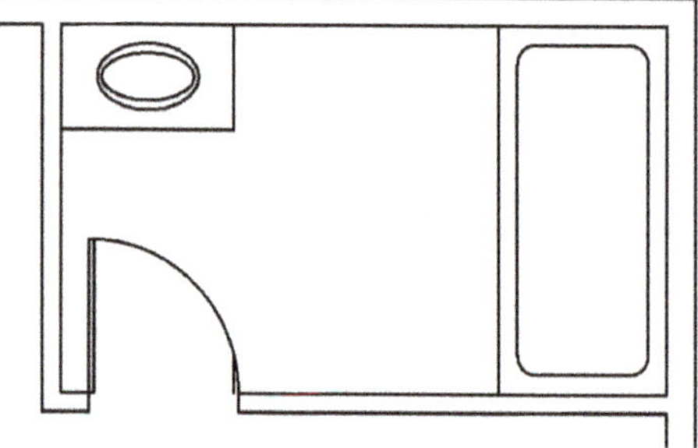

- Select the outer ellipse, and then click on its center point.

- Move the pointer up and type-in **1**, and then press Enter. The outer ellipse moves up.

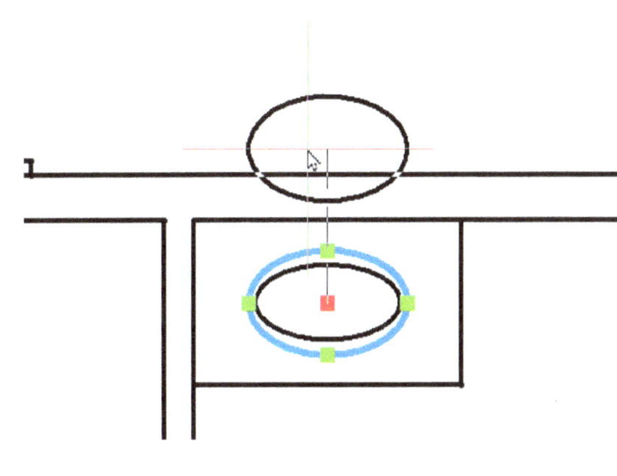

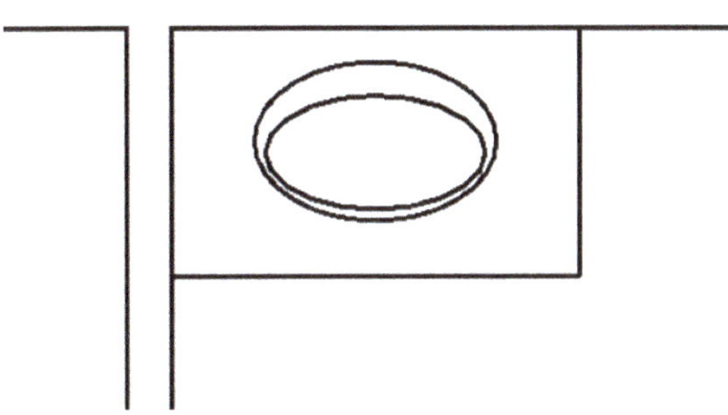

- Move the rectangle up to **19.5** rightwards and **1** downwards.

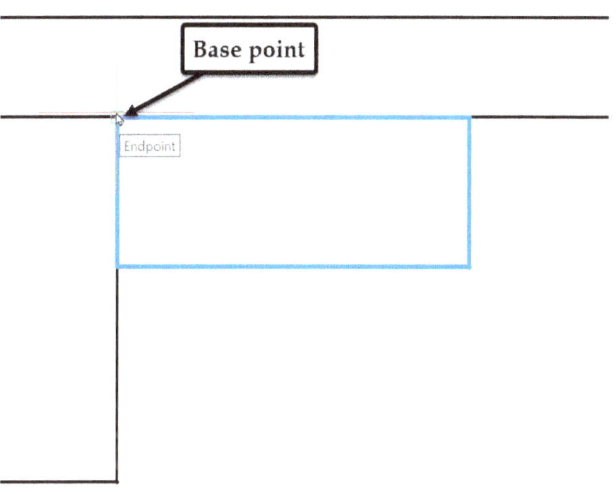

- On the ribbon, click **Home** > **Draw** > **Rectangle**.
- Select the Dimensions option from the command line.
- Type **22** and press ENTER.
- Type **9** and press ENTER.
- Select the top-right corner of the washbasin.

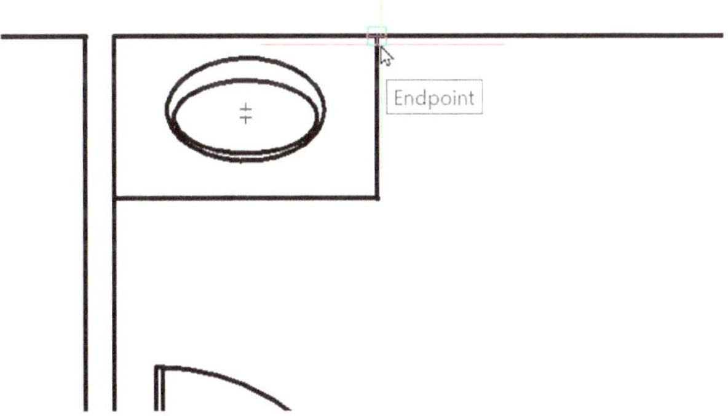

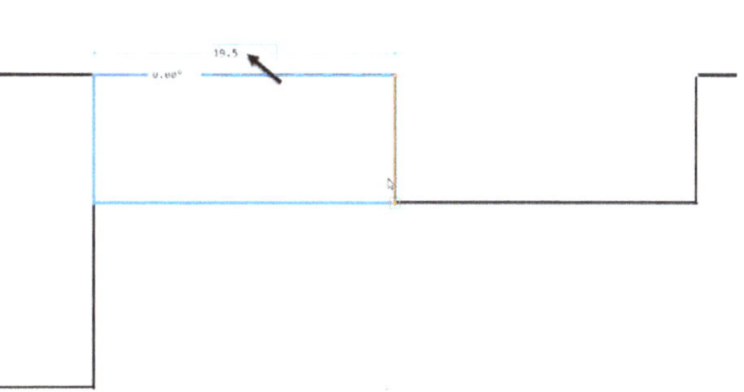

- Move the cursor toward right and click.

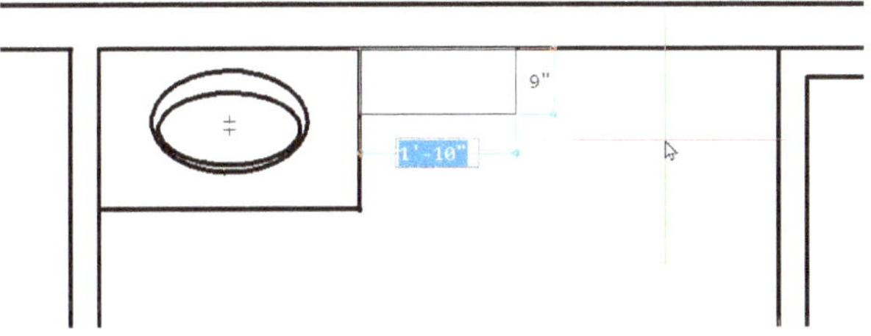

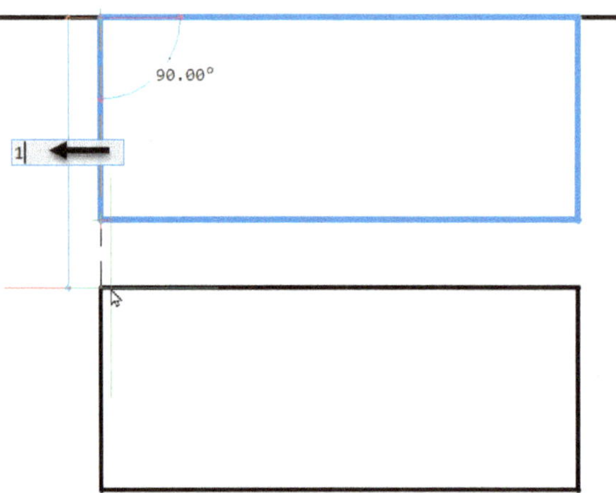

- On the ribbon, click **Home** >**Draw > Ellipse > Ellipse**.
- Select the midpoint of the lower horizontal line of the rectangle.

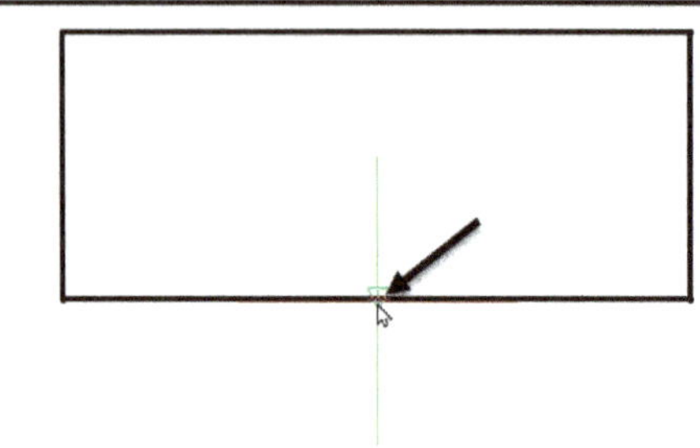

- Move the pointer downward and type in **18**, and then press Enter.

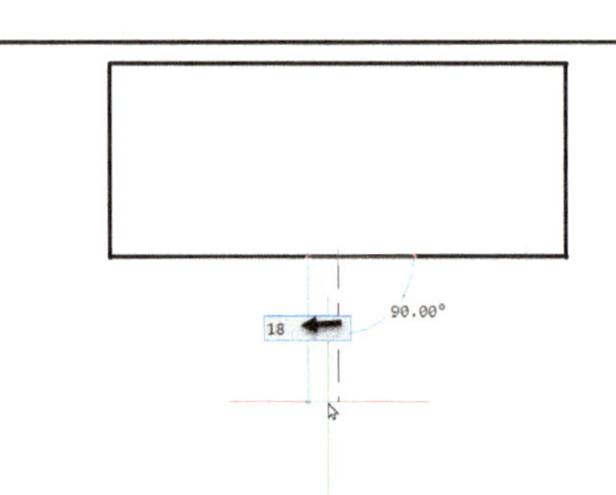

- Move the pointer towards right and type-in **6** as the minor axis and press Enter.

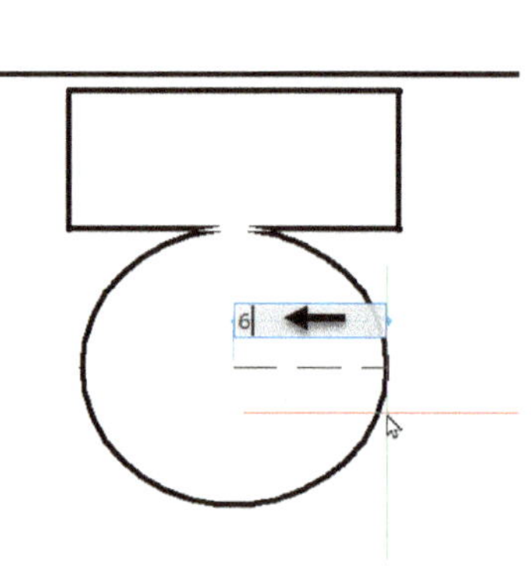

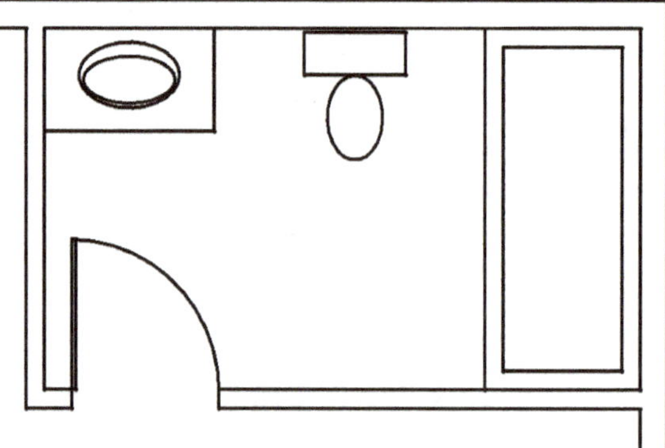

Adding Furniture using Blocks

- On the ribbon, click **Home** > **Draw** > **Rectangle**.
- Select **Dimensions** from the command line.
- Type **72** as the length of the rectangle and press ENTER.
- Type **36** as the width of the rectangle and press ENTER.
- Click in the empty space to specify the first corner of the rectangle.
- Click to create the rectangle.

- On the ribbon, click Home > **Draw** > **Rectangle**.
- Select the **Dimensions** option from the command line.

- Type **18** as the length of the rectangle and press ENTER.
- Type **18** as the width of the rectangle and press ENTER.
- Click in the empty space to specify the first corner of the rectangle.
- Click to create the rectangle.

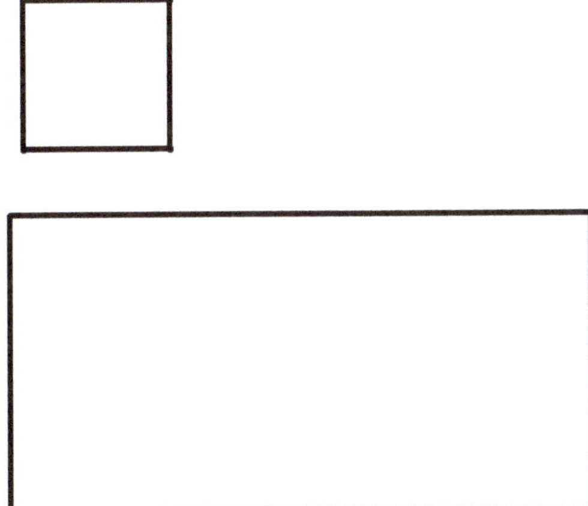

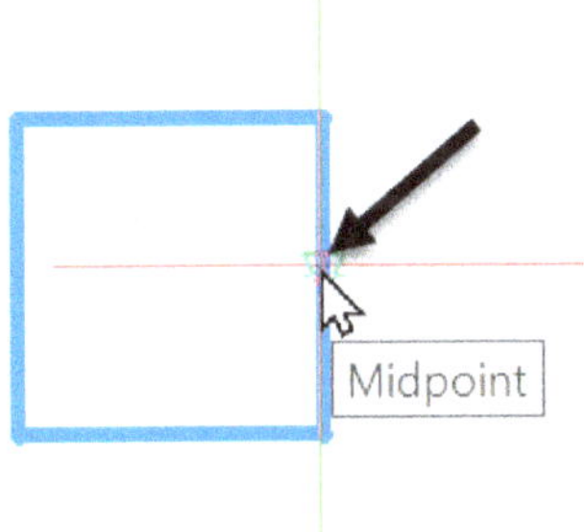

- Type **ALIGN** in the command line and press ENTER. Next, select the second rectangle and press ENTER.
- Select the midpoint of the right vertical line as the first source point, as shown.

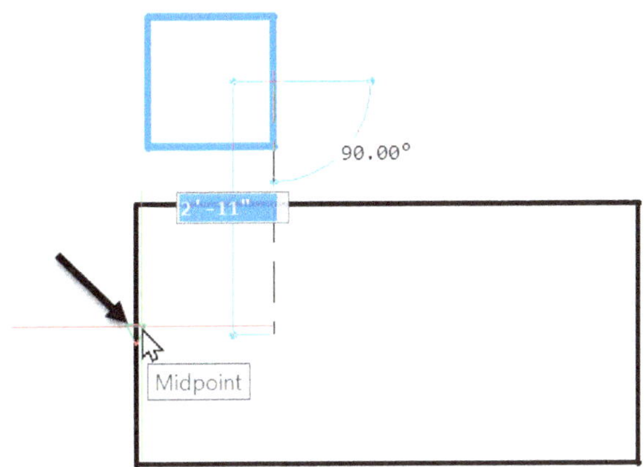

- Select the midpoint of the left vertical line of the first rectangle, as shown.

- Press ENTER to align the midpoints of the two rectangles.

- Type M in the command line and press Enter to activate the **Move** command. Next, select the second rectangle and press Enter.
- Select the midpoint of the vertical line as a Basepoint, as shown.

- Move the pointer horizontally towards left and type 1. Press Enter.

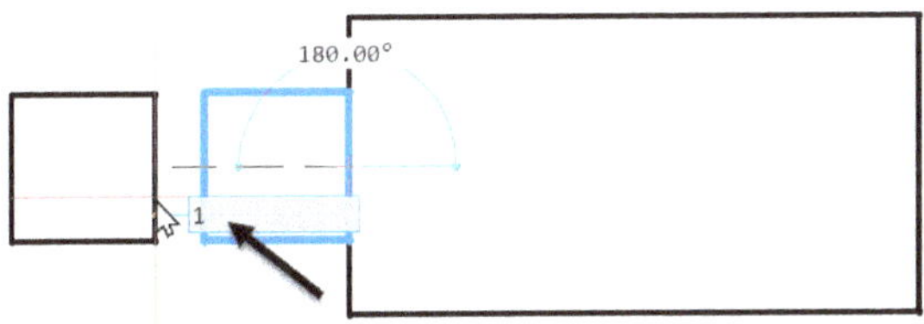

- On the ribbon, click **Home > Modify > Chamfer**.

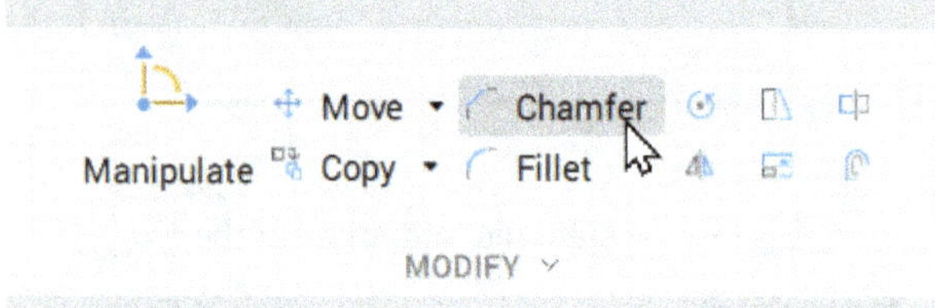

- Select the **Distance** option from the command line.
- Type **2** and press ENTER to define the distance on the first entity.
- Type **18** and press ENTER to define the distance on the second entity.
- Select the left vertical and bottom horizontal edges of the rectangle, as shown.

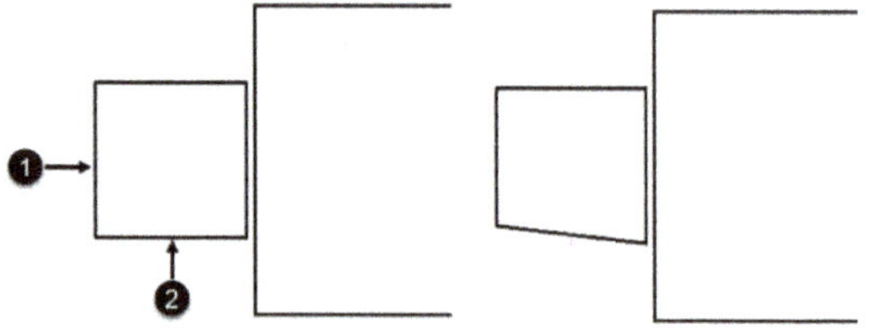

- Press ENTER to activate the Chamfer command.
- Select the left vertical and top horizontal edges of the rectangle. Next, press ESC to deactivate the command.

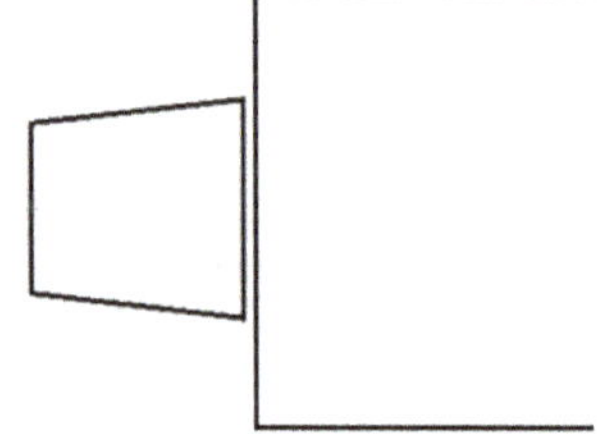

- Select the chamfered rectangle and click **Modify > 2D Mirror** on the Quad.

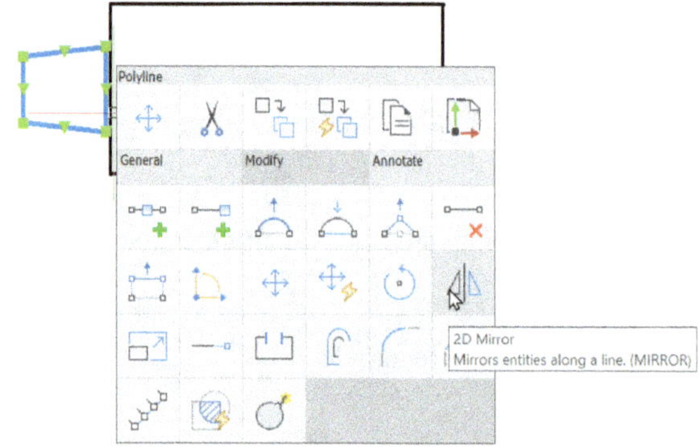

- Select the midpoint of the lower horizontal edge of the large rectangle.
- Move the pointer vertically upward and click to define the mirror line.

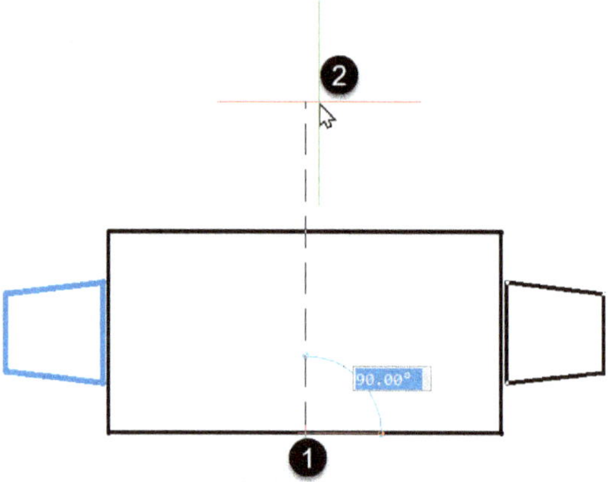

- Next, select **No-keep entities** option from the command line to keep the original object.
- Select the chamfered rectangle on the left side.
- Click **Modify > 2D Rotate** on the Quad.

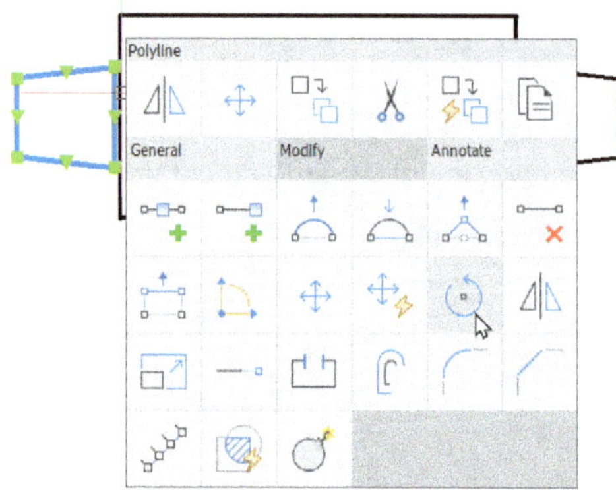

- Select the midpoint of the top horizontal edge of the large rectangle.

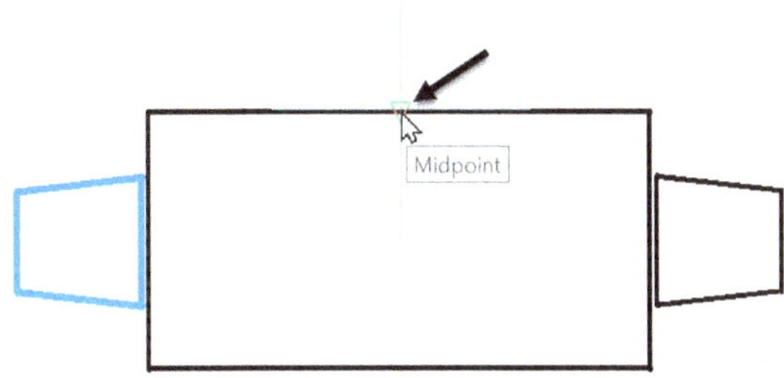

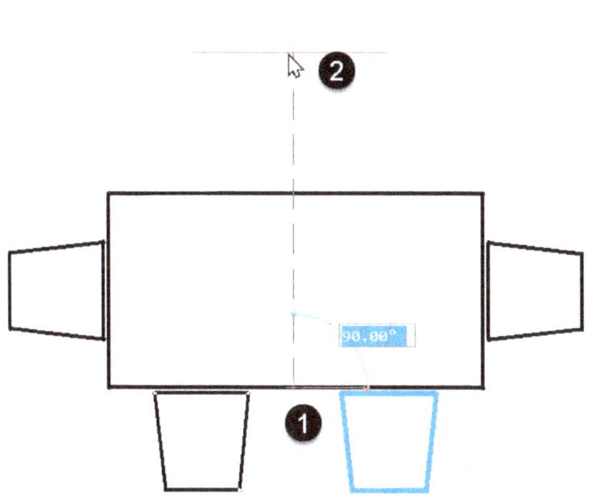

- Select the **Copy** option from the Command Line.
- Move the pointer vertically upward and click to copy the selected entity.

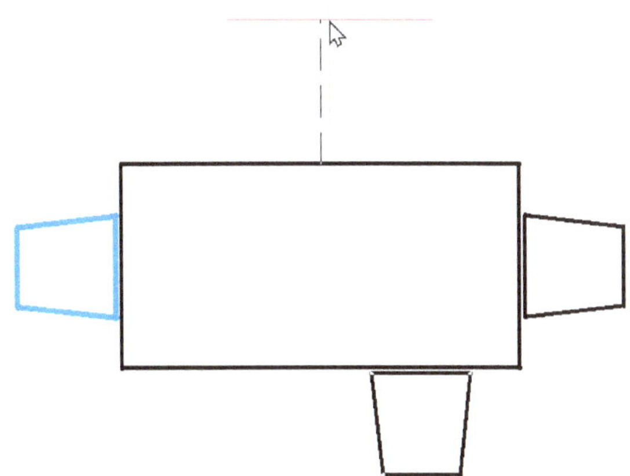

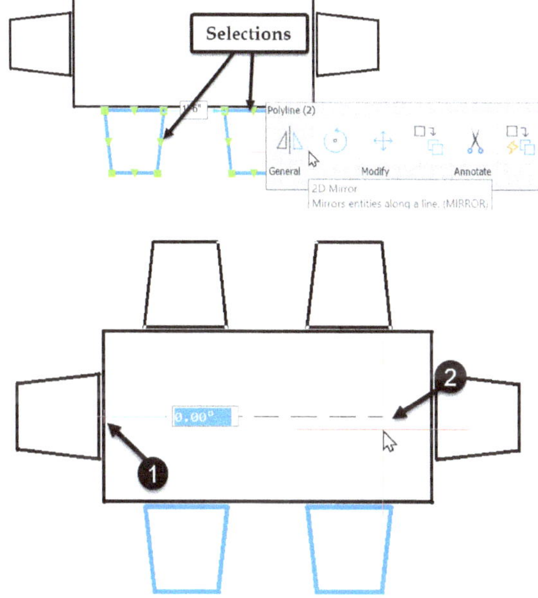

- Mirror the rotated rectangle, as shown.

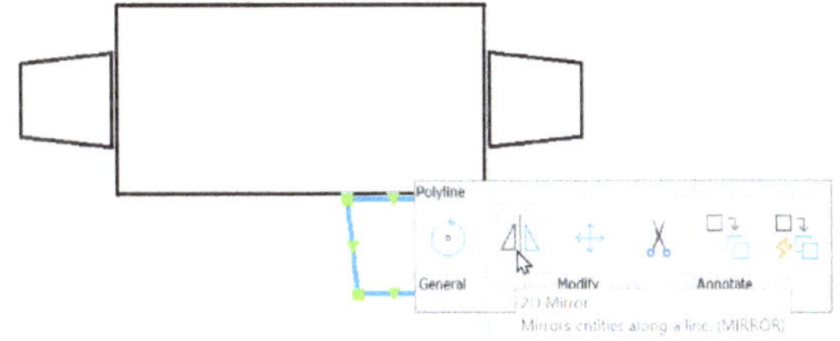

- On the ribbon, click **Home > Draw > Rectangle**.
- Select **Dimensions** from the command line.
- Type **80** as the length of the rectangle and press ENTER.
- Type **62** as the width of the rectangle and press ENTER.
- Click in the empty space.
- Move the cursor and to create the rectangle.

- Press ENTER and select the midpoint of the right vertical edge of the rectangle.
- Type **15** as the length of the rectangle and press TAB.
- Type **20** as the width of the rectangle and press ENTER to create another rectangle, as shown.

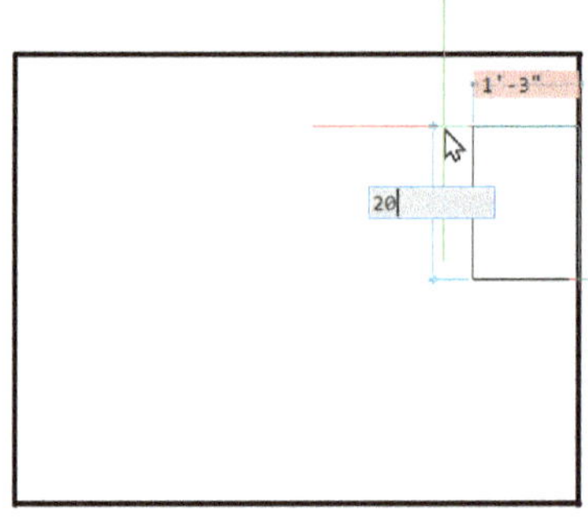

- Select the newly created rectangle.
- Click **Modify > Move** on the Quad.
- Click on the lower right corner of the rectangle as a Basepoint.
- Move the pointer towards left and type **2** in the command line. Press Enter.

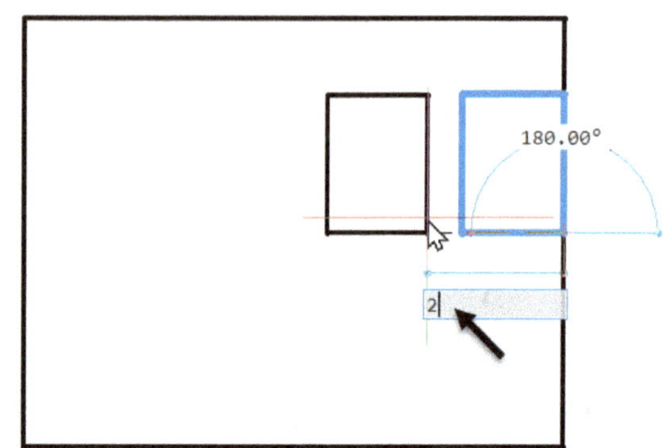

- Likewise, move the rectangle upwards by **2** inches, as shown.

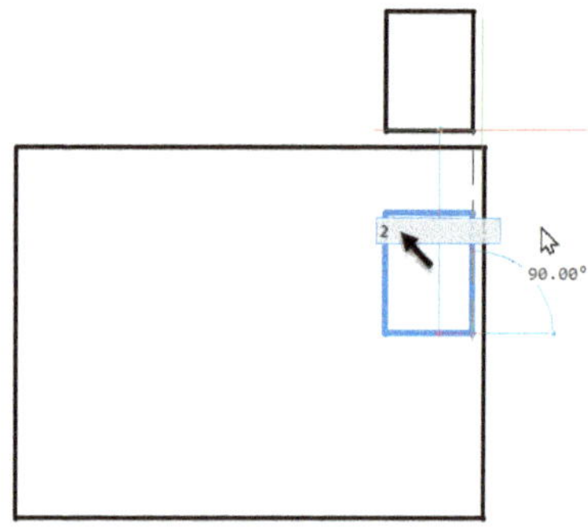

- Create a mirrored copy of the rectangle, as shown.

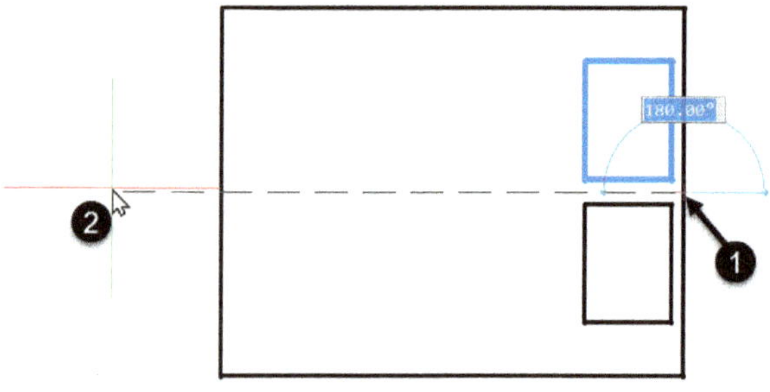

- Select the large rectangle of the bed and click **Modify > Explode** on the Quad.

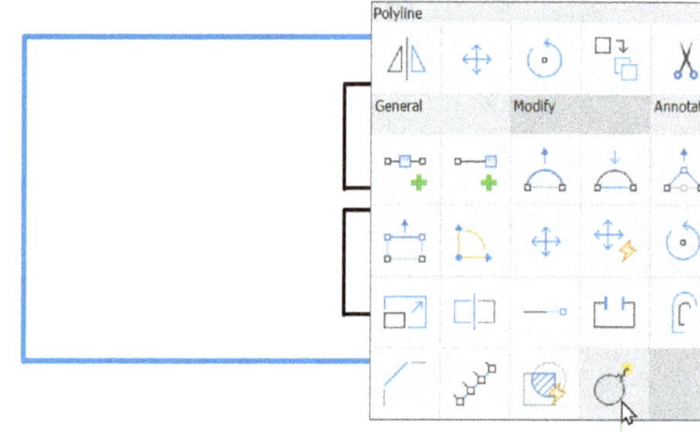

- Select the right vertical line of the exploded rectangle and click **Modify** > **Offset** on the Quad.
- Next, move the pointer toward the left.
- Type **14** in the command line and press ENTER.

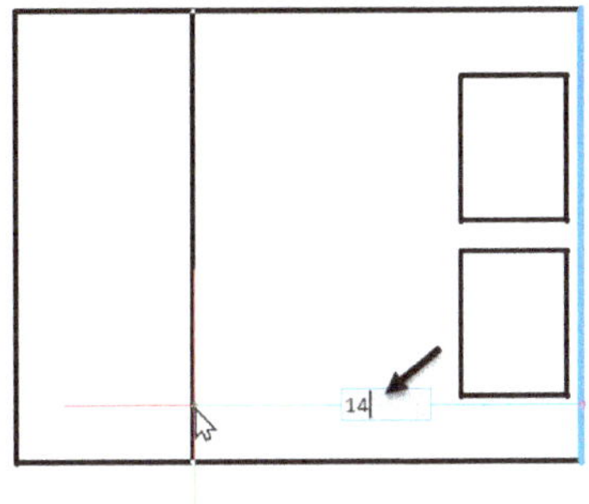

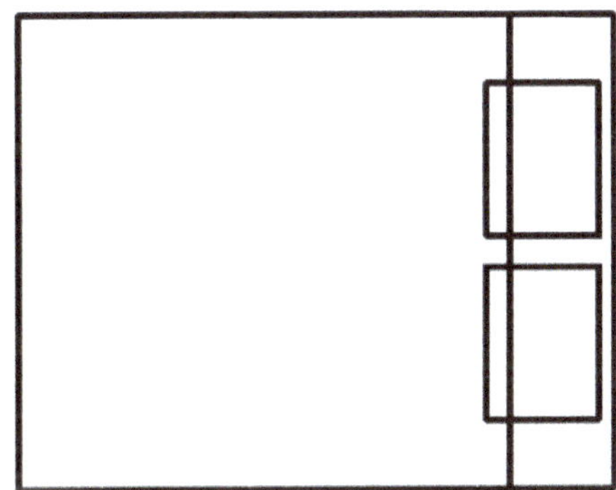

- Press ENTER to activate the **Offset** command. Type **4** in the command line and press ENTER.
- Select the offset line and move the pointer toward the left. Next, click to create another offset line.

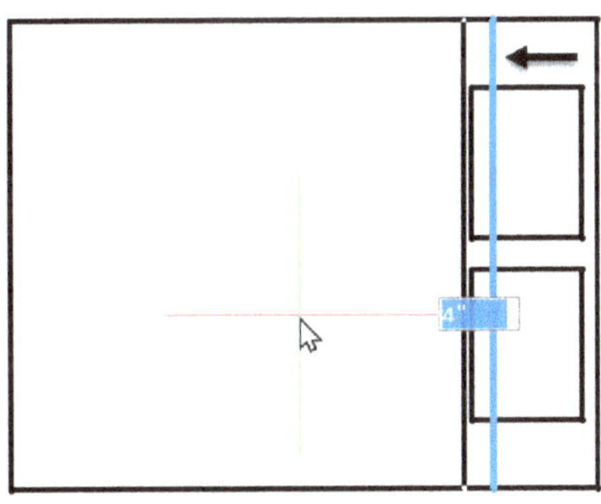

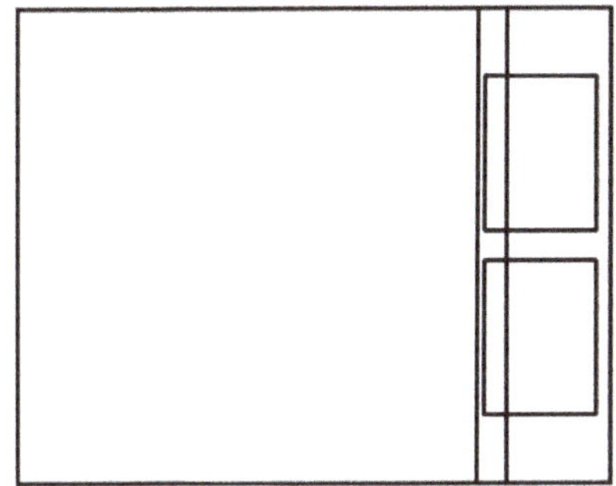

- Click **Home** > **Draw** > **Rectangle** on the ribbon.
- Select the lower endpoint of the first offset line.
- Move the pointer upward.

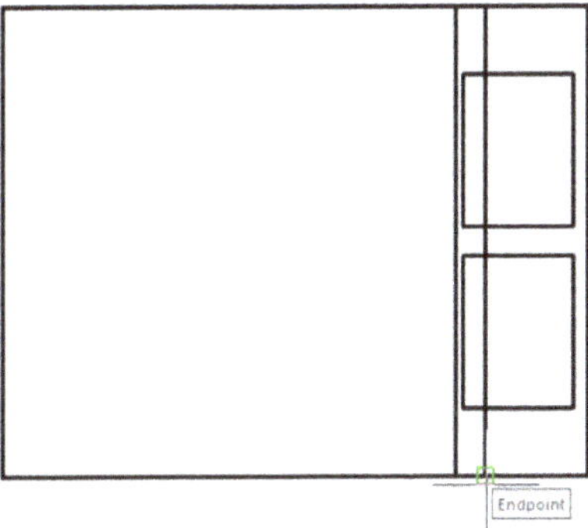

- Type **15** and press TAB to define the length of the rectangle.
- Type **15** and press ENTER to define the width of the rectangle.

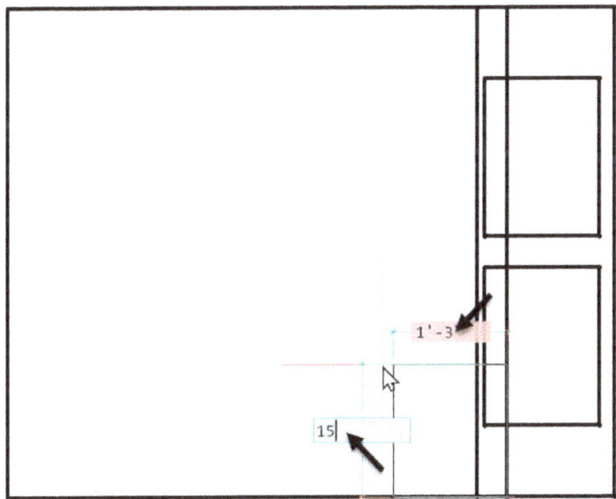

- On the ribbon, click **Home** > **Draw** > **Line**. Next, select the top-right and bottom-left corners of the newly created rectangle.

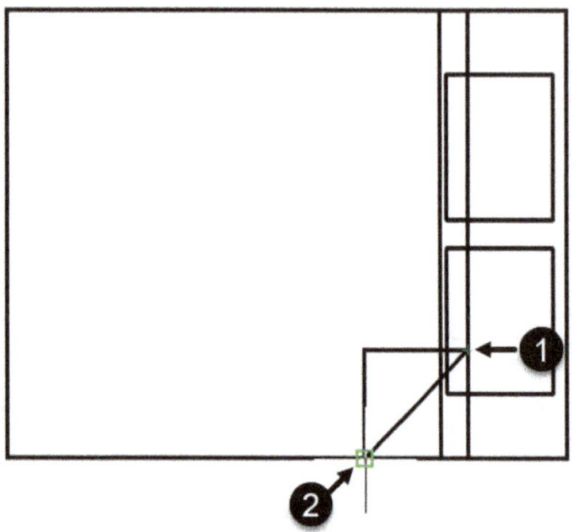

- Press **Esc** to deactivate the **Line** command.
- Select the newly created rectangle and click **Modify > Explode** on the Quad.

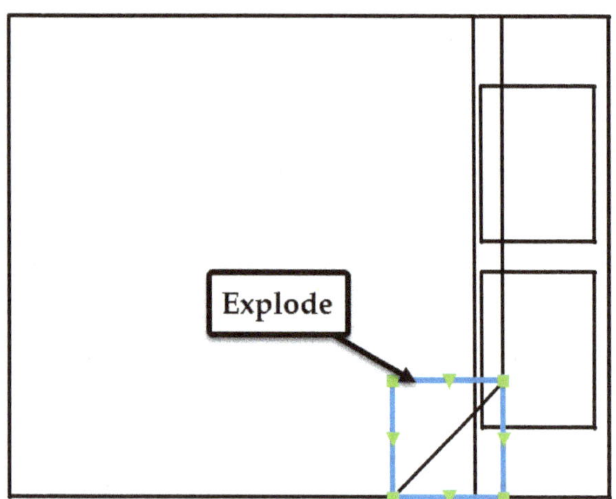

- Select the right vertical edge of the exploded rectangle and press DELETE.

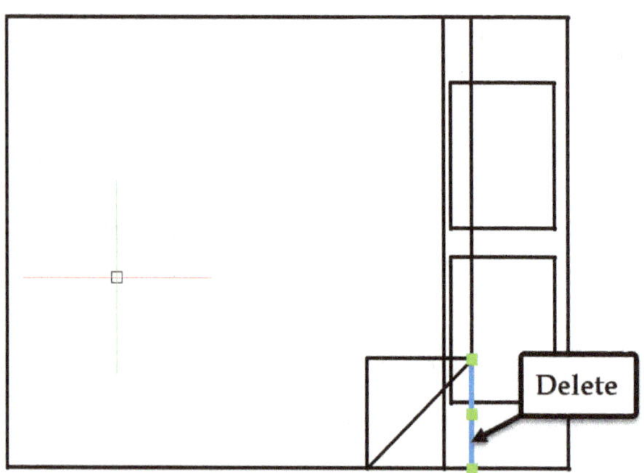

- Likewise, delete the bottom horizontal edge of the exploded rectangle.

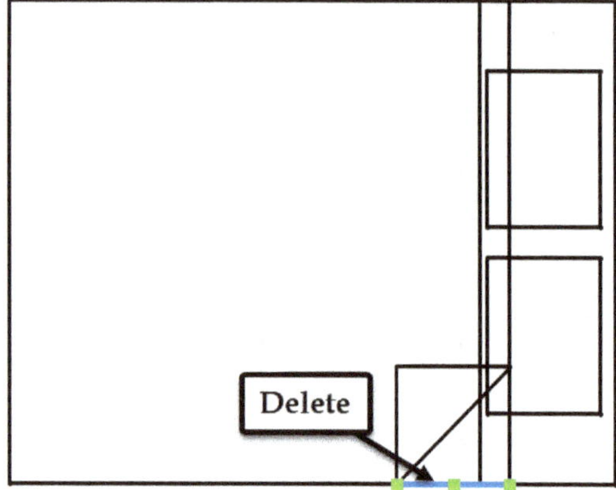

- On the ribbon, click **Modify > Trim**. Next, press ENTER.
- Trim the unwanted portions of the rectangles and offset lines, as shown.

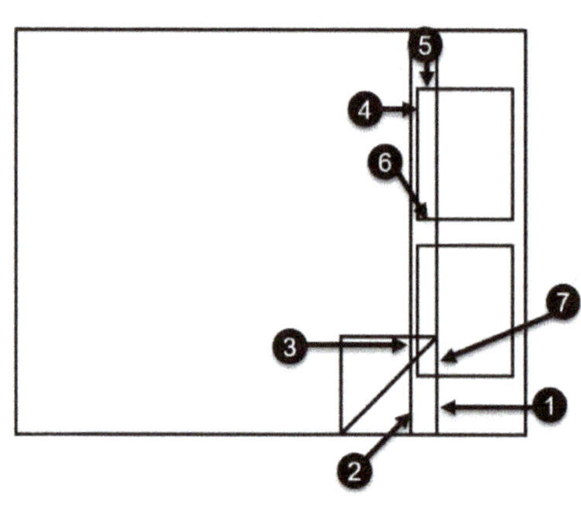

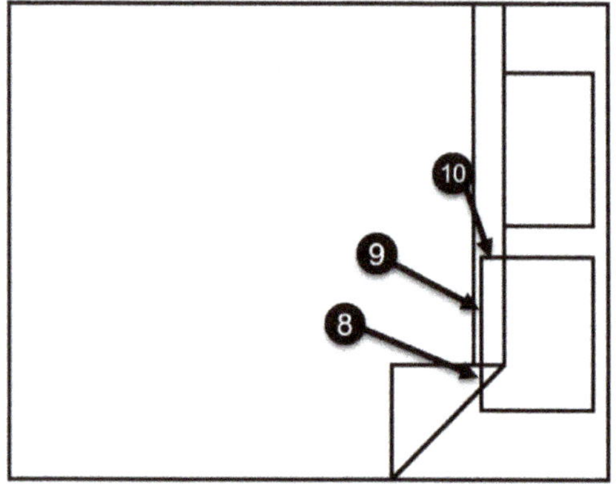

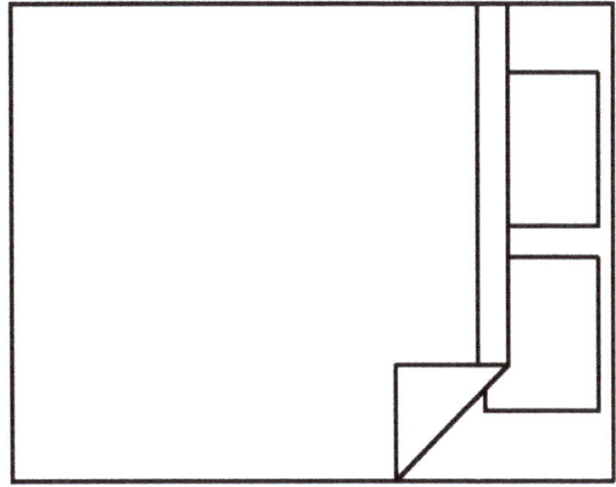

- On the ribbon, click **Home** > **Block** > **Create Block**.

Create
Block

BLOCK ∨

- Next, type **Dining Set** in the **Block Name** box on the **Create Block Definition** dialog.

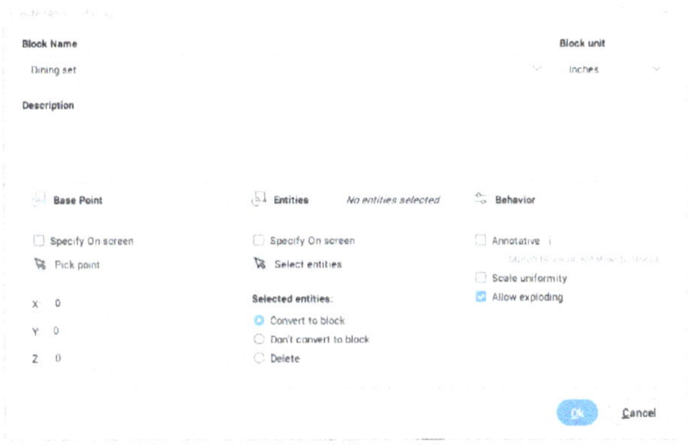

- Click the **Select entities** icon in the **Entities** section. Next, create a selection window across the dining set.
- Press ENTER and click the **Pick point** icon in the **Base point** section.

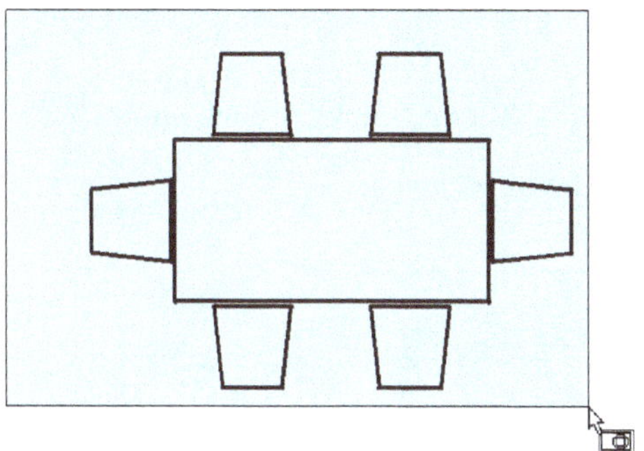

- Select the lower-left corner of the rectangle, as shown.

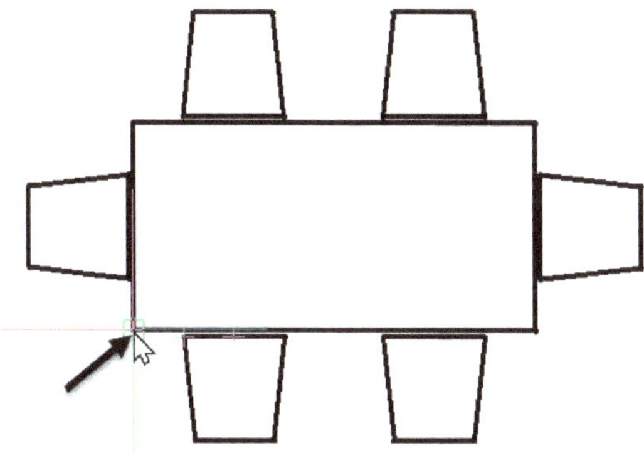

- Select the **Convert to Block** option in the **Entities** section and click **OK**.
- Select the Dining set block, and then click on the grip located at the bottom-left corner.
- Move the block and place it at the location shown below.

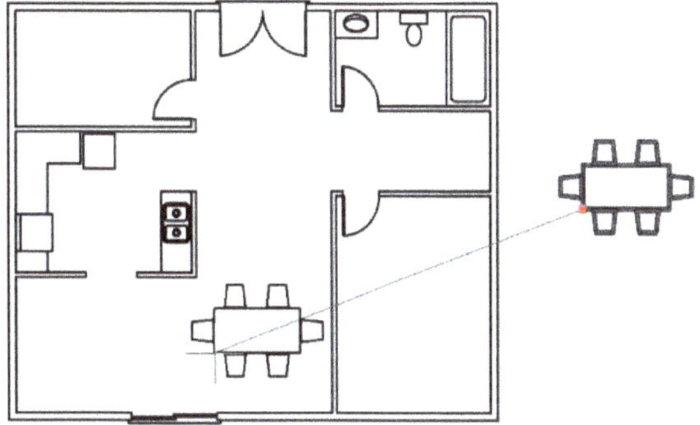

- On the ribbon, click **Home** > **Block** > **Create Block**.
- Next, type **Bed** in the **Block Name** box on the **Create Block Definition** dialog.
- Click the **Select entities** icon in the **Entities**

section. Next, create a selection window across the bed.

- Press ENTER and click the **Pick point** icon in the **Base point** section.

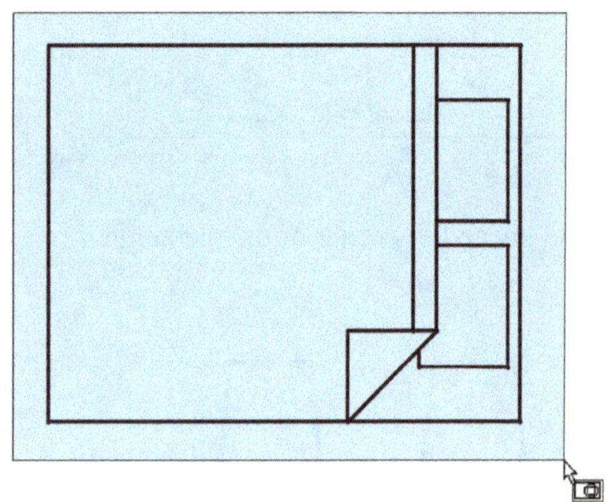

- Select the lower-left corner of the rectangle, as shown.

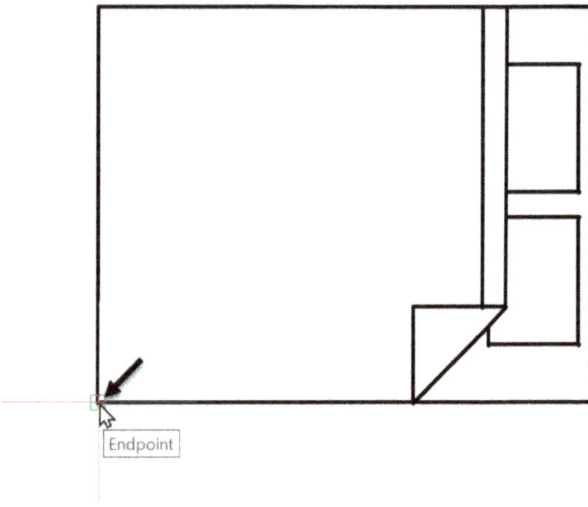

- Select the **Convert to Block** option and click **OK**.
- Activate the **Rectangle** command and select the corner point of the bedroom, as shown.
- Move the pointer downward.
- Type 86 and press the TAB key.
- Type 27.5 and press ENTER.

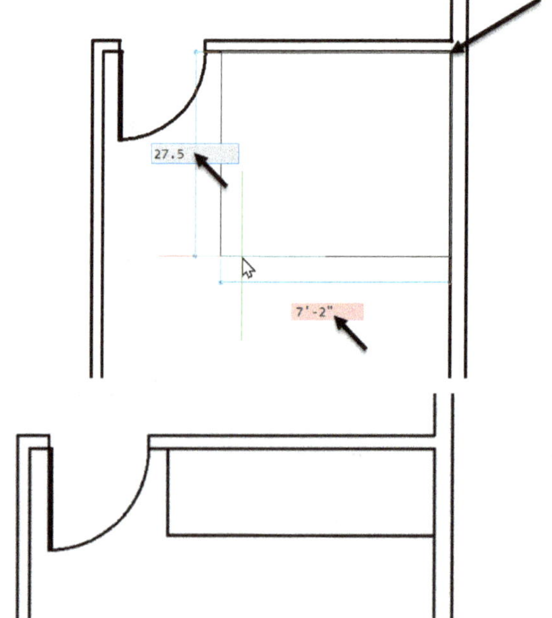

- Create another rectangle by selecting the corner points, as shown below.

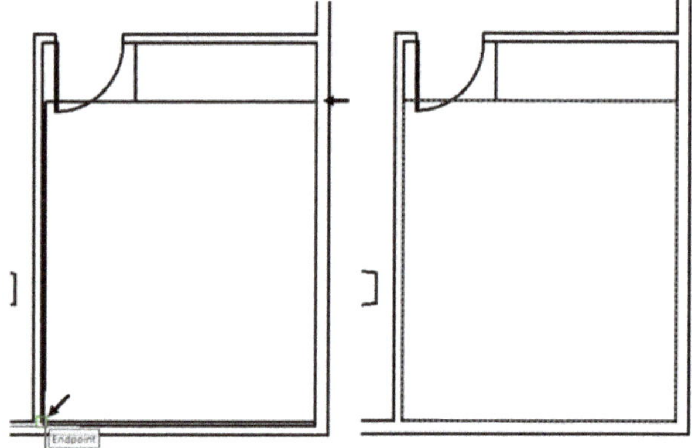

- Offset the rectangle by a distance of **47.5** inwards. Next, delete the original rectangle.

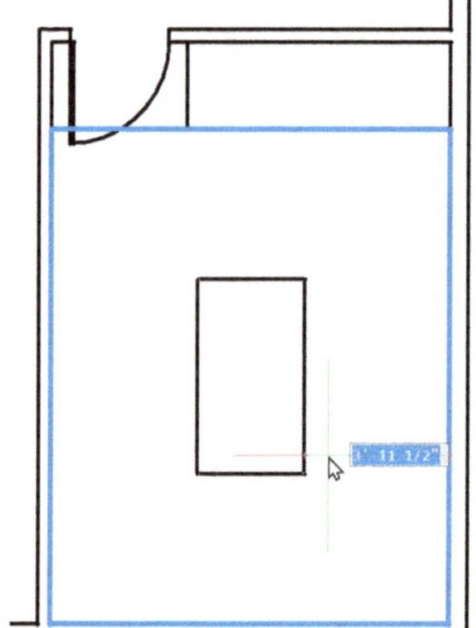

- Select the bed and click on the grip located at the bottom left corner.
- Move the pointer and select the bottom left corner of the offset rectangle to define the destination point.

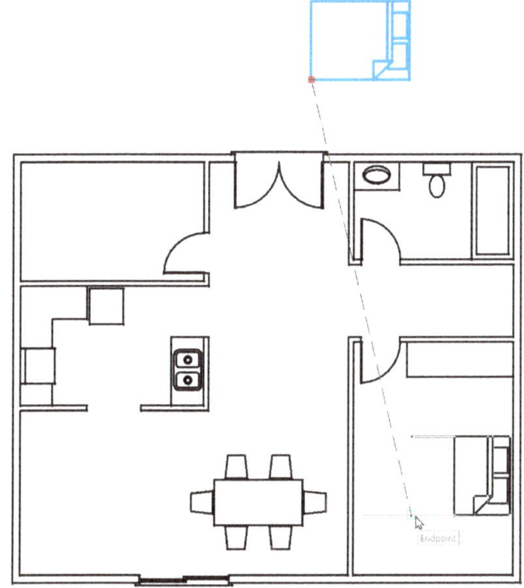

- Press Esc and delete the offset rectangle.

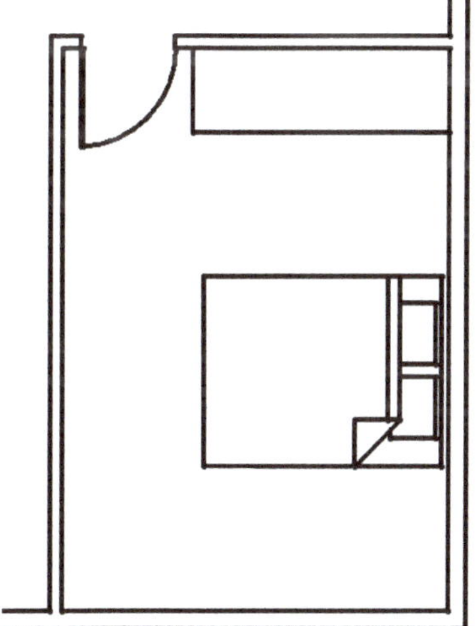

Adding Windows

- In the empty space, create the window using the **Line** command, as shown below.

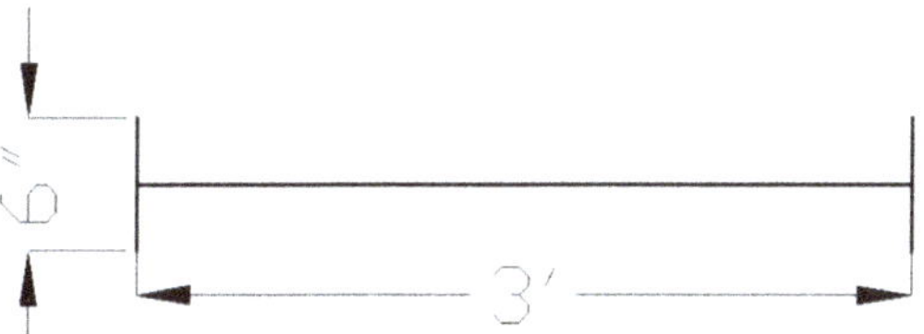

- On the ribbon, click **Home > Block > Create Block**.
- Type **Window** in the **Block Name** box on the **Create Block Definition** dialog.
- Click the **Select objects** area icon in the **Entities** section. Next, create a selection window across all the newly created elements.
- Press ENTER and click the **Pick point** icon in the **Base point** section.
- Select the lower-left corner of the window.

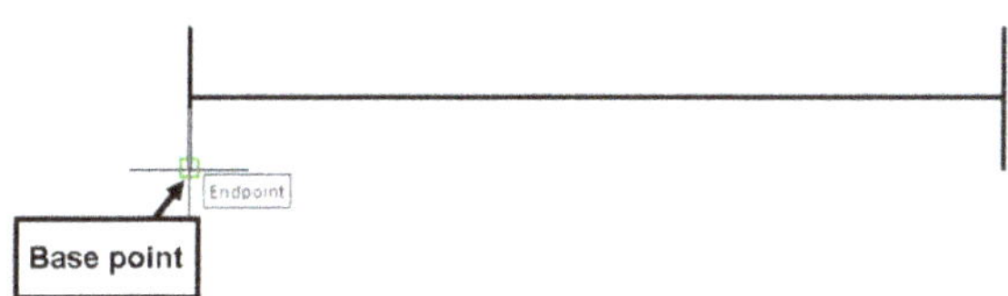

- Make sure that the **Convert to Block** option is selected under the **Entities** section.
- Click **OK** on the **Create Block Definition** dialog.
- On the ribbon, click **Home** > **Draw** > **Infinite Line**.
- Select **Parallel** from the command line. Next, type 95, and press ENTER.
- Select the right vertical line, as shown.

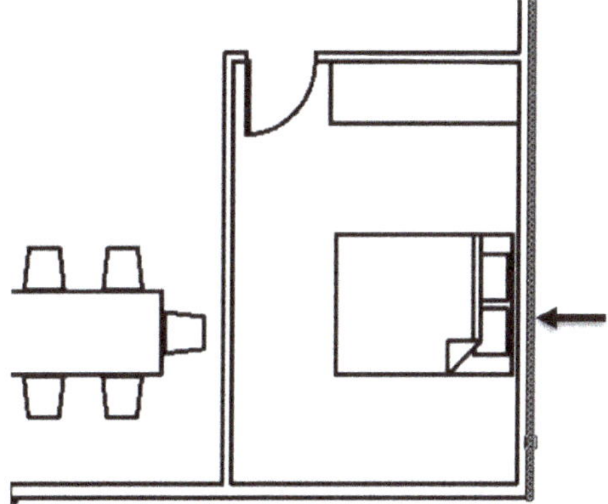

- Next, move the pointer toward the left and click.

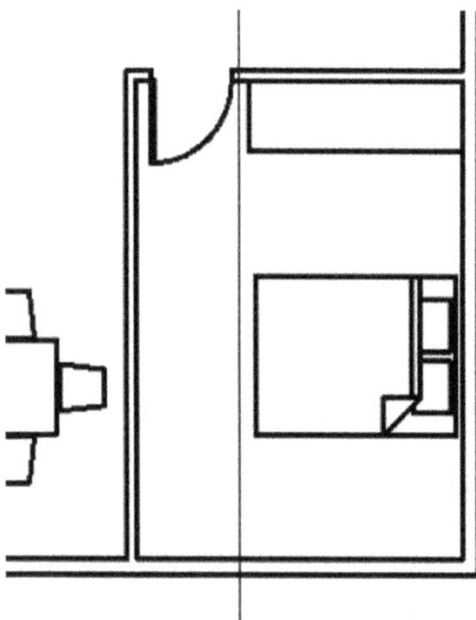

- Press ENTER twice. Next, select **Parallel** from the command line.
- Type 26 and press ENTER. Next, select the horizontal line of the kitchen wall, as shown.
- Move the pointer upward and click.

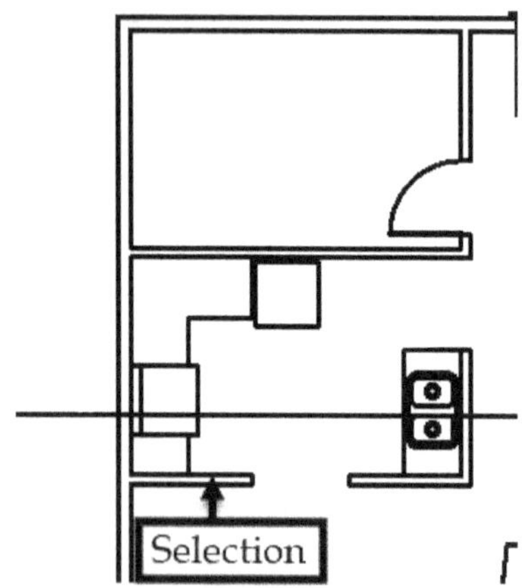

- Press ENTER twice. Next, select **Parallel** from the command line.
- Type 29 and press ENTER. Next, select the horizontal line, as shown.
- Move the pointer upward and click.

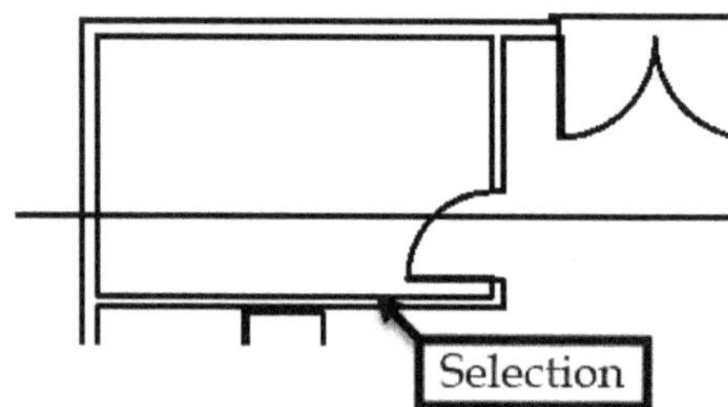

- Press ENTER twice. Next, select **Parallel** from the command line.
- Type 16 and press ENTER. Next, select the horizontal line, as shown.
- Move the pointer upward and click.

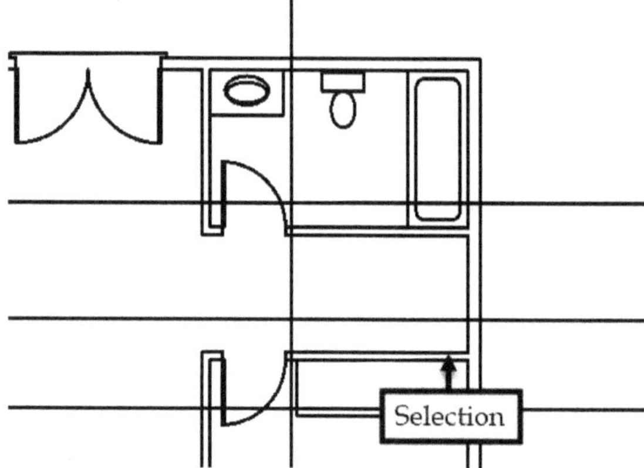

- Press ENTER twice. Next, select **Parallel** from the command line.
- Type 54 and press ENTER. Next, select the vertical line, as shown.
- Move the pointer toward the right and click.

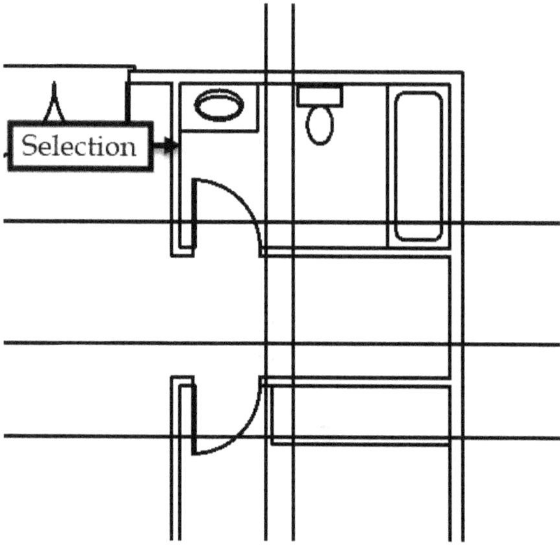

- On the ribbon, click **Home > Block > Insert Block**.

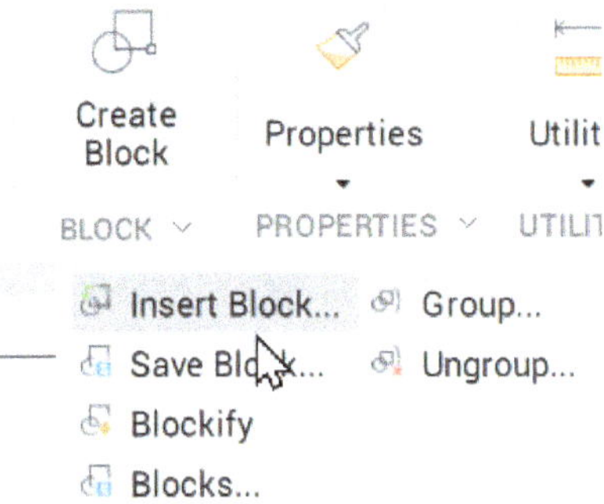

- Select **Window** from the **Name** drop-down.

- Type 1.5 in the **X** box available in the **Scale** section.

- Check the **Specify On-screen** option in the **Insertion Point** section. Next, click **OK**.

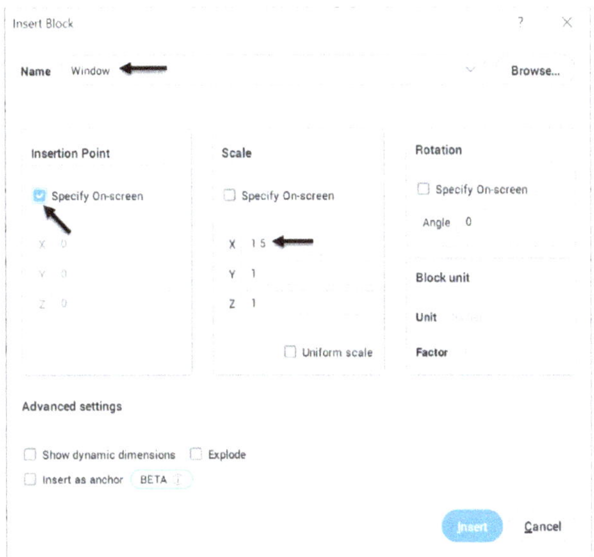

- Select the intersection point between the construction line and the horizontal line, as shown. The **Window** block will be placed at the specified location.

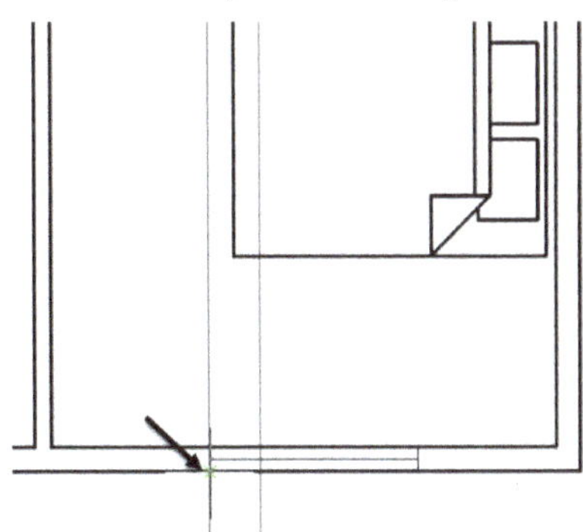

- Press ENTER and select **Window** from the **Name** drop-down.

- Type 0.72 in the **X** box available in the **Scale** section.

Next, click **OK**.

- Select the intersection point between the infinite line and the horizontal line, as shown.

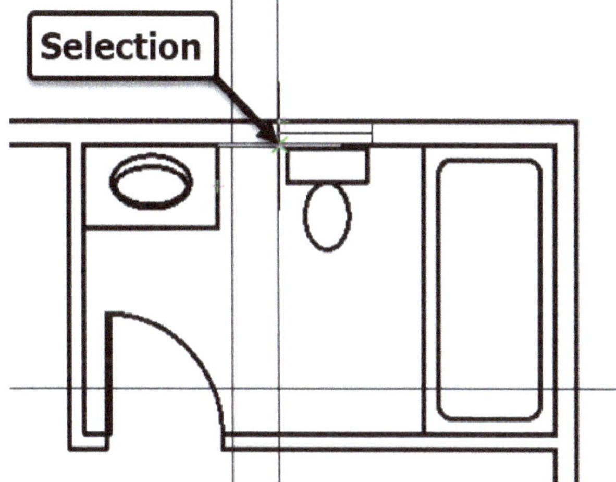

- On the ribbon, click **Home > Block > Insert Block**. Next, select **Window** from the **Name** drop-down.

- Type-in **90 Angle** box in the **Rotation** section and click **OK**.

- Place the **Window** block on the kitchen wall, as shown below.

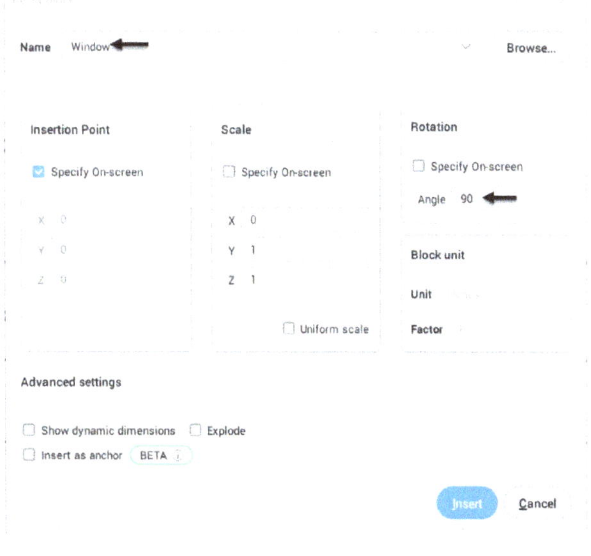

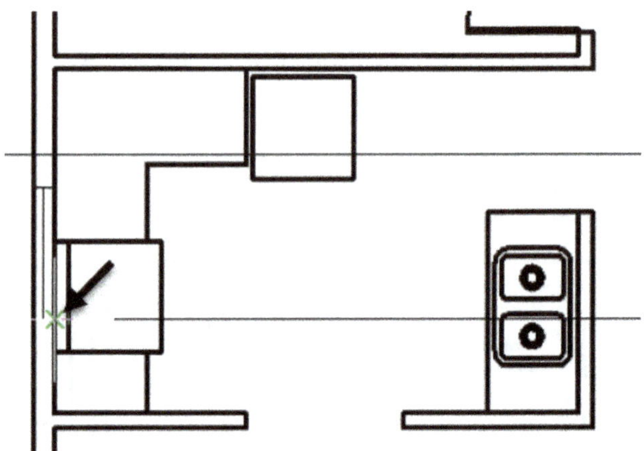

- Likewise, place the window blocks, as shown below.

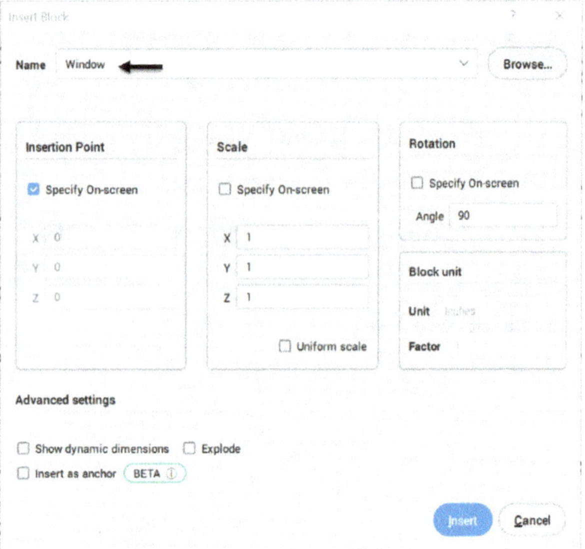

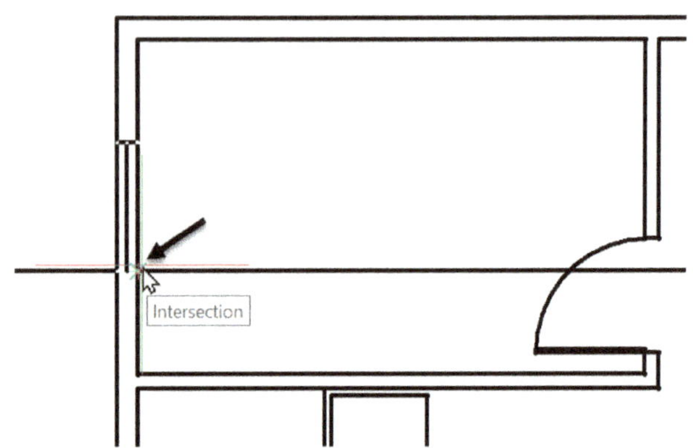

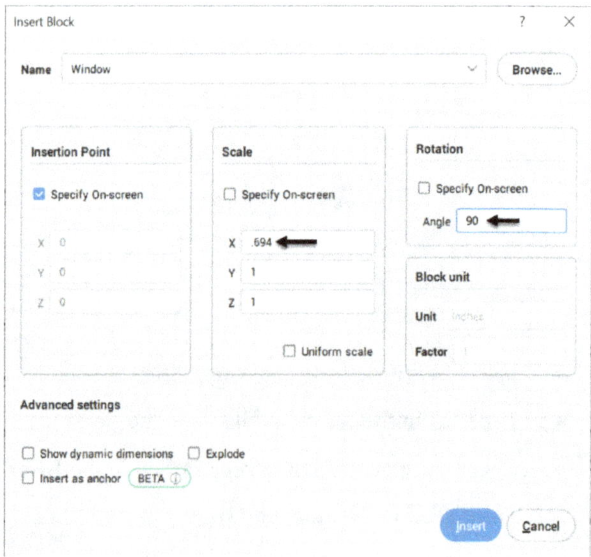

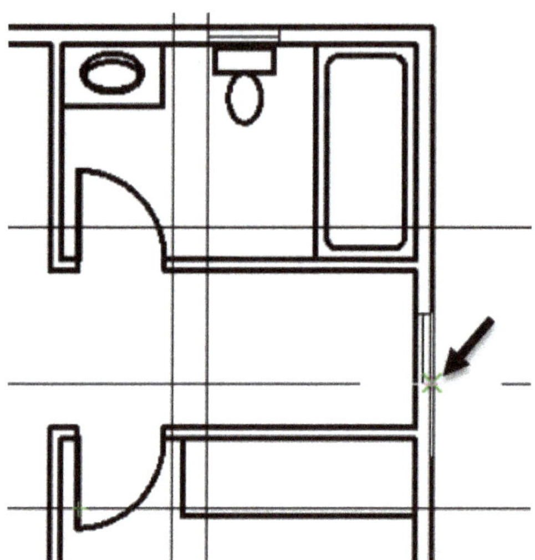

- Select all the construction lines and press DELETE.

Arranging Objects of the drawing in Layers

- On the ribbon, click **Home > Layers > Layers**. It displays the **Layers** palette.

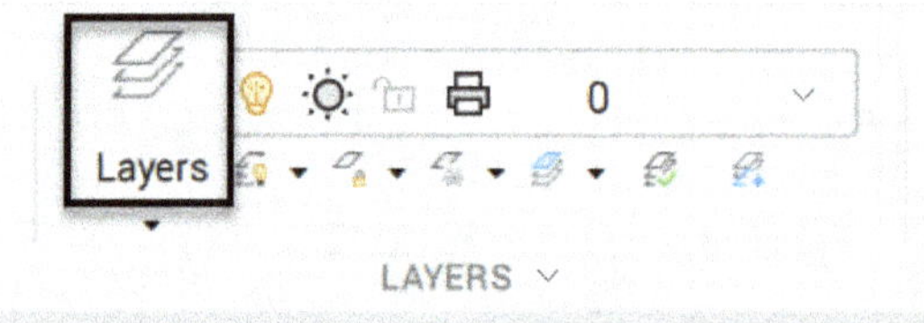

- On the **Layers** palette, click the **Add** button.

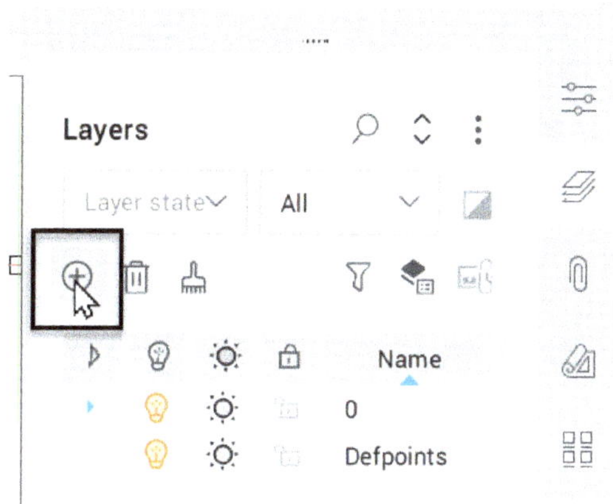

- Type **Wall** in the layer **Name** box and press Enter.

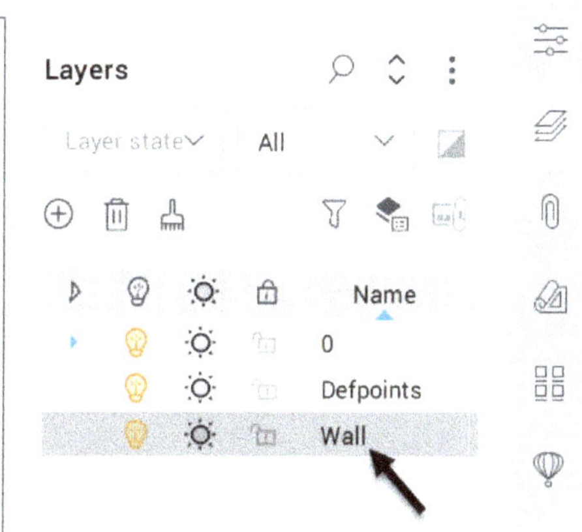

- Create another layer, and then type-in **Door** — press Enter.
- Likewise, create other layers, as shown below.

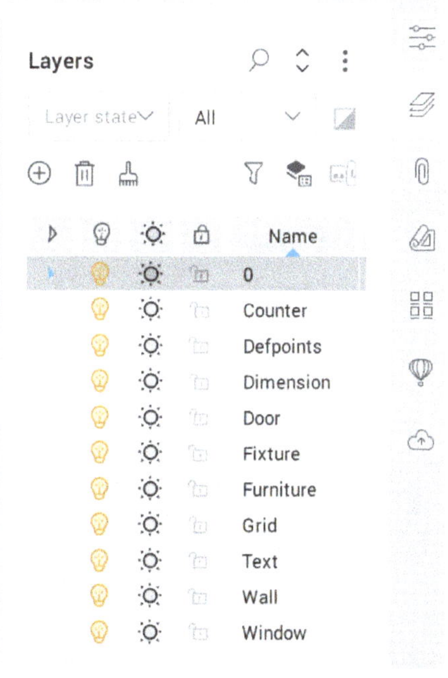

- Click the **Color** swatch of the **Counter** layer.
- Select the **Index color 1** from the **Color** dialog. Next, click **OK**.

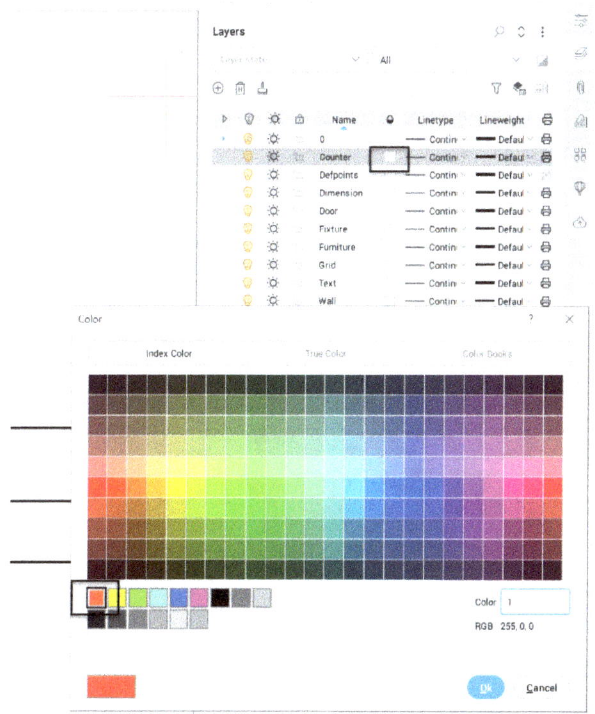

- Click the **Color** swatch of the **Dimensions** layer.
- Select the **Index color 8** from the **Color** dialog. Next, click **OK**.

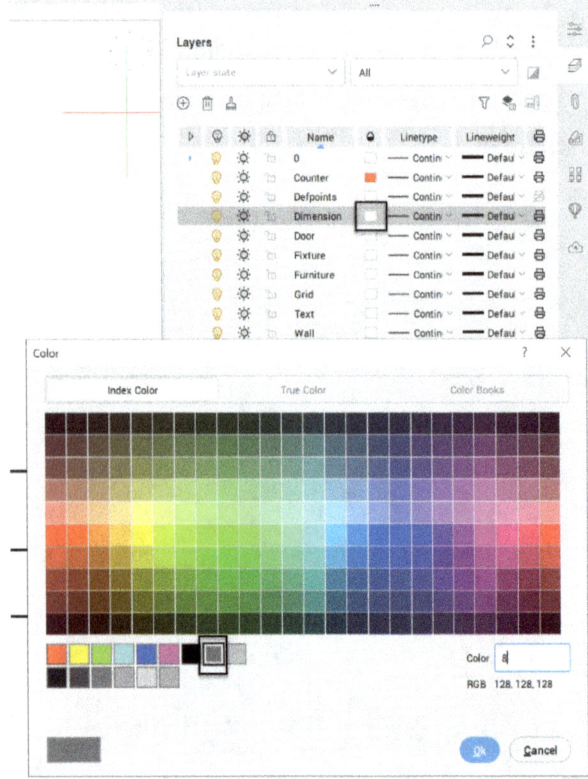

- Likewise, change the line colors of the remaining layers, as shown.

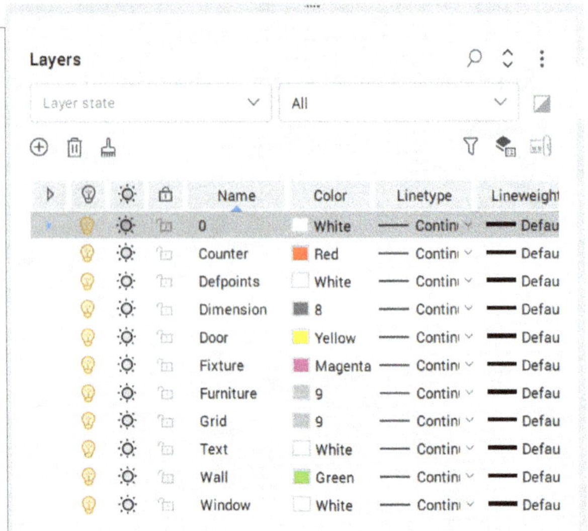

- Click the **Line Type** drop-down of the **Grid** layer, and then select **Load**.

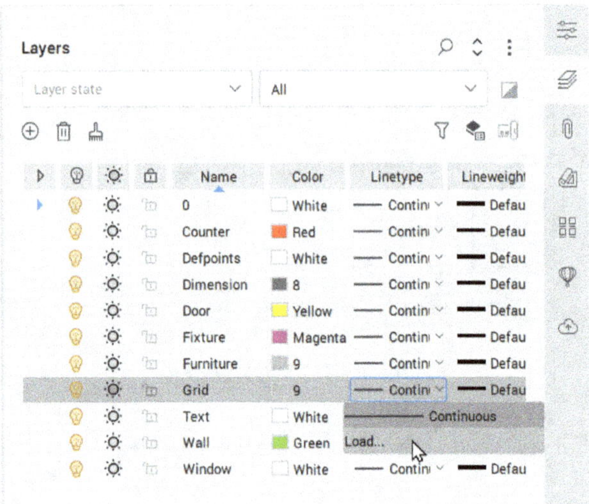

- Select the **DASHED** Linetype from the **Load Linetypes** dialog. Next, click **OK**.

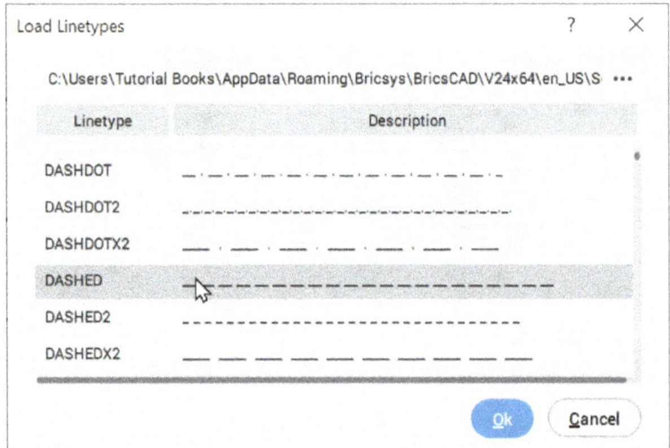

- Click the **Line Weight** drop-down of the **Counter** layer and select 0.35 mm.

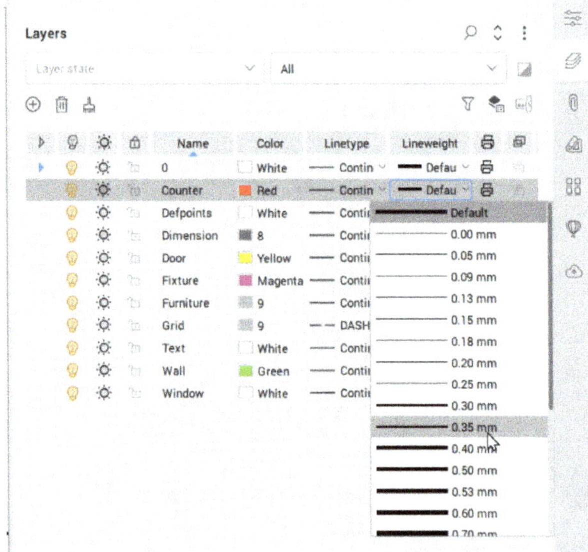

- Likewise, change the Line weights of the remaining

layers, as shown.

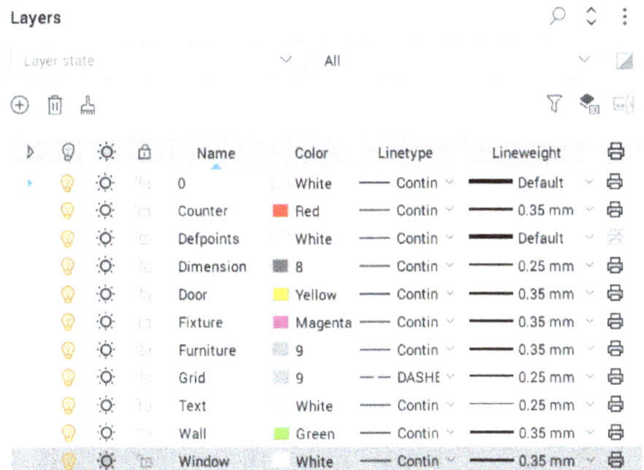

- Click the **Layers** button on the right side to hide the **Layers** palette.

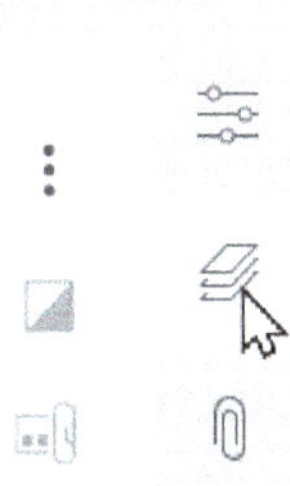

- Press and hold the SHIFT key and select the Dining set, cupboard, and bed.

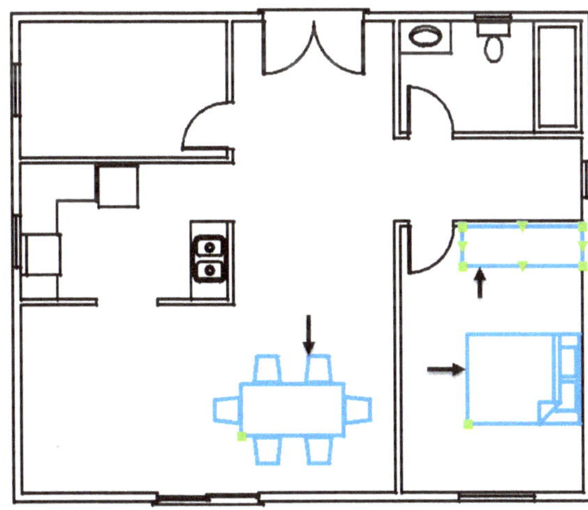

- On the ribbon, click **Home > Layers > Layers Control > Furniture**. The selected objects will be transferred to the **Furniture** layer.

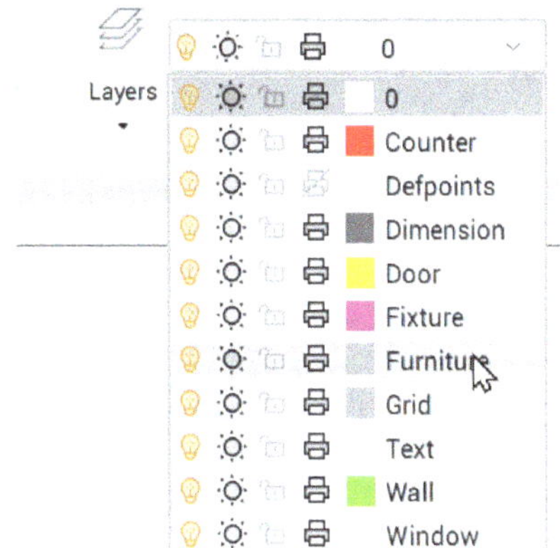

- Press Esc to deselect the selected objects.
- Press and hold the SHIFT key and select the kitchen and bathroom fixtures.

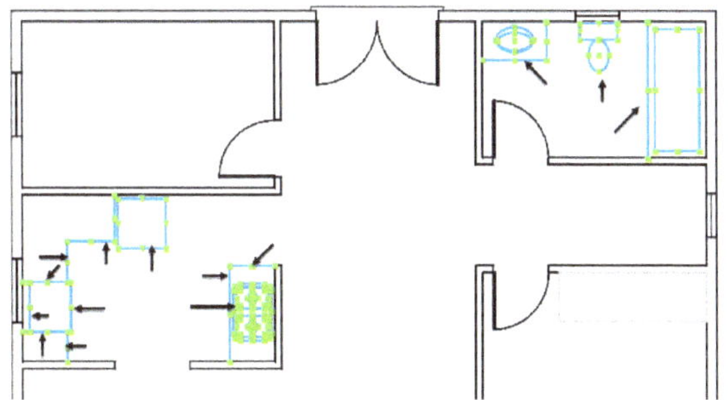

- Click **Home > Layers > Layers Control > Fixtures** on the ribbon.

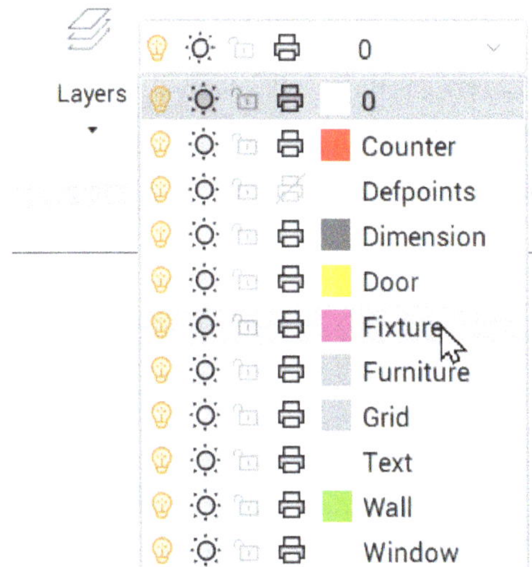

- Press Esc.
- Likewise, transfer the remaining objects onto their respective layers, as shown.

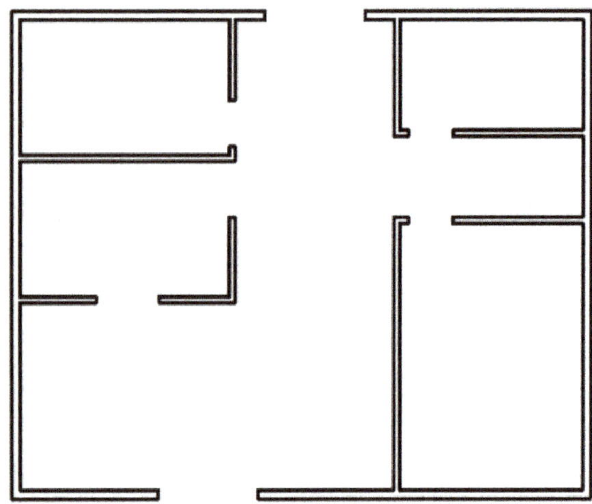

- Create a selection window and select all the walls.

- On the **Access** toolbar, click **Layers Control > Wall**. All the walls will be transferred to the **Wall** layer.

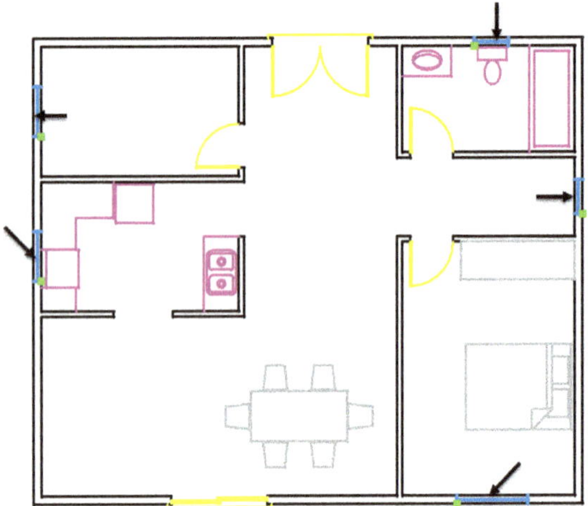

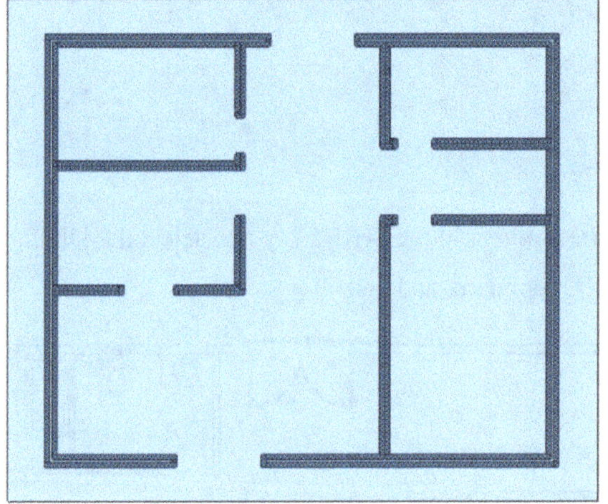

- Open the **Layers** palette and click the bulb icons associated with Door, Window, Fixtures, Furniture, and Counter layers. It will hide the corresponding layers.

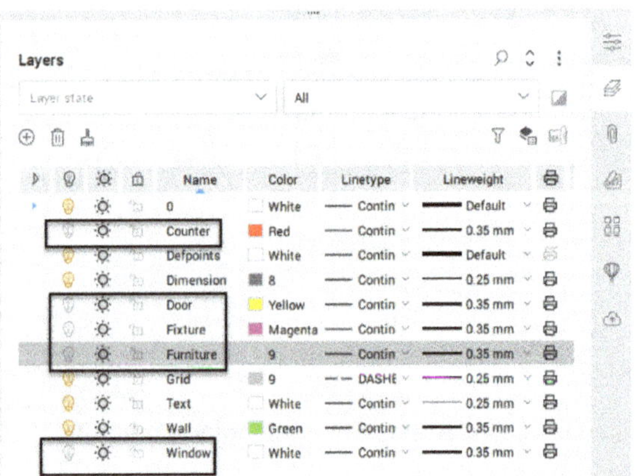

- Now, turn ON the hidden layers by clicking the bulb symbols on the **Layers Control** drop-down of the **Access** toolbar.

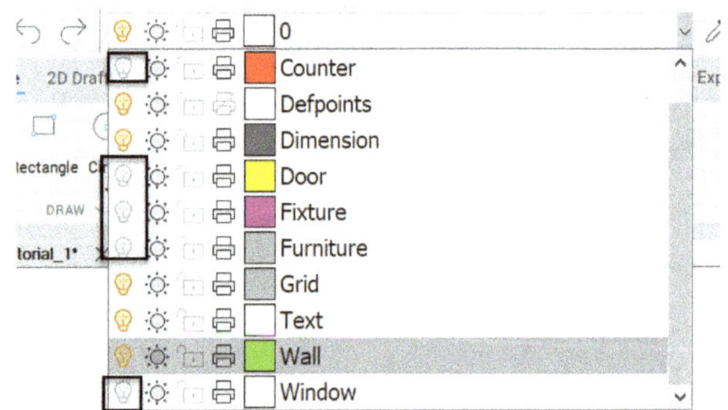

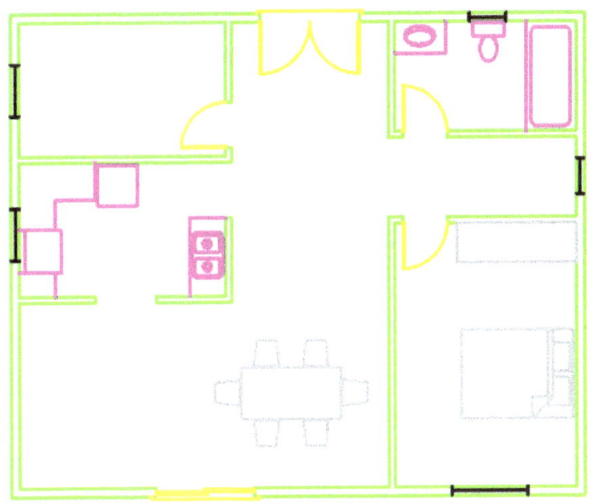

Creating Grid Lines

- On the **Access** toolbar, click **Layers Control > Grid**. The **Grid** layer becomes active.

- Click **Home > Draw > Infinite Line** on the ribbon. Next, select the **Vertical** option from the command line.
- Select the endpoint of the window left outer wall, as shown.

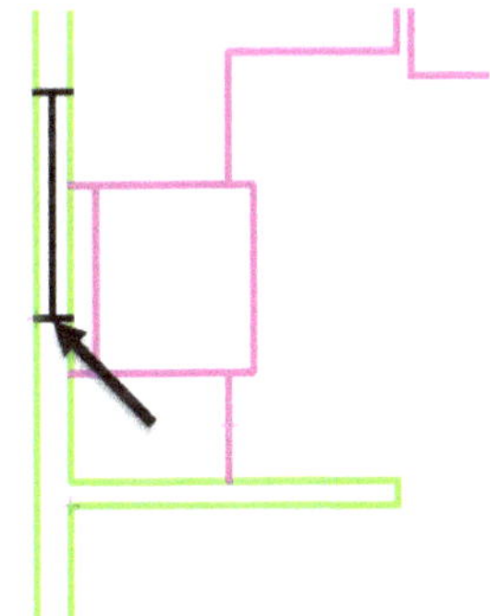

- Zoom to the top portion of the drawing and selected midpoint of the horizontal edge of the inner wall.

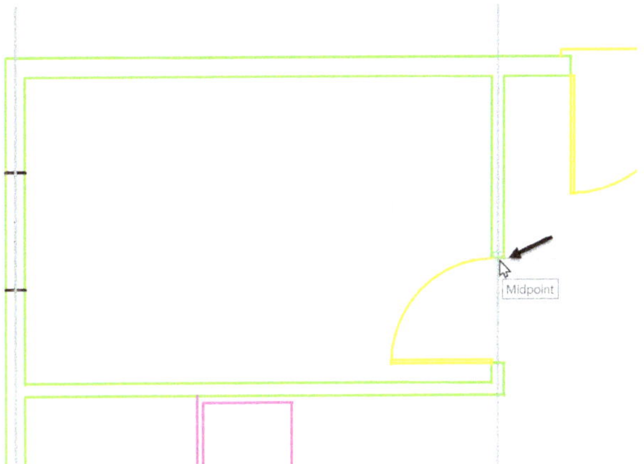

- Select the endpoint of the window of the right outer wall.

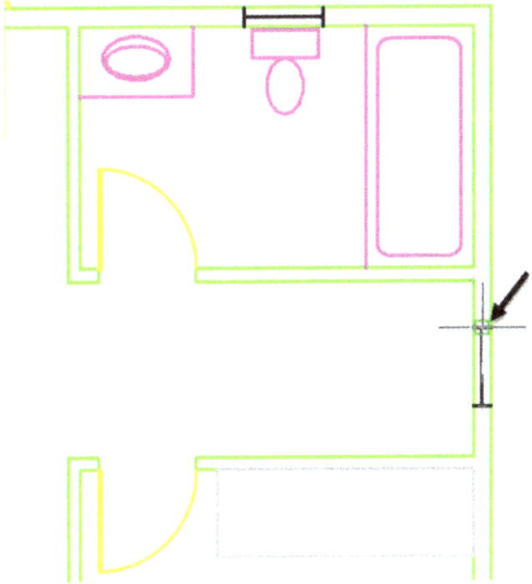

- Press ENTER twice and select the **Parallel** option from the command line.
- Type **2** in the command line and press ENTER.
- Select the vertical edge of the inner wall, as shown. Next, move the pointer toward right and click.

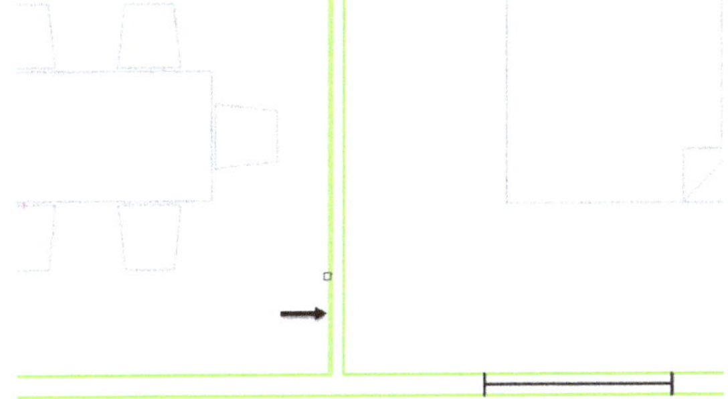

- Select the horizontal edge of the inner wall, as shown. Next, move the pointer downward and click.

- Select the horizontal edge of the inner wall, as shown. Next, move the pointer downward and click.

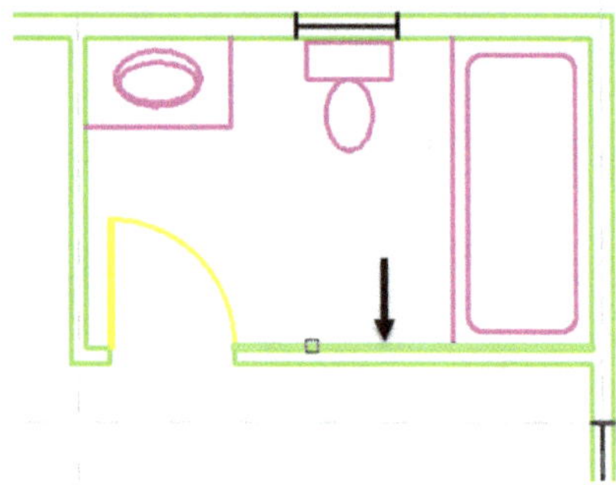

- Select the horizontal edge of the inner wall, as shown. Next, move the pointer downward and click.

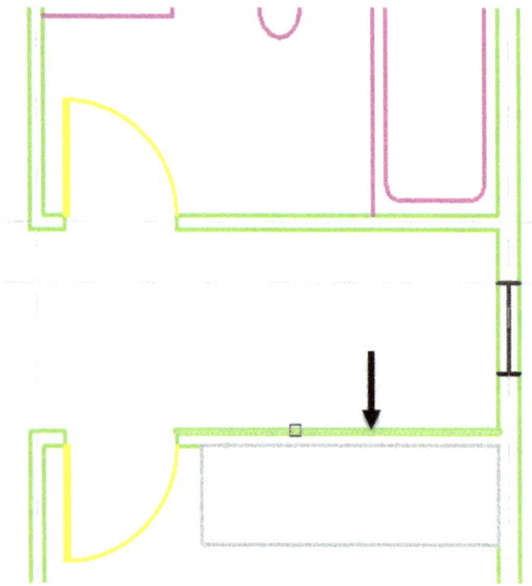

- Select the horizontal edge of the inner wall, as shown. Next, move the pointer downward and click.

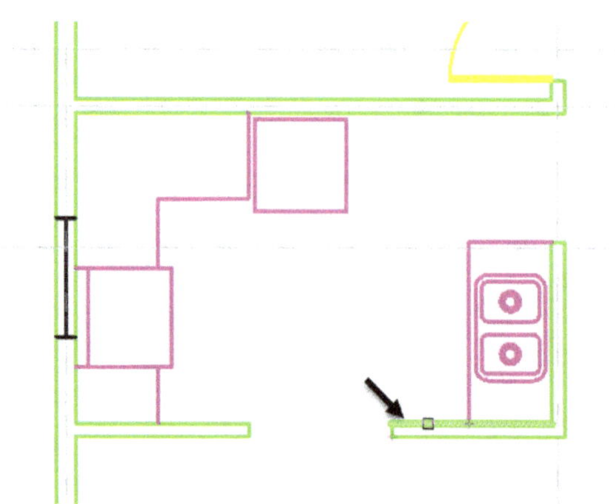

- Press ENTER twice and select the **Horizontal** option from the command line.
- Select the endpoints of the windows of the outer walls, as shown. Next, press ENTER twice.

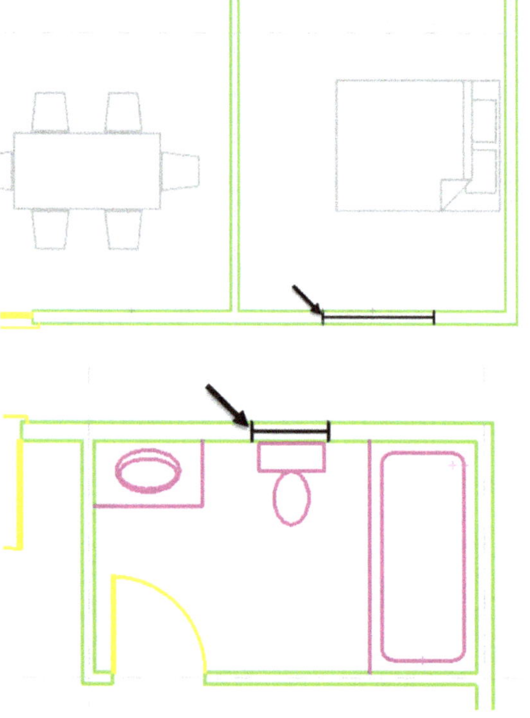

- Select the **Parallel** option from the command line. Next, type 36 and press ENTER.
- Select the left vertical dotted line. Next, move the pointer toward left and click.

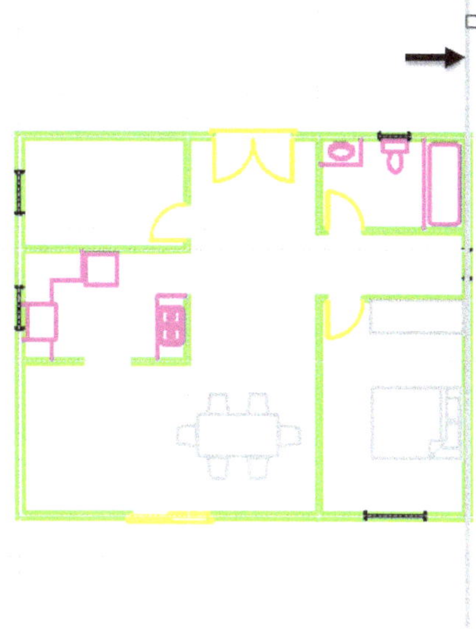

- Select the top horizontal dotted line. Next, move the pointer upward and click.

- Select the bottom horizontal dotted line. Next, move the pointer downward and click.

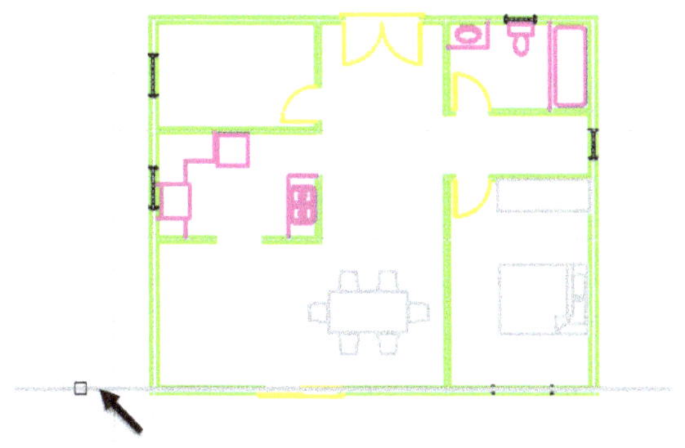

- Select the right vertical dotted line. Next, move the pointer toward right and click.

- On the ribbon, click **Home** > **Modify** > **Trim**. Next, press ENTER to select all the elements as the cutting edges.

- Press and hold the left mouse button and drag the pointer from right to left across the top portions of the vertical dotted lines.

- Press and hold the left mouse button and drag the pointer from right to left across the right portions of the horizontal dotted lines.

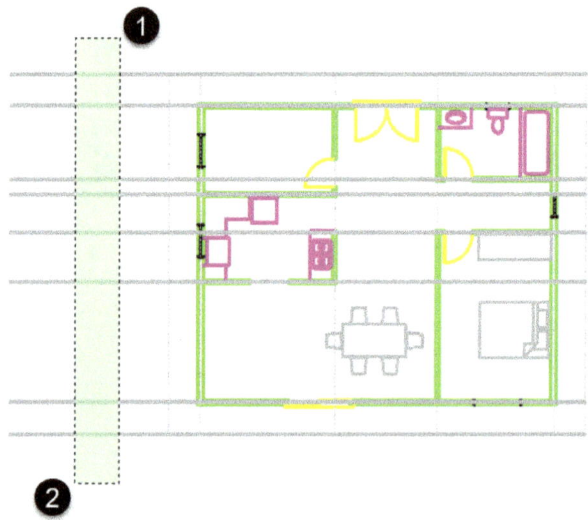

- Press and hold the left mouse button and drag the pointer from right to left across the bottom portions of the vertical dotted lines.

- Select the eRase option from the command line.

- Select the line forming the outer boundary and press ENTER to delete them.

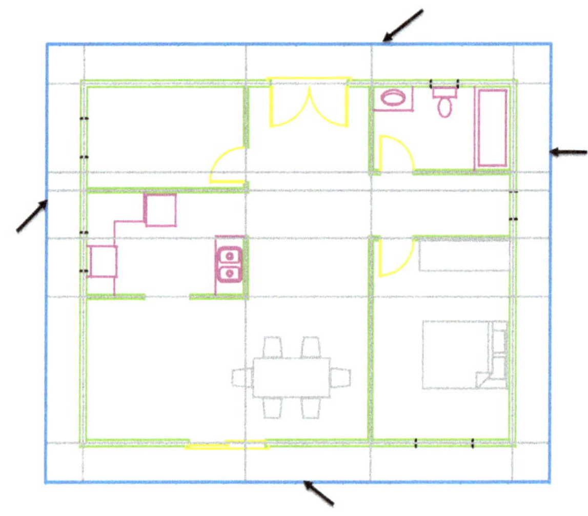

- Press and hold the left mouse button and drag the pointer from right to left across the left portions of the horizontal dotted lines.

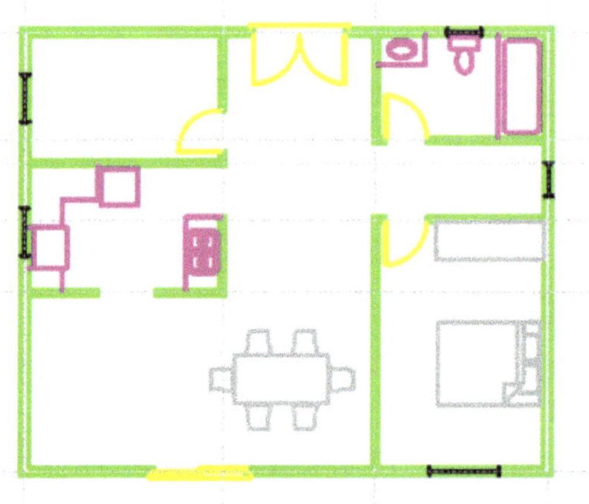

- Create a new layer called **Grid Bubble**. Make sure that all its parameters are same as the Grid layer.

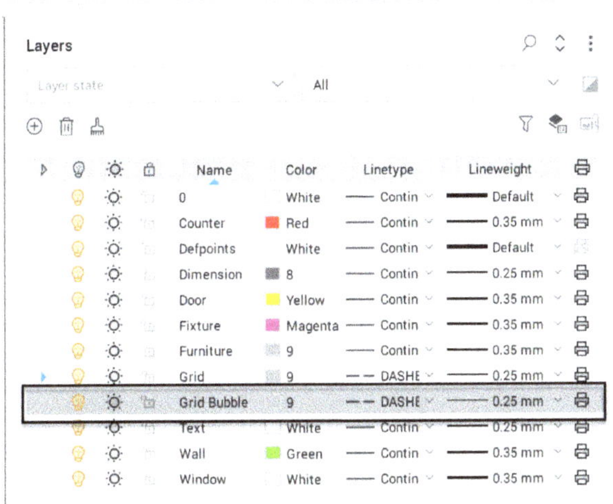

- Next, right-click on the **Grid Bubble** layer and select **Set Current**.

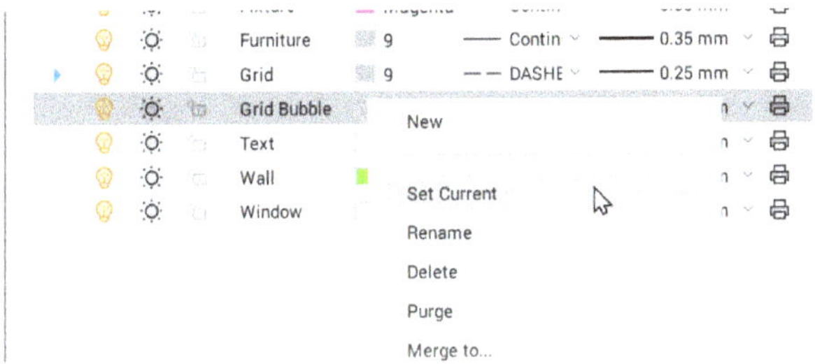

- Hide the **Layers** palette.
- Create a circle of 12 diameter.
- On the ribbon, click **Insert > Blocks > Define Attributes**.

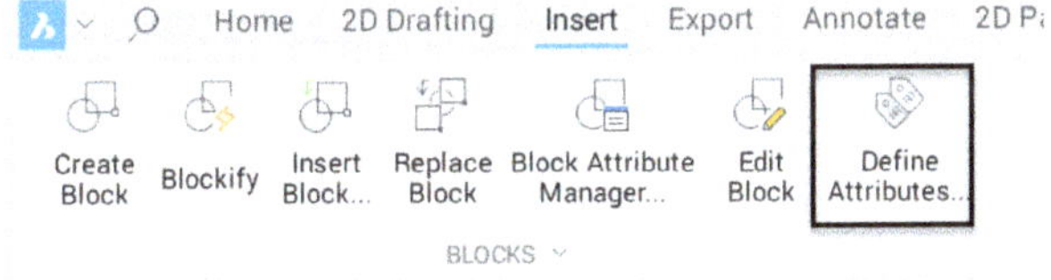

- On the **Define Attribute** dialog, type-in GRIDBUBBLE in the **Tag** box and select **Justification > Middle center**.
- Type-in **6** in the **Height** box.

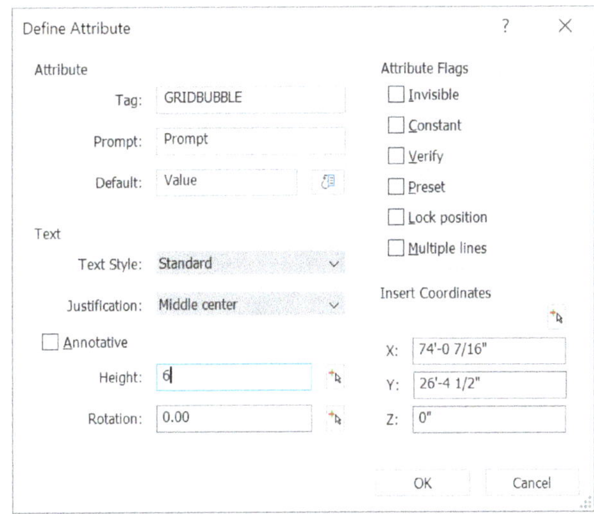

- Click the **Pick point** button in the **Insert Coordinates** section.
- Select the center point of the circle. The attribute text will be placed at its center.

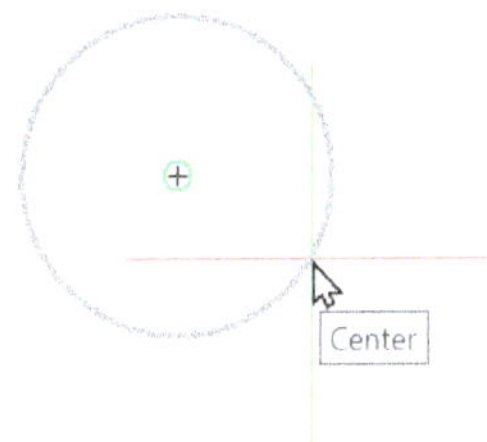

- Click **OK** to create attribute.

- On the ribbon, click **Insert > Blocks > Create Block**.
- Type-in Grid bubble in the **Block Name** box and click the **Select entities** button under the **Entities** section.
- Draw a crossing window to select the circle and attribute. Press Enter to accept the selection.

- Click the **Pick point** icon under the **Base point** section.

- Press and hold the SHIFT key and right-click. Next, select the **Snap to Quadrant** option.

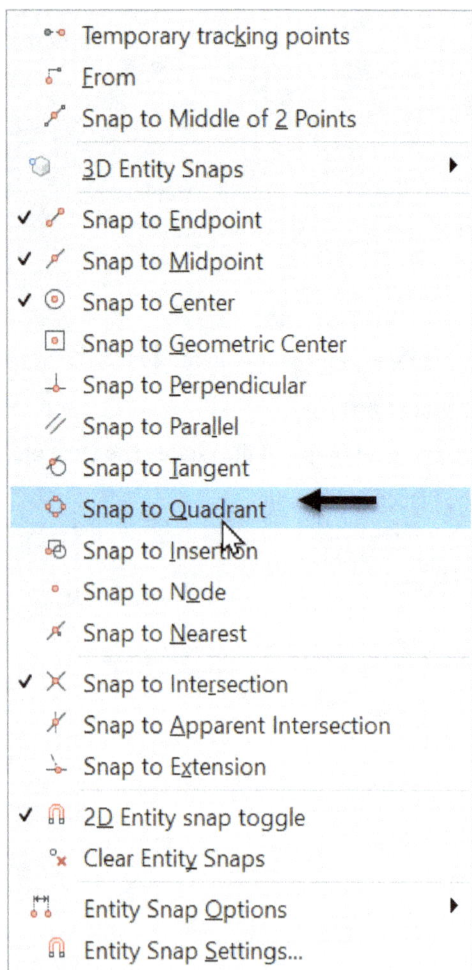

- Select the lower quadrant point of the circle to define the base point of the block.

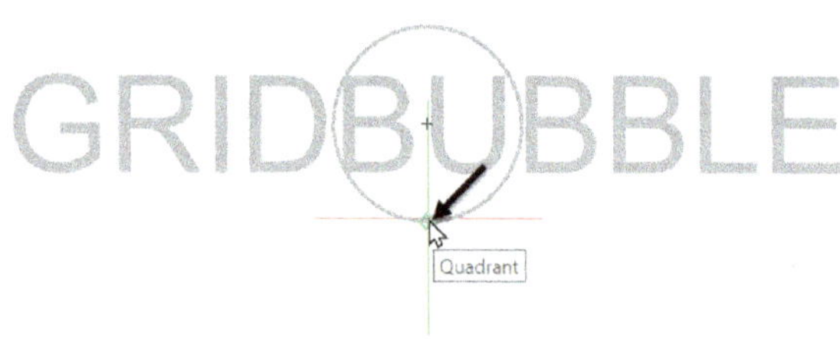

- Select the **Delete** option from the **Entities** section and click **OK**.

- On the ribbon, click **Insert > Blocks > Insert Block**. Next, select the **Grid Bubble** block from the **Name** drop-down.

- Type **0** in the **Angle** box and click **Insert**.

- Select the top endpoint of the first vertical grid line.

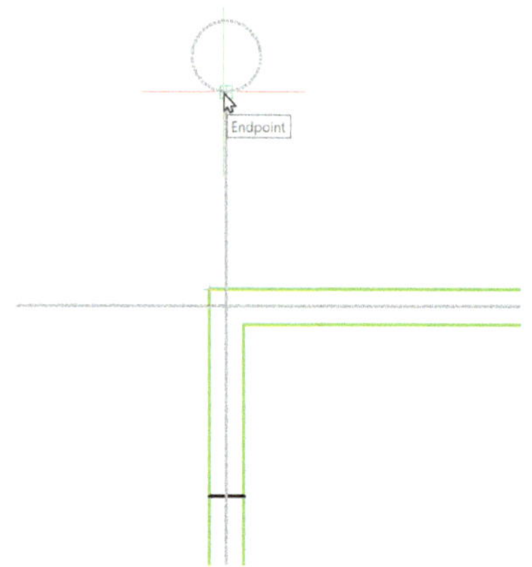

- Type-in **A** in the command line and press ENTER.

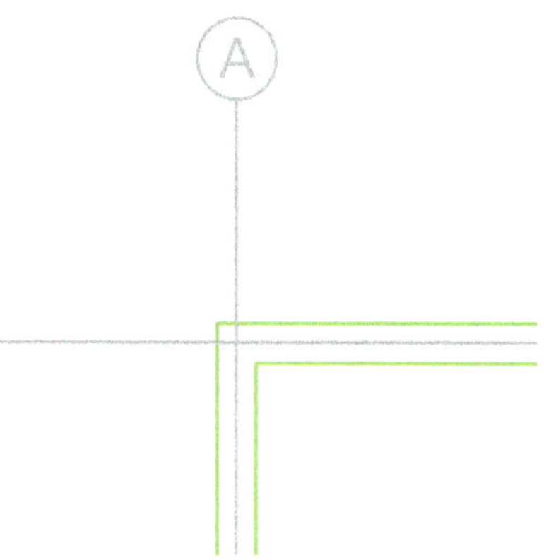

- Likewise, add other grid bubbles to the vertical grid lines.

- Create another block with the name **Vertical Grid bubble**. Make sure that you select the right quadrant point of the circle as the base point.

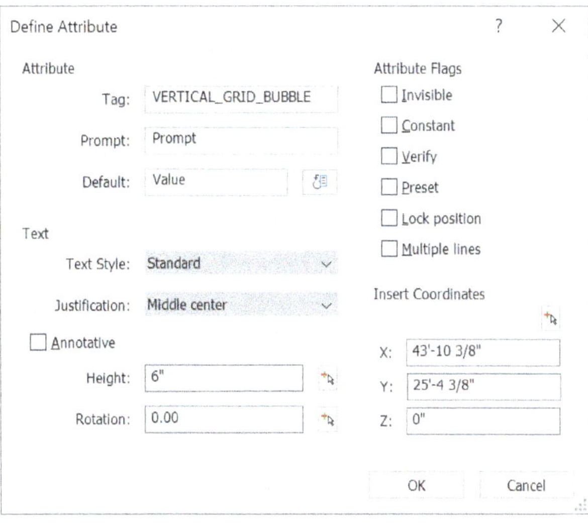

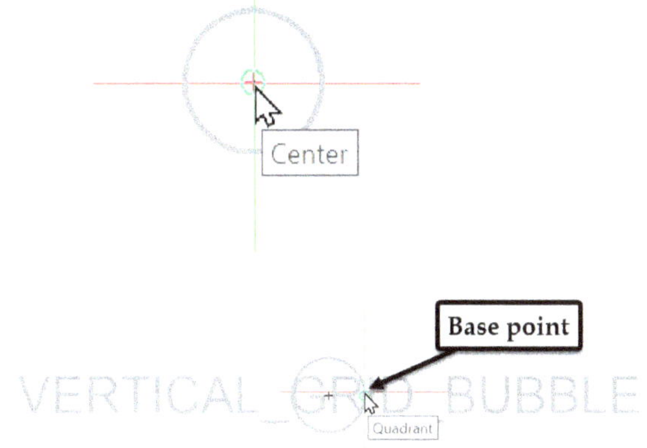

- Insert the vertical grid bubbles, as shown below.

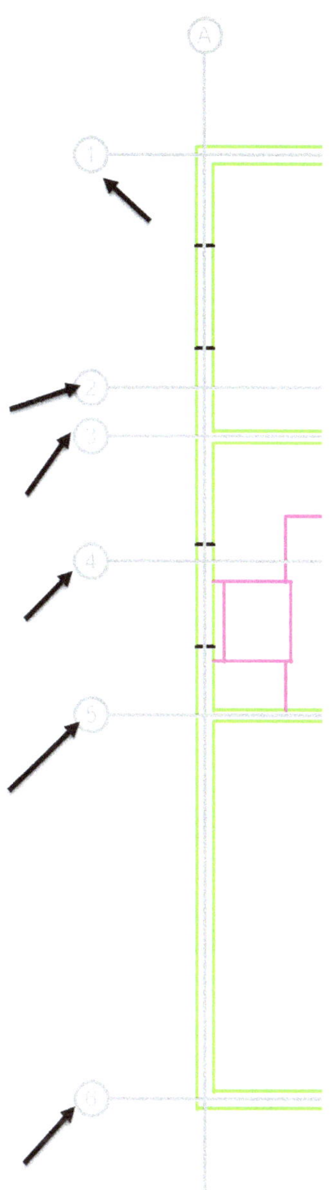

Adding Dimensions

- On the **Access** toolbar, click **Layers Control > Dimension** to make it current.

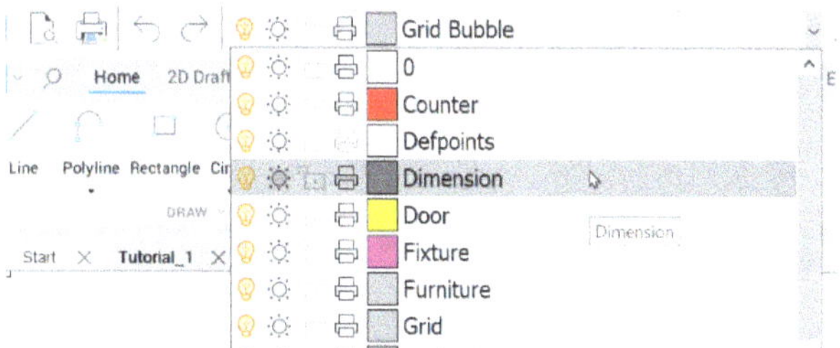

- Click **Annotate** > **Dimension** > **Dimension Styles** on the ribbon.

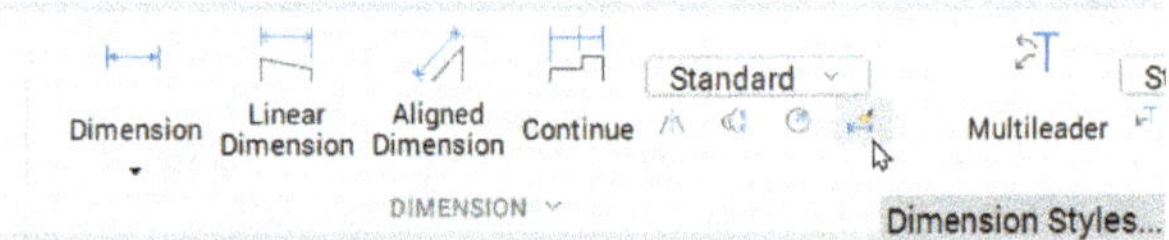

- On the **Drawing Explorer** dialog, right-click the **Standard** dimension style from the **Dimension Styles** section, and select the **New** option.

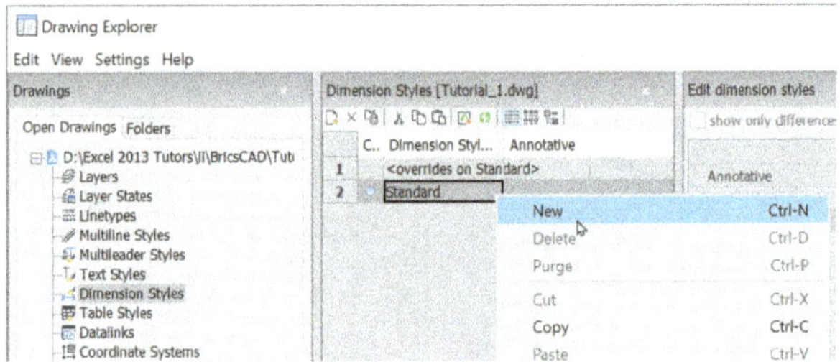

- Type-in **Floor Plan** in the **Dimension Style Name** box.

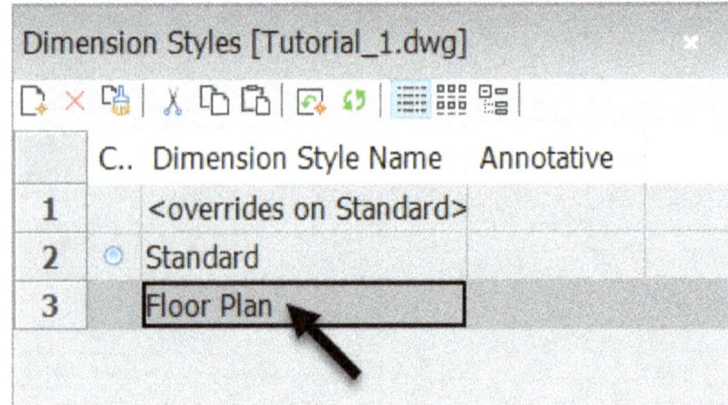

- Scroll to the **Primary Units** section and select **Dim units > Architectural**.
- Set **Dim precision** to **0'-01/16"**.
- Set **Fractional type** to **Horizontal**.
- Uncheck the **Suppress zero inches** option.

Primary units	
Dim units	Architectural
Dim precision	0'-0 1/16"
Fractional type	Horizontal
Decimal separator	.
Dim round	0
Dim prefix	
Dim suffix	
Dim sub-units suffix	
Dim scale linear	1
Dim sub-units scale	100
Suppress leading zeros	☐ Suppress leading ze...
Suppress trailing zeros	☐ Suppress trailing ze...
Suppress zero feet	☑ Suppress zero feet
Suppress zero inches	☐ Suppress zero inches
Dim angle units	Decimal degrees
Dim angle precision	0
Suppress angle leading zeros	☐ Suppress leading ze...
Suppress angle trailing zeros	☐ Suppress trailing ze...

- Scroll to the **Lines and arrows** section.
- Select **Arrow > Architectural tick**.
- Select **Arrow 1 > Architectural tick**.
- Select **Arrow 2 > Architectural tick**.
- Select **Leader arrow > Closed Filled**.
- Enter 1/4′ in the **Arrow Size** box.

Dim break size	1/8"
Lines and Arrows	
Tick size	0"
Arrow size	3/16"
Arrowheads	☐ Arrowheads
Arrow	➤ Closed filled
Arrow 1	✓ Architectural tick
Arrow 2	✓ Architectural tick
Leader arrow	➤ Closed filled
Dim line color	■ ByBlock
Dim line type	——— ByLayer
Dim line LW	——— ByBlock

- Set **Ext line ext** and **Ext line offset** to 3″.

Ext line ext	3"
Ext line offset	3"
Ext line 1	☐ Suppress first exten...

- Scroll to the **Text** section set and **Text height** to 6″.
- Set **Text position vertical > Centered**.
- Set **Text position horizontal > Centered**.
- Scroll to the **Fit** section, and select **Arrow ans text fit > Best fit**.

- Select **Text movement > Move text, no leader**.

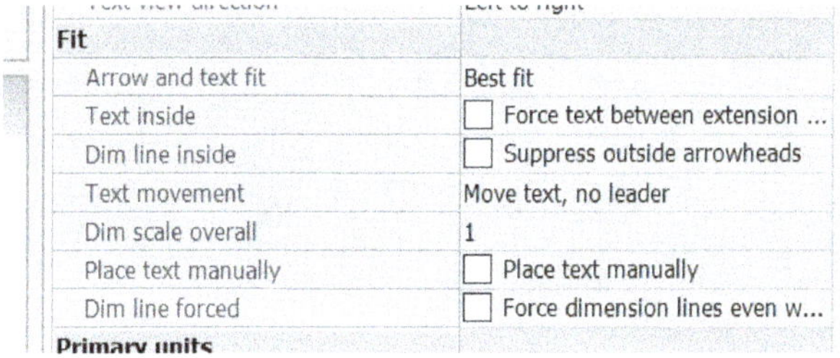

- Right-click on the **Floor Plan** dimension style in the **Dimension Styles** section, and then select **Set Current**.

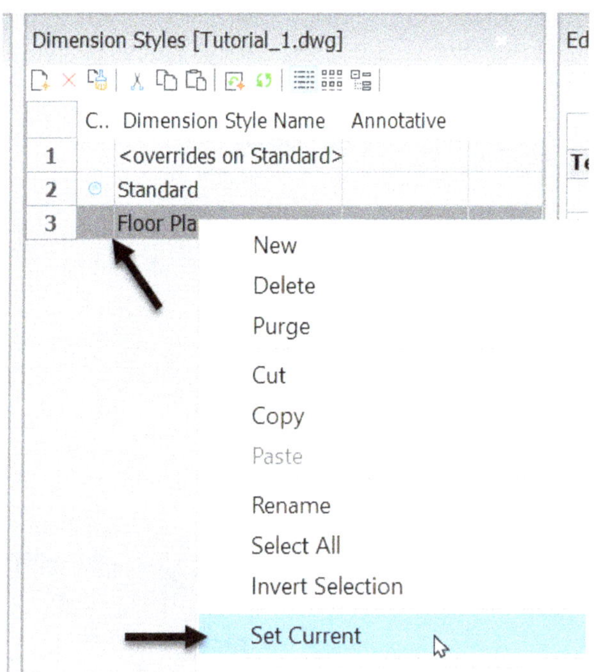

- Close the **Drawing Explorer** dialog.
- On the ribbon, click **Home > Annotation > Dimension** drop-down > **Linear Dimension**.

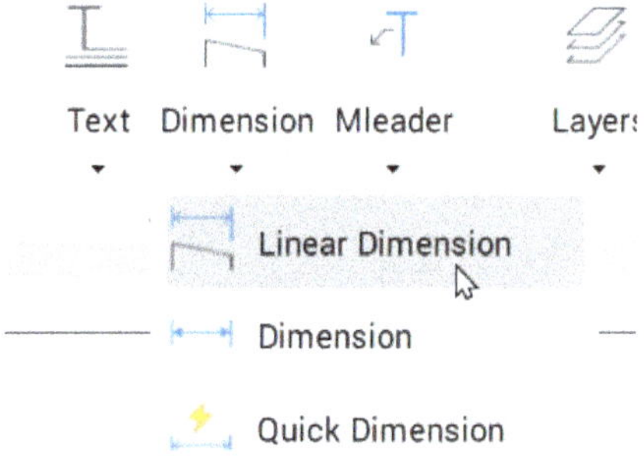

- Select the points on the vertical grid lines, as shown below.
- Move the pointer and click to locate the dimension.

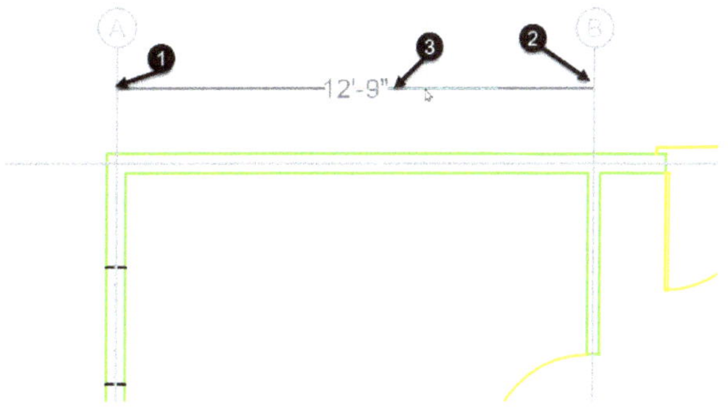

- On the ribbon, click **Annotation > Dimension Continue**. Next, select the existing dimension; you will notice that a dimension is attached to the pointer.

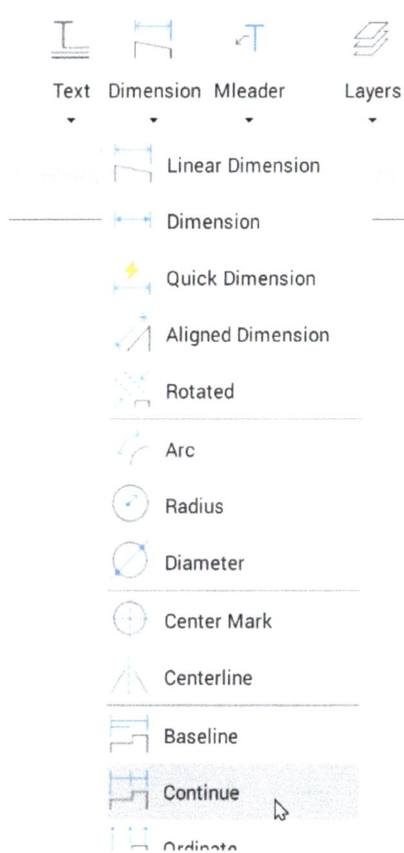

- Move the pointer and click on the next grid line.

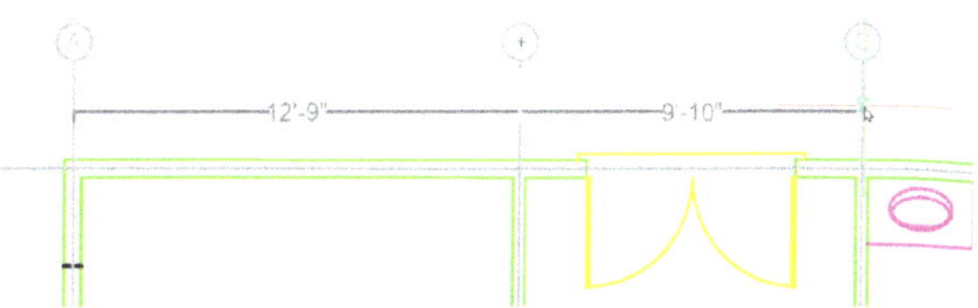

- Likewise, move the pointer and click on the next grid line.

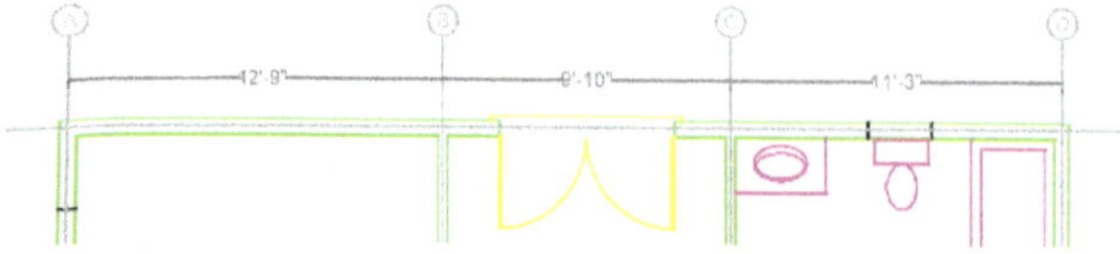

- On the ribbon, click **Annotation > Dimension drop-down > Baseline**. Select last dimension of the dimension chain.
- Move the pointer and select the left vertical grid line. Next, press ESC.

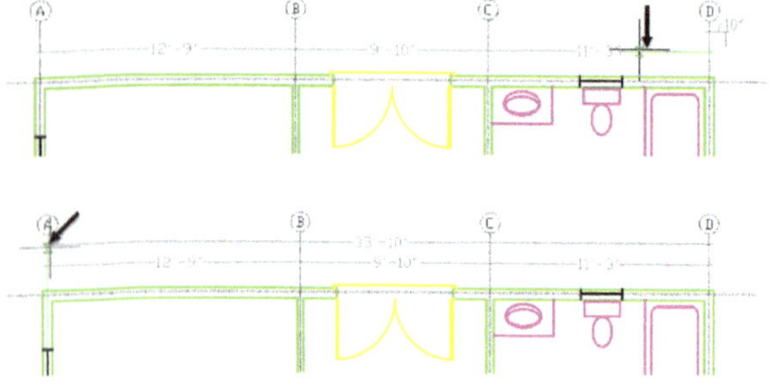

- Likewise, add vertical dimensions to the grid lines.

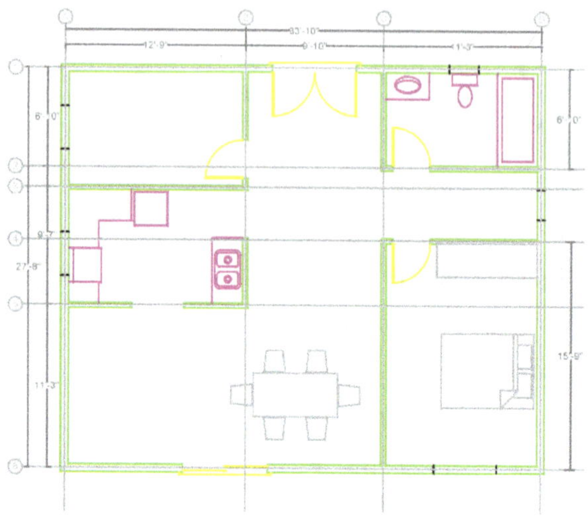

- Save and close the drawing.

Tutorial 2: Creating the Stairs

In this tutorial, you will draw stairs.

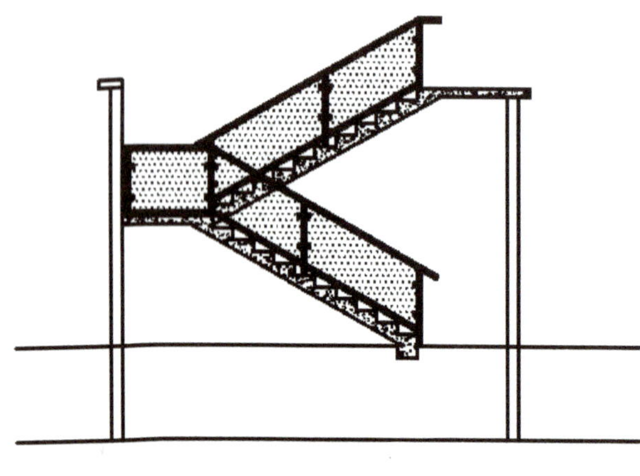

Staircase Nomenclature

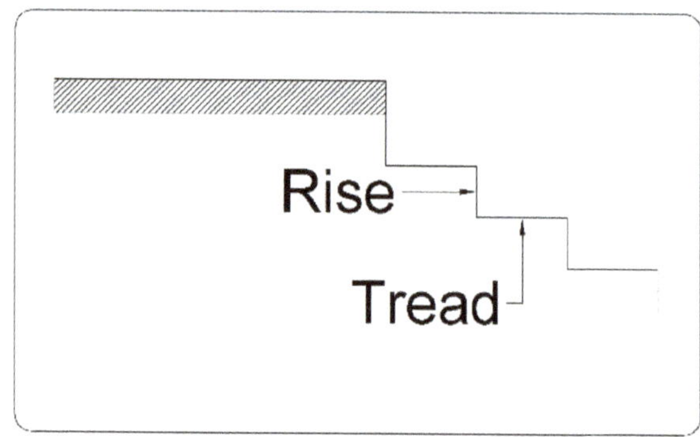

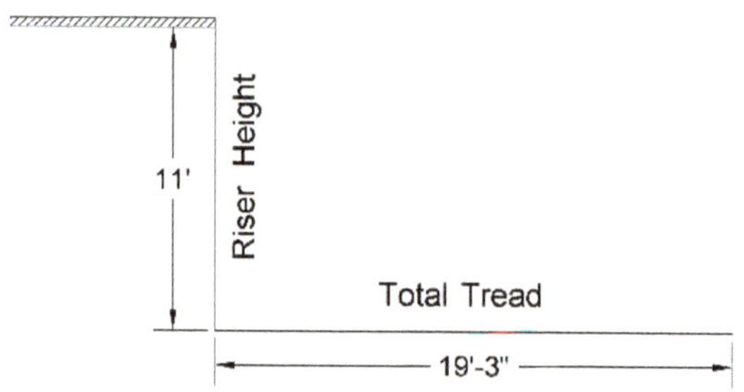

Creating the Stairs

- Start the BricsCAD application and click the **Default Imperial** button under the **Start from Template** section on the **Home** page.

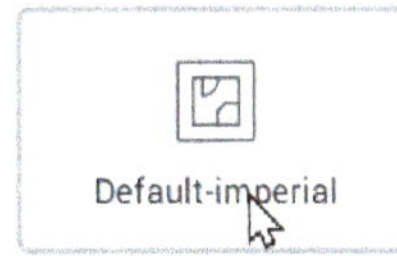

- Type LIMITS in the command line and press Enter.

- Press Enter to accept 0, 0 as the lower limit.

- Type 50', 40' in the command line, and press Enter. The program sets the upper limit of the drawing.

- On the ribbon, click the **View** > **Views** > **Zoom** > **Zoom Extents**.

- Deactivate the **GRID** icon on the status bar.

- Activate the **ORTHO** icon on the Status bar.

- Click **Home** > **Draw** > **Polyline** on the ribbon.

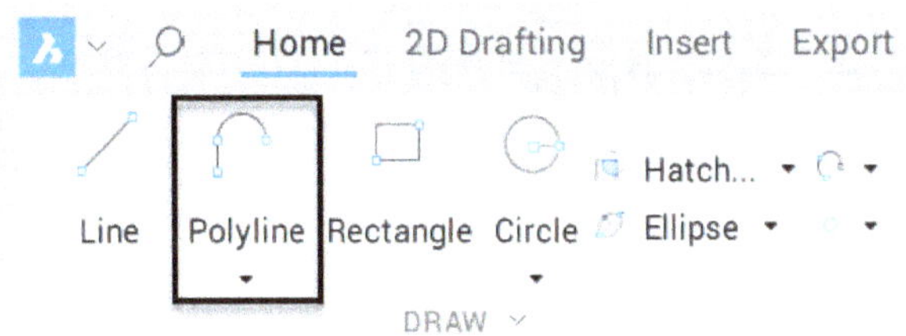

- Click to define the start point of the line. Next, move the pointer toward the left.
- Type 17'8" and press ENTER.

- Move the pointer upward. Next, type 7' and press ENTER.

- Move the pointer toward the right. Next, type 17'2" and press ENTER.

- Move the pointer downward. Next, type 3'6" and press ENTER.

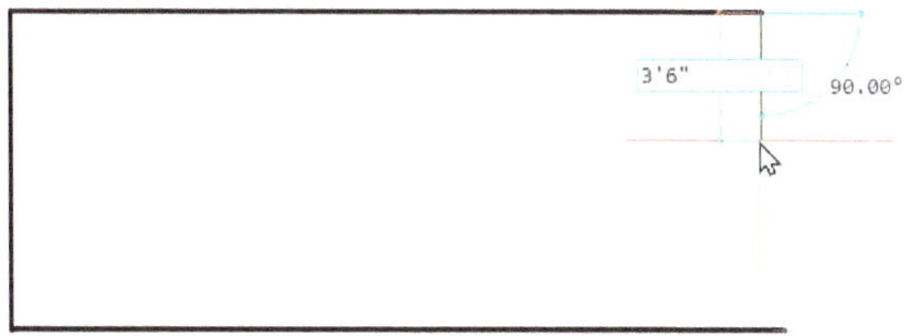

- Press Esc.

- On the ribbon, click the **Home** > **Modify** > **Offset** tool. Next, type 6" and press ENTER.
- Select the polyline. Next, move the pointer outward and click.

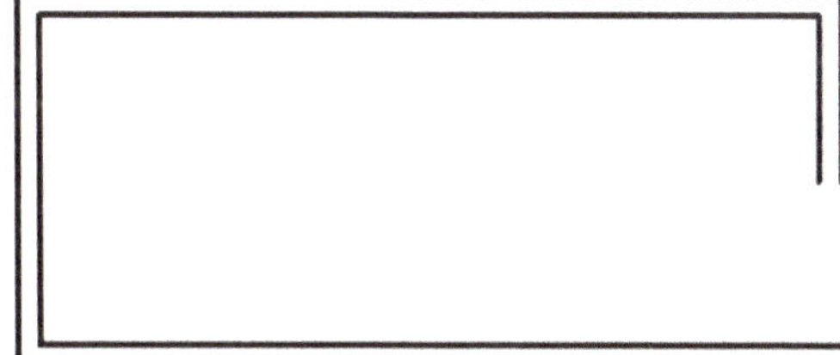

- Click the **Line** tool on the **Draw** panel of the **Home** ribbon tab and close the open ends of the drawing, as shown.

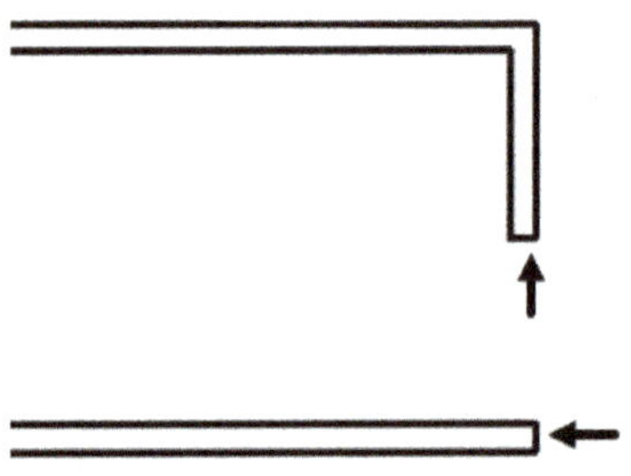

- Create a selection window across all the elements of the drawing.

- Click the **Explode** tool on the **Modify** panel of the **Home** ribbon tab. The polylines are exploded into lines.
- On the ribbon, click the **Home** > **Modify** > **Offset** tool. Next, type 4' and press ENTER.
- Select the left vertical inner edge. Next, move the pointer toward the right and click.

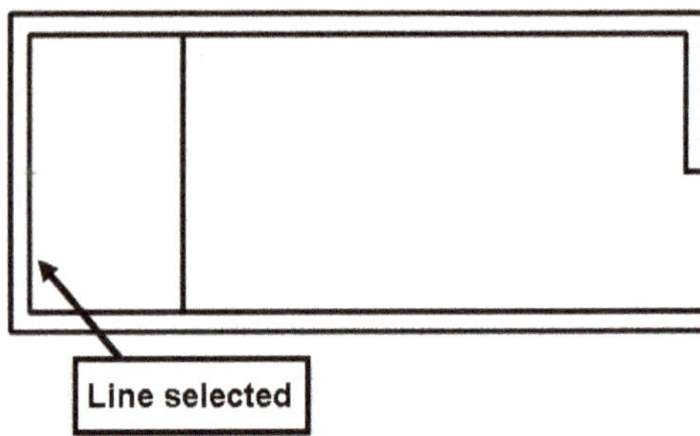

- Press ENTER.
- On the ribbon, click **Home** > **Modify** > **Rectangular Array**.
- Select the offset line and press Enter.
- Select the Rows option from the command line.
- Type 1 in the command line and press ENTER to define the number of rows.
- Press ENTER to accept the default value for the distance between rows.
- Press ENTER to accept the default value for the incrementing elevation between rows.
- Select the **COlumns** option from the command line.

- Type 11 in the command line and press ENTER to define the number of columns.
- Type **11** and press ENTER to accept the default value for the distance between columns.
- Select the **ASociative** option from the command line.
- Select the **No** option.
- Select the **eXit** option from the command line.

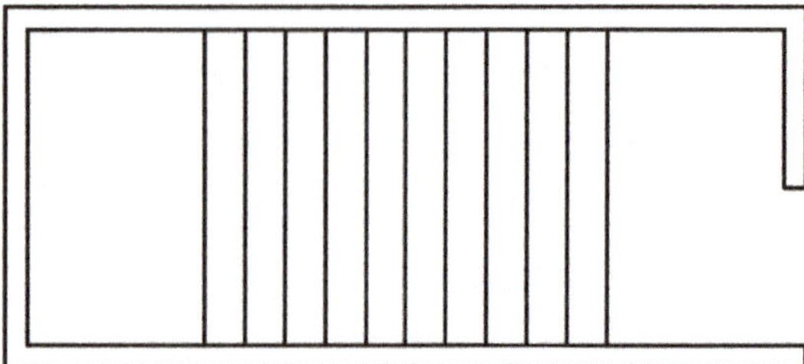

- Activate the **Offset** command and select the **Through point** option from the command line.
- Select the inner horizontal line, as shown. Next, move the pointer upward and select the corner point, as shown.

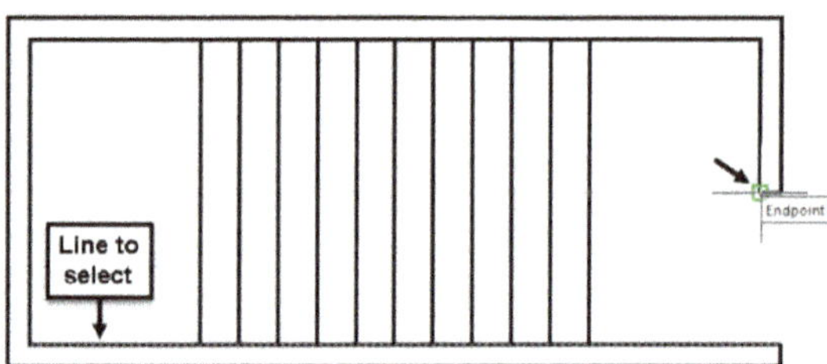

- Again, activate the **Offset** command and type **1** in the command line. Press Enter.
- Select the newly created offset line and then click on the bottom portion of the drawing.

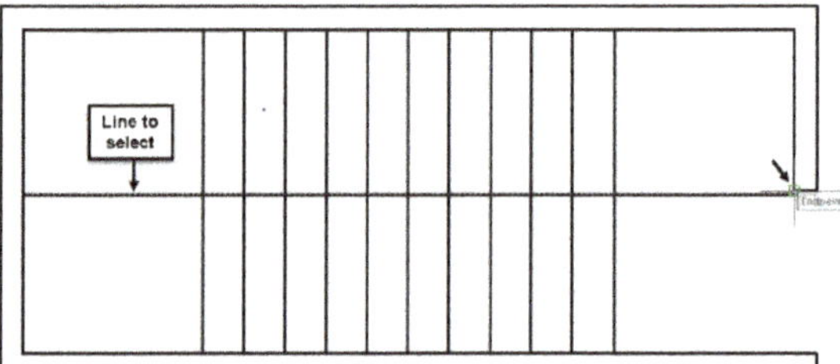

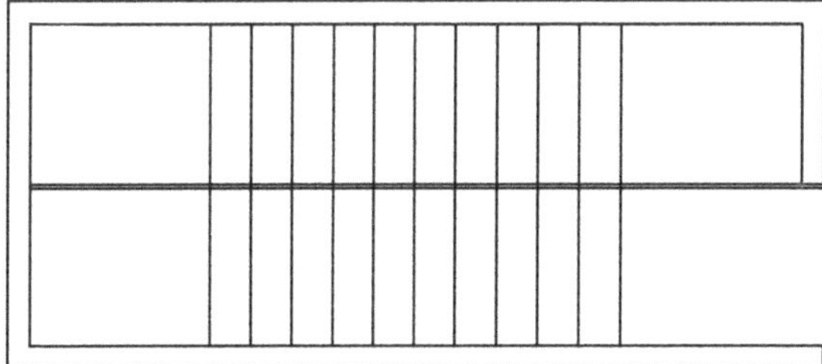

- On the ribbon, click **Home** tab > **Modify** panel > **Trim**. Next, press Enter to select all the objects.
- Create a crossing window from right to left across the unwanted portions of the horizontal lines, as shown.

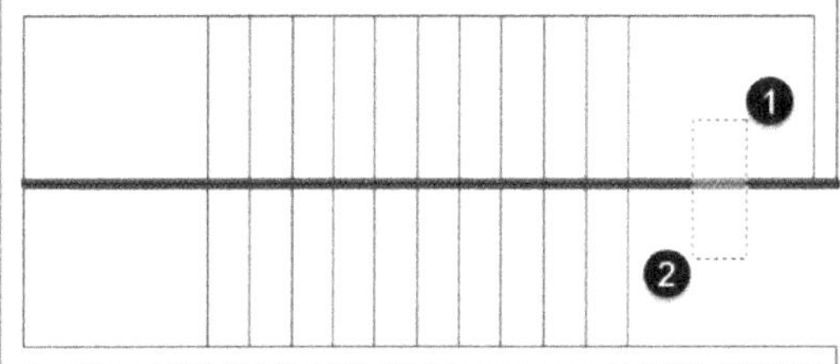

- Likewise, trim the unwanted portions of the horizontal lines, as shown.

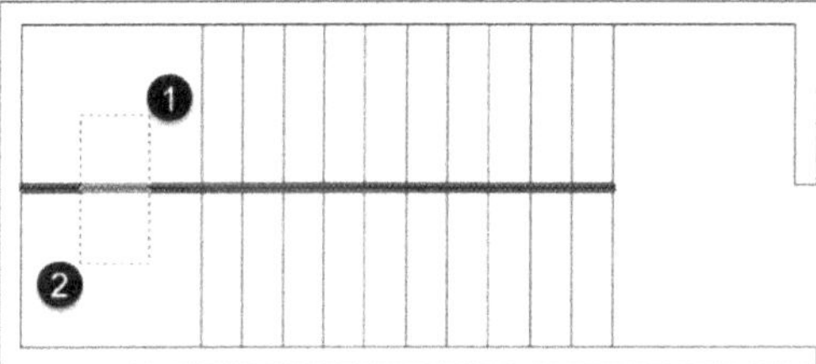

- Zoom-in to the center portion of the stairs.

- Click on the portions of the vertical lines, as shown.

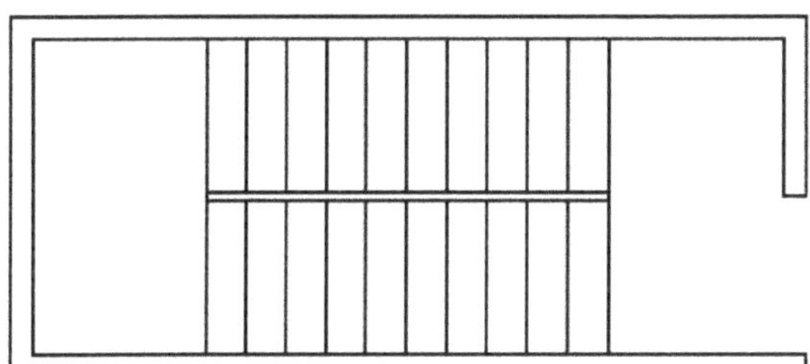

Creating the Section elevation of the Staircase

- Create a horizontal line above the staircase, as shown.

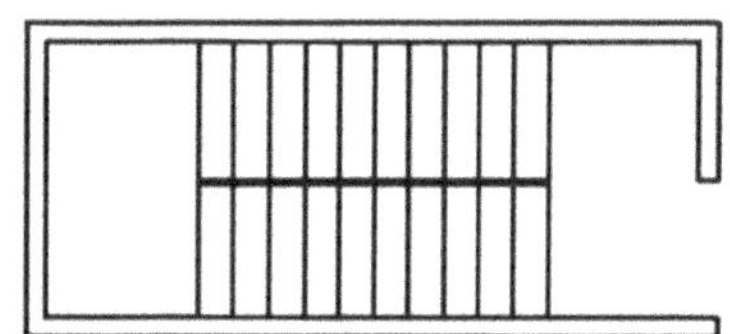

- Click the **Modify > Offset** on the **Home** ribbon tab. Next, type **4'** and press ENTER.
- Select the newly created horizontal line. Move the pointer upward and click to create the offset line.

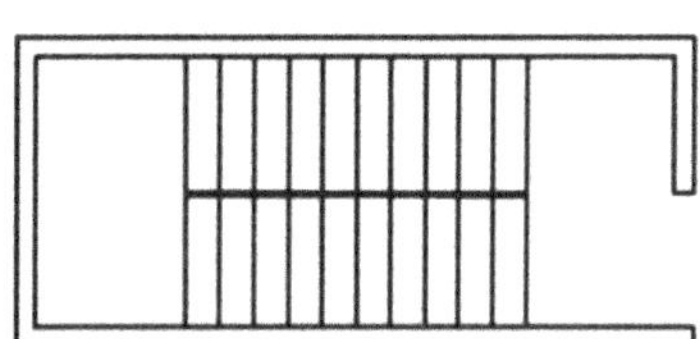

- On the ribbon, click **Home > Draw > Infinite Line**. Next, select the **Vertical** option from the command line.
- Select the endpoints of the left vertical line, as shown.
- Likewise, select the endpoints of the lines, as shown. Next, press ESC.

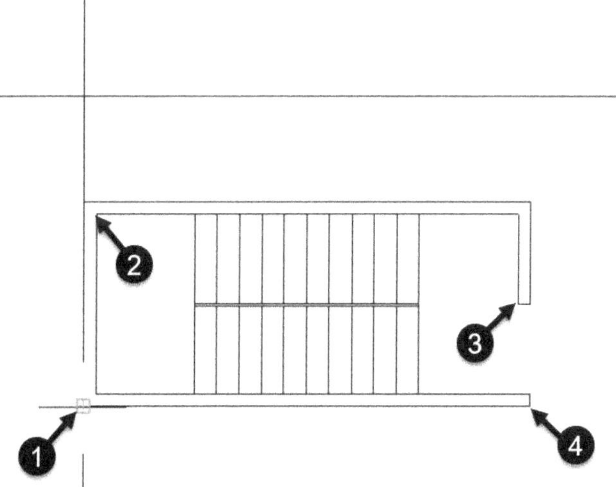

- Click **Home > Modify > Offset** on the ribbon. Next, type 10'8" and press ENTER.
- Select the offset horizontal line.

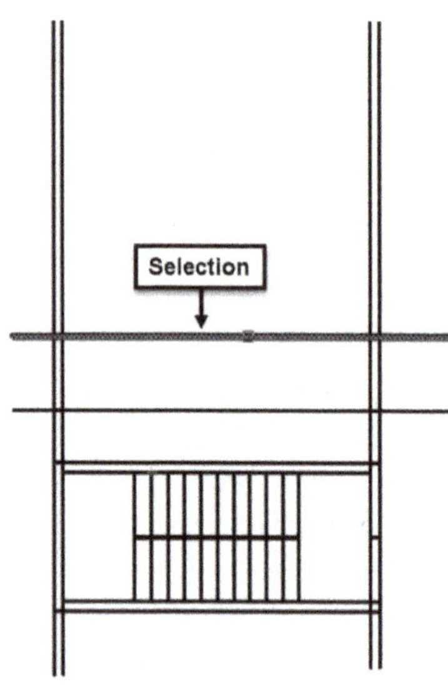

- Move the pointer upward and click.

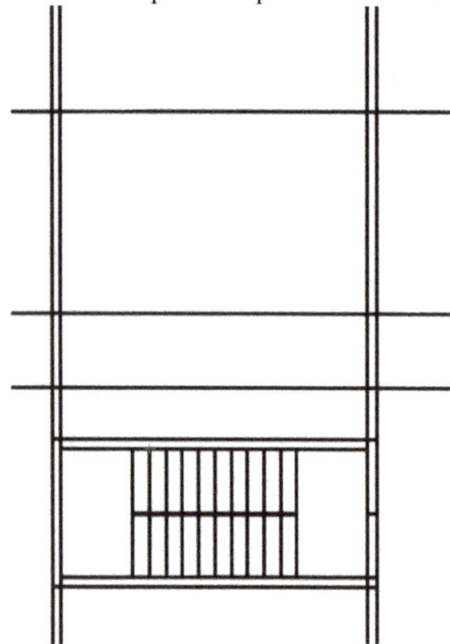

- Press ENTER twice to deactivate the **Offset** tool and then activate it again. Next, type 4" and press ENTER.
- Select the newly created offset line. Next, move the pointer upward and click.

- Press **Esc** to deactivate the **Offset** tool.

- On the ribbon, click **Home** > **Modify** > **Trim**. Press ENTER.
- Press and hold the left mouse button and drag the selection box from the right to left across the portions of the construction lines, as shown.

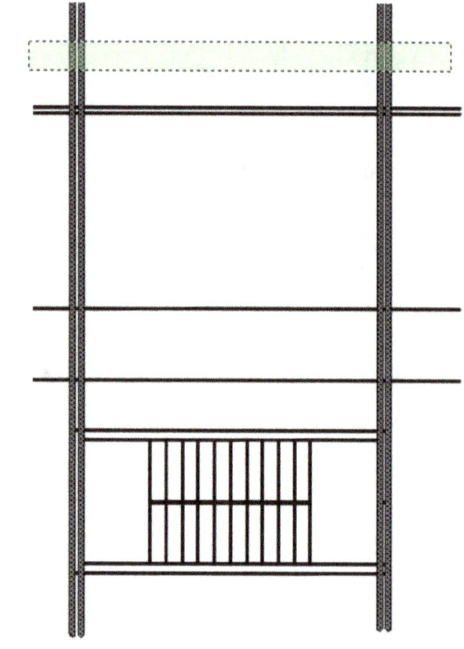

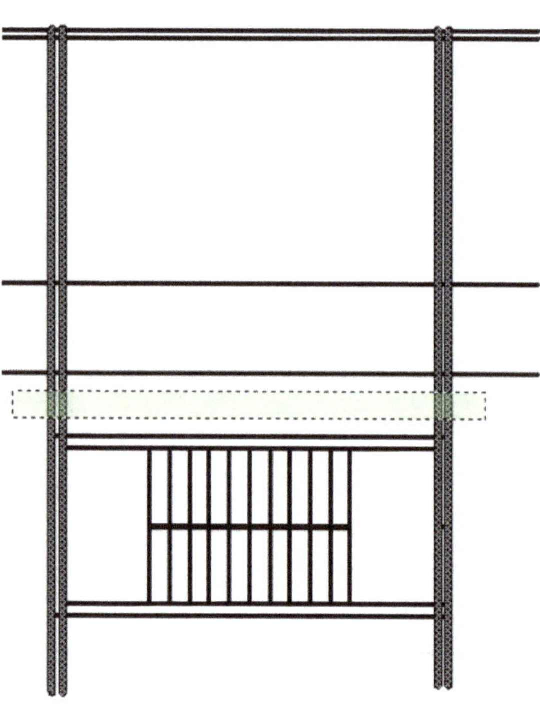

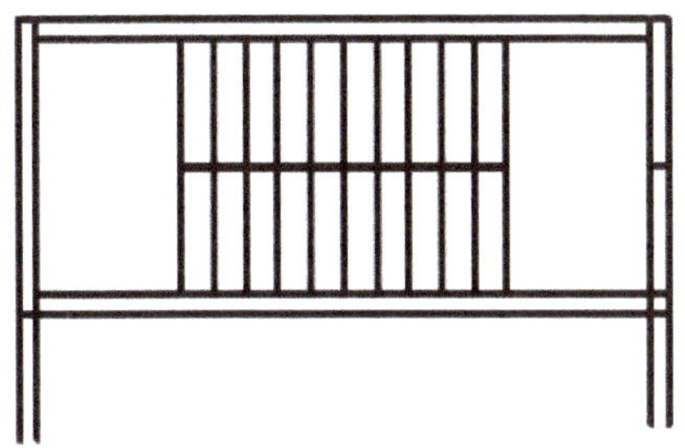

- Click **Home** > **Modify** > **Offset** on the ribbon. Next, type **6"** and press ENTER.
- Offset the outer vertical lines on both sides.

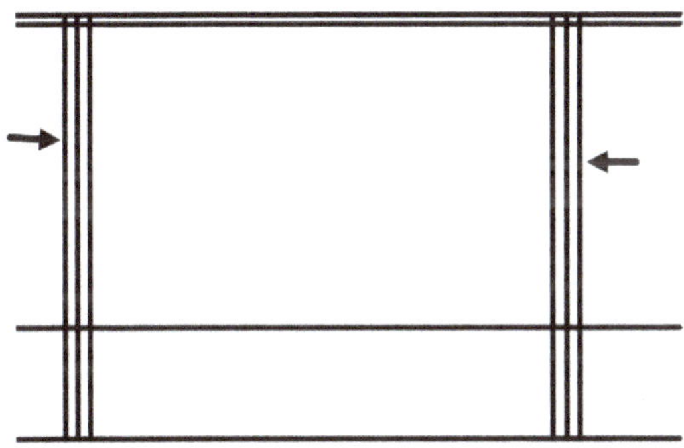

- On the ribbon, click **Home** > **Modify** > **Trim**. Next, press ENTER.
- Trim the portions of the vertical and horizontal lines, as shown.

- On the ribbon, click **Home** > **Modify** > **Extend**.

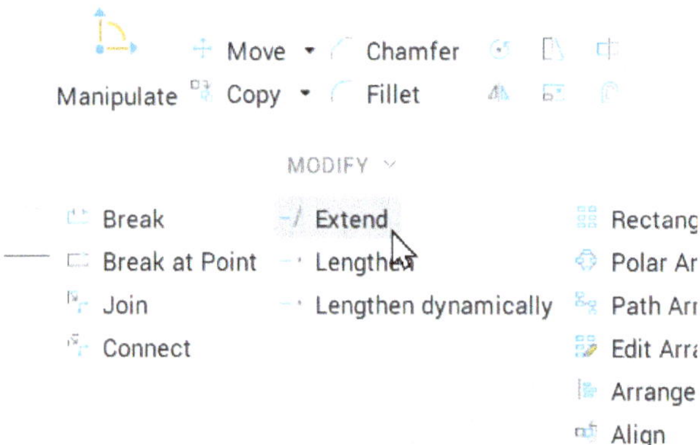

- Select the lower horizontal edge of the roof, as shown. Next, press ENTER.

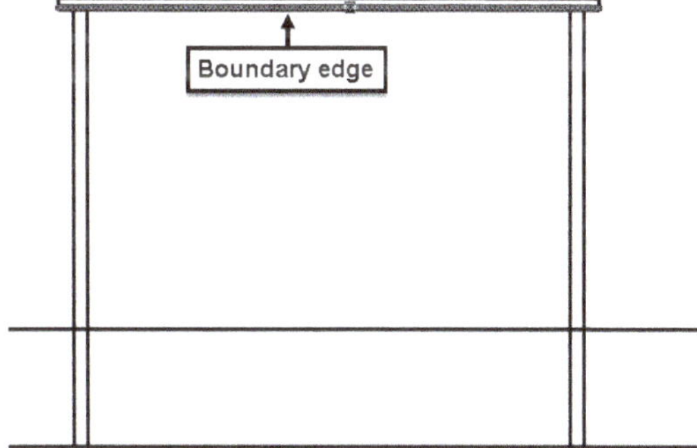

- Press and hold the left mouse button.
- Create a selection window across the lines of the staircase from right to left; the lines are extended up to the boundary edge.

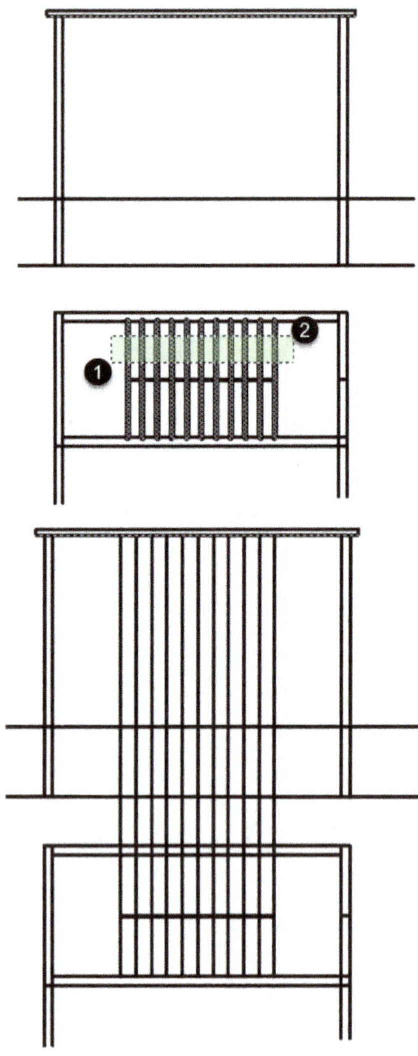

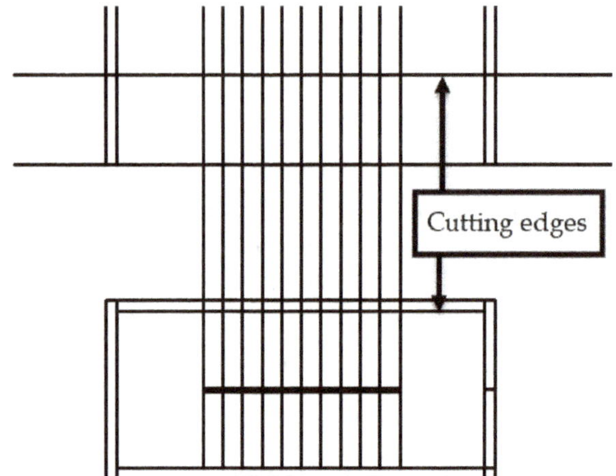

- On the ribbon, click **Home** > **Modify** > **Trim**.
- Press and hold the CTRL key and select the horizontal lines, as shown. Next, press ENTER.

- Create a selection window across the vertical lines, as shown.

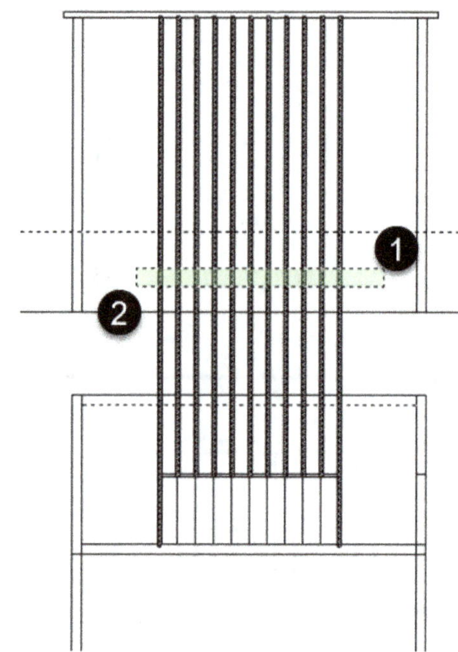

- On the ribbon, click **Home** > **Draw** > **Polyline** .
- Select the first point of the polyline.

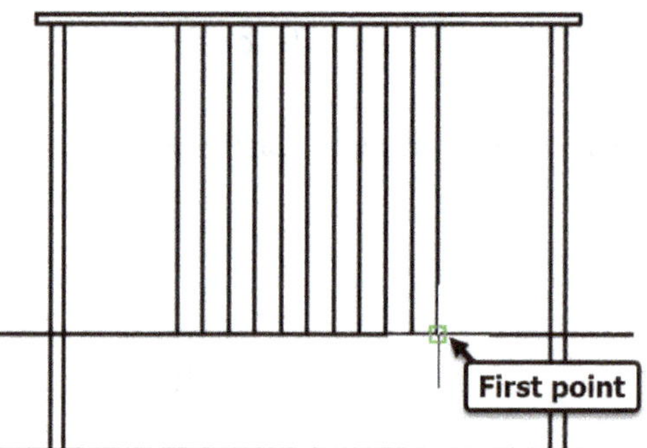

- Move the pointer upward. Next, type 6" and press ENTER.

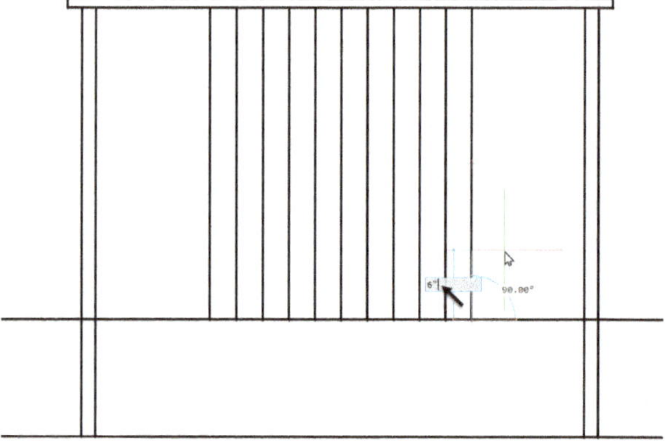

- Move the pointer toward left. Next, type 11" and press ENTER.

- Press Esc.

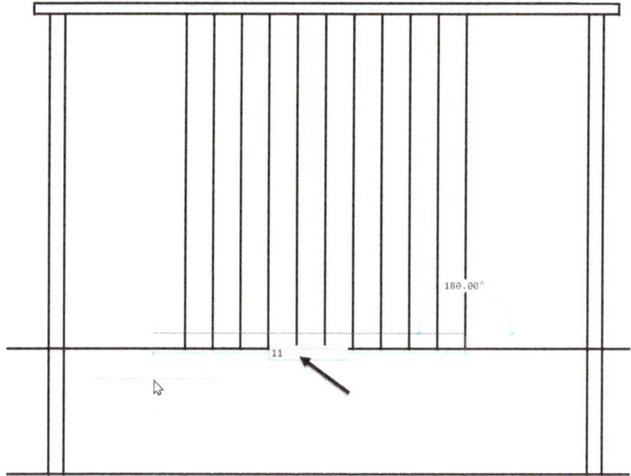

- Deactivate the **ORTHO** icon on the status bar.
- Select the polyline and click the **Copy** icon on the **Modify** panel of the **Home** tab of the ribbon.
- Select the first point of the polyline as the base point.

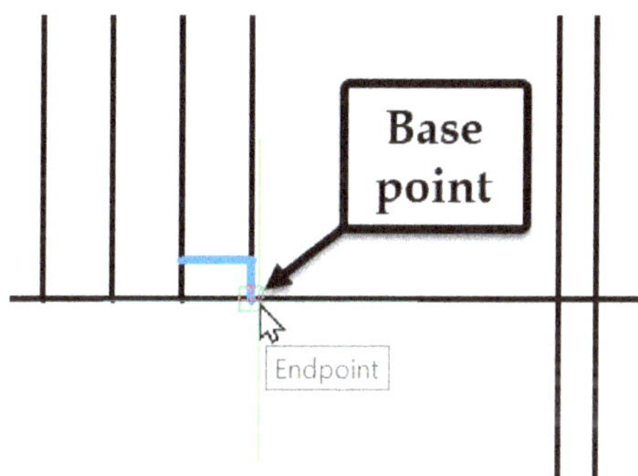

- Move the pointer upward and select the endpoint of the polyline. The polyline is copied.

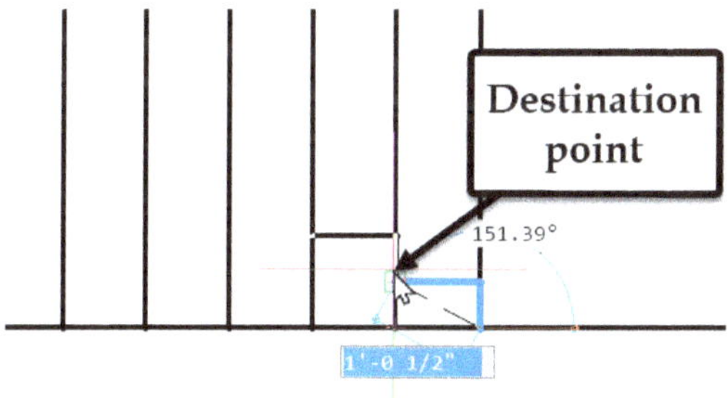

- Likewise, create copies of the polylines, as shown. Next, press ESC.

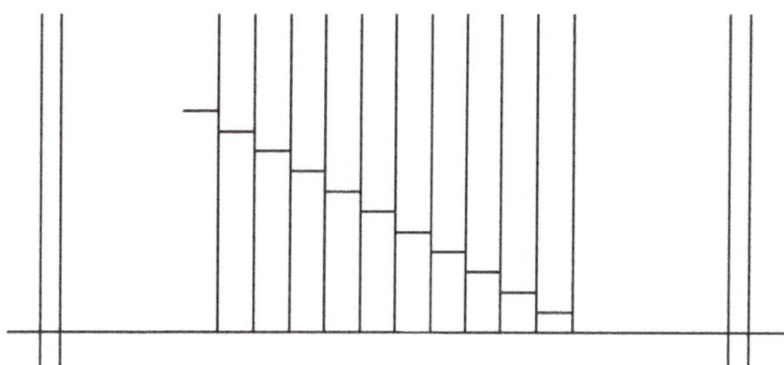

- Click the **Join** icon on the **Modify** panel on the **Home** ribbon tab.

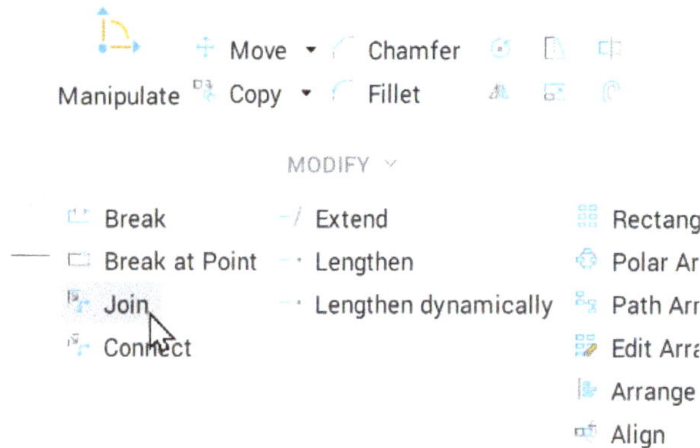

- Press and hold the Shift key and select all the polylines and press ENTER. All the polylines are joined.

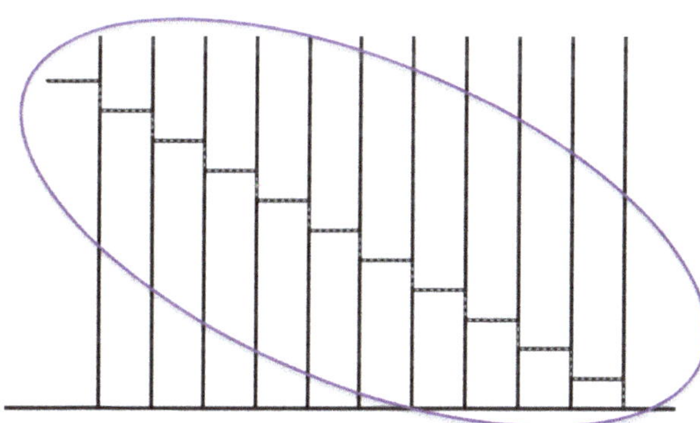

- On the **Home** ribbon tab, click **Modify** > **Extend**. Next, press ENTER.
- Click on the end portion of the polyline to extend it up to the left vertical line. Press Esc.

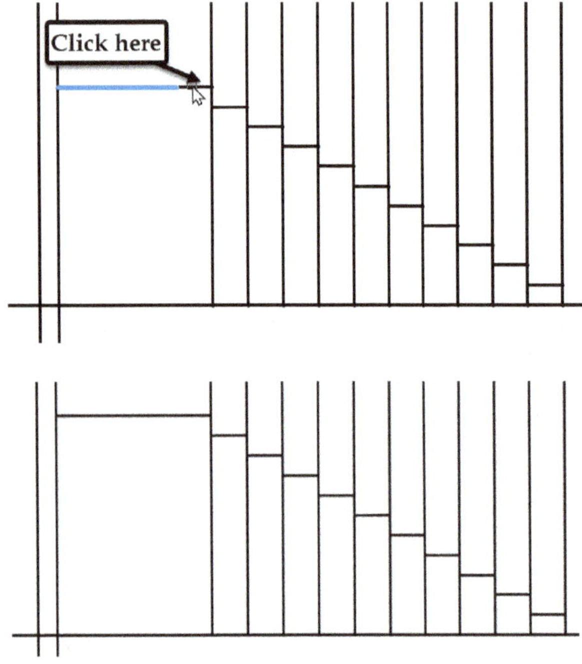

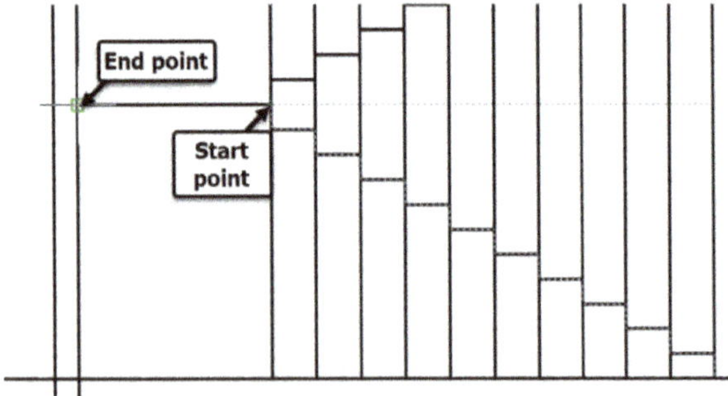

- Select the stairs and click **Modify** > **Mirror** on the **Home** ribbon tab.
- Specify the start point of the mirror line, as shown.
- Move the pointer toward the left and specify the endpoint of the mirror line, as shown.

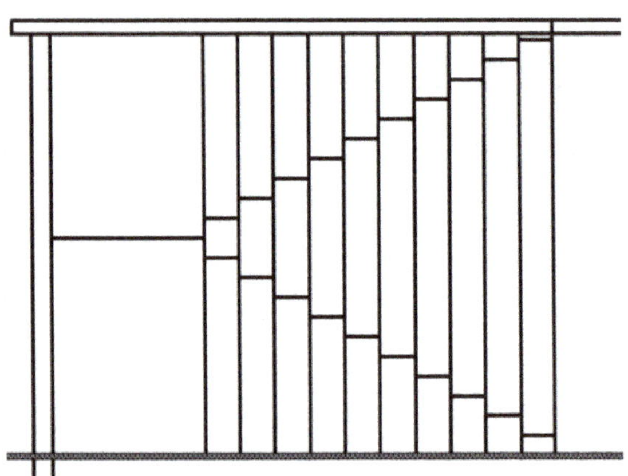

- Next, select **No-keep entities**.

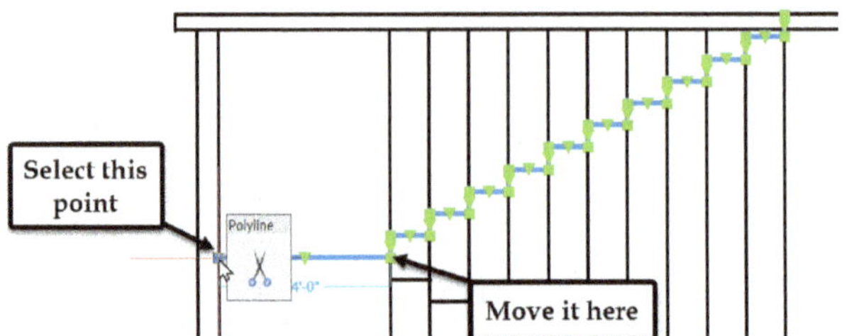

- Select the mirrored polyline. Next, click on the endpoint of the polyline.

- Move the pointer toward the right and select the vertex point, as shown. The polyline is shortened.

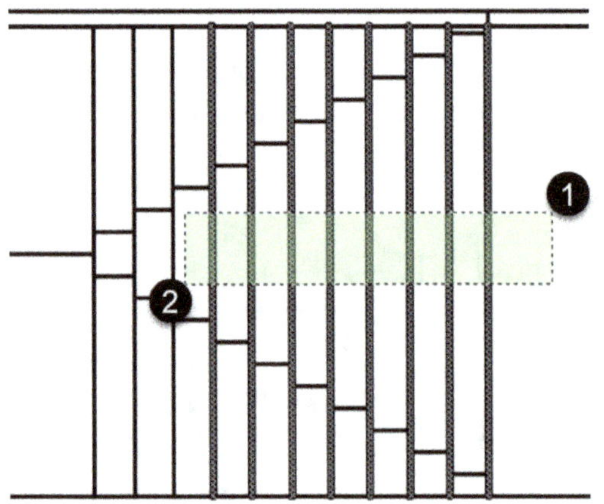

- Press Esc to deselect the mirrored polyline.
- Drag a selection window across the vertical lines from right to left, as shown.

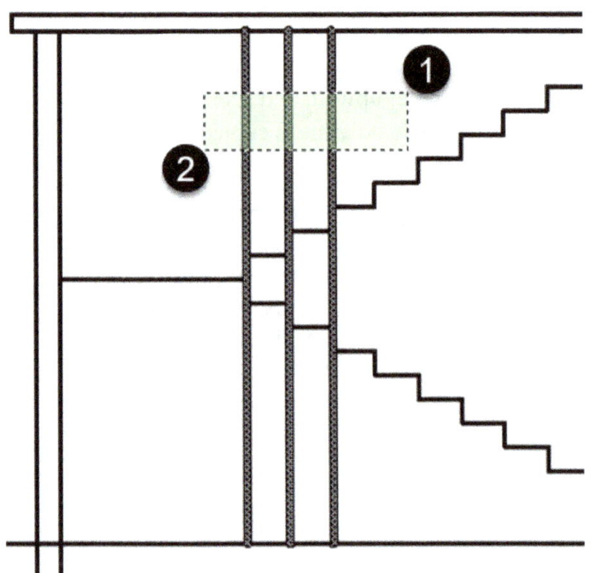

- Press Delete on your keyboard.
- On the ribbon, click **Home** > **Draw** > **Line**. Next, select the corner points, as shown.

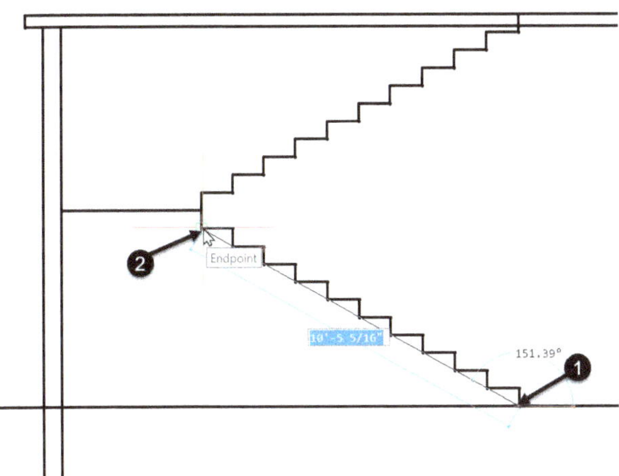

- Offset the newly created line by 4".

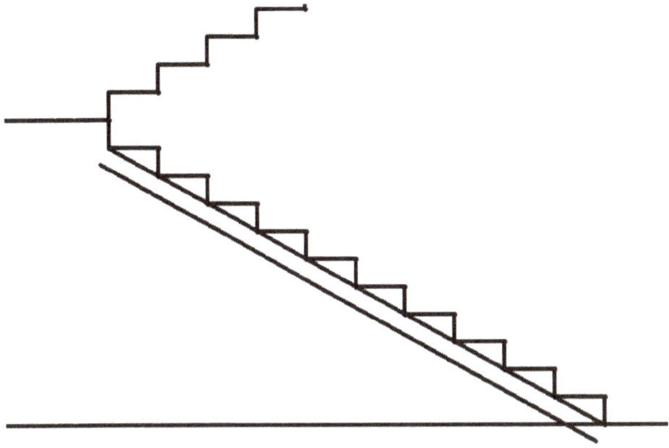

- On the ribbon, click **Home** > **Draw** > **Line**. Next, select the two points, as shown.

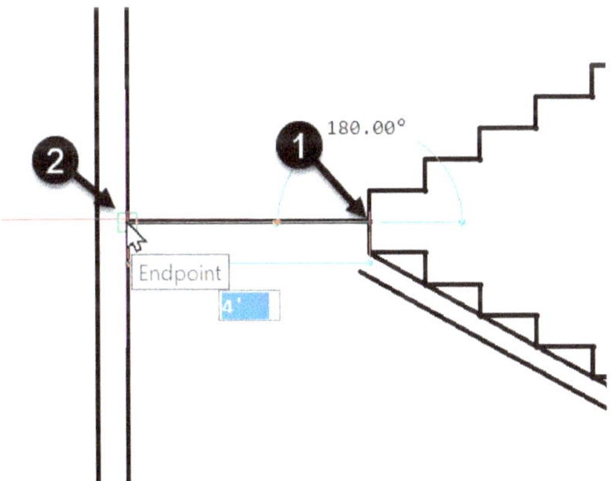

- Press ESC and click on the newly created line.

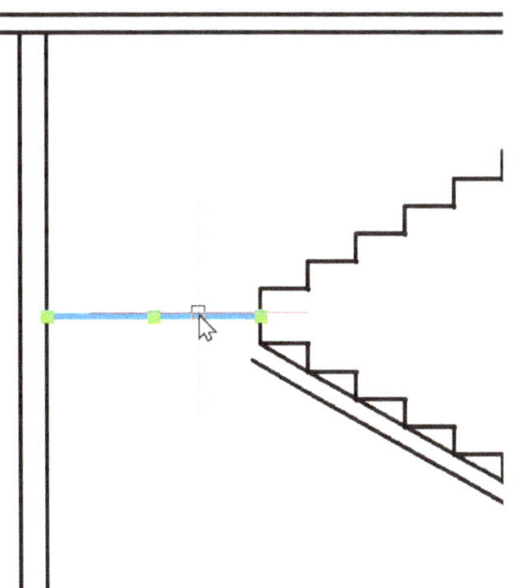

- Click on the midpoint of the selected line.

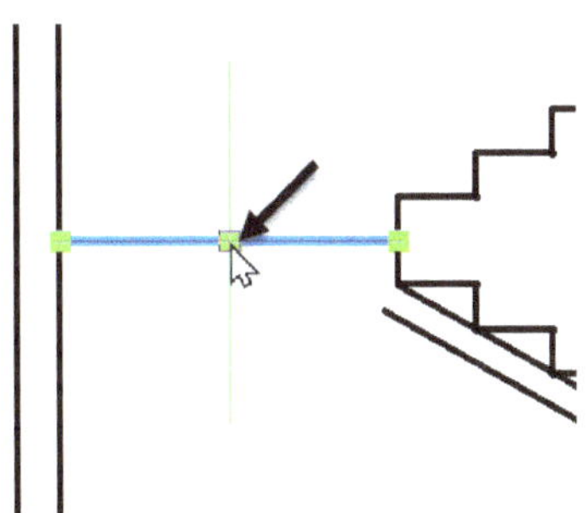

- Next, move the pointer downward and type 4. Next, press ENTER.

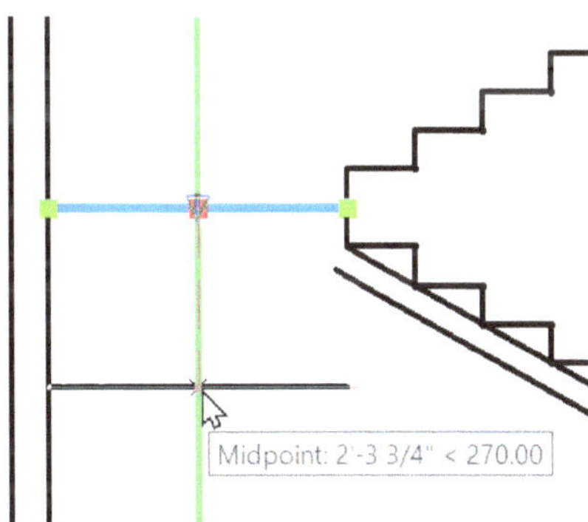

- Click the **Fillet** icon on the **Modify** panel on the **Home** ribbon tab.
- Select the **Radius** option from the command line.
- Type **0** in the command line and press ENTER.
- Select the horizontal and inclined lines, as shown.

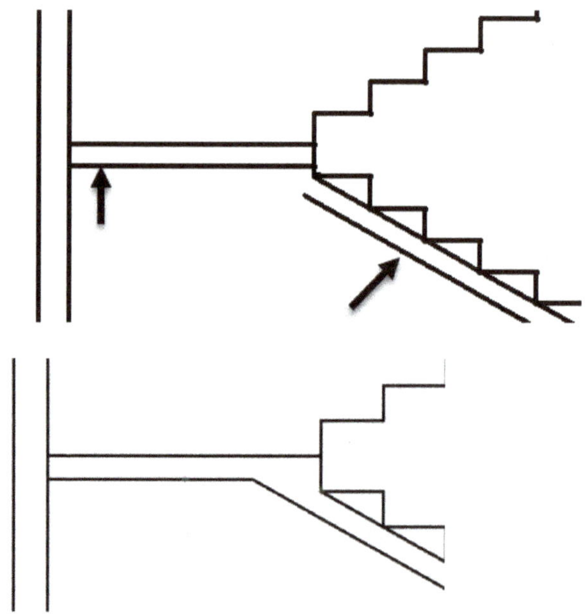

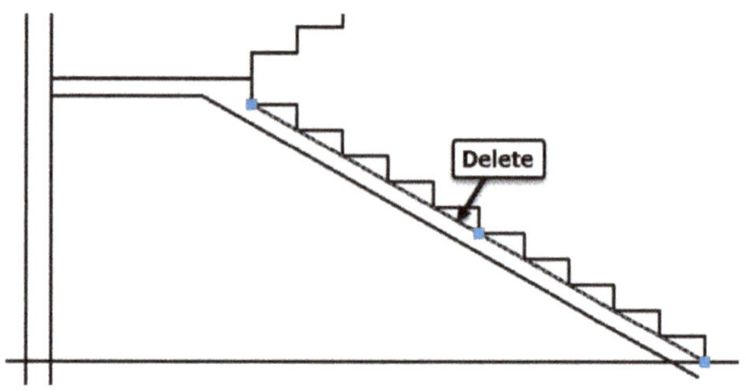

- Delete the inclined line, as shown.

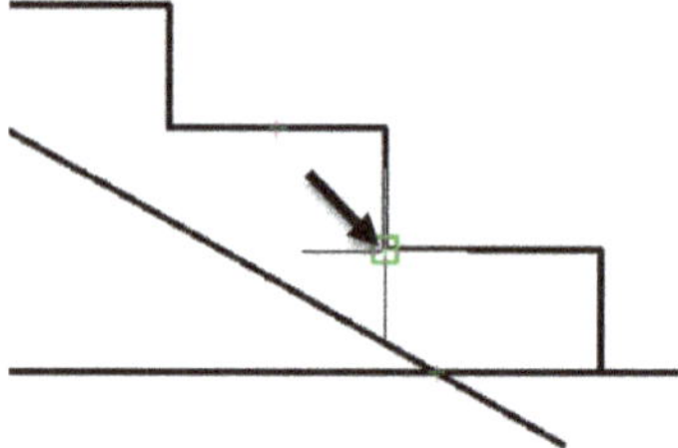

- On the ribbon, click **Home** > **Draw** > **Line**.
- Select the corner point of the stair, as shown.

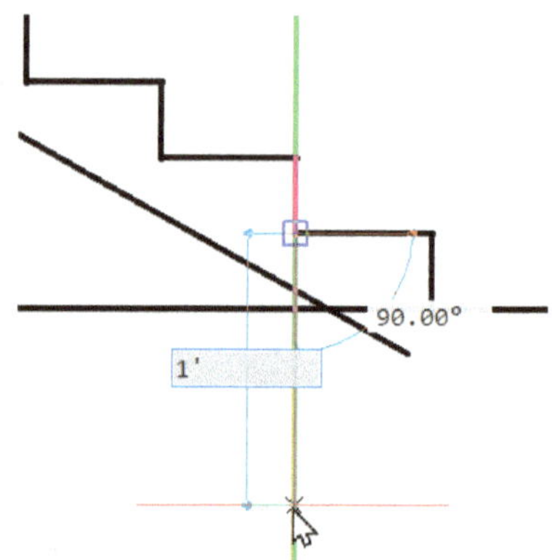

- Move the pointer downward. Next, type 1' and press ENTER.

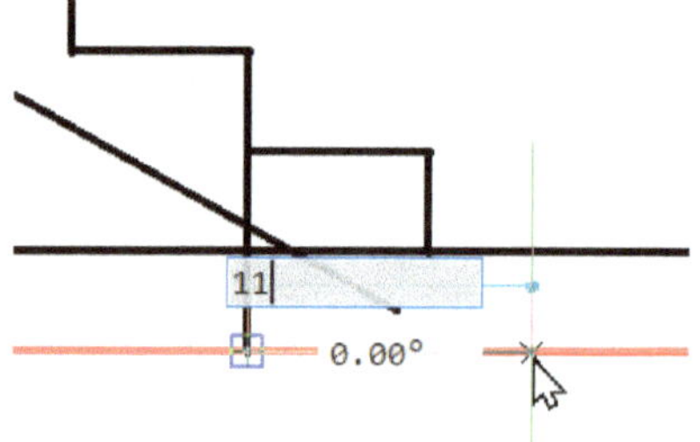

- Move the pointer toward the right. Next, type 11" and press ENTER.

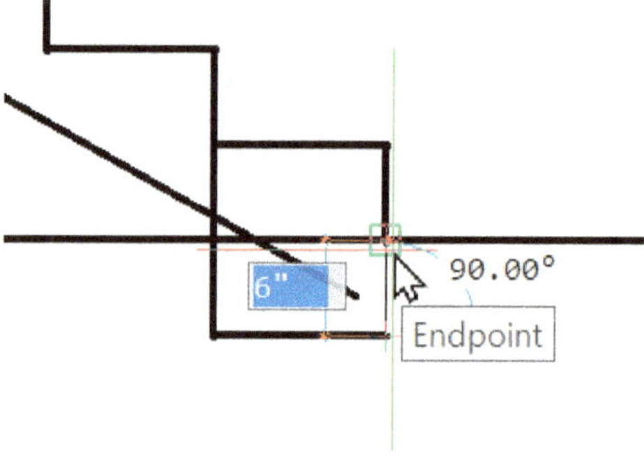

- Move the pointer upward. Next, type 6" and press ENTER.

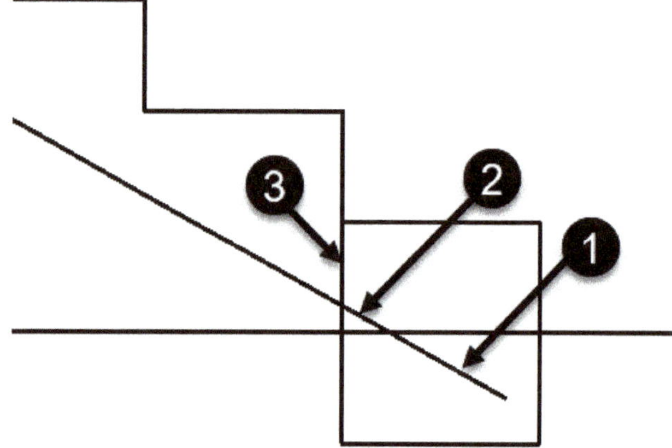

- On the ribbon, click **Home** > **Modify** > **Trim**. Next, press ENTER.
- Select the portions of the lines, as shown.

- On the ribbon, click **Home** > **Draw** > **Line**.
- Select the corner points, as shown.

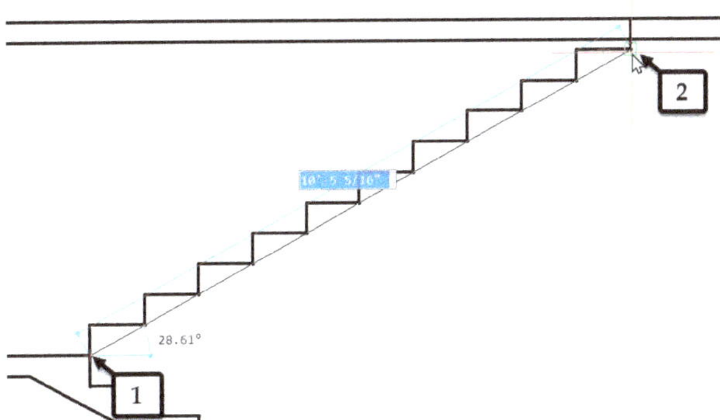

- Offset the newly created line by 4".

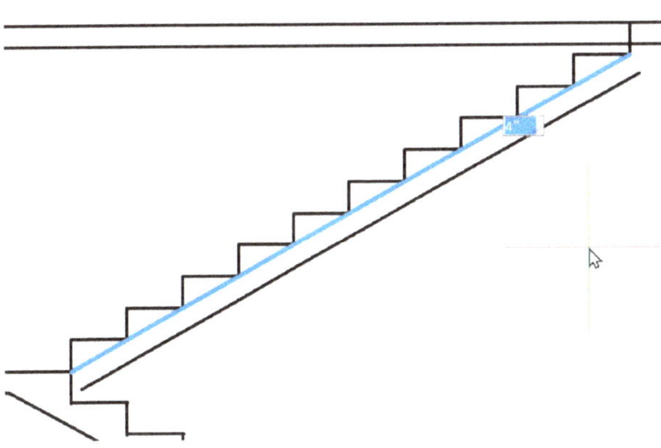

- On the ribbon, click **Home** > **Modify** > **Extend**. Next, press ENTER.
- Select the inclined line, as shown.

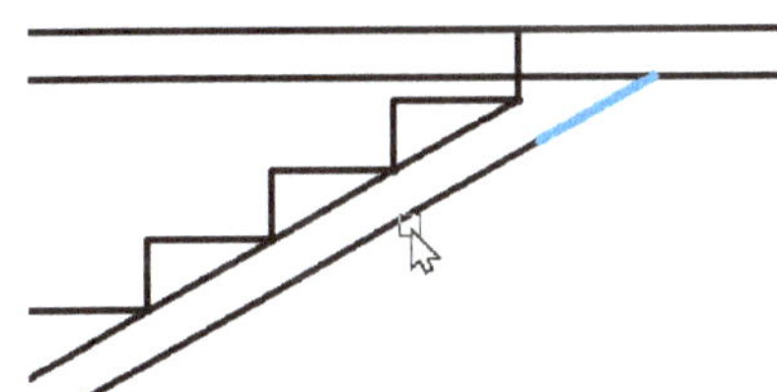

- Extend the inclined line up to the horizontal line, as shown.

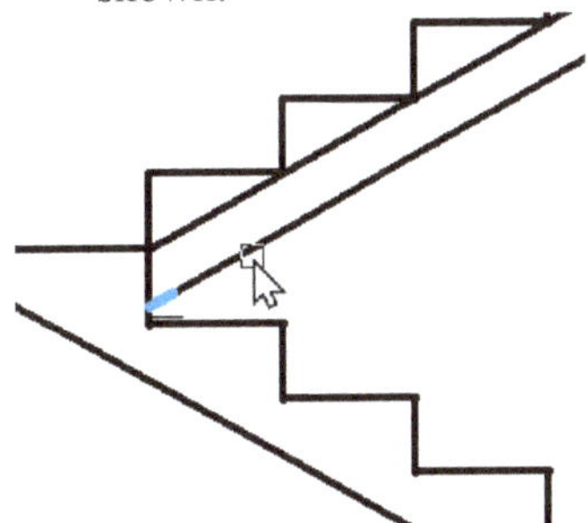

- Extend the vertical line, as shown. Next, press Esc.

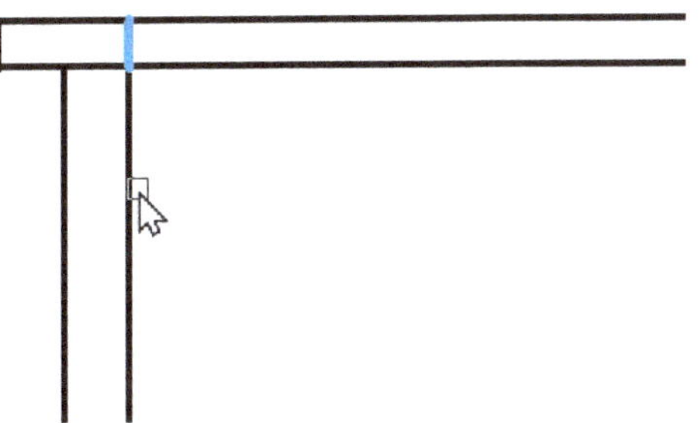

- Select the inclined line, as shown. Next, press Delete.

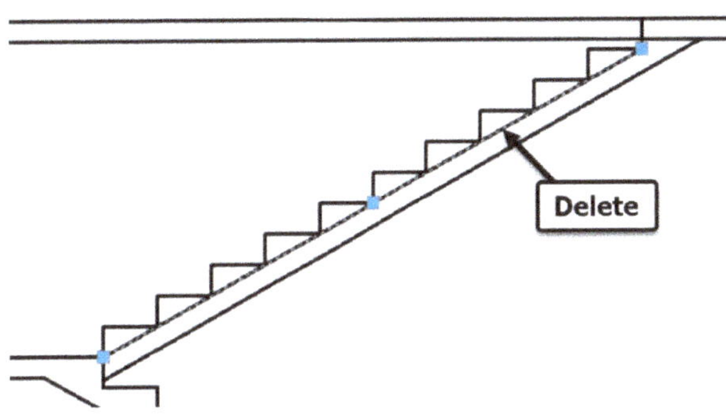

- On the ribbon, click **Home** > **Modify** > **Trim**. Next, press ENTER.
- Click and drag the pointer across the entities, as shown.

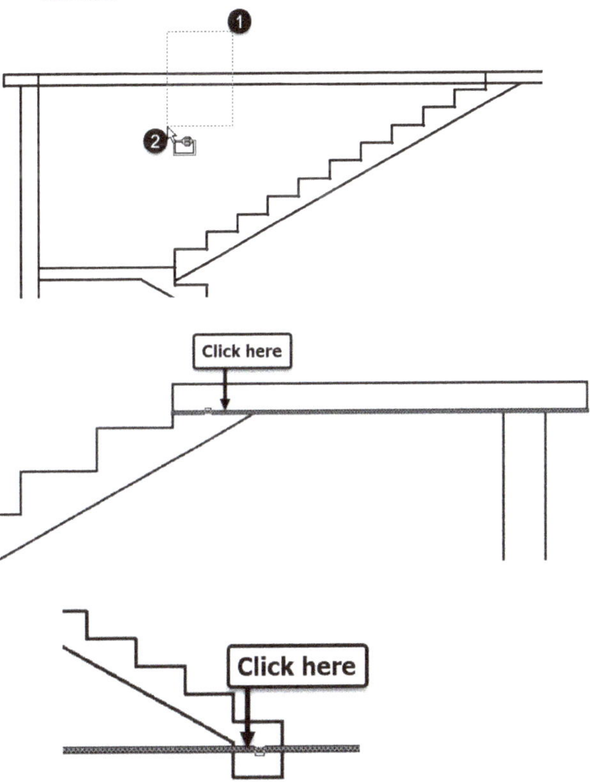

- On the ribbon, click **Home** > **Draw** > **Hatch**.

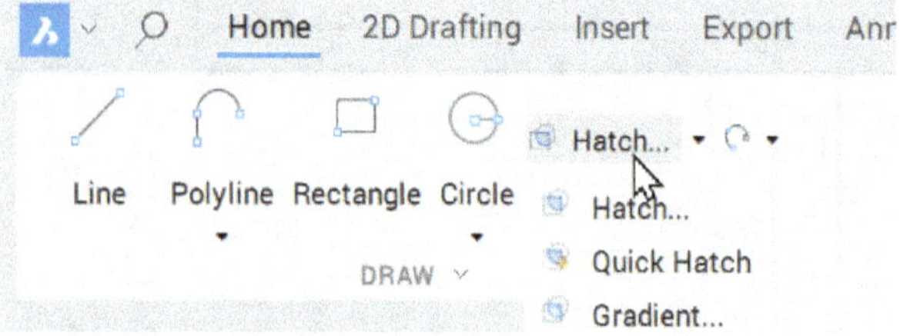

- On the **Hatch and Gradient** dialog, click the

  Browse [...] icon next to the **Name** box.

- Select the **CONCRETE2** hatch from the **Hatch Pattern Palette** and click **OK**.

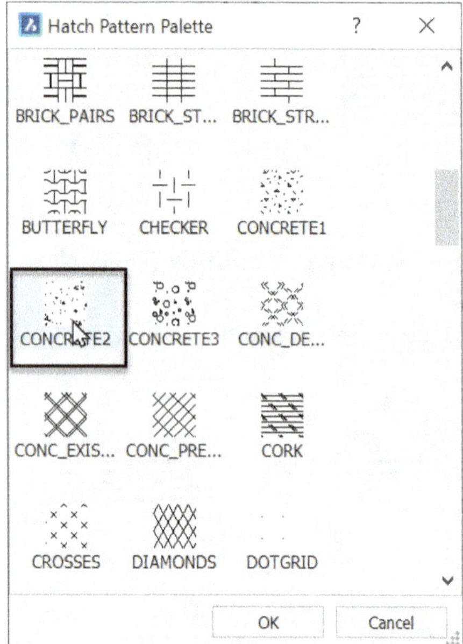

- Click the **Pick points in boundaries** icon under the **Boundaries** section. Next, pick points in the areas, as shown.

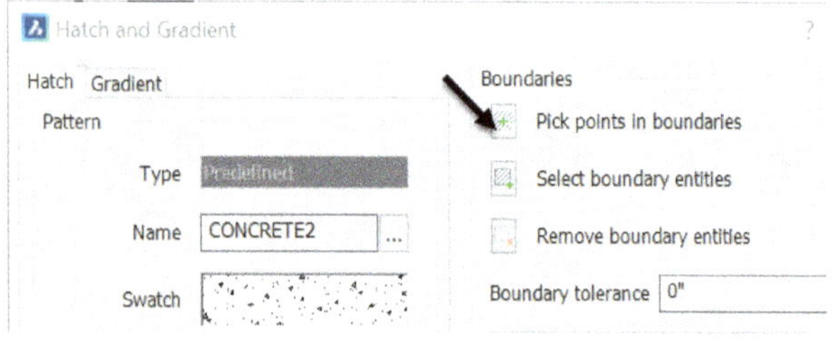

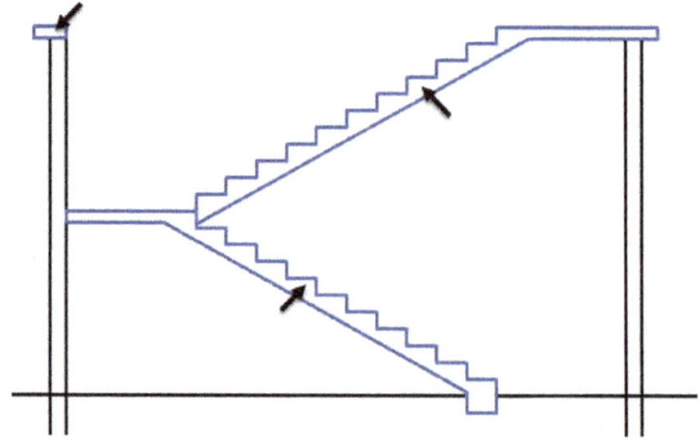

- Press ENTER.
- Type **10** in the **Scale** box and click **OK** on the **Hatch and Gradient** dialog.

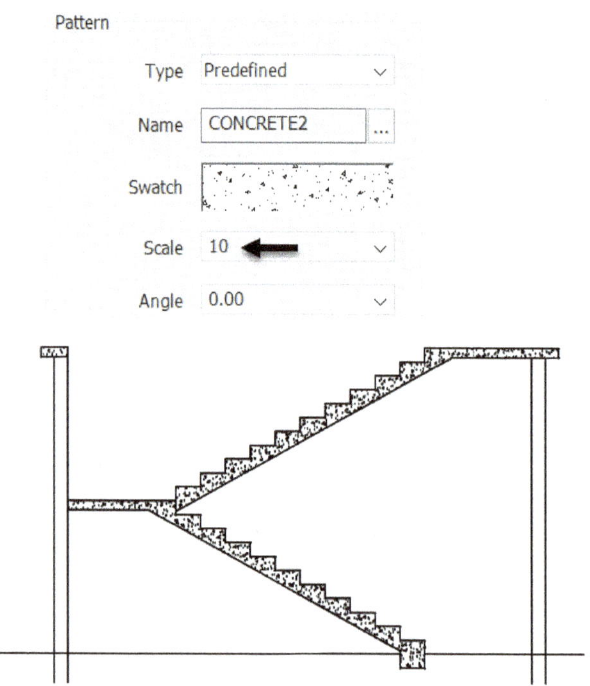

Creating the Handrail

- Activate the **ORTHO** icon on the status bar.
- On the ribbon, click **Home > Draw > Line**.
- Create two vertical lines of 3' length each at the locations, as shown.

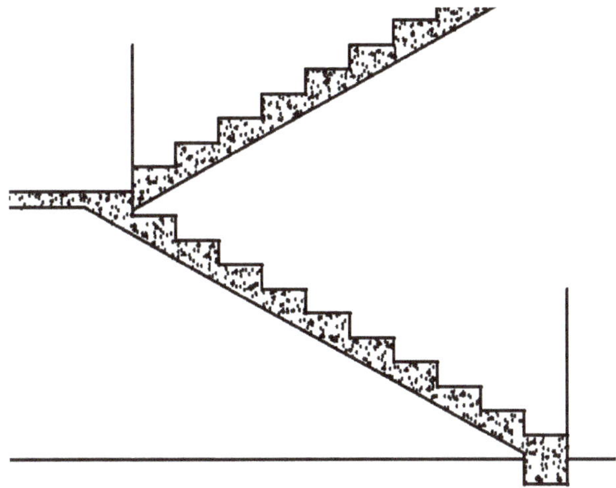

- Activate the **Line** tool and connect the endpoints of the two vertical lines, as shown.

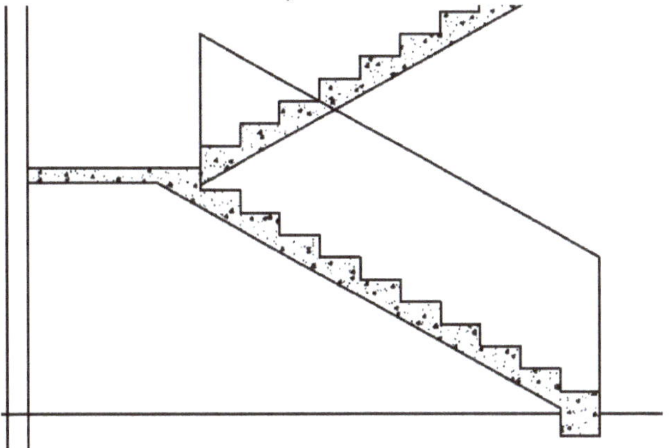

- On the ribbon, click **Home** > **Modify** > **Lengthen**.

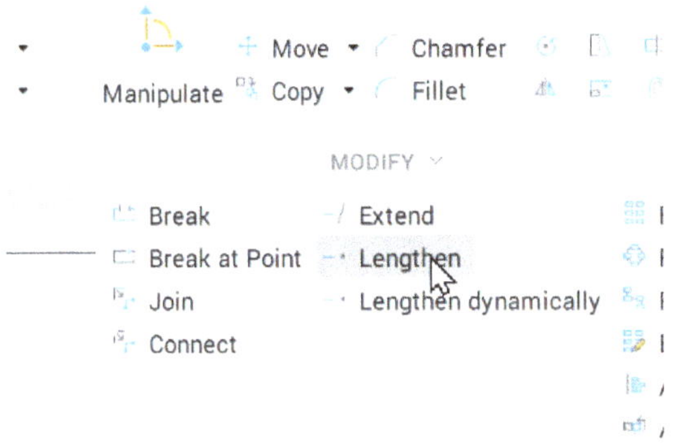

- Select the **Increment** option from the command line.
- Type 12" and press ENTER.
- Click near the endpoint of the inclined line. The inclined line is lengthened.

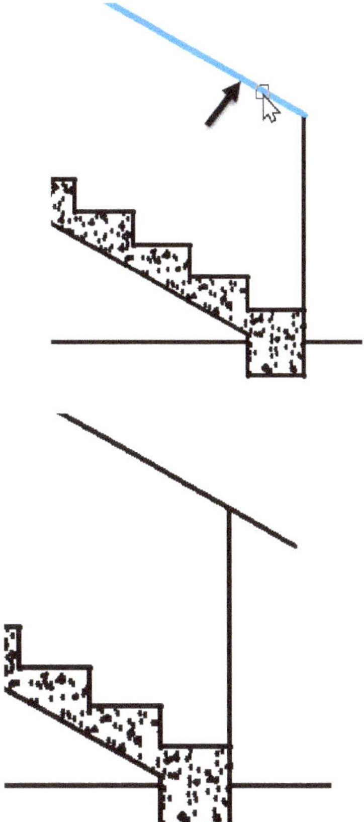

- Create a horizontal line of a random length, as shown.

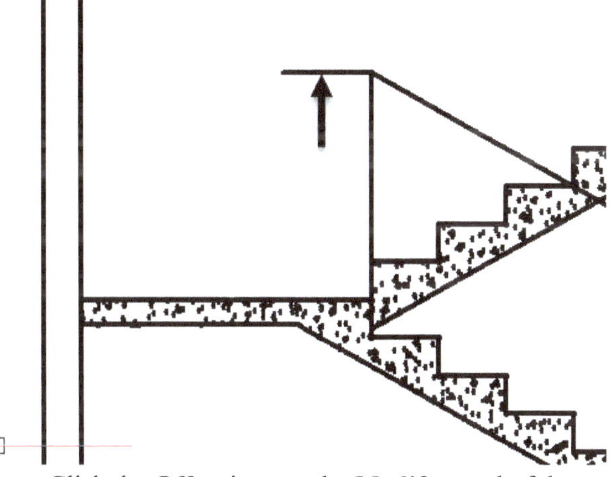

- Click the **Offset** icon on the **Modify** panel of the Home ribbon tab. Next, offset the newly created lines by 2" distance, as shown.

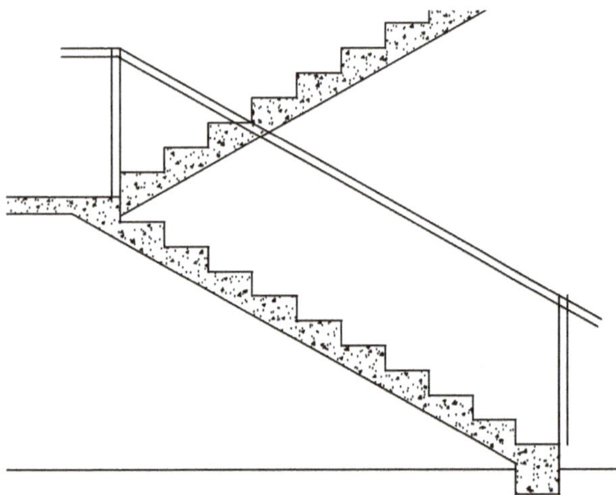

- On the ribbon, click **Home** > **Modify** > **Extend**. Next, press ENTER.
- Extend the two vertical lines up to the bottom horizontal edge, as shown.

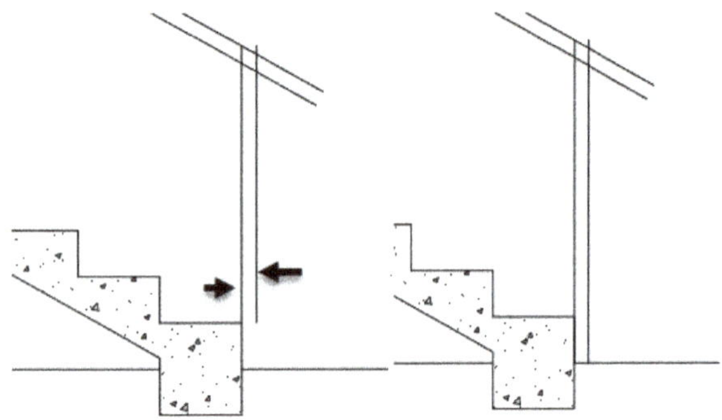

- Activate the **Line** tool. Next, zoom to the fifth step from the top.
- Select the midpoint of the horizontal line, as shown.

- Next, move the pointer upward and click.

- Click the **Offset** icon on the **Modify** panel on the **Home** ribbon tab. Offset the newly created line by 1" on both sides, as shown.
- Delete the middle line.

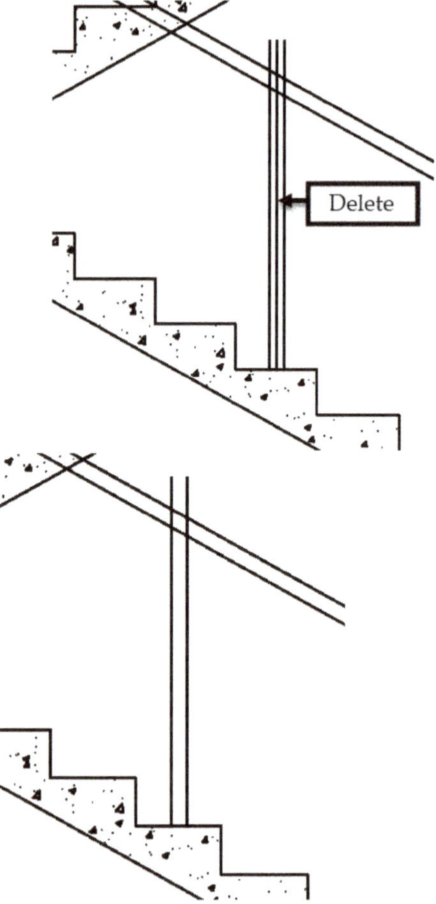

- On the ribbon, click **Home** > **Modify** > **Trim**.

- Press and hold the CTRL key and select the lower inclined and horizontal lines of the handrail. Next, press ENTER.

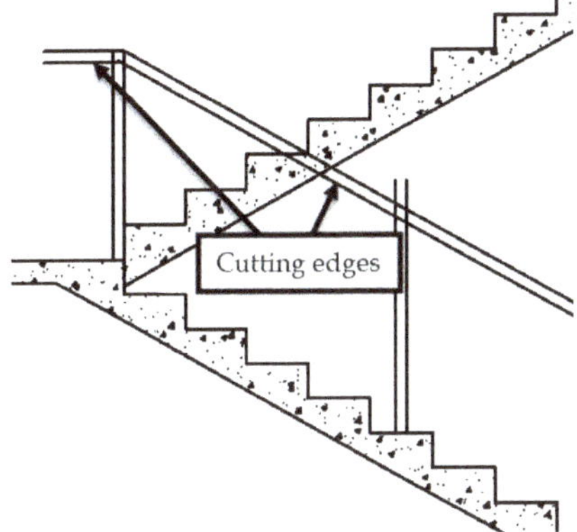

- Trim the portions of the vertical lines, as shown.

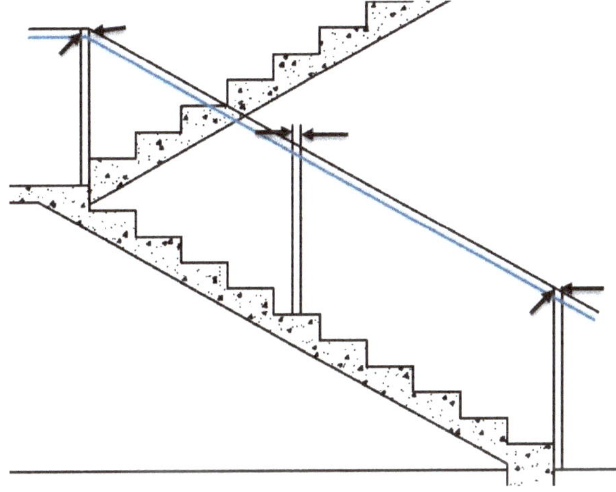

- Click the **Fillet** icon on the **Modify** panel on the **Home** tab.
- Select the **Radius** option from the command line.
- Type 0 and press ENTER.
- Select the horizontal and inclined lines, as shown.

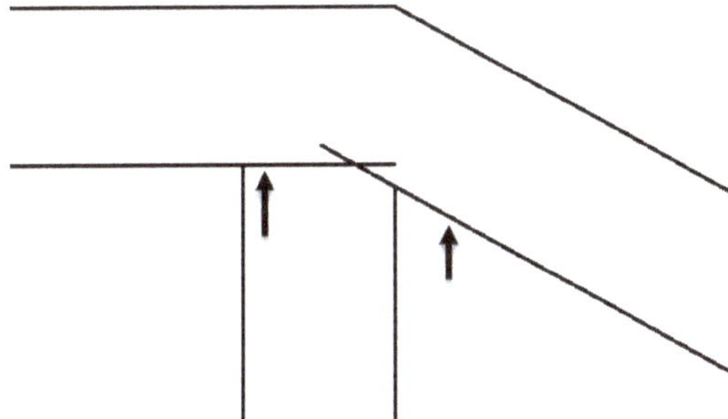

- On the ribbon, **Modify** > **Break at Point**.
- Select the vertical line, as shown.

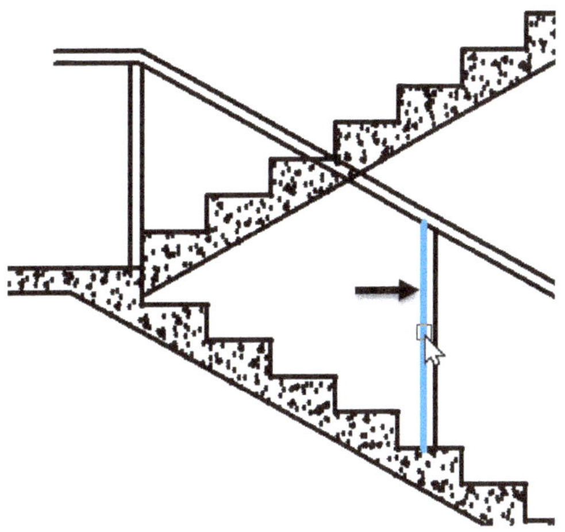

- Select the midpoint of the vertical line, as shown. The vertical line is broken at the midpoint.

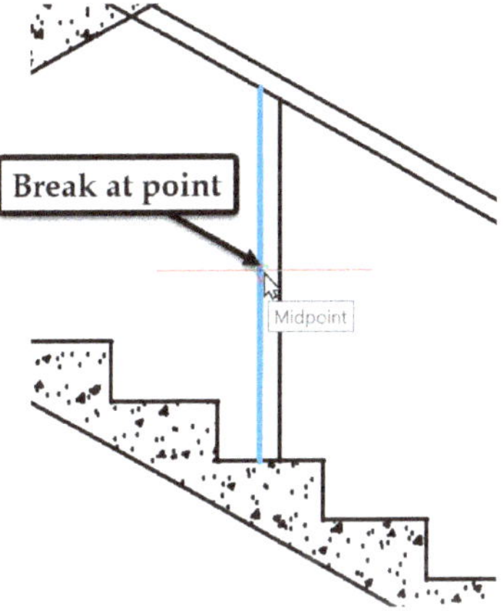

- On the ribbon, click **Home** > **Draw** > **Rectangle**.
- Select the midpoint of the lower portion of the broken line, as shown.

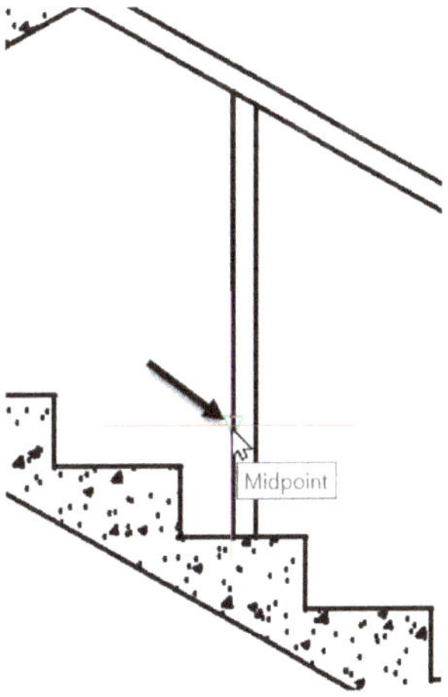

- Move the cursor upward.
- Next, type 2 and press TAB.
- Type 2 and press ENTER.

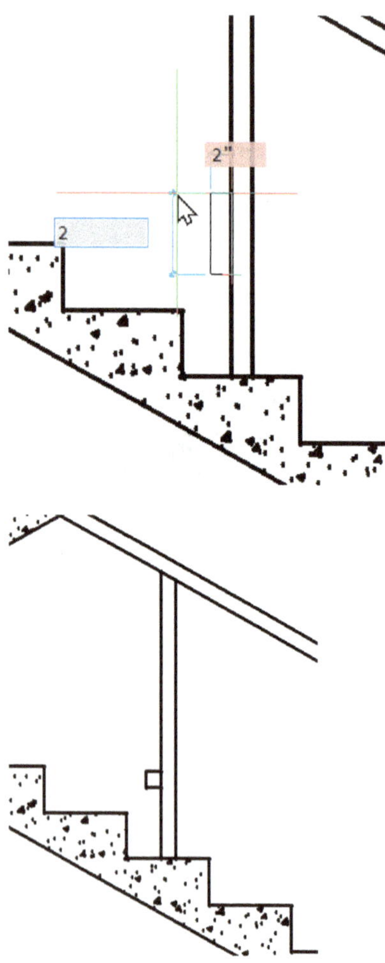

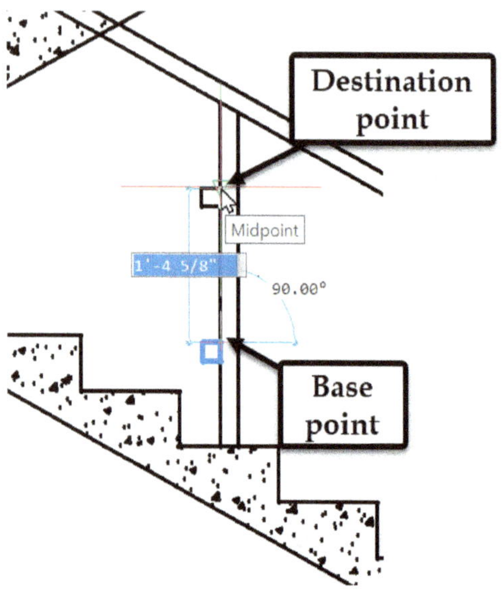

- Select the rectangle and click the **Copy** icon on the **Modify** panel on the **Home** ribbon tab.
- Select the top right corner point of the rectangle. Next, move the pointer upward.
- Select the midpoint of the upper portion of the broken line, as shown. Press ESC.

- Select the two rectangles and click the **Copy** icon on the **Modify** panel on the **Home** ribbon tab.
- Select the top right corner point of anyone of the rectangles.

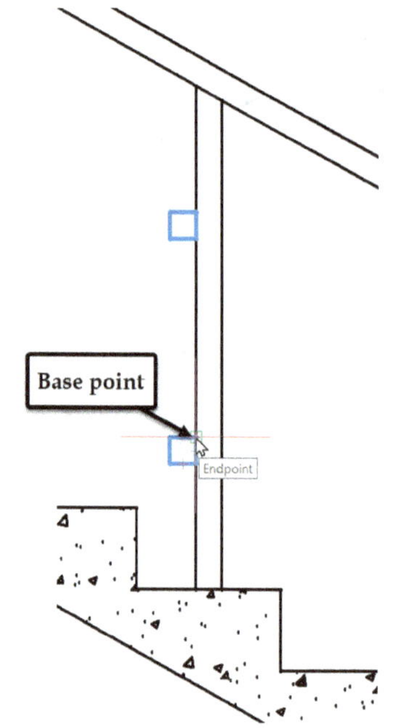

- Move the pointer toward the right. Next, type 4" and press ENTER.
- Press ESC.

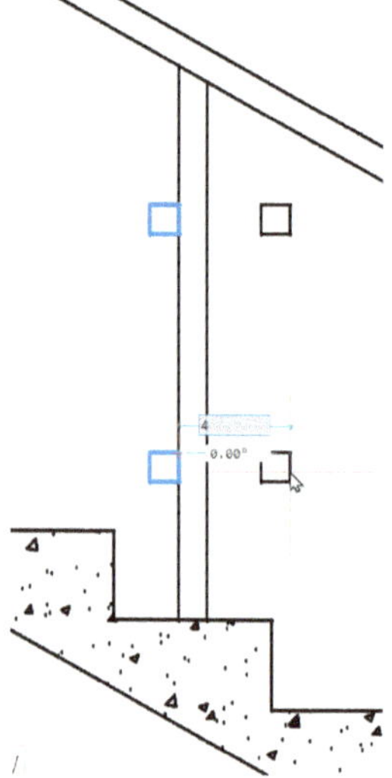

- Deactivate the ORTHO icon on the status bar.
- Select the four rectangles and click the **Copy** icon on the **Modify** panel on the **Home** ribbon tab.

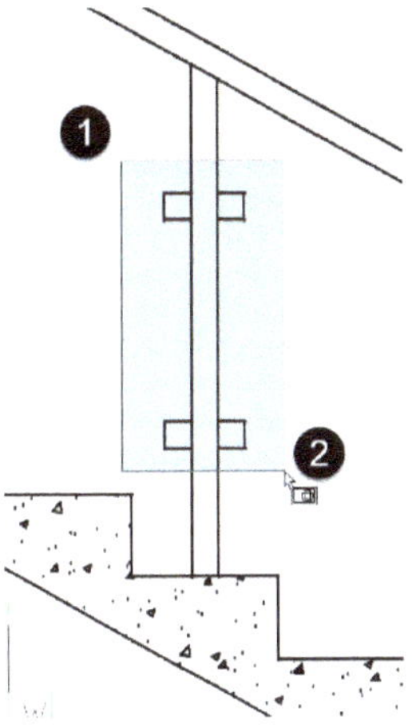

- Select the midpoint of the right vertical line.

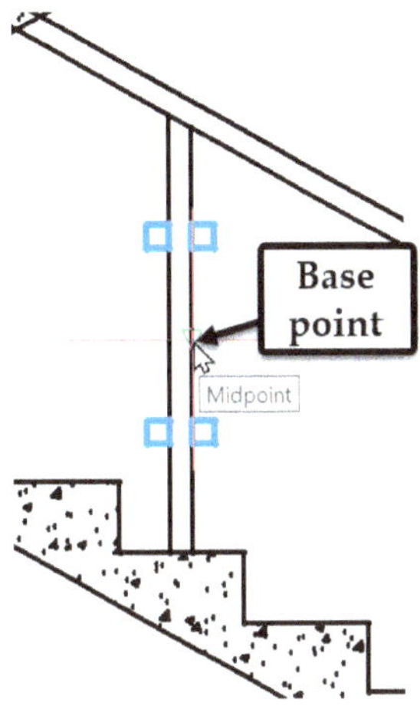

- Move the pointer toward the right and select the midpoint of the vertical line, as shown.

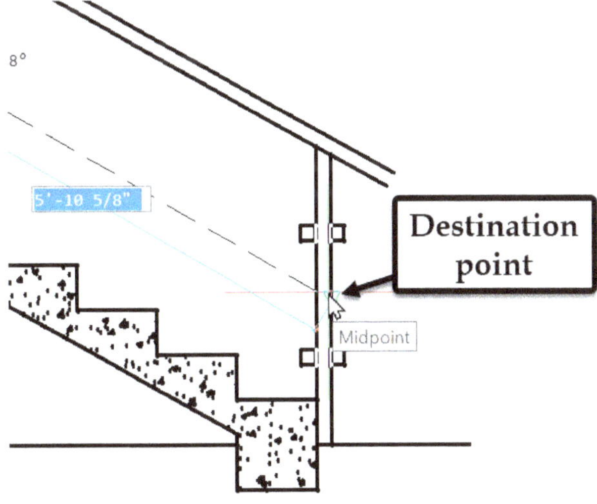

- Move the pointer toward the left and select the midpoint of the vertical line, as shown. Press Esc.

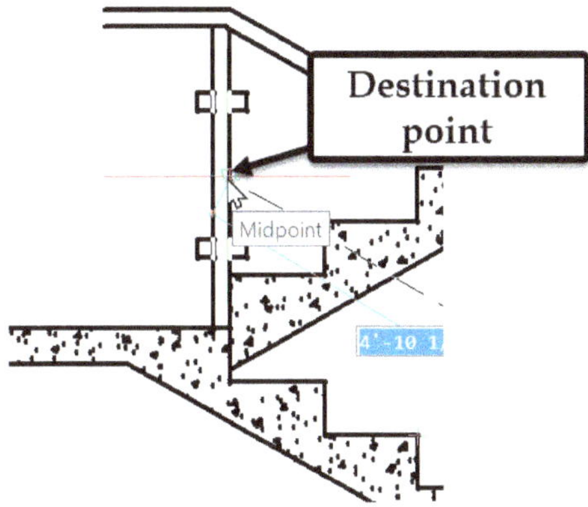

- Delete the two rectangles, as shown.

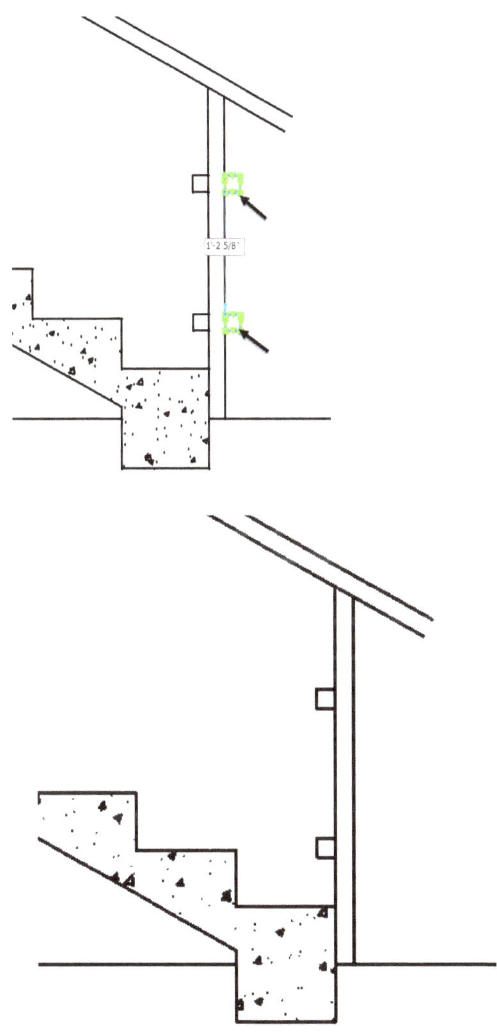

- Select the vertical line and click the **Offset** icon on the **Modify** panel on the **Home** ribbon tab.
- Type 3'8" and press ENTER. Next, move the pointer toward the left and click.

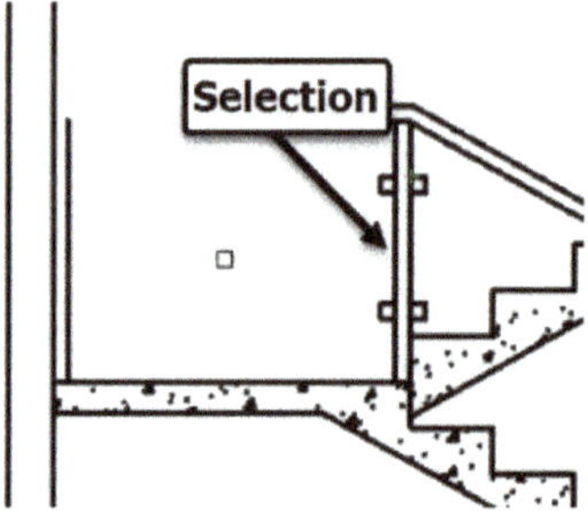

- Press ENTER twice.
- Type 2" and press ENTER. Next, select the newly offset line.
- Move the pointer toward the right and click.

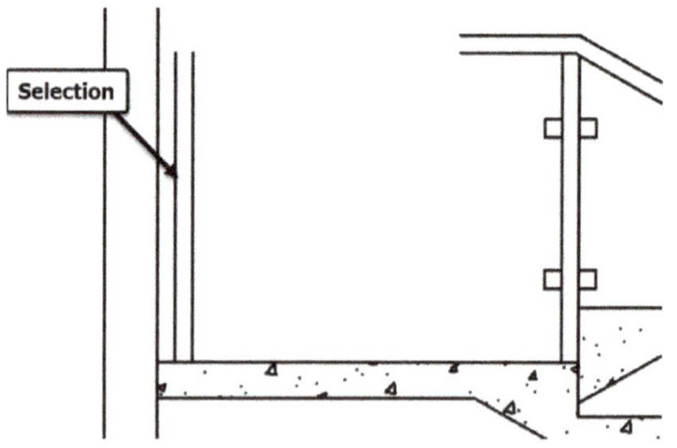

- Click the **Fillet** icon on the **Modify** panel on the **Home** ribbon tab.
- Select the **Radius** option from the command line.
- Type 0 and press ENTER.
- Select the left vertical and top horizontal line, as shown.

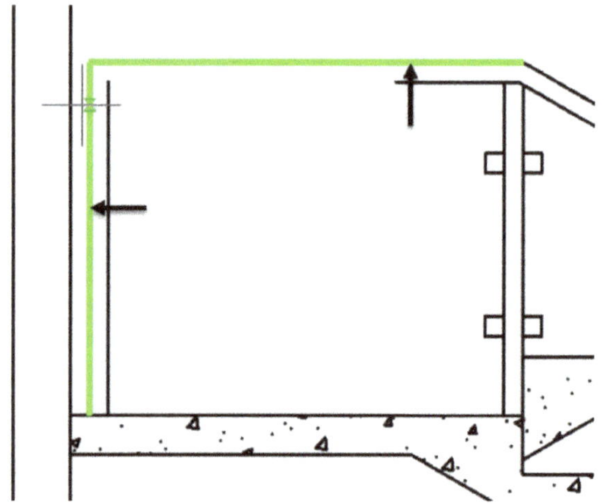

- On the ribbon, click **Home** > **Modify** > **Extend**.
- Extend the horizontal line up to the vertical line. Press Esc

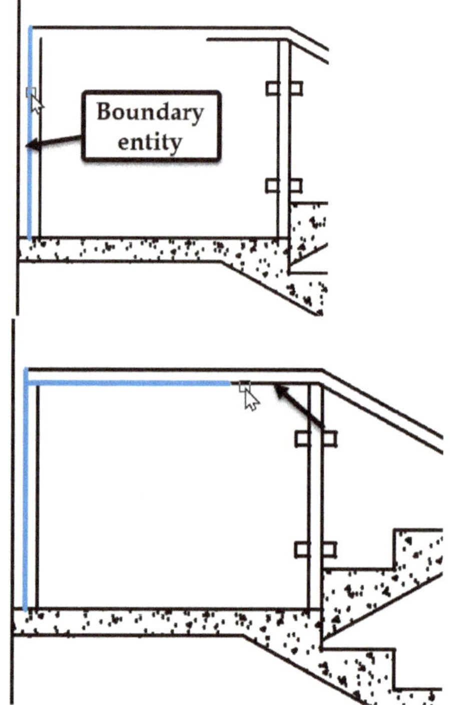

- Select the two rectangles.
- Click the **Copy** icon on the **Modify** panel on the **Home** ribbon tab.
- Specify the base and destination points, as shown.

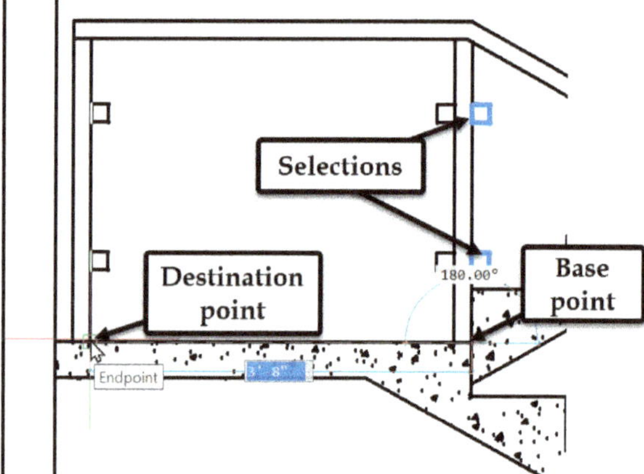

- Click the **Line** icon on the **Draw** panel on the **Home** ribbon tab. Next, select the corner points of the top and bottom steps, as shown.

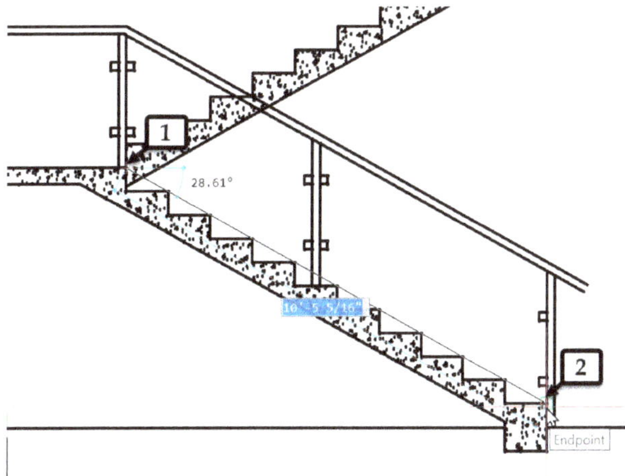

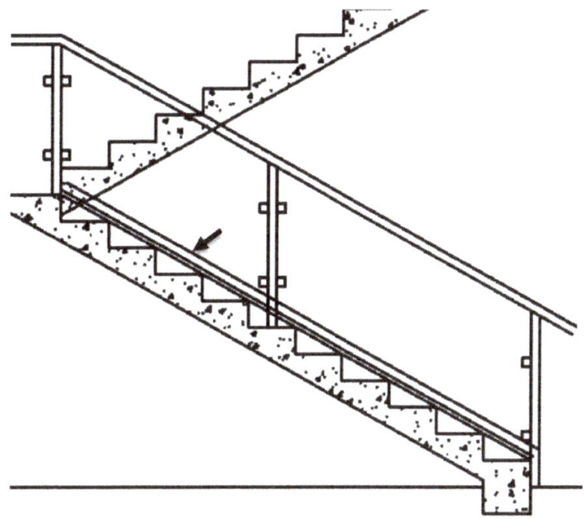

- Press Esc.
- Select the newly created line and click the **Offset** icon on the **Modify** panel on the **Home** ribbon tab.
- Type 1" and press ENTER. Move the pointer upward and click.

- On the ribbon, click **Home** > **Modify** > **Trim**. Press ENTER.
- Trim the intersecting portions of the lines, as shown. Press Esc.

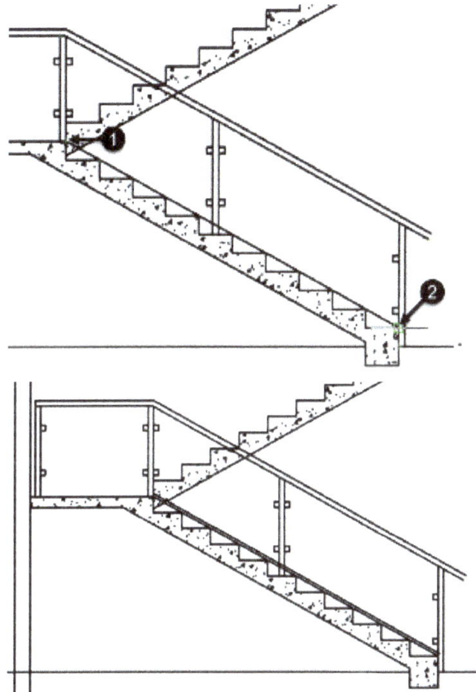

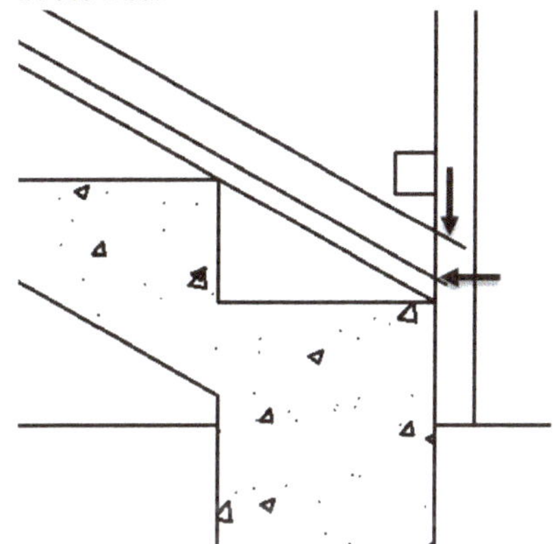

- Press ENTER twice. Next, type 2" and press ENTER.
- Select the newly offset line. Next, move the pointer upward and click.

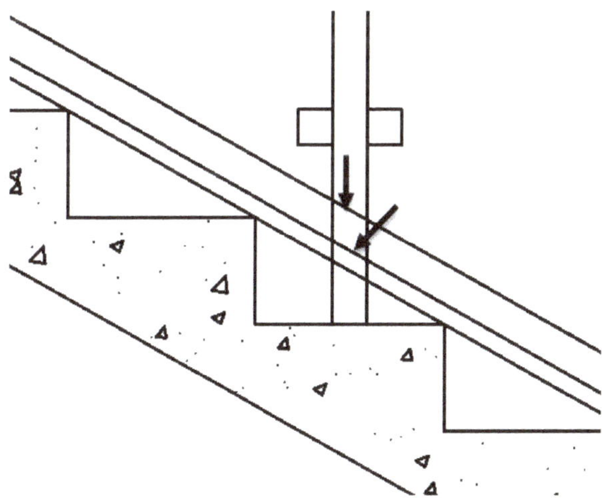

- Activate the ORTHO icon on the status bar.
- Select the rectangles, as shown.
- Click **Move** on the **Modify** panel on the **Home** ribbon tab.

- Specify the base point, as shown.

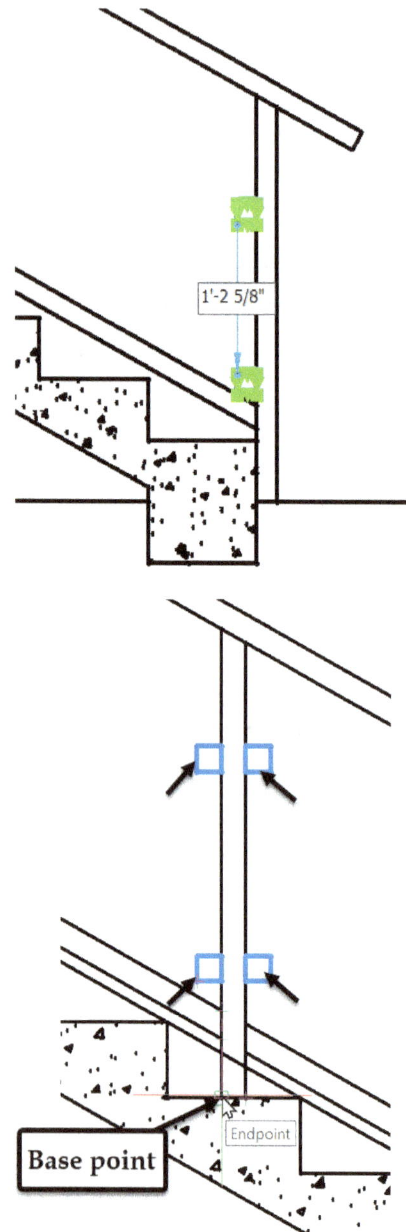

- Move the pointer upward. Next, type 4" and press ENTER.

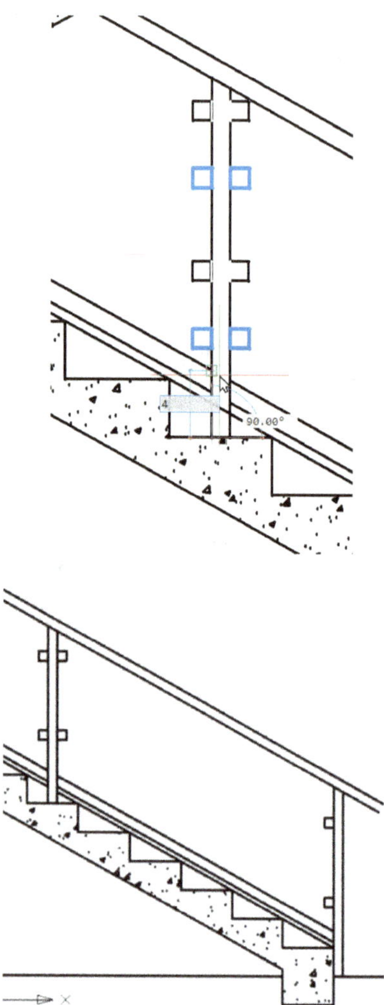

- Select the horizontal line, as shown. Next, click the **Offset** icon on the **Modify** panel on the **Home** ribbon tab.
- Type 33" and press ENTER. Next, move the pointer downward and click.

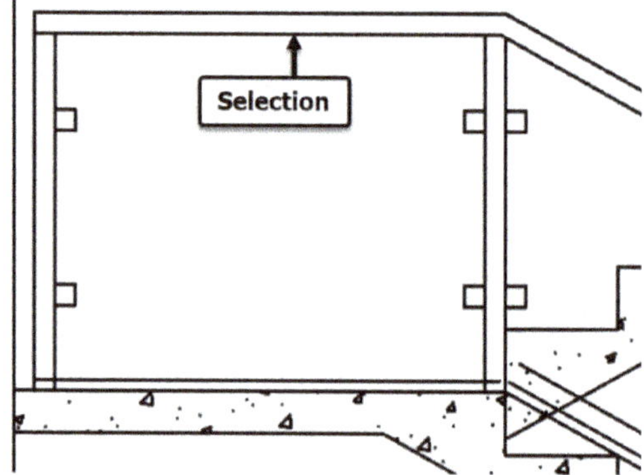

- Press ENTER twice. Next, type 2" and press ENTER.
- Select the newly offset line. Next, move the pointer upward and click.

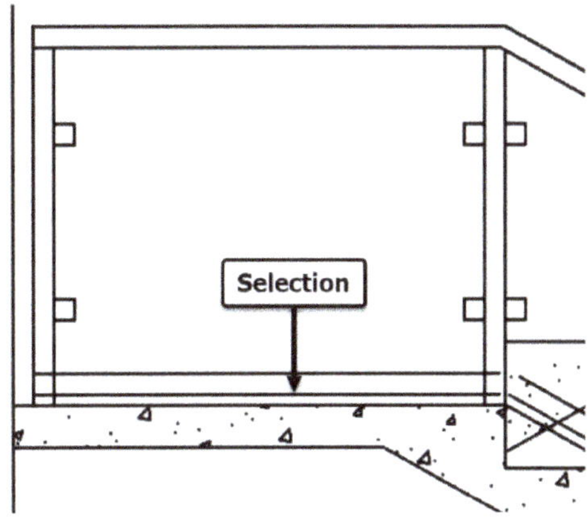

- Click **Fillet** on the **Modify** panel on the **Home** ribbon tab.
- Type 0 in the command line and press ENTER.
- Select the horizontal and inclined lines, as shown.
- Press ENTER and select the horizontal and inclined lines, as shown.

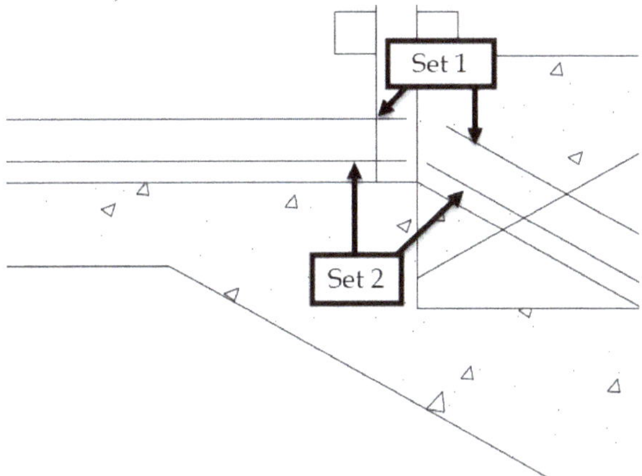

- Click **Trim** on the **Modify** panel on the **Home** ribbon tab. Next, press ENTER.
- Select the portions of the horizontal and inclined line, as shown.

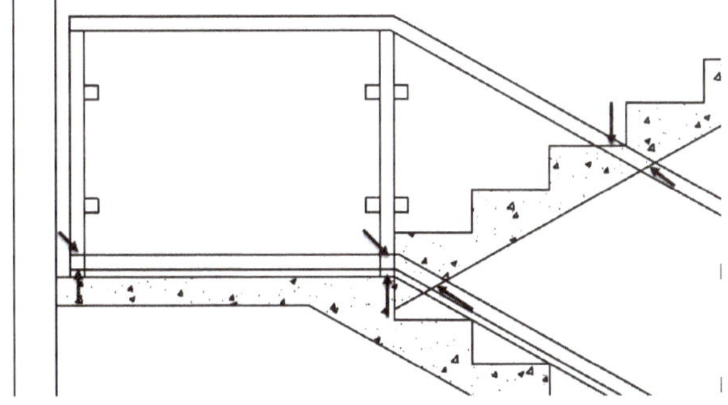

- Select the **eRase** option from the command line.
- Press and hold the SHIFT key and select the inclined lines, as shown. Next, press ENTER.

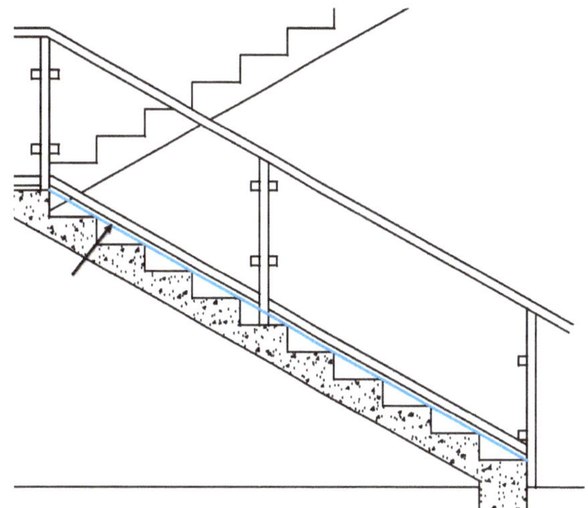

- Close the end of the offset lines using the **Line** tool.

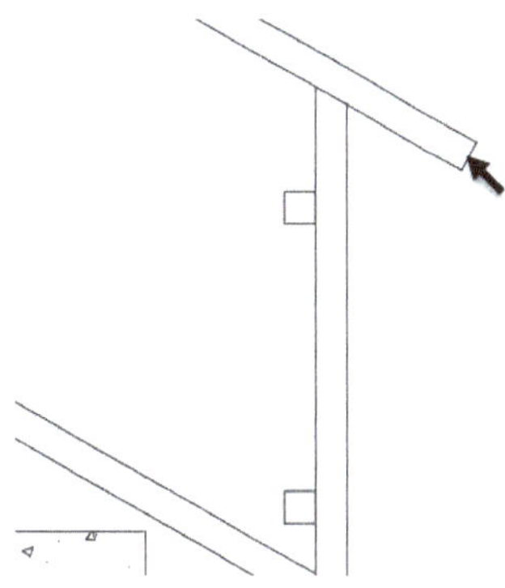

- Press and hold the SHIFT key and select the elements of the handrail.

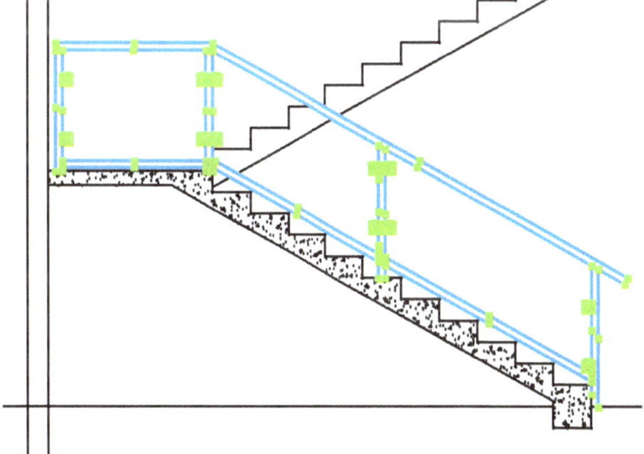

- Click **Copy** on the **Modify** panel on the **Home** ribbon tab. Next, Specify the base point, as shown.

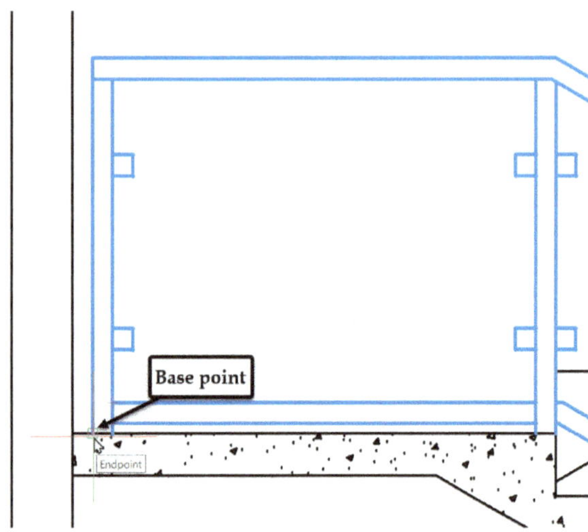

- Move the pointer toward the right and click to create the copy.

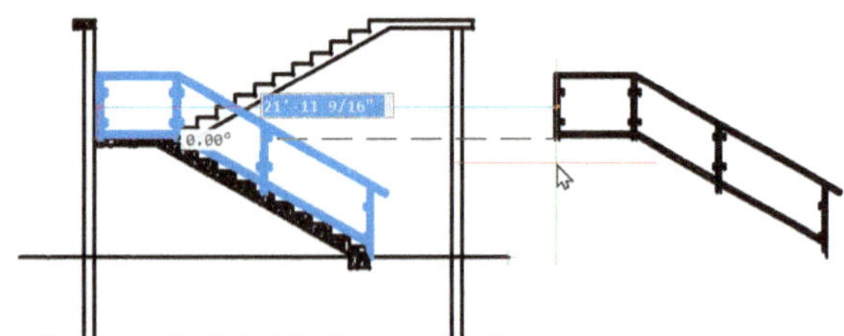

- Click **Mirror** on the **Modify** panel on the **Home** ribbon tab.
- Create a selection window covering all the copied entities of the handrail. Next, press ENTER.

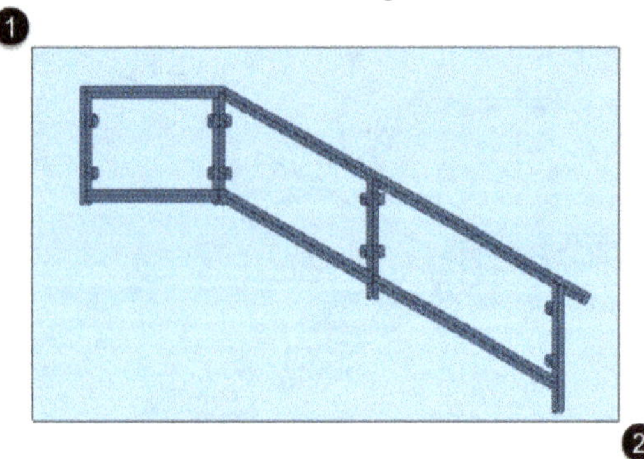

- Select the base point, as shown. Next, move the pointer vertically upward and click. Next, select **Yes-delete entities**.

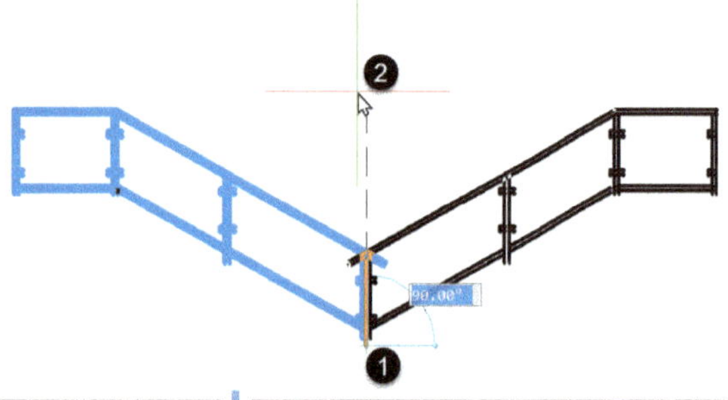

- Create a selection window across all the mirrored entities.
- Click **Move** on the **Modify** panel on the **Home** ribbon tab.
- Next, specify the base point, as shown.

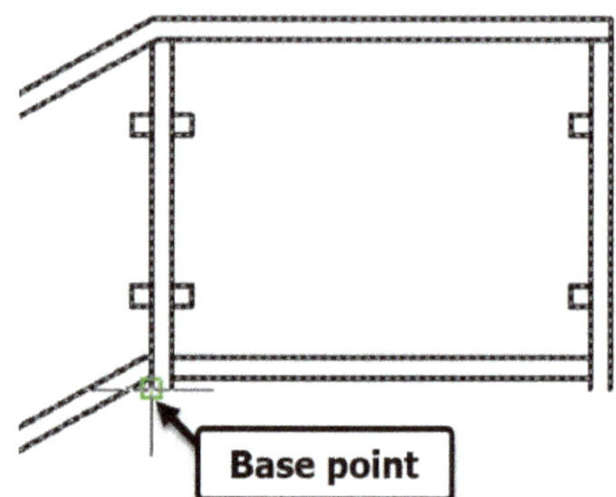

- Move the pointer toward the right and select the destination point.

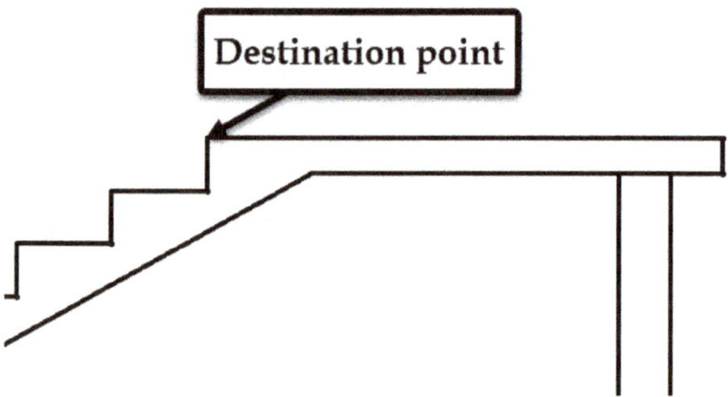

- Select the elements of the handrail, as shown. Next, press Delete.

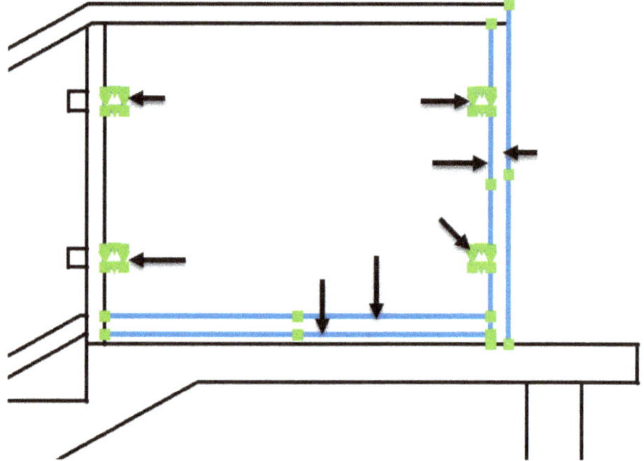

- Click the **Line** icon on the **Draw** panel on the **Home** ribbon tab.
- Select the endpoint of the vertical line, as shown.

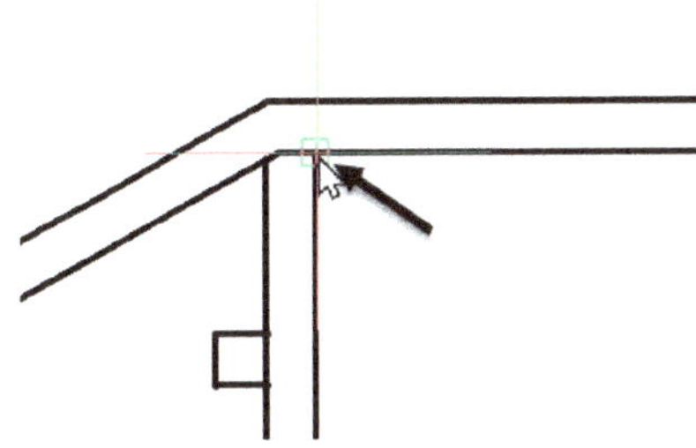

- Move the pointer upward, type 2, and then press ENTER.

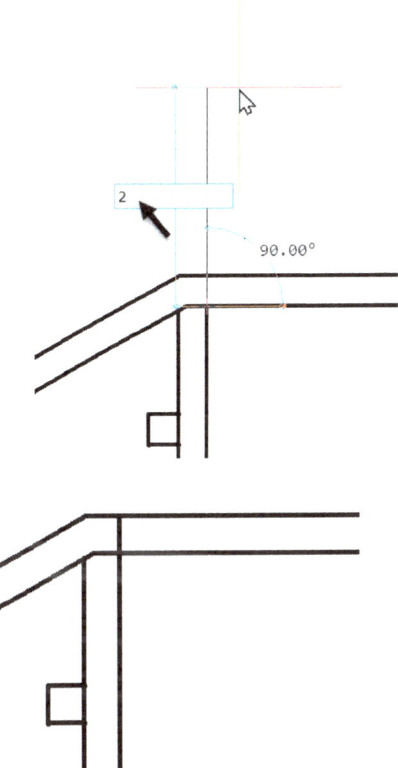

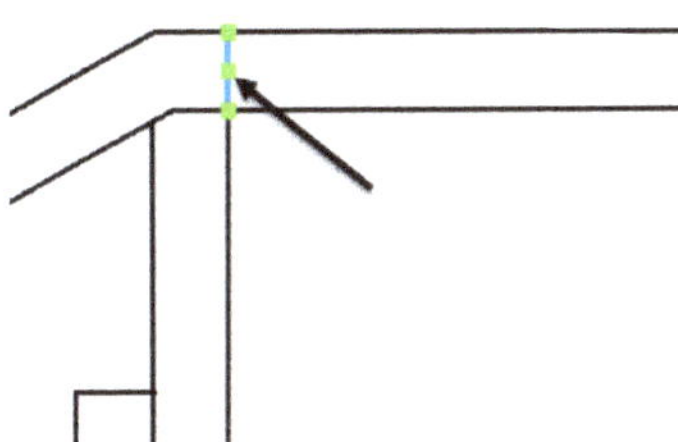

- Select the newly created line. Next, click on the midpoint of the selected line.

- Move the pointer toward right.

- Type 12 and press ENTER.

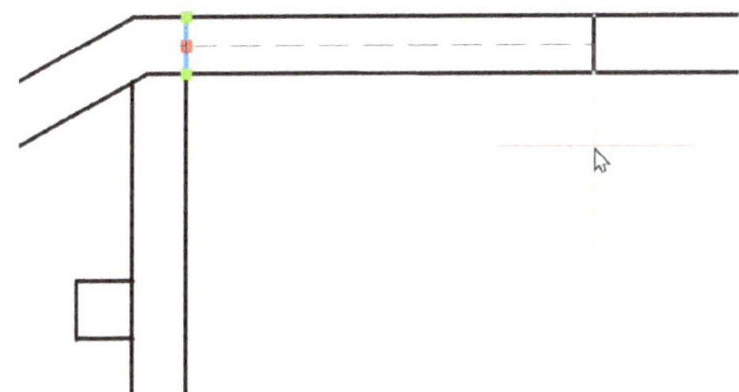

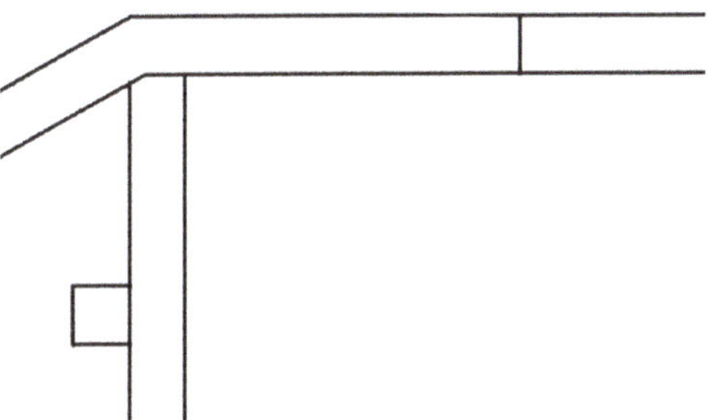

- Click **Trim** on the **Modify** panel on the **Home** ribbon tab. Next, press ENTER.
- Trim the unwanted elements.

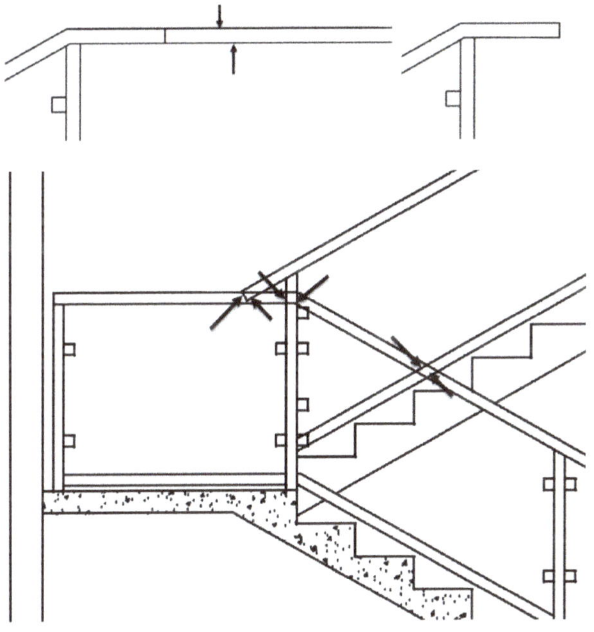

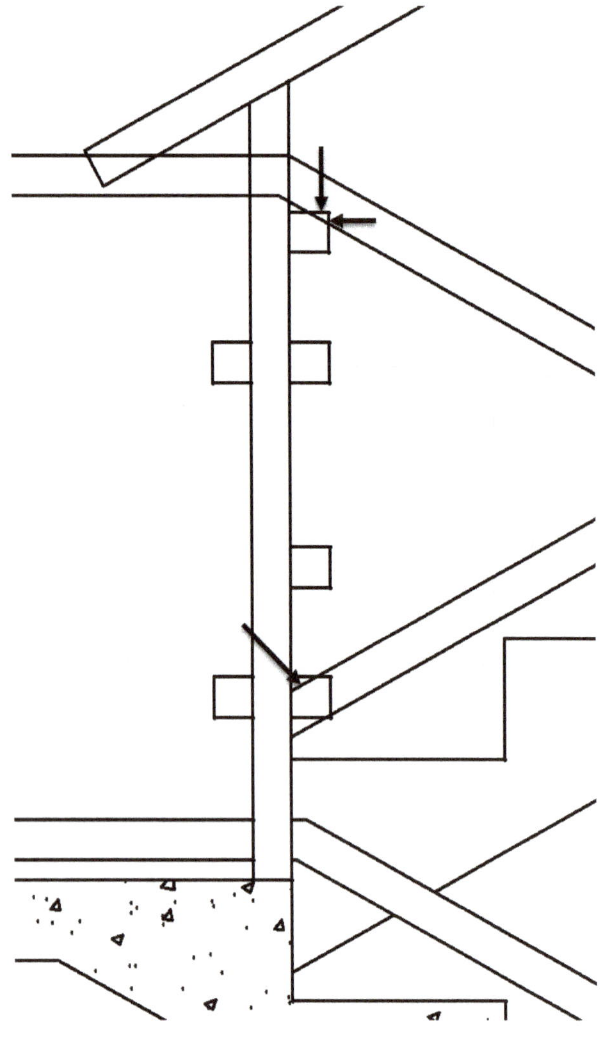

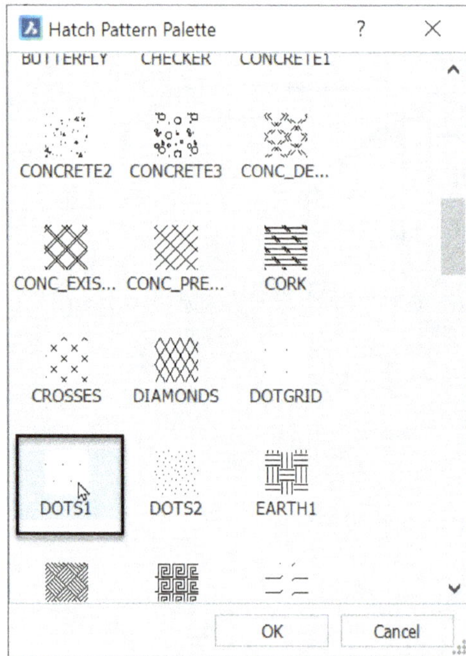

- On the ribbon, click **Home** > **Draw** > **Hatch**.
- On the **Hatch and Gradient** dialog, click the

  Browse [...] icon next to the **Name** box.

- Select the **DOTS1** hatch from the **Hatch Pattern Palette** and click **OK**.

- Click the **Pick points in boundaries** icon under the **Boundaries** section. Next, pick points in the areas, as shown.

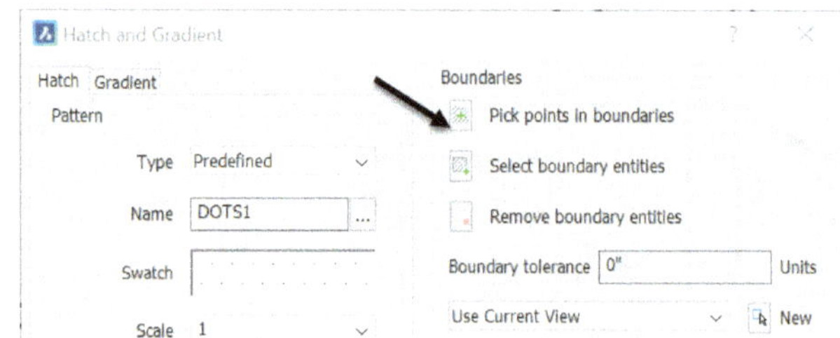

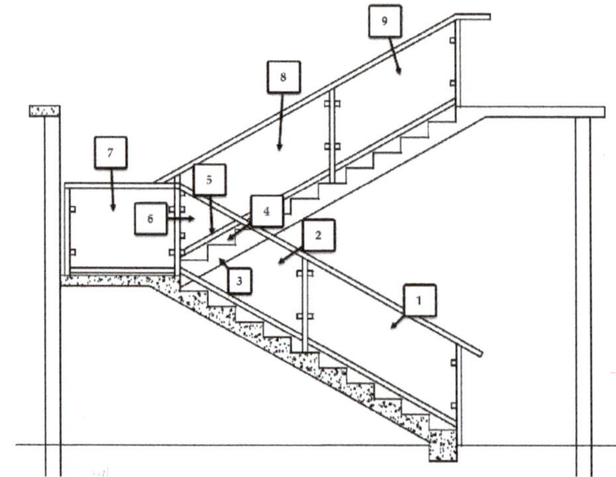

- Press ENTER.
- Type **30** in the **Scale** box and click **OK** on the **Hatch and Gradient** dialog.

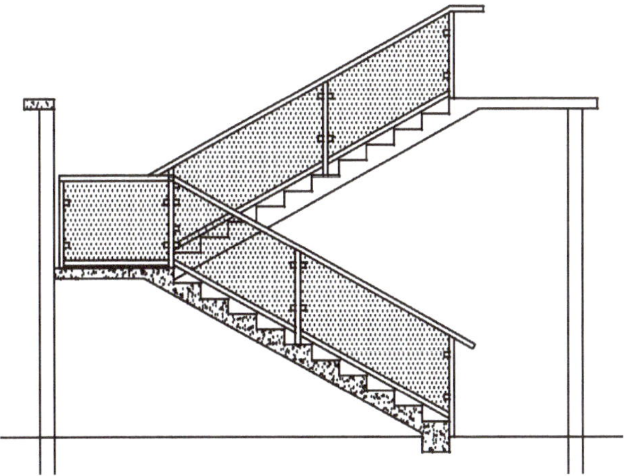

- On the ribbon, click **Home** > **Draw** > **Hatch**.
- On the **Hatch and Gradient** dialog, click the **Browse** [...] icon next to the **Name** box.
- Select the **CONCRETE2** hatch from the **Hatch Pattern Palette** and click **OK**.
- Click the **Pick points in boundaries** icon under the **Boundaries** section. Next, pick points in the areas, as shown.

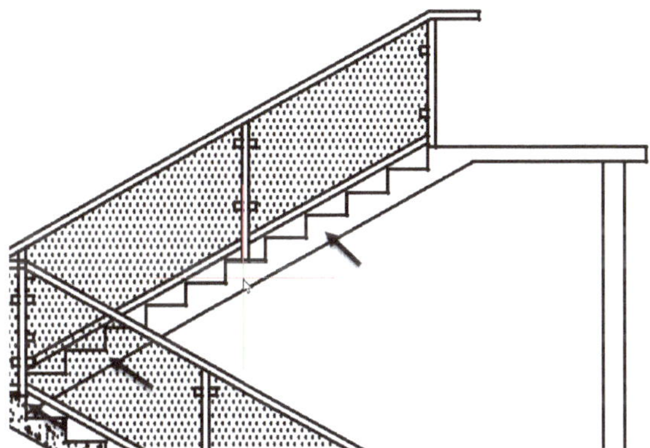

- Press ENTER.
- Type **10** in the **Scale** box and click **OK** on the **Hatch and Gradient** dialog.

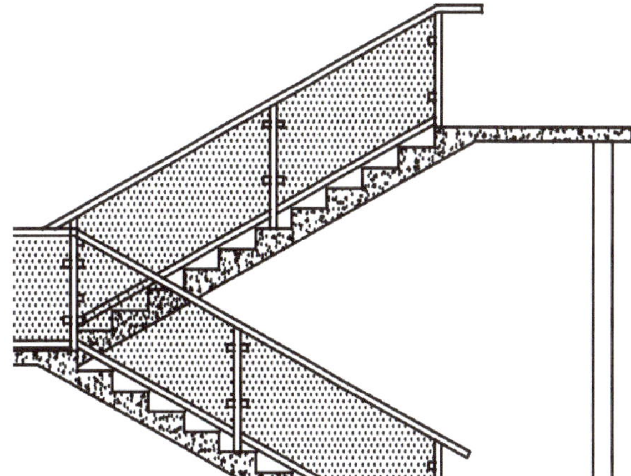

- Delete the construction lines, as shown.

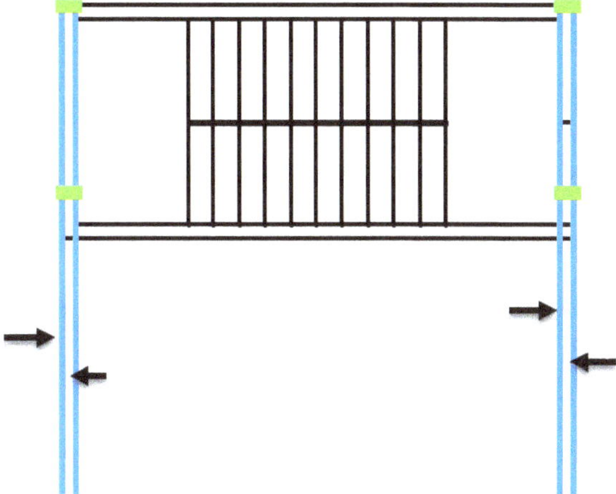

- Save and close the file.

Tutorial 3: Creating the Elevation View

In this tutorial, you will create the elevation view using the floor plan.

- Download the Elevation_plan from the companion website.
- Start the BricSCAD V24 application.
- Click the **2D drafting** button on the **BricsCAD Launcher** dialog.
- Click the Open files button on the Home page.
- Browse to the location of the downloaded file and double-click on it.
- Click the **Layers** icon on the right pane.
- Click the **Add layer** ⊕ icon on the **Layers** palette. Next, type Elevation as the layer name.
- Double-click on the Elevation layer. Next, hide the **Layers** palette.

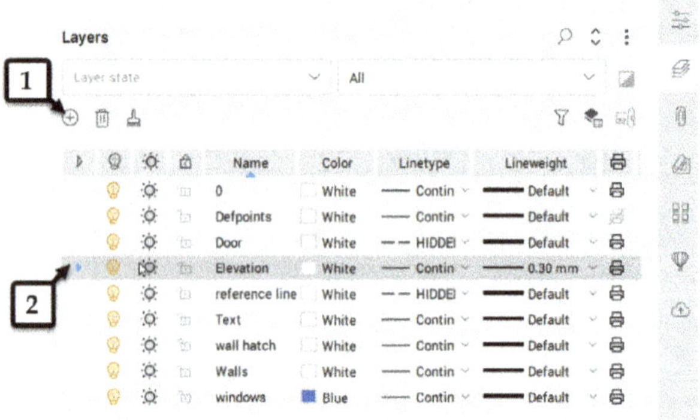

- Draw a horizontal line above the floor plan, as shown.

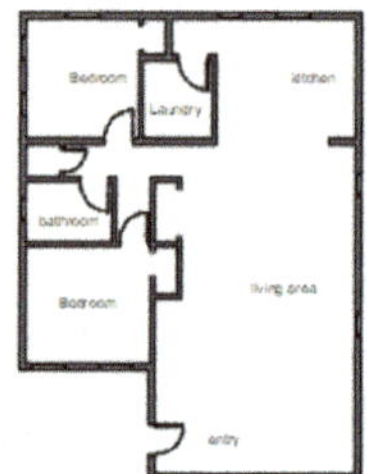

- On the ribbon, click **Home > Draw > Ray**.

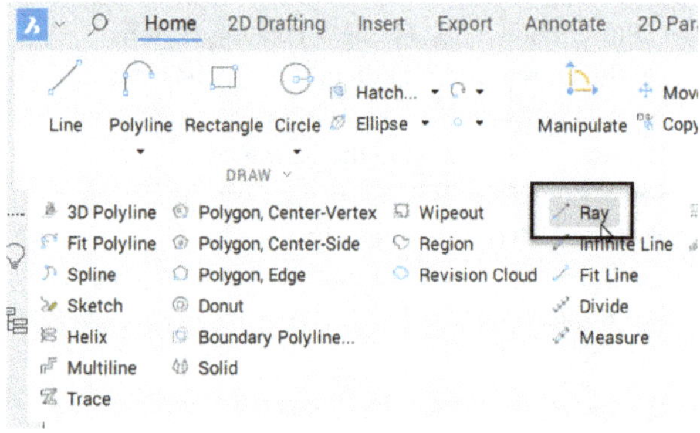

- Select the top-left corner of the floor plan. Next, move the pointer upward and click.

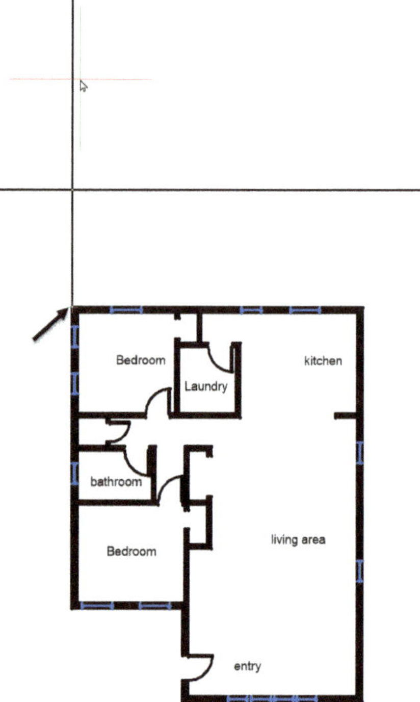

- Press ENTER twice.

- Select the top-right corner of the floor plan. Next, move the pointer upward and click.

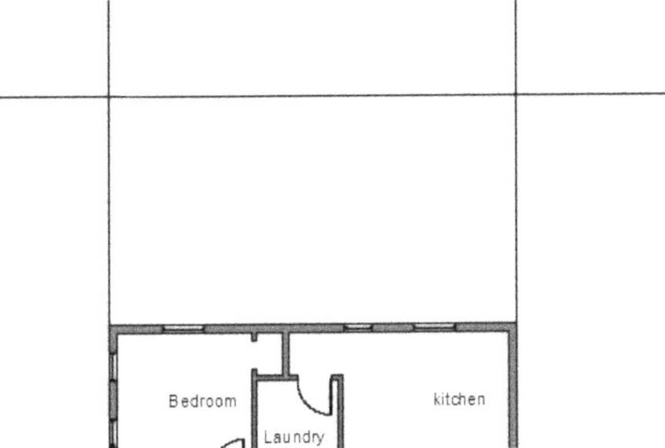

- Click the **Offset** tool on the **Modify** panel on the **Home** ribbon tab.
- Type 6" and press ENTER. Next, select the horizontal line.
- Move the pointer upward and click to create an offset line. Next, press ENTER twice.

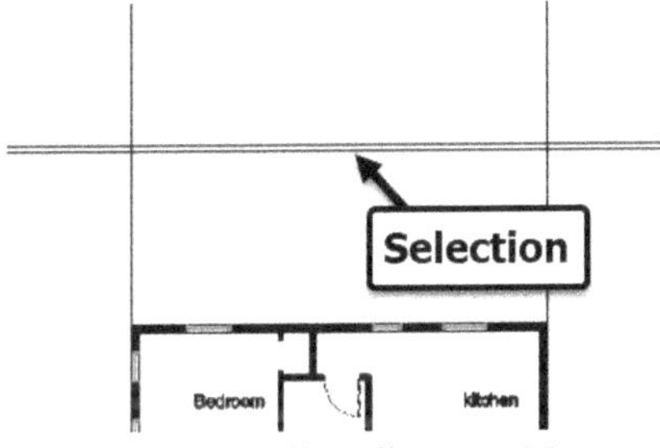

- Type 9' as the offset distance. Next, press ENTER.
- Select the offset line created previously. Move the pointer upward and click.

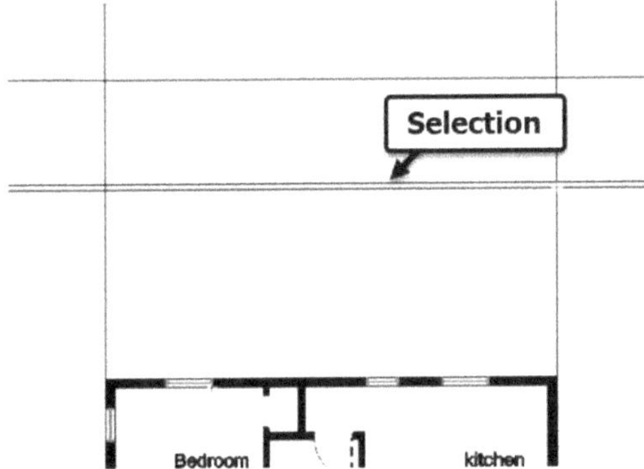

- Press ENTER twice.
- Type 10' as the offset distance. Next, press ENTER.
- Select the offset line created previously. Next, move the pointer upward and click.

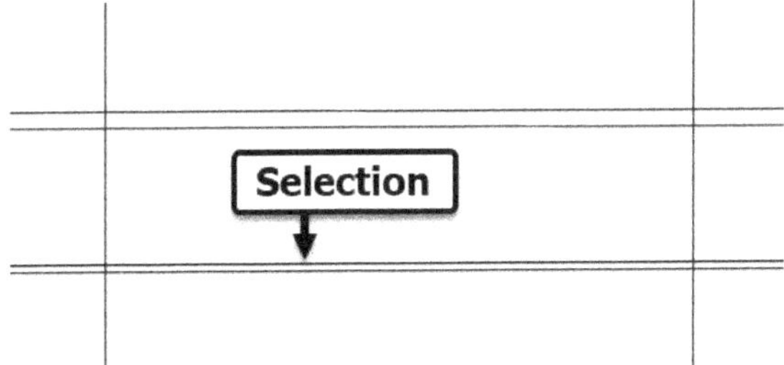

- Press ENTER twice.
- Type 6' as the offset distance. Next, press ENTER.
- Select the offset line created previously. Move the pointer upward and click.

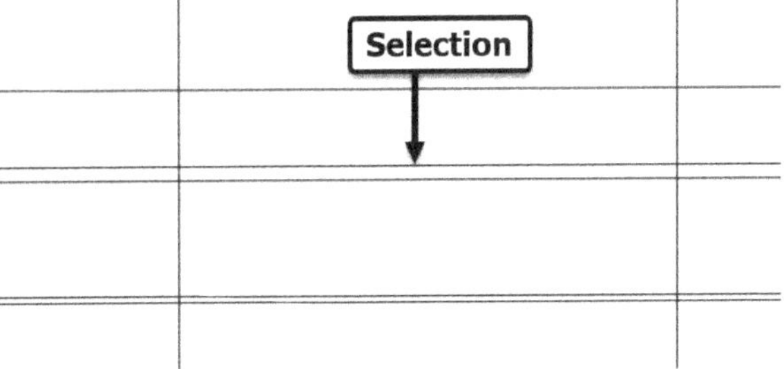

- On the ribbon, click **Draw** > **Infinite Line**.
- Select the **Parallel** option from the shortcut menu.
- Type 16" as the offset distance. Next, press ENTER.
- Select the right exterior wall. Next, move the pointer toward the right and click.
- Select the left exterior wall. Move the pointer toward the left and click.

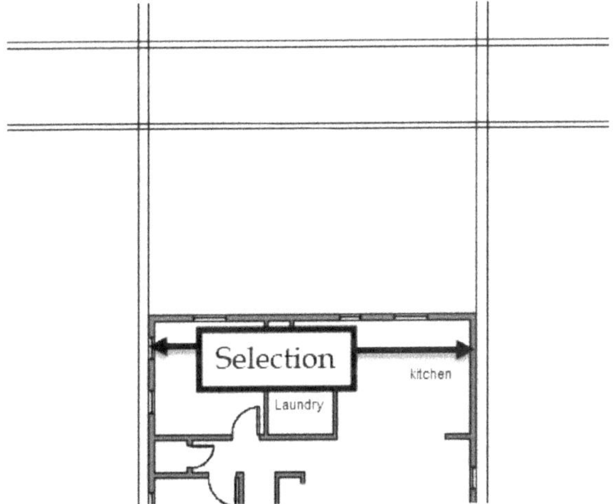

- Press ENTER twice.
- Select the **Vertical** option from the command line.
- Select the corner point of the exterior wall, as shown.

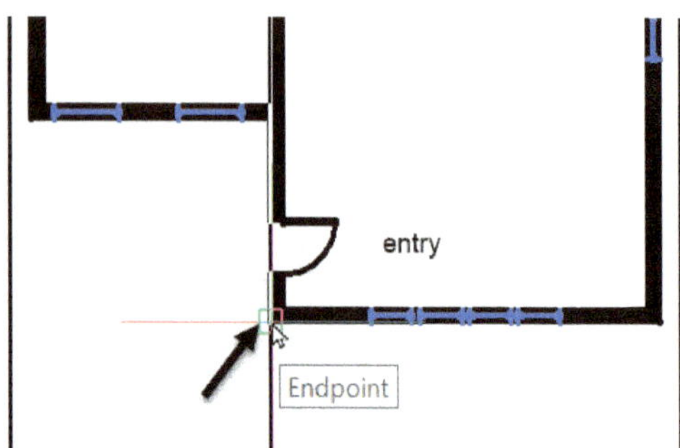

- Press ENTER twice.
- Select the **Parallel** option from the shortcut menu.
- Type 16" as the offset distance. Next, press ENTER.
- Select the construction line created in the last step. Next, move the pointer toward the left and click.

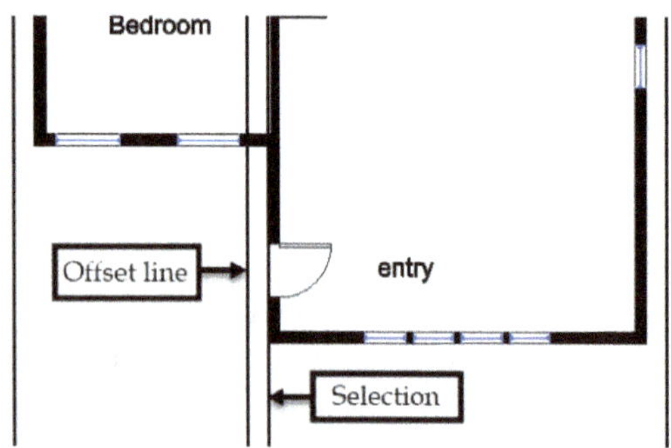

- On the ribbon, click **Home > Modify > Break at Point**.

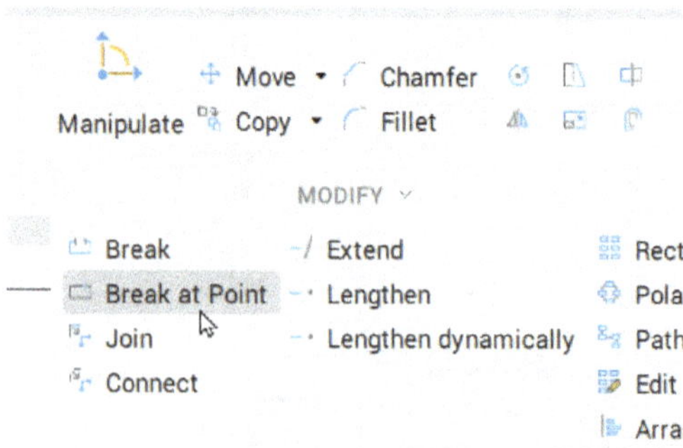

- Select the horizontal line, as shown.

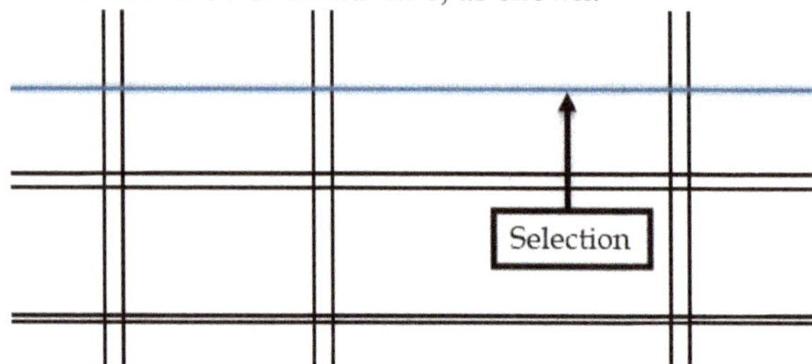

- Select the intersection point between the horizontal and vertical lines, as shown.

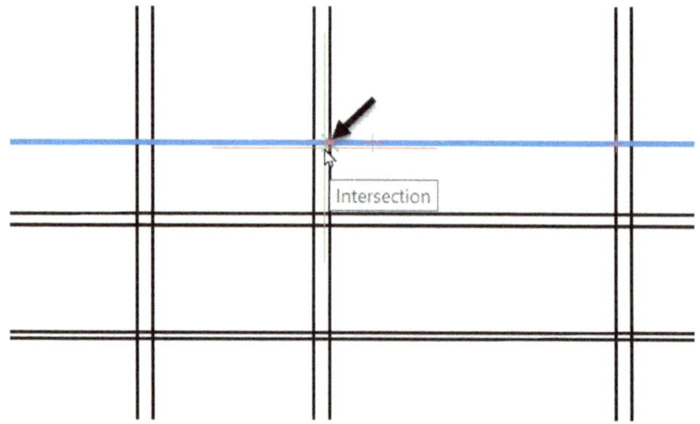

- Press ENTER to activate the **Break at Point** tool.
- Select the right portion of the broken line.
- Select the intersection point between the horizontal and vertical lines, as shown.

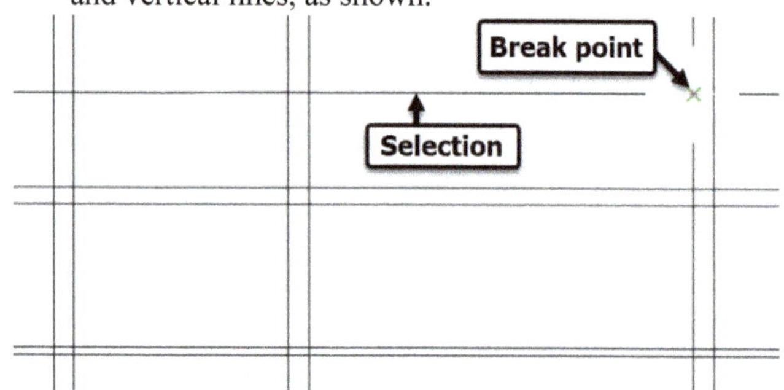

- Click the **Line** tool on the **Draw** panel on the **Home** ribbon tab.
- Select the midpoint of the broken line, as shown.

- Select the intersection point between the horizontal and vertical lines, as shown.

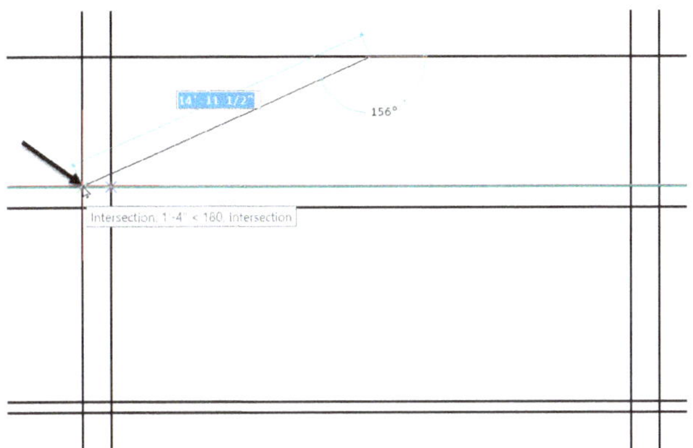

- Press ENTER twice. Next, select the start point of the line created in the last step.
- Select the intersection point between the horizontal and vertical lines, as shown.

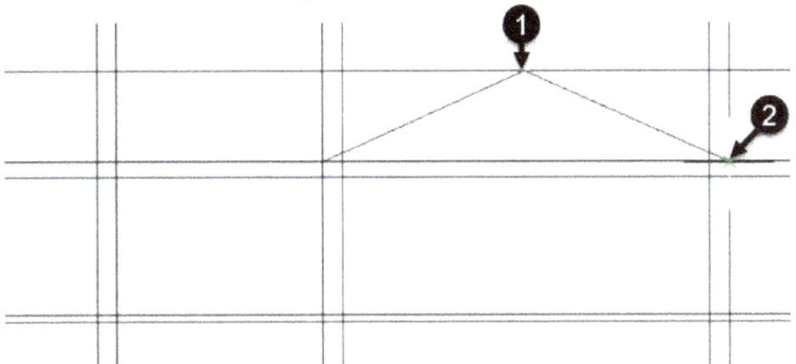

- Click **Trim** on the **Modify** panel on the **Home** ribbon tab. Next, press ENTER.
- Select the portions of the vertical lines, as shown.

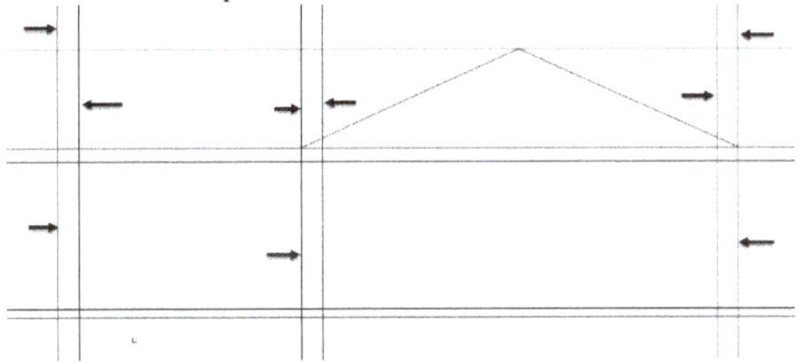

- Select **eRase** option from the command line.
- Click and drag the mouse pointer across the vertical lines, as shown.

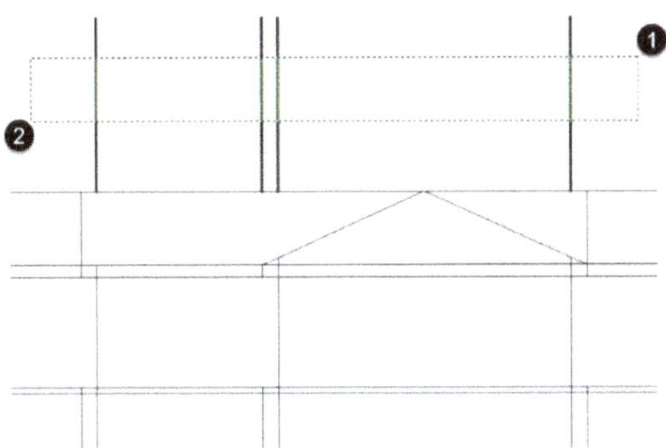

- Press ENTER.
- Click the Trim tool on the Modify panel.

- Press ENTER and drag a selection window across the vertical lines, as shown.

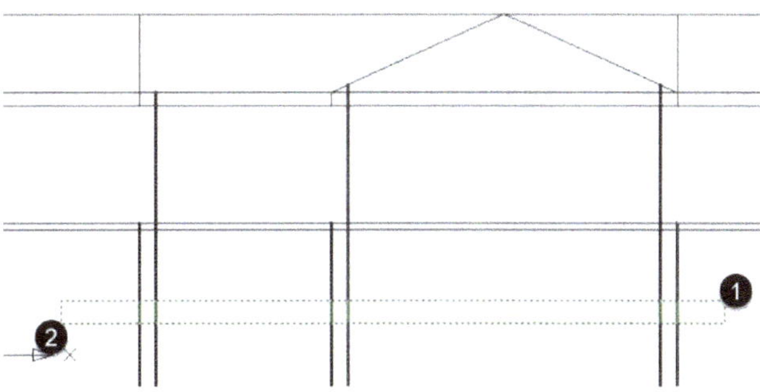

- Trim the horizontal and vertical lines, as shown.

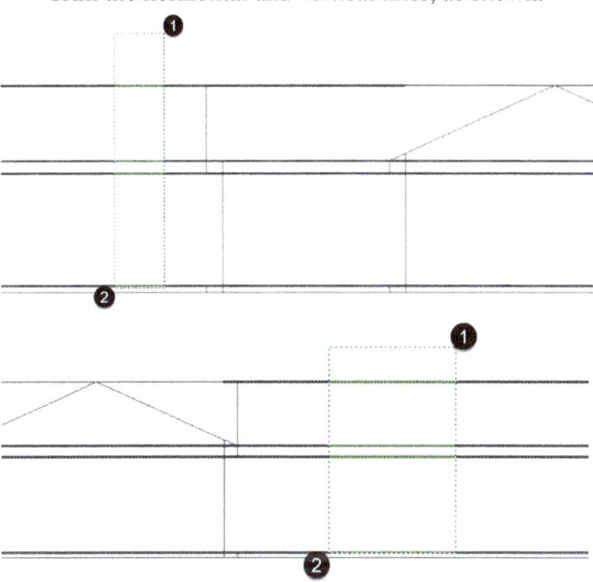

- Trim the small portions, as shown.

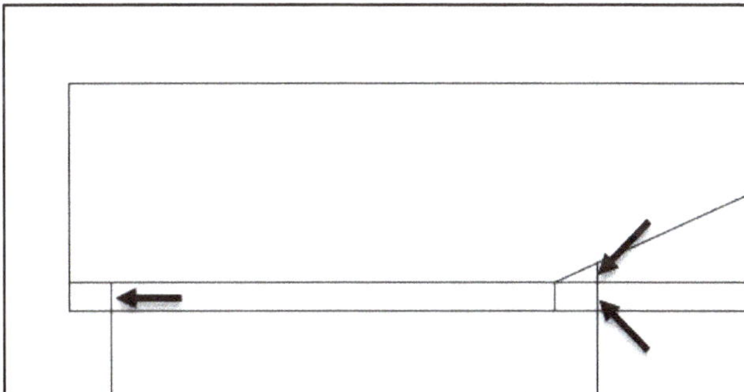

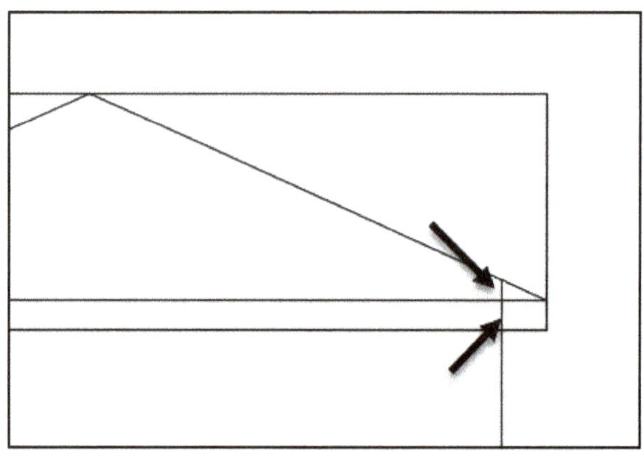

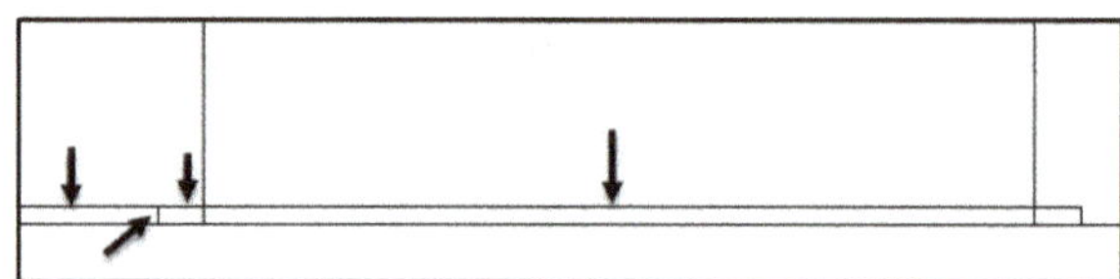

- Press Esc. Next, select the inclined line, as shown.
- Click the **Move** tool on the **Modify** panel. Next, specify the base point, as shown.

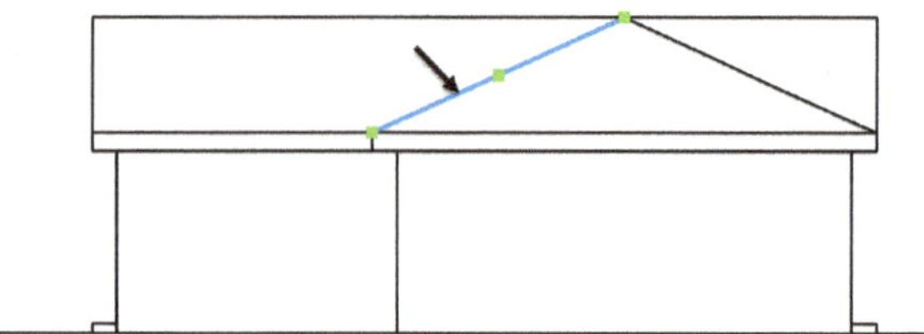

- Move the pointer downward and select the intersection point, as shown.

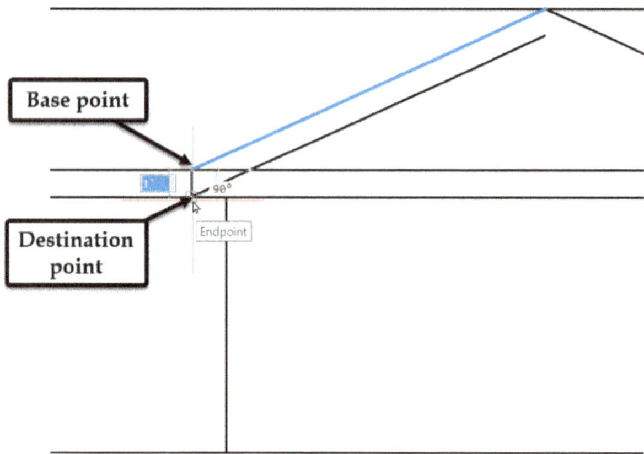

- Press Esc.
- Likewise, copy the other inclined line, as shown.

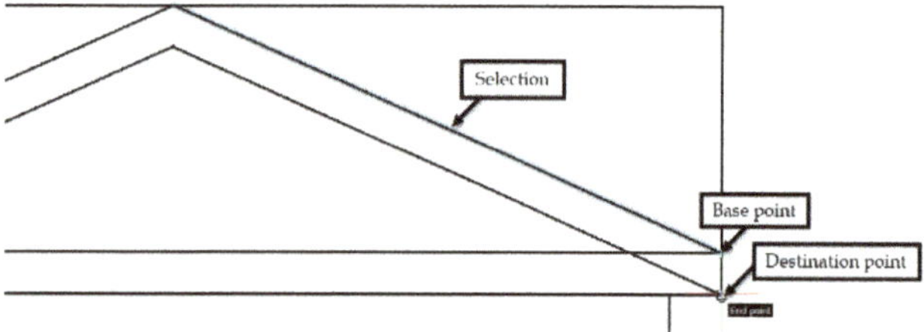

- Click the **Trim** icon on the **Modify** panel of the Home ribbon tab. Next, press ENTER.
- Select the portions of the horizontal line from right to left, as shown.

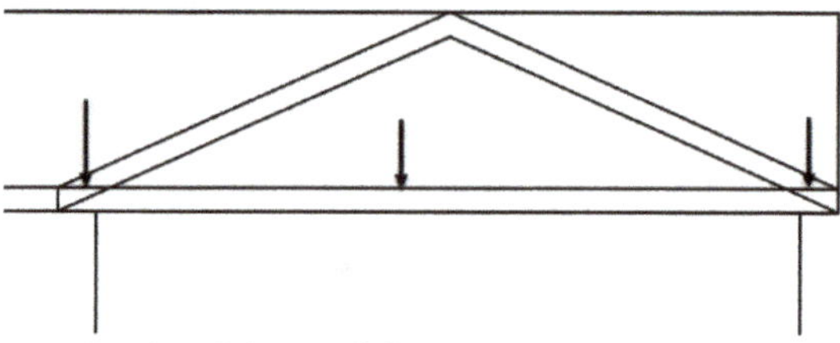

- On the ribbon, click **Modify** > **Break at Point**.
- Select the horizontal line, as shown. Next, select the intersection point, as shown.

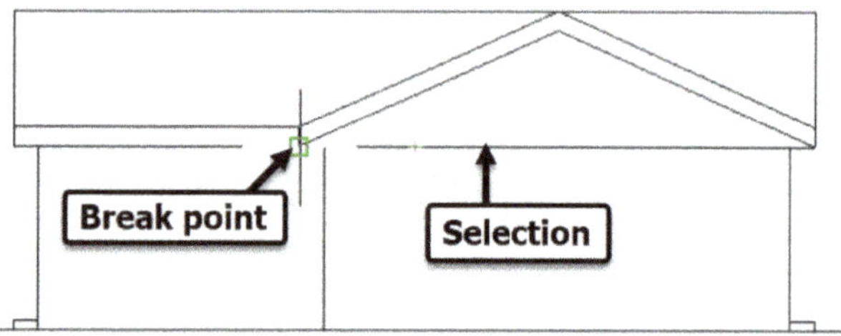

- On the ribbon, click **Modify** > **Break Vectors at Point**.
- Select the vertical line, as shown. Next, select the intersection point, as shown.

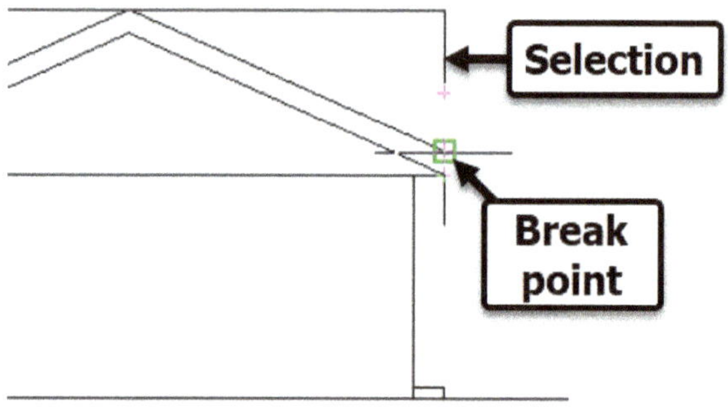

- On the ribbon, click **Modify** > **Break Vectors at Point**.
- Select the vertical line, as shown. Next, select the intersection point, as shown.
- Select the horizontal line, as shown. Next, press Delete.

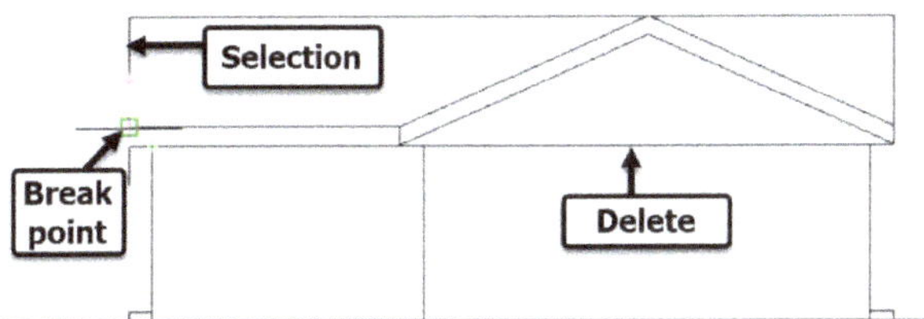

- Click the **Extend** icon on the **Modify** panel on the Home ribbon tab. Next, press ENTER.
- Select the two vertical lines, as shown.

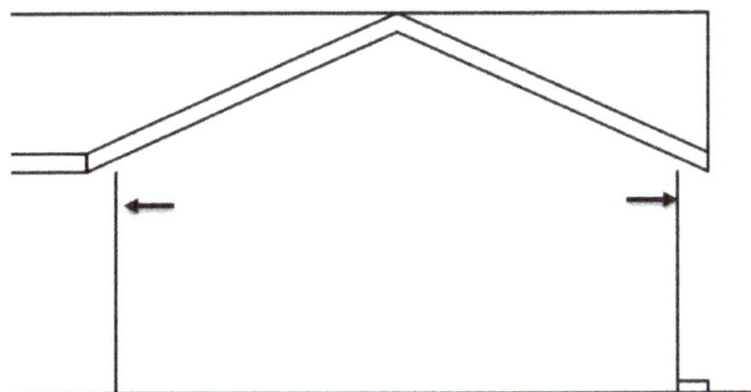

- Create a horizontal line connecting the endpoints of the two vertical lines.

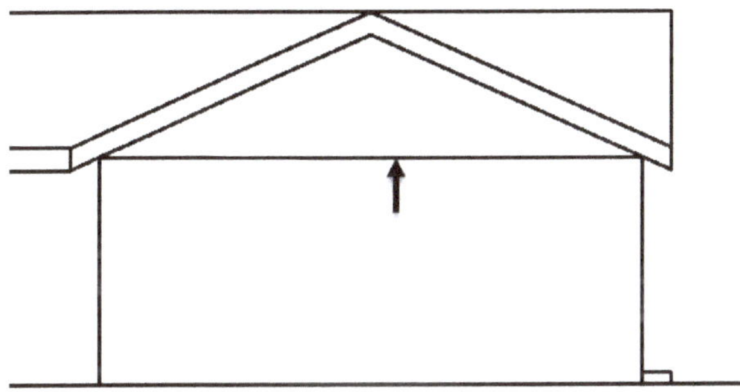

- Select the two construction lines, as shown.
- Press Delete.

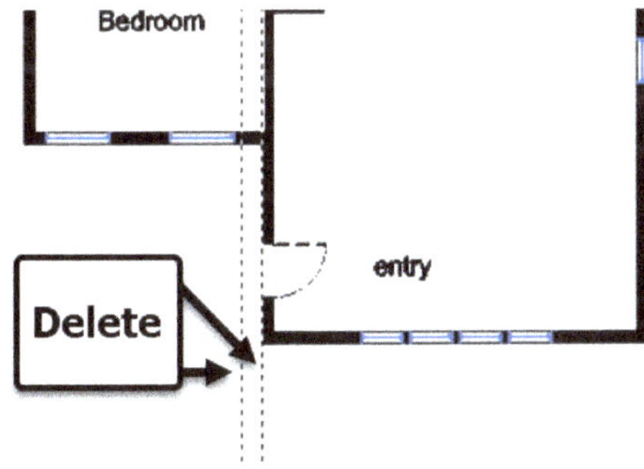

- On the ribbon, click **Home > Draw > Infinite Line** tool.
- Select the **Vertical** option from the command line.
- Zoom to the lower portion of the floor plan and select the vertex points on the window, as shown.

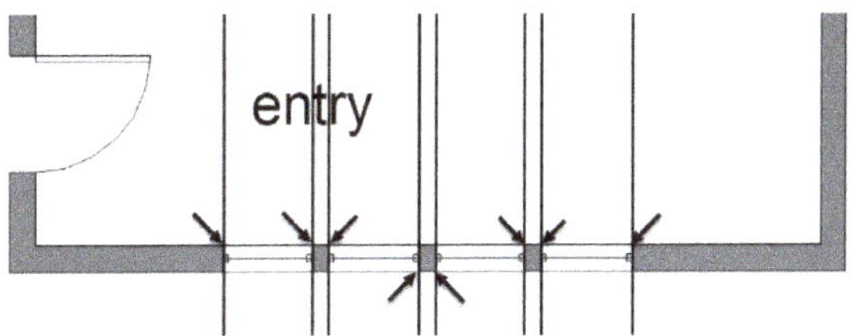

- Click the **Offset** tool on the **Modify** panel on the **Home** ribbon tab.
- Type 3' as the offset distance. Next, press ENTER.
- Select the horizontal line, as shown.
- Next, move the pointer upward and click.

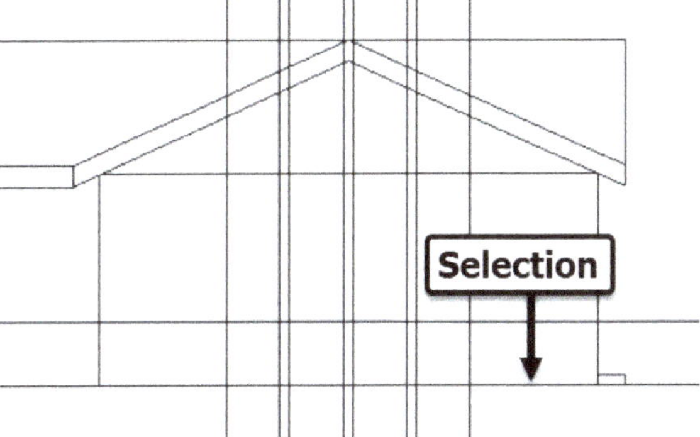

- Click the **Home > Draw > Rectangle** on the ribbon.
- Select the **Dimensions** option from the command line.
- Select the two intersection points, as shown.

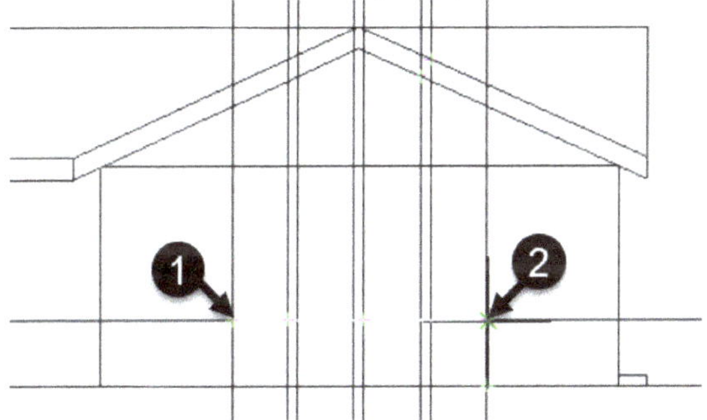

- Type 54 as the rectangle width and press ENTER.
- Select the intersection point, as shown.

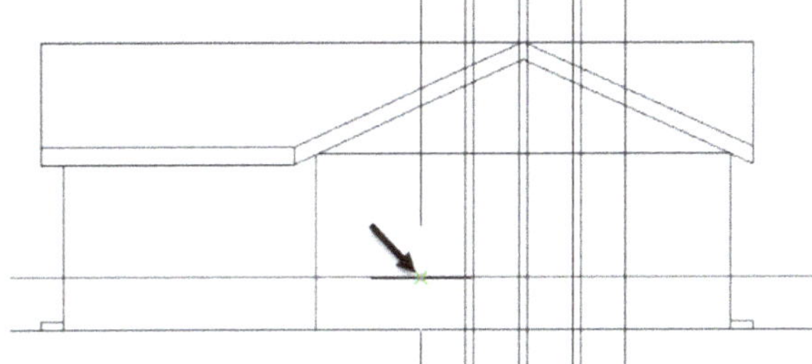

- Next, move the pointer upward and click.

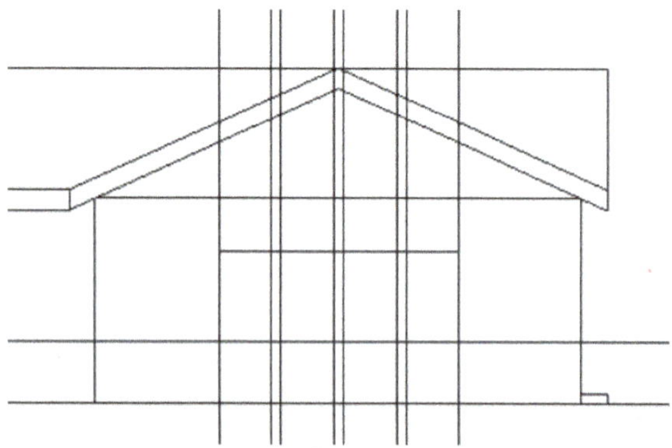

- Click the **Offset** tool on the **Modify** panel.
- Type 4" as the offset distance. Next, press ENTER.
- Select the rectangle. Next, move the pointer outward and click.

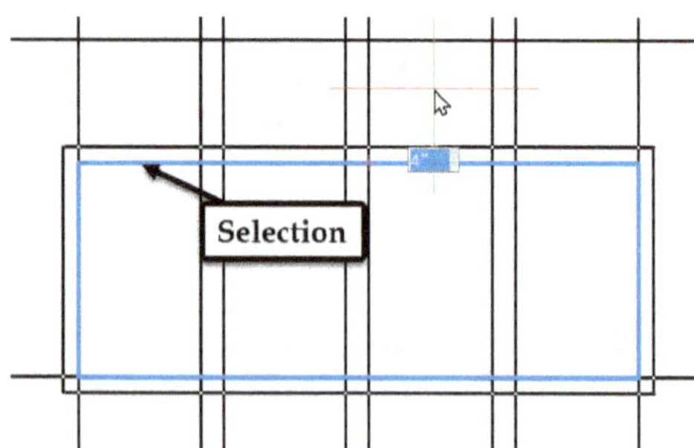

- Click the **Trim** icon on the **Modify** panel. Next, press ENTER.
- Click and drag the pointer across the vertical lines, as shown.

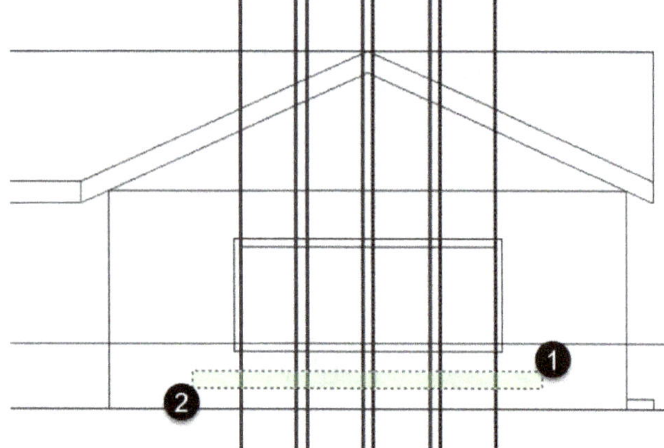

- Select the portions of the vertical lines, as shown.

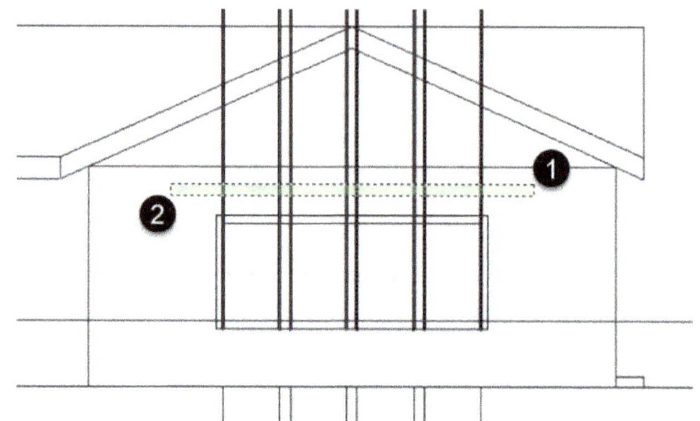

- Press ENTER.
- Select the vertical and horizontal construction lines. Next, press Delete.

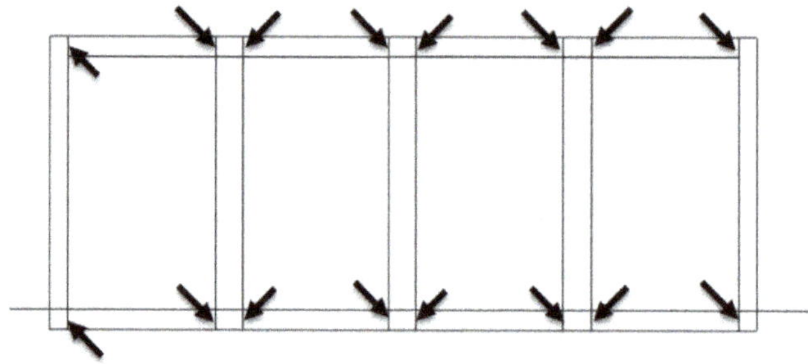

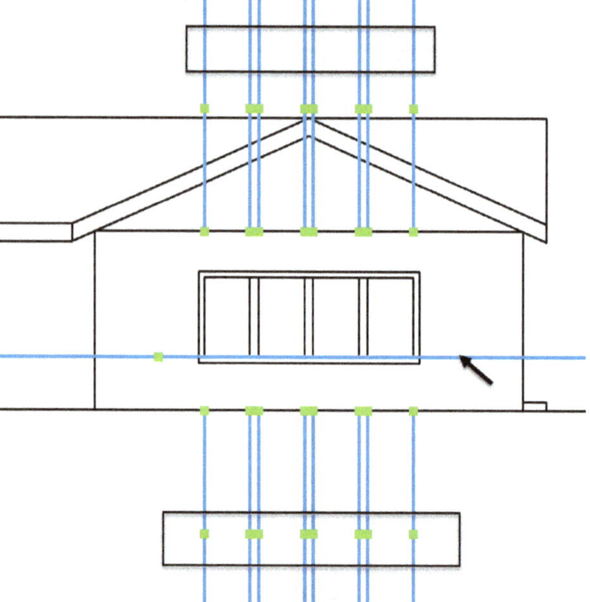

- Select the two rectangles and click the **Explode** tool on the **Modify** panel of the **Home** ribbon tab.

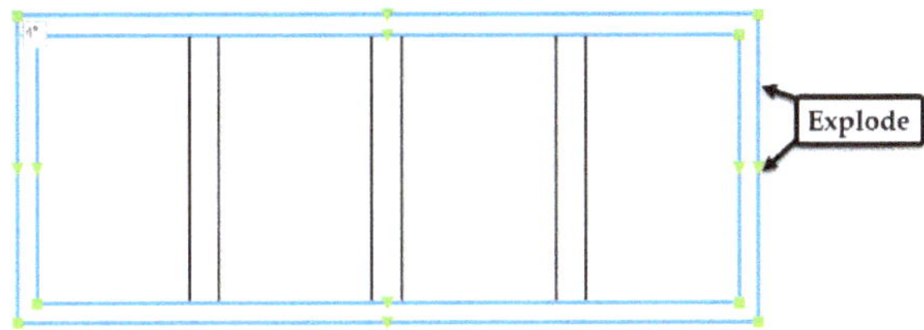

- On the ribbon, click **Home** tab > **Draw** panel > **Multiline**.

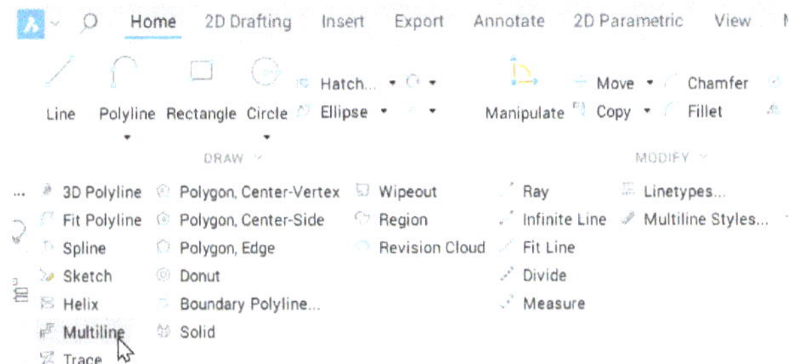

- Select the **Justification** option from the command line.
- Select the **Zero** option.
- Select the **Scale** option from the command line.
- Type 0.25, and press ENTER.
- Press and hold the Shift key, and then right click.
- Select the **Snap to Middle of 2 Points** option.

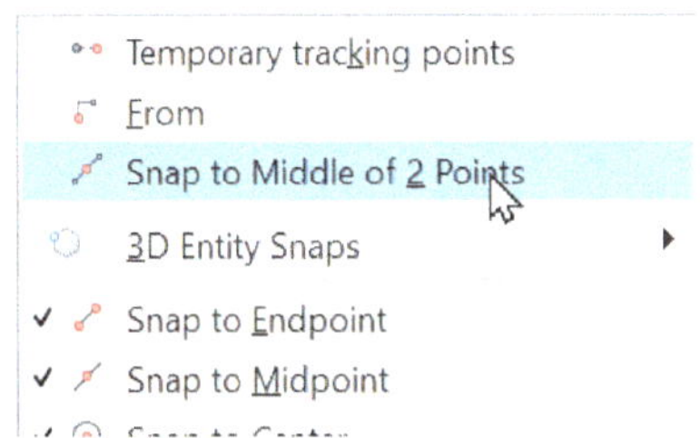

- Select the two points, as shown.

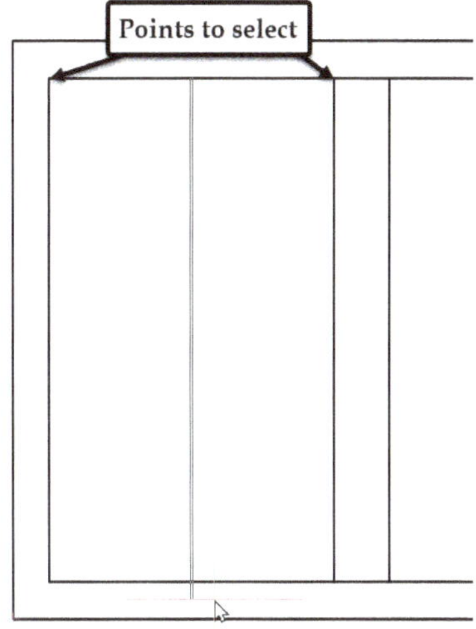

- Move the pointer downward and click.
- Press ENTER.
- Select the midpoint of the vertical line, as shown.

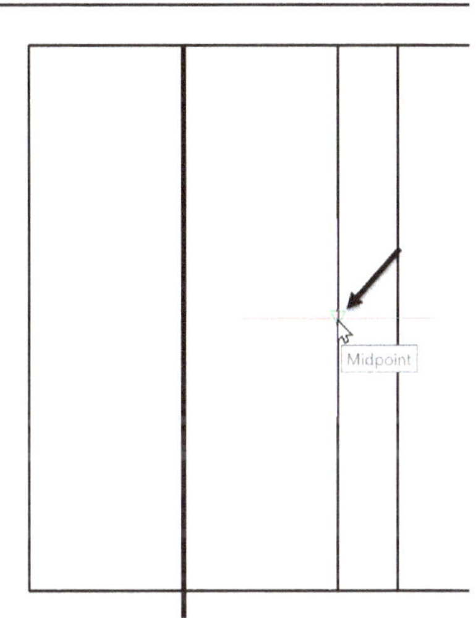

- Move the pointer toward the left and select the midpoint of the vertical line.

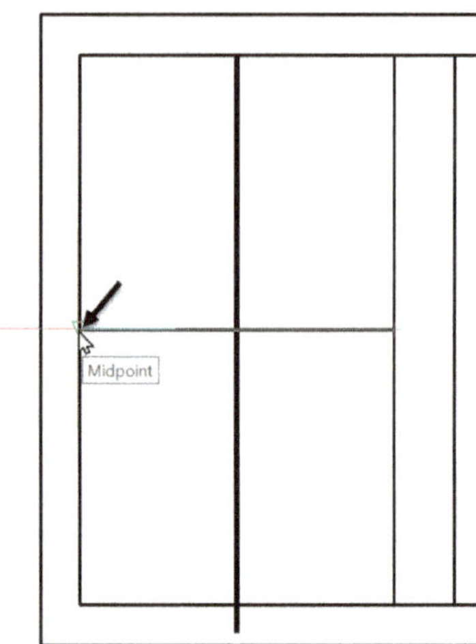

- Press Esc.
- Select the two multilines.
- On the ribbon, click **Home** tab > **Modify** panel > **Explode**.
- On the ribbon, click **Home** tab > **Modify** panel > **Trim**.
- Press ENTER and click in the portions of the exploded lines, as shown.

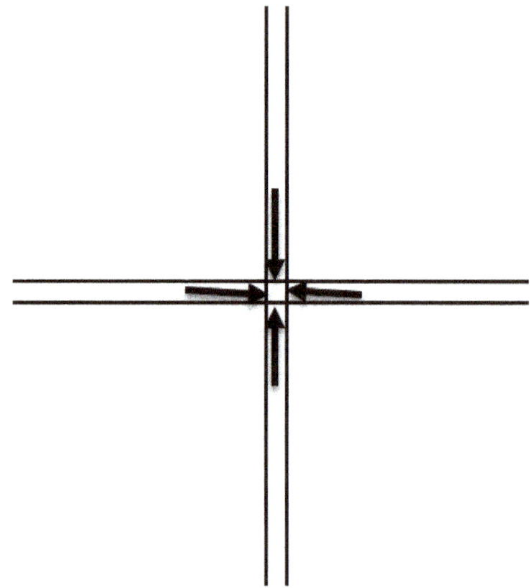

- Click the **Copy** tool on the **Modify** panel of the **Home** ribbon tab.
- Select the lines and press ENTER, as shown.

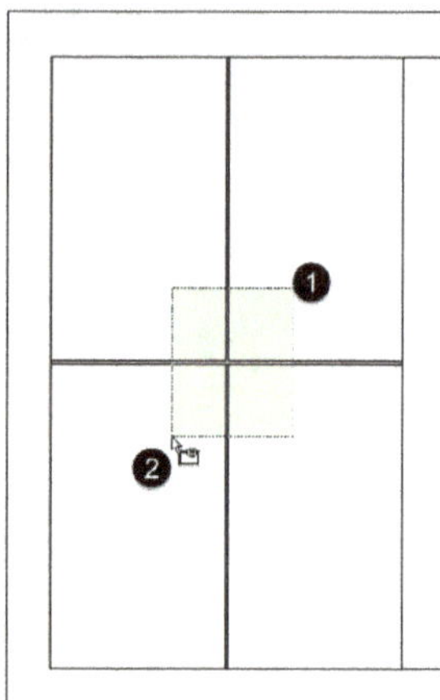

- Select the lower-left corner point.
- Move the pointer toward the right and select the corner point, as shown.

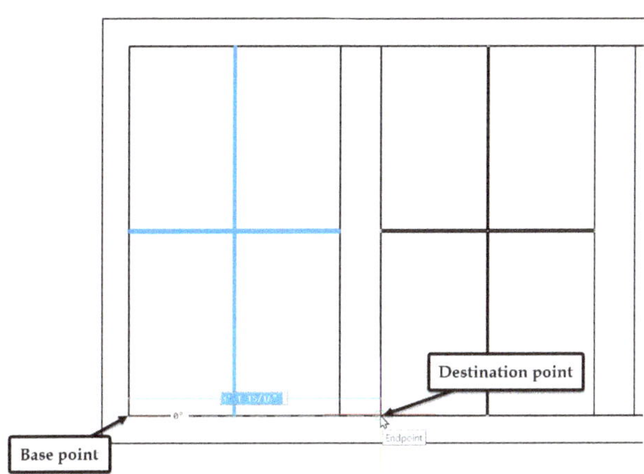

- Likewise, create two more copies of the multi-lines, as shown.

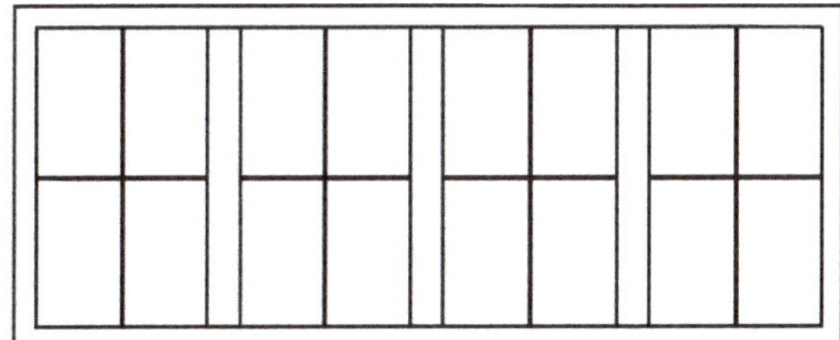

- Likewise, create two windows on the left side.

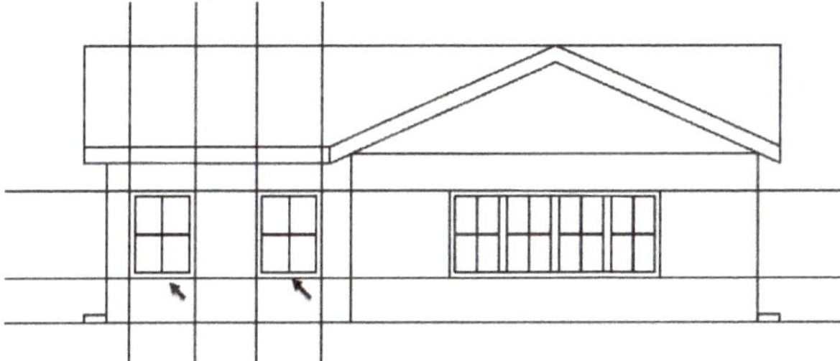

- Delete the construction lines.

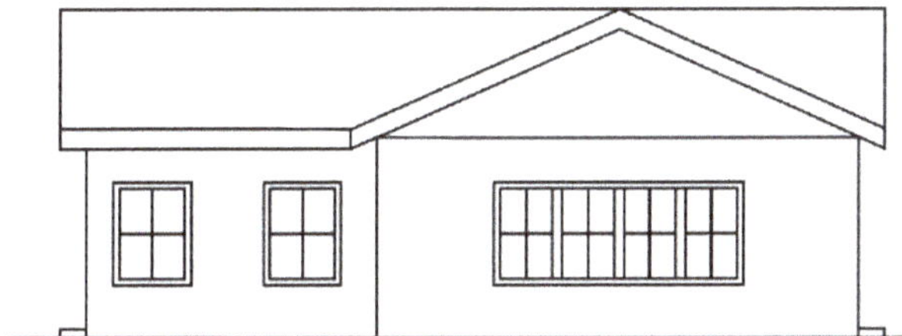

- Click the **Hatch** tool on the **Draw** panel of the **Home** ribbon tab.
- On the **Hatch and Gradient** dialog, click the

  Browse icon next to the **Name** box.

- Select the **SHAKES** hatch from the **Hatch Pattern Palette** and click **OK**.

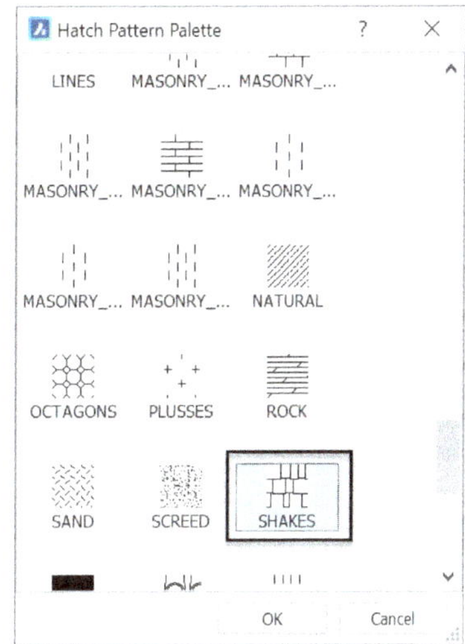

- Click the **Pick points in boundaries** icon under the **Boundaries** section. Next, pick points in the areas, as shown.

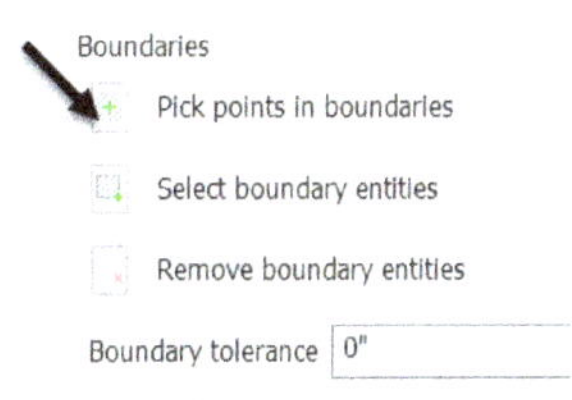

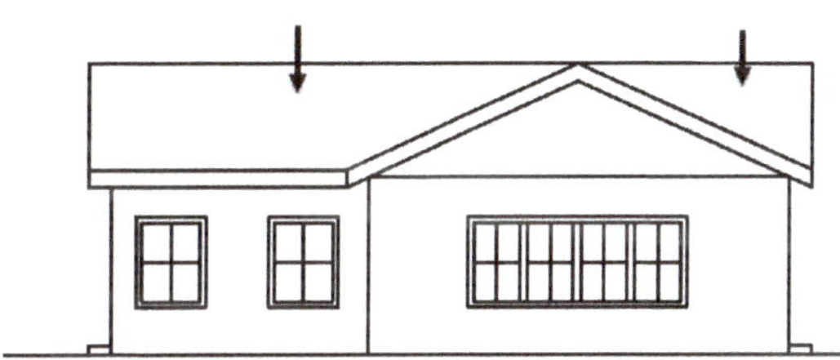

- Press ENTER.
- Type **10** in the **Scale** box and click **OK** on the **Hatch and Gradient** dialog.
- Click the **Hatch** tool on the **Draw** panel of the **Home** ribbon tab.
- On the **Hatch and Gradient** dialog, click the

  Browse icon next to the **Name** box.

- Select the **BRICK_STRBOND** hatch from the **Hatch Pattern Palette** and click **OK**.

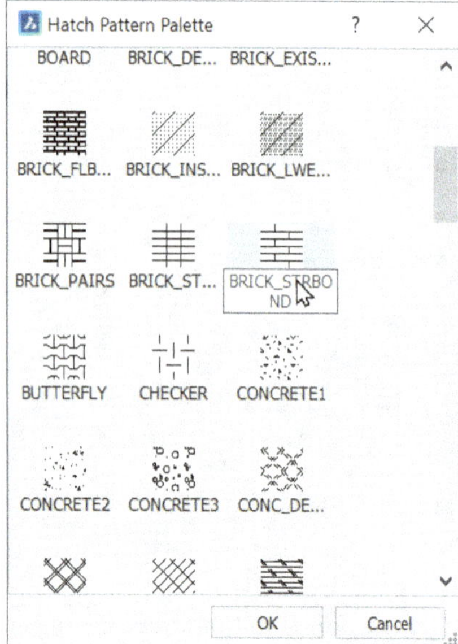

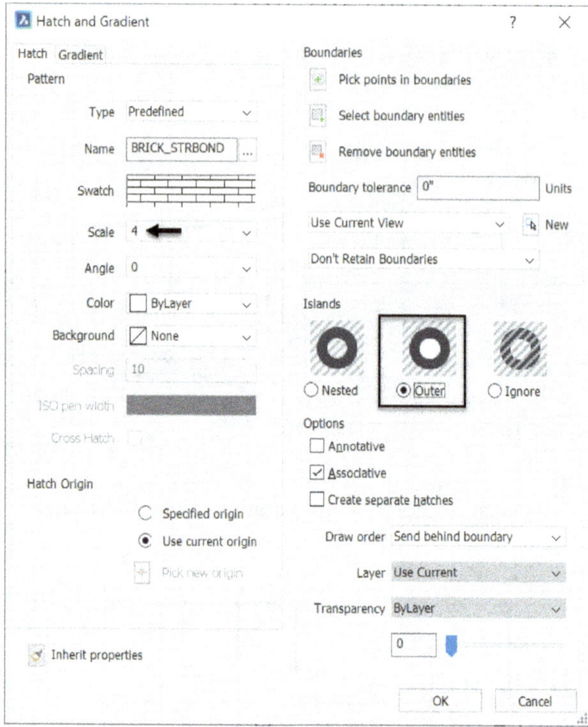

* Click the **Pick points in boundaries** icon under the **Boundaries** section. Next, pick points in the areas, as shown.

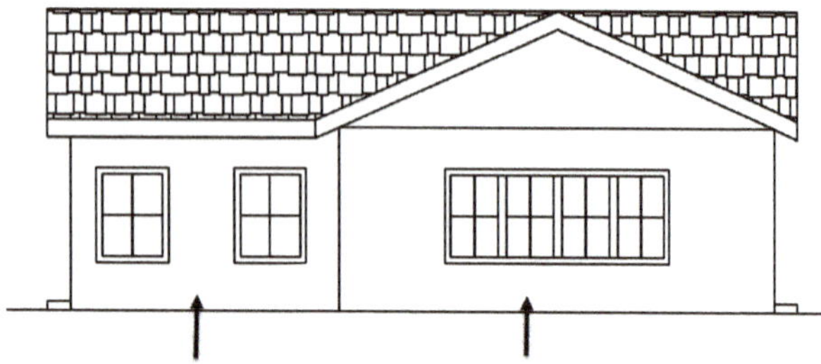

* Press ENTER.
* Type **4** in the **Scale** box.
* Under the **Islands** section, select the **Outer** option.

* Click **OK** on the **Hatch and Gradient** dialog.

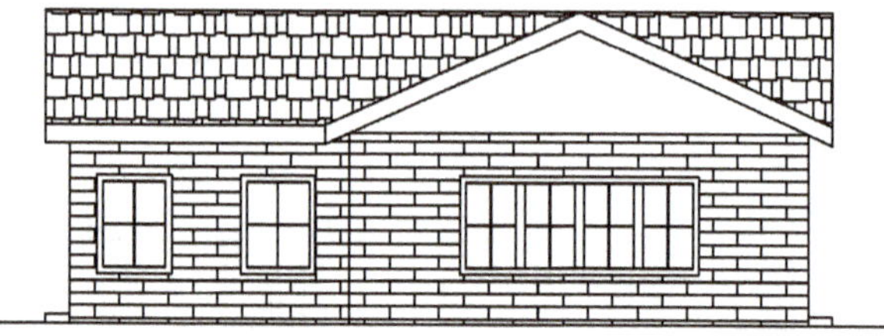

* Click the **Hatch** tool on the **Draw** panel of the **Home** ribbon tab.
* On the **Hatch and Gradient** dialog, click the **Browse** icon next to the **Name** box.

* Select the **ANSI31** hatch from the **Hatch Pattern Palette** and click **OK**.

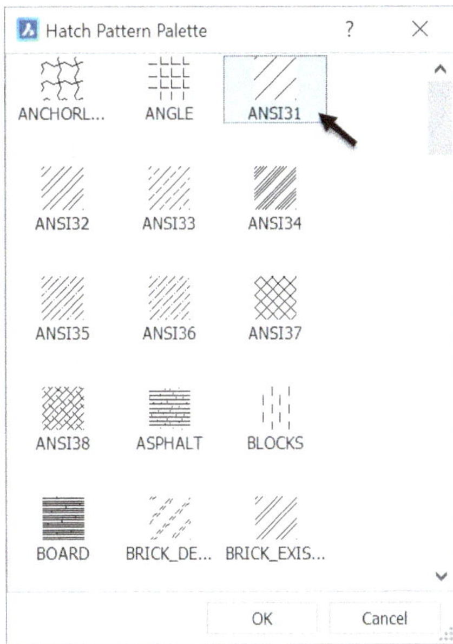

- Enter **135** and **50** in the **Angle** and **Scale** boxes, respectively.
- Click in the region, as shown.

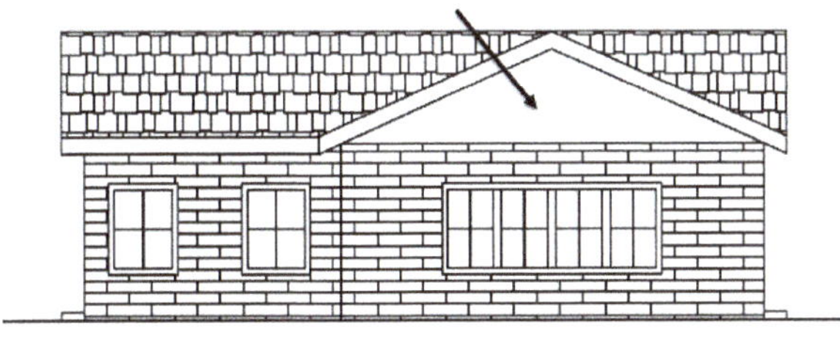

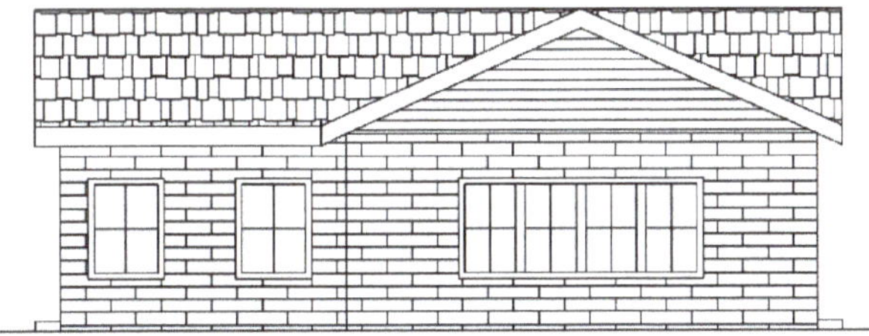

- Press ENTER twice.
- Save and close the file.

Tutorial 4: Creating the Roof Plan

In this tutorial, you will create the Roof plan using the floor plan.

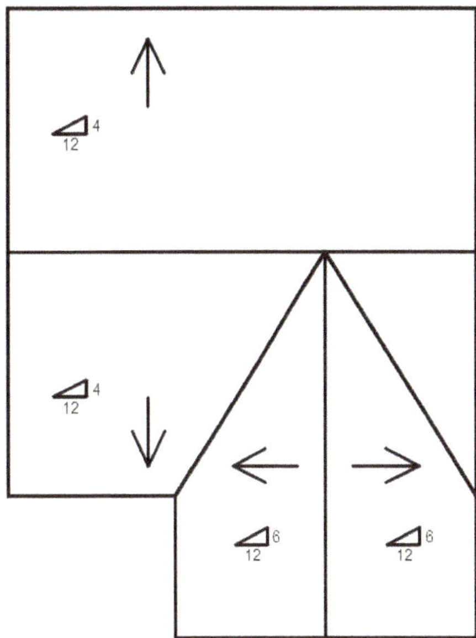

- Download the Floor_plan.dwg from the companion website.
- Start a new drawing using the **Default-imperial** template.
- Click the **Attach Xref** tool on the **XREFS** panel of the **Insert** ribbon tab.

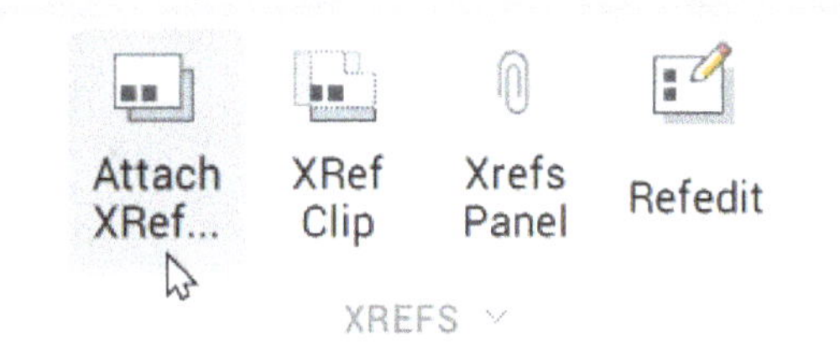

- On the **Select Reference File** dialog, go to the location of the Floor_plan.dwg file and double-click on it.
- Check the **Specify On-screen** option from the **Insertion Point** section.
- Click **Insert** on the **Attach External Reference** dialog.

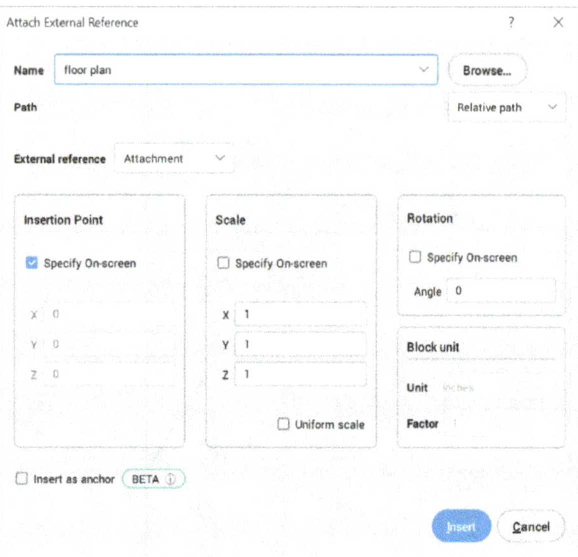

- Click in the graphics window.
- Click **View** > **Views** > **Zoom** > **Zoom Extents** on the ribbon.

- Click the **Polyline** tool on the **Draw** panel of the **Home** ribbon tab.
- Select the corner points of the floor plan.
- Select the **Close** option from the command line.

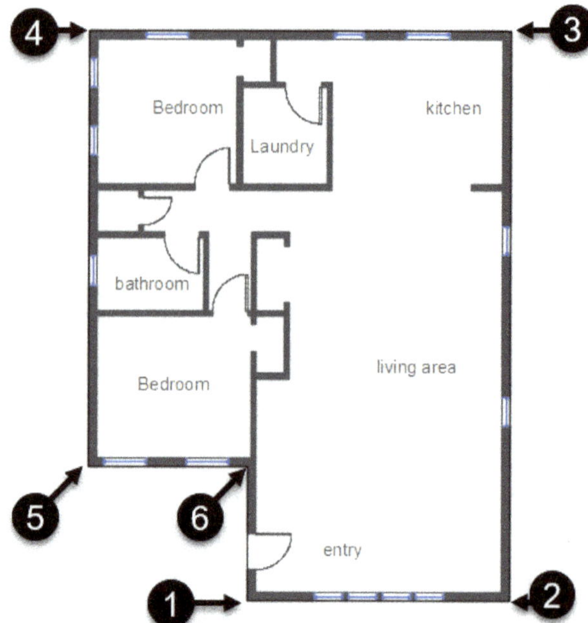

- Click the **Offset** tool on the **Modify** panel of the **Home** ribbon tab.
- Type 16 and press ENTER. Next, select the newly created polyline.
- Move the pointer outward and click.

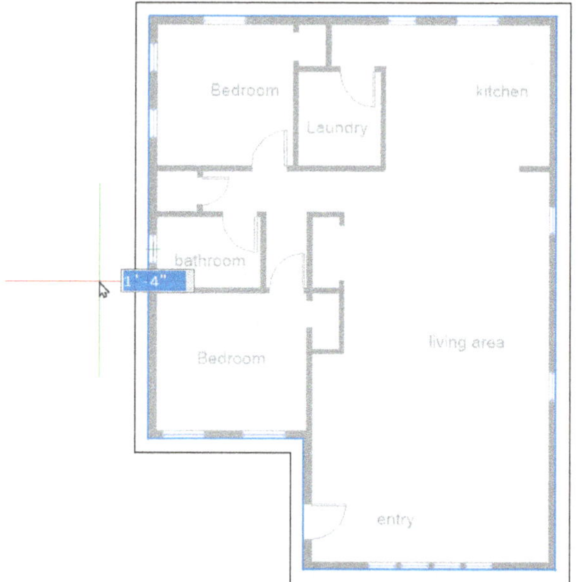

- Click the **Erase** tool on the **Modify** panel of the **Home** ribbon tab.

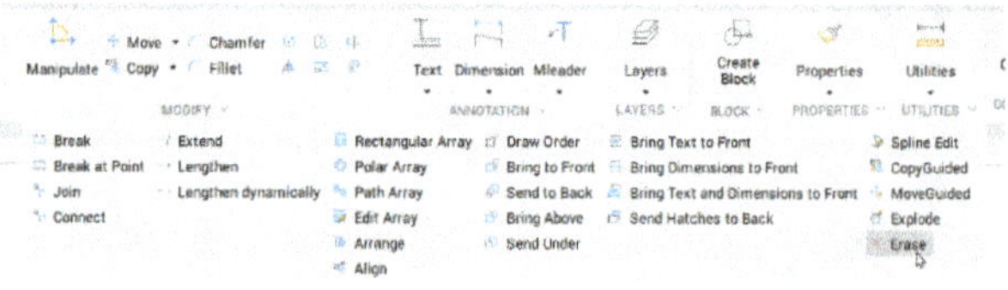

- Select the polyline used to create the offset. Next, press ENTER.

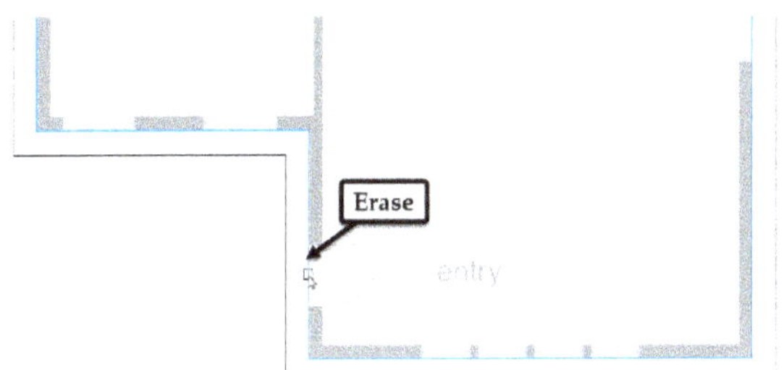

- Click the **Line** tool on the **Draw** panel of the **Home** ribbon tab.
- Select the midpoint of the left vertical line.

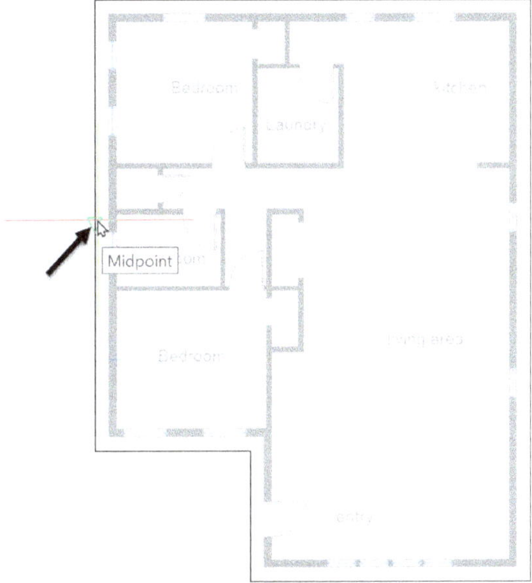

- Make sure the ORTHO icon is active on the status bar.
- Move the pointer toward the right and click. Next, press ENTER twice.

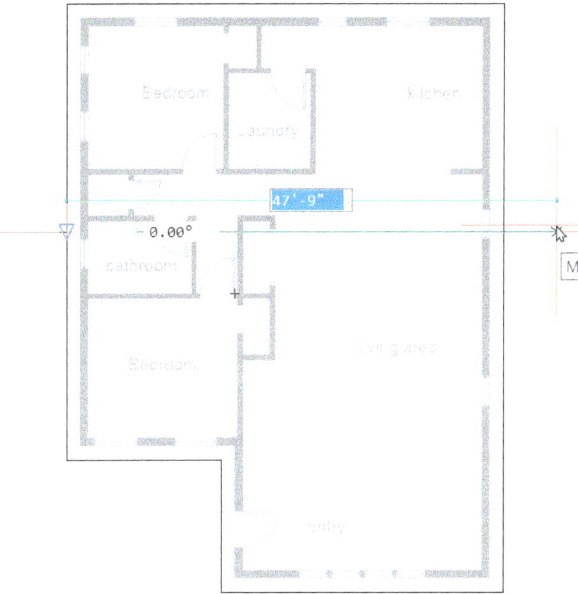

- Select the midpoint of the lower horizontal line, as shown.

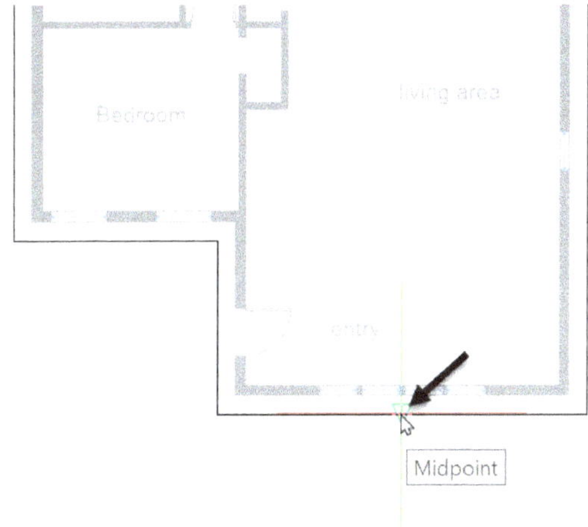

- Move the pointer upward and click.

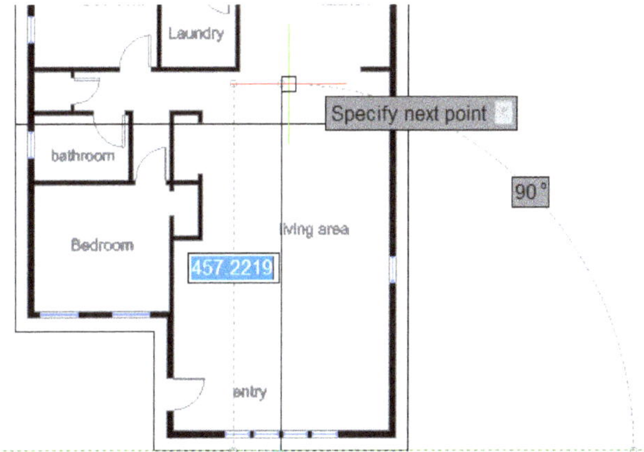

- Click the **Trim** tool on the **Modify** panel of the **Home** ribbon tab. Next, press ENTER.

- Select the unwanted portions of the lines, as shown.

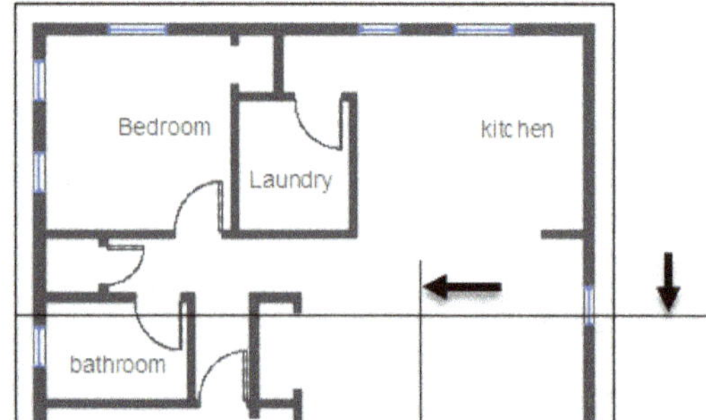

- Click the **Line** tool on the **Draw** panel of the **Home** ribbon tab.
- Select the corner point of the polyline.
- Select the intersection point of the vertical and horizontal lines. Next, press ESC.

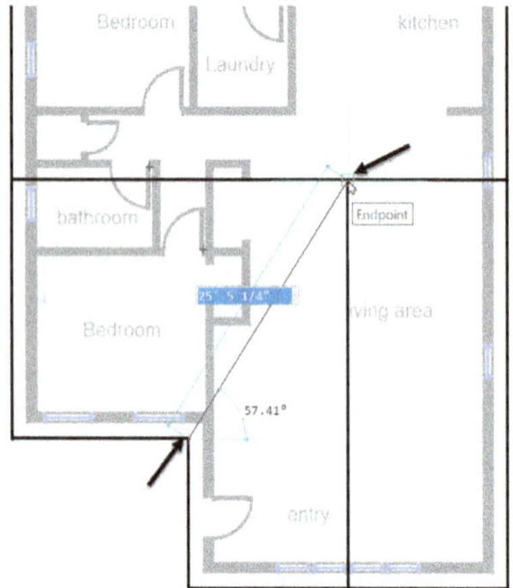

- Select the inclined line.
- Click the **Mirror** tool on the **Modify** panel of the **Home** ribbon tab.
- Select the endpoints of the vertical line. Next, select the **No-keep entities** option from the command line.

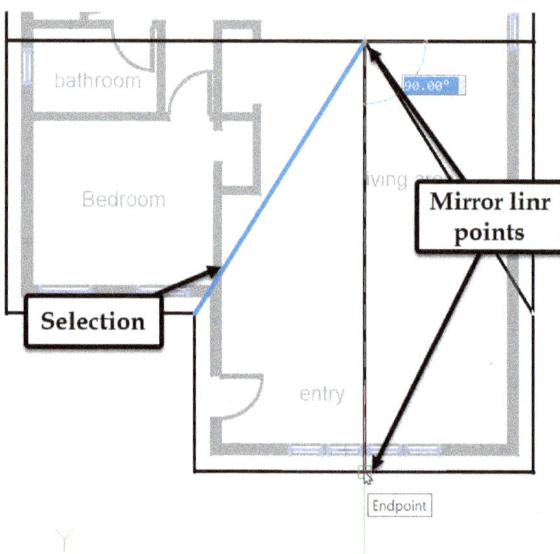

- Select the attachment.
- Click on the origin point of the attachment, and then move the pointer upward.

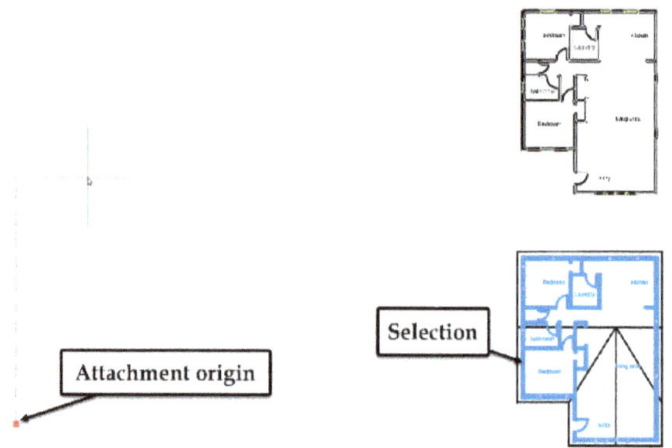

- Click the **Line** tool on the **Draw** panel of the **Home** ribbon tab. Next, click in the graphics window.
- Move the pointer toward the right. Next, type 36, and press ENTER.

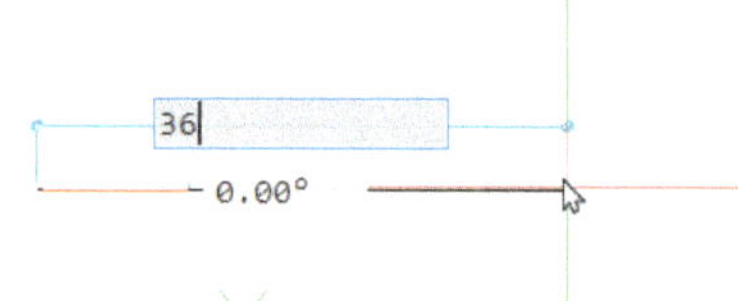

- Move the pointer upward. Next, type 18, and press ENTER.

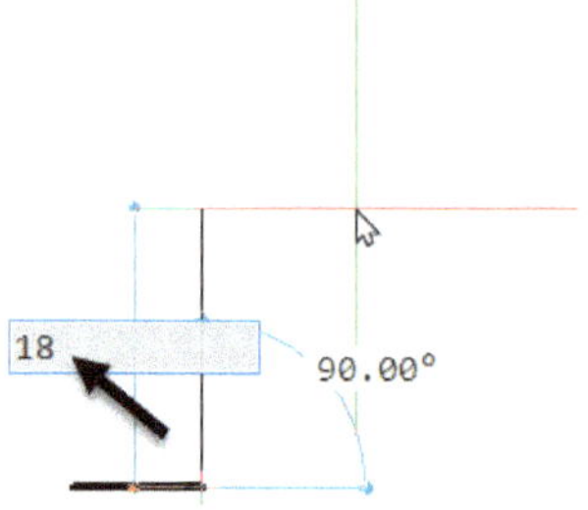

- Select the Close option from the command line.
- Click the **Text** drop-down > **Text** on the **Annotations** panel of the **Home** ribbon tab.

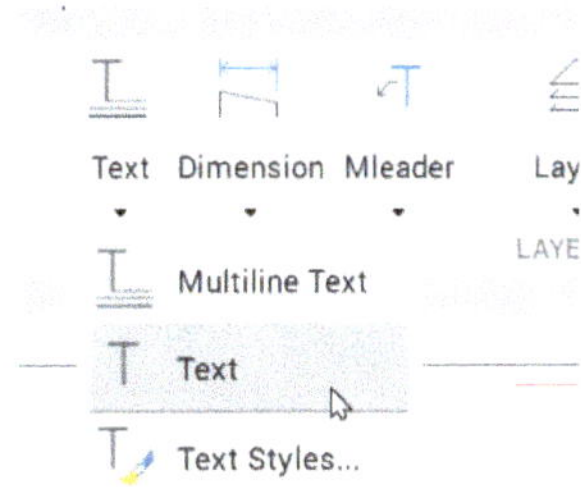

- Click in the graphics window.
- Type **12** as the text height. Next, press ENTER.

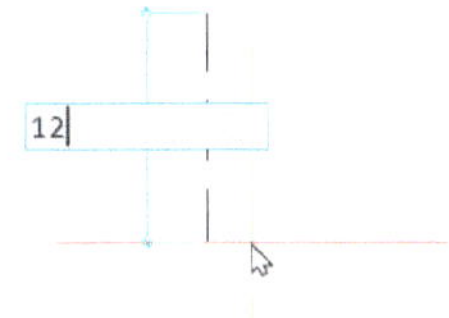

- Type 0 as the rotation angle, and then press ENTER.
- Type 4 and click in the graphics window.
- Type 12 and click in the graphics window. Next, press ESC.
- Select the 4 text and click on its base point. Next, move the pointer and click at the location, as shown.

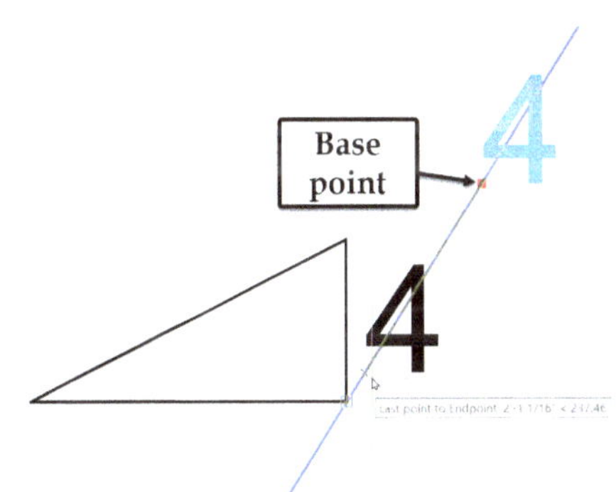

- Likewise, position the 12 text at the location, as shown.

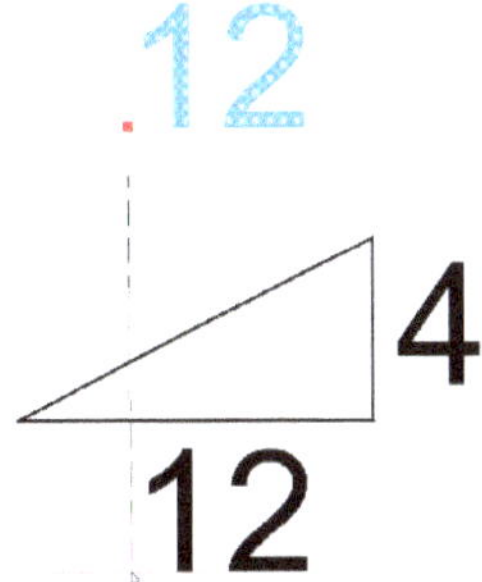

- Create a selection window across the triangle and the texts.

- Click the **Copy** tool on the **Modify** panel of the **Home** ribbon tab. Next, select the base point, as shown.

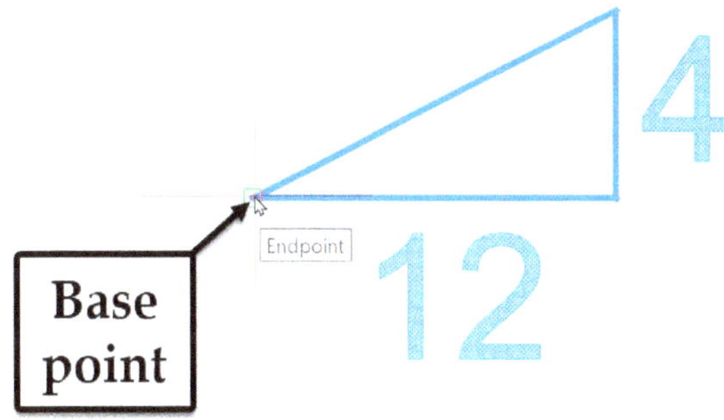

- Place the copies at the locations, as shown.

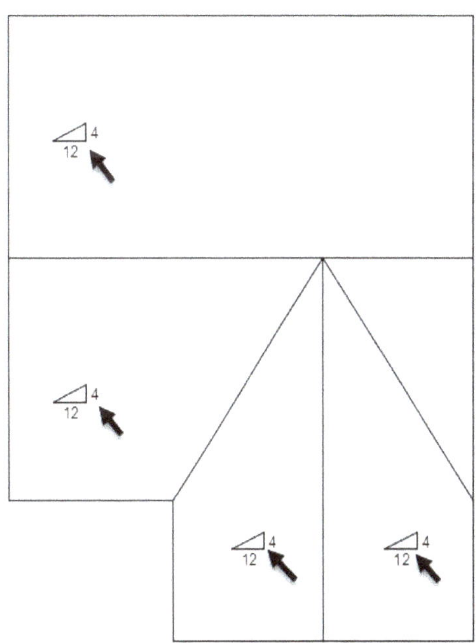

- Zoom the lower portion of the drawing. Next, double-click on 4.
- Type 6 and click in the graphics window.
- Likewise, change the text on the right side to 6. Next, press ESC.

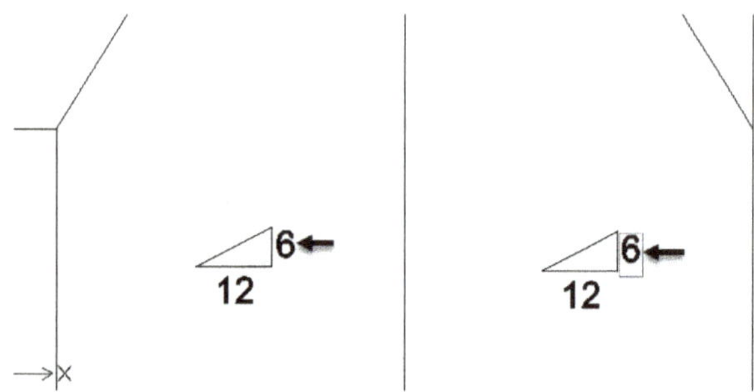

- Click the **Rectangle** on the **Draw** panel of the **Home** ribbon tab.
- Select the **Dimensions** option from the command line.
- Type 36 and press ENTER.
- Type 72 and press ENTER.
- Click at the location, as shown. Next, right-click.

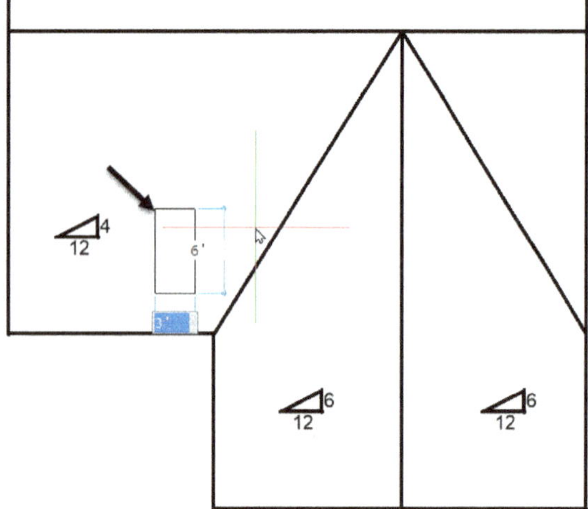

- Click the **Line** tool on the **Draw** panel of the **Home** ribbon tab.
- Select the midpoints of the horizontal edges of the rectangle.

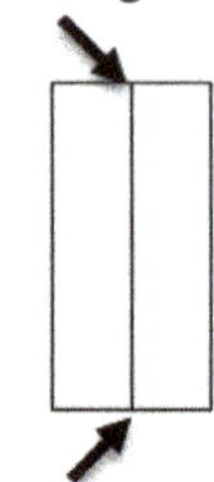

- Press ENTER twice. Next, select the midpoint of the left vertical edge of the rectangle.
- Select the lower endpoint of the vertical line. Next, select the midpoint of the right vertical edge of the rectangle.

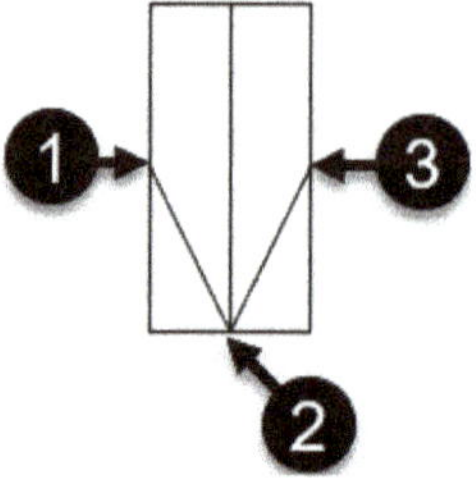

- Press ESC.
- Select the rectangle and press Delete.

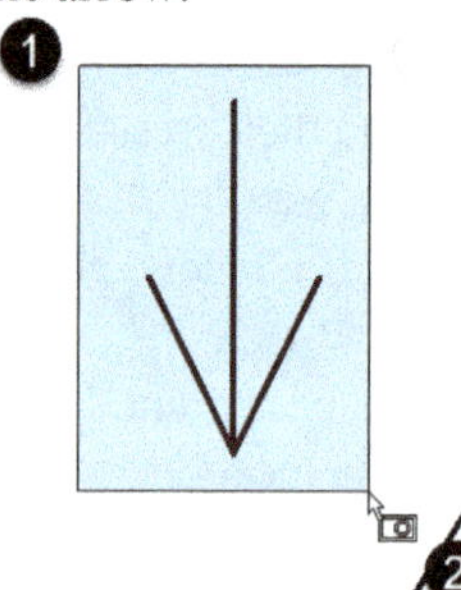

- Create a selection window across all the elements of the arrow.

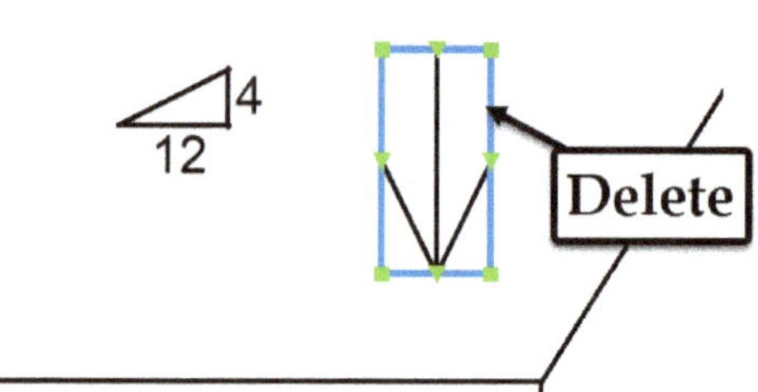

- Click the **Mirror** on the **Modify** panel of the **Home** ribbon tab.
- Select the endpoints of the horizontal line to define the mirror line.
- Next, right-click and select **NO-keep entities**.

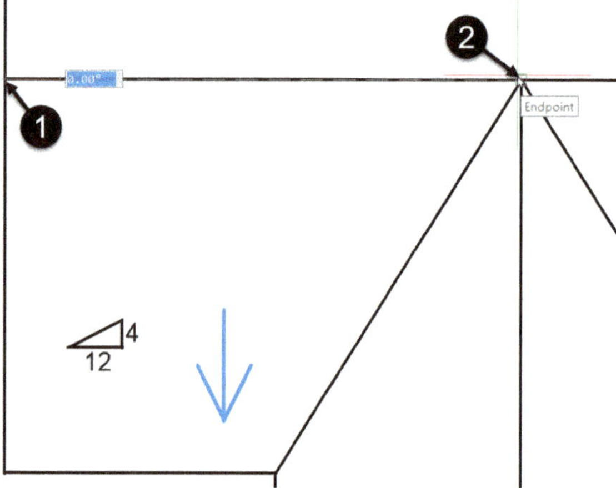

- Activate the **ORTHO** icon on the status bar.
- Create a selection window across all the elements of the arrow.
- Click the **2D Rotate** tool on the **Modify** panel of the **Home** ribbon tab.

- Select the rotation point, as shown.

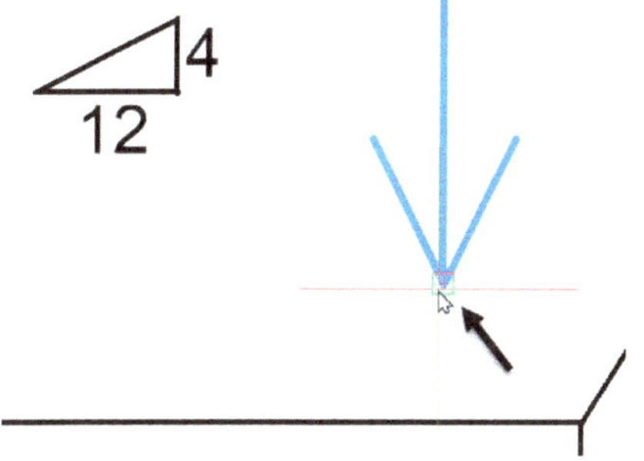

- Select the **Copy** option from the command line.
- Move the pointer vertically downward and click.

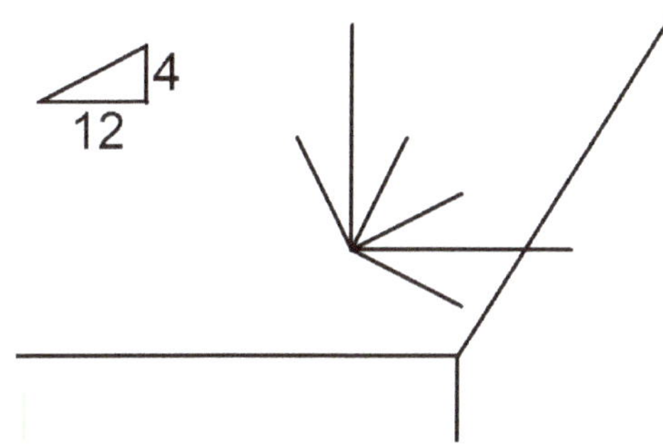

- Select the elements of the rotated arrow.
- Click **Move** tool on the **Modify** panel of the **Home** ribbon tab.
- Select the base point, as shown.

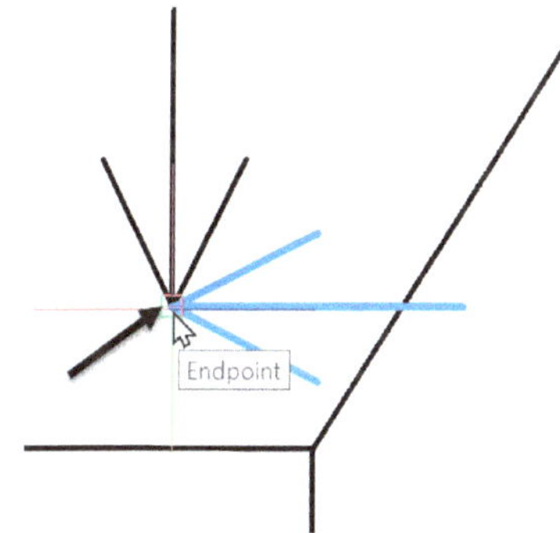

- Move the pointer toward the right and click.

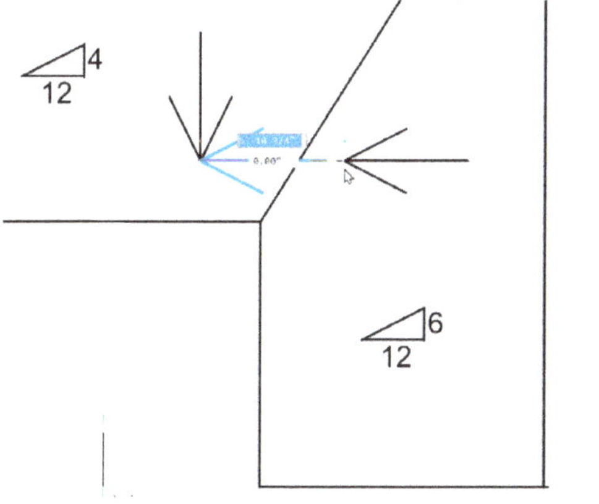

- Select the elements of the arrow moved in the previous step.
- Click the **Mirror** tool on the **Modify** panel of the **Home** ribbon tab.
- Select the endpoints of the vertical line, as shown.

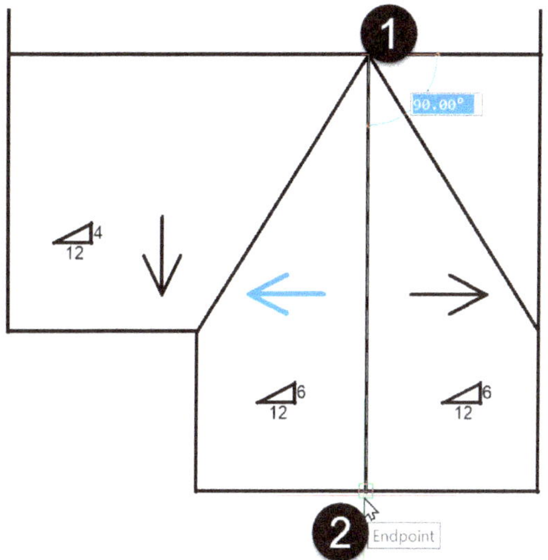

- Right-click and select **No-keep entities**.
- Save and close the drawing file.

Tutorial 5: Creating the Wall and Roof Detail

In this tutorial, you will create the Roof and wall detail.

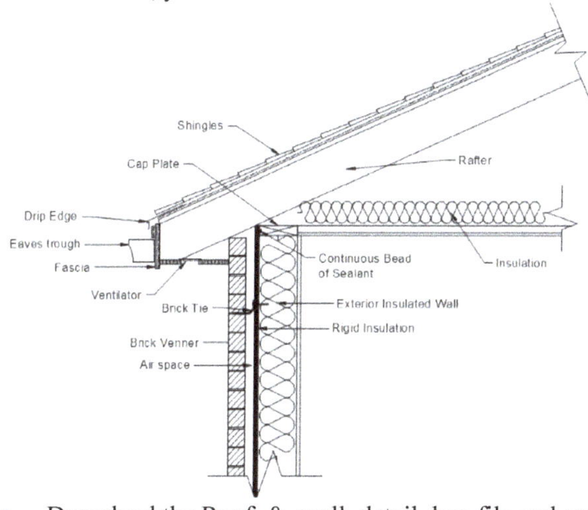

- Download the Roof_&_wall_detail.dwg file and open it.
- Click the **Layers** tool on the **Layers** panel of the **Home** ribbon tab.
- Create a new layer and name it as Roof_wall_detail. Next, make the new layer are current.

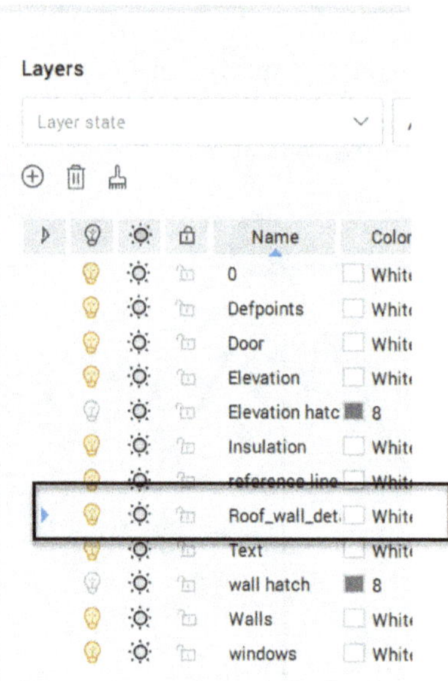

- Close the **Layers** palette.
- On the **Home** ribbon tab, click > **Draw** panel > **Line** drop-down > **Ray** tool.
- Create the projection lines from the elevation view, as shown.
- Create a vertical line, as shown.

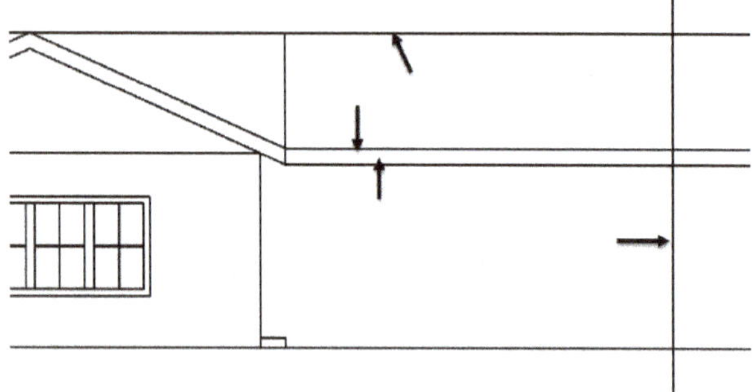

- Select the two inclined lines of the roof, as shown.
- Select the two vertical lines, as shown.

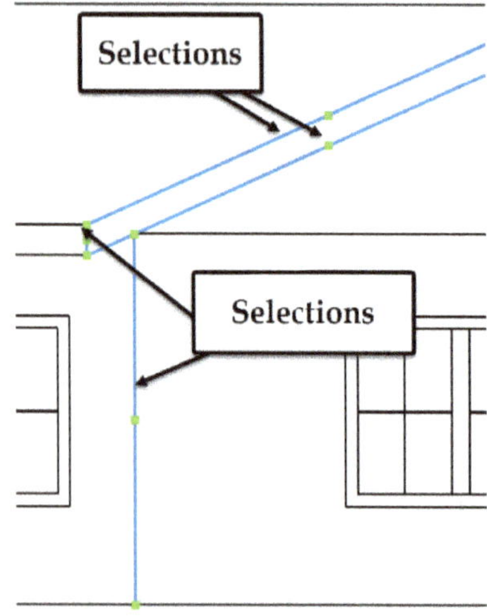

- Click the **Copy** tool on the **Modify** panel of the **Home** ribbon tab.
- Select the base point, as shown.

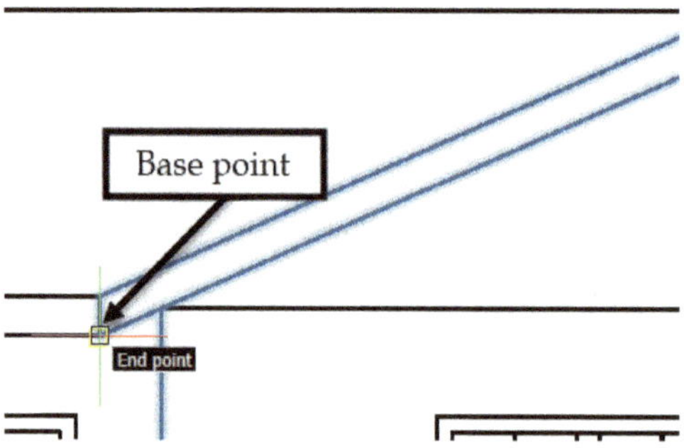

- Move the pointer toward the right and select the intersection point, as shown.

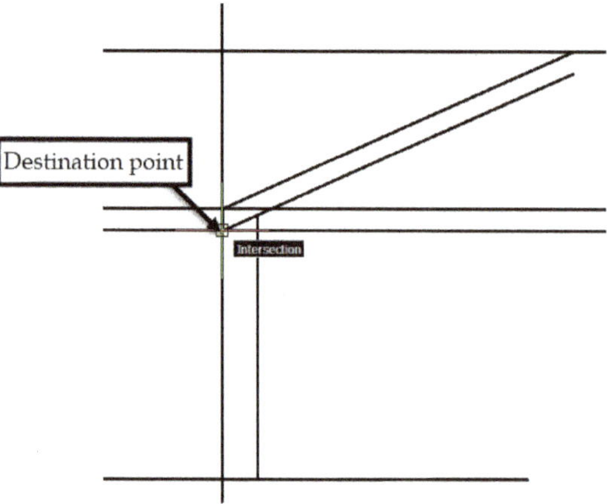

- Delete the reference lines, as shown.

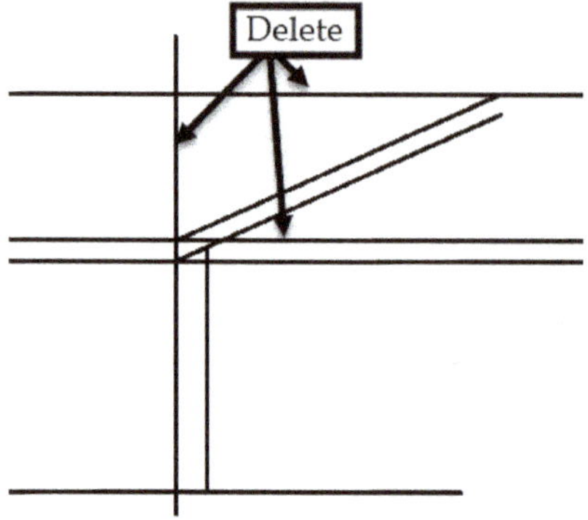

- Click the **Trim** tool on the **Modify** panel of the **Home** ribbon tab. Next, press ENTER.
- Select the portion of the horizontal line, as shown.

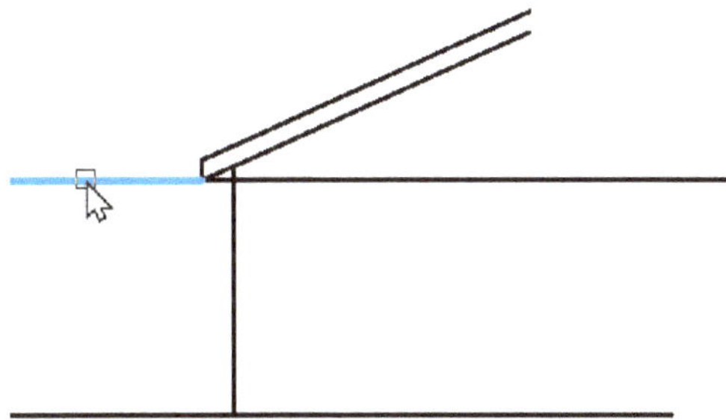

- Click the **Offset** tool on the **Modify** panel of the **Home** ribbon tab. Next, type 4, and press ENTER.
- Select the vertical line. Next, move the pointer toward the right and click.

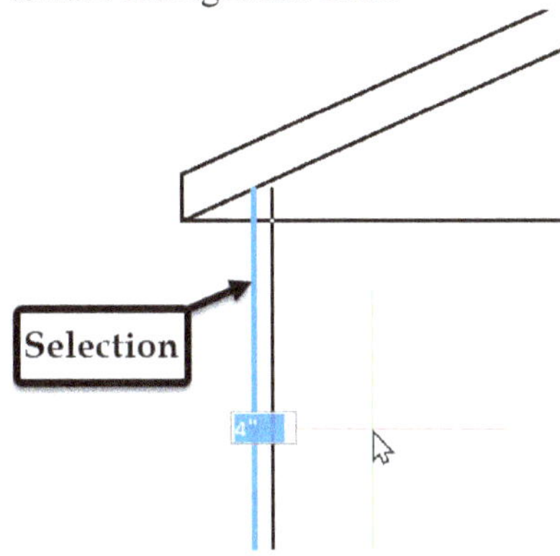

- Press ENTER twice. Next, type 2, and press ENTER.
- Select the offset line. Next, move the pointer toward the right and click.

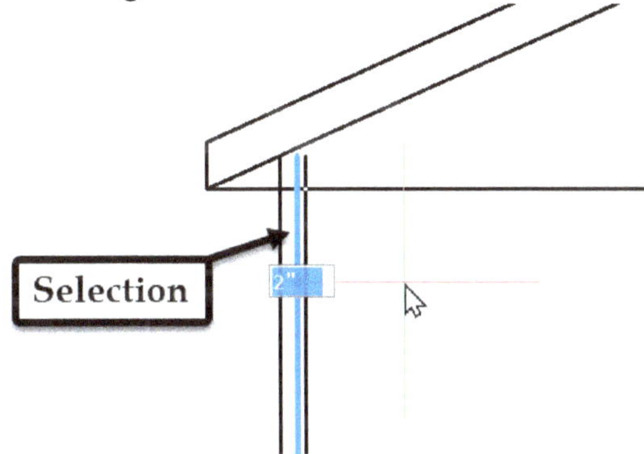

Creating the Brick Veneer

- Click the **Rectangle** on the **Draw** panel of the **Home** ribbon tab.
- Specify the corner point, as shown.

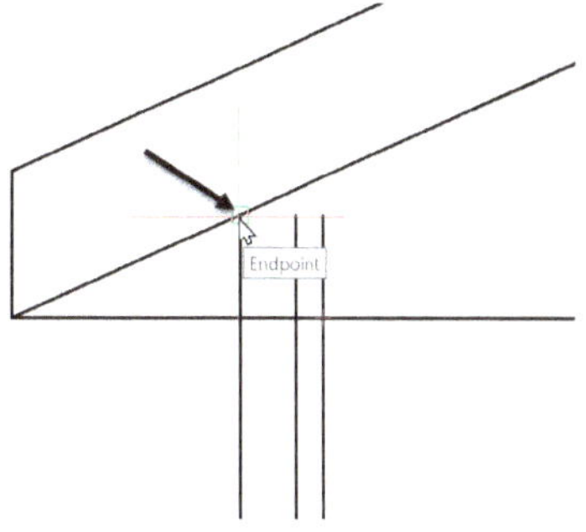

- Type 4, and press TAB.
- Type 4 and press ENTER.

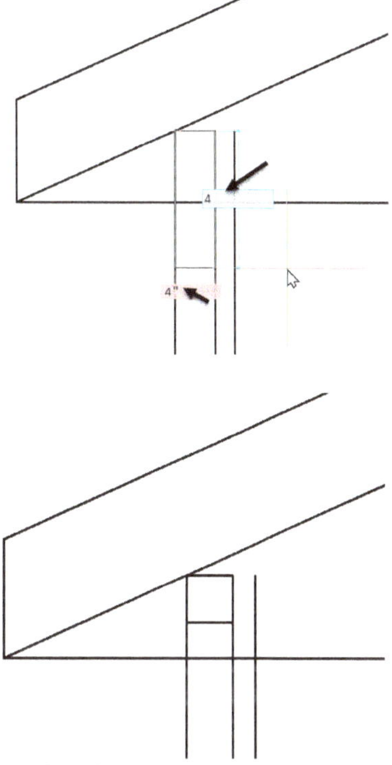

- Select the rectangle.
- Click the **Path Array** icon on the **Modify** panel of the **Home** ribbon tab.

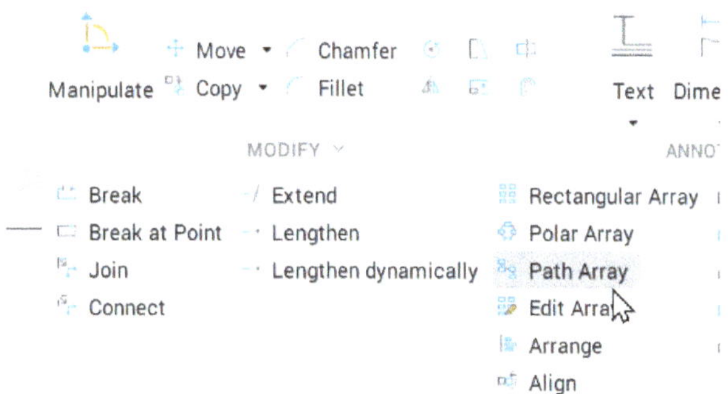

- Select the left vertical line to define the path.

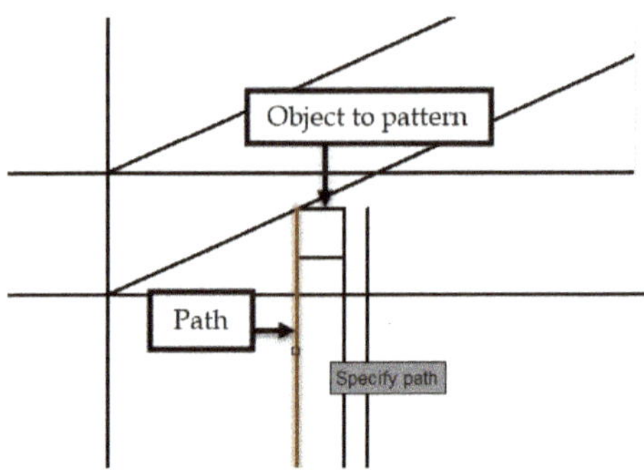

- Select the **Associative** option from the command line.
- Select the **No** option from the command line.
- Select the **Method** option from the command line.
- Select the **Measure** option from the command line.
- Select **Items** from the command line.
- Type **4.25** and press ENTER to define the distance between items along path.
- Type **14** and press ENTER to define the number of items.

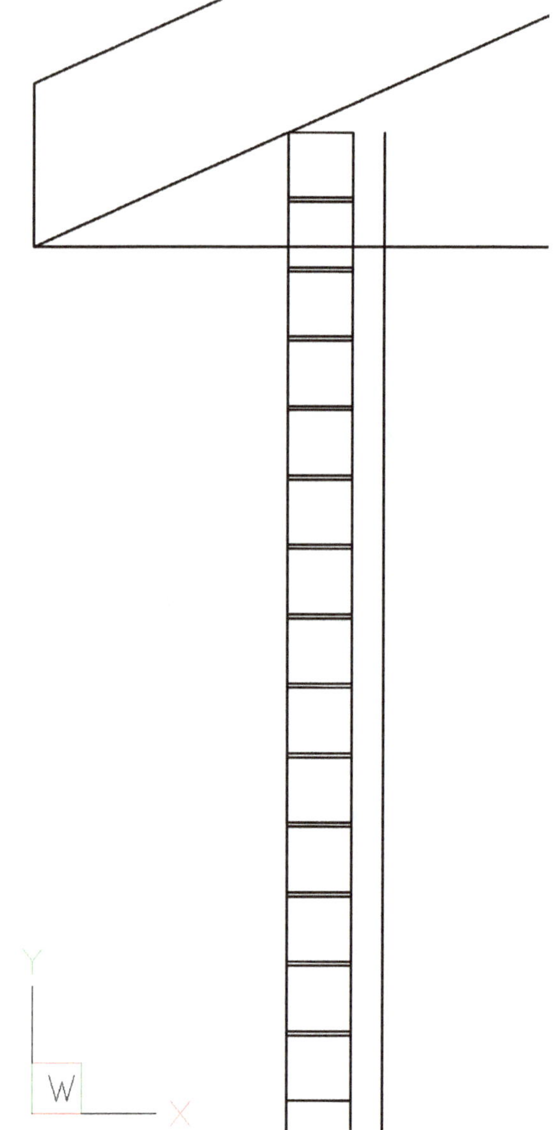

- Select the **eXit** option from the command line.
- Select any one of the rectangles.
- On the Quad, click **General > Select Similar**. All the rectangles are selected.

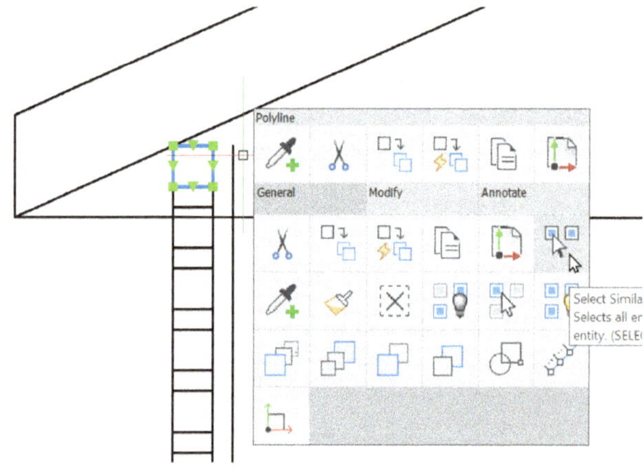

- Click the **Explode** tool on the **Modify** panel of the **Home** ribbon tab. All the rectangles are exploded into individual objects.
- Click the **Line** tool on the **Draw** panel of the **Home** ribbon tab. Next, zoom to the top portion of the drawing.
- Create a line by selecting the two points, as shown. Next, press ESC.

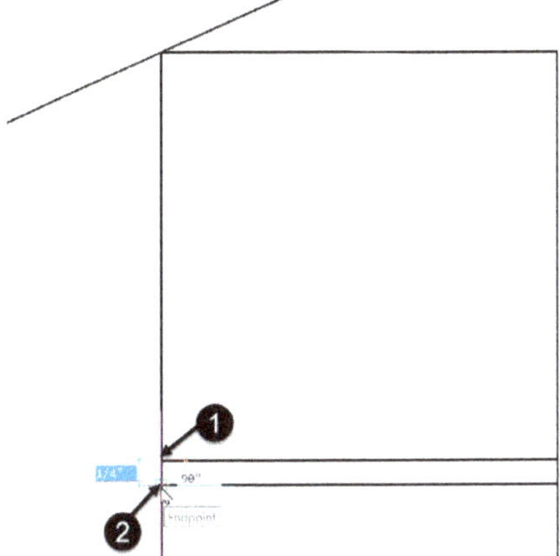

- Select the newly created line.
- Click the **Move** tool on the **Modify** panel of the **Home** ribbon tab.
- Select the top endpoint of the selected line. Next, move the pointer toward the right.
- Type 0.125, and press ENTER.

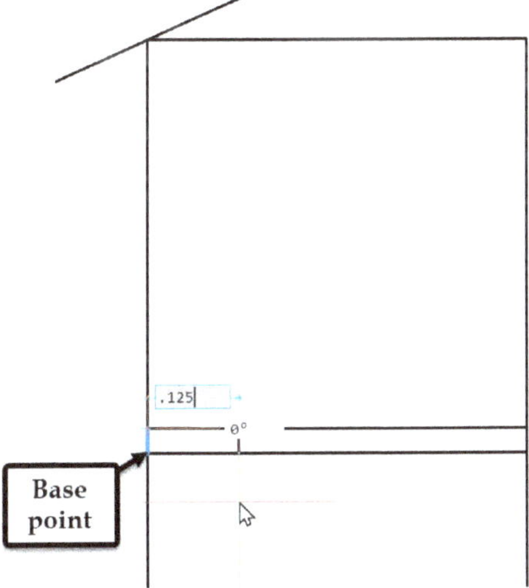

- Select the line moved in the last step.
- Click the **Rectangular Array** icon on the **Modify** panel of the **Home** ribbon tab.
- Select the **Associative** option from the command line.
- Select the **No** option from the command line.
- Select the **Columns** option from the command line.
- Type **2** and press ENTER to specify the number of columns.
- Type **3.75** and press ENTER to specify the distance between the columns.

- Select the **Rows** option from the command line.
- Type **13** and press ENTER to specify the number of rows.
- Type -4.25 and press ENTER to specify the distance between the rows.
- Select the **eXit** option from the command line.

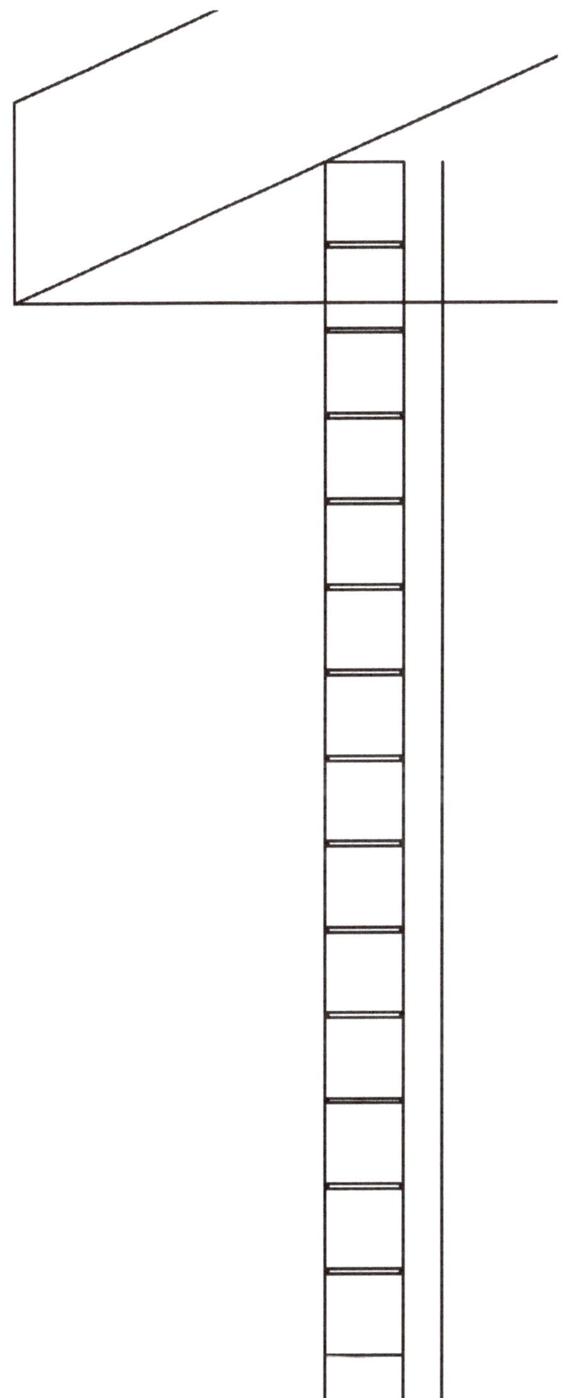

- Select the two vertical lines, as shown. Next, press Delete.

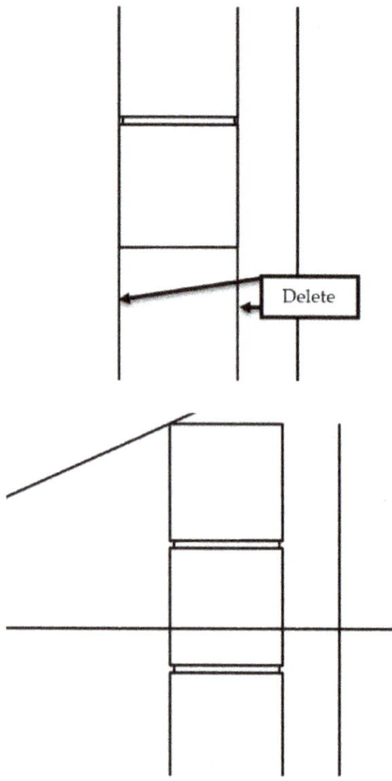

- Click the **Hatch** tool on the **Draw** panel of the **Home** ribbon tab.
- Make sure that the **ANSI31** pattern is selected from the **Name** selection box.
- Type 8 in the **Scale** box.
- Click the **Pick points in boundaries** icon in the **Boundaries** section and click in the regions, as shown.

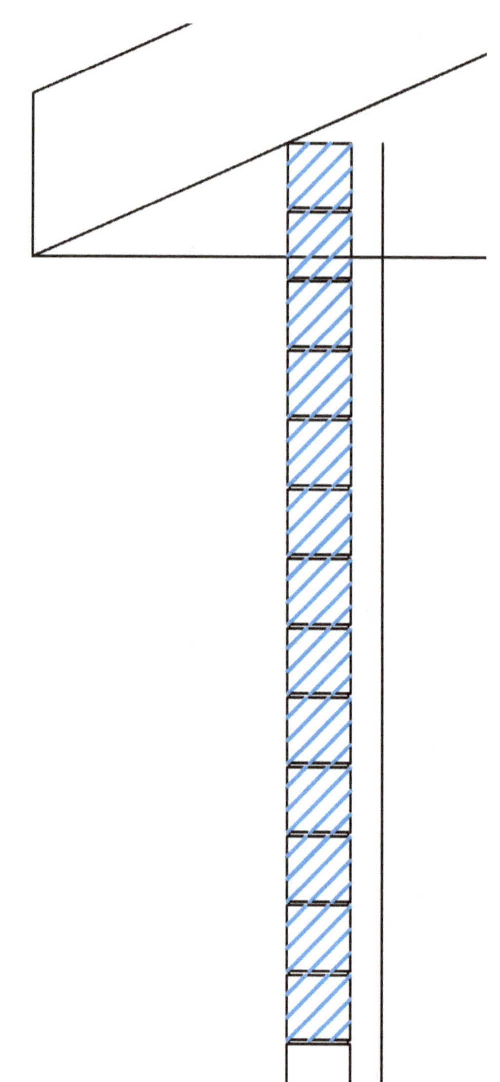

- Press and ENTER and click **OK**.

Creating the Brick Tie

- On the ribbon, click **View** tab > **Views** panel > **Zoom** drop-down > **Zoom Window**.
- Create a zoom window at the location, as shown.

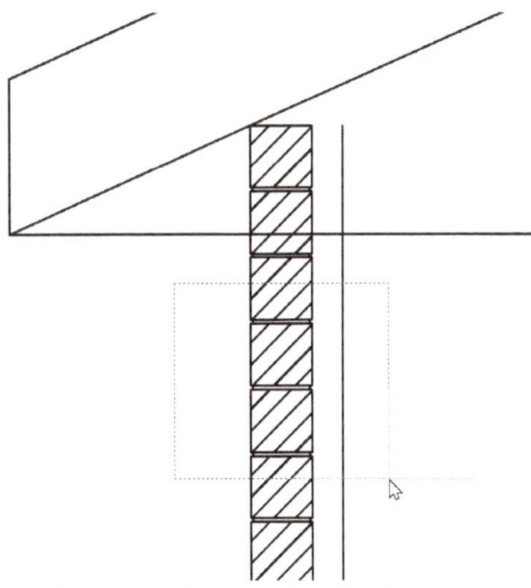

- Click the **Offset** tool on the **Modify** panel of the **Home** ribbon tab.
- Type 0.025, and press ENTER. Next, offset the two horizontal lines in the inward direction.

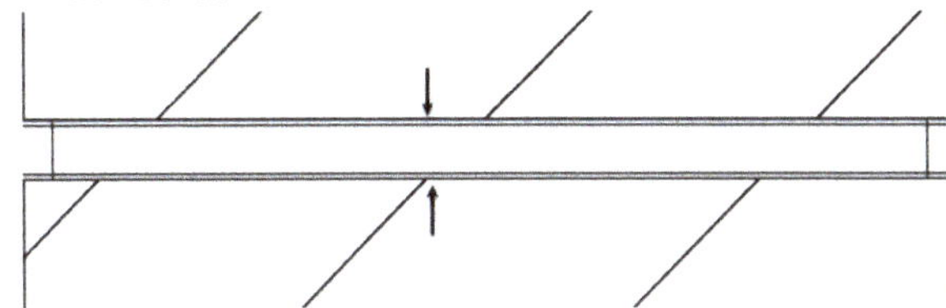

- Press ENTER twice.
- Type 1 and press ENTER. Next, offset the left vertical line towards the right.

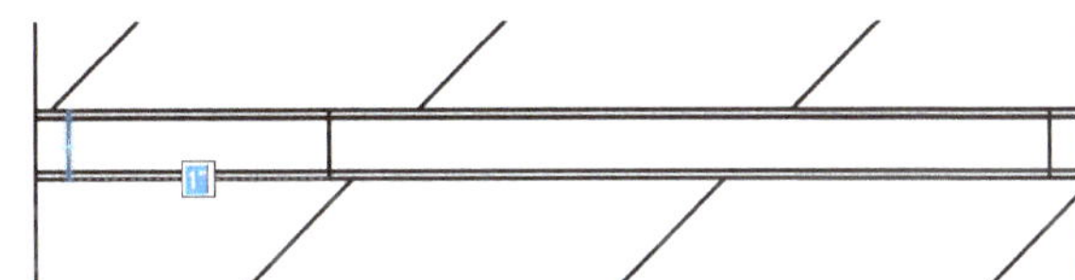

- Click the **Trim** tool on the **Modify** panel of the **Home** ribbon tab. Next, press ENTER.
- Trim the portions of the lines, as shown.

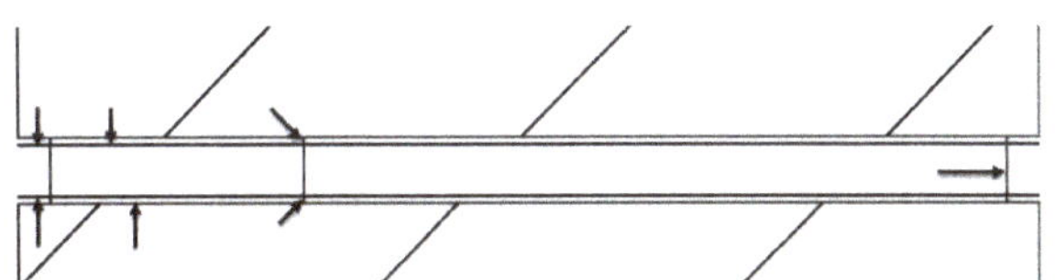

- Click the **Extend** on the **Modify** panel of the **Home** ribbon tab. Next, press ENTER.
- Select the ends of the horizontal lines, as shown. The horizontal lines are extended up to the right vertical line.

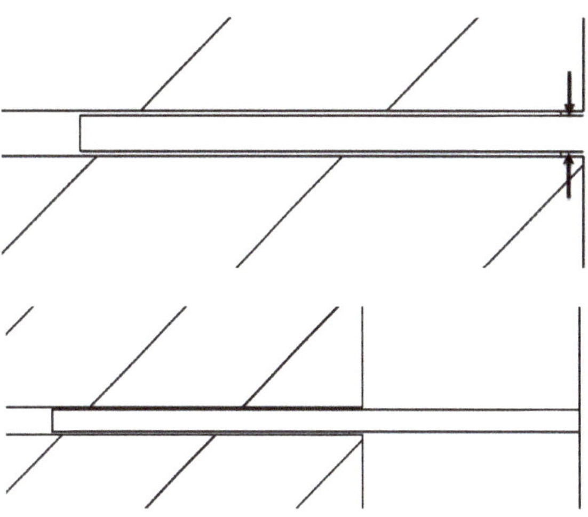

- Click the **Line** tool on the **Draw** panel of the **Home** ribbon tab.
- Select the endpoint of the lower horizontal line. Next, move the pointer vertically upward.
- Type 3 and press ENTER.

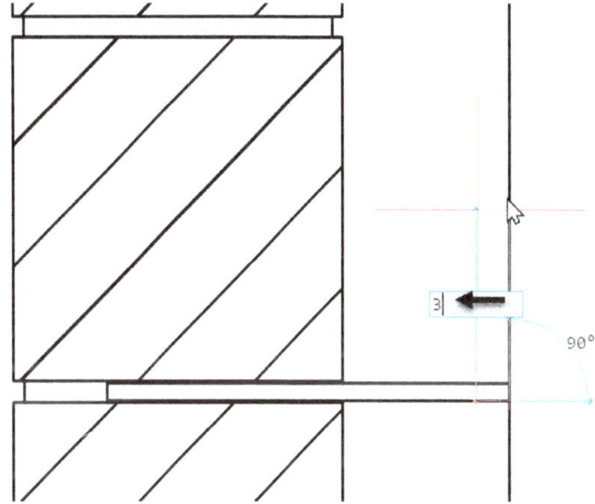

- Click the **Offset** tool on the **Modify** panel of the **Home** ribbon tab.
- Type 0.2 and press ENTER.
- Select the vertical line created in the last step.
- Move the pointer toward the left and click.

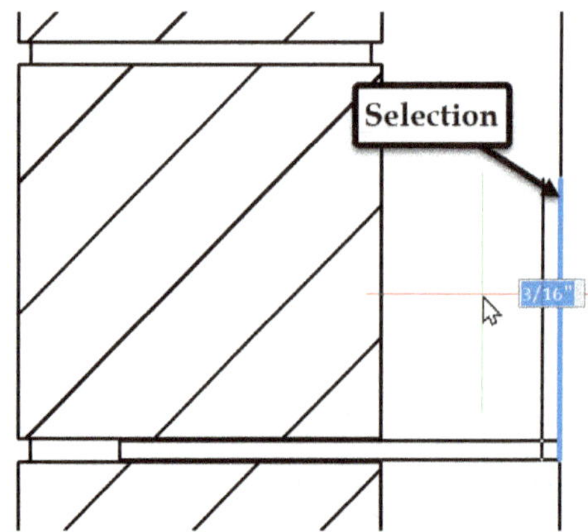

- Click the **Chamfer** on the **Modify** panel of the **Home** ribbon tab.
- Select the **Angle** option from the command line. Next, type 1 as the chamfer length.
- Type 45 as the chamfer angle. Next, select horizontal and vertical lines, as shown.

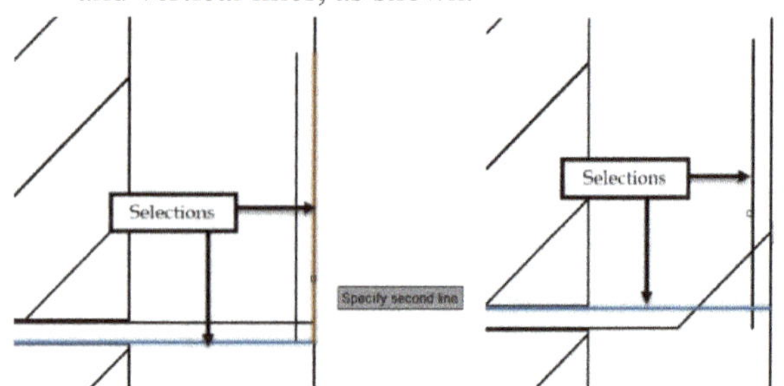

- Likewise, create another chamfer, as shown.
- Click the **Line** tool on the **Draw** panel of the **Home** ribbon tab. Next, cap the ends of the offset lines, as shown.

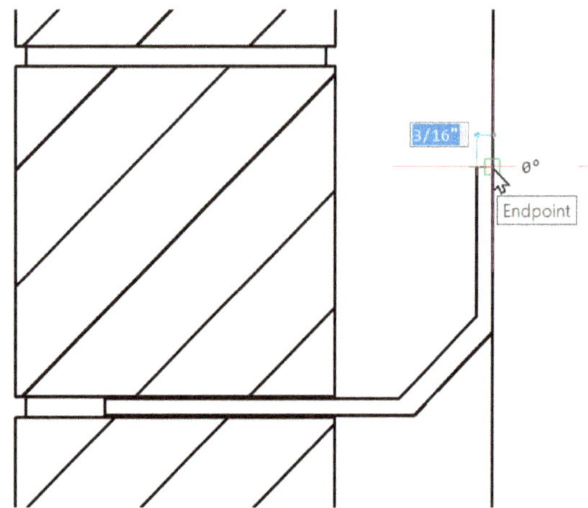

- Click the **Rectangle** on the **Draw** panel of the **Home** ribbon tab. Next, click in the graphic window.
- Type 0.2, and press TAB.
- Type 0.5 and press ENTER.
- Select the rectangle and click the **Move** tool on the **Modify** panel of the **Home** ribbon tab.

- Select the midpoint of the right vertical edge of the rectangle.

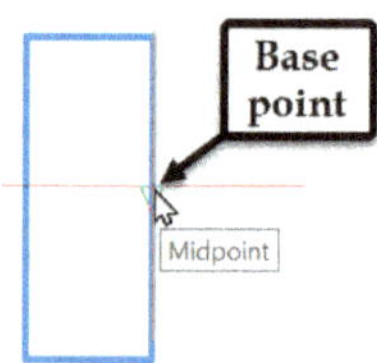

- Move the pointer and select the midpoint of the vertical line, as shown.

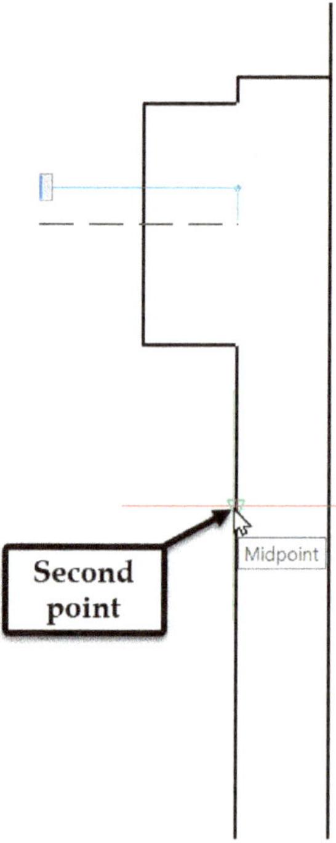

- Click the **Line** tool on the **Draw** panel of the **Home** ribbon tab.
- Select the midpoint of the right vertical edge of the rectangle. Next, move the pointer toward the right.
- Type 3.5 and press ENTER.

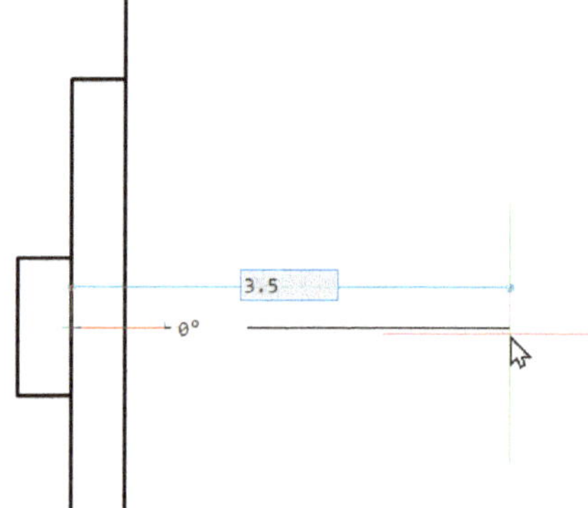

- Click the **Offset** tool on the **Modify** panel of the **Home** ribbon tab.
- Type 0.1 and press ENTER. Next, offset the newly created horizontal line on both sides.

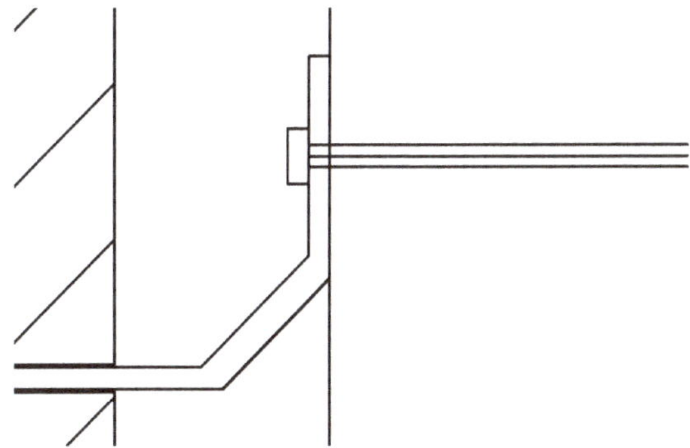

- Select the center line and press Delete.
- Click the **Arc** drop-down > **Arc Start-End-Direction** on the **Draw** panel of the **Home** ribbon tab.

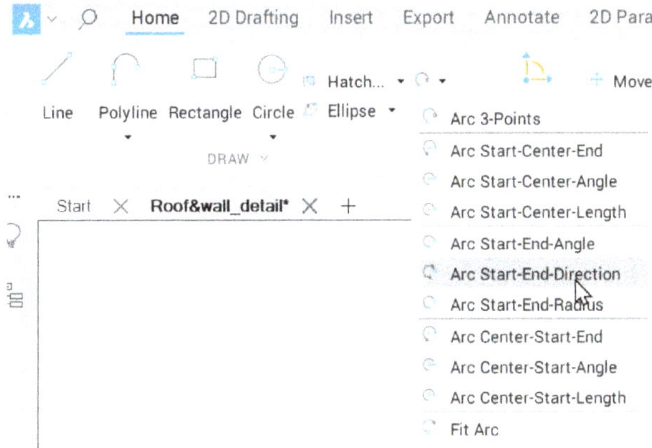

- Select the endpoints of the offset lines.
- Move the pointer toward the right and click.

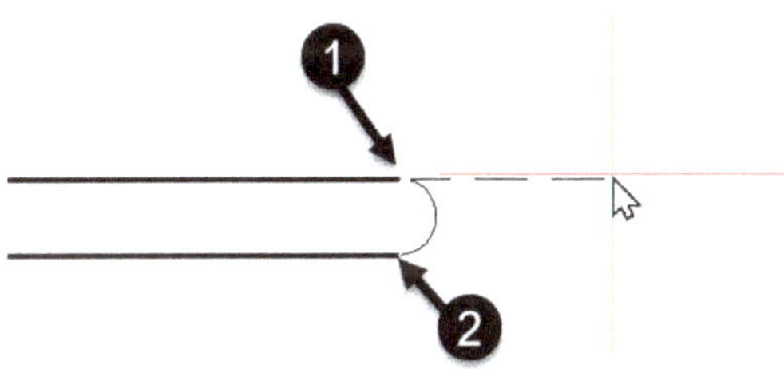

- Click the **Trim** tool on the **Modify** panel of the **Home** ribbon tab. Next, press ENTER.
- Trim the portions of the lines, as shown.

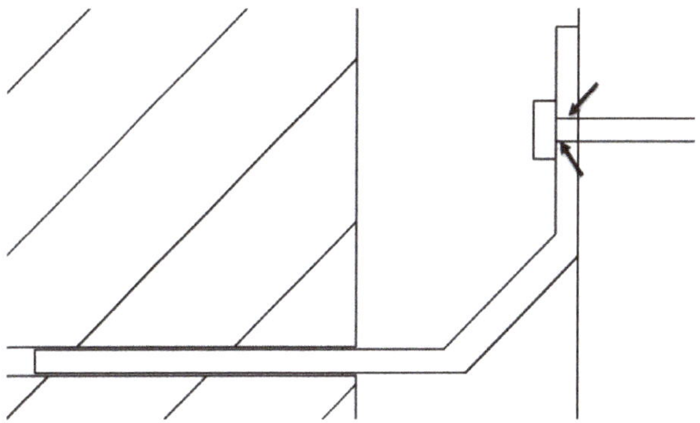

- Click the **Hatch** tool on the **Draw** panel of the **Home** ribbon tab.
- On the **Hatch and Gradient** dialog, click the **Browse** icon next to the **Name** box.
- Select the **SOLID** hatch from the **Hatch Pattern Palette** and click **OK**.

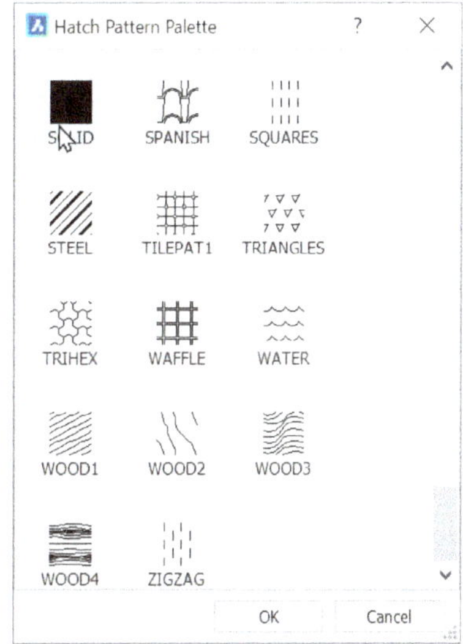

- Click the **Pick points in boundaries** icon and click in the regions, as shown. Press ENTER and click **OK**.

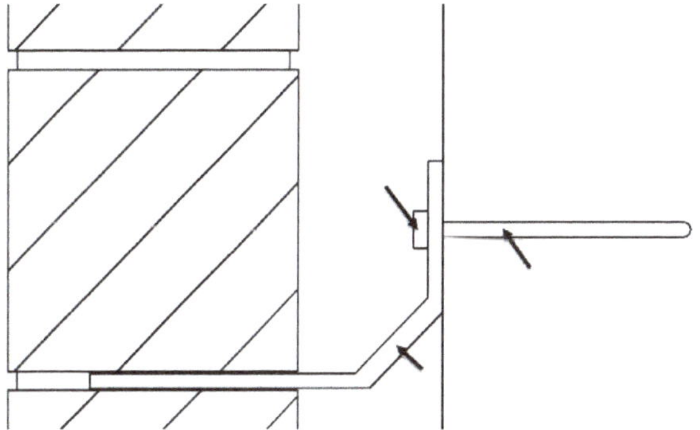

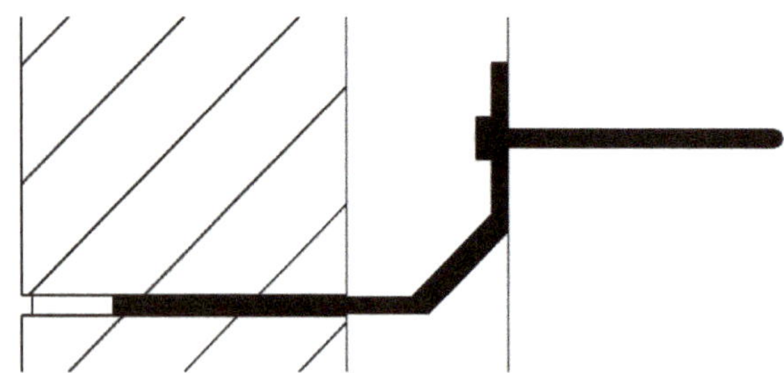

Creating the Insulation

- Click the **Offset** tool on the **Modify** panel of the **Home** ribbon tab. Next, type 1, and press ENTER.
- Select the vertical line, as shown. Next, move the pointer toward the right and click.

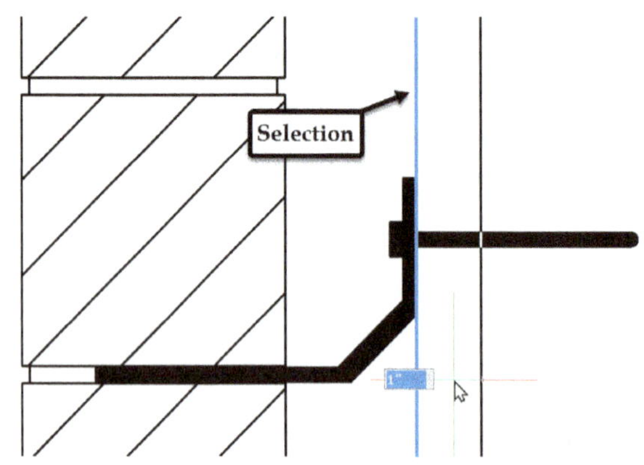

- Press ENTER twice. Next, type 9, and press ENTER.
- Select the offset line. Next, move the pointer toward the right and click.

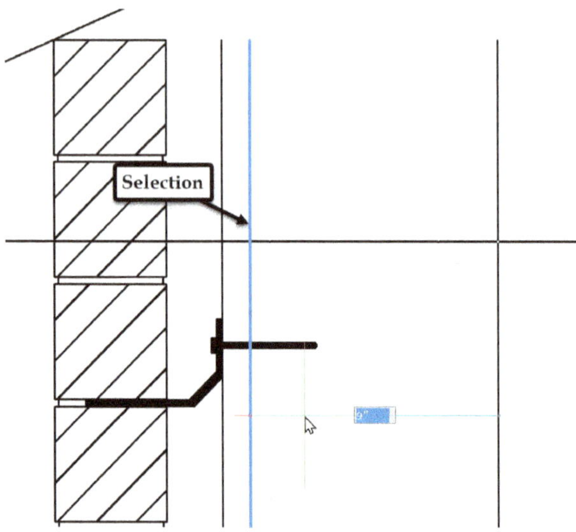

- Press ENTER twice. Next, type 0.75, and press ENTER.
- Select the offset line. Next, move the pointer toward the right and click.

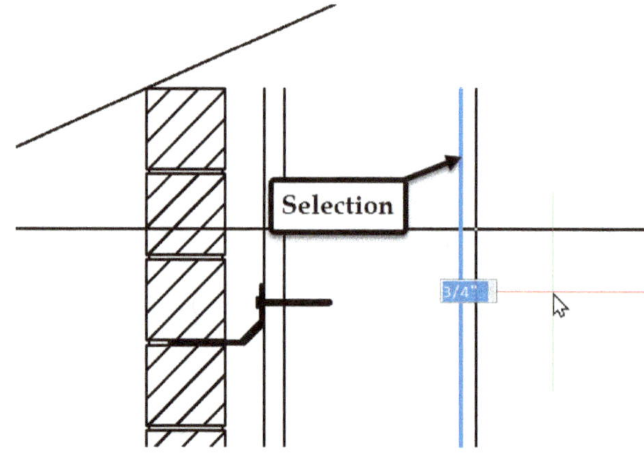

- Click the **Extend** on the **Modify** panel of the **Home** ribbon tab. Next, press ENTER.
- Click and drag a selection window across the ends of the vertical lines, as shown.

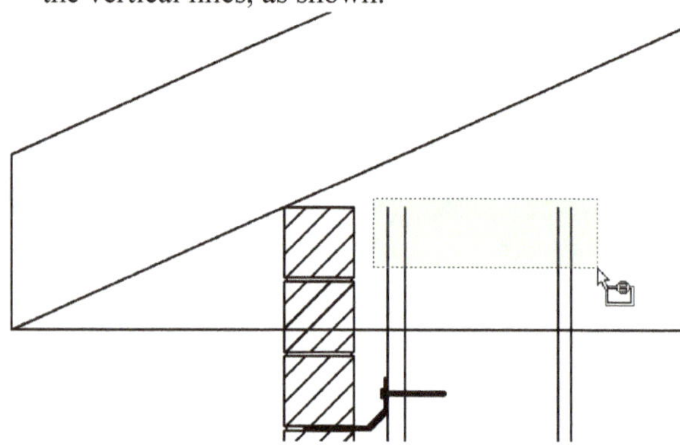

- Create the two horizontal lines, as shown.

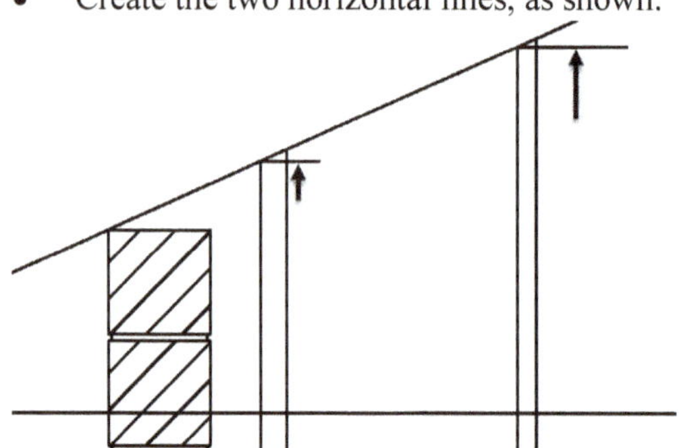

- Trim the extending portions.

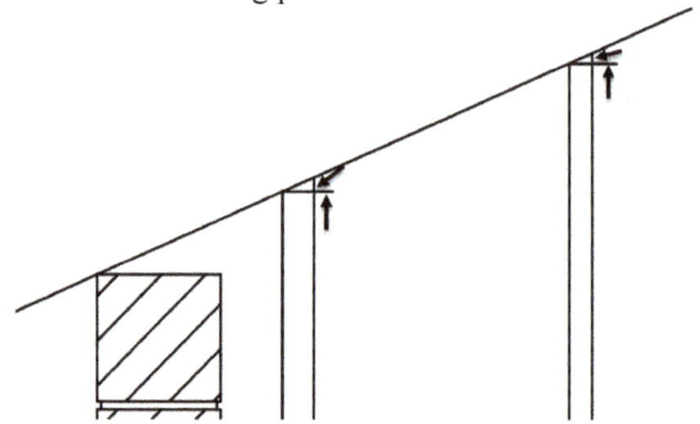

- Click the **Rectangle** on the **Draw** panel of the **Home** ribbon tab.

- Select the corner point, as shown.

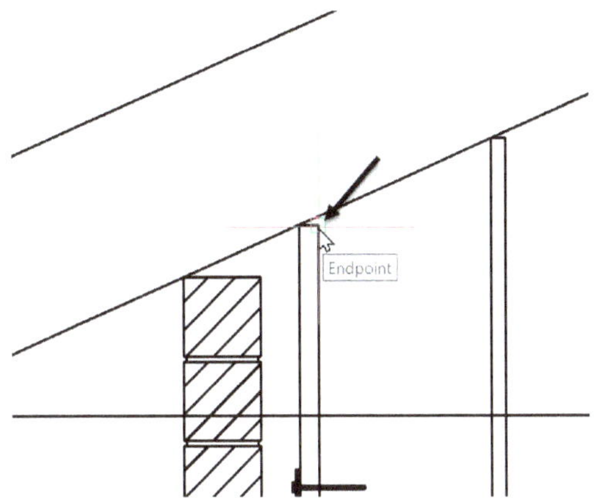

- Type 9, and press TAB.
- Type -2.25 and press ENTER.

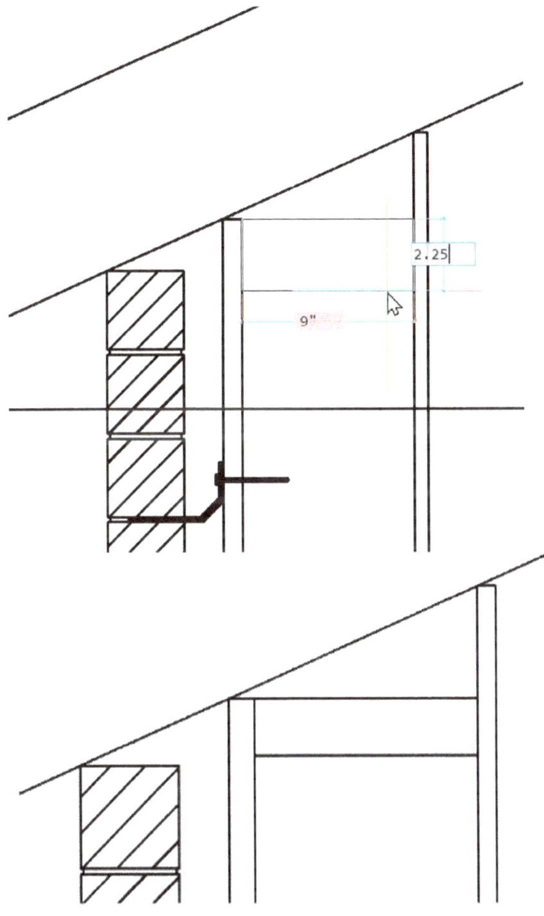

- Click the **Line** tool on the **Draw** panel of the **Home** ribbon tab.
- Create the diagonal lines by selecting the corner points of the rectangle.

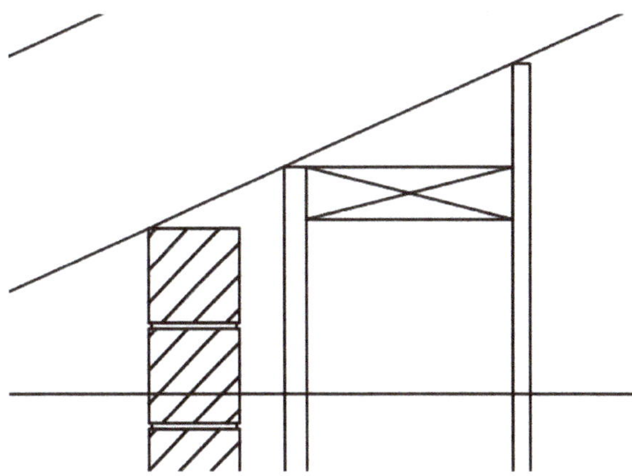

- Click **Circle** drop-down > **Circle Center-Diameter** on the **Draw** panel on the **Home** ribbon tab.
- Select the midpoint of the left vertical edge of the rectangle.

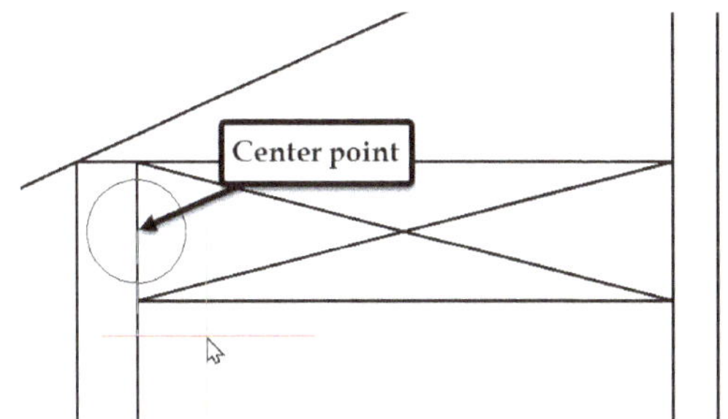

- Next, type 1, and press ENTER.

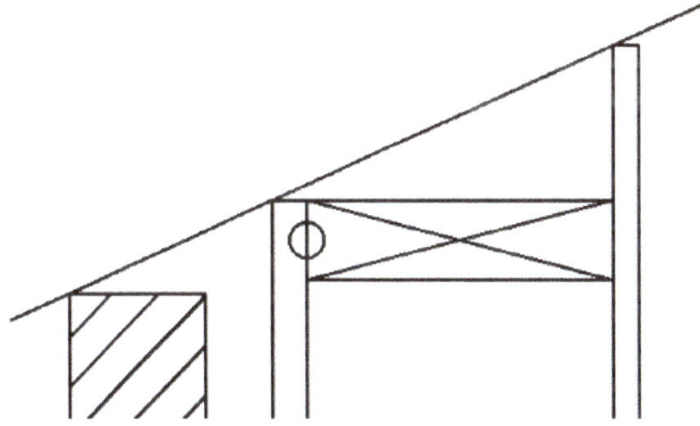

- Click the **Hatch** tool on the **Draw** panel of the **Home** ribbon tab.
- On the **Hatch and Gradient** dialog, click the **Browse** icon next to the **Name** box.

- Select the **SOLID** hatch from the **Hatch Pattern Palette** and click **OK**.

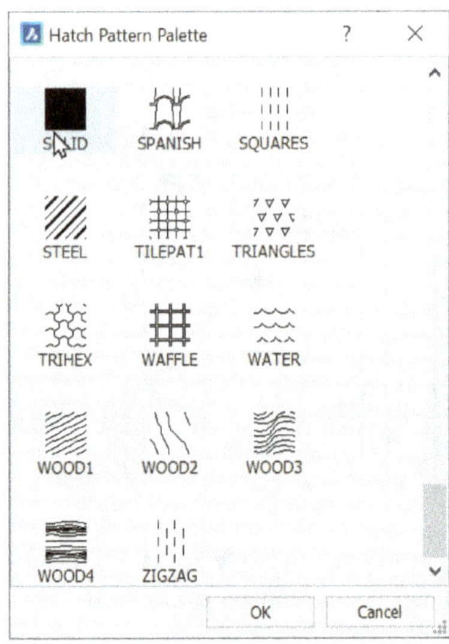

- Click the **Select boundary entities** icon and select the circle, as shown. Press ENTER and click **OK**.

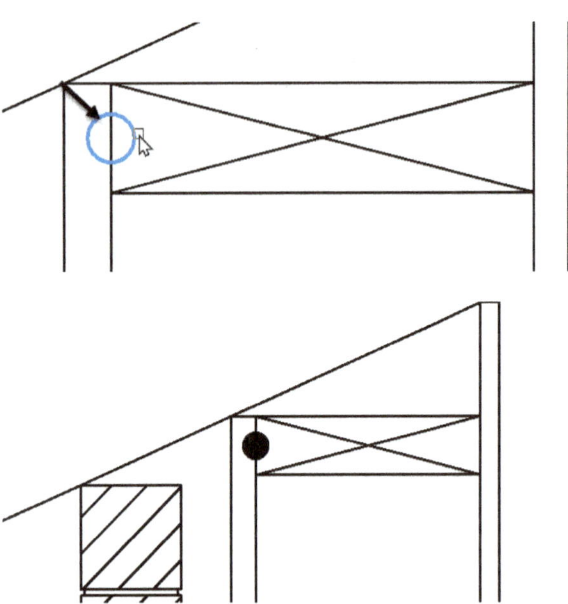

- Click the **Line** tool on the **Draw** panel of the **Home** ribbon tab. Next, create a horizontal line, as shown.

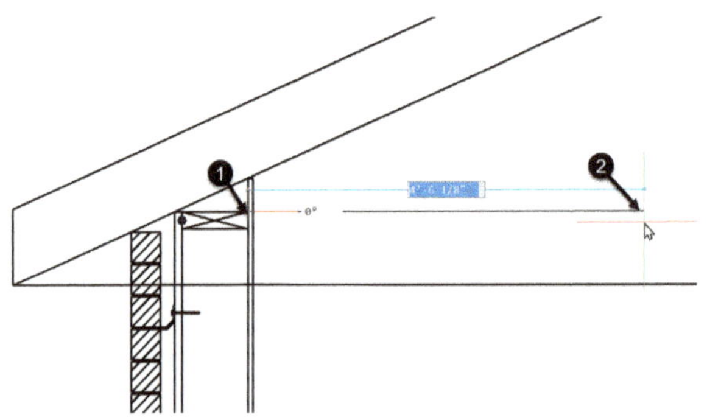

- Click the **Offset** tool on the **Modify** panel of the **Home** ribbon tab. Next, type 1.5, and press ENTER.
- Select the newly created line. Next, move the pointer downward and click.

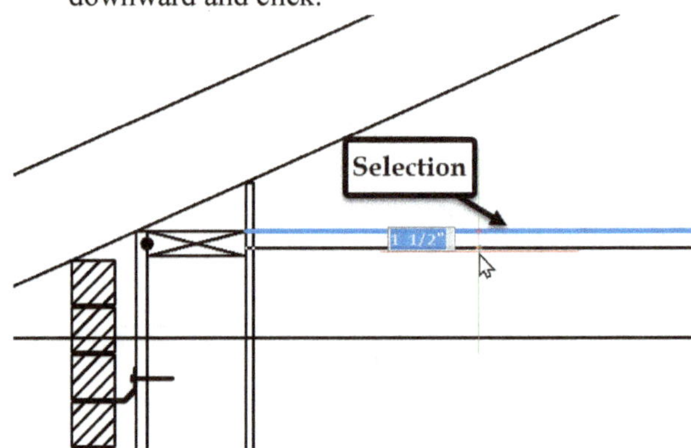

- Press ENTER twice. Next, type 0.75, and press ENTER.
- Select the offset line. Next, move the pointer downward and click.

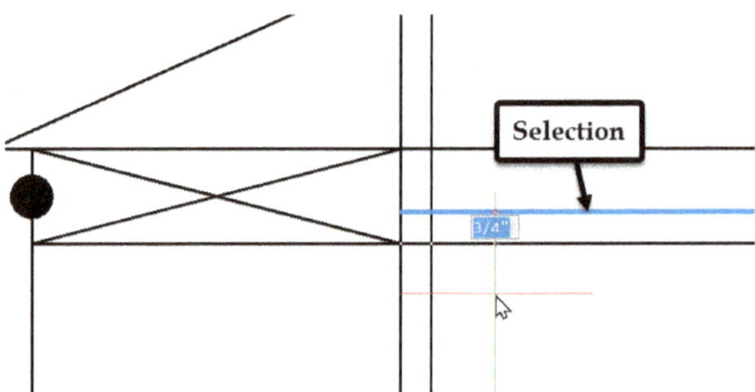

- Click the **Trim** tool on the **Modify** panel of the **Home** ribbon tab.
- Trim the elements, as shown.

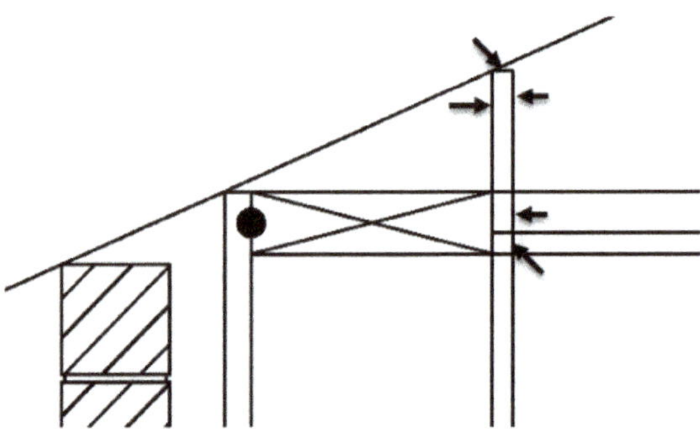

- Click the **Hatch** tool on the **Draw** panel of the **Home** ribbon tab.
- On the **Hatch and Gradient** dialog, click the **Browse** icon next to the **Name** box.

- Select the **ANSI37** hatch from the **Hatch Pattern Palette** and click **OK**.

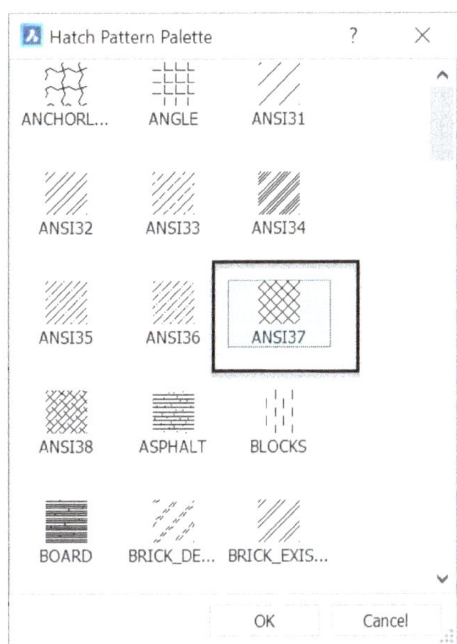

- Type **2** in the **Scale** box. Next, type **45** in the **Angle** box.
- Click **Pick points in boundaries** icon and click in the regions, as shown.

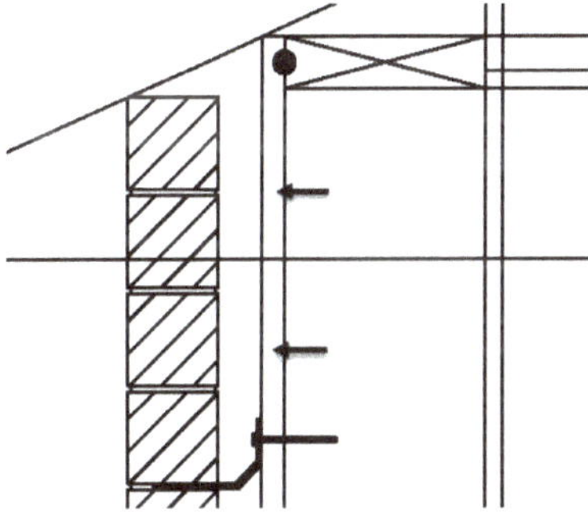

- Press ENTER.
- Click the **Select boundary entities** icon and select the three lines, as shown.

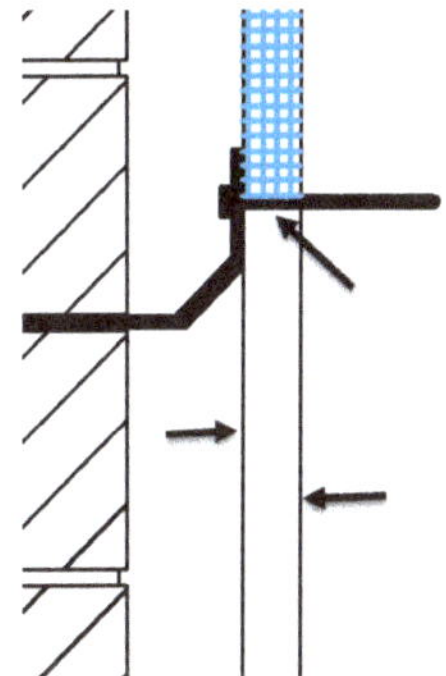

- Pan to the bottom portion and select the horizontal line, as shown.

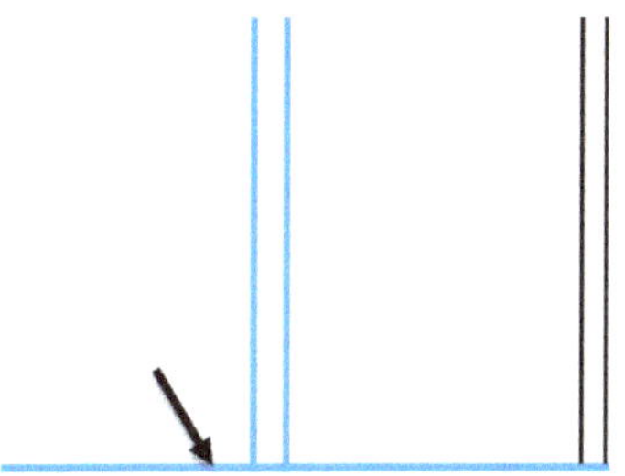

- Press ENTER and click **OK**.

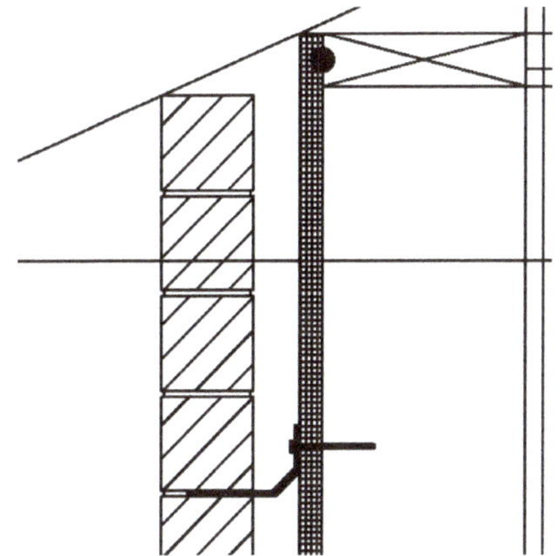

- Click the **Line** tool on the **Draw** panel of the **Home** ribbon tab.
- Select the midpoint of the horizontal line, as shown.
- Move the pointer downward and click. Next, press ESC.

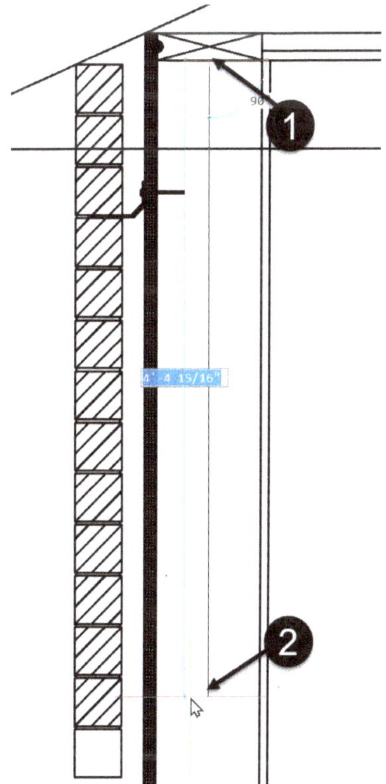

- Click the **Layers** icon on the **Layers** panel of the **Home** ribbon tab.
- Click the **Add Layer** icon on the **Layers Manager**. Next, type **Insulation** as the layer name.
- Click in the **Linetype** column on the Layers palette, and then select **Load**.
- Click the **Load** button on the **Line Style** dialog.
- Select the **BATTING** linetype from the **Load Linetypes** dialog. Next, click **OK**.
- Select the newly created line.

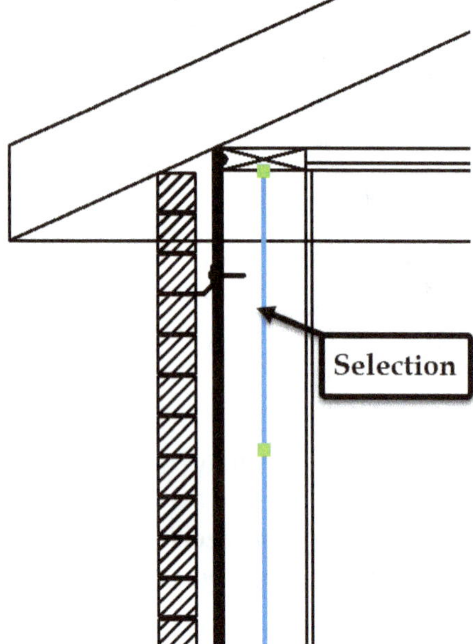

- Select **Insulation** from the **Layer Control** drop-down on the **Access** toolbar.
- Select the newly created line.
- Click the **Properties** tab on the right side of the graphics window.
- Type 10 in the **Linetype scale** box and press ENTER. Next, press ESC.

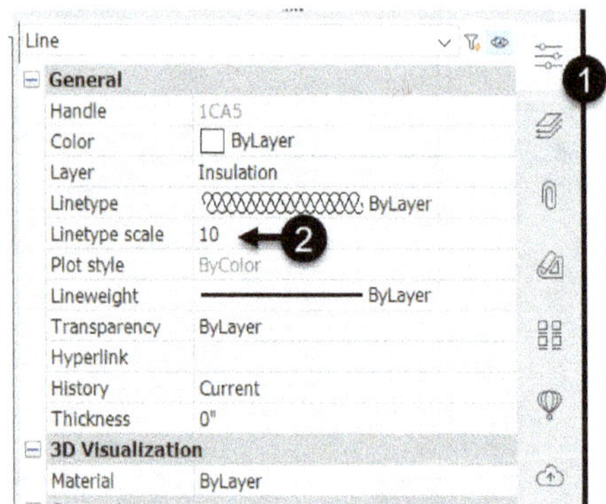

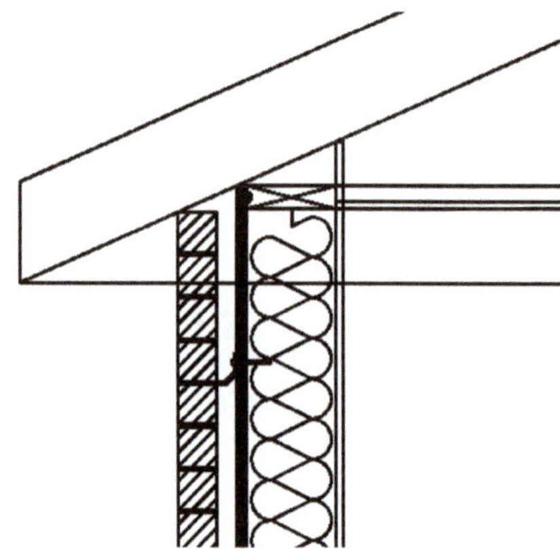

- Click the **Offset** tool on the **Modify** panel of the **Home** ribbon tab. Next, type 3, and press ENTER.
- Select the horizontal line, as shown. Next, move the pointer upward and click.

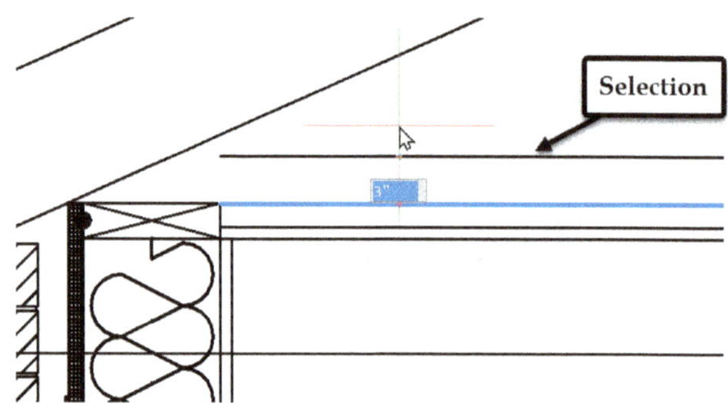

- Press ESC.
- Select the newly created line. Next, select **Insulation** from the **Layer Control** drop-down on the **Access** toolbar.
- Click the **Properties** tab on the graphics window. Next, type 6 in the **Linetype scale** box and press ENTER.
- Press ESC.

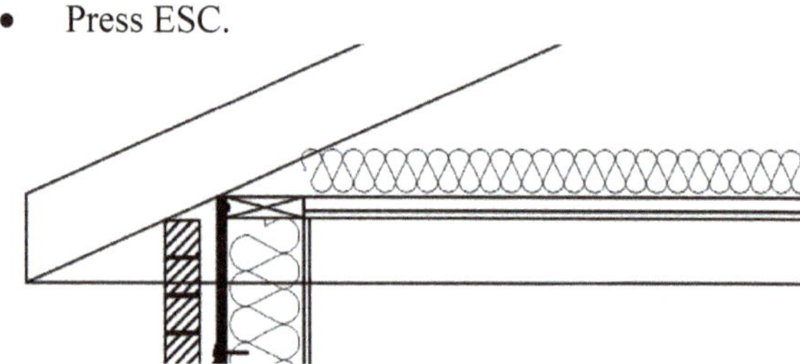

Creating the Roof Detail

- Offset the inclined line by 1". Next, close the end of the offset lines.

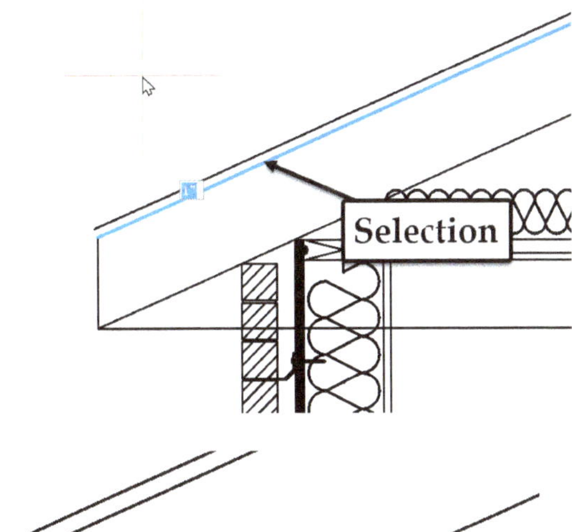

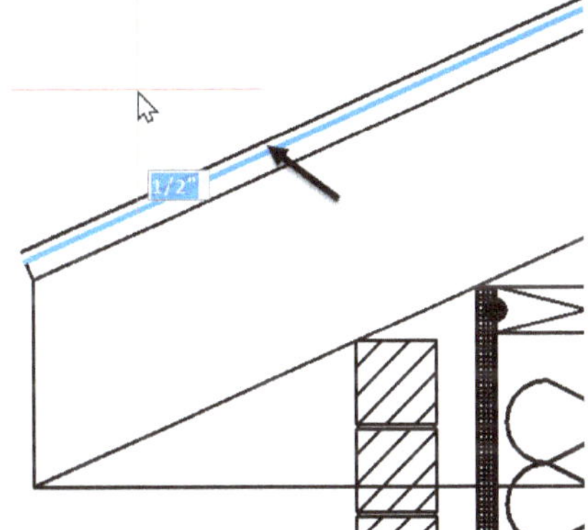

- Offset the new line by 0.5".

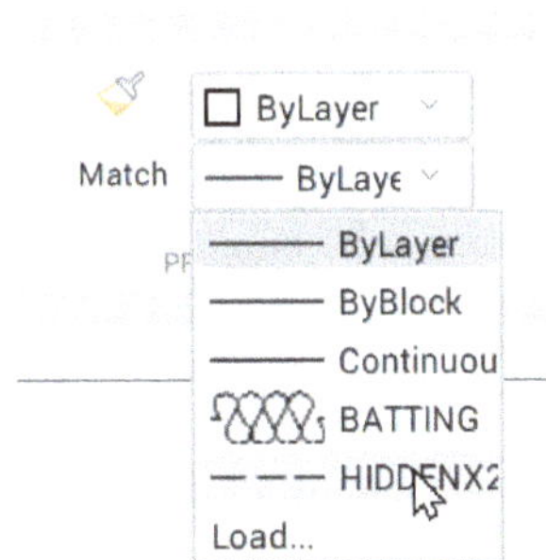

- Select the newly created offset line.
- Select HIDDENX2 from the **Line Type Combo** drop-down on the **Properties** panel.

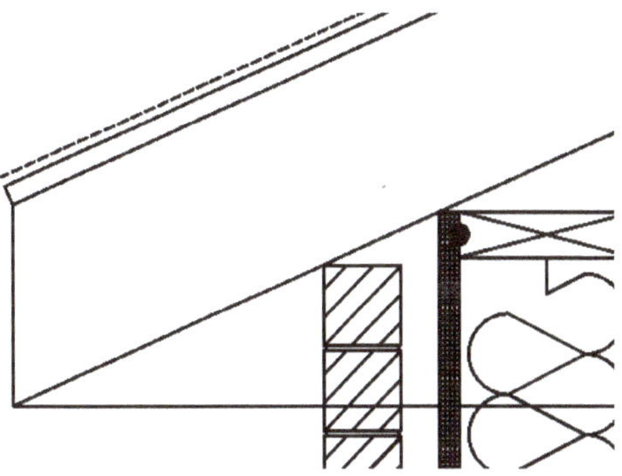

- Create another line with the offset distance of 0.75".

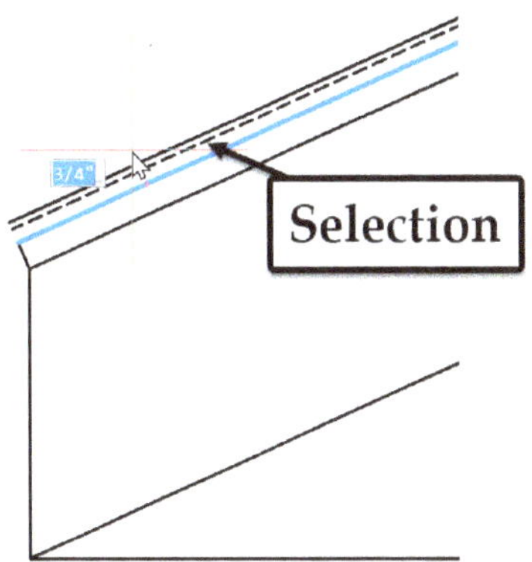

- On the **Modify** panel and click the **Lengthen** tool.

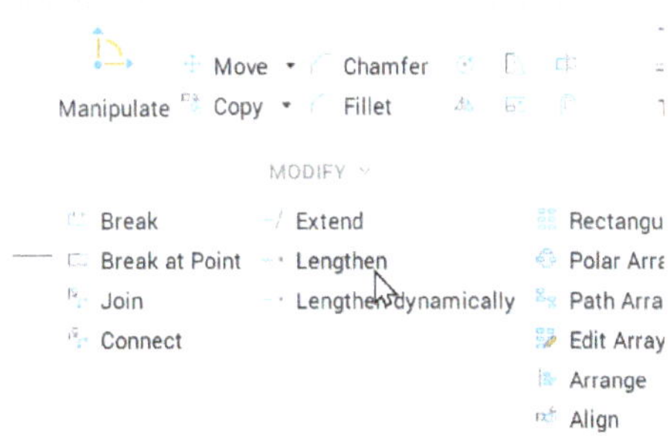

- Select the **Increment** option from the command line.
- Type 2.5, and press ENTER.
- Select the newly offset line.

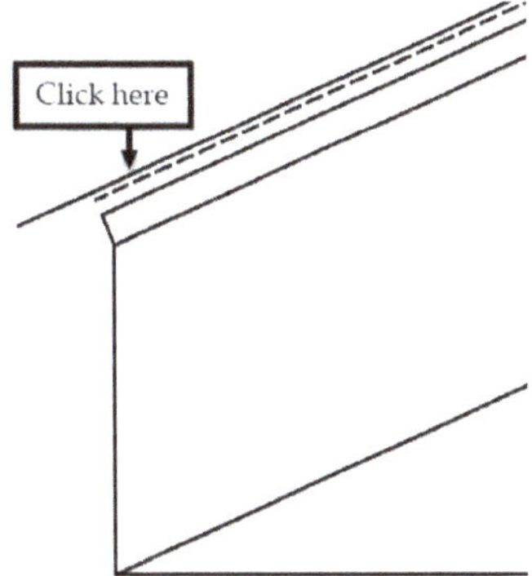

- Deactivate the **Ortho** button on the status bar.
- On the ribbon, click **View** tab > **Coordinates** panel > **UCS** icon.

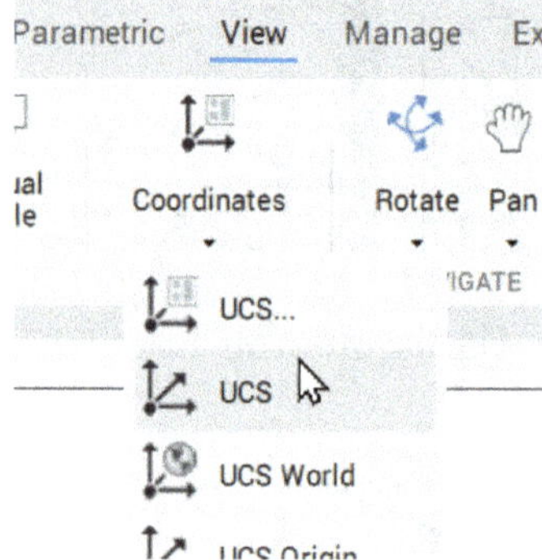

- Select the endpoint of the inclined line, as shown. Next, select a point of the inclined, and then press ENTER.

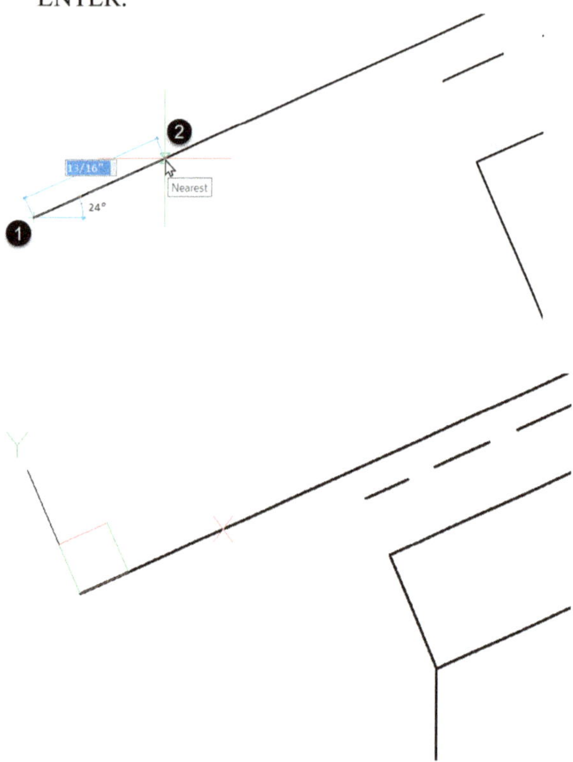

- Activate the **Ortho** button on the status bar.
- Click the **Line** tool on the **Draw** panel of the **Home** ribbon tab.
- Select the endpoint of the inclined line, as shown. Next, move the pointer downward.
- Type 0.25 and press ENTER. Next, move the pointer toward the right.

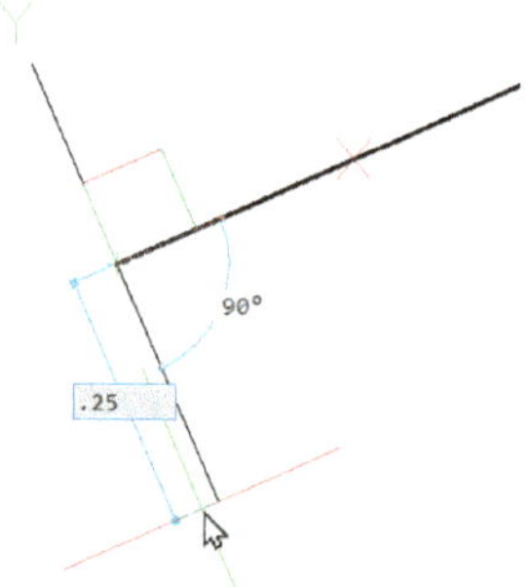

- Type 0.375, and press ENTER.

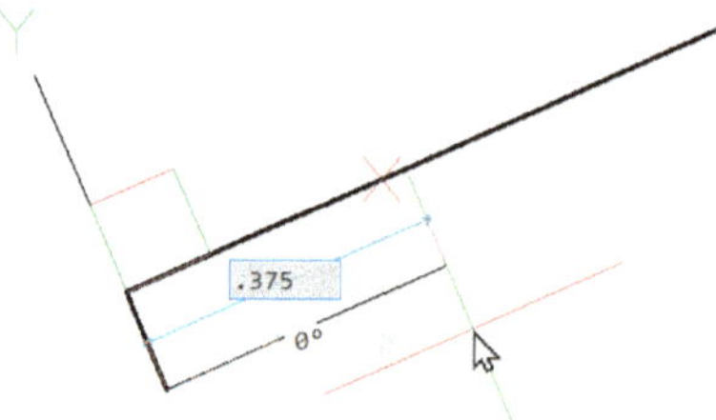

- On the ribbon, click **View** tab > **Coordinates** panel > **UCS, World** icon; the coordinate system is restored to its default location.

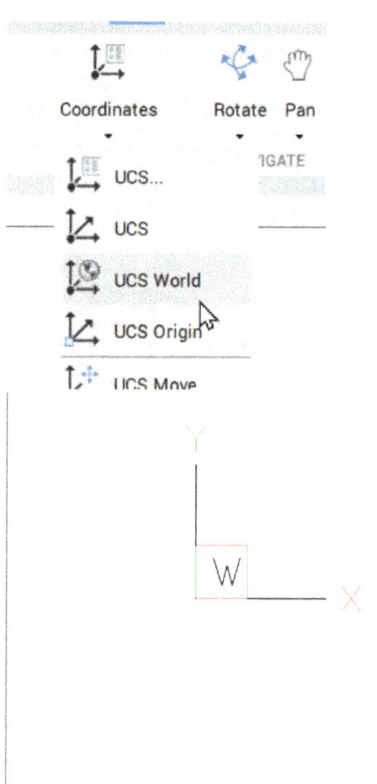

- Click the **Line** tool on the **Draw** panel of the **Home** ribbon tab. Next, select the endpoint of the last line.
- Move the pointer downward. Next, type 1.5, and press ENTER.

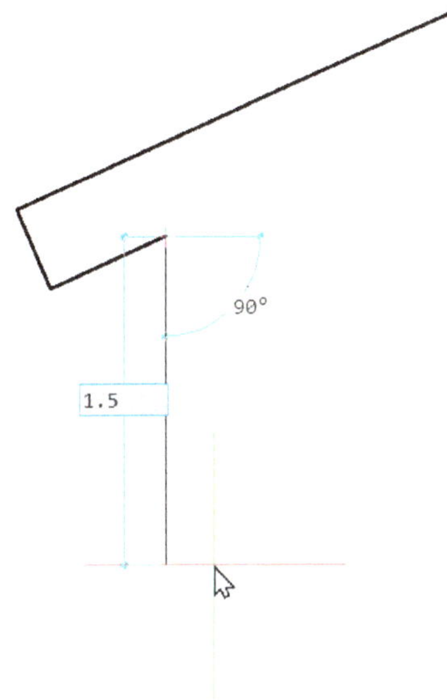

- Type @.375<225 in the command line and press ENTER.
- Press Esc.

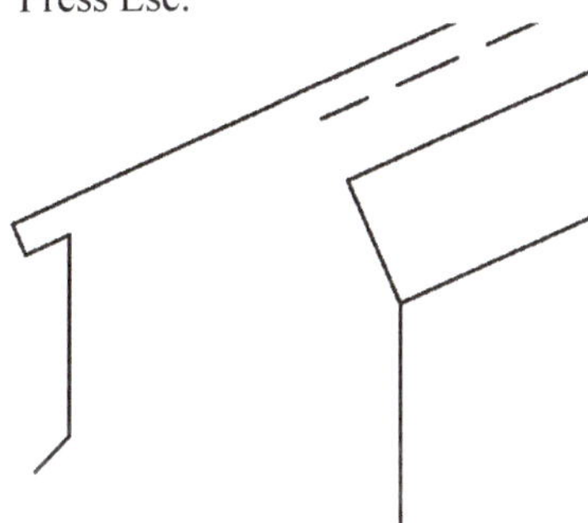

- On the **Draw** panel, click **Arc** drop-down > **Arc Start-Center-End**. Next, select the endpoint of the line, as shown.
- Select the centerpoint of the line. Next, select the other endpoint of the line, as shown

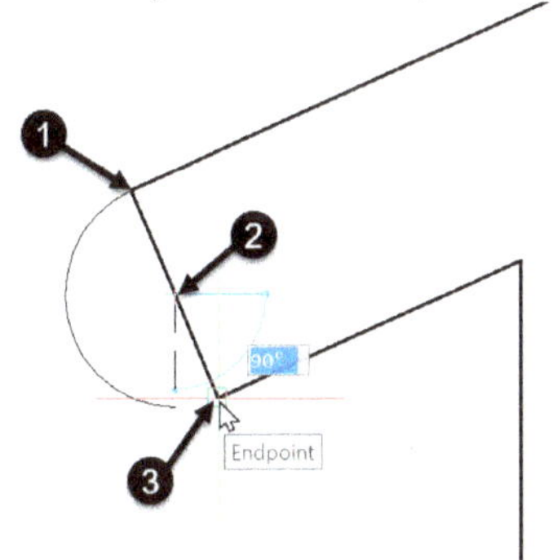

- Delete the line between the endpoints of the arc.

- On the ribbon, click **Home** tab > **Modify** panel > **Weld** drop-down > **Break at point**.

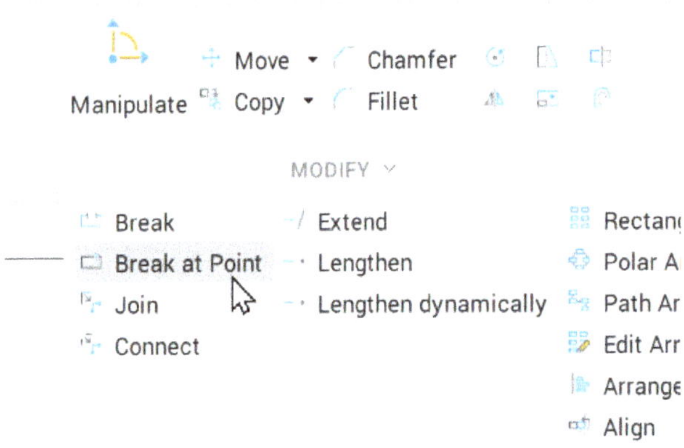

- Next, select the inclined line.

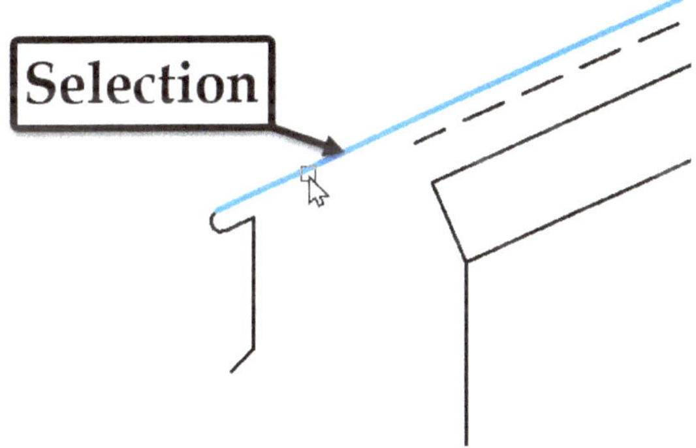

- Press and hold the SHIFT key, and then right click. Next, select the **From** option from the shortcut menu.

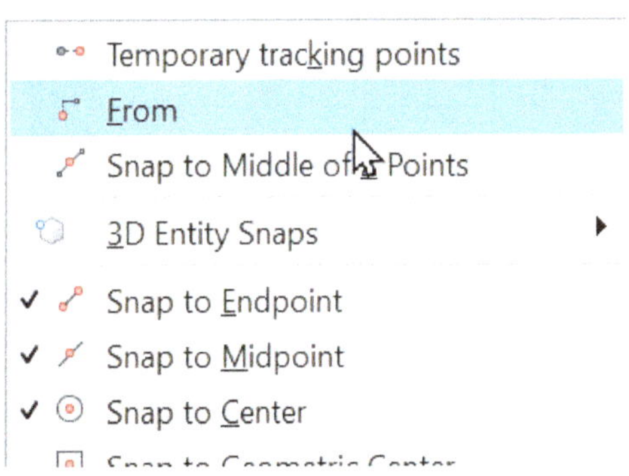

- Select the endpoint of the selected line.

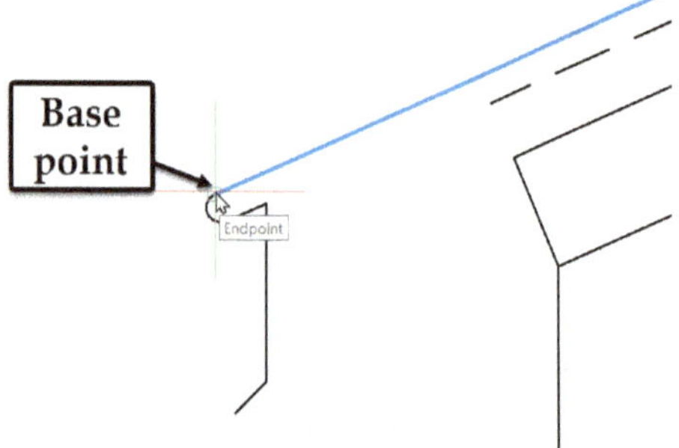

- Move the pointer on the selected line.

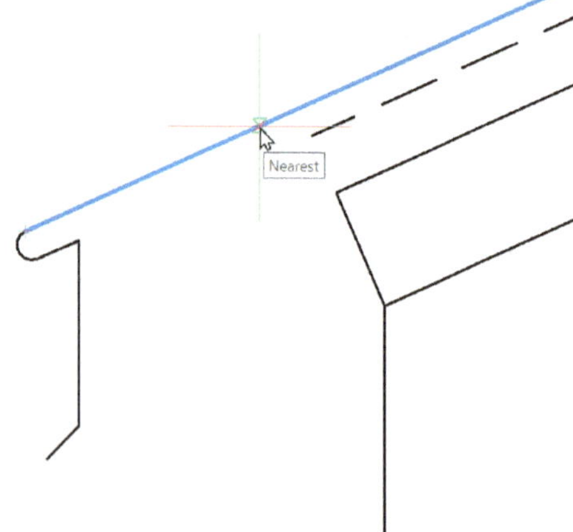

- Type 9 and press ENTER; the line is broken at the specified distance.
- Delete the right-side portion of the line.

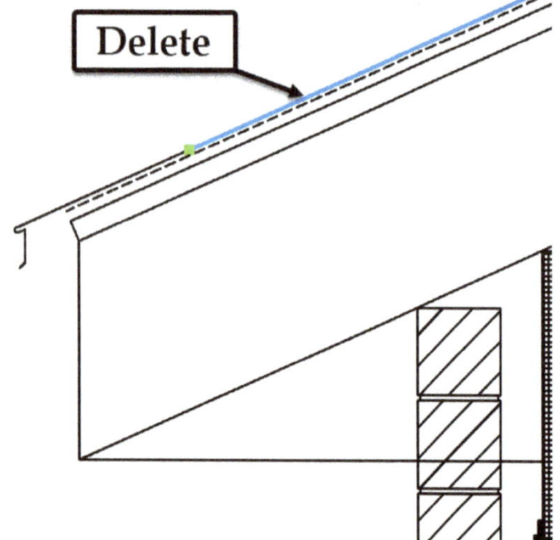

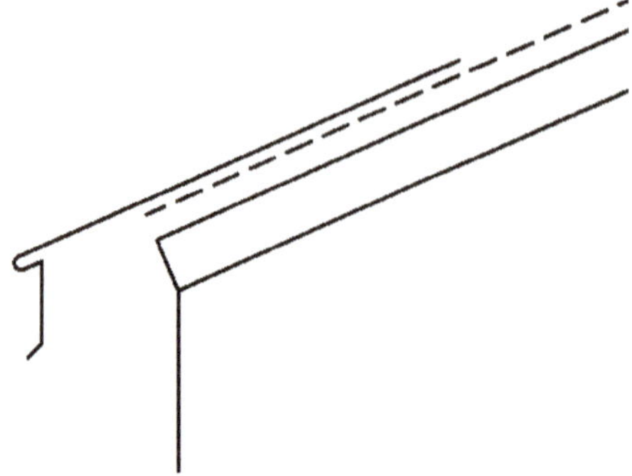

- Click the **Rectangle** on the **Draw** panel of the **Home** ribbon tab.
- Select the corner point, as shown.
- Type 1 and press TAB.
- Next, type 10 and press ENTER.

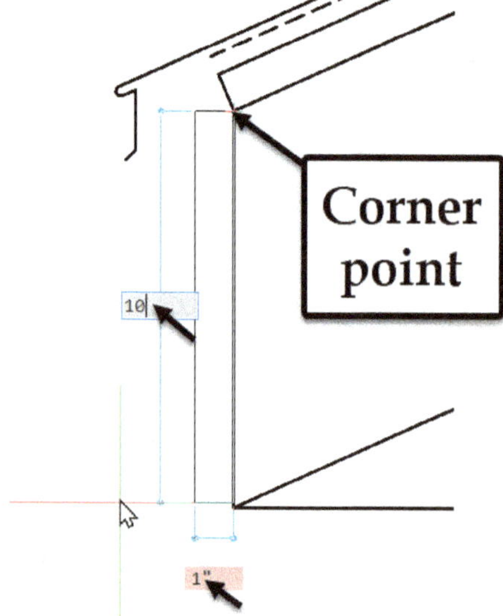

- Click the **Rectangle** on the **Draw** panel of the **Home** ribbon tab.
- Select the top-left corner of the rectangle, as shown.
- Move the pointer downward.
- Type 1 and press TAB.
- Type 2.5 and press ENTER.

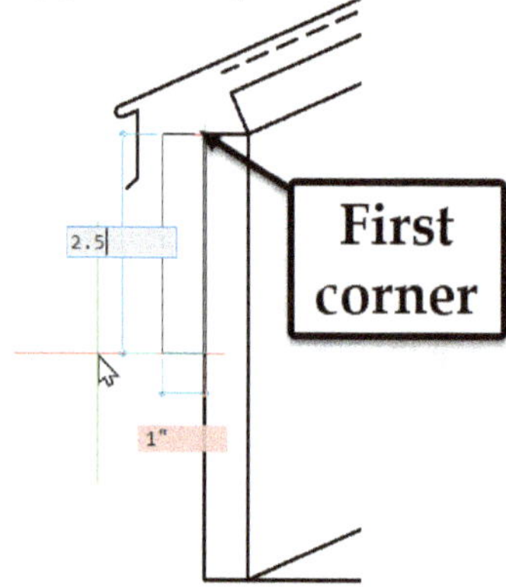

- Move the newly created rectangle downward by 0.5".

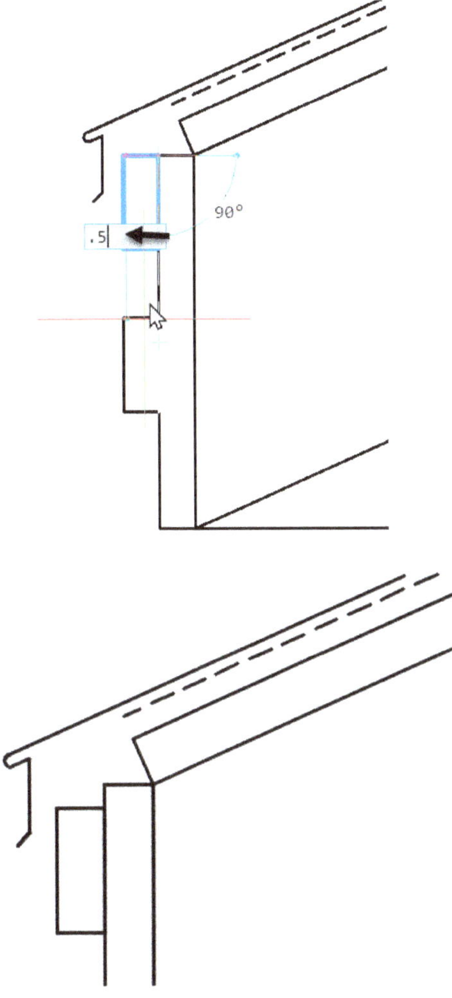

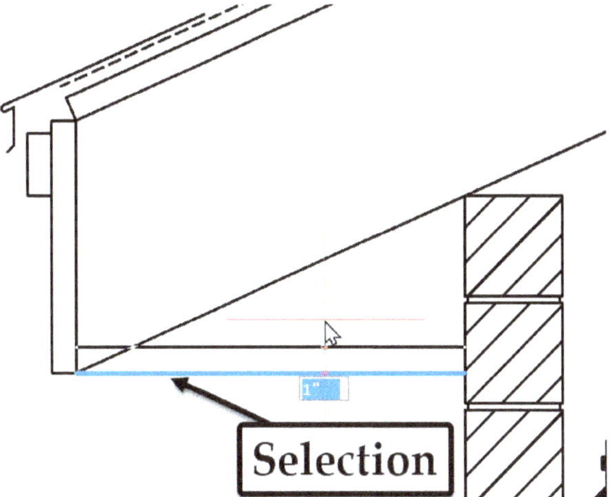

- Select the offset line. Next, move the pointer upward and click.

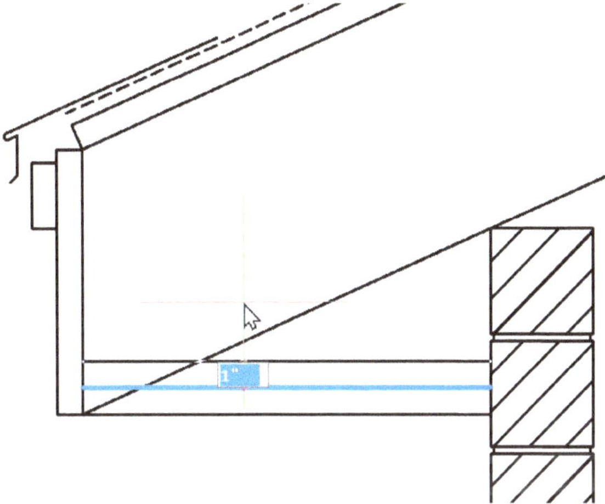

- Click the **Trim** on the **Modify** panel of the **Home** ribbon tab.
- Select the vertical edge of the brick, as shown. Next, press ENTER.
- Click on the horizontal line on the right side.

- Click the **Trim** tool on the **Modify** panel of the **Home** ribbon tab. Next, press ENTER.
- Select the portions of the lines, as shown.

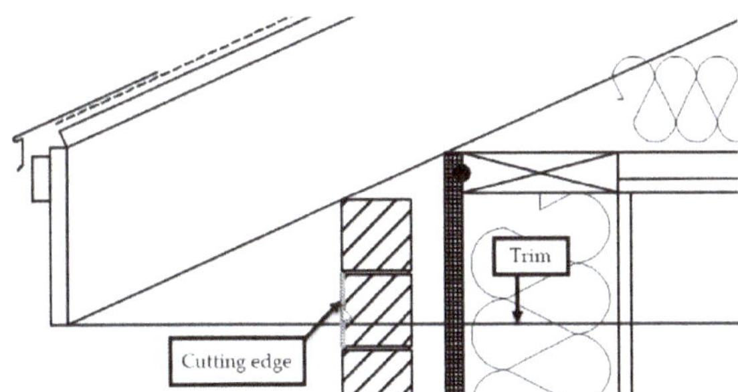

- Click the **Offset** tool on the **Modify** panel of the **Home** ribbon tab. Next, type 1, and press ENTER.
- Select the horizontal line trimmed in the last step.
- Move the pointer upward and click.

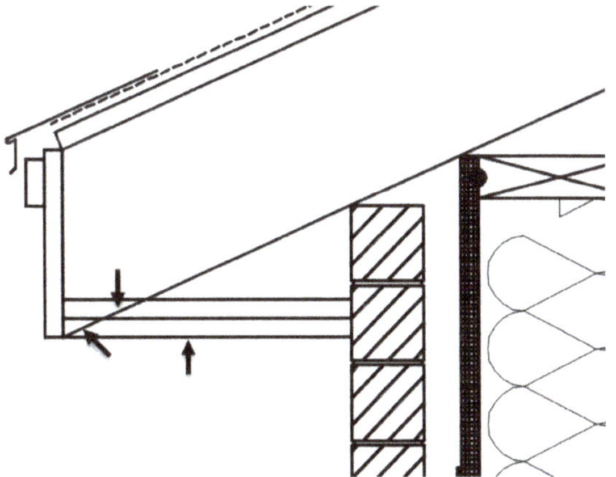

- Click the **Offset** tool on the **Modify** panel of the **Home** ribbon tab. Next, type 7, and press ENTER.
- Select the left vertical line of the veneer brick.
- Move the pointer toward the left and click.

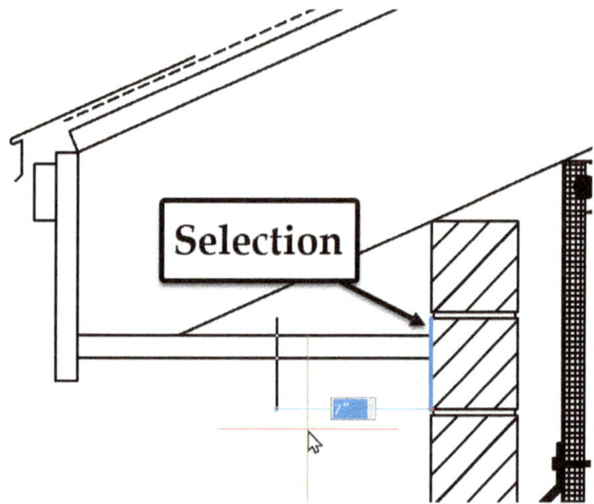

- Press ENTER twice.
- Type 4 and press ENTER. Next, select the offset line.
- Move the pointer toward the left and click.

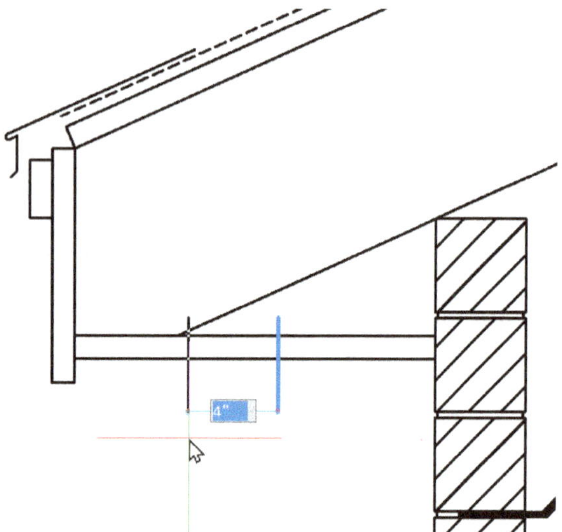

- Click the **Trim** tool on the **Modify** panel of the **Home** ribbon tab.
- Press ENTER.
- Select the portions of the lines, as shown.

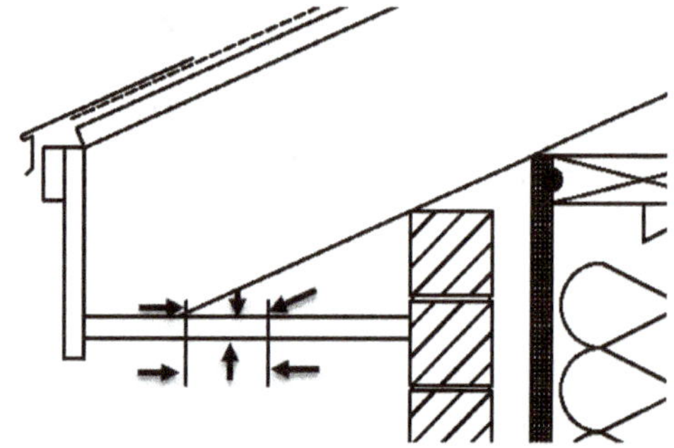

- Create a line by selecting the corner points of the opening, as shown.

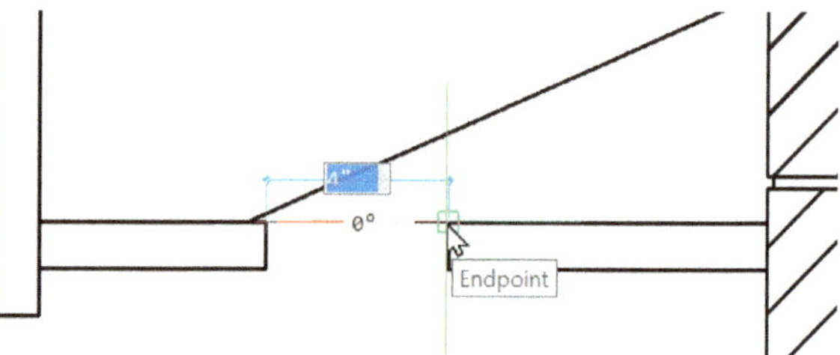

- Press ESC.
- Activate the **Ortho** icon on the status bar.
- Select the newly created line and click **Scale** on the **Modify** panel of the **Home** ribbon tab.

- Select the midpoint.

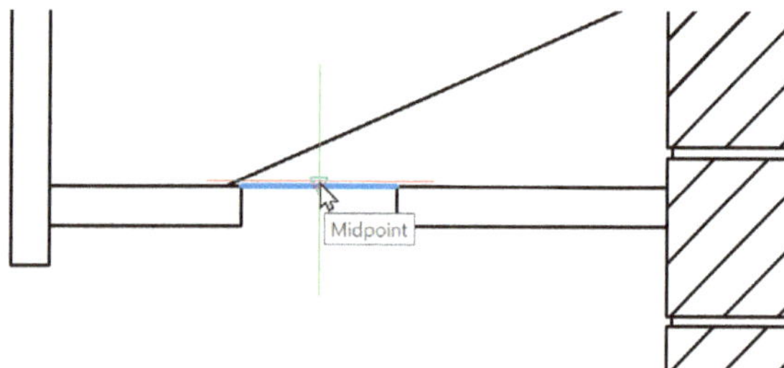

- Next, move the pointer vertically downward.

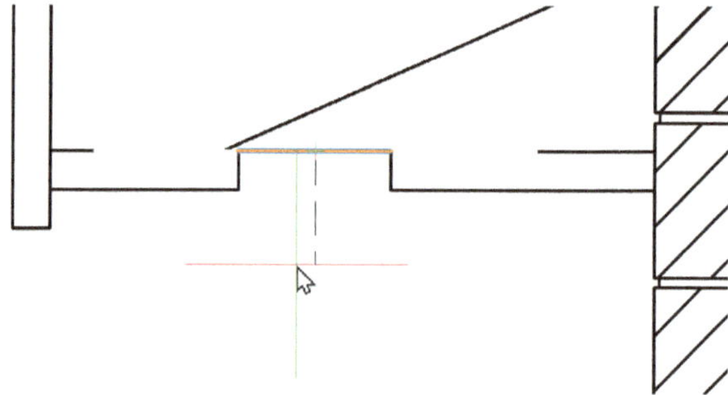

- Type 1.25 as the scale factor, and then press ENTER.
- Select the horizontal line and click on its midpoint grip.
- Move the pointer upward. Next, type 0.2, and press ENTER.

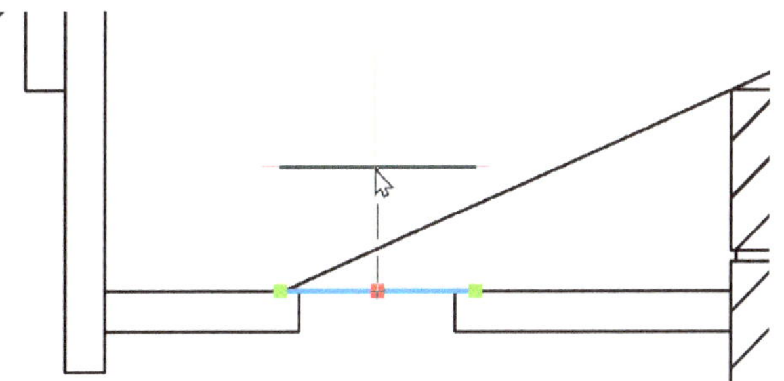

- Create an inclined line and array it, as shown.

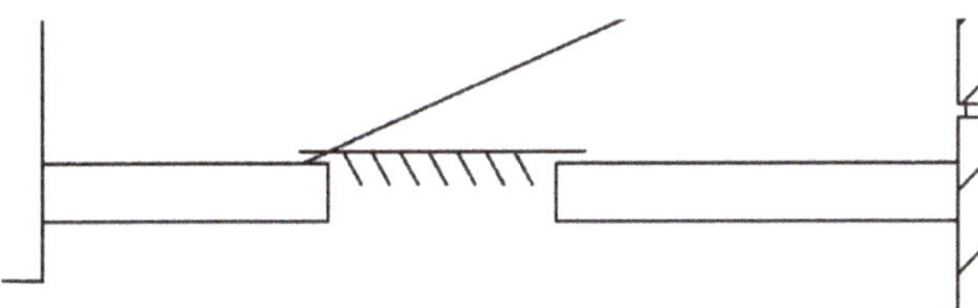

- Click the **Hatch** tool on the **Draw** panel of the **Home** ribbon tab.
- On the **Hatch and Gradient** dialog, click the Browse [...] icon next to the **Name** box.
- Select the **NATURAL** hatch from the **Hatch Pattern Palette** and click **OK**.

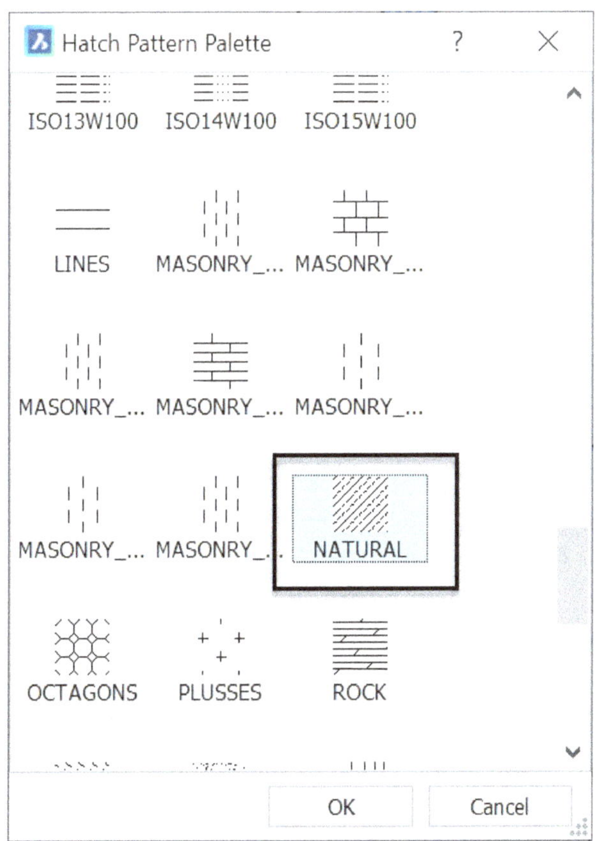

- Click the **Pick points in boundaries** icon under the **Boundaries** section.
- Pick points in the areas, as shown. Next, press ENTER.

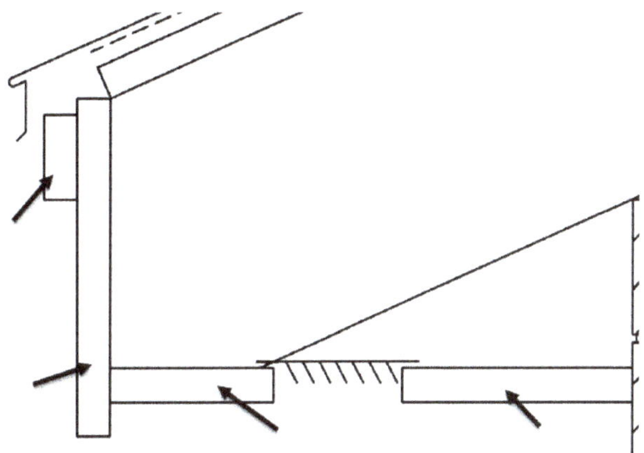

- Type **45** and **2** in the **Angle** and **Scale** boxes, respectively. Next, click **OK**.

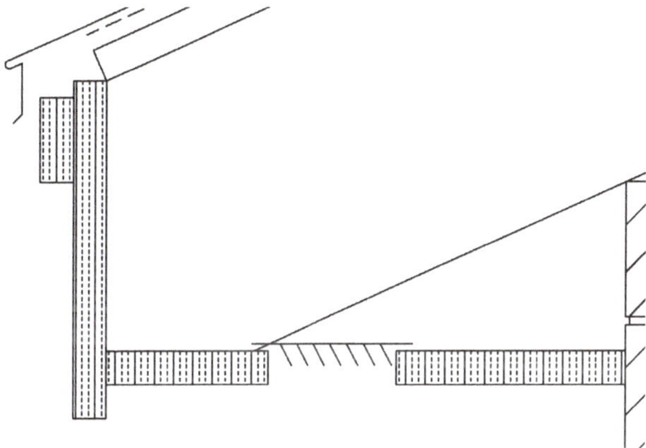

- On the **Home** tab of the ribbon, click **Draw** panel > **Rectangle**.
- Select the lower right corner of the rectangle, as shown.
- Move the pointer downward.
- Type 6 and press TAB.
- Type 5 and press ENTER.

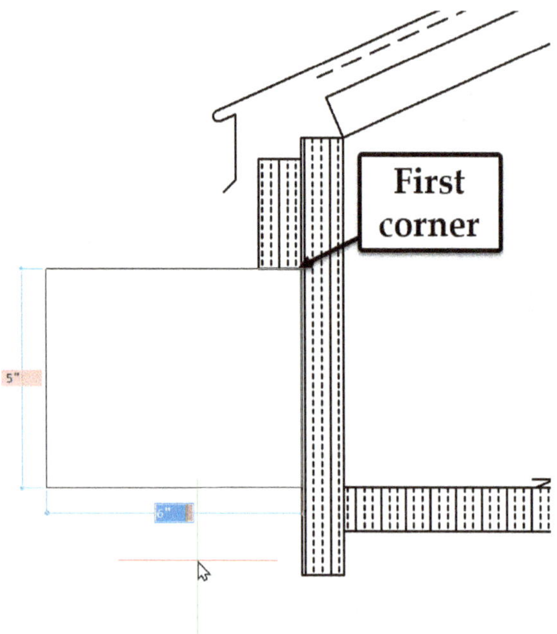

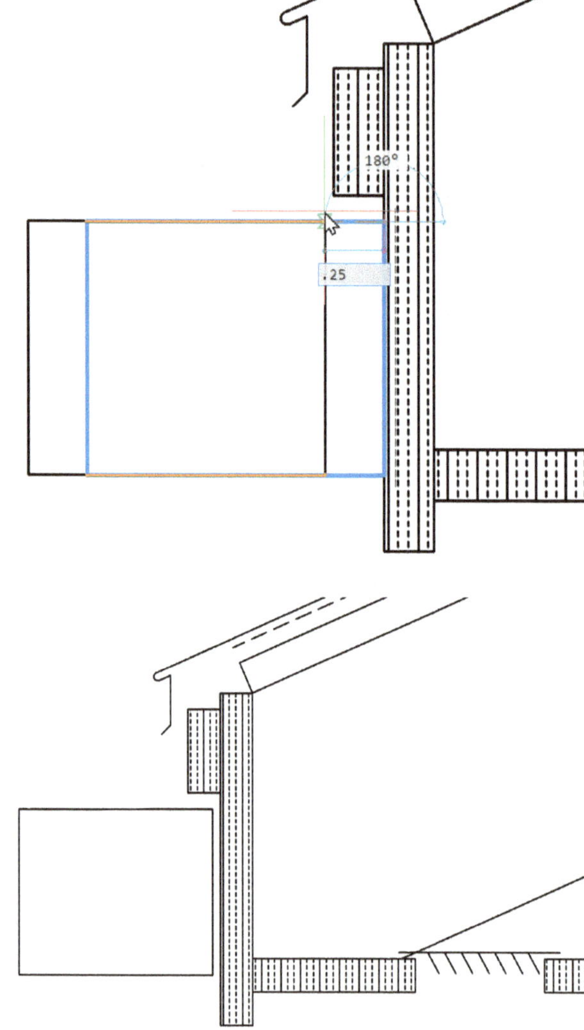

- Select the rectangle and click **Move** tool on the **Modify** panel.
- Select the top right corner point of the rectangle.
- Move the pointer downward. Next, type 0.5, and press ENTER.

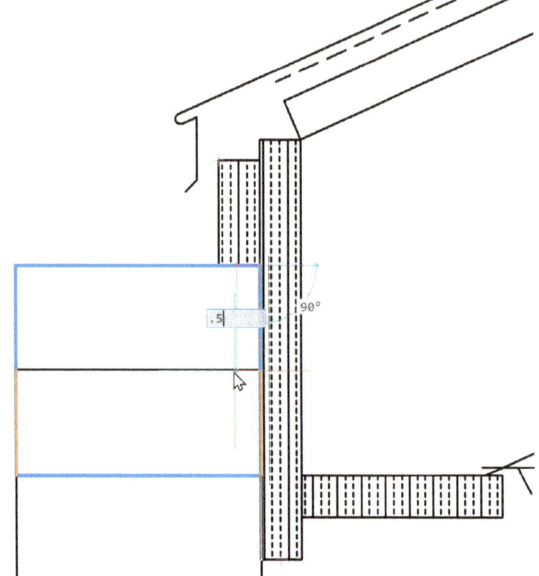

- Select the rectangle and click the **Move** tool on the **Modify** panel.
- Select the top right corner point of the rectangle.
- Move the pointer toward left. Next, type 0.25, and press ENTER.

- Click **Circle** drop-down > **Circle Center-Radius** on the **Draw** panel of the **Home** ribbon tab.
- Select the lower-left corner of the rectangle.
- Type 8 and press ENTER.

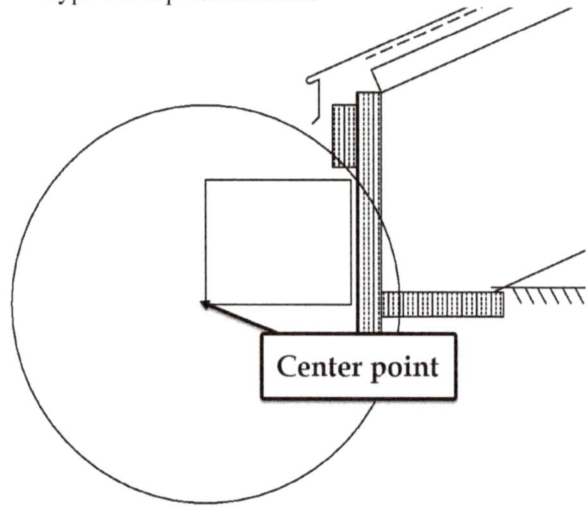

- Select the circle. Next, click on the centerpoint of the circle.
- Move the pointer toward left. Next, type 7, and press ENTER.

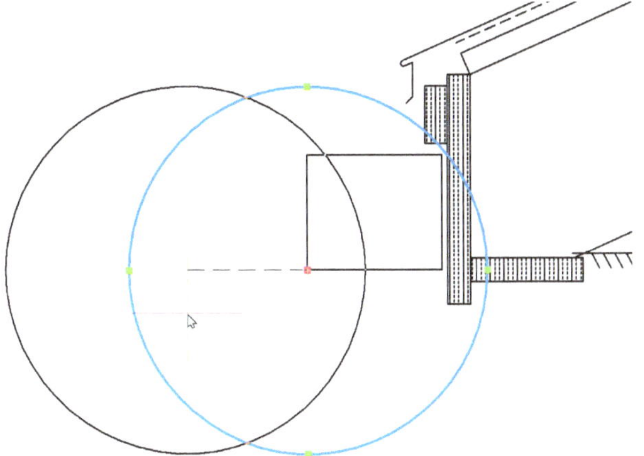

- Click the **Trim** on the **Modify** panel. Next, press ENTER.
- Trim the edges of the circle and rectangle, as shown.

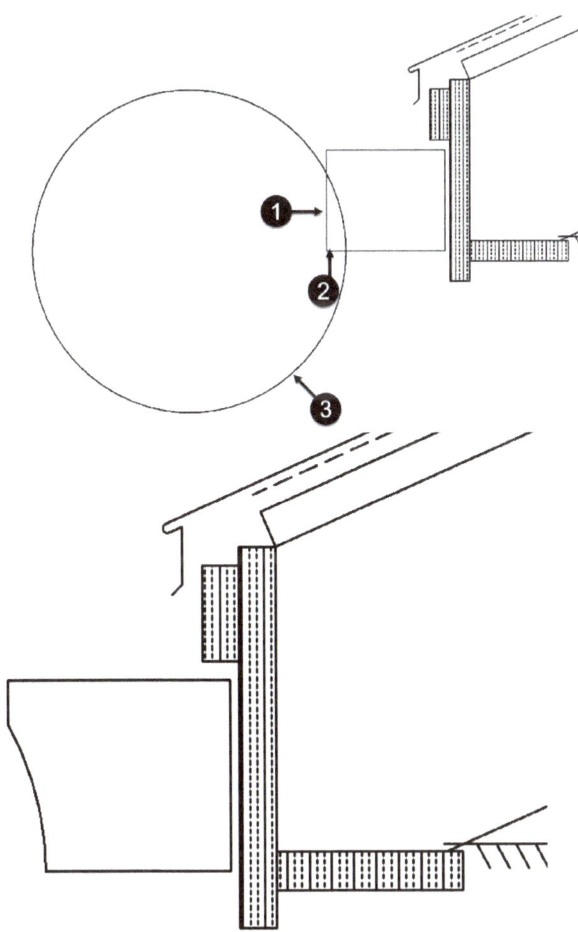

- Press ESC.
- Select the rectangle and click the **Explode** tool on the **Modify** panel.

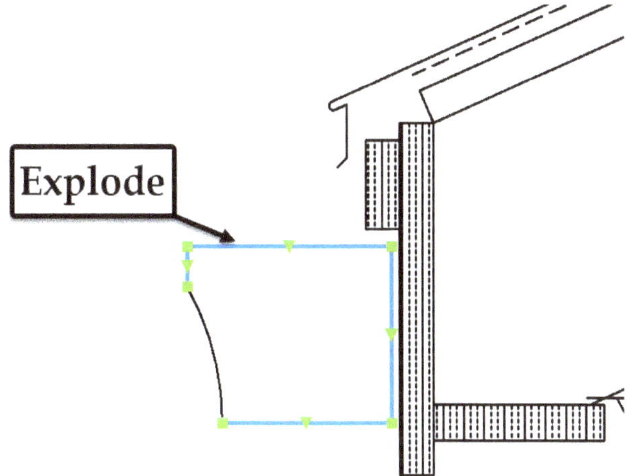

- Select the lines and arcs, as shown in the figure.

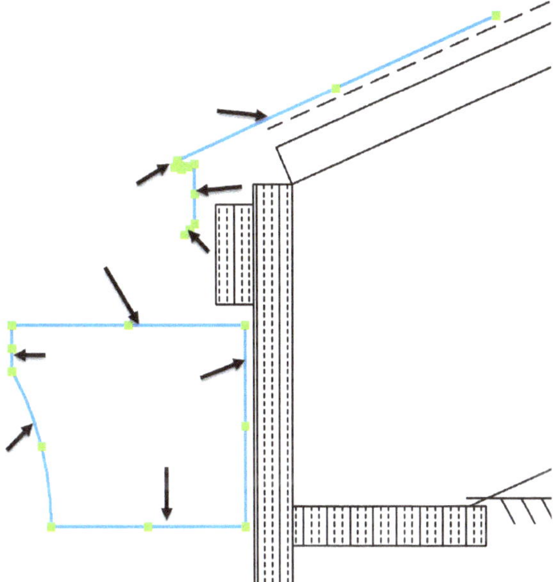

- On the **Home** ribbon tab, click the **Line Weight Control** drop-down on the **Properties** panel, and then select 0.70.

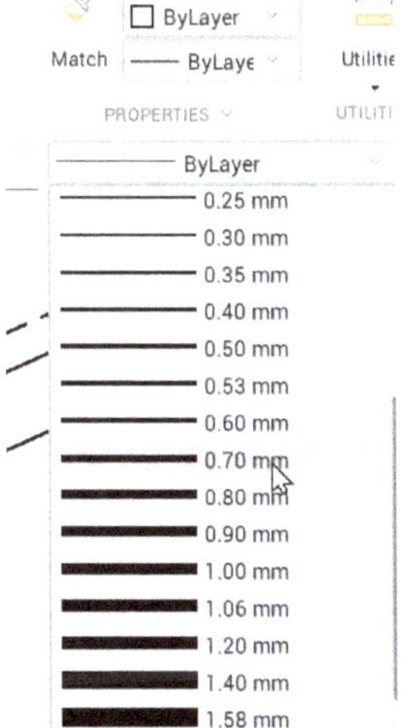

- Press Esc.
- Click the **Offset** tool on the **Modify** panel. Next, type 1.25, and press ENTER.
- Select the offset line, as shown in the figure. Next, move the pointer upward and click.

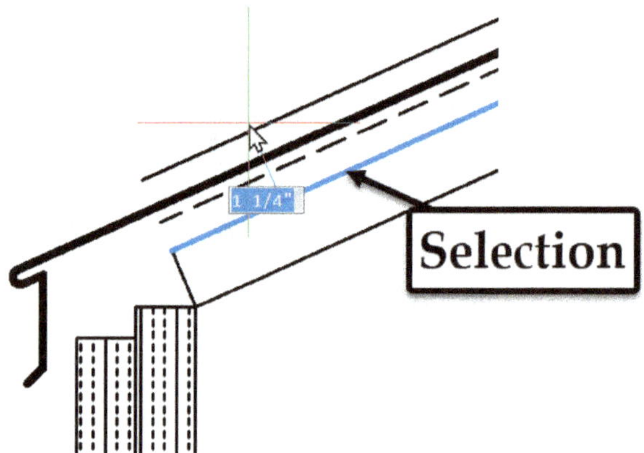

- Deactivate the **Ortho** button on the status bar.
- On the ribbon, click **View** tab > **Coordinates** panel > **UCS** icon.

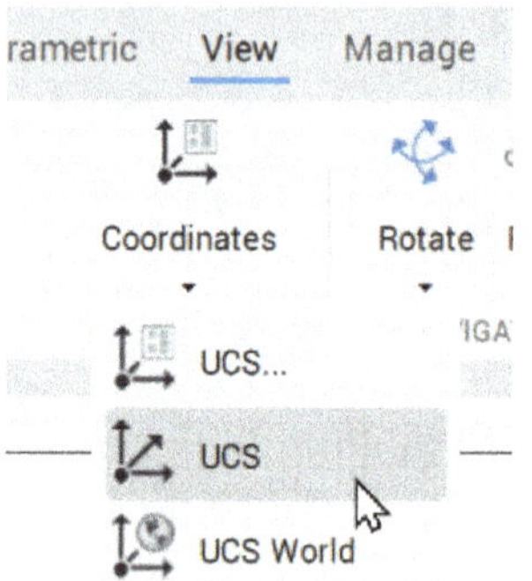

- Select the endpoint of the inclined line, as shown. Next, select a point of the inclined, and then press ENTER.

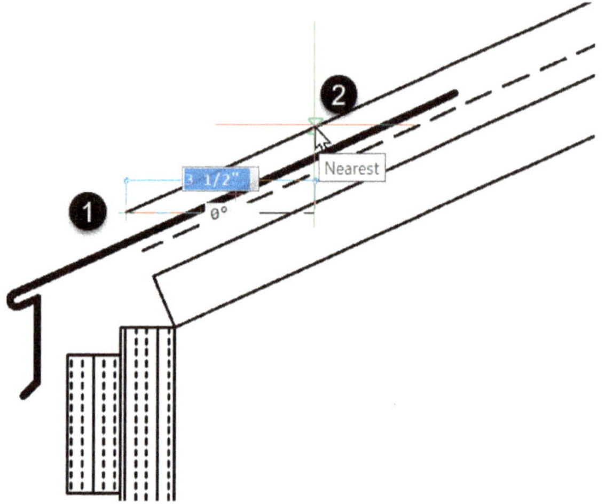

- Activate the **Ortho** button on the status bar.
- Click the **Line** tool on the **Draw** panel of the **Home** ribbon tab.
- Select the endpoint of the offset line. Move the pointer upward.
- Type 2 and press ENTER.
- Type @7<355 in the command line and press ENTER.

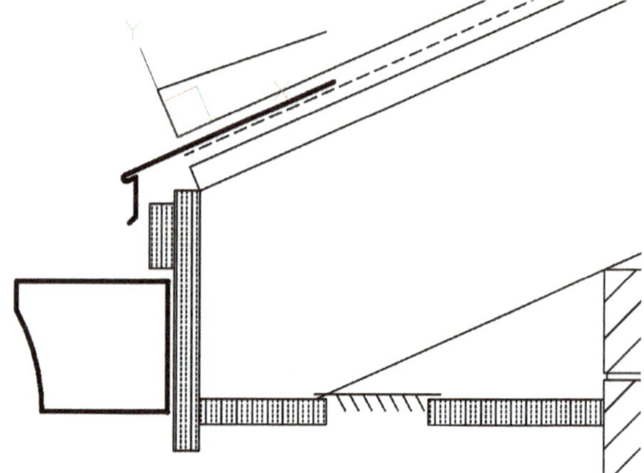

- On the ribbon, click **View** tab > **Coordinates** panel > **UCS World** icon; the coordinate system is restored to its default location.
- Select the two newly created lines.
- Click the **Path Array** tool on the **Modify** panel.

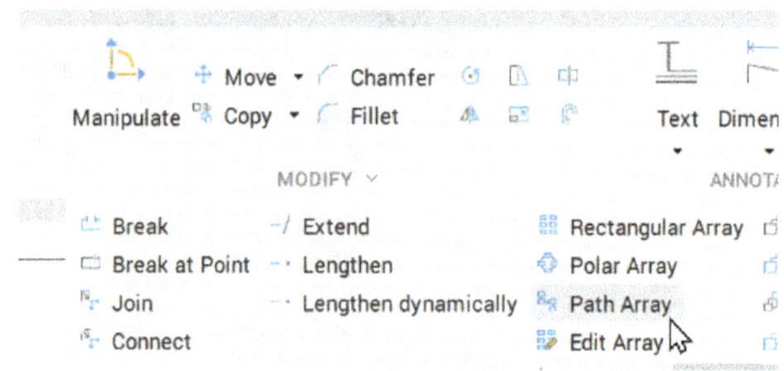

- Next, select the offset to define the path.

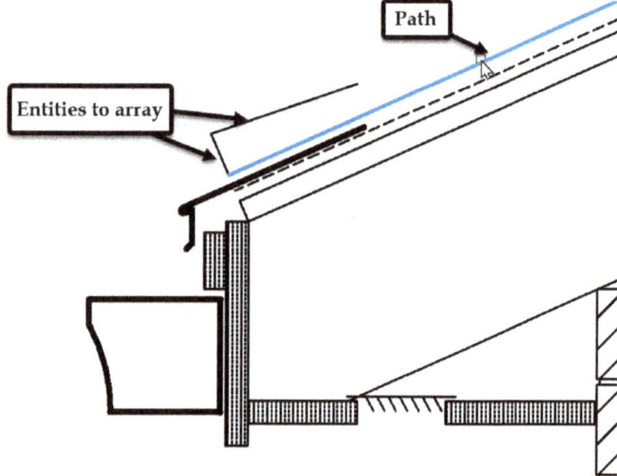

- Select the **Items** option from the command line.

- Type **7** and press ENTER to define the distance between items along path.
- Select the **Full entire path** option from the command line.
- Select the **eXit** option from the command line.

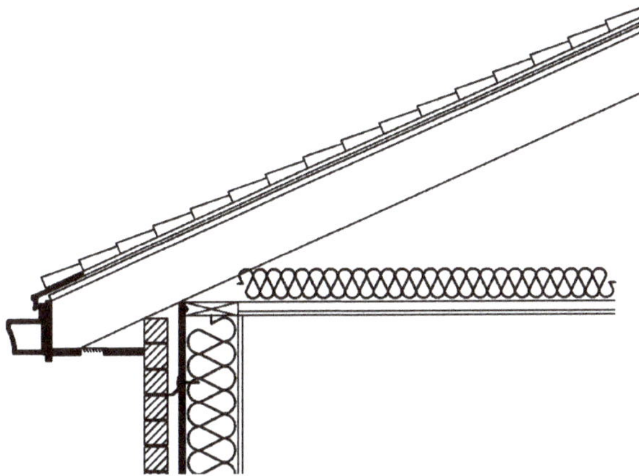

Adding Annotations

- On the **Home** ribbon tab, click **MLeader** drop-down > **Multileader** on the **Annotations** panel.

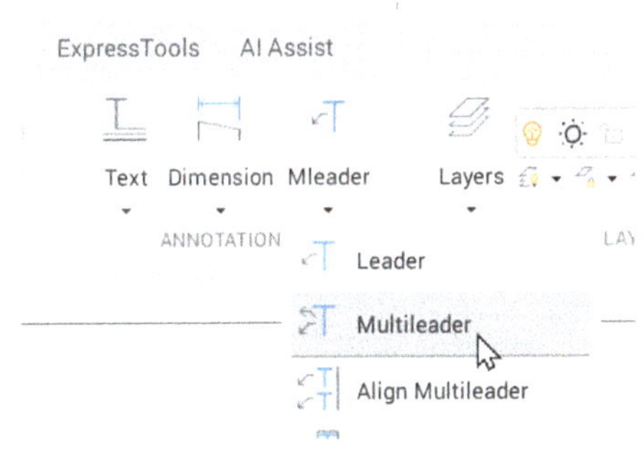

- Deactivate the **Ortho** button on the status bar.
- Specify the start point of the leader on the insulation, as shown.
- Move the pointer diagonally toward the bottom right corner, and then click.

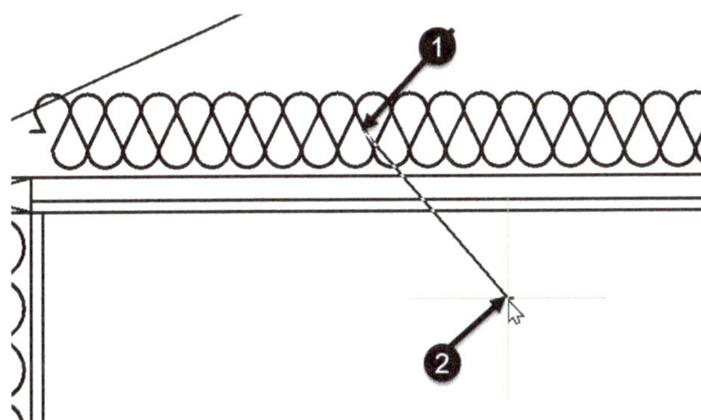

- Type **2** in the **Text Height** box and press ENTER.

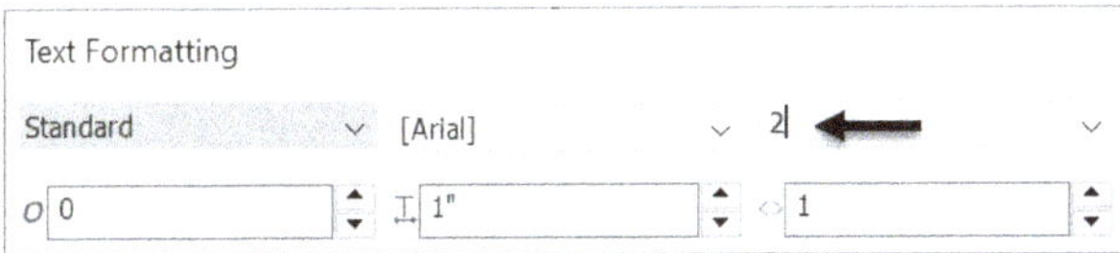

- Type **Insulation** and click in the graphics area.

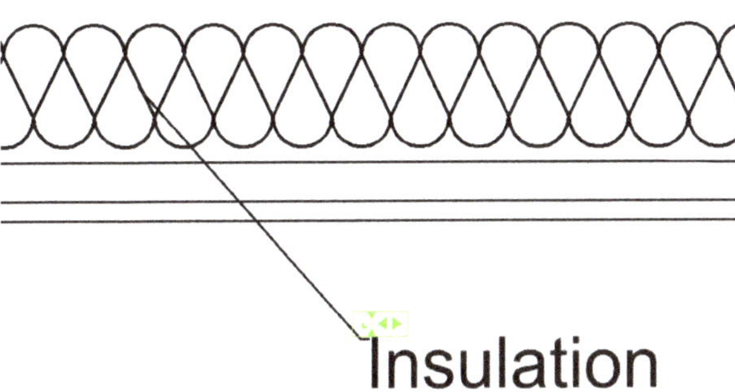

- Select the leader and click the **Properties** tab on the right side of the graphics window.
- On the **Properties** palette, scroll to the **Leaders** section and enter **2** in the **Arrow size** and **Landing distance** boxes, respectively.

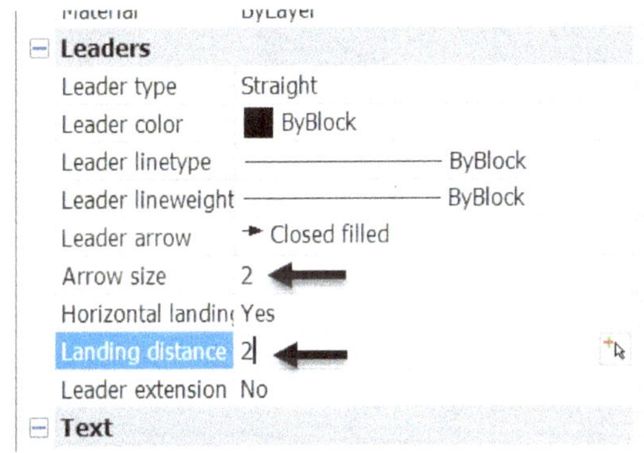

- Scroll to the **Text** section, and then **1** in the **Landing gap** box.

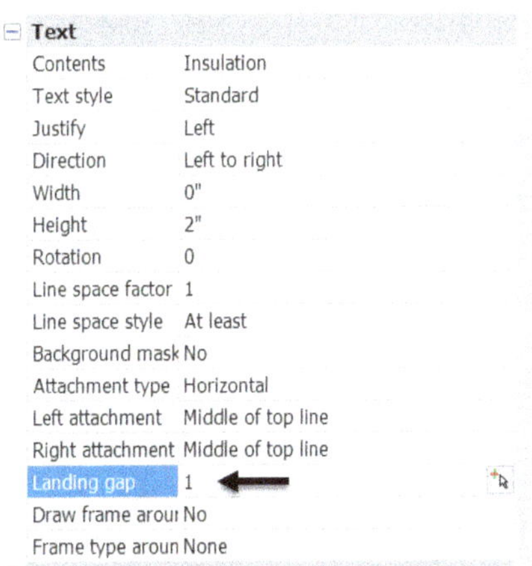

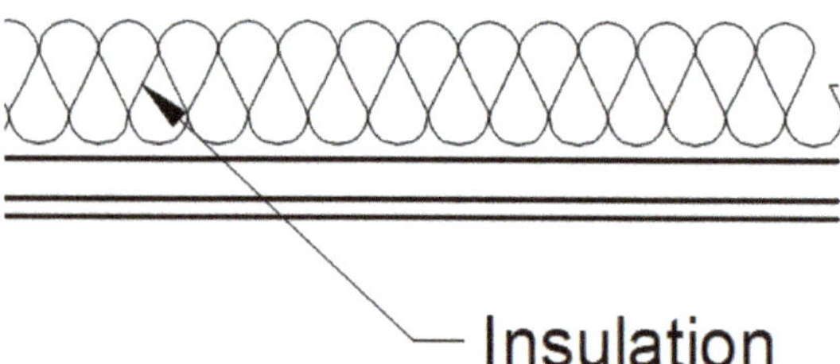

- On the **Home** ribbon tab, click **MLeader** drop-down > **Multileader** on the **Annotation** panel.
- Specify the start point of the leader on the circle, as shown.
- Move the pointer diagonally toward the bottom right corner, and then click.

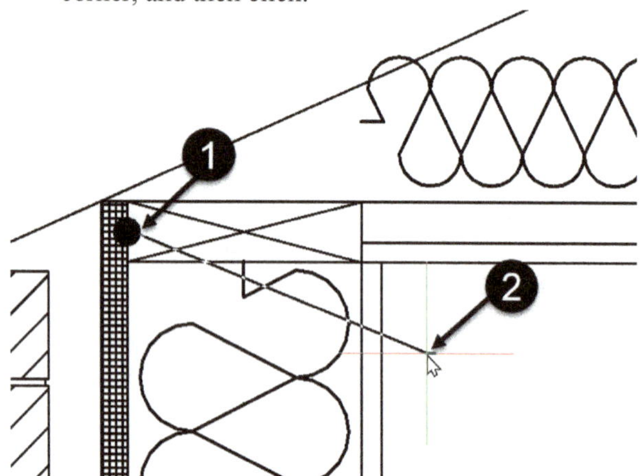

- Type **Continuous Bead of Sealant** and click in the graphics area.
- Click the **Match** tool on the **Properties** panel.

- Select the **Insulation** leader to specify the source object.

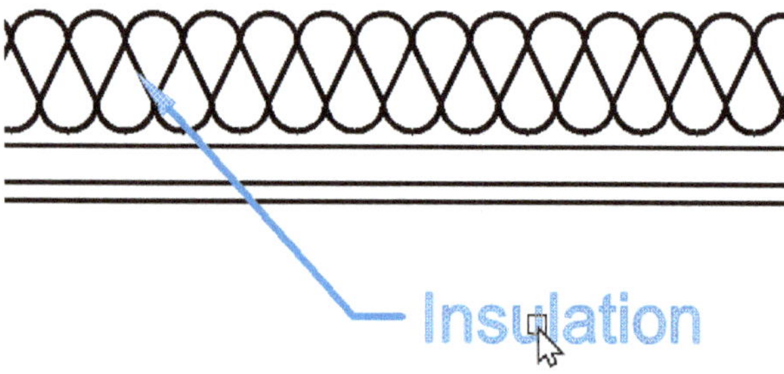

- Select the newly created leader; the properties of the source object are matched with the destination object.

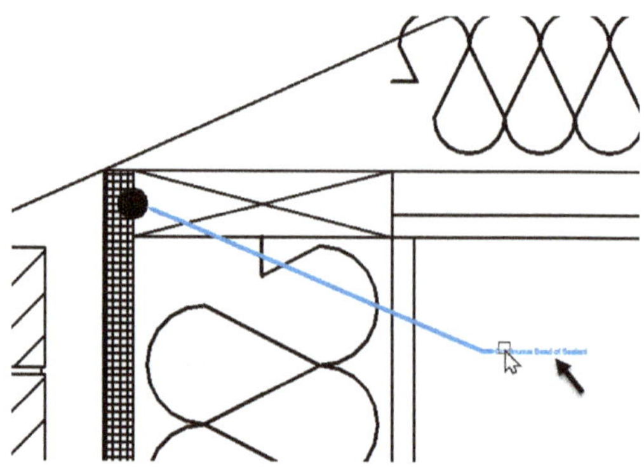

- Likewise, create the remaining leaders, as shown.

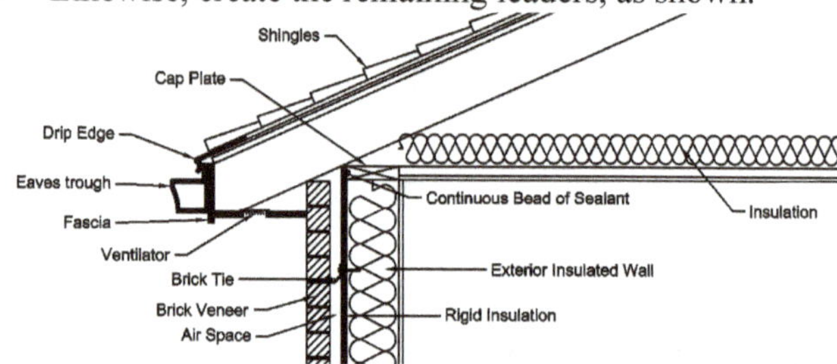

- Activate the **Ortho** button on the status bar.
- On the ribbon, click the **Express Tools** tab > **Draw** > **Breakline**.

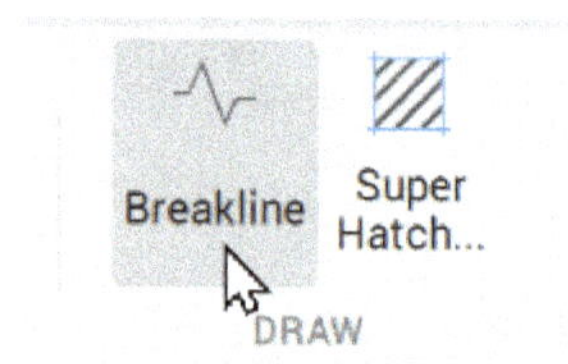

- Select the **Size** option from the command line.
- Type **8** and press ENTER.
- Zoom to the bottom portion and specify the start and endpoints of the break line.

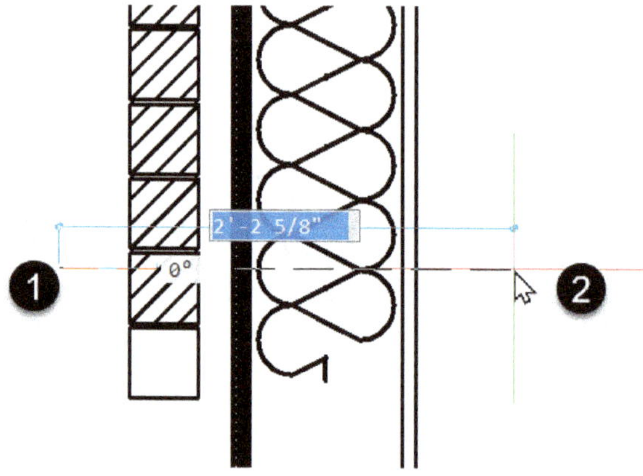

- Select the midpoint of the break line; the break line symbol is placed.

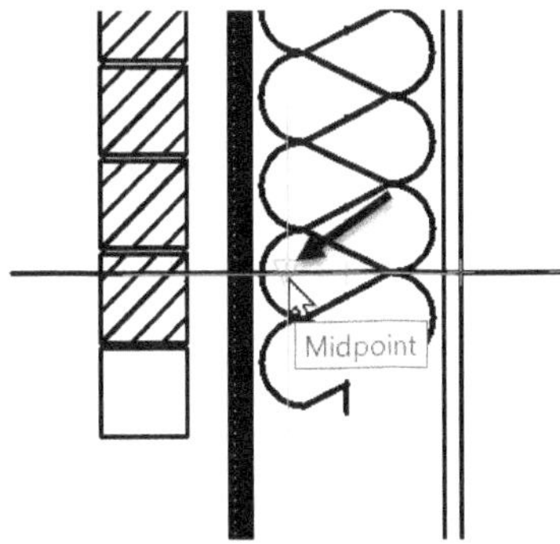

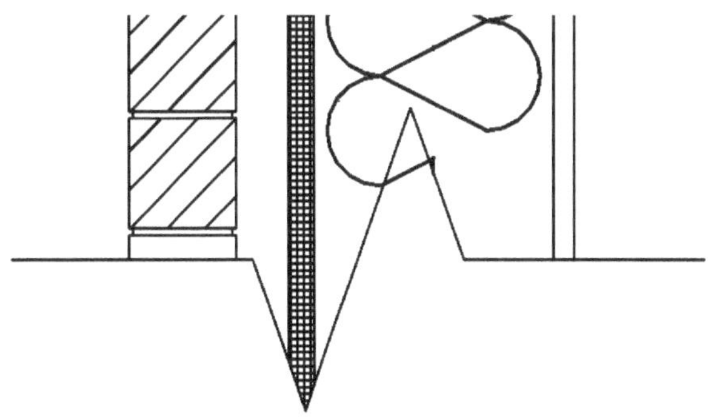

- On the **Home** ribbon tab, click **Trim** on the **Modify** panel.
- Select the break line and press ENTER.

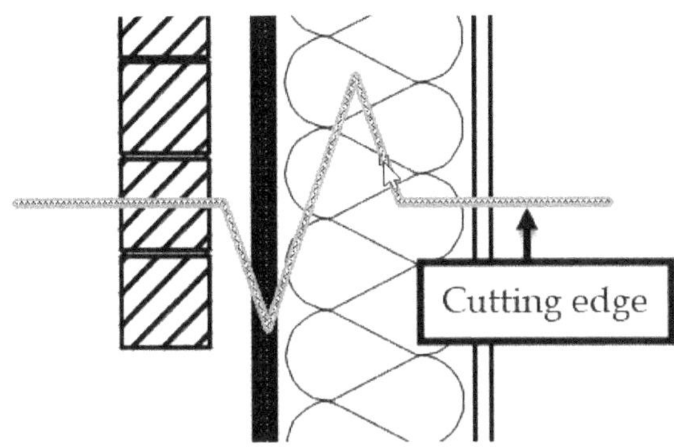

- Trim the elements on the bottom side of the drawing. Make sure that the hatch patterns trimmed first.

- Likewise, create the break lines and trim the elements, as shown.

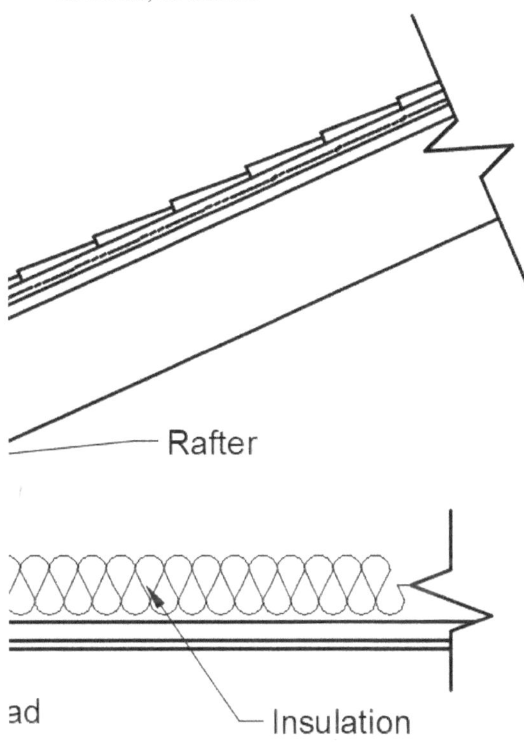

- Save and close the drawing file.

Tutorial 6: Sheets and Title Block

- Open the Tutorial 1 drawing file.

- Click the **Layout 1** tab at the bottom of the graphics window.

Notice that a white paper is displayed with a viewport created automatically. The components of a sheet are shown in the figure below.

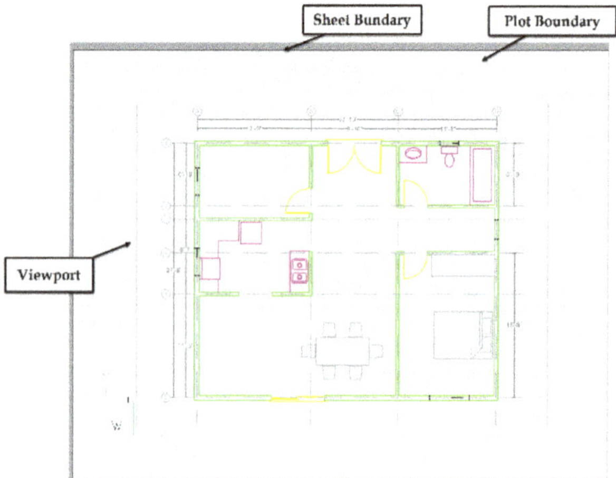

- Click **Export > Print > Plotter Manager** on the ribbon; the **PlotConfig** folder is opened in the explorer.

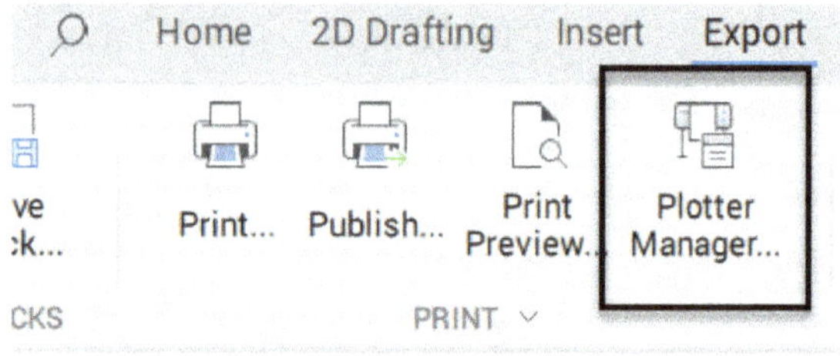

- Click the **Create a new plotter configuration** icon in the **PlotConfig** folder; the **Plotter Configuration Editor** dialog appears.

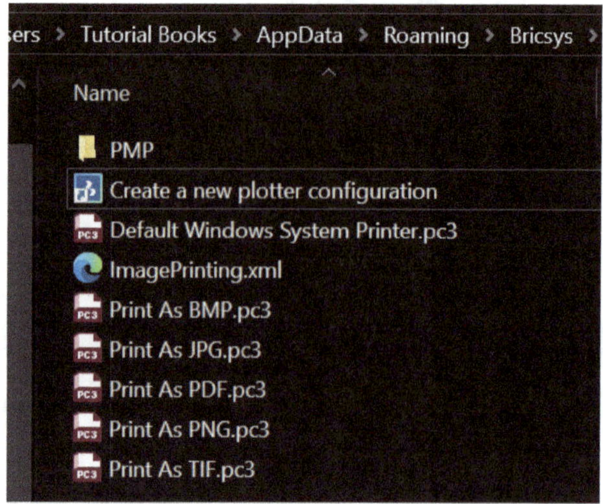

- Select the **Print As PDF** option from the **Printer name** drop-down on the **New Print Configuration** dialog, and then click **OK**.

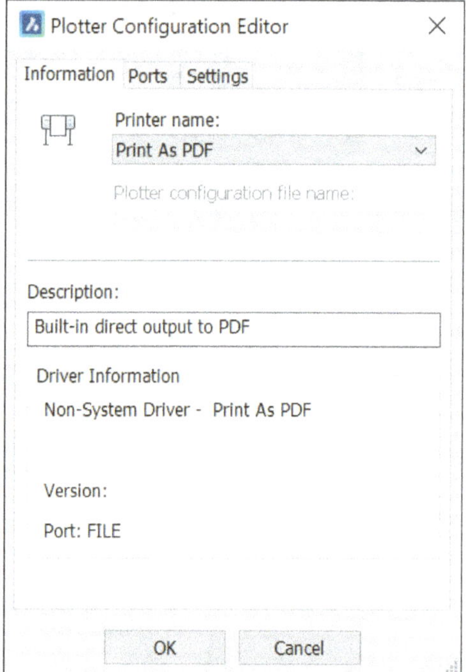

- On the **Save Plotter Configuration As** dialog, type **ARCH D** in the **File name** box. Next, click **Save.**

- Right-click on the **Layout1** tab and select **Page Setup**.

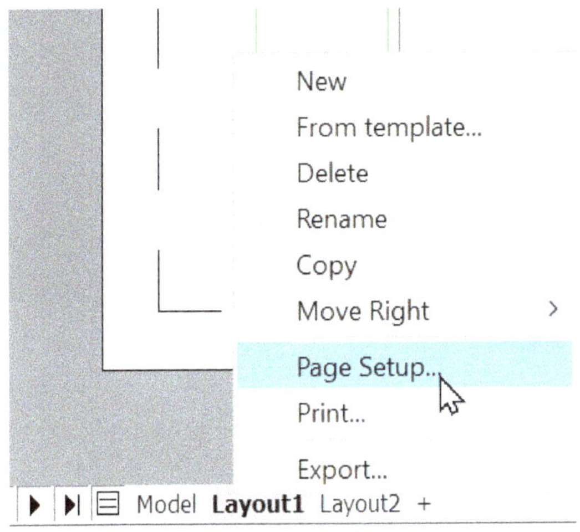

- On the **Page Setup** dialog, select **ARCH D.pc3** from the **Printer/Plotter configuration** drop-down under the **Printer/Plotter** group.

- Set the **Paper size** to **ARCH D (36.00 x 24.00 inches)**. Next, set the **Scale** to **1:1**.

- Set the **Plot style table** to **default.ctb**.

- Select **Drawing orientation > Landscape**.

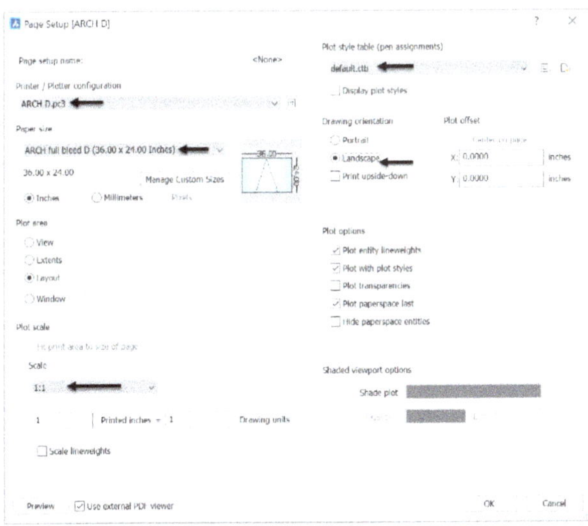

- Click **OK** on the **Page Setup** dialog.

- Double-click on the **Layout1** tab and enter **ARCH D** in the **Rename Layout** dialog.

- Click **OK**; the **Layout1** is renamed.

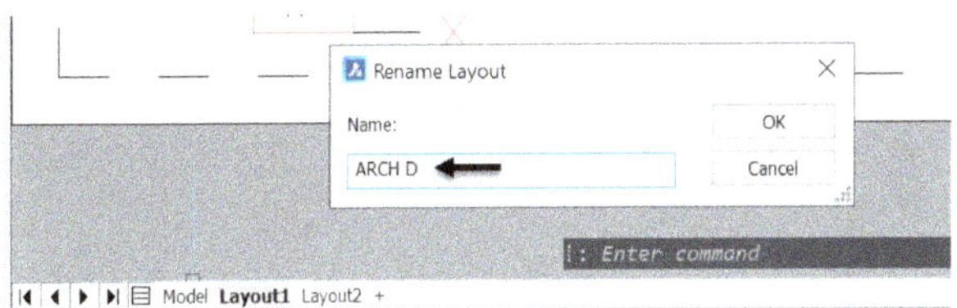

Creating the Title Block on the Layout

You can draw objects on layouts to create title blocks, borders, and viewports. However, it is not recommended to draw the actual drawing on layouts. You can also create dimensions on layouts.

- Click the **ARCH D** layout tab.

- Create the **Title Block** layer and make it current.

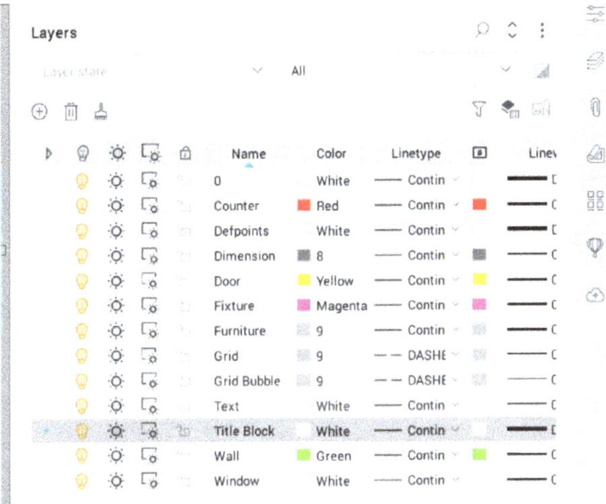

- Select the viewport on the sheet and press Delete.

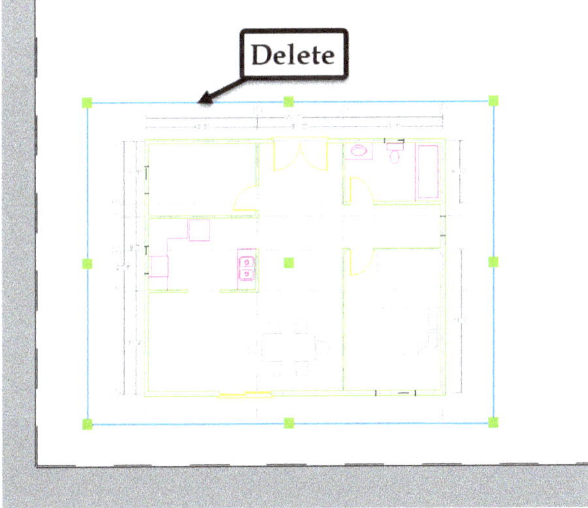

- Create the border and title block, as shown. Insert text inside the title block, as shown.

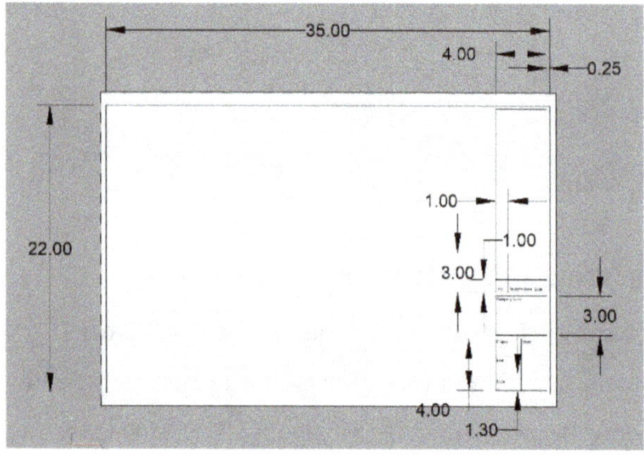

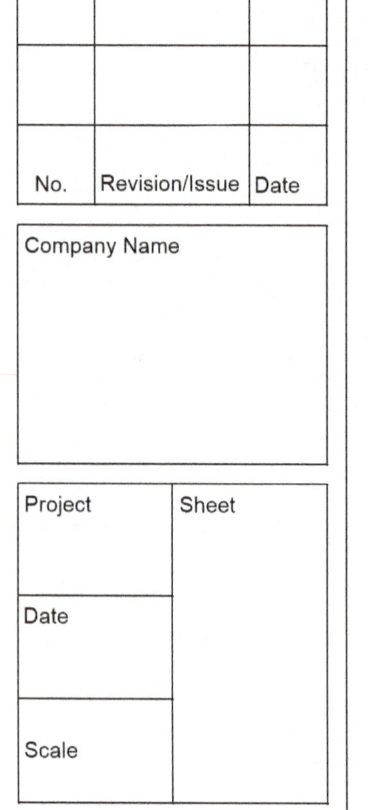

* On the ribbon, click **Insert > Blocks > Create Block**. Next, type **Title Block** in the **Block Name** box of **Create Block Definition** dialog.
* Click the **Select entities** icon under the **Entities** section. Next, select the elements of the title block, and then press ENTER.

* Click the **Pick point** icon under the **Base point** section. Next, select the lower right corner point of the title block.

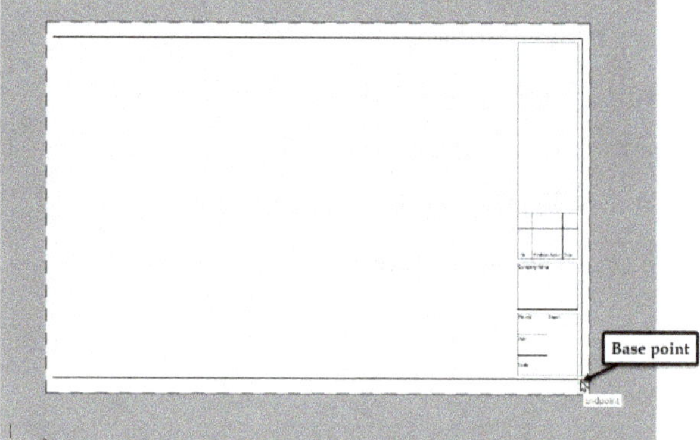

* Select the **Convert to block** option from the **Entities** section, and then click **OK**.

Creating Viewports in the Paper space

The viewports that exist in the paper space are called floating viewports. Because you can position them anywhere in the sheet, and modify their shape size concerning the sheet.

* Open the **ARCH D** layout, if not already open.
* Click **View > Layout > Paper Space Views** on the ribbon.

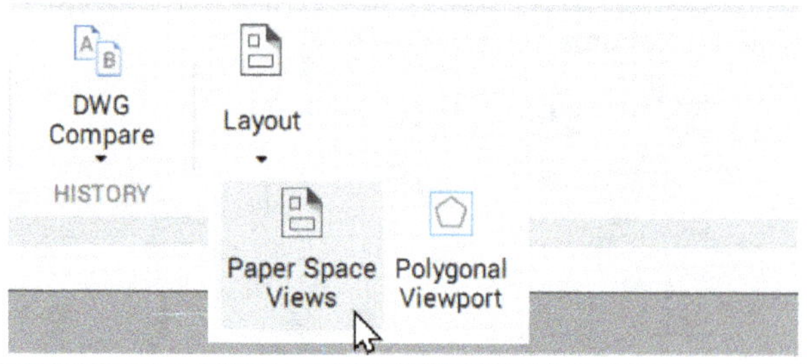

- Create the rectangular viewport by picking the first and second corner points, as shown in the figure.

- Click inside the viewport; the model space inside the viewport is activated. Also, the viewport frame becomes thicker when you are in model space.
- On the ribbon, click Views > Zoom drop-down > Zoom scale.
- Type 0.6 in the command line and press ENTER.

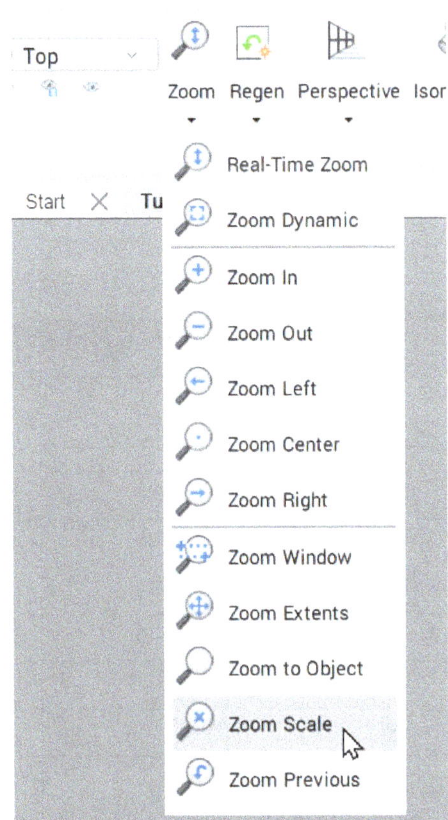

- Press ESC.

- Click in the area outside the viewport to switch back to paper space.

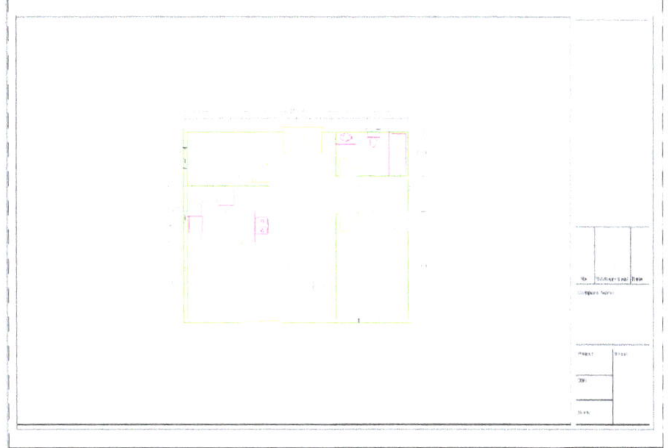

To hide viewport frames while plotting a drawing, follow the steps given below.

- Click the **Layers** tab on the right side of the graphics area.
- In the **Layers** palette, create a new layer called **Hide Viewports** and make it current.

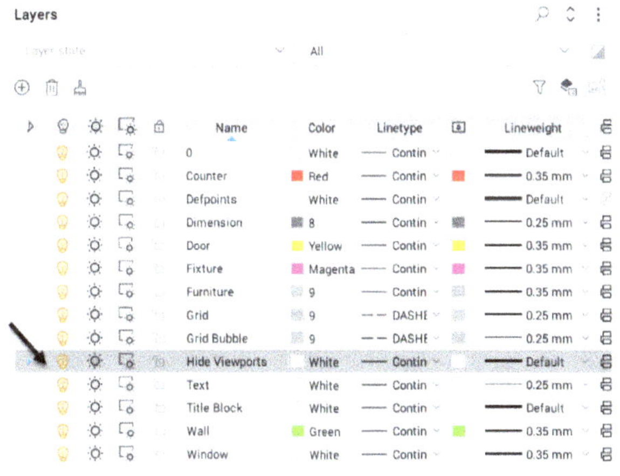

- Deactivate the plotter symbol  under the **Print** column of the **Hide Viewports** layer; the object on this layer will not be print. Close the **Layers Manager**.

- On the ribbon, click **Home** tab > **Layers** panel >
  Active Layer drop-down > **Move to Current Layer**
  button.

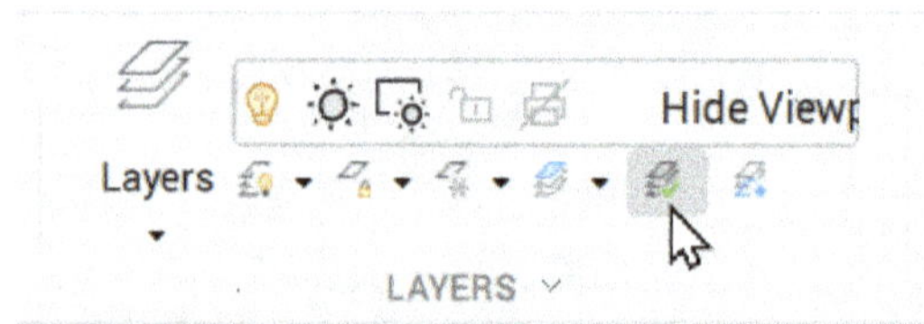

- Select the viewport in the **ARCH D** sheet and press
  ENTER; the viewport frames are unplottable.

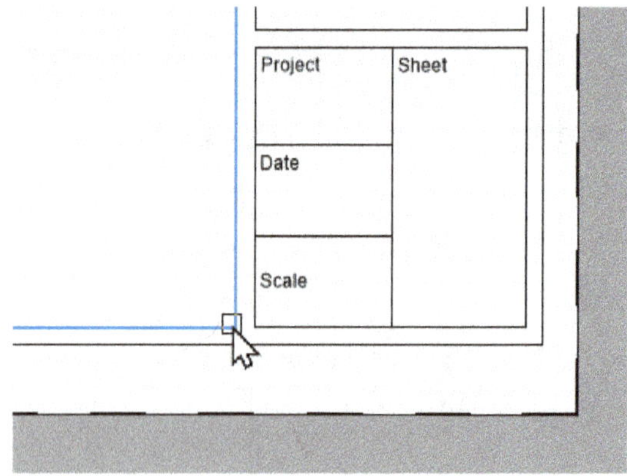

- Press ESC.
- Save the drawing file.

Tutorial 7: Printing

- Open the Tutorial 1 file.
- On the ribbon, click **Export > Print > Print**.

- Select the **default.ctb** option from the **Print style
  table** section, and then click the **Edit plot style**
  button.

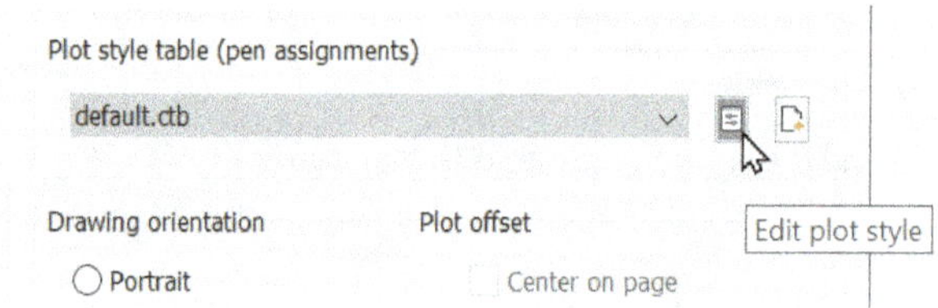

- On the **Plot Style Table Editor** dialog, click the
  Form View tab on **Plot Style Table Editor** dialog.
- Select **Color 1** from the **Plot Styles** list. Next, set the
  Lineweight to 0.1000 mm. Likewise, change the
  lineweights of the other colors, as shown.

Color	Lineweight
Color 1	0.1 mm
Color 2	0.2 mm
Color 3	1.0 mm
Color 4	0.5 mm
Color 5	0.7 mm
Color 6	0.5 mm
Color 8	0.09 mm
Color 9	0.05 mm

- Press and hold the Shift key and select Color 1 and
  Color 9. Set **Color** to **Black**. Click **Save & Close** on
  the **Plot Style Table Editor** dialog.

- On the **Print** dialog, uncheck the Use external PDF viewer option and click **Preview**; the print preview of the drawing appears.

- Click **Close** on the top right corner.

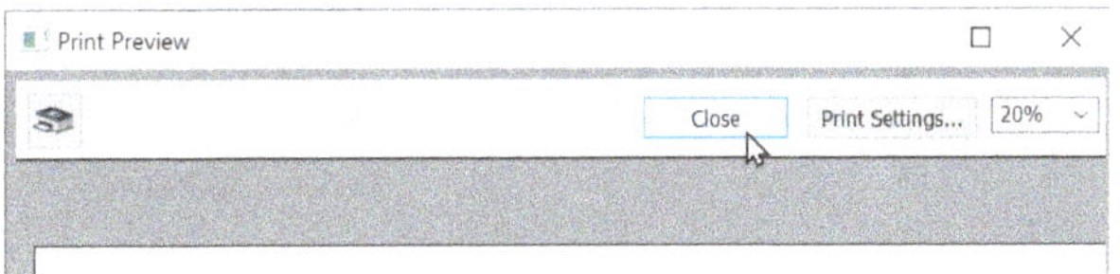

- Click **Print** to print the drawing. Next, browse to the desired location and save the PDF file.

- Save and close the drawing.

Exercise

27'-7"
23'-0"
4'-0"
8'-0"
6'-0"
8'-0"
18'-0"
Down
4'-6"
49'-6"
13'-3"
8'-0"
13'-3"
8'-0"
13'-3"
8'-0"
10'-2"
2'-8"
14'-7"
5'-7 5/16"
8'-0"
28'-6"
4'-2"
8'-0"
54'-0"
2'-9"
12'-3"
5'-2"
4'-6"
16'-6"
4'-0"
8'-0"
8'-0"
8'-0"
24'-0"

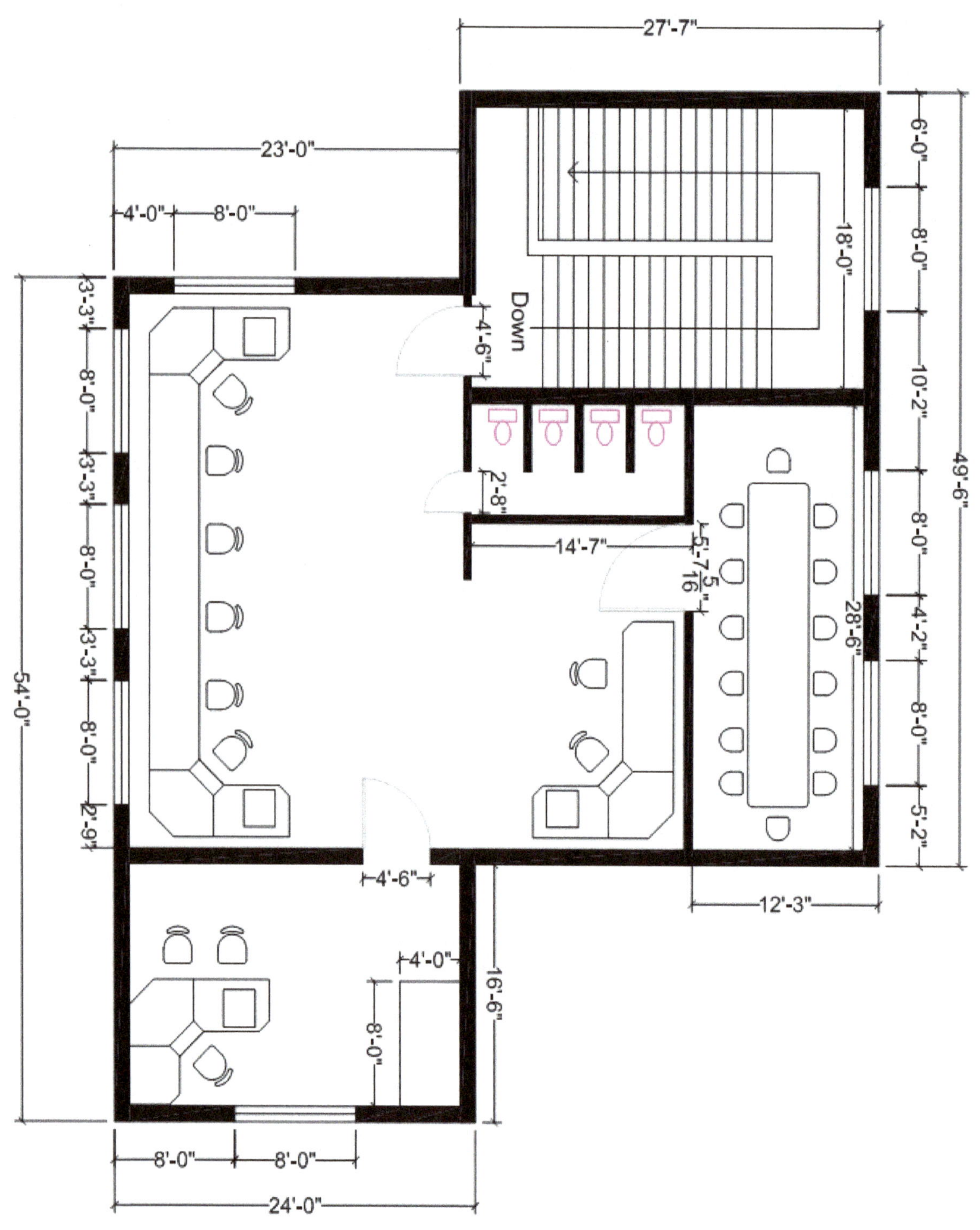

Tutorial 8

In this example, you will learn to create drawing shown in figure.

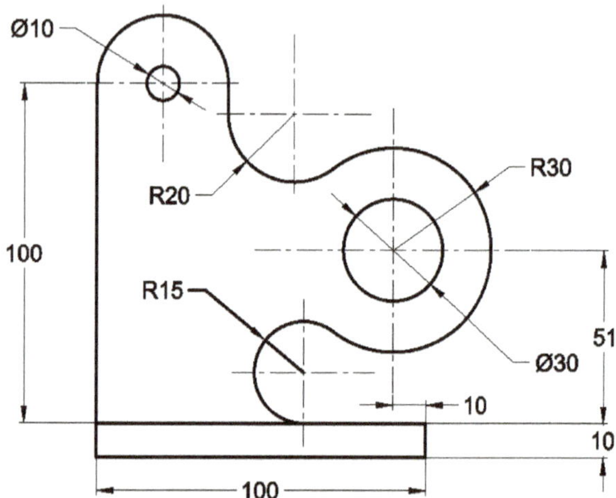

- Double-click on the **BricsCAD V24(x64) en_US** icon on your desktop.
- Click the **Start** button in the **2D Drafting** section on the **BricsCAD Launcher** pop up window.
- Click **Start from Template > Default-mm**; a new document is created.
- Type LIMITS in the command line and press Enter.
- Press Enter to accept 0, 0 as the lower limit.
- Type 420, 297 in the command line, and press Enter. The program sets the upper limit of the drawing.
- Make sure that the **Grid** icon is turned OFF on the status bar.
- On the ribbon, click **View > Views > Zoom** drop-down > **Zoom Extents**.
- On the Status bar, turn ON the **Ortho** icon.
- On the ribbon, click **Home > Draw > Rectangle**. Next, click at an arbitrary location.
- Type-in 100 and press Enter. It defines the horizontal distance of the rectangle.
- Type-in 10 and press Enter. It defines the vertical distance of the rectangle.

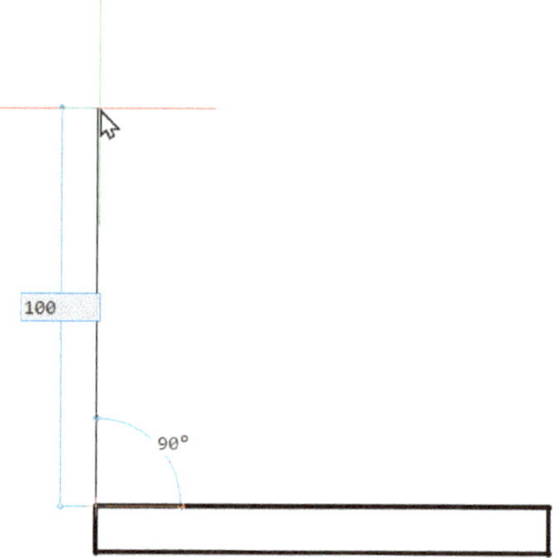

- Click the **Polyline** tool on the **Draw** panel of the **Home** ribbon tab.
- Select the top left corner of the rectangle. Next, move the pointer up.
- Type 100 and press ENTER.

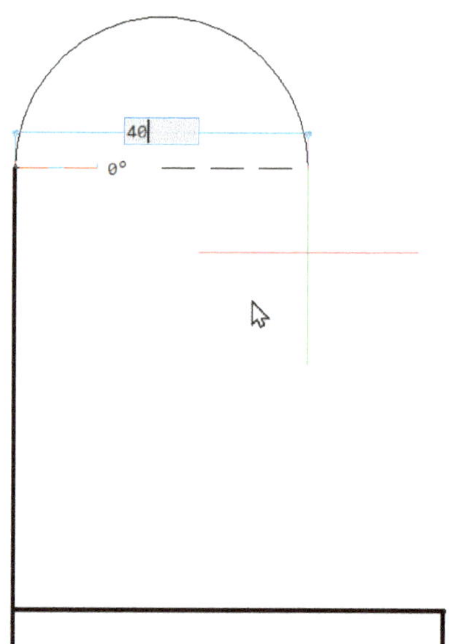

- Select the **draw Arcs** option from the command line.
- Move the pointer toward right. Next, type 40 and press ENTER.

- Select the **draw Lines** option from the command line.
- Move the pointer downward up to a random distance and click. Next, press ESC.

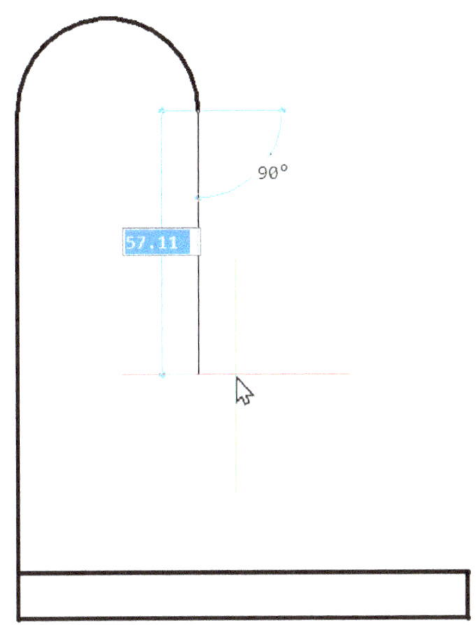

- On the **Home** ribbon tab, click **Draw** panel > **Infinite Line** tool.
- Select the **Parallel** option from the command line.
- Type **10** and press ENTER. Next, select the right vertical line.

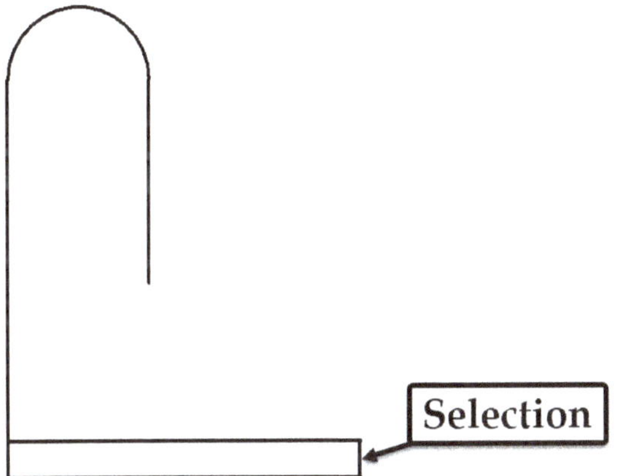

- Click on the left side of the selected line; a vertical infinite line is created.

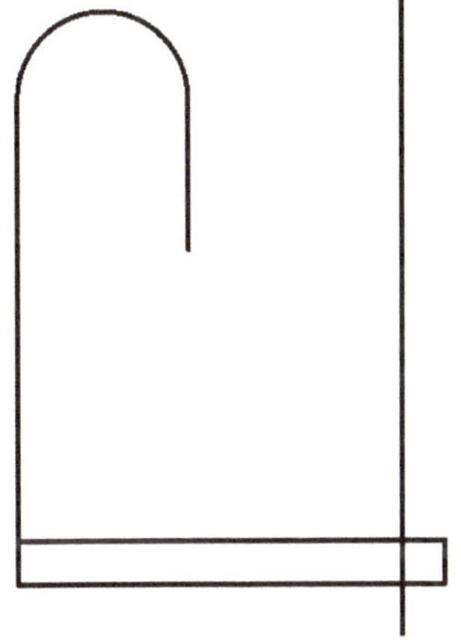

- Press ENTER twice.
- Select the **Parallel** option from the command line.
- Type **51** and press ENTER.
- Select the top horizontal line of the rectangle, as shown.

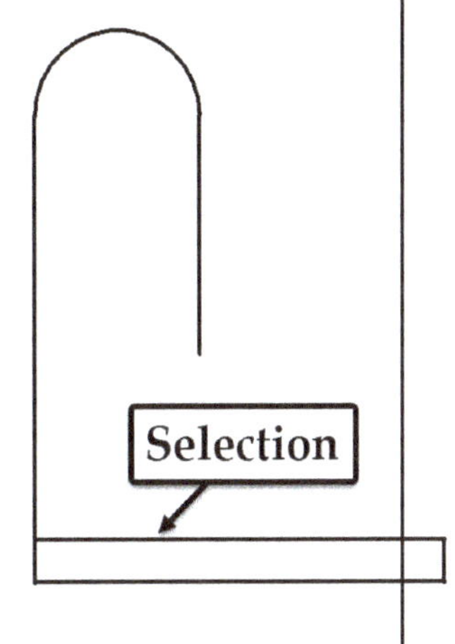

- Move the pointer upward and click.

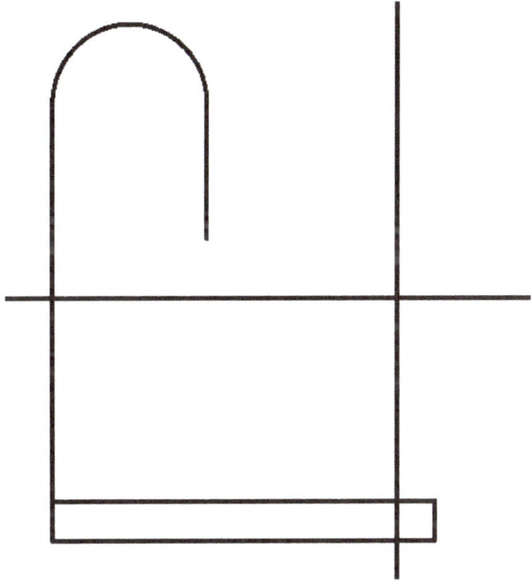

- Click **Circle** drop-down > **Circle Center-Radius** on the **Draw** panel on the **Home** ribbon tab.
- Select the intersection point of the vertical and horizontal infinite line. Next, type 30, and press ENTER.

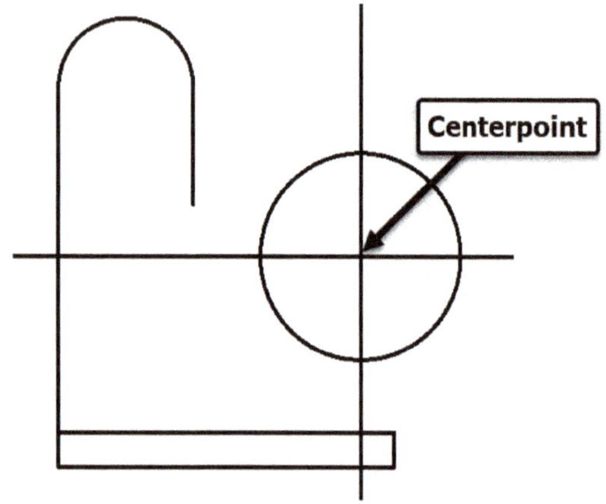

- On the ribbon, click **Home > Draw > Circle drop-down > Circle Tangent, Tangent, Radius**.

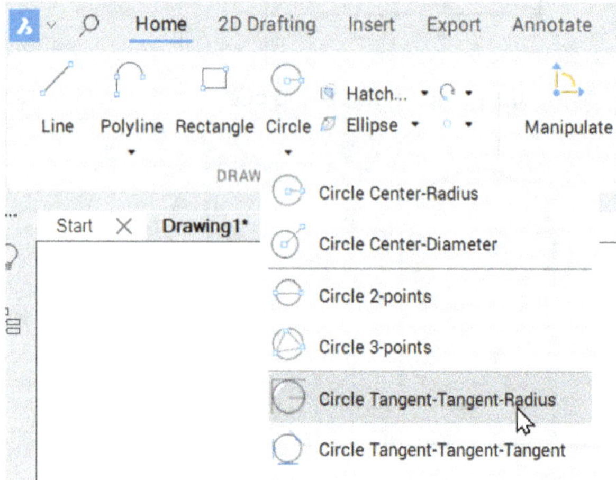

- Select the vertical line and the circle, as shown.

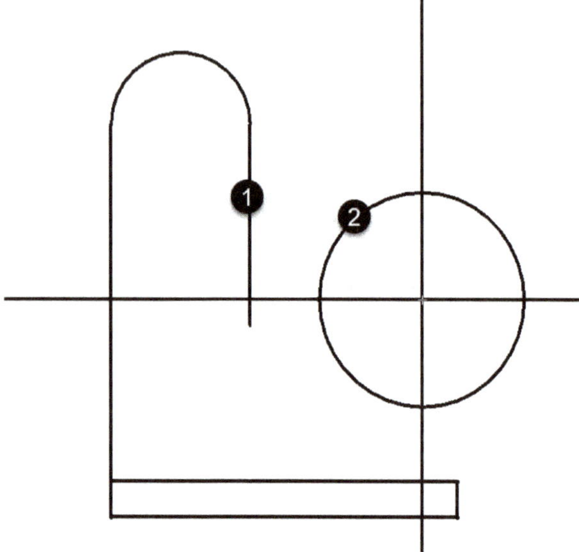

- Type 20 and press ENTER.

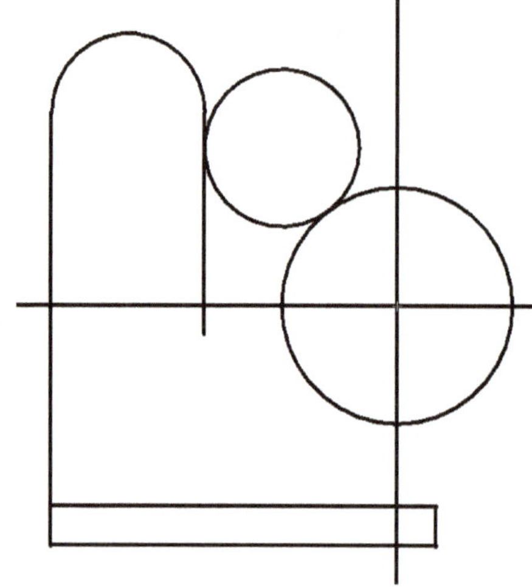

- On the ribbon, click **Home > Draw > Circle drop-down > Circle Tangent, Tangent, Radius**.
- Select the circle and the horizontal line of the rectangle, as shown.

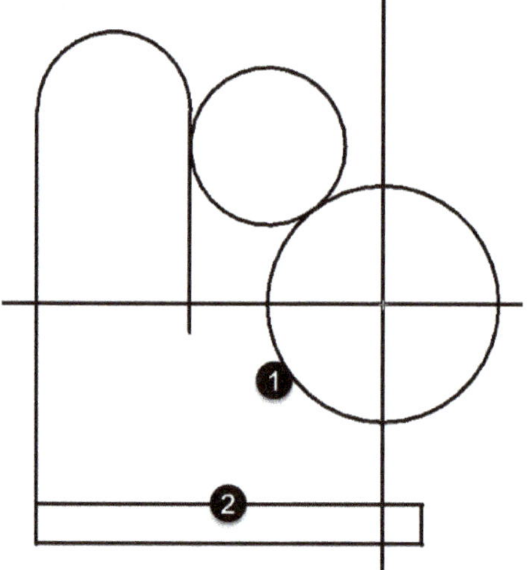

- Type 15 and press ENTER.

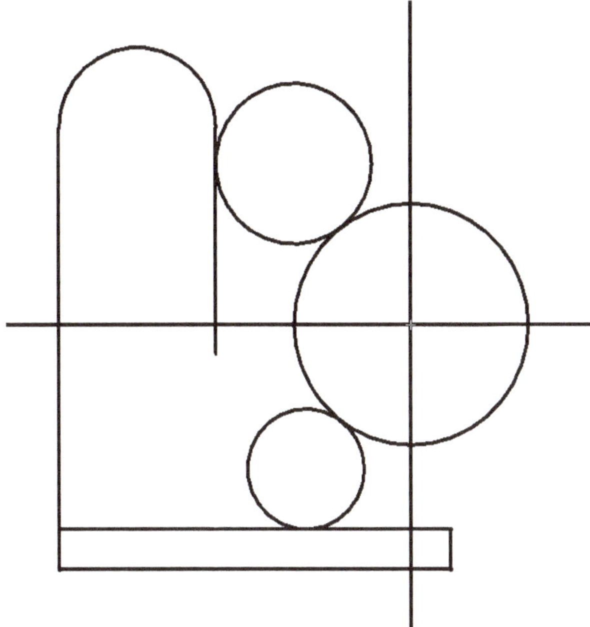

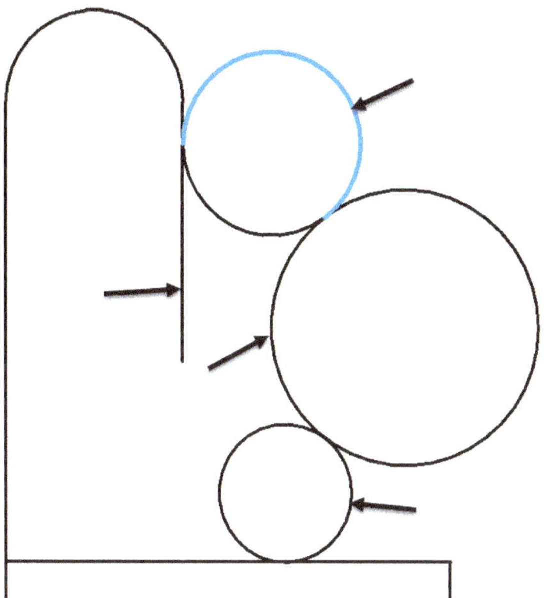

- Select the two infinite lines. Press the DELETE key.

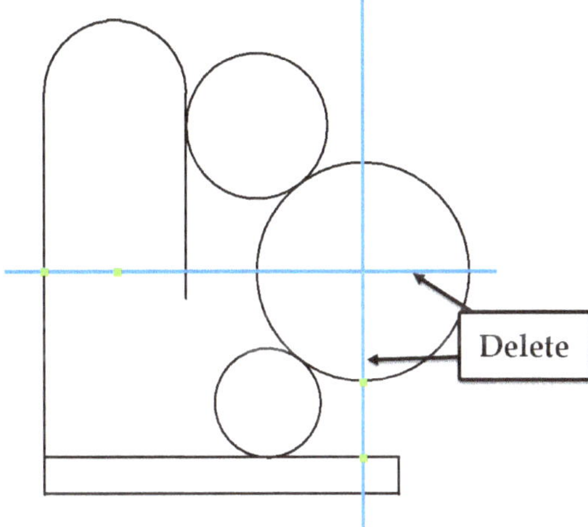

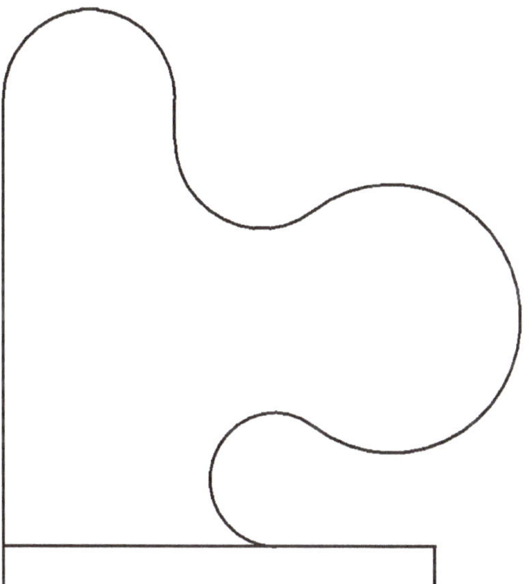

- Click **Home** tab > **Modify** panel > **Trim** on the ribbon.
- Press ENTER to select all the entities as cutting edges.
- Select the entities, as shown. Press ESC.

- On the ribbon, click **Home** tab > **Draw** panel > **Circle** drop-down > **Circle Center-Diameter**.
- Select the center point of the large arc. Move the pointer outward, type 30 and press ENTER.
- Activate the Circle Center-Diameter command.
- Select the center point of the top arc. Move the pointer outward, type 10 and press ENTER.

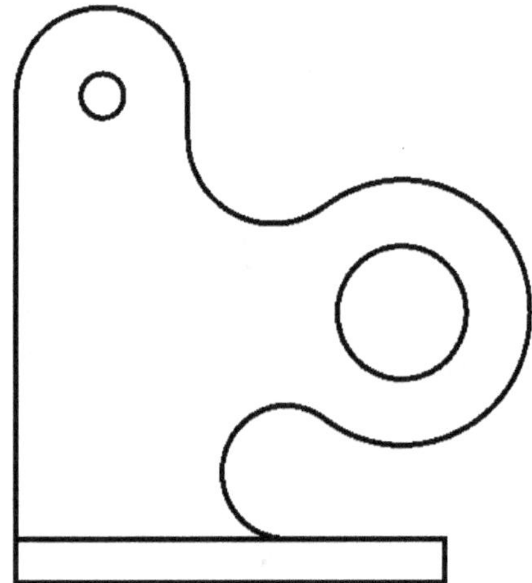

Tutorial 9

In this example, you will learn to create drawing shown in figure.

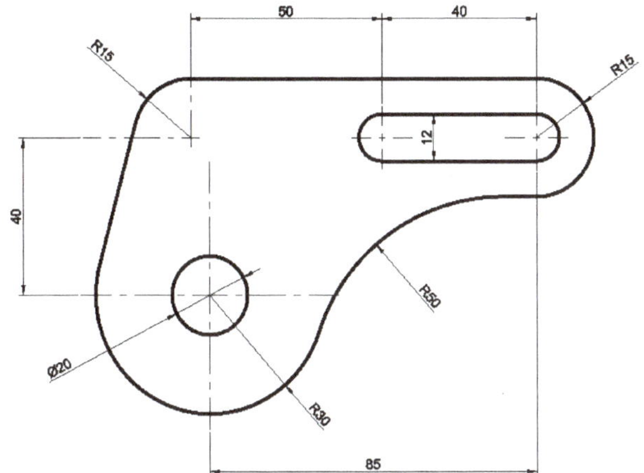

- Double-click on the **BricsCAD V24(x64) en_US** icon on your desktop.
- Click the **Start** button in the **2D Drafting** section on the **BricsCAD Launcher** pop up window.
- Click **Start from Template > Default-mm**; a new document is created.
- On the ribbon, click **Home > Draw > Rectangle**. Next, click at an arbitrary location.
- Type-in 90 and press TAB. It defines the horizontal distance of the rectangle.
- Type-in 30 and press Enter. It defines the vertical distance of the rectangle.

- Click **Circle** drop-down > **Circle 2-points** on the **Draw** panel on the **Home** ribbon tab.

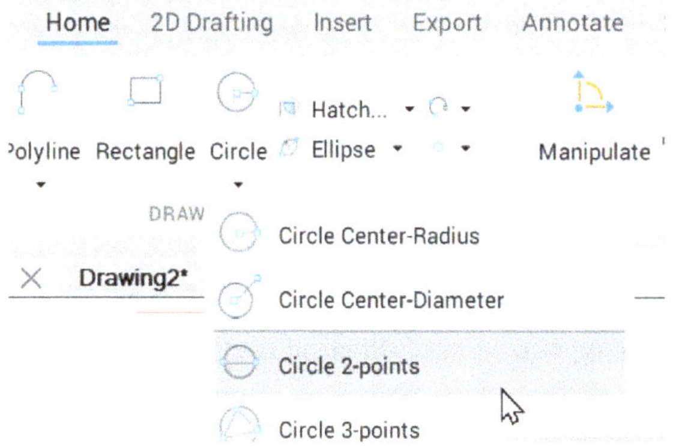

- Select the top-left and bottom-left corners of the rectangle.

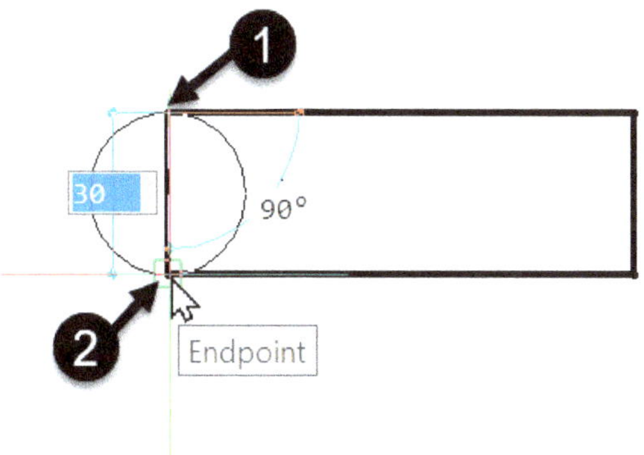

- Click **Circle** drop-down > **Circle 2-points** on the **Draw** panel on the **Home** ribbon tab.
- Select the top-right and bottom-right corners of the rectangle.

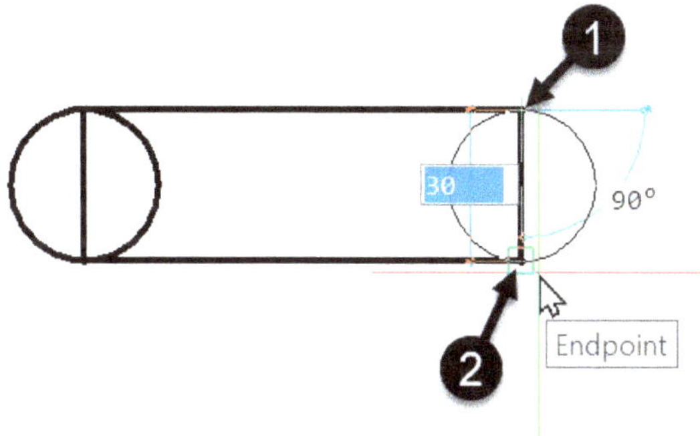

- Click **Home** tab > **Modify** panel > **Trim** on the ribbon.
- Press ENTER.
- Select the entities, as shown. Press ESC.

- On the ribbon, click **Home > Modify > Offset**.

- Next, type-in 9 in the command line and press Enter.

- Select the right arc of the slot. Next, click inside the slot.

- Likewise, offset the other entities, as shown below.

- On the ribbon, click **Home > Modify > Stretch**.

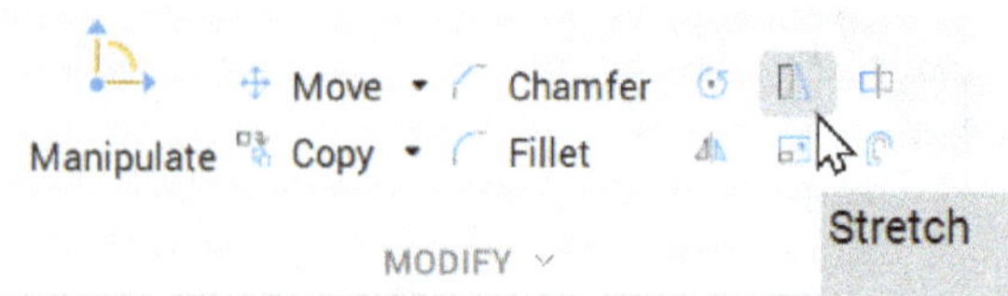

- Click and drag a selection window from the midpoint of the inner slot. Next, release the pointer outside the left arc of the inner slot.

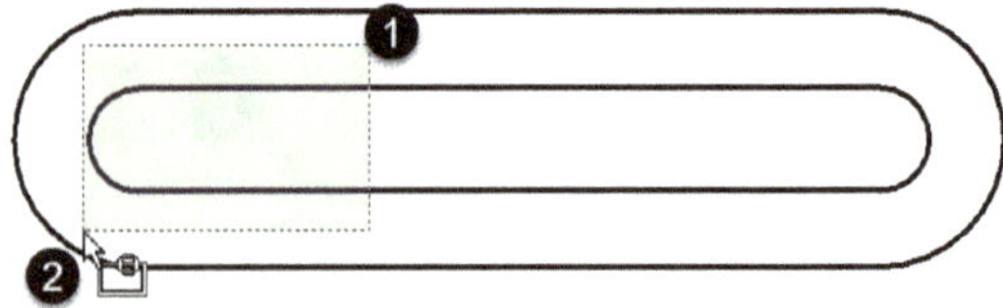

- Press ENTER. Next, place the pointer of the left arc, and then select its center point.

- Click the **Ortho** icon on the Status bar.
- Move the pointer horizontally toward right. Type 50 and press ENTER.

- On the **Home** ribbon tab, click **Draw** panel > **Infinite Line** tool.
- Select the **Vertical** option from the command line.
- Select the centerpoint of the right arc of the slot.

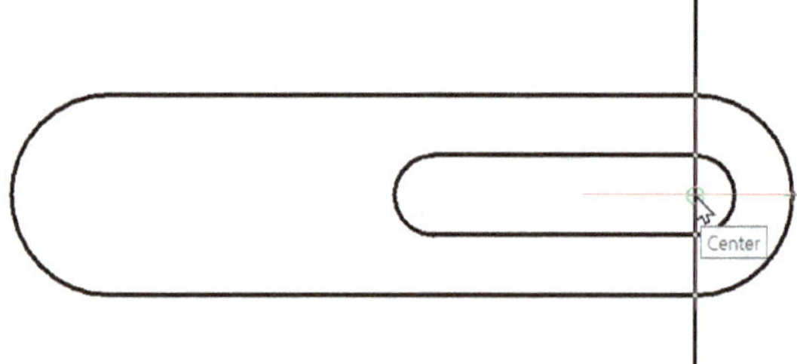

- Press ENTER twice.
- Select the **Parallel** option from the command line.
- Type 85 as the offset distance. Next, press ENTER.
- Select the newly created infinite line. Next, move the pointer toward the left and click.

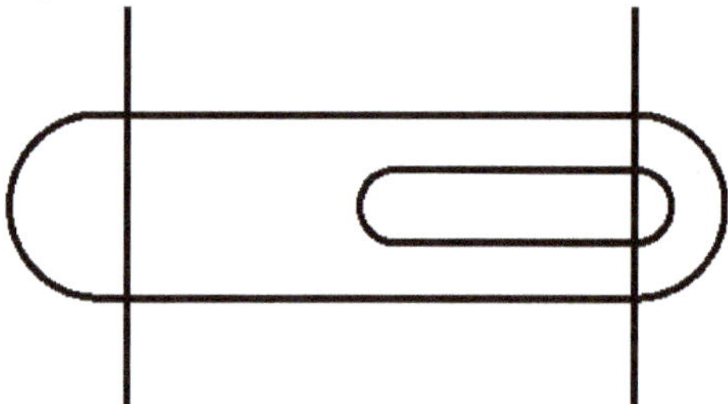

- Press ENTER twice.
- Select the **Parallel** option from the command line.
- Type 25 as the offset distance. Next, press ENTER.
- Select the lower horizontal line of the outer slot. Next, move the pointer downward and click.

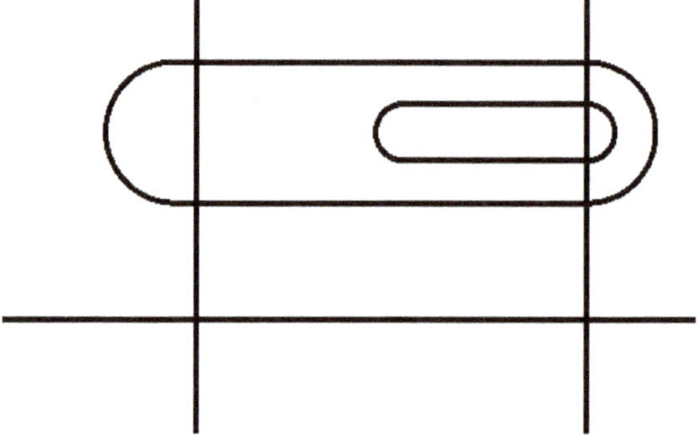

- Click **Circle** drop-down > **Circle Center-Radius** on the **Draw** panel on the **Home** ribbon tab.

- Select the intersection point of the vertical and horizontal infinite line. Next, type 30, and press ENTER.
- Press ENTER and select the intersection point of the vertical and horizontal infinite lines.
- Type 10 and press ENTER.

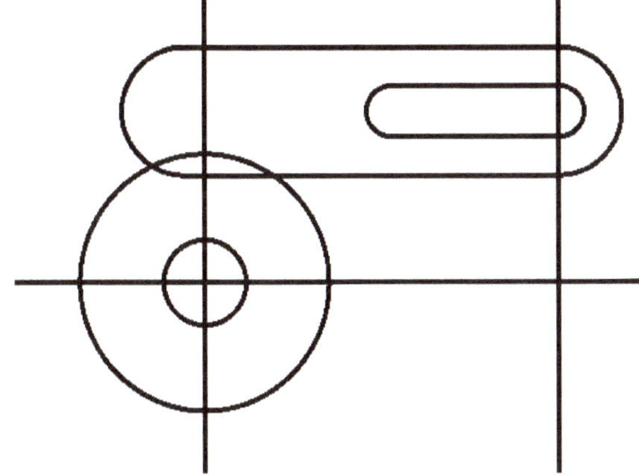

- Select all the infinite lines and press DELETE.

- On the ribbon, click **Home > Draw > Circle** drop-down > **Circle Tangent-Tangent-Radius**.

- Select the horizontal line and the circle, as shown.

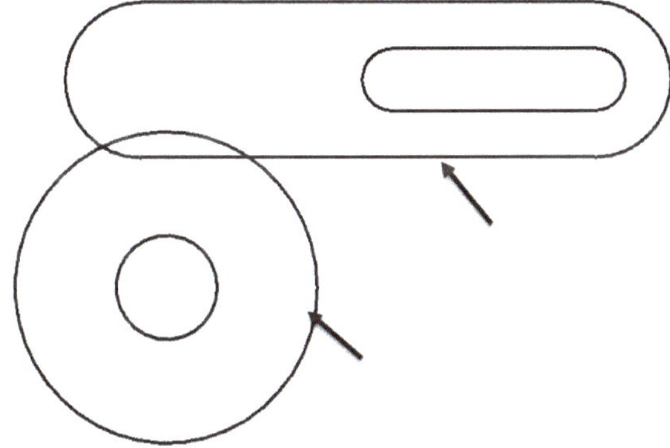

- Type 50 and press ENTER.

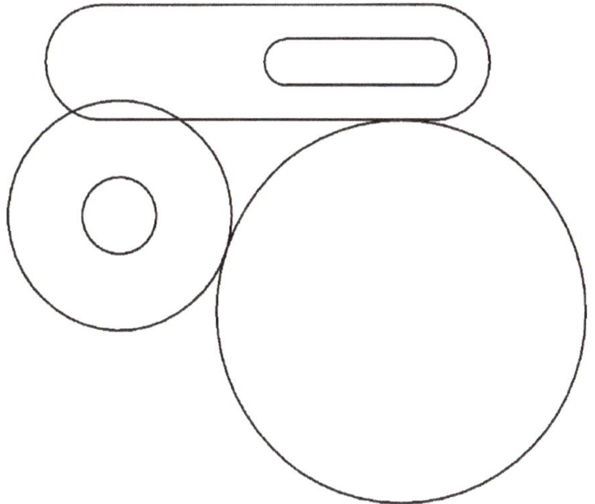

- Click the **Line** icon on the **Draw** panel.
- Press and hold the SHIFT key, right-click and select **Snap to Tangent**.

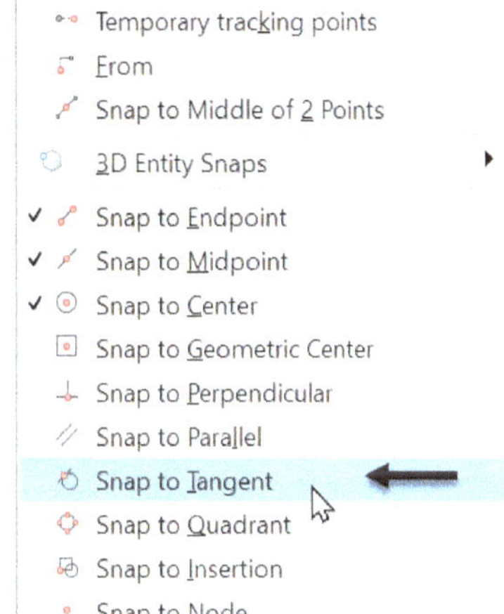

- Select the left arc of the large slot.

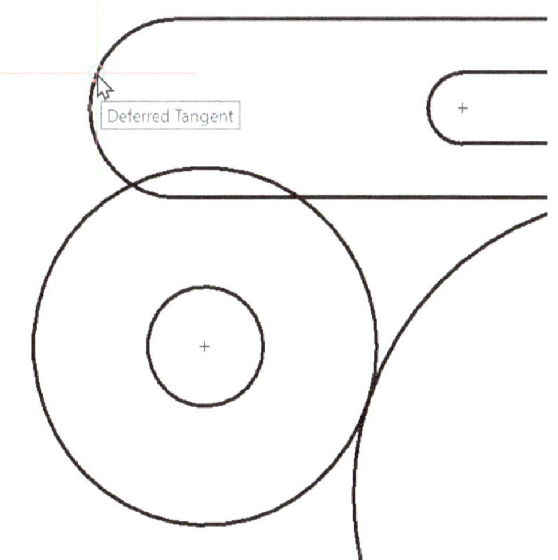

- Press and hold the SHIFT key, right-click and select **Snap to Tangent**.
- Next, click on the left side of the large circle.

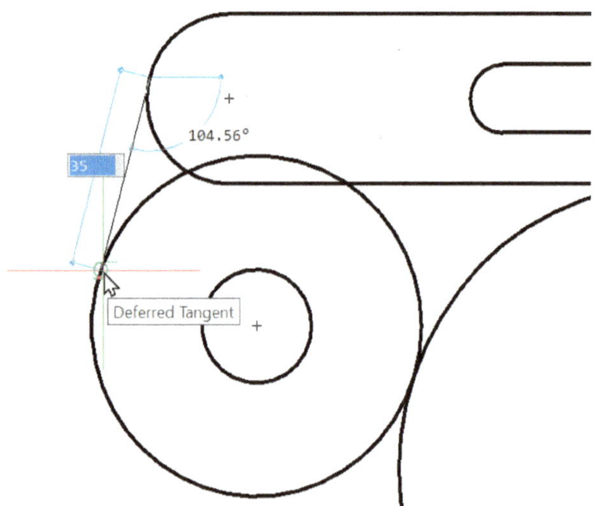

- Press ESC.
- Trim the unwanted portions, as shown.

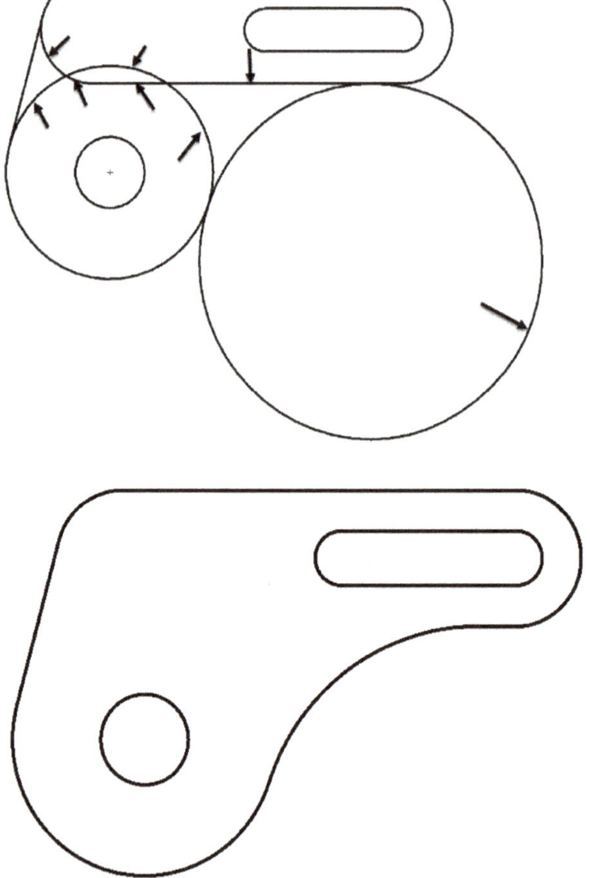

- Save and close the drawing file.

Tutorial 10

In this example, you will learn to create drawing shown in figure.

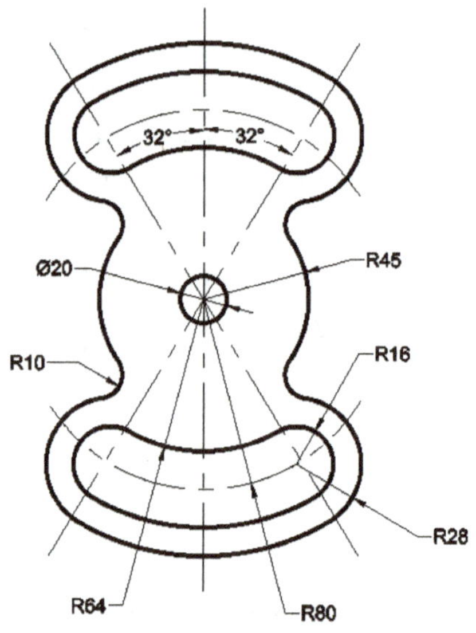

- Double-click on the **BricsCAD V24(x64) en_US** icon on your desktop.
- Click the **Start** button in the **2D Drafting** section on the **BricsCAD Launcher** pop up window.
- Click **Start from Template > Default-mm**; a new document is created.
- On the **Home** ribbon tab, click **Draw** panel > **Infinite Line** tool.
- Right click and select the **Angle** option from the shortcut menu.
- Type **120** and press ENTER. Next, click in the graphics window to place the infinite line.
- Press ENTER twice. Next, type **A** in the command line and press ENTER.
- Type 60 and press ENTER. Next, click in the graphics window.

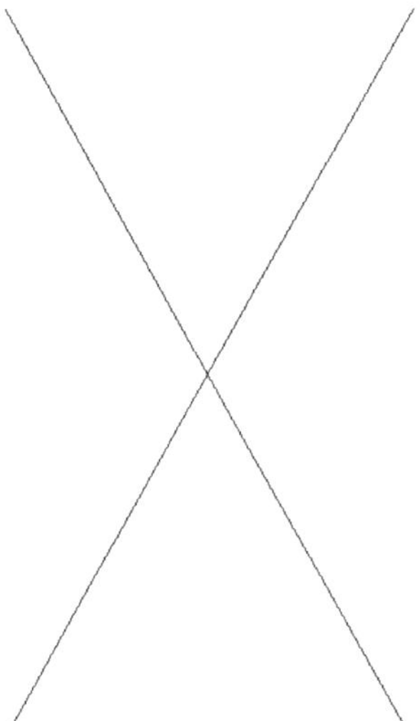

- On the ribbon, click **Home** tab > **Draw** panel > **Circle** drop-down > **Circle Center-Diameter**.

- Select the intersection point of the two infinite lines. Next, type 20, and press ENTER.

- Likewise, create six more circles, as shown.

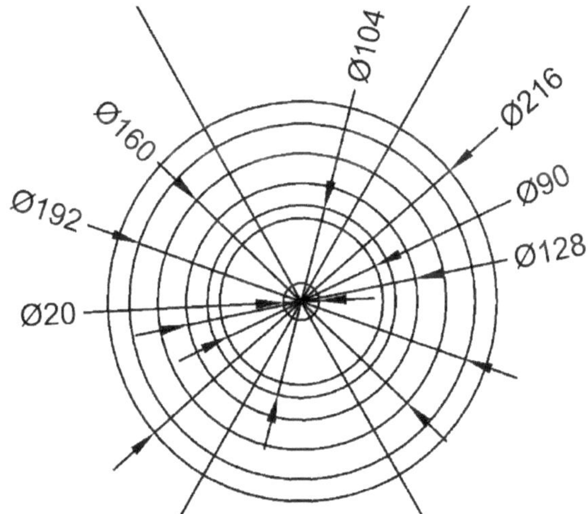

- Click **Home** tab > **Modify** panel > **Trim** on the ribbon.

- Press ENTER.

- Drag a selection window across the portions of the circles, as shown. Press ESC.

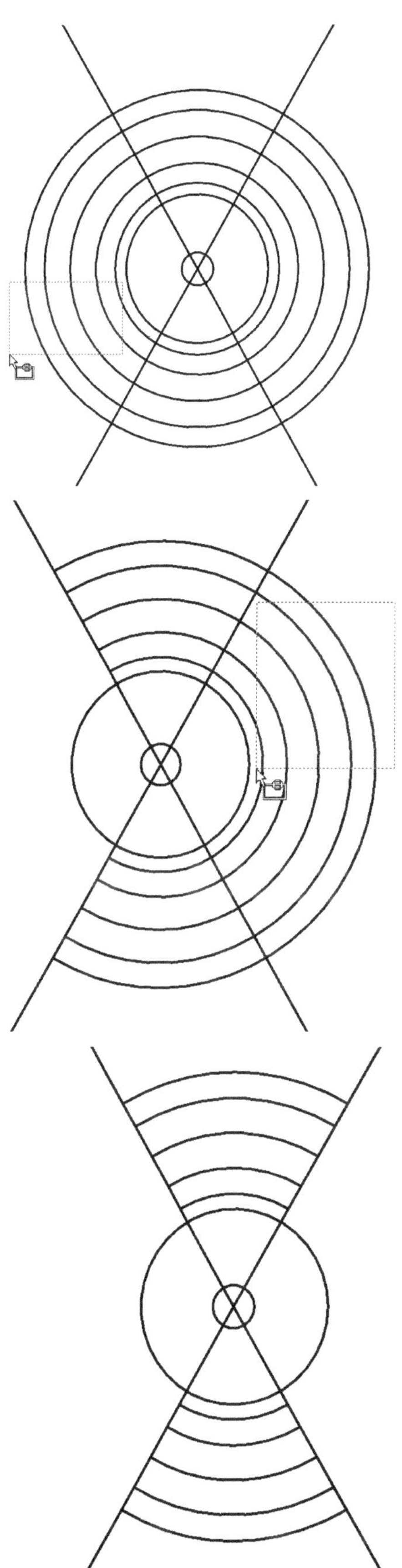

- On the ribbon, click **Home > Draw > Arc drop-down > Arc Start-Center-End**.

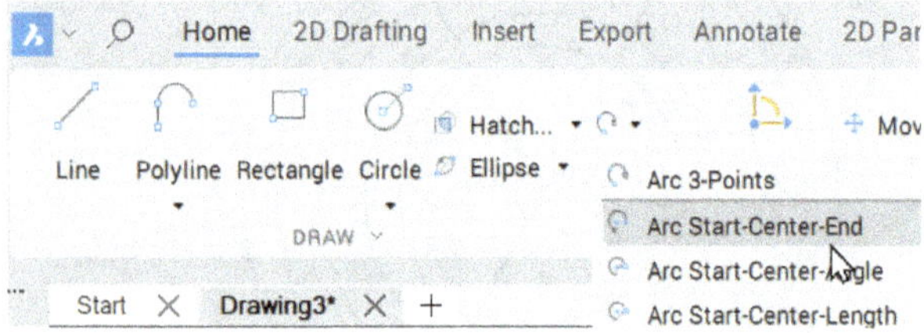

- Specify the start, center, and end points of the arc.

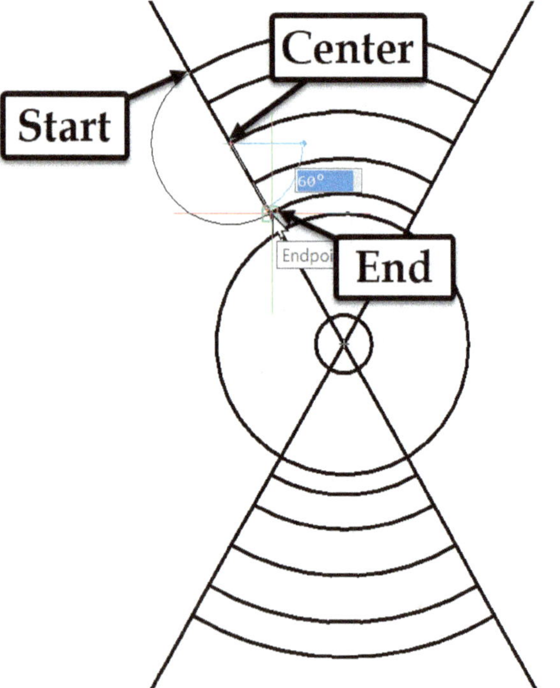

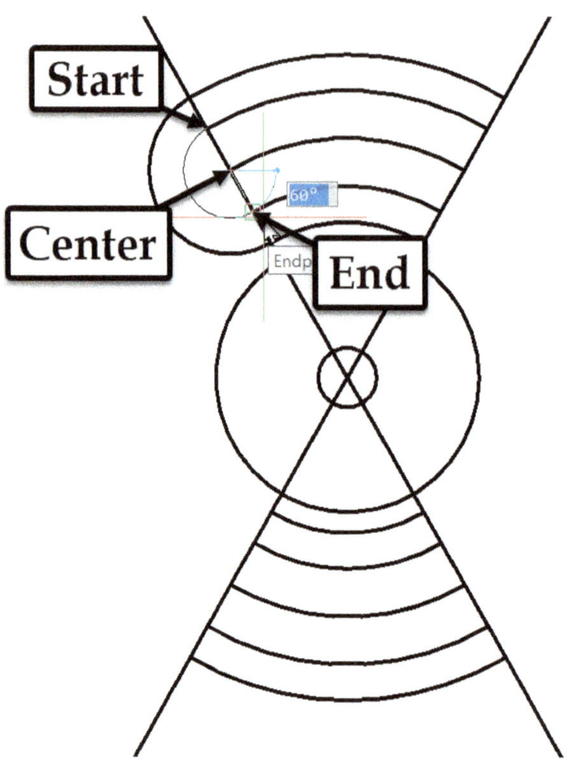

- Likewise, create another arc using the **Arc Start-Center-End** command.

- On the ribbon, click **Home > Modify > Mirror**, and then select the two newly created arcs. Press Enter to accept the selection.

- Click the **Ortho** icon on the Status bar.

- Select the center point of the circle located at the center. Next, move the pointer upward and click.

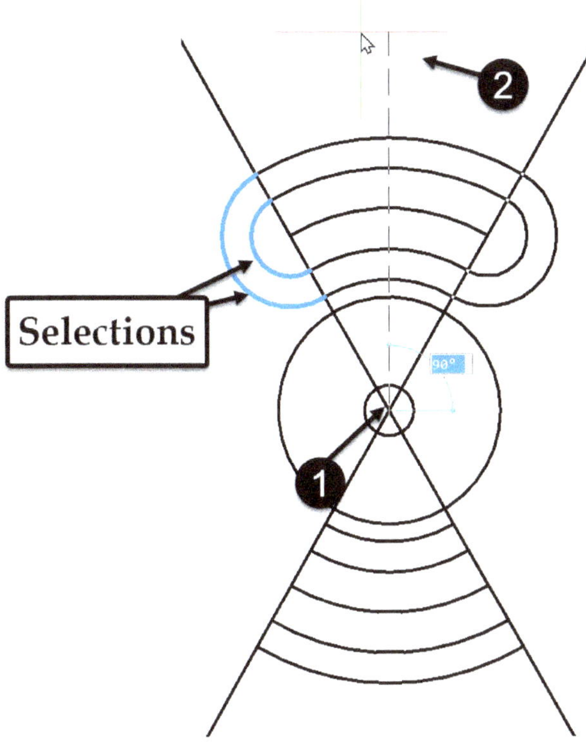

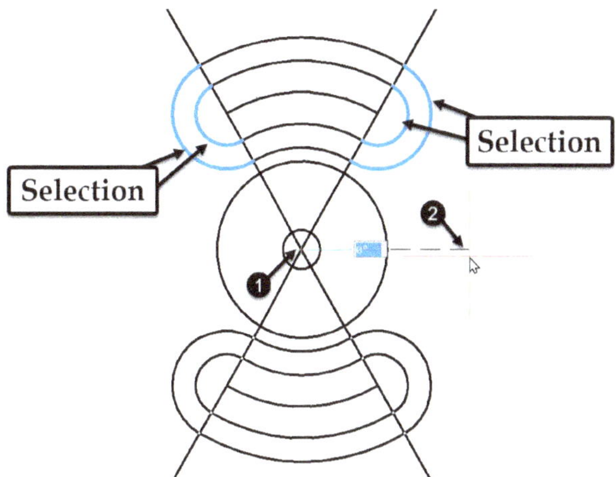

- Select **No-keep entities** to keep the original objects.

- On the ribbon, click **Home > Modify > Mirror**, and then select the two newly created arcs. Press Enter to accept the selection.

- Click the **Ortho** icon on the Status bar.

- Select the center point of the circle located at the center. Next, move the pointer toward right and click.

- Select **No-keep entities** to keep the original objects.

- On the ribbon, click **Home > Draw > Circle** drop-down > **Circle Tangent-Tangent-Radius**.

- Select the arc and the circle, as shown.

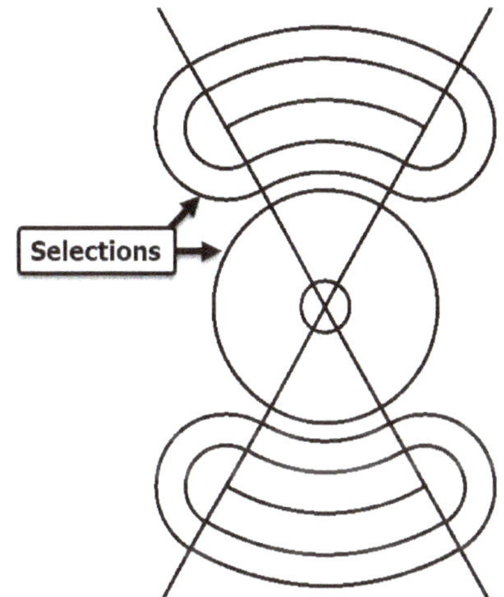

- Next, type 10 and press ENTER.

- Likewise, create three more circles using the **Circle**

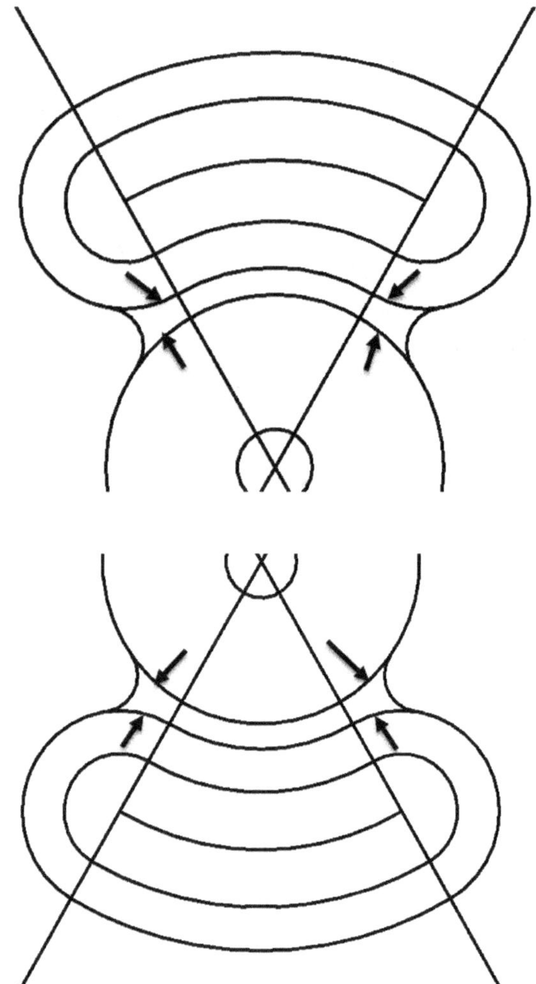

- Click **Home** tab > **Modify** panel > **Trim** on the ribbon.
- Press ENTER.
- Select the entities, as shown below. Press ESC.

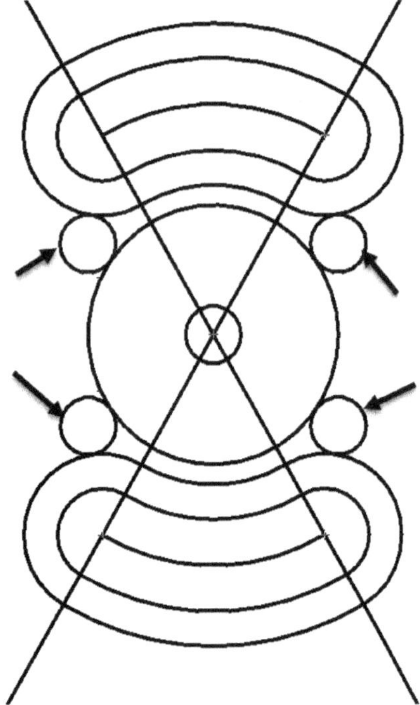

- Press ESC and select the entities of the drawing, as shown. Next, press DELETE.

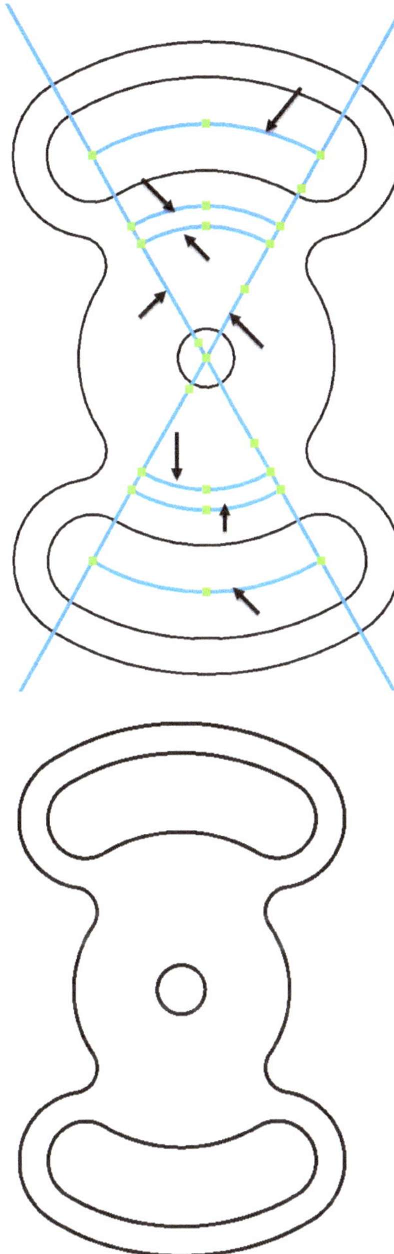

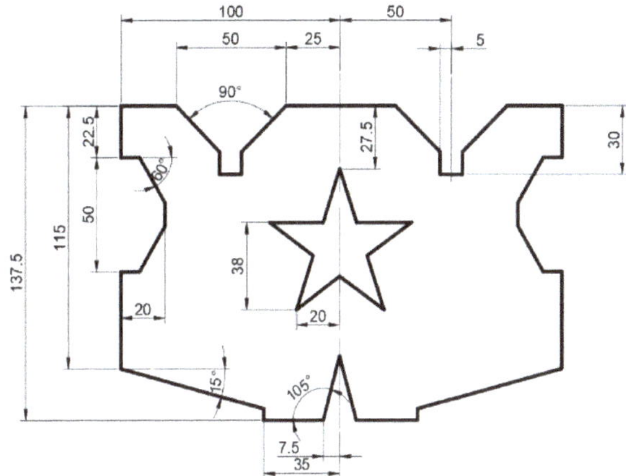

- Save and close the drawing file.

Tutorial 11

In this example, you will create the drawing shown in the figure.

- Start a new drawing file.

- Activate the **Ortho** icon on the Status bar.

- On the **Draw** panel, click **Line**. Next, pick a point in the graphics area.

- Move the pointer toward the right and type 35 and press ENTER.

- Move the pointer upward. Type 22.5 and press ENTER.

- Move the pointer toward the right. Type 65 and press ENTER.

- Move the pointer upward. Type 42.5 and press ENTER.

- Move the pointer toward left. Type 20 and press ENTER.

- Move the pointer upward. Type 50 and press ENTER.

- Move the pointer toward the right. Type 20 and press ENTER.

- Move the pointer upward. Type 22.5 and press ENTER.

- Move the pointer toward left. Type 45 and press ENTER.

- Move the pointer downward. Type 30 and press ENTER.

- Move the pointer toward left. Type 10 and press ENTER.

- Move the pointer upward. Type 30 and press ENTER.

- Move the pointer toward left. Type 45 and press ENTER.

- Move the pointer downward and select the start point of the drawing.

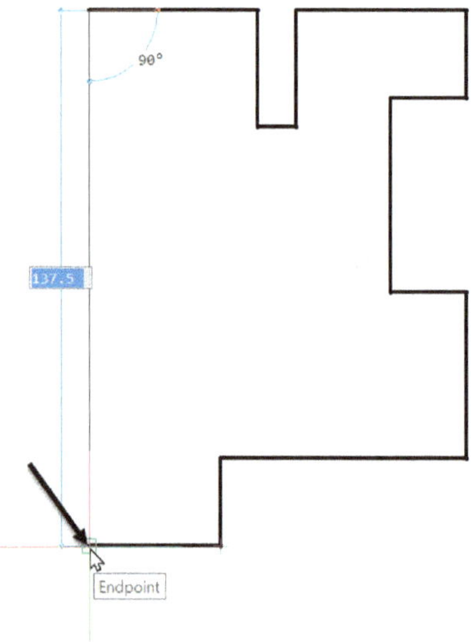

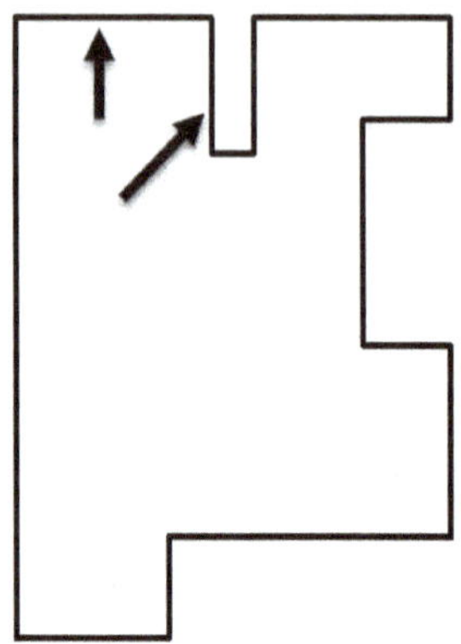

- Press ESC.

- On the ribbon, click **Home** tab > **Modify** panel > **Chamfer**.

- Select **Angle** from the command line.

- Type 20 and press ENTER.

- Type 45 and press ENTER.

- Select the vertical line on the right-side.

- Select the horizontal and vertical lines, as shown in the figure.

- Press ENTER to activate the **Chamfer** command. Next, select the horizontal and vertical lines, as shown.

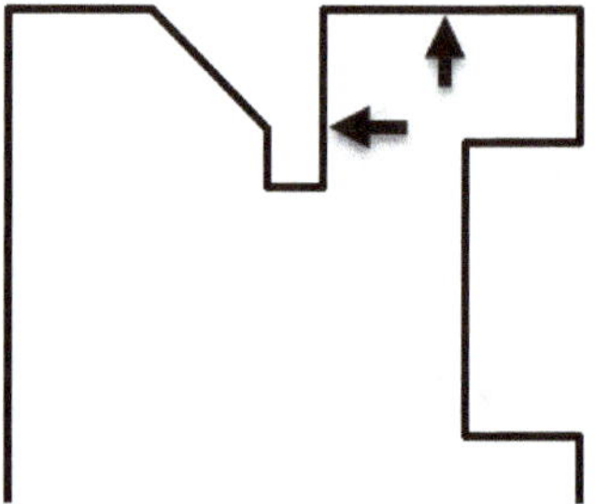

- Press ENTER to activate the **Chamfer** command.

- Select **Angle** from the command line.

- Type 20 and press ENTER.

- Type 30 and press ENTER.

- Select the vertical and horizontal lines, as shown in the figure.

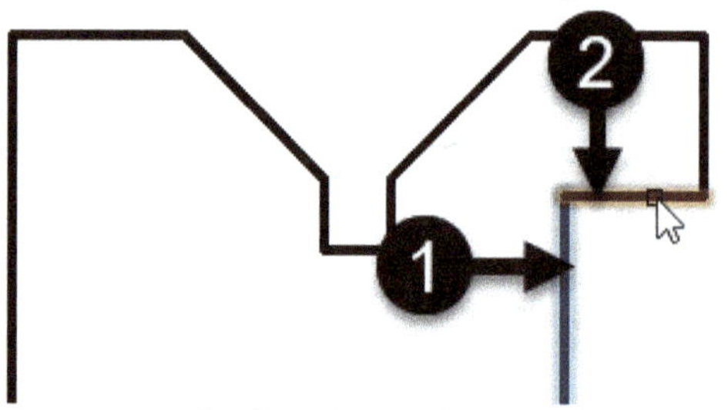

- Press ENTER and select the vertical and horizontal lines, as shown in the figure.

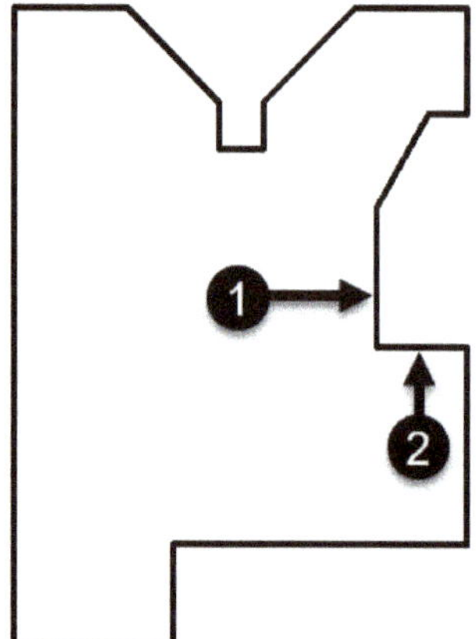

- Press ENTER to activate the **Chamfer** command.

- Select **Angle** from the command line.

- Type 65 and press ENTER.

- Type 15 and press ENTER.

- Select the horizontal and vertical lines, as shown in the figure.

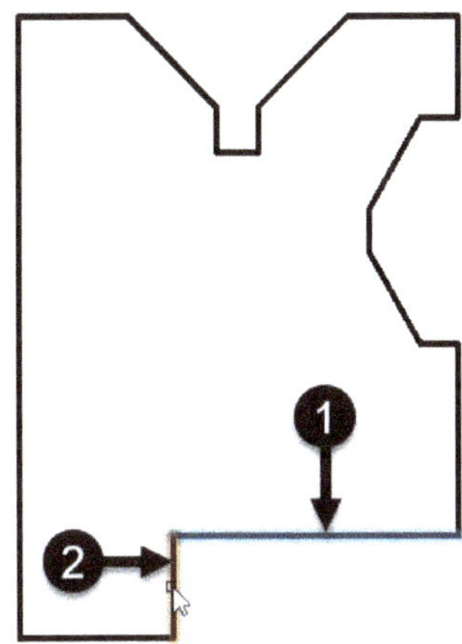

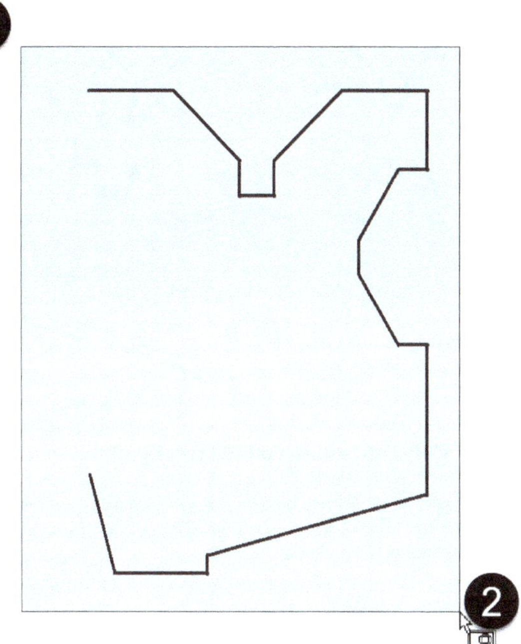

- Press ENTER to activate the **Chamfer** command.

- Select **Angle** from the command line.

- Type 7.5 and press ENTER.

- Type 75 and press ENTER.

- Select the horizontal and vertical lines, as shown in the figure.

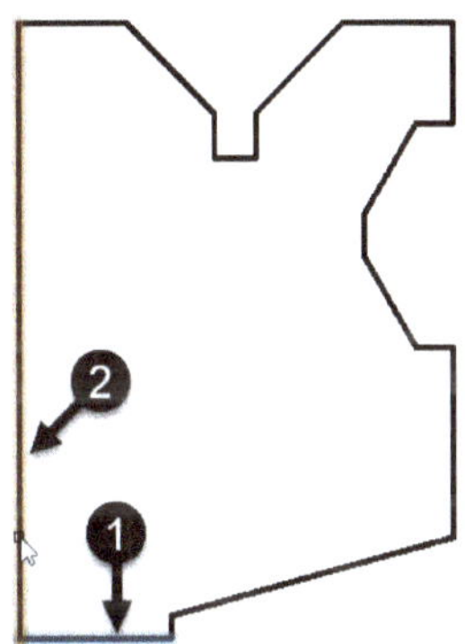

- Select the left vertical line and press **Delete**.

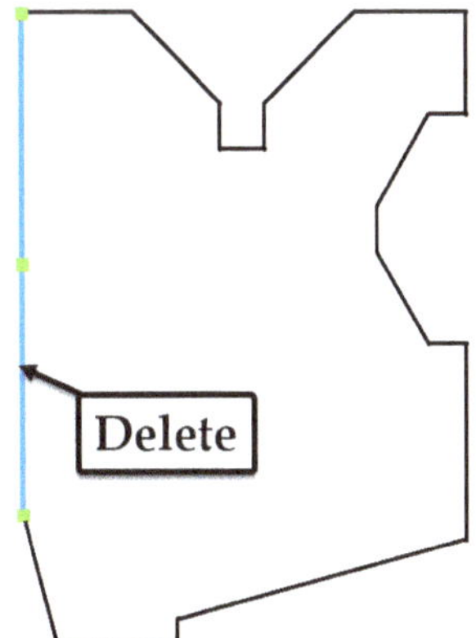

- Create a selection window across all the objects.

- Click **Mirror** on the **Modify** panel of the **Home** ribbon tab.

- Make sure that the **Ortho** mode is activated on the Status bar.

- Select the lower-left endpoint of the lines, as shown.

- Move the pointer upward and click to create the mirror line, as shown below.

- Select the points, as shown. The mirror line is defined.

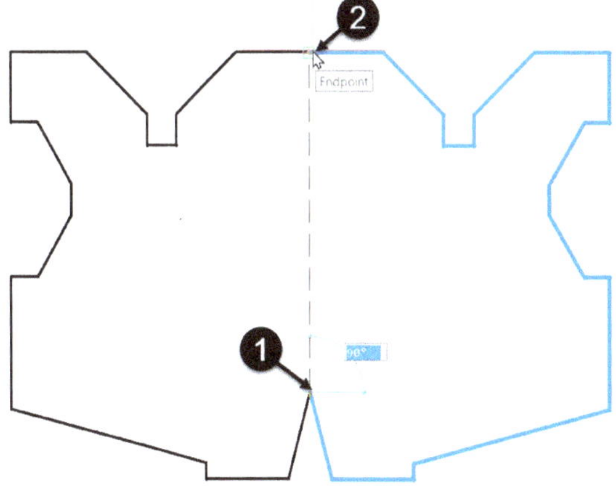

- Type N and press ENTER. The selected objects are mirrored about the mirror line.

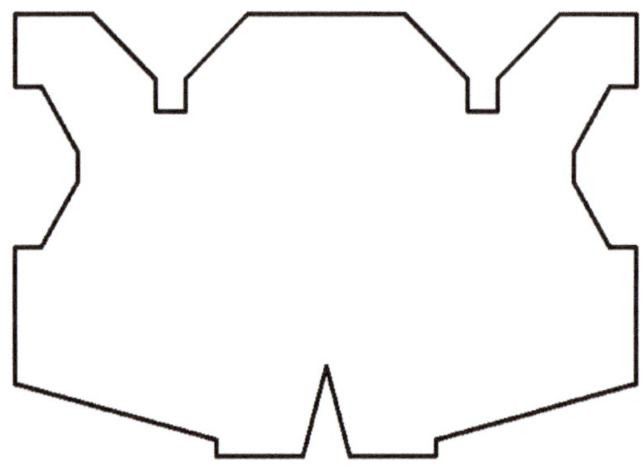

- Click **Polygon, Edge** on the **Draw** panel.

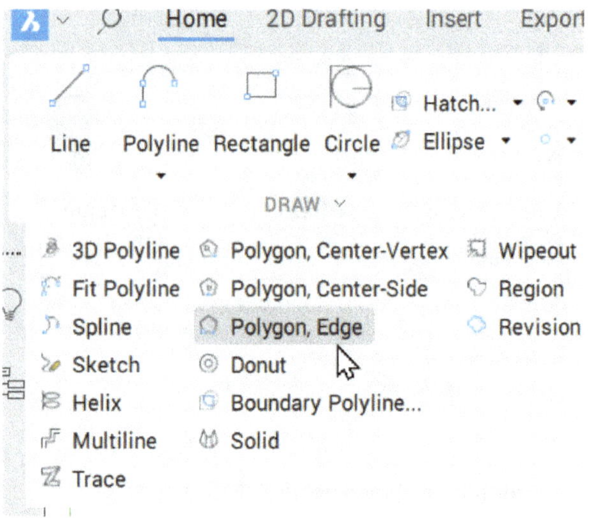

- Type **5** as the number of sides and press ENTER.
- Make sure that the **Ortho** button is activated on the Status bar.
- Click in the empty space. Next, move the pointer toward right. Type 40 and press ENTER.

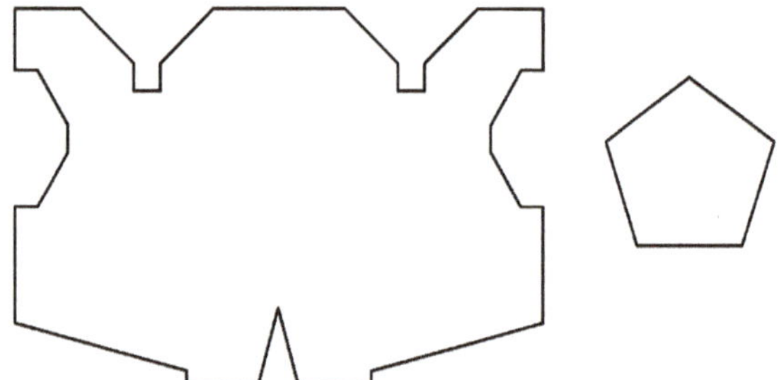

- Select the polygon and click the **Move** icon on the **Modify** panel of the **Home** ribbon tab.
- Select the vertex point of the polygon, as shown.

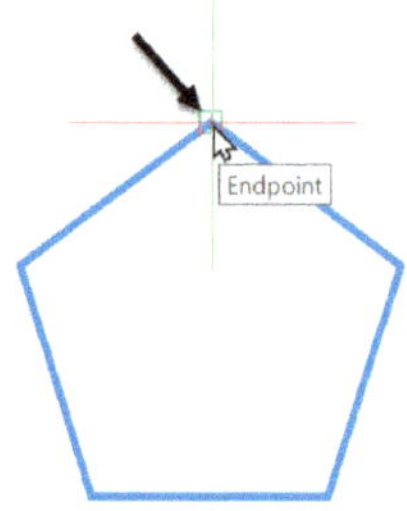

- Move the pointer and select the endpoint of the line, as shown.

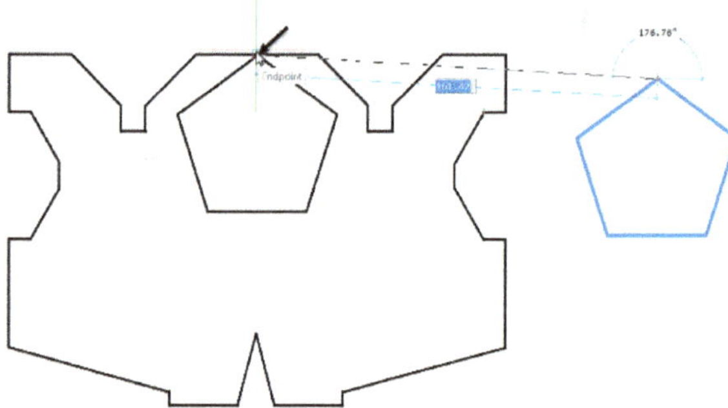

- Select the polygon and click the **Move** icon on the **Modify** panel of the **Home** ribbon tab.
- Select the vertex point of the polygon, as shown.

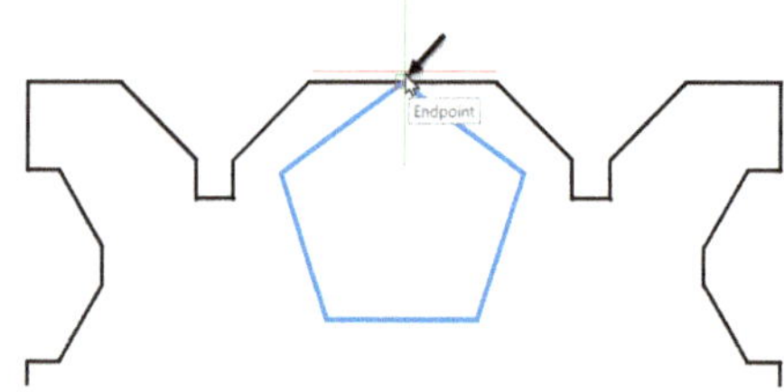

- Move the pointer downward. Next, type 27.5 and press ENTER.

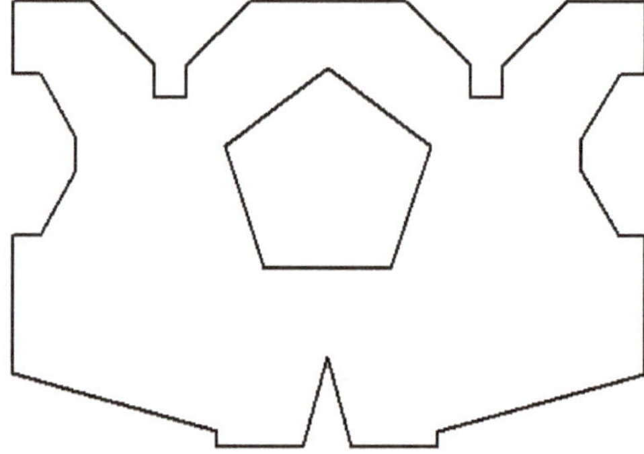

- Click **Line** on the **Draw** panel. Next, deactivate the **Ortho** mode on the status bar.
- Select the vertices of the polygon, as shown.

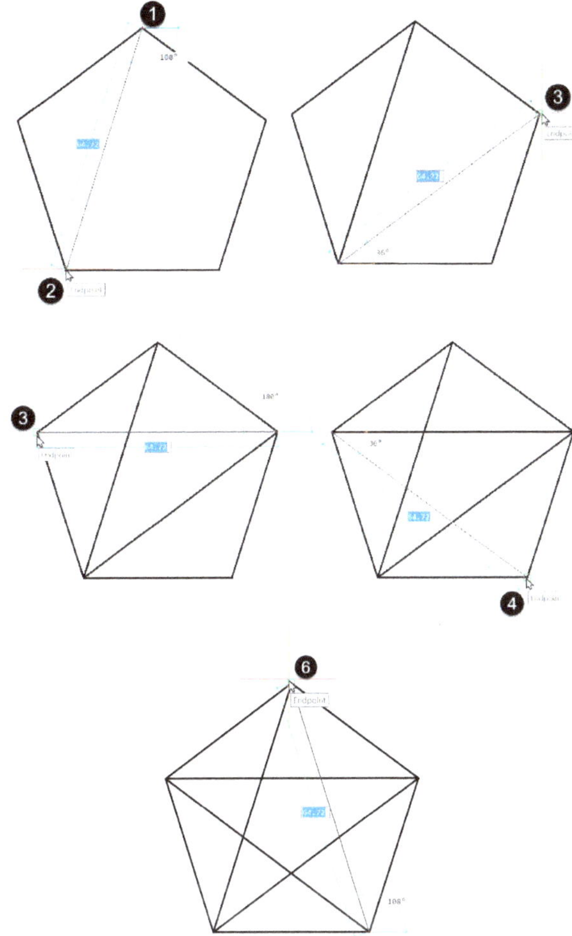

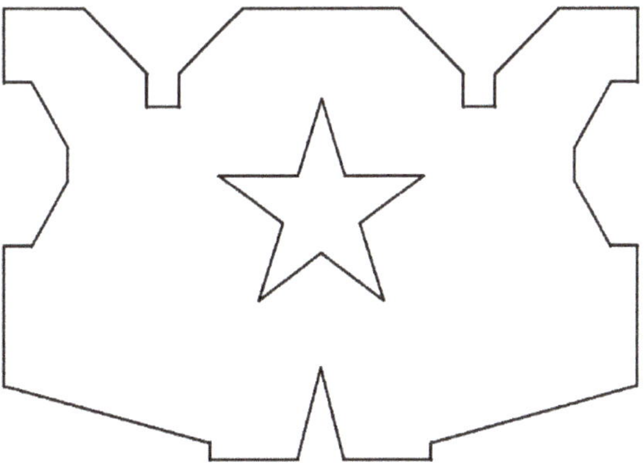

- Press ESC.
- Save and close the drawing file.

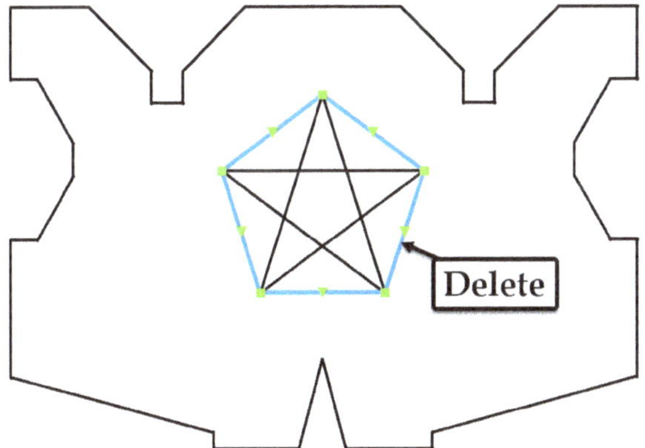

- Select the polygon and press Delete.

- Click **Trim** on the **Modify** panel. Next, press ENTER.
- Select the inner lines of the star, as shown.

Tutorial 12

In this example, you will create the drawing shown in the figure.

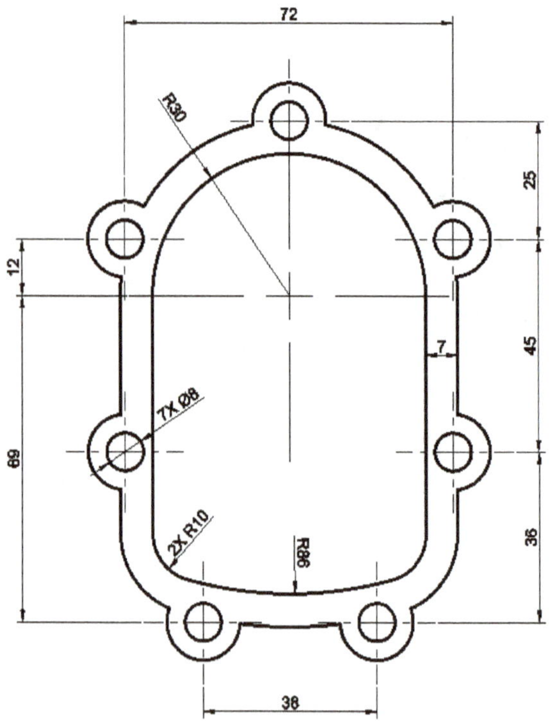

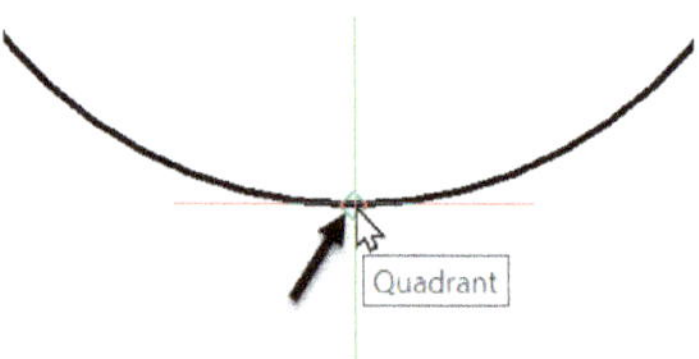

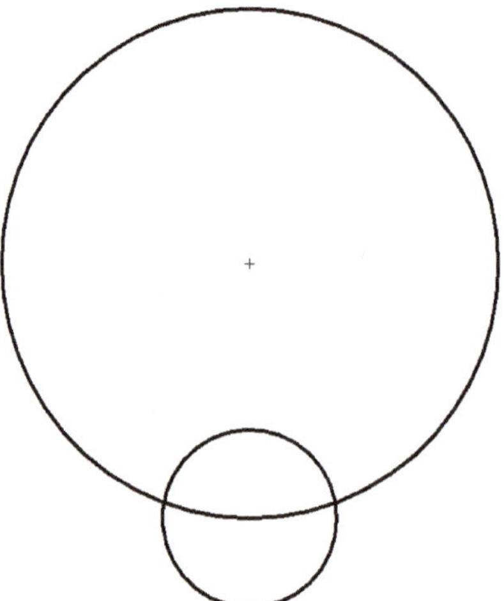

- Start a new drawing file.
- Activate the **Ortho** icon on the Status bar.
- Click the right-mouse button on the ESNAP button on the status bar, and then select **Quadrant**.
- Click **Circle** drop-down > **Circle Center-Radius** on the **Draw** panel on the **Home** ribbon tab. Next, pick a point in the graphics area.
- Type 86, and press ENTER.
- Press ENTER to activate the **Circle** command. Next, select the lower quadrant point of the existing circle.

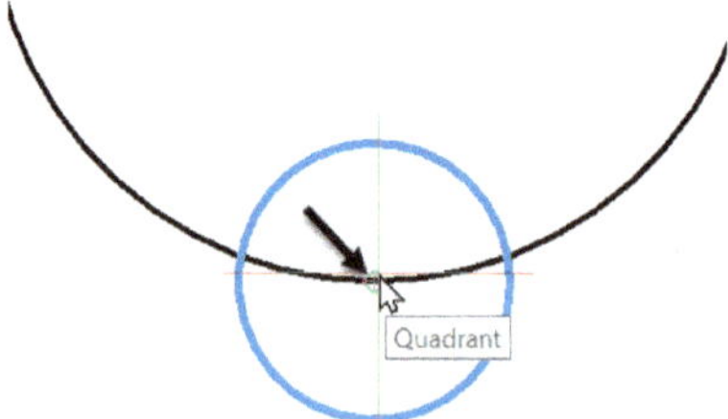

- Type 30 and press ENTER.

- Select the circle and click the **Move** icon on the **Modify** panel of the **Home** ribbon tab.
- Select the centerpoint of the small circle.

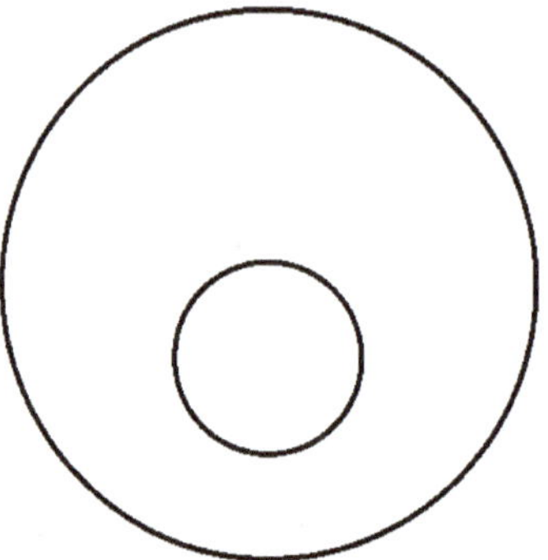

- Move the pointer upward, type 63 and press ENTER.

- On the **Draw** panel, click **Line**. Next, select the left quadrant point of the small circle.
- Move the pointer downward and click outside the large circle.

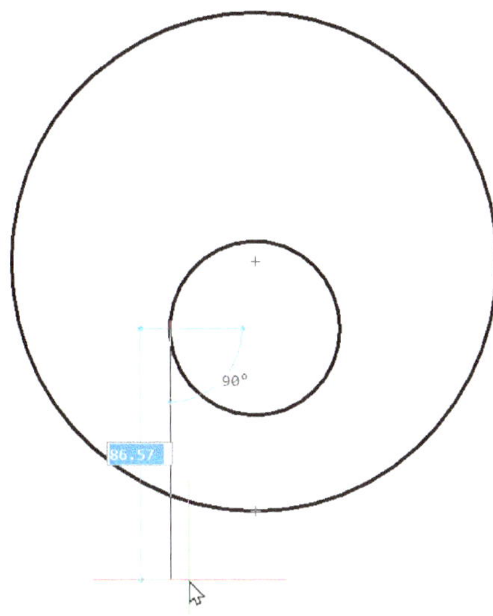

- Likewise, create another line, as shown.

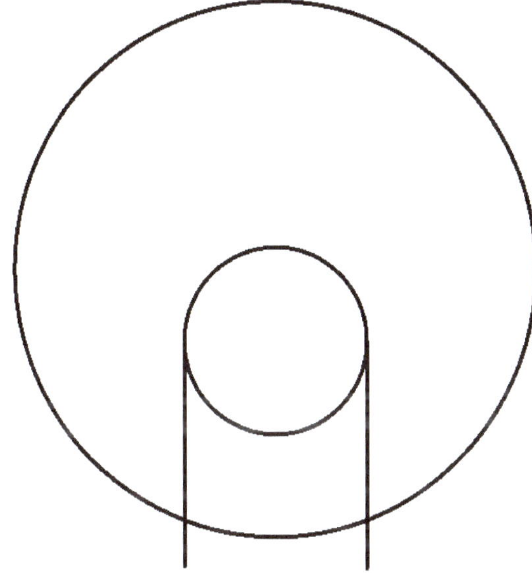

- Click **Home** tab > **Modify** panel > **Trim** on the ribbon.

- Press ENTER and select the entities, as shown below. Press ESC.

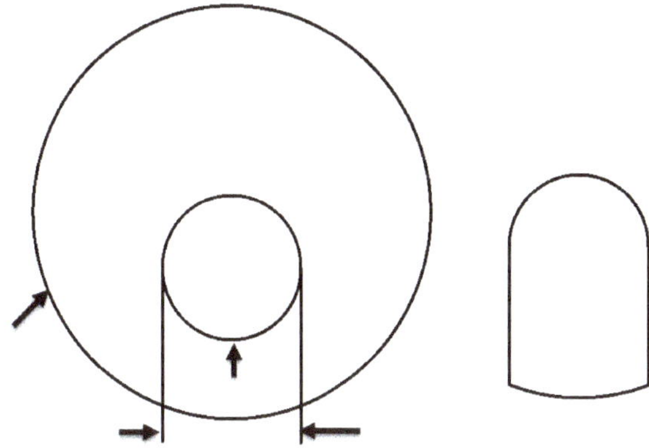

- On the ribbon, click **Home** > **Modify** > **Fillet**.

- Select the **Radius** option on the command line. Next, type in 10 — press Enter.

- Select the bottom arc and the left vertical line.

- Press ENTER and select the bottom arc and the right vertical line.

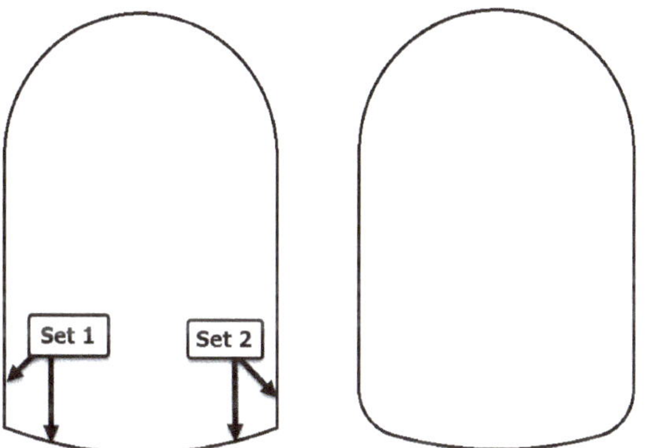

- On the ribbon, click **Home** > **Modify** > **Offset**. Next, type-in 7 in the command line and press Enter.

- Select the large arc. Click outside to create an offset arc.

- Likewise, offset the other entities, as shown below.

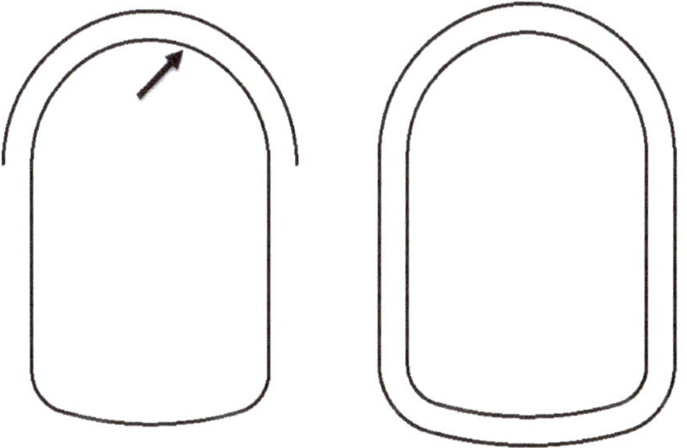

- Create two circles at the center point of the large arc. The diameters of the two circles are 16 mm and 8 mm, respectively.

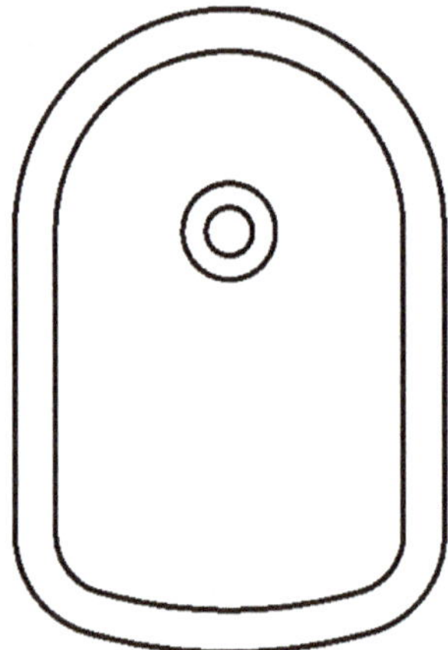

- Select the two newly created circles. Next, click the **Move** icon on the **Modify** panel.
- Select the centerpoint of the circles to define the base point.

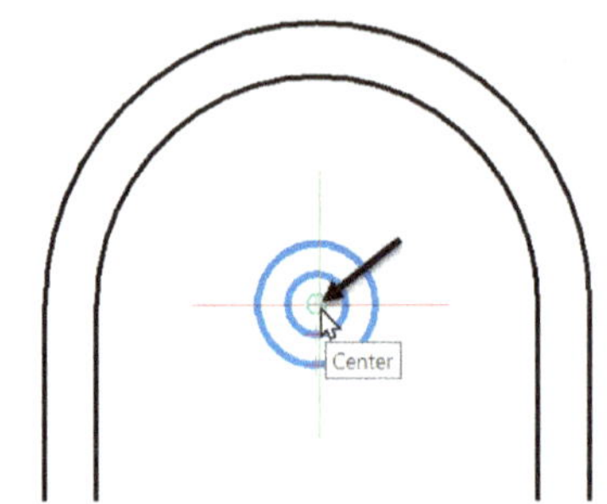

- Move the pointer toward the left and type 36 and press ENTER.

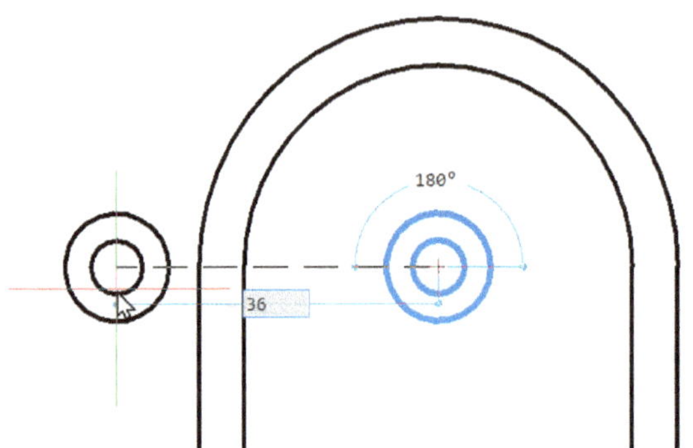

- Again, select the circles. Next, right-click and select **Move**.
- Select the centerpoint of the circles.
- Move the pointer upward. Type 12 and press ENTER.

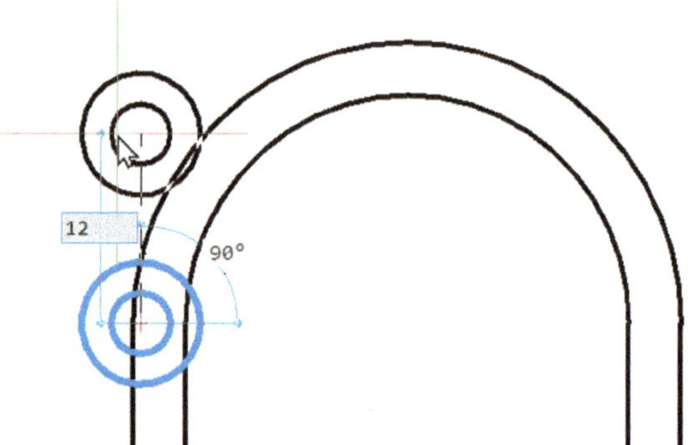

- Select the two newly created circles. Next, click **Copy** on the **Modify** panel of the **Home** tab of the ribbon.
- Select the centerpoint of the circles to define the base point.
- Select the top quadrant point of the arc, as shown.

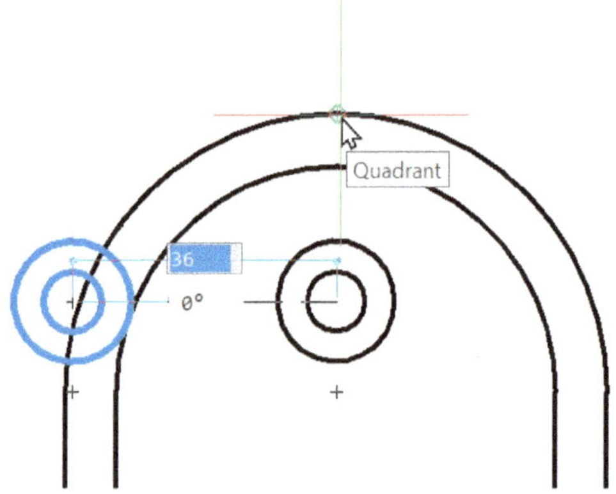

- Move the pointer downward, type 45 and press ENTER.

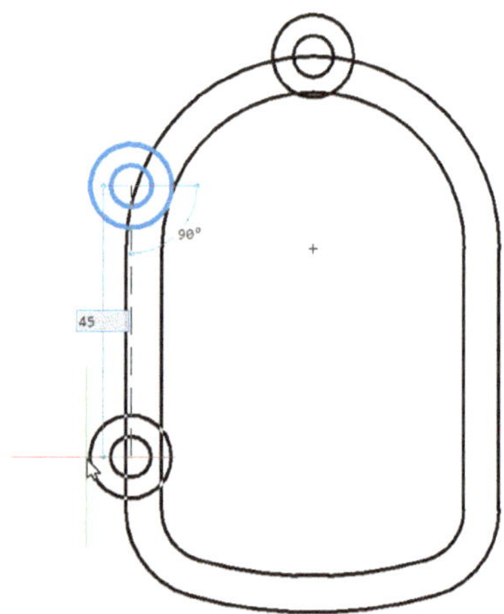

- Move the pointer downward, type 81 and press ENTER. Next, press ESC.

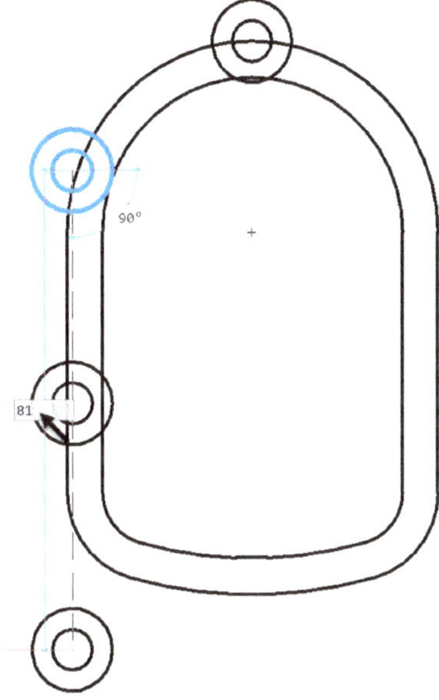

- Select the bottom circles. Next, click **Move** on the **Modify** panel of the **Home** tab of the ribbon.
- Select the centerpoint of the selected circles.

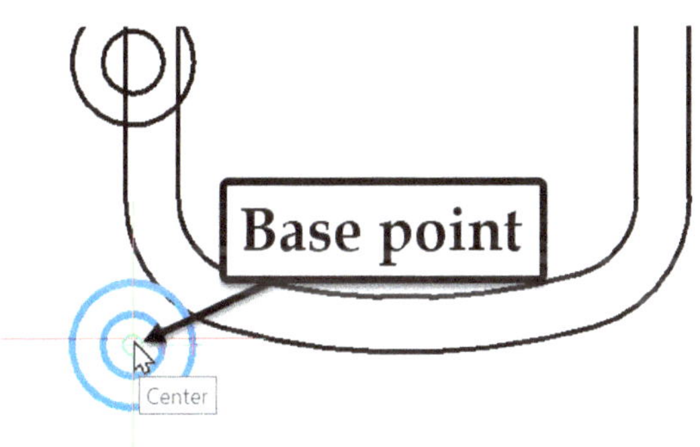

- Next, move the pointer toward right, type 17, and then press ENTER.

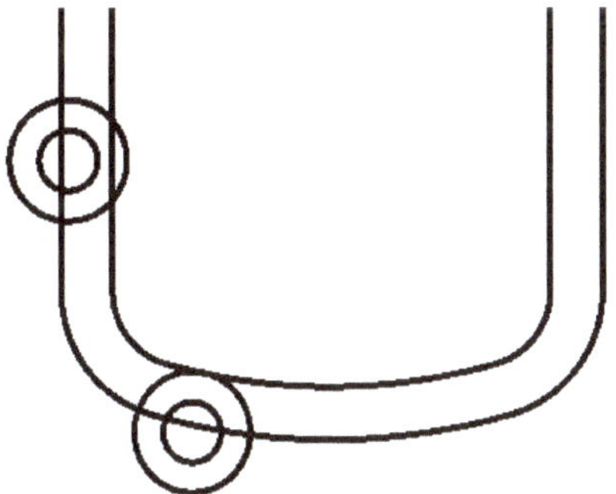

- On the ribbon, click **Home > Modify > Mirror**, and then select the circles, as shown. Press Enter to accept the selection.

- Define the mirror line by selecting the points, as shown below.

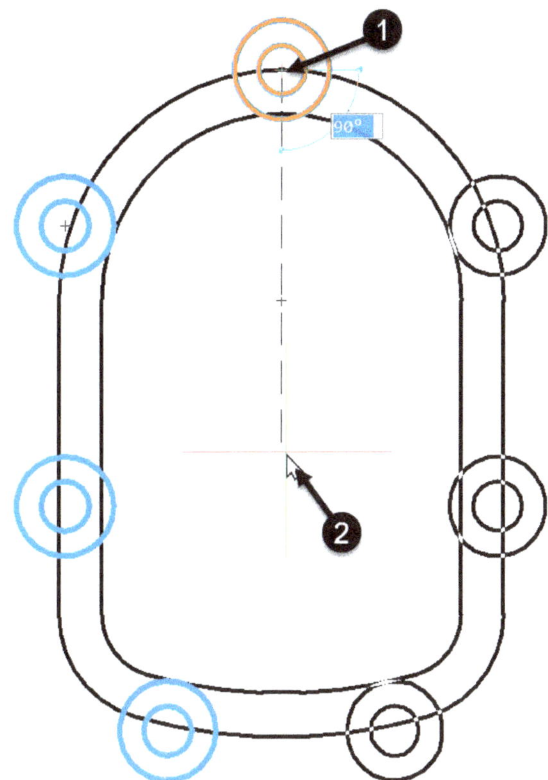

- Right-click and select **No-keep entities** to keep the original objects.

- Click **Trim** on the **Modify** panel. Next, select the outer loop of the drawing and press ENTER.

- Select the lower portions of the large circles, as shown.

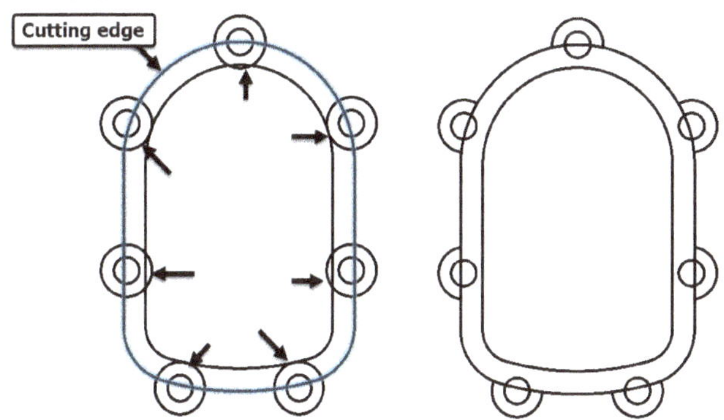

- Press ENTER twice and select the trimmed circles as the cutting edges, as shown.
- Select the portions of the arcs and lines to trim, as shown.

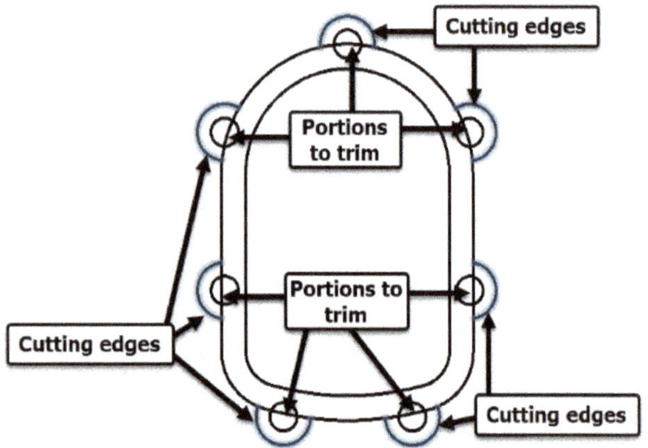

- Zoom to the bottom portion of the drawing and select the two untrimmed edges, as shown.

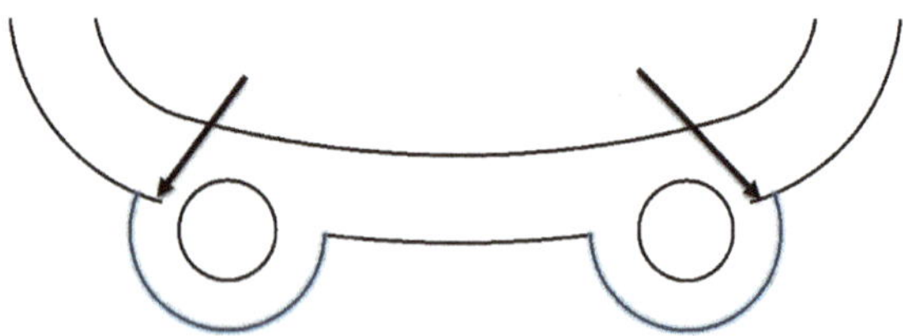

- Save and close the drawing file.

Tutorial 13

In this tutorial, you will draw the exhaust fan shown in figure.

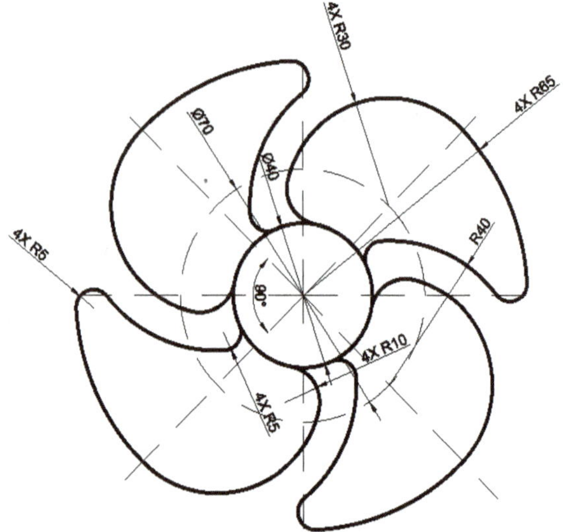

- Double-click on the **BricsCAD V24(x64) en_US** icon on your desktop.
- Click the **Start** button in the **2D Drafting** section on the **BricsCAD Launcher** pop up window.

- Click **Start from Template > Default-mm**; a new document is created.
- On the ribbon, click the **View** tab > **Views** panel > **Zoom** drop-down > **Zoom Extents**.
- Deactivate the **Grid** icon on the status bar.
- On the **Home** tab, click the **Layers** button on the **Layers** panel.
- On the **Layers** palette, click the **Add layer** button.
- Type **Dimension** in the **Name** box and press Enter.
- Click the **Lineweight** drop-down of the **Dimension** layer and select **0.25 mm**.
- Click the **Add layer** button and type **Construction** in the **Layer Name** box and press Enter.
- Select **0.15 mm** from the **Lineweight** drop-down of the **Construction** layer.
- Click the **Linetype** drop-down of the **Construction** layer and select the **Load** option; the **Load Linetypes** dialog appears.
- On the **Load Linetypes** dialog, select the **DASHED** option and click **OK.**
- Select **DASHED** on the **Load Linetypes** dialog and click **OK**.

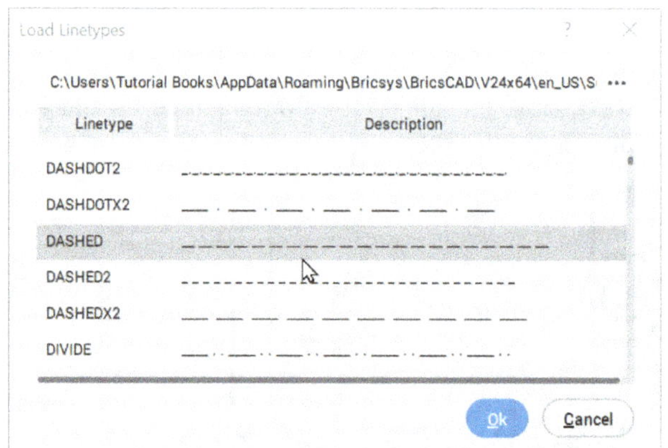

- Close the **Layers** Palette.
- On the ribbon, click **Home > Draw > Circle Center-Radius**. Click in the graphics window and move the pointer outwards.
- Type **20** and press Enter.

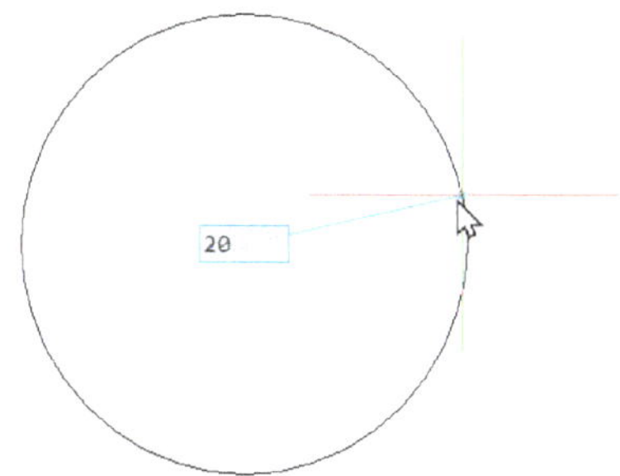

- Select the **Construction** layer from the **Layer Control** drop-down **Access** toolbar.
- Activate the **Circle** command.
- Select the center point of the previous circle.
- Move the pointer and type **35** and press Enter.

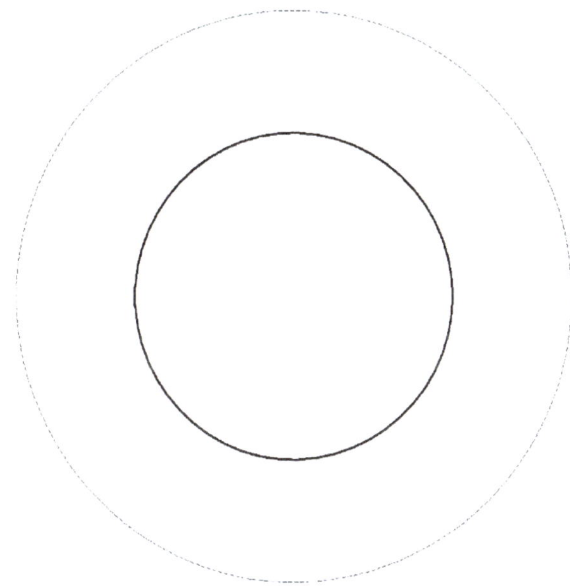

- On the ribbon, click **Home > Draw > Line**.
- Click on the center point of the circle and move the pointer upwards. Type 90 and press ENTER, as shown.

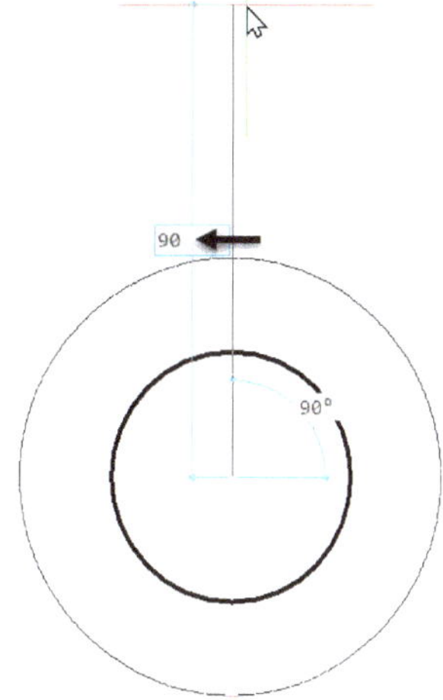

- Press Esc.
- On the ribbon, click **Home > Modify > Polar Array**.
- Select the vertical line and press Enter.
- Select the center point of the circle, as shown.

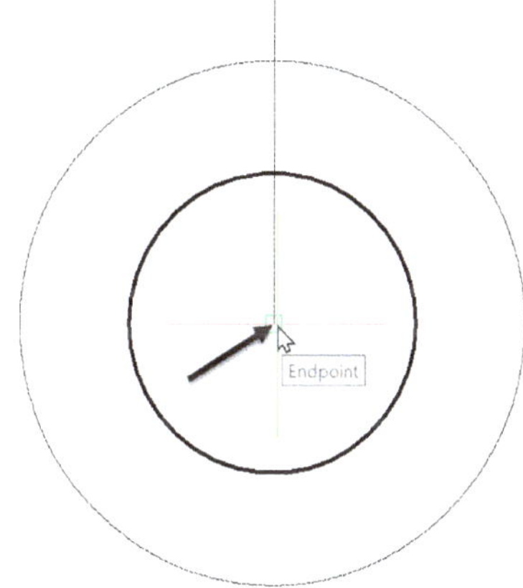

- Select the **Items** option from the command line.
- Type **8** in the command line.
- Select the **Angle between** option from the command line.
- Type **45** in the command line and press ENTER.
- Select the **ASsociative** option from the command line.
- Select the **No** option from the command line.
- Select the **eXit** option from the command line.

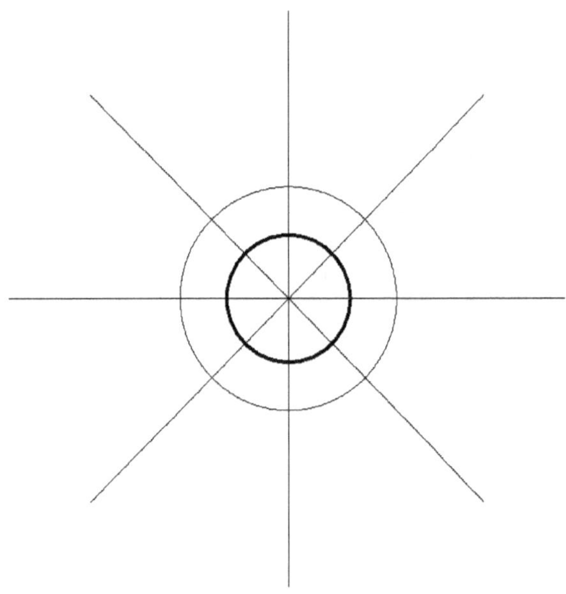

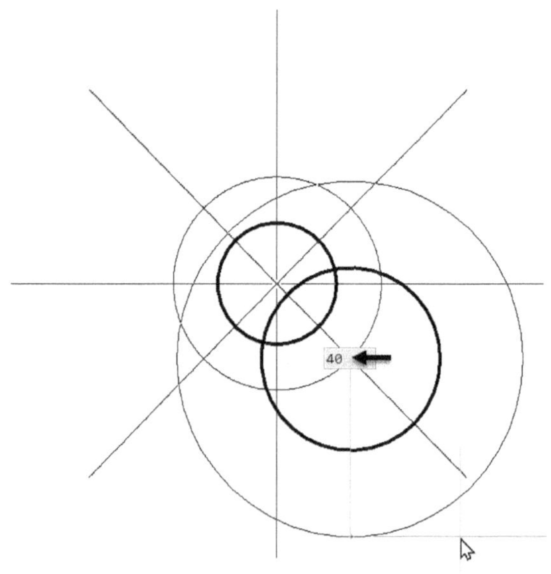

- On the **Layers** panel, select **0** from the **Layer Control** drop-down.
- Activate the **Circle** command.
- Click on the intersection point of the large circle and the inclined line at the lower right corner, as shown.

- On the ribbon, click **Home > Modify > Trim**.
- Select the inner circle and the inclined line, and then press ENTER.
- Select the unwanted portions, as shown.

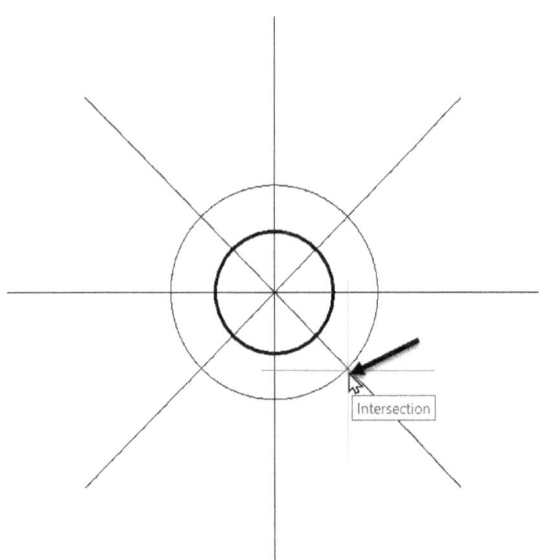

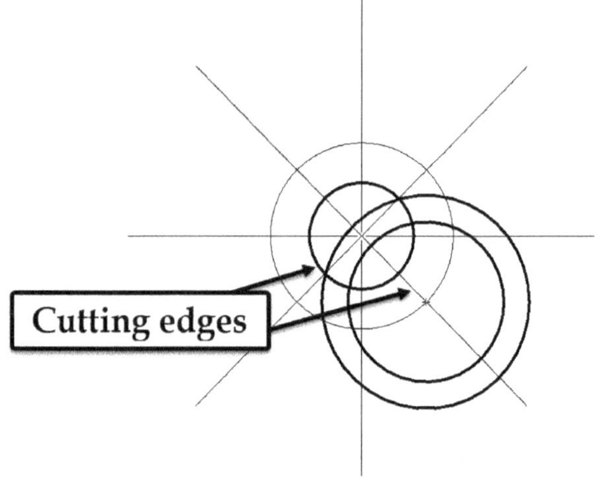

- Move the pointer and type **30**. Press Enter.
- Likewise, create another circle of radius **40** at the same intersection point, as shown.

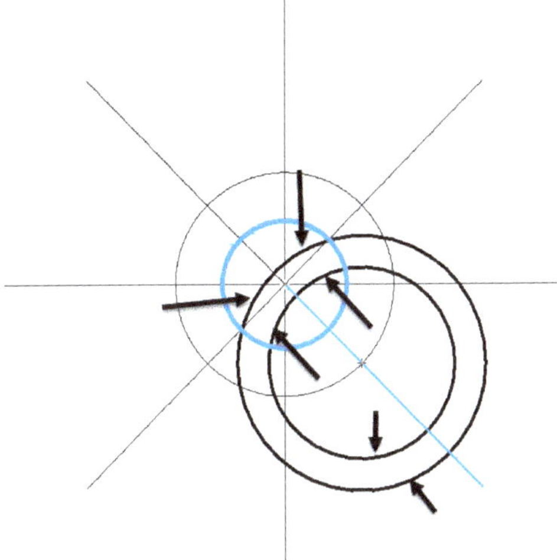

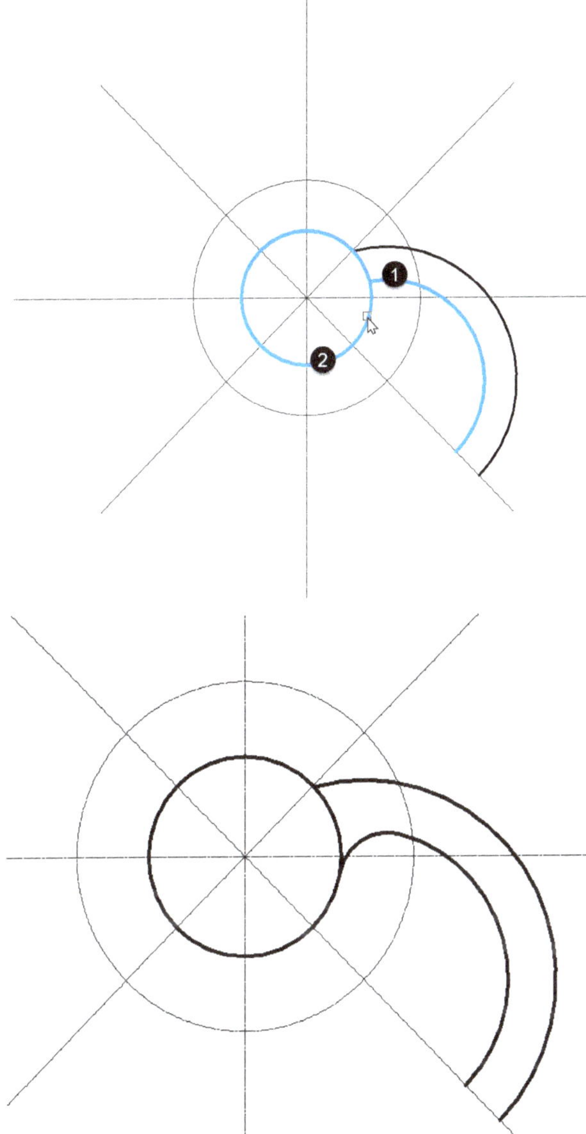

- Press Esc.

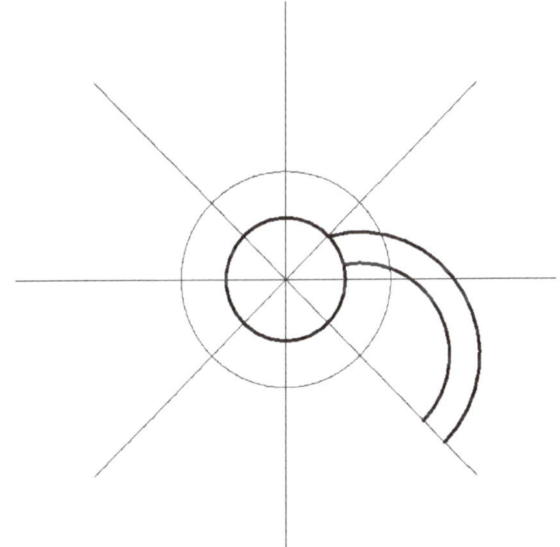

- Click the **Fillet** command on the **Home** tab of the **Modify** panel. Next, select **Radius** from the command line.

- Type-in **10** and press Enter.

- Select the small arc and select the small circle, as shown.

- Click **Home >Modify > Polar Array** on the ribbon.

- Select the arcs and fillet, as shown. Press Enter.

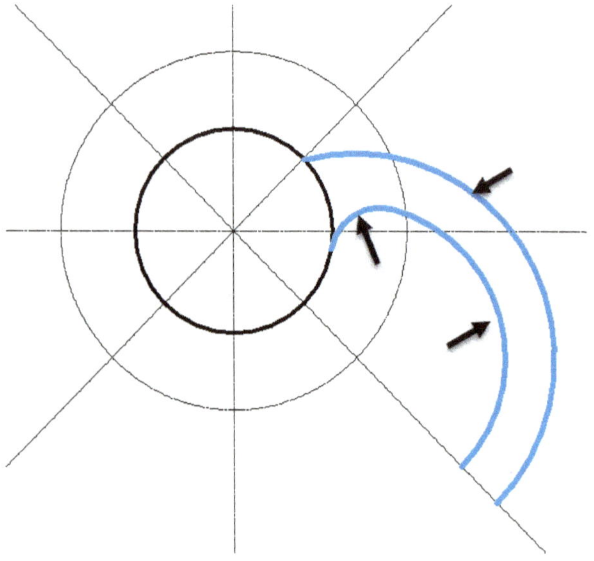

- Select the center point of the circle, as shown.

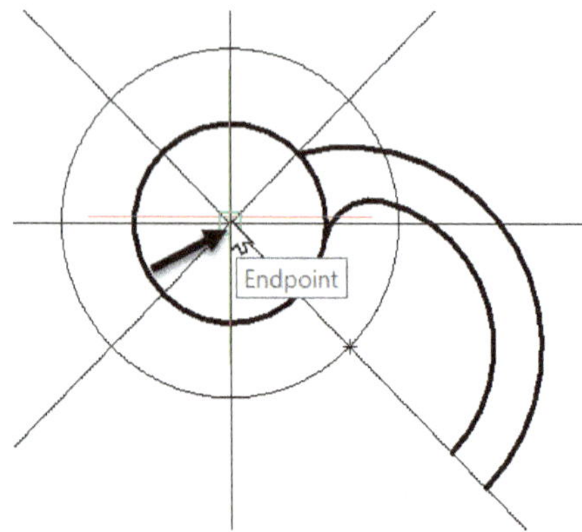

- Select the Items option from the command line.
- Type **4** in the command line and press ENTER.
- Select the **ASsociative** option from the command line.
- Select the **No** option.
- Select the **eXit** option.

- On the **Home** tab, click the **Circle Center-Radius** command on the **Draw** panel.
- Click on the center point of the circle and move the pointer outwards.
- Type **65** in the **Radius** box and press Enter.

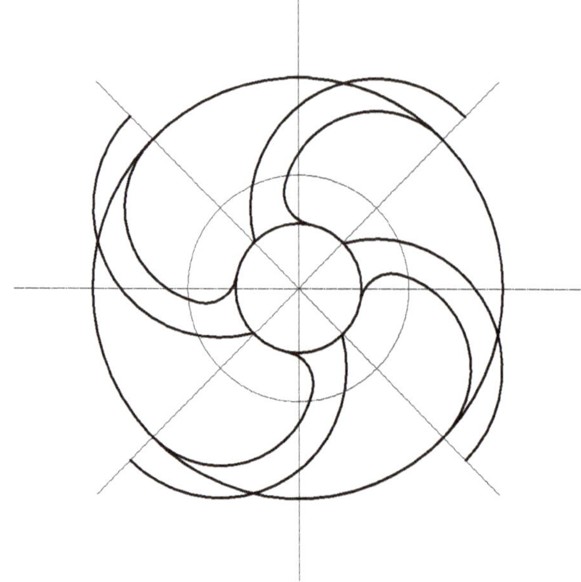

- Click **Home > Modify > Trim** on the ribbon. Press Enter.
- Trim the unwanted portions, as shown.

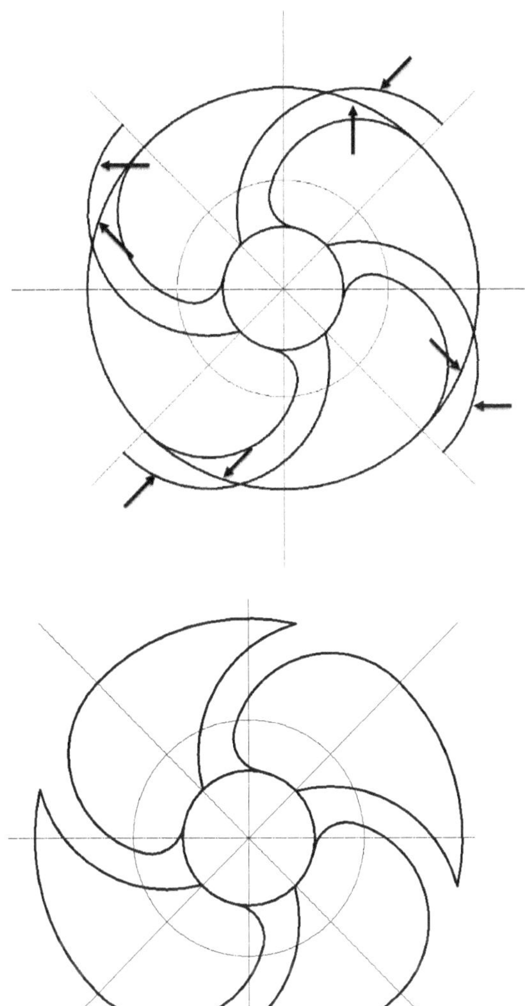

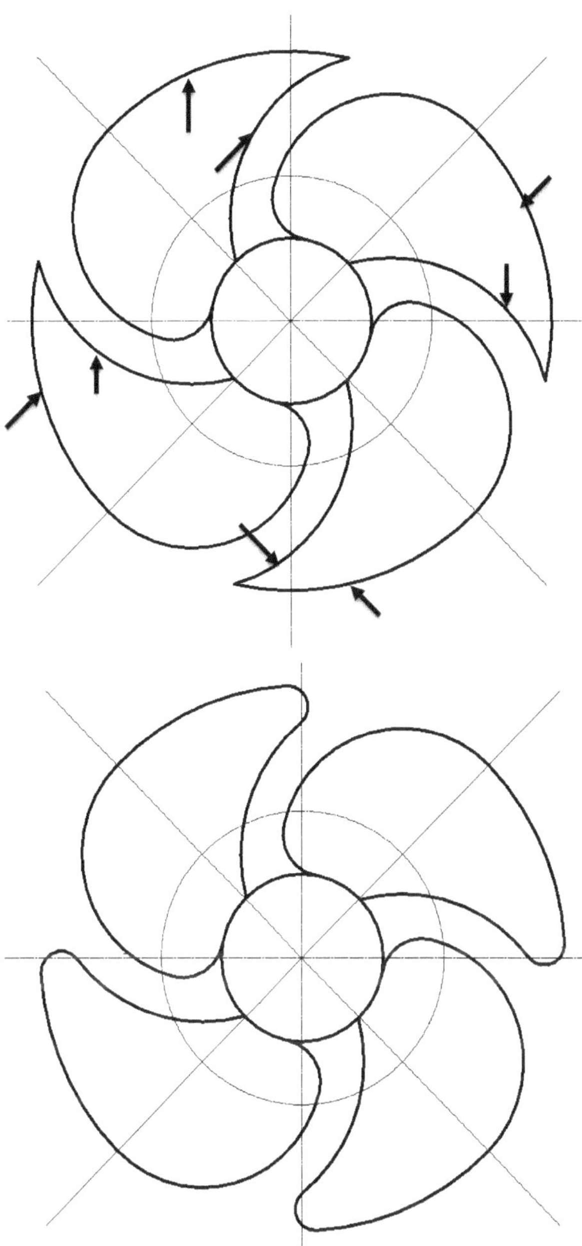

- Click the **Fillet** command on the **Home** tab of the **Modify** panel.

- Select **Radius** from the command line. Next, type **5** and press Enter.

- Select the large arc and the small arc, as shown.

- Likewise, fillet the other corners, as shown.

- Press Enter to activate the **Fillet** command.

- Select the arc and small circle, as shown. Likewise, create other fillets, as shown.

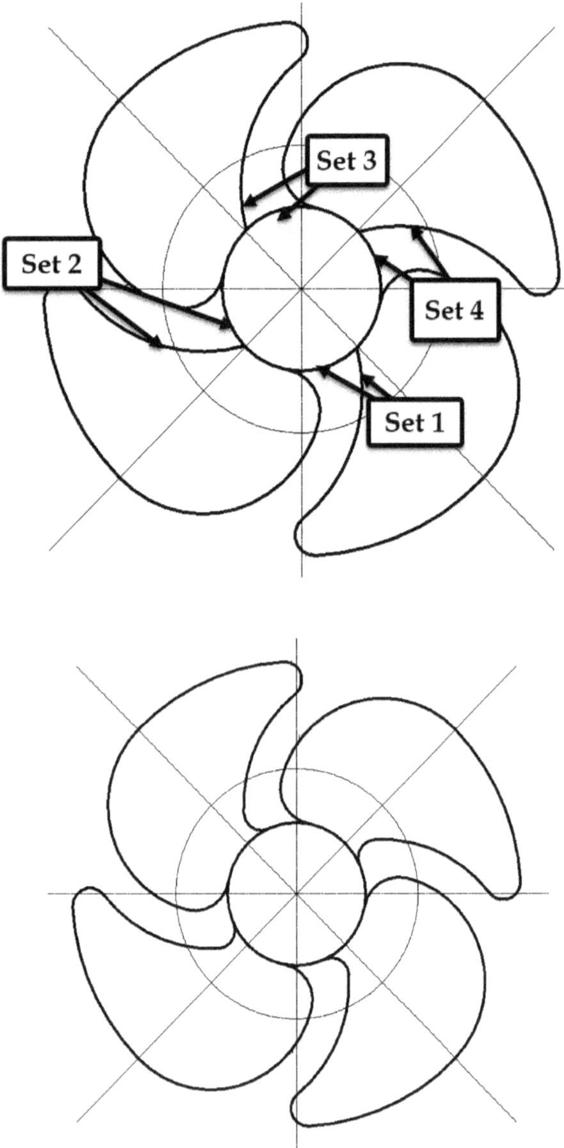

*   Save and close the file.

Tutorial 14 (Creating Orthographic views)

Orthographic Views are standard representations of an object on a sheet. These views are created by projecting an object onto three different planes (top, front, and side planes). You can project an object by using two different methods: **First Angle Projection** and **Third Angle Projection**. The following figure shows the orthographic views that will be created when an object is projected using the **First Angle Projection** method.

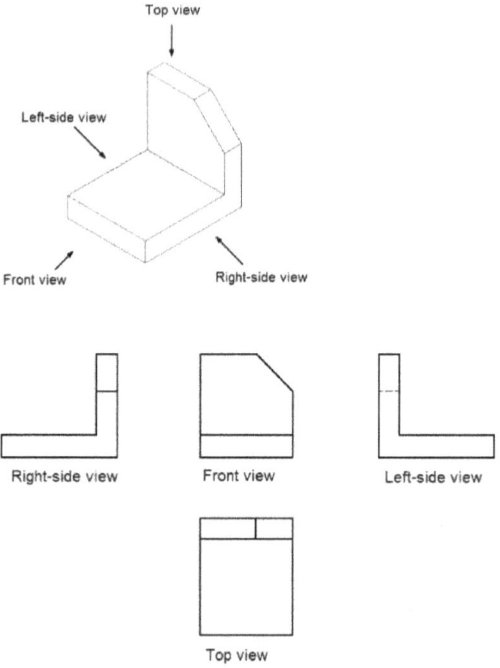

The following figure shows the orthographic views that will be created when an object is projected using the **Third Angle Projection** method.

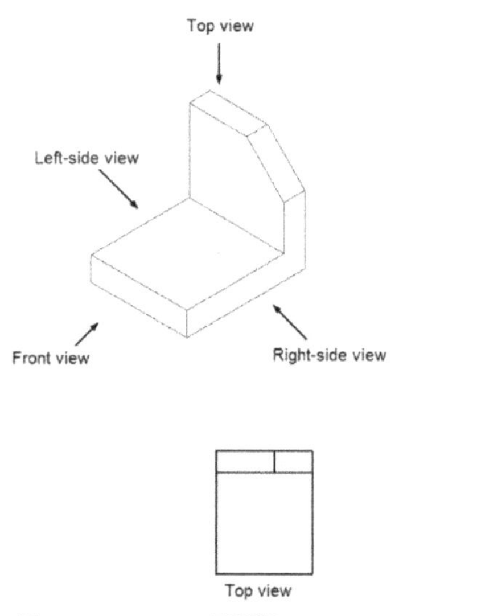

In this tutorial, you will create the orthographic views of the part shown below. The views will be created by using the **Third Angle Projection** method.

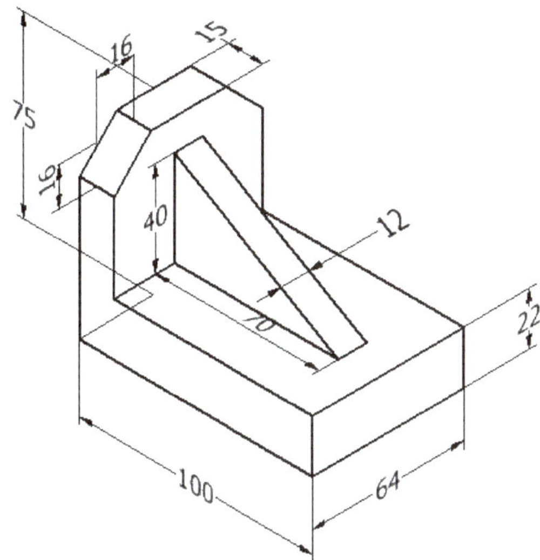

- Open a new drawing using the **standardiso** template.
- On the ribbon, click the **Home > Layers > Layers**. It displays the Layers palette.
- Create two new layers with the following properties.

Layer Name	Lineweight	LineStyle
Construction	0.00 mm	Continuous Solid Line
Object	0.30 mm	Continuous Solid Line

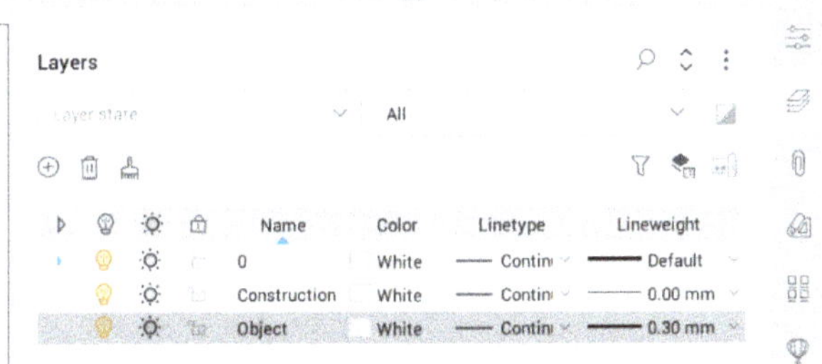

- Double-click in the **Current** column of the **Construction** layer to activate it.
- Close the **Layers palette**.
- Activate the **Ortho** icon on the status bar.

- Click **View** > **Views** > **Zoom** > **Zoom Extents** on the ribbon.
- On the ribbon, click **Home** tab > **Draw** panel > **Infinite Line**.
- Click anywhere in the lower left corner of the graphics window.
- Move the pointer upward and click to create a vertical construction line.
- Move the pointer toward the right and click to create a horizontal construction line.
- Press ENTER twice.
- Select the **Parallel** option from the command line. Next, type 100 as the offset distance and press ENTER.
- Select the vertical construction line.
- Move the pointer toward the right and click to create an offset line.

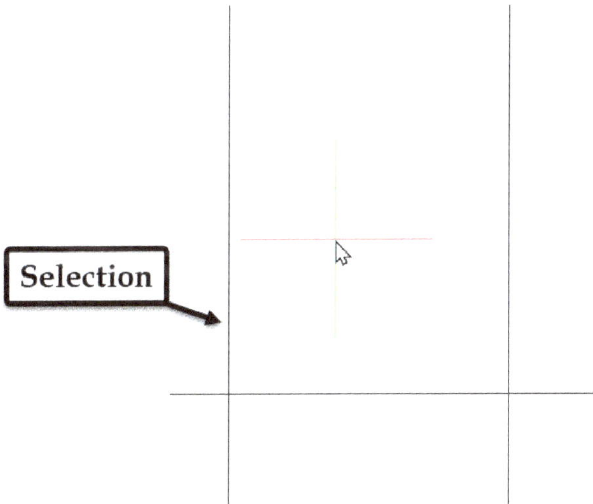

- Click **Draw** > **Modify** > **Offset** on the ribbon. Type 75 as the offset distance and press ENTER.
- Select the horizontal construction line. Move the pointer above and click to create the offset line.
- Press ENTER to exit the **Offset** tool.
- Likewise, create other offset lines as shown below. The offset dimensions are displayed in the image. Do not add dimensions to the lines.

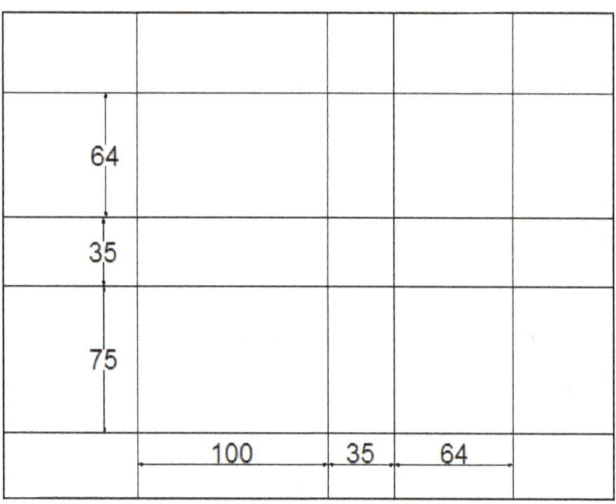

- Activate the **Object** layer.

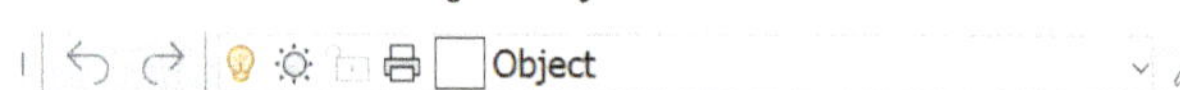

- Next, activate the **LWT** button on the status bar.

- Click the **Line** on the **Draw** panel. Next, select the intersection points of the construction lines, as shown.

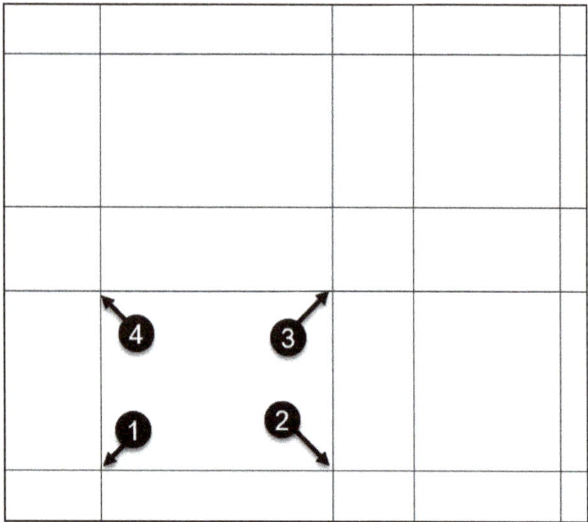

- Select the **Close** option from the command line to create the outline of the front view.

- Likewise, create the outlines of the top and side views.

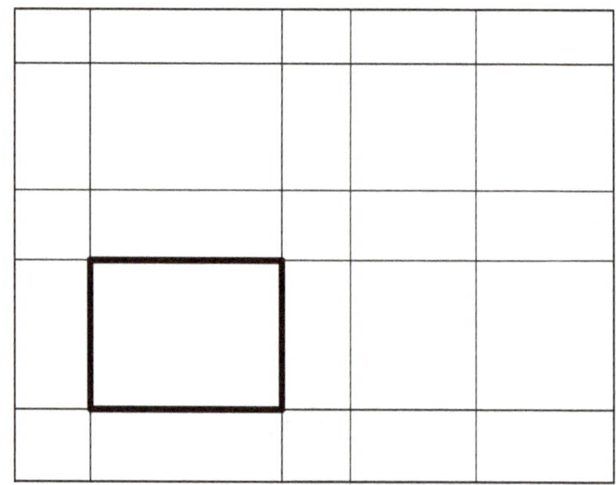

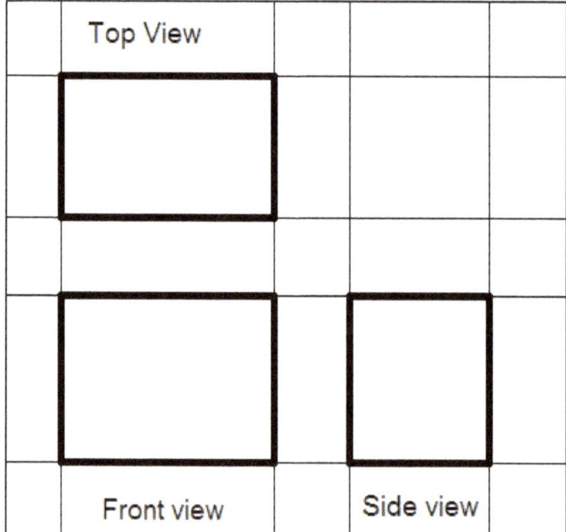

Next, you must turn off the **Construction** layer.

- Click on the **Layer Control** drop-down in the **Layers** panel.

- Click the bulb icon of the **Construction** layer; the layer will be turned off.

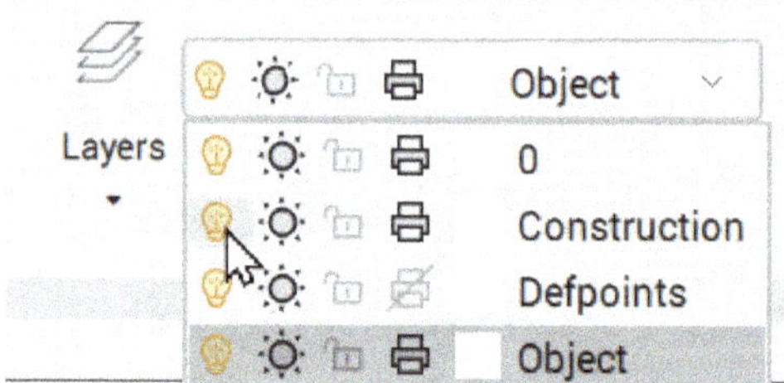

- Use the **Offset** tool and create two parallel lines on the front view, as shown below.

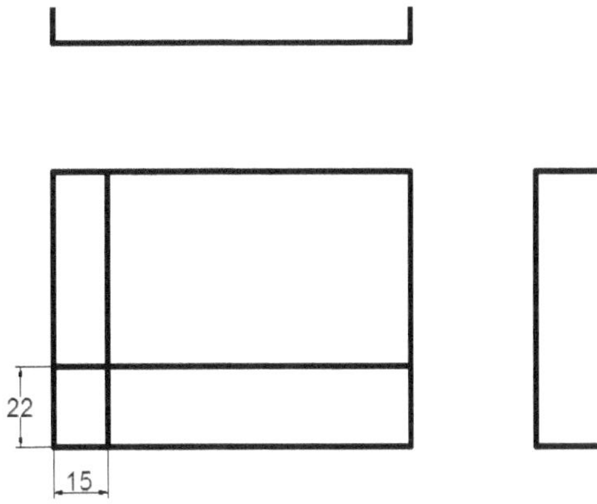

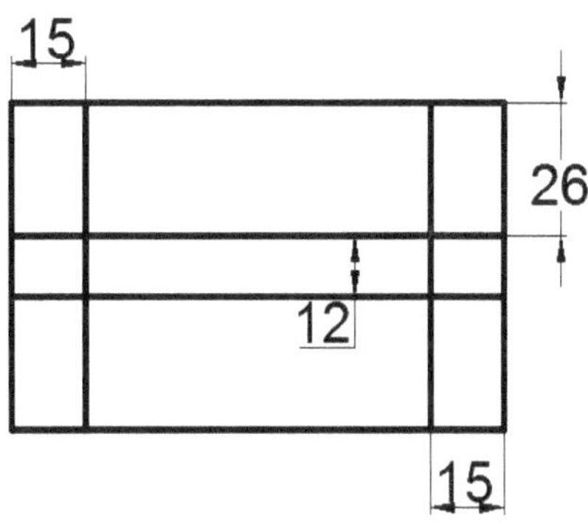

- Use the **Trim** tool and trim unwanted objects.

- Use the **Trim** tool and trim the unwanted lines of the front view as shown below.

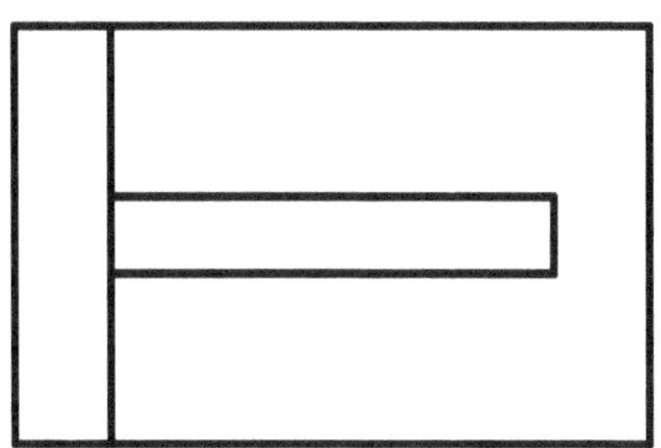

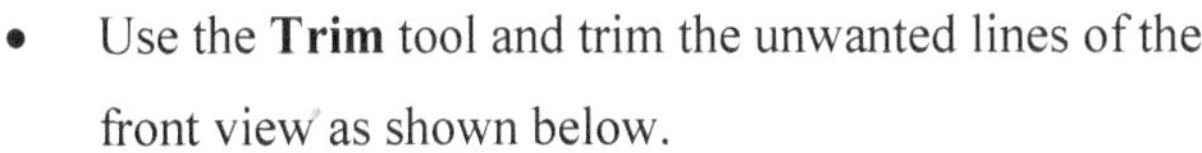

- Create other offset lines and trim the unwanted portions as shown below.

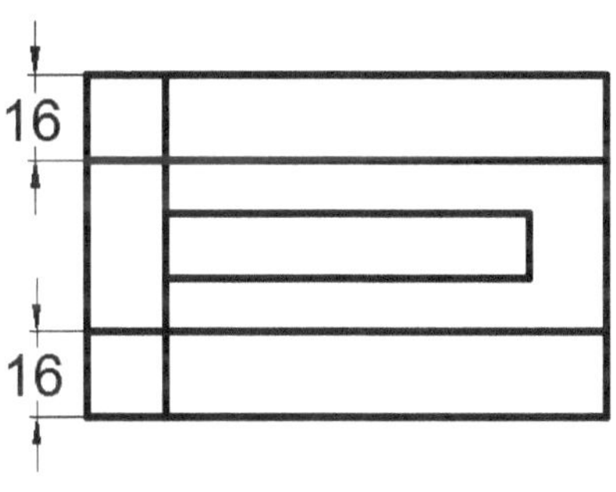

- Use the **Offset** tool to create the parallel line as shown below.

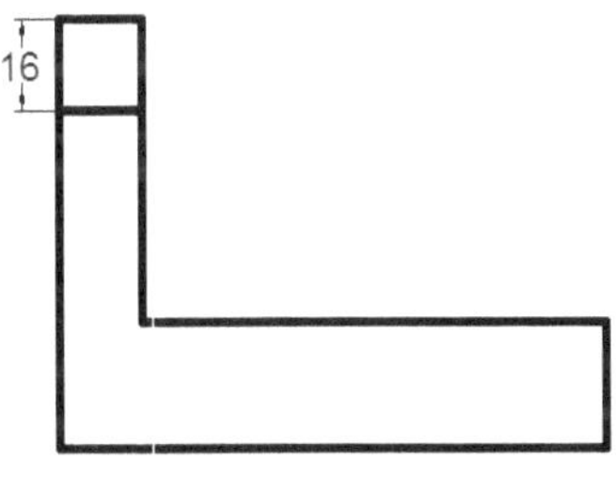

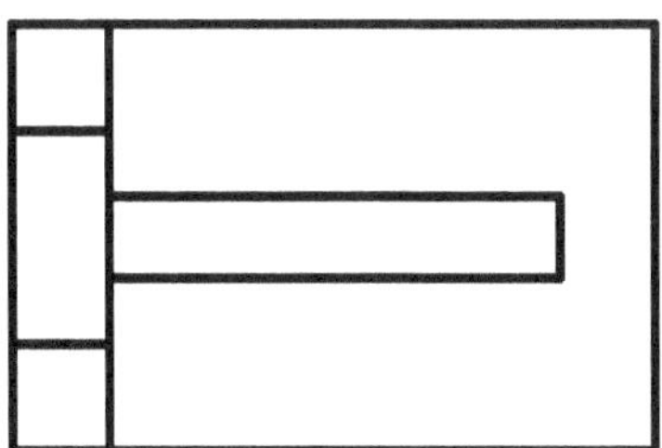

- Use the **Offset** tool and create offset lines in the Top view as shown below.

- Deactivate the **Ortho** icon on the status bar.
- Click the **Line** button on the **Draw** panel.
- Press and hold the SHIFT key and right-click. Select the **From** option.

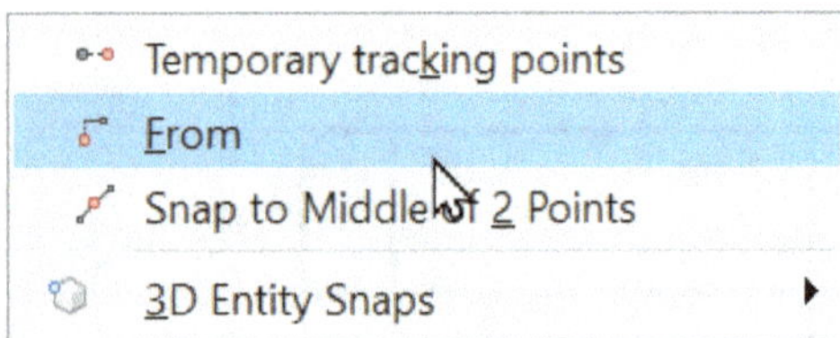

- Select the endpoint of the line in the front view as shown below.

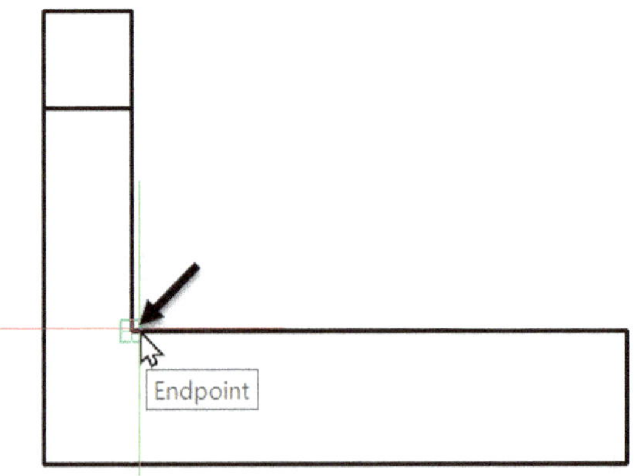

- Move the pointer on the vertical line and enter **40** in the command line; the first point of the line is specified at a point 40 mm away from the endpoint. Also, a rubber band line will be attached to the pointer.

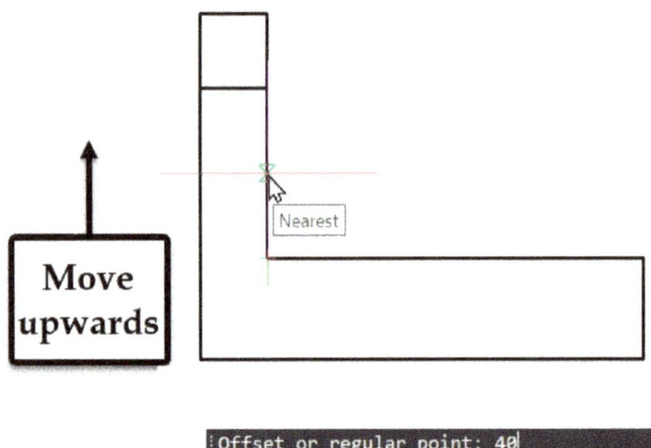

- Move the pointer onto the endpoint on the top view as shown below.

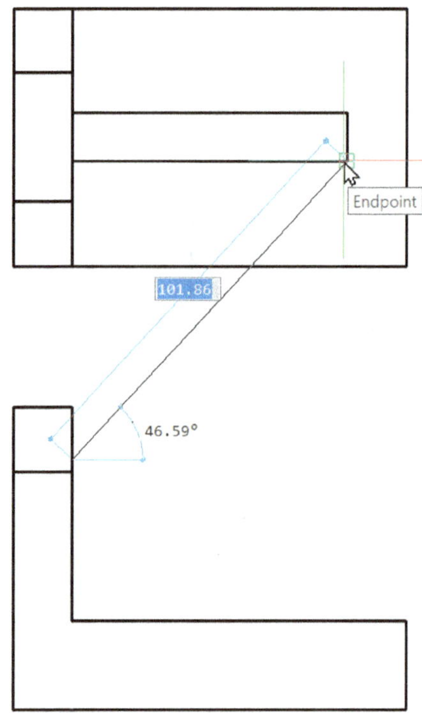

- Move the pointer vertically downward; you will notice the track lines.
- Move the pointer near the horizontal line of the front view and click at the intersection point as shown below. Press ENTER to exit the tool.

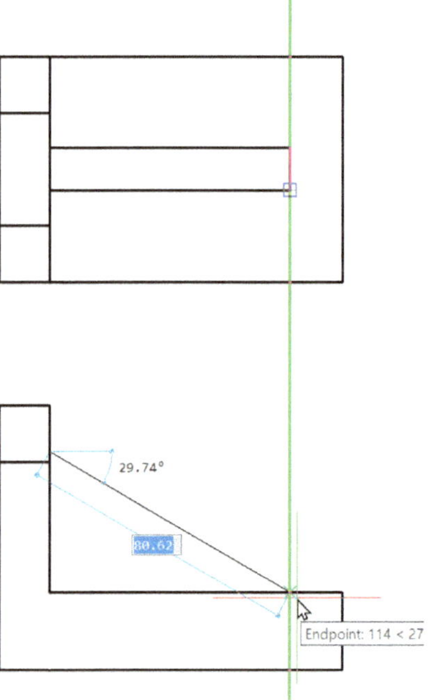

Next, you must create the right side view. To do this, you must draw a 45- degree miter line and project the measurements of the top view onto the side view.

- Click on the **Layer** drop-down in the **Layers** panel.
- Click the grey bulb of the **Construction** layer; the **Construction** layer is turned on.

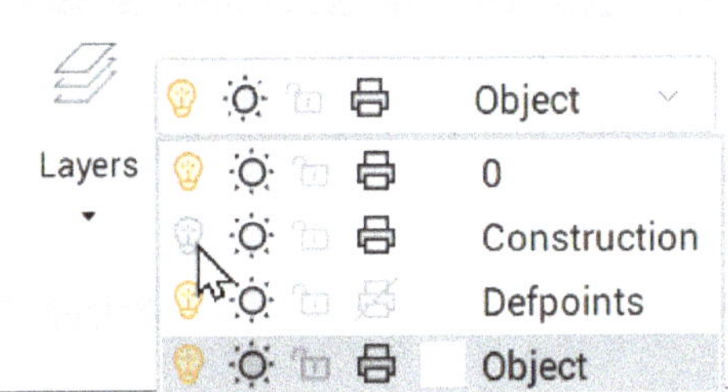

- Select the **Construction** layer from the **Layer** drop-down to set it as the current layer.
- Draw an inclined line by connecting the intersection points of the construction lines as shown below.

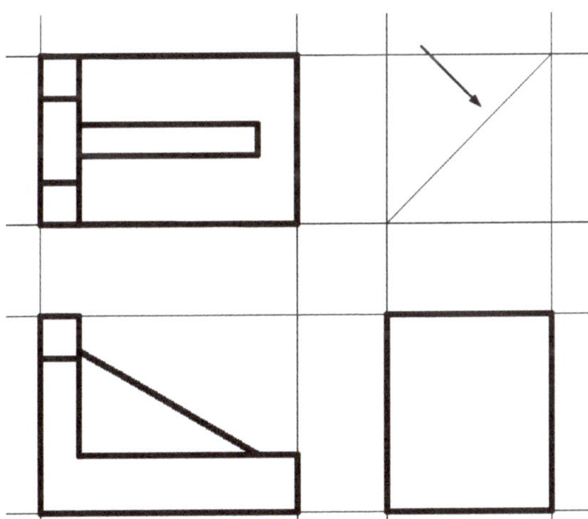

- Click the **Infinite Line** on the **Draw** panel.
- Select the **Horizontal** option from the command line. Next, select the points on the top and front views, as shown below.

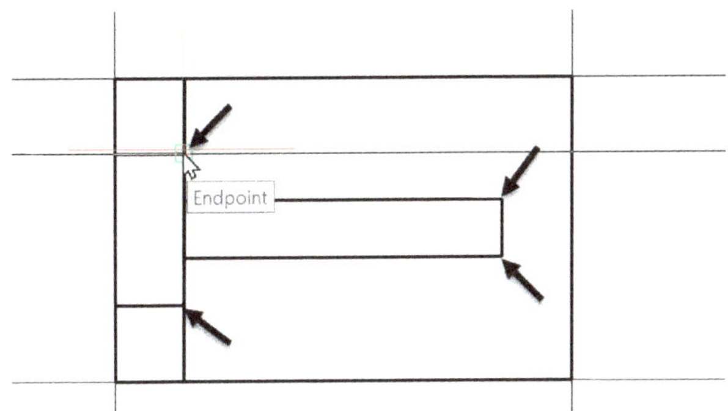

The projection lines are created, as shown below.

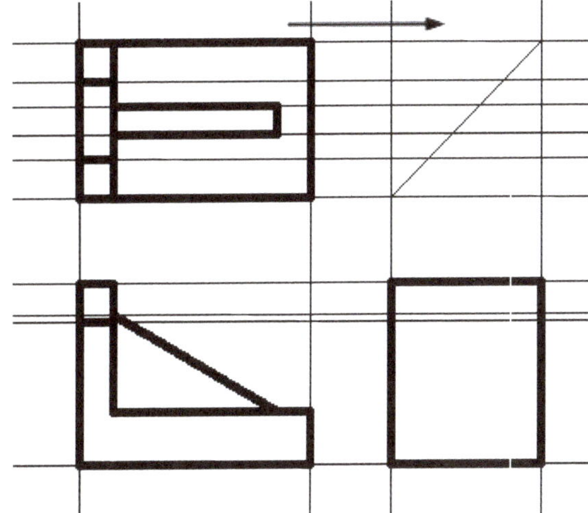

- Press ENTER twice.
- Right-click and select the **Vertical** option from the shortcut menu.
- Create the vertical projection lines as shown below.

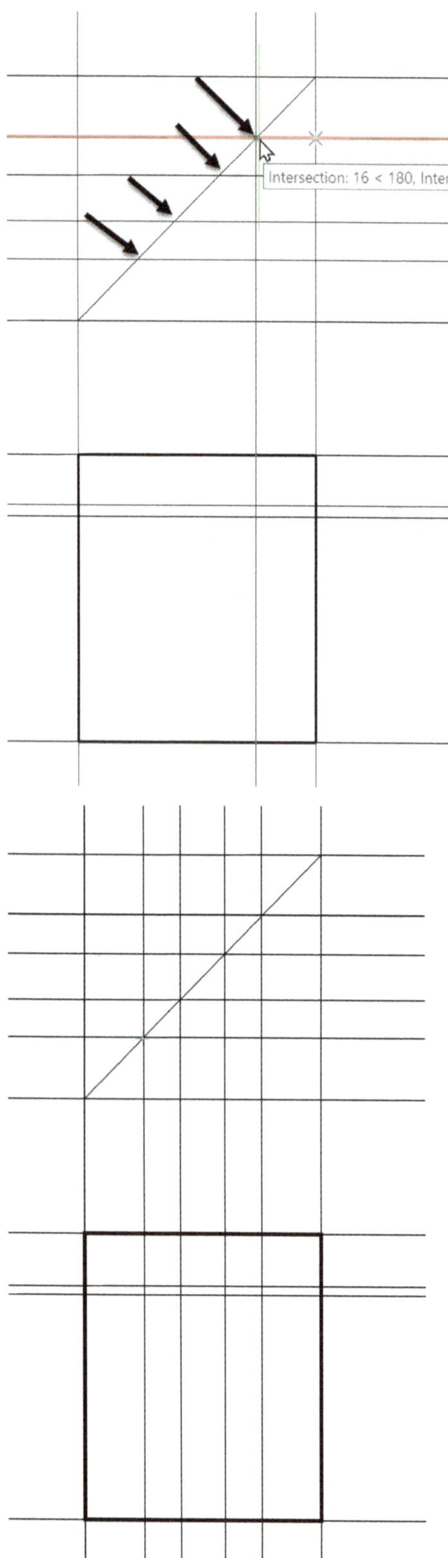

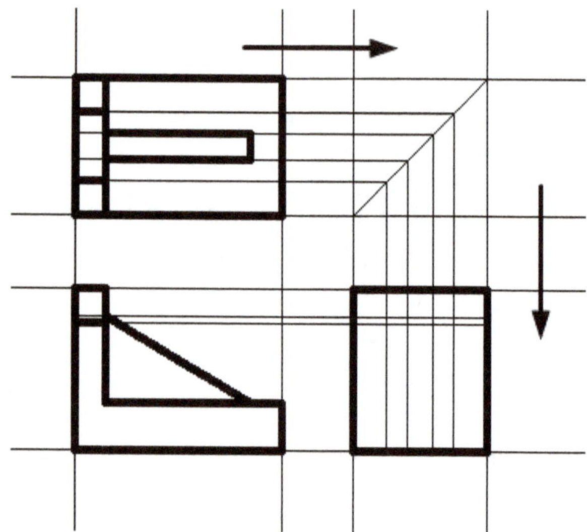

- Use the **Trim** tool and trim the extended portions of the infinite lines.

- Set the **Object** layer as current.

- Click the **Offset** button on the **Modify** panel. Next, select the **Through point** option from the command line.

- Select the lower horizontal line of the side view.

- Select the endpoint on the front view to define the through point, as shown below. Next, press ESC.

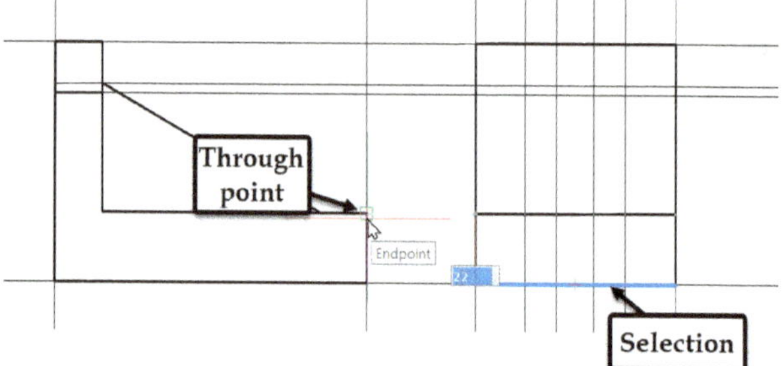

- Use the **Line** tool and create the objects in the side view as shown below.

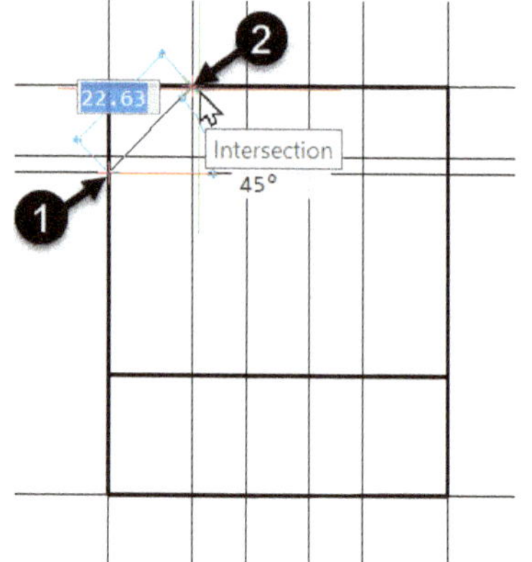

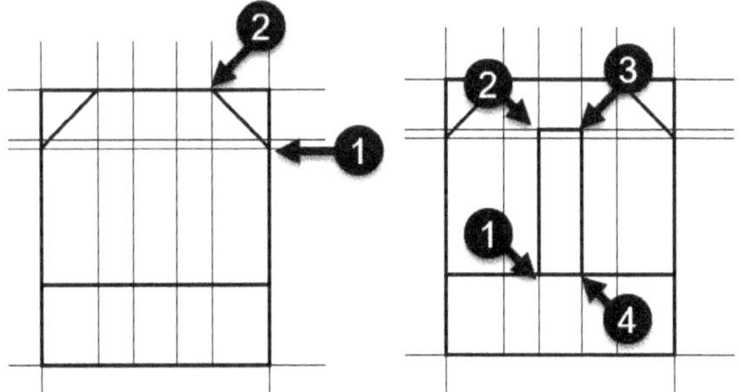

- Turn off the **Construction** layer by clicking on the green circle of the **Construction** layer.

- Trim the unwanted portions on the right side view.

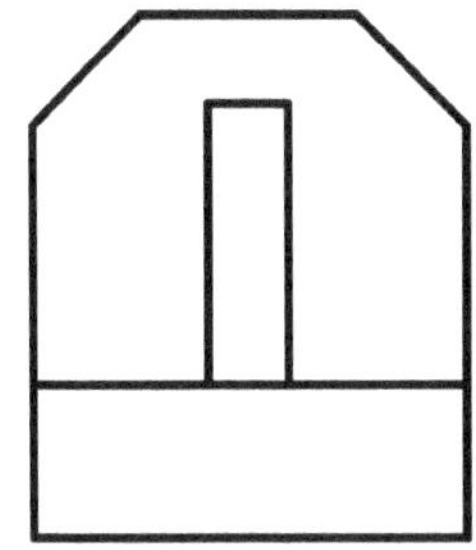

The drawing after creating all the views is shown below.

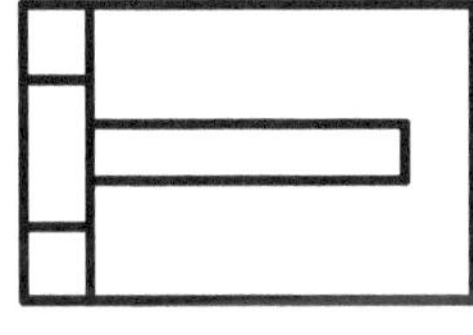

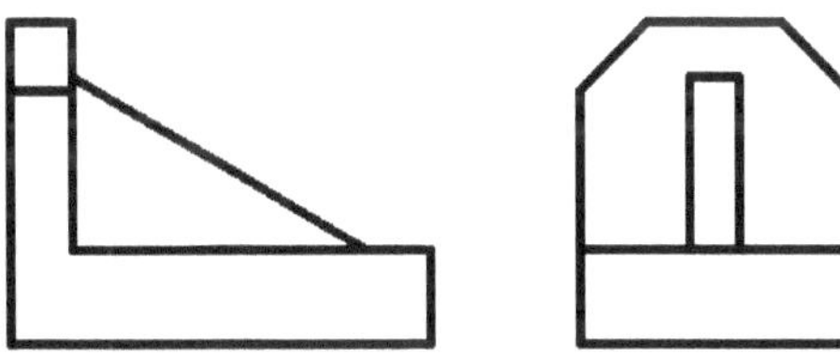

- Save the file as **ortho_views.dwg**. Close the file.

Tutorial 15 (Creating Auxiliary Views)

Most of the components are represented by using orthographic views (front, top and/or side views). But many components have features located on inclined faces. You cannot get the true shape and size for these features by using the orthographic views. To see an accurate size and shape of the inclined features, you must create an auxiliary view. An auxiliary view is created by projecting the component onto a plane other than horizontal, front or side planes. The following figure shows a component with an inclined face. When you create orthographic views of the component, you will not be able to get the true shape of the hole on the inclined face.

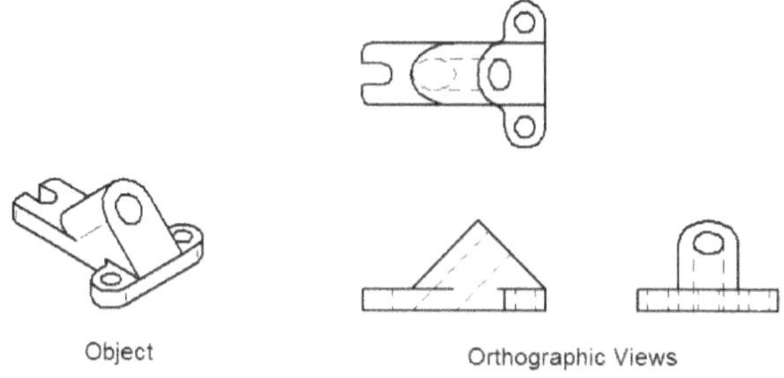

To get the actual shape of the hole, you must create an auxiliary view of the object as shown below.

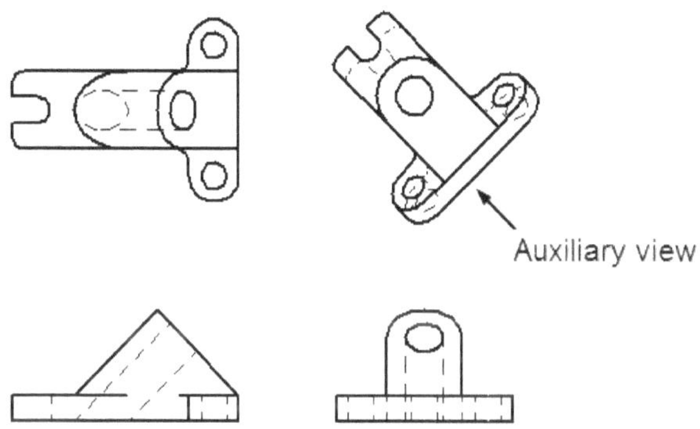

In this tutorial, you will create an auxiliary view of the object shown below.

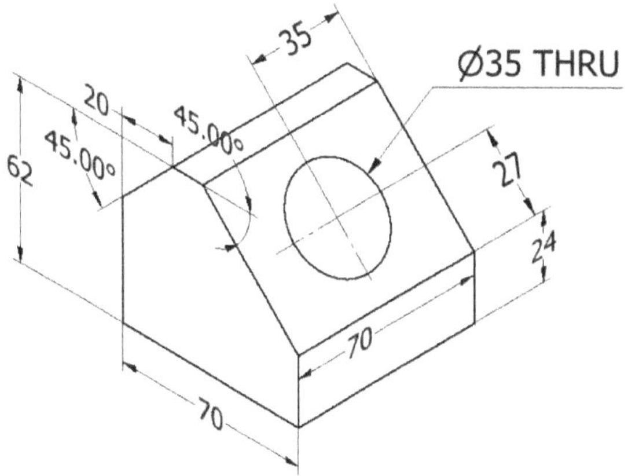

- Open a new BricsCAD file.

- Create four new layers with the following properties.

Layer Name	Lineweight	Linetype
Construction	0.00 mm	Continuous
Object	0.50 mm	Continuous
Hidden	0.30 mm	HIDDEN
Centerline	0.30 mm	CENTER

- Select the **Construction** layer from the **Layer Control** drop-down in the **Layers** panel.
- Create a rectangle at the lower left corner of the graphics window, as shown in the figure.

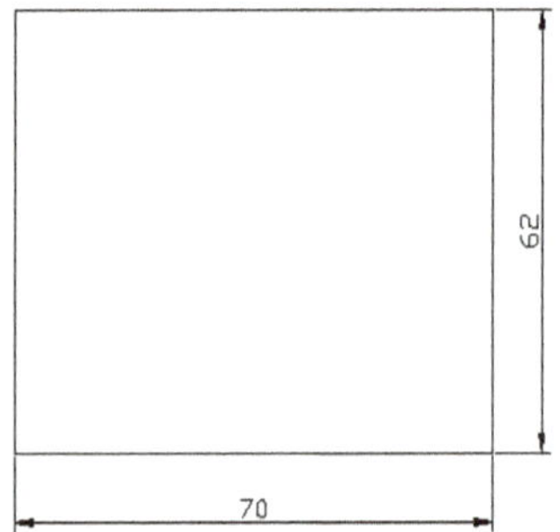

- Select the rectangle and click the **Copy** on the **Modify** panel.
- Select the lower left corner of the rectangle as the base point.

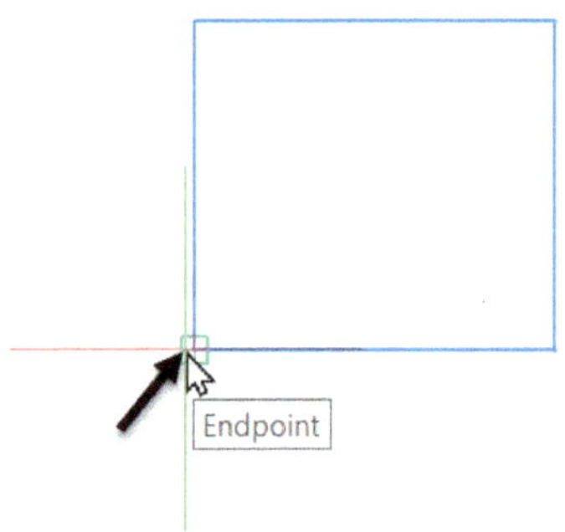

- Make sure that the **Ortho** mode is activated.
- Move the pointer upward and type **25** in the command line — next, press ENTER.
- Press ESC to exit the **Copy** tool.

- Click the **2D Rotate** button on the **Modify** panel and select the copied rectangle. Press ENTER to accept.
- Select the lower right corner of the copied rectangle as the base point.

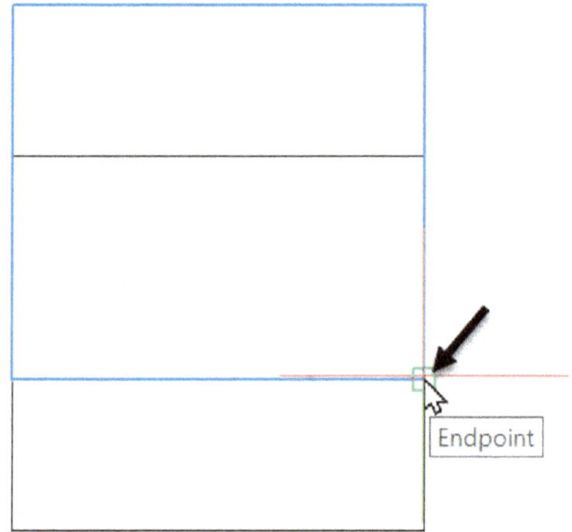

- Type 45 as the angle and press ENTER.

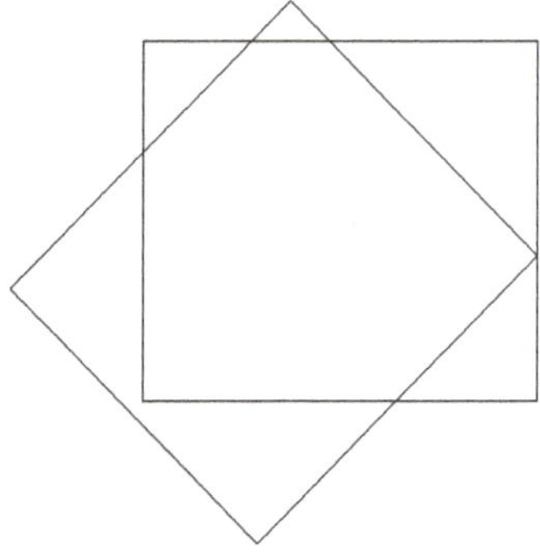

- Activate the **STrack** button on the Status Bar.
- Right-click on the **ESnap** button, and then select **Settings** from the shortcut menu.

- On the **Settings** dialog, make sure that the **Endpoint** option is checked under the **Entity snap mode** section. Next, close the **Settings** dialog.

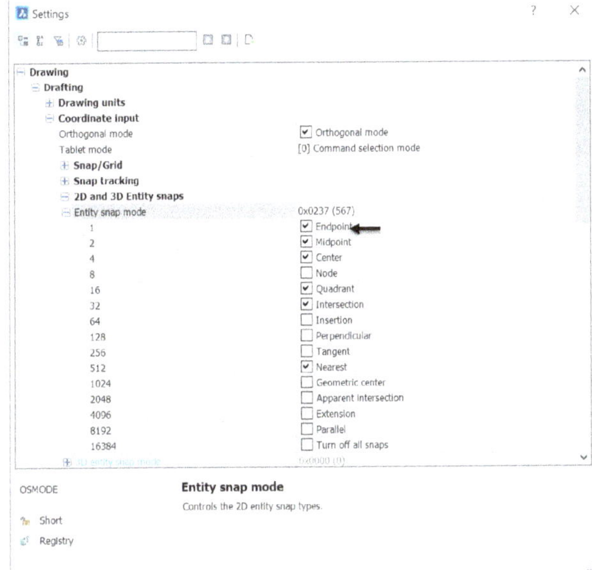

- Activate the **Rectangle** command.
- Place the pointer on the top left corner of the existing rectangle.
- Move the pointer vertically upward, and then notice a vertical tracking line from the top left corner of the rectangle.
- Move the pointer along the tracking line up to an approximate distance of 60 mm.

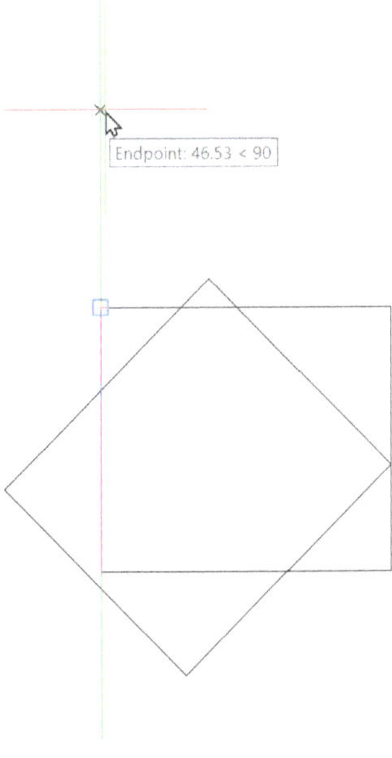

- Click to specify the first corner of the rectangle.
- Select **Dimensions** from the command line. Type 70 and press Enter to specify the length of the rectangle.
- Again, type 70 and press Enter to specify the width of the rectangle. Move the pointer up and click to position the rectangle.

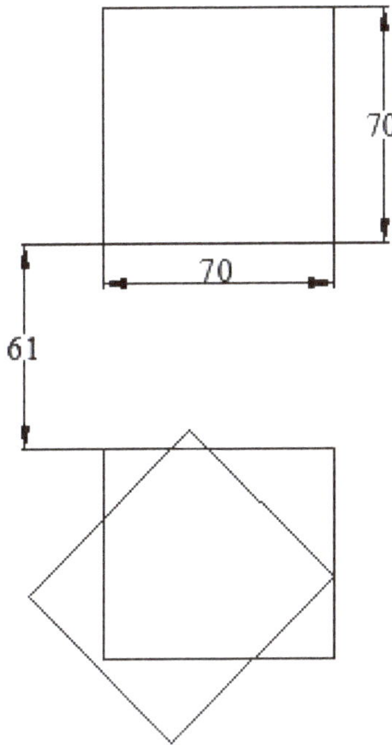

The rectangle located at the top is considered as top view and the below one as the front view.

- Click the **Explode** button on the **Modify** panel and select the newly created rectangle. Next, right-click to explode the rectangle.
- Activate the **Offset** tool.
- Select the **Through point** option from the command line.
- Select the left vertical line of the top rectangle.
- Select any one of the through points, as shown; the selected vertical line is offset through the selected point.
- Again, select the left vertical line.
- Move the pointer, and then select the remaining through point.

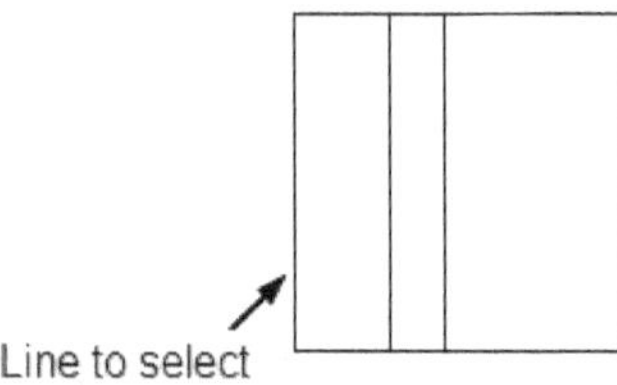

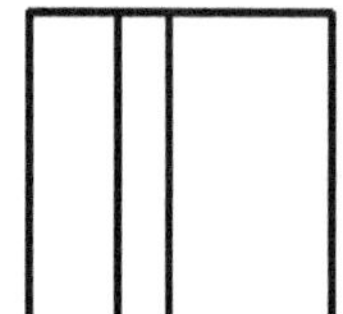

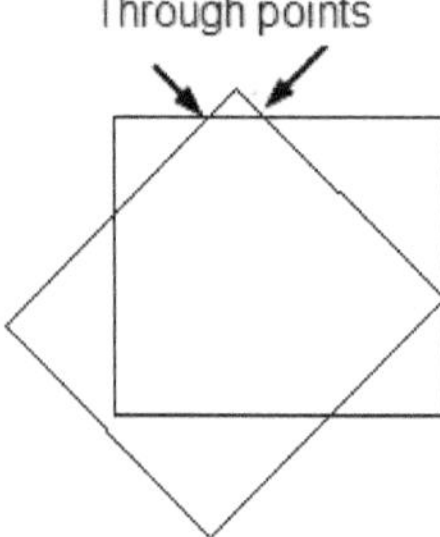

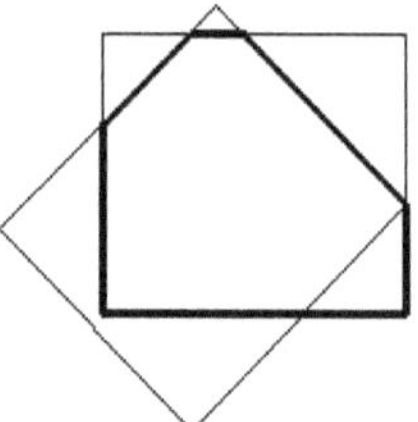

- Press Esc to deactivate the **Offset** tool.

- Select the **Object** layer from the **Layer Control** drop-down in the **Layers** panel.

- Activate the **LWT** button on the status bar.

- Activate the **Line** tool and select the intersection points on the front view, as shown.

- Select the **Construction** layer from the **Layers** panel.

- On the **Home** ribbon tab, click **Draw** panel > **Infinite Line** tool.

- Select the **Parallel** option from the command line.

- Select the **Through** option.

- Select the inclined line on the front view.

- Select the intersection point as shown below.

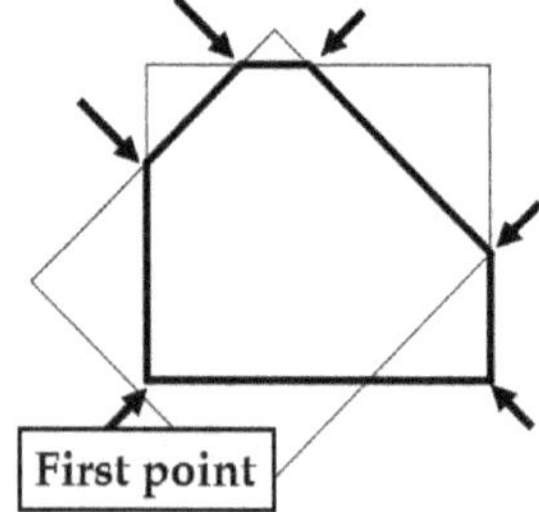

- Likewise, create the object lines in the top view, as shown below.

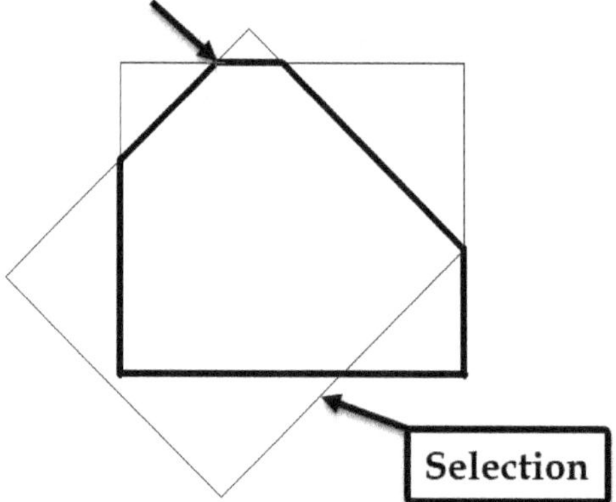

- Activate the **Offset** command and create other construction lines as shown below.

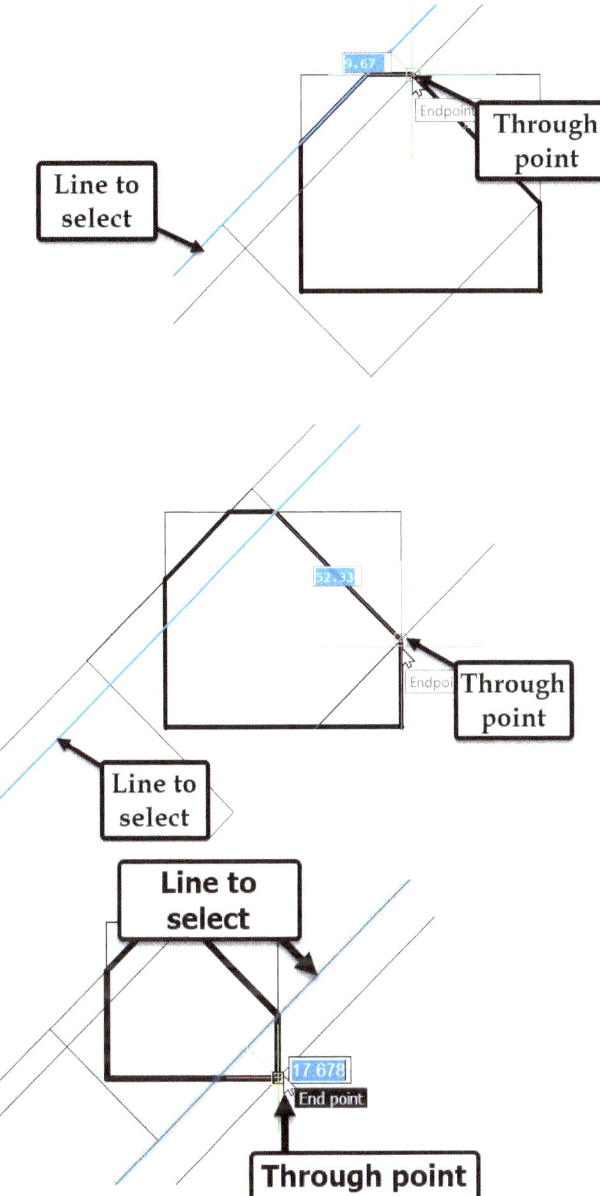

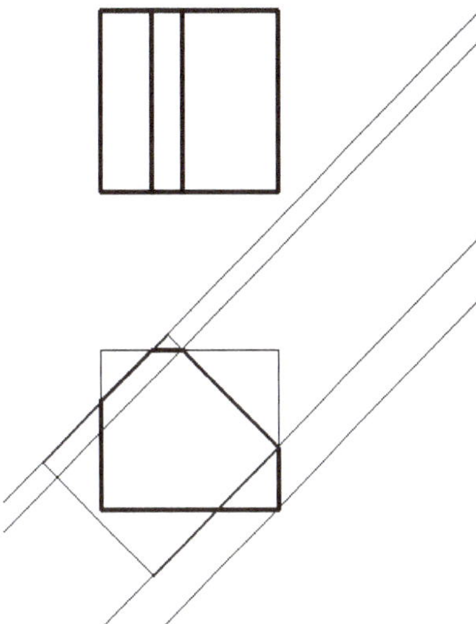

- Press Esc to deactivate the **Infinite Line** command.
- Activate the **Infinite Line** command.
- Select **Parallel** from the command line.
- Type 80 and press ENTER. Select the inclined line of the front view, as shown.
- Move the pointer toward the right and click to create the construction line.

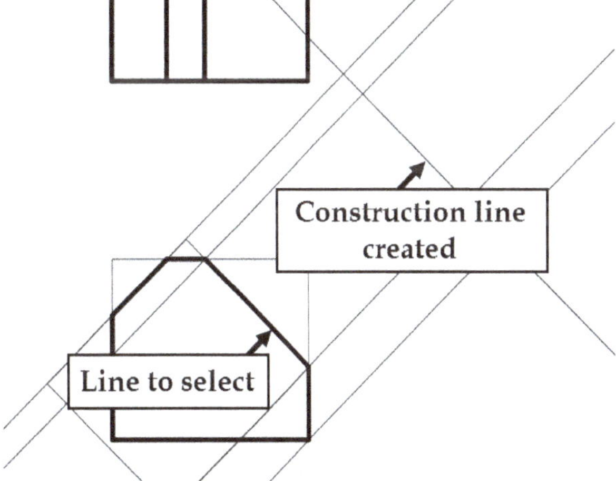

- Create other construction lines, as shown. The offset dimensions are given in the figure.

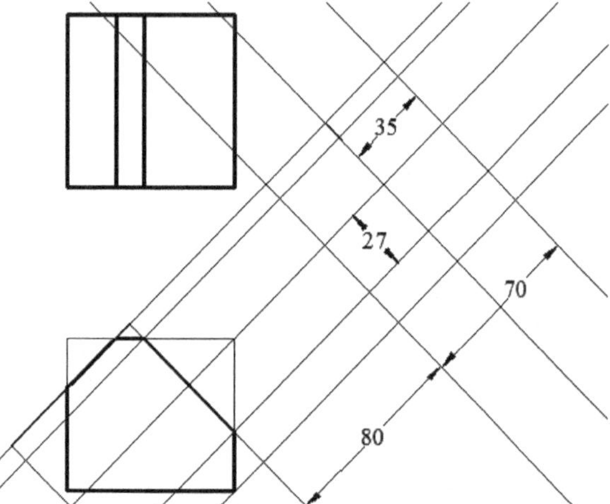

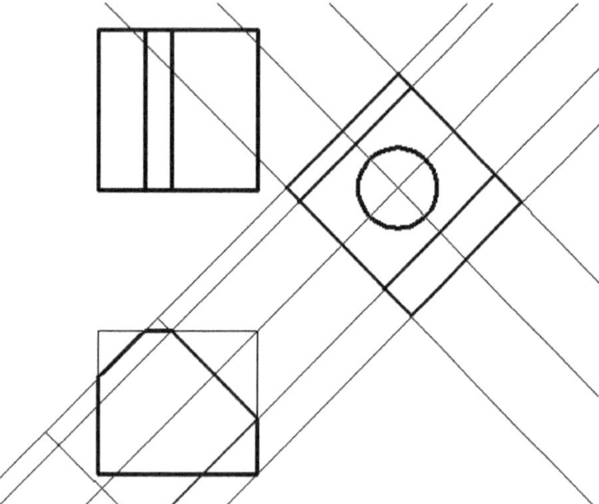

- Set the **Object** layer as the current layer. Next, create the object lines using the intersection points between the construction lines.
- Use the **Circle** tool and create a circle of 35 mm in diameter.

- Set the **Construction** layer as the current layer. Next, create projection lines from the circle.

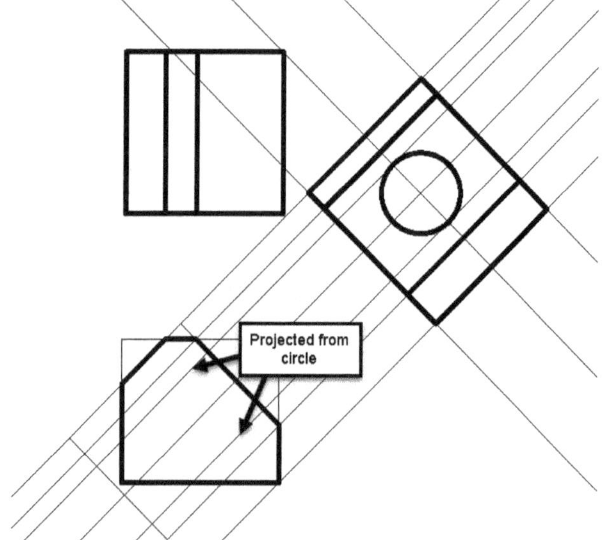

- Set the **Hidden** layer as the current layer. Next, create the hidden lines, as shown.

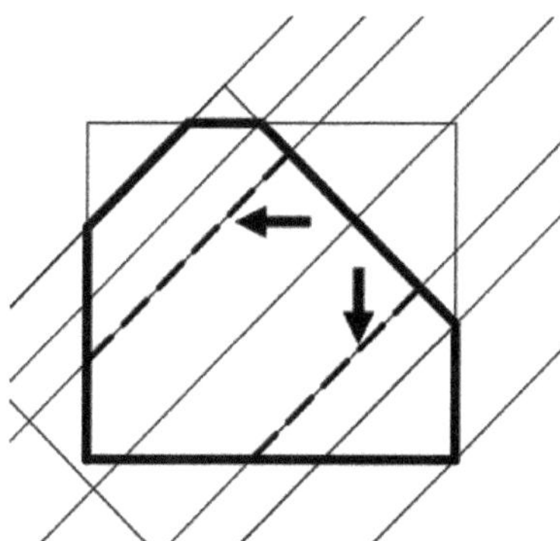

- Set the **Centerline** layer as the current layer.
- Activate the **Line** tool. Next, create the centerlines, as shown.

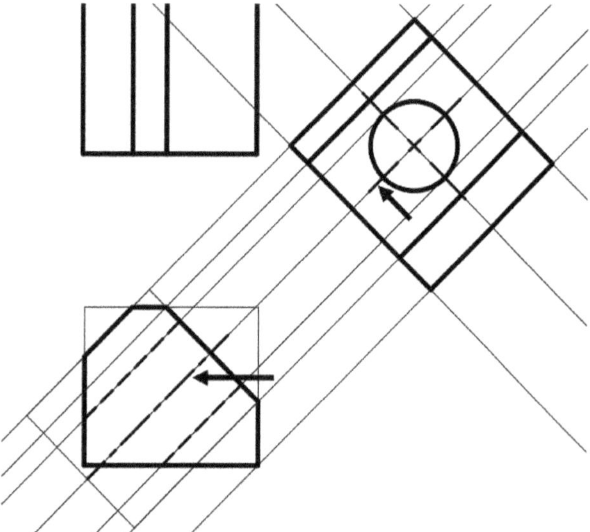

- Set the **Construction** layer as the current layer.

- On the ribbon, click **Home > Draw > Ray**.

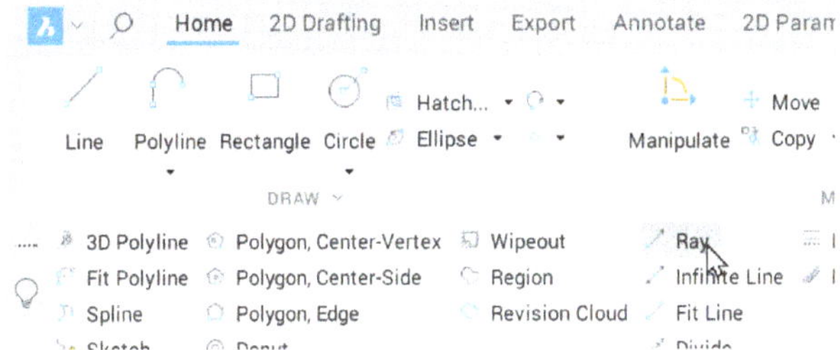

- Select the intersection point of the centerline and object line, as shown.

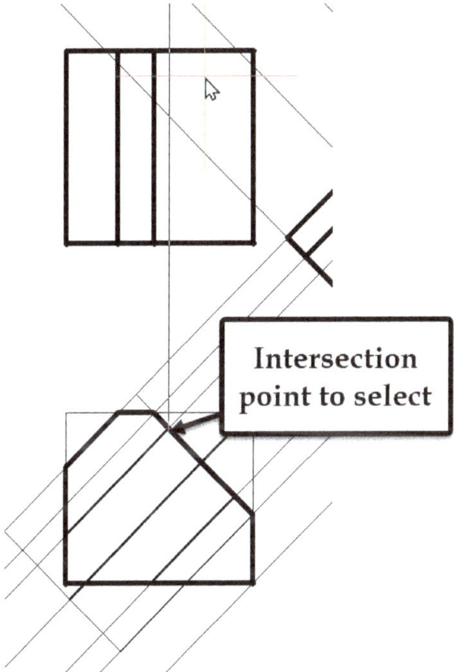

- Move the pointer upward and click to create a ray.

- Press ENTER twice.

- Likewise, create two more rays, as shown.

- Create a horizontal construction line passing through the midpoint of the top view, as shown.

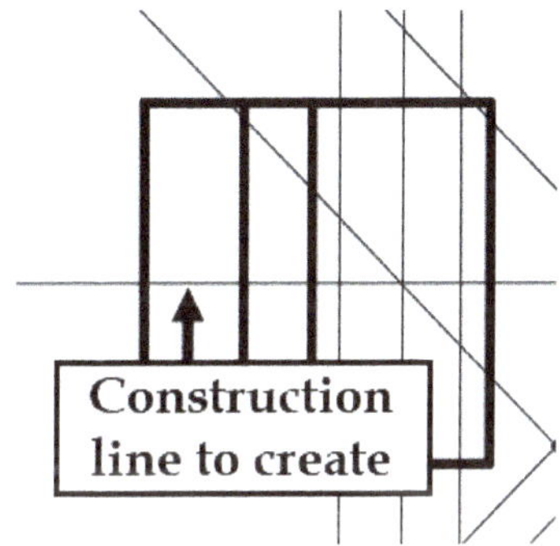

- Set the **Object** layer as the current layer,

- On the ribbon, click **Home > Draw > Ellipse drop-down > Ellipse Axis-Axis**.

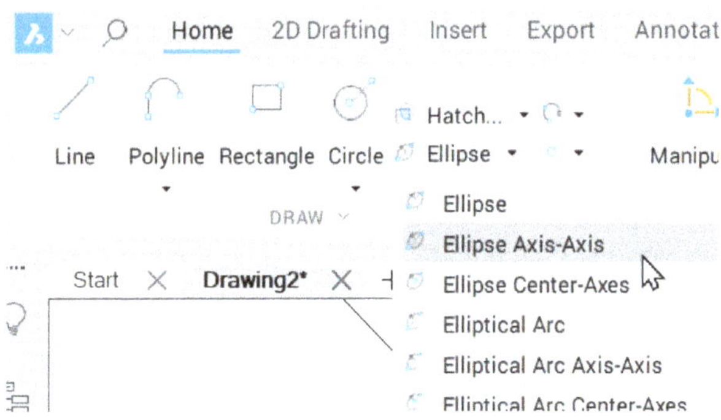

- Specify the first and second points, as shown. Move the point downward, type-in 17.5, and then press ENTER.

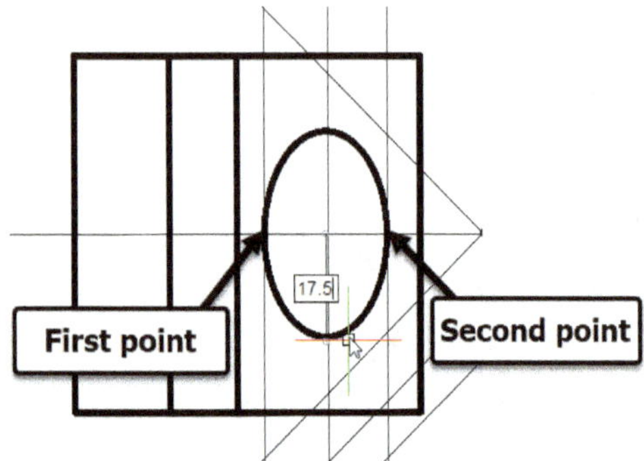

- Set the **Centerline** layer as current layer. Next, create the remaining centerlines.
- The drawing after hiding the **Construction** layer is shown next.
- Save the file as auxiliary_views.dwg.

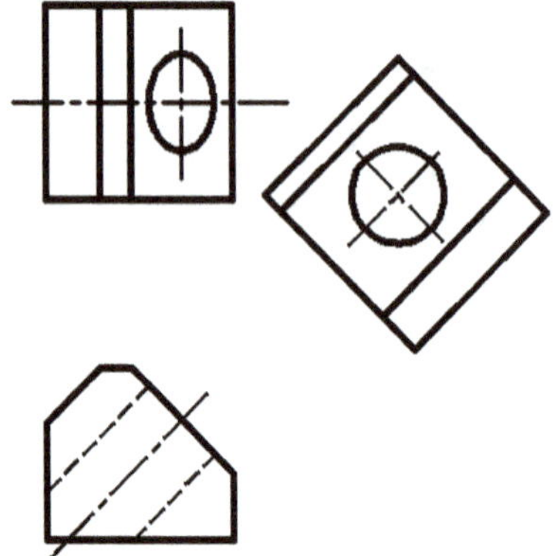

Tutorial 16 (Creating Named views)

While working with a drawing, you may need to perform numerous zoom and pan operations to view key portions of a drawing. Instead of doing this, you can save these portions with a name. Then, restore the named view and start working on them.

- Open the **ortho_views.dwg** file (The drawing file created in the Orthographic Views section of this chapter).
- To create a named view, click **View > Views > Views** on the ribbon; the **Drawing Explorer** dialog appears with **Views** page active.

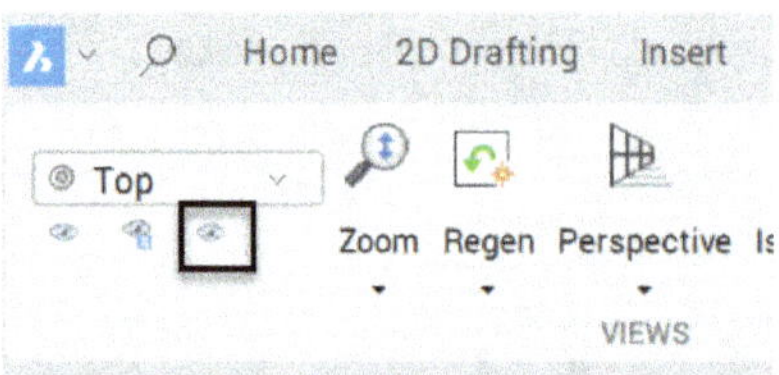

- Click the **New** button on the **Views** page of the Drawing Explorer.
- Select the **Window** option from command line.
- Create a window on the front view, as shown below.

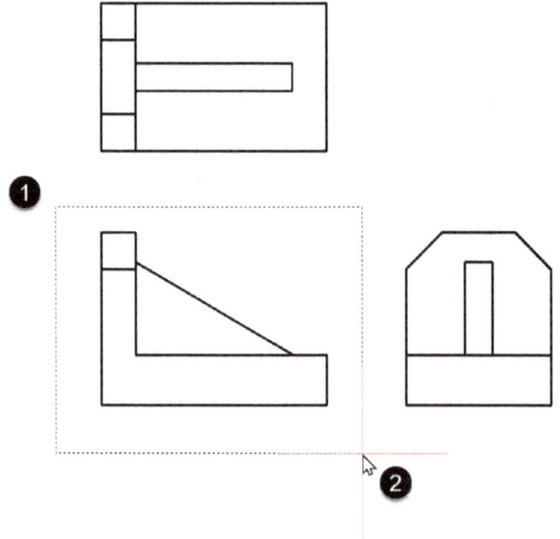

- On the **Drawing Explorer** dialog, click the right mouse button on the **NewView1** view under the **Views** section.
- Select the **Rename** option from the shortcut menu.

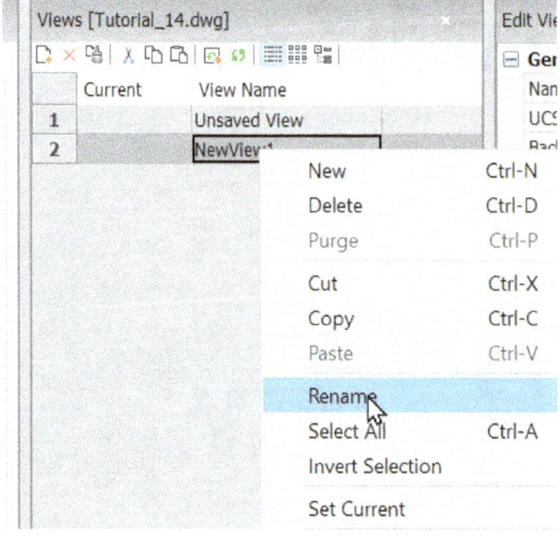

- Type **Front** in the **View Name** box.

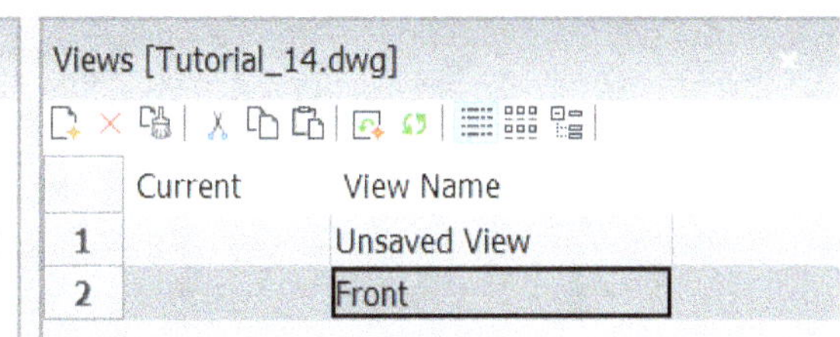

- Likewise, create the named views for the top and right views of the drawing.
- To set the **Top** view to current, double-click on it in the **Views** section; the **Top** view will be zoomed and fitted to the screen.

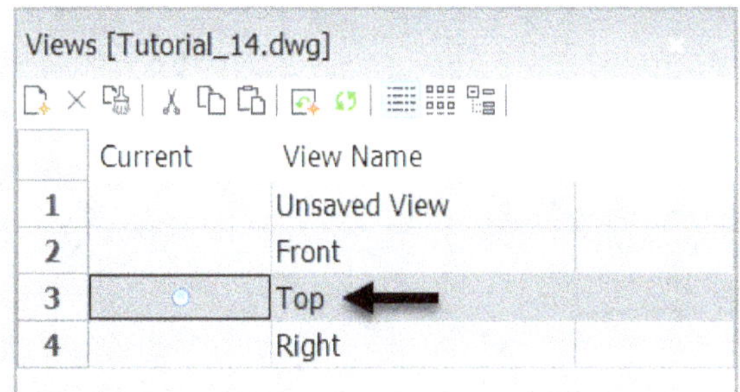

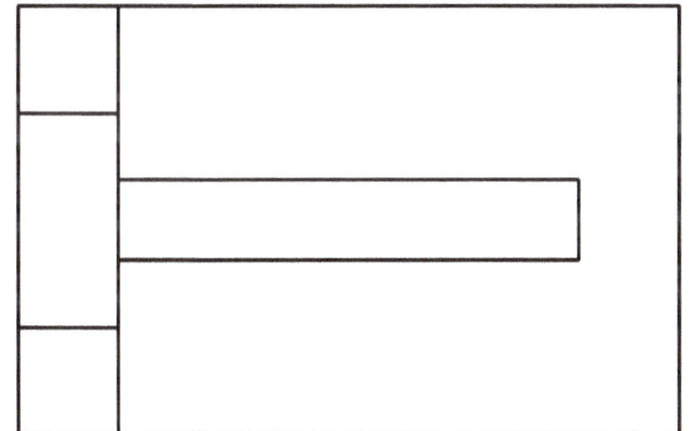

- Close the **Drawing Explorer** dialog.
- Save and close the file.

Tutorial 17

In this example, you will create the drawing as shown in the figure and add dimensions to it.

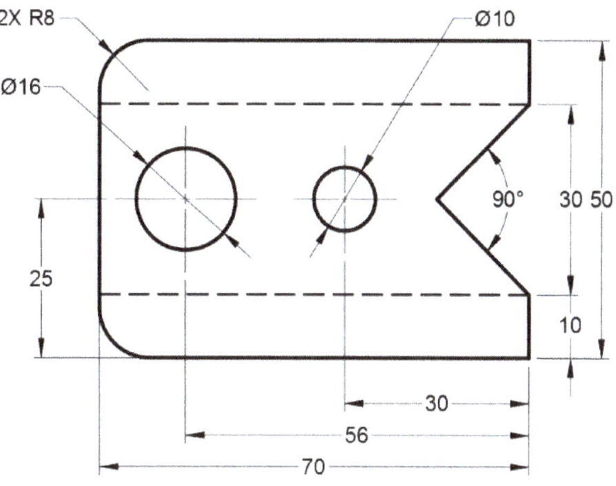

- Create four new layers with the following settings.

Layer	Lineweight	LineStyle
Construction	0.00 mm	Continuous
Object	0.50 mm	Continuous
Hidden	0.30 mm	HIDDEN
Dimensions	0.30 mm	Continuous

- Type LIMITS and press ENTER. Next, type 0,0 and press ENTER.
- Type 100, 100 and press ENTER to set the maximum limit of the drawing.
- On the ribbon, click **View > Views > Zoom** drop-down > **Zoom Extents**.
- Create the drawing on the **Object** and **Hidden** layers.

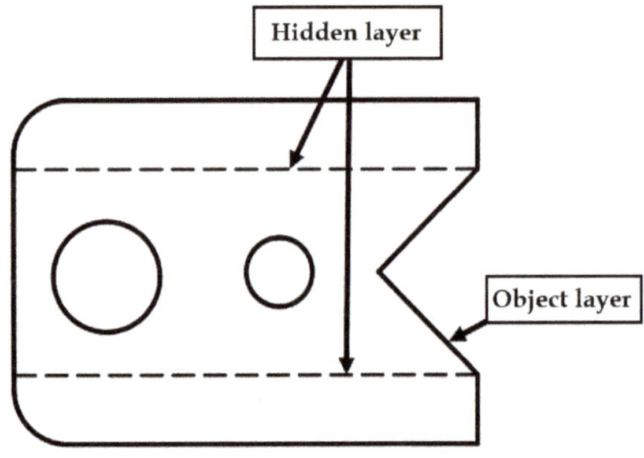

- Select the **Dimensions** layer from the **Layers Manager** drop-down in the **Layers** panel.

Creating a Dimension Style

The appearance of the dimensions depends on the dimension style that you use. You can create a new dimension style using the **Dimensions Styles** settings on the **Drawing Explorer** dialog. In this dialog, you can specify various settings related to the appearance and behavior of dimensions. The following example helps you to create a dimension style.

- On the ribbon, click **Annotate > Dimension > Dimensions Styles**.

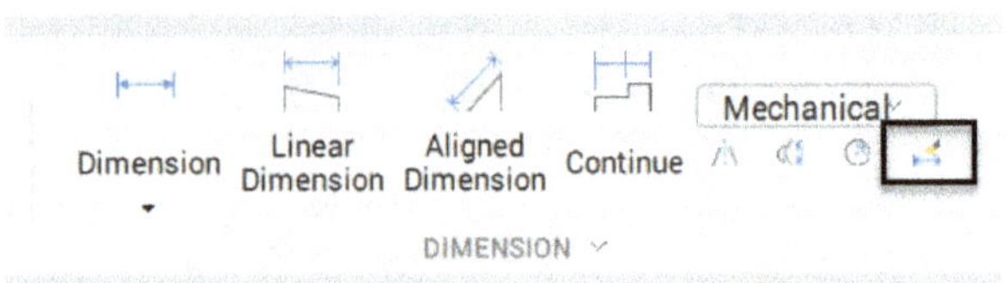

The **Dimension Styles** page appears on the **Drawing Explorer** dialog.

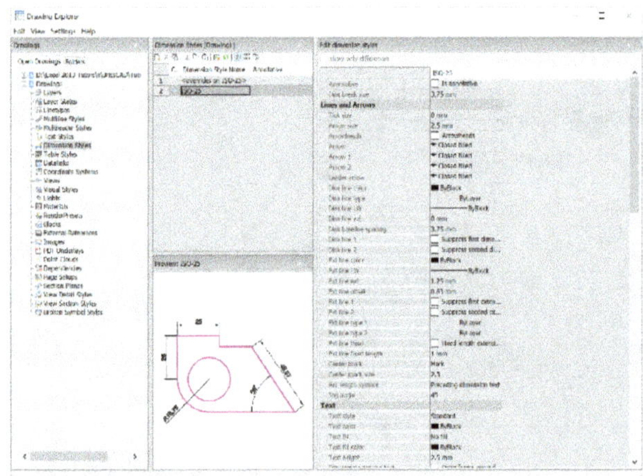

The basic nomenclature of dimensions is given below.

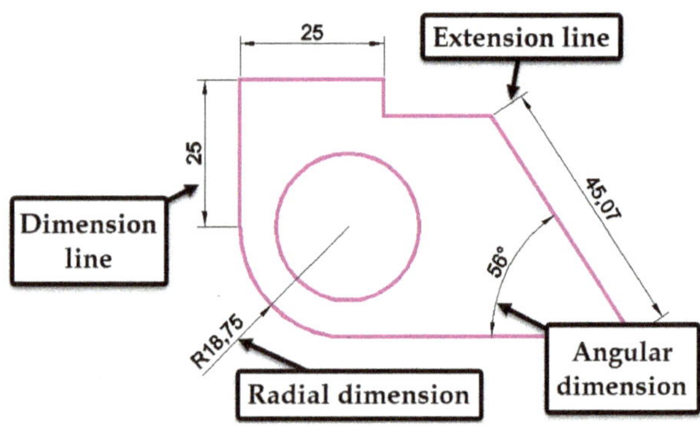

By default, the **ISO-25** or the **Standard** dimension style is active. If the default dimension style does not suit the dimensioning requirement, you can create a new dimension style and modify the nomenclature of the dimensions.

- To create a new dimension style, click the **New** button in the **Dimension Styles** section.

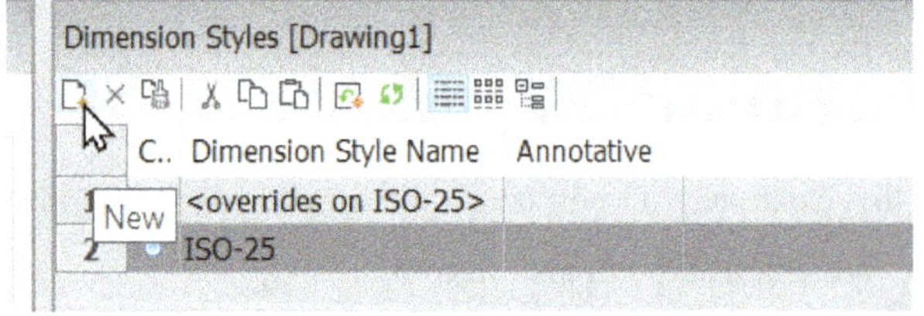

- Double-click on the **New Dimension Style 1**, and the type Mechanical. Next, click in the empty area on the **Drawing Explorer** dialog.

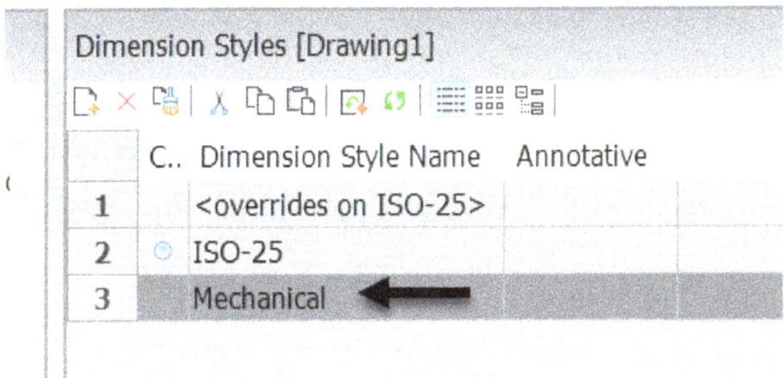

- Under the **Primary Units** section, select **Dim units** > Decimal.

- Set **Dim precision** to **0**. Next, set **Decimal separator** to '**.**'.

Primary units	
Dim units	Decimal
Dim precision	0
Fractional type	Horizontal
Decimal separator	.
Dim round	0
Dim prefix	
Dim suffix	

Study the other options in the **Primary units** section. Most of them are self-explanatory.

- Scroll to the **Text** section.

- Ensure that the **Text height** is set **2.5**.

- Select **Text position vertical > Centered**.

- Select **Text position horizontal > Centered**.

- Check the **Text Inside align** and **Text outside align** options.

Text	
Text style	Standard
Text color	ByBlock
Text fill	No fill
Text fill color	ByBlock
Text height	2.5 mm
Draw frame around text	Draw frame around…
Text position vertical	Centered
Text position horizontal	Centered
Text offset	0.625
Text vertical offset	0
Text inside align	☑ Text inside align
Text outside align	☑ Text outside align
Text view direction	Left to right

Study the other options in the **Text** section. These options let you change the appearance of the dimension text.

- In the **Lines and Arrows** section, set the **Ext line ext** to **1.25**.

- Set the **Ext line offset** value to **2**.

- Set the **Arrow size** to **3**.

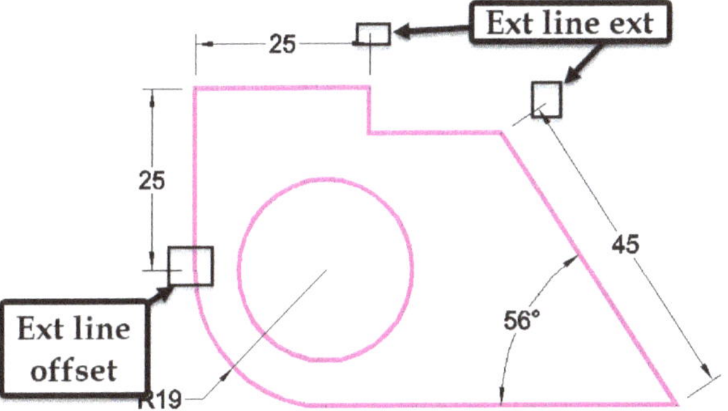

- Enter **3** in the **Center mark Size** box.

- Select **Center mark > Line**.

Lines and Arrows	
Tick size	0 mm
Arrow size	3
Arrowheads	☐ Arrowheads
Arrow	Closed filled
Arrow 1	Closed filled
Arrow 2	Closed filled
Leader arrow	Closed filled
Dim line color	ByBlock
Dim line type	ByLayer
Dim line LW	ByBlock
Dim line ext	0 mm
Dim baseline spacing	3.75 mm
Dim line 1	☐ Suppress first dimension line
Dim line 2	☐ Suppress second dimension line
Ext line color	ByBlock
Ext line LW	ByBlock
Ext line ext	1.25
Ext line offset	2
Ext line 1	☐ Suppress first extension line
Ext line 2	☐ Suppress second extension line
Ext line type 1	ByLayer
Ext line type 2	ByLayer
Ext line fixed	☐ Fixed length extension lines
Ext line fixed length	1
Center mark	Line
Center mark size	3
Arc length symbol	Preceding dimension text
Jog angle	45

Study the different options in this section. The options in this tab are used to change the appearance and behavior of the dimension lines and extension lines.

- Double-click on the **Mechanical** dimension style in the **Dimension Styles** section.

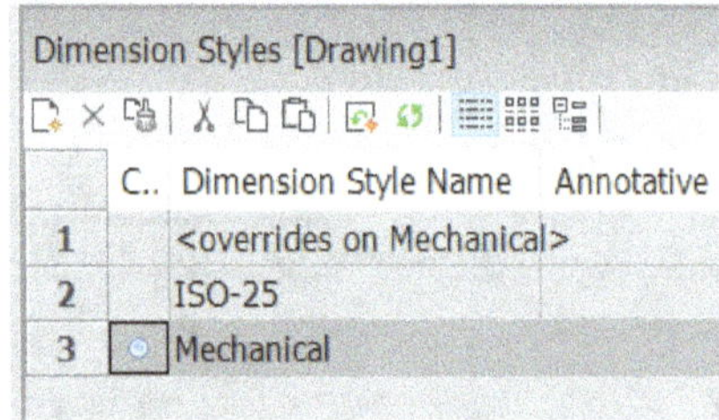

- Close the **Drawing Explorer** dialog.

- On the **Annotate** tab of the ribbon, click **Dimension > Center Mark** .

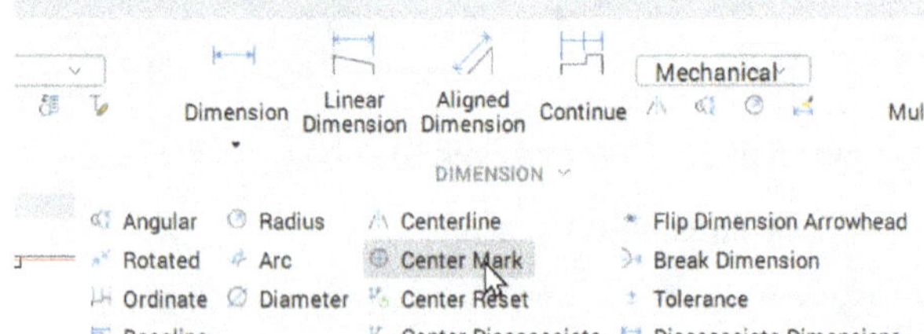

- Select the circle from the drawing to apply the center mark to it. Next, press ENTER and select the remaining circle.

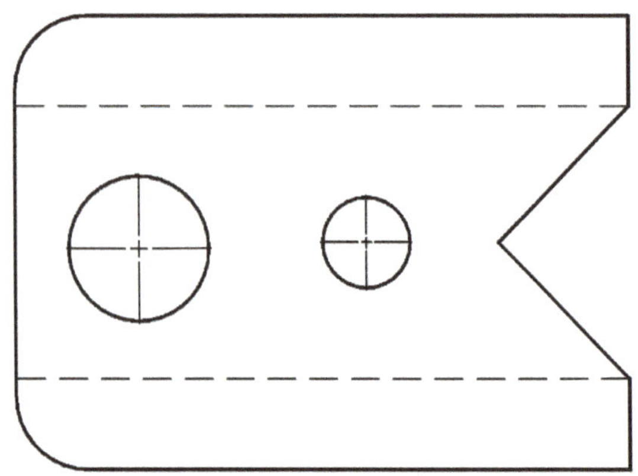

- On the ribbon, click **Annotate > Dimension > Linear Dimension**.

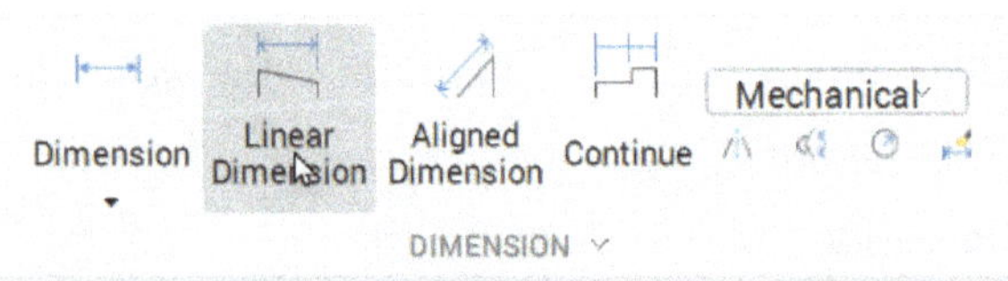

- Make sure that the **ESNAP** button is turned on the status bar.

- Select the lower right corner of the drawing.

- Select the endpoint of the center mark of the small circle; the dimension is attached to the pointer.

- Move the pointer vertically downwards and position the dimension, as shown below.

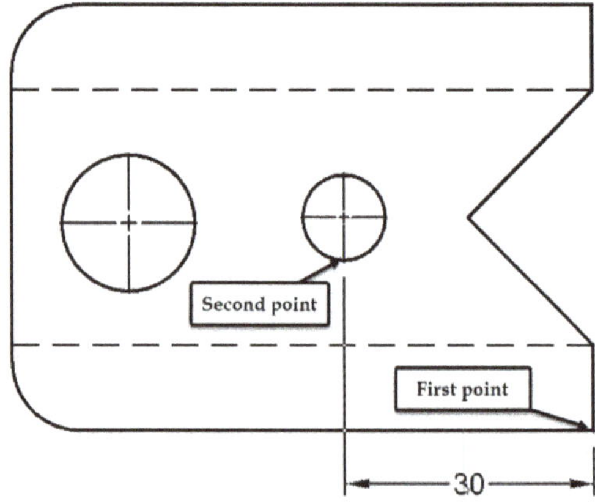

- On the ribbon, click **Annotate > Dimension > Baseline**.

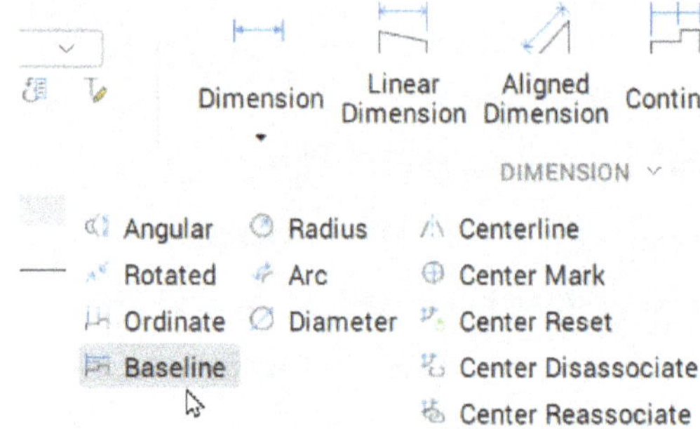

- Select the right extension line of the linear dimension if not already selected; a dimension is attached to the pointer.

- Select the endpoint of the center mark of the large circle; another dimension is attached to the pointer.

- Select the lower left corner of the drawing.

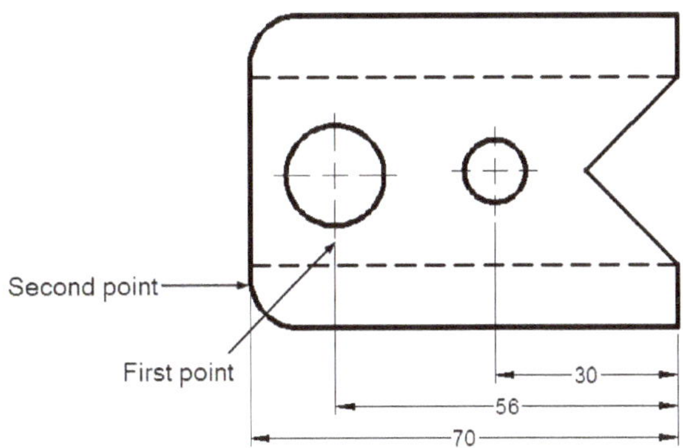

- Press ENTER twice.
- On the ribbon, click **Annotate > Dimension > Angular**.

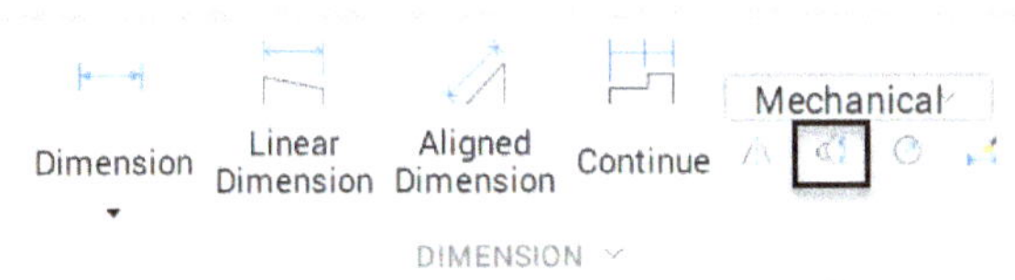

- Select the two angled lines of the drawing and position the angle dimension.

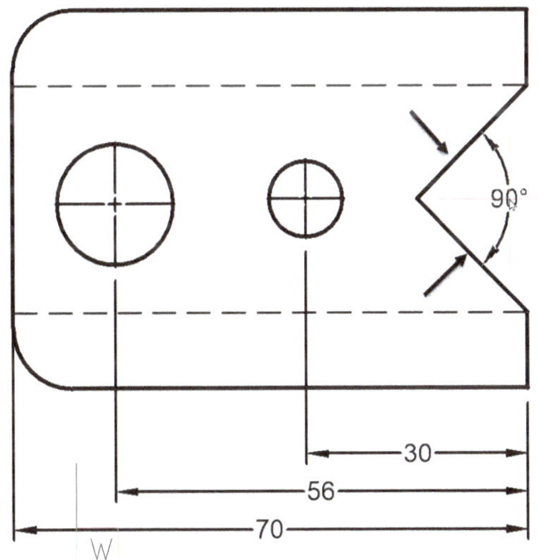

- On the ribbon, click **Annotate > Dimensions > Diameter**.

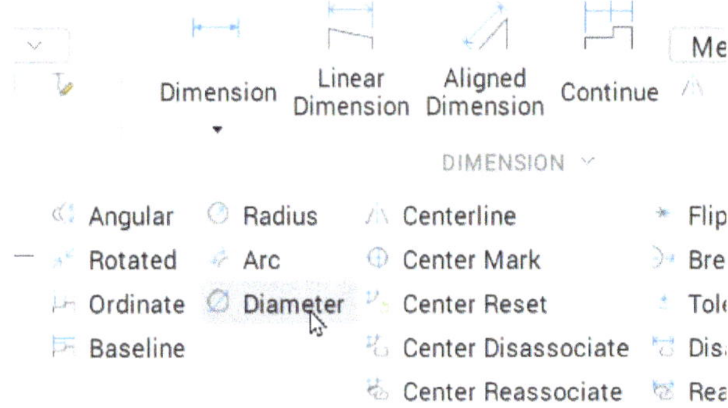

- Select the large circle and position the diameter dimension, as shown.

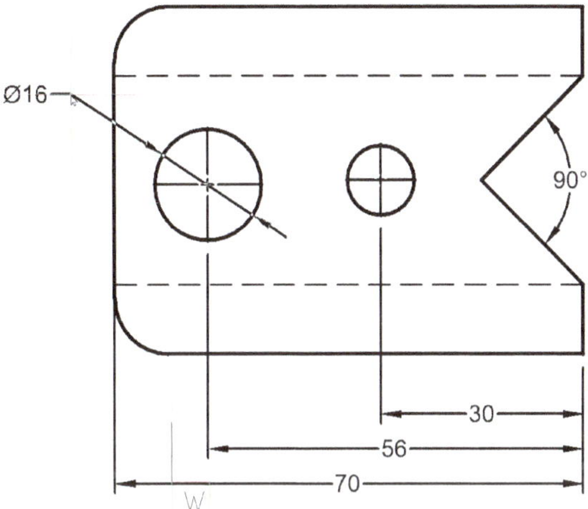

- Press ENTER and select the small circle and position the dimension.

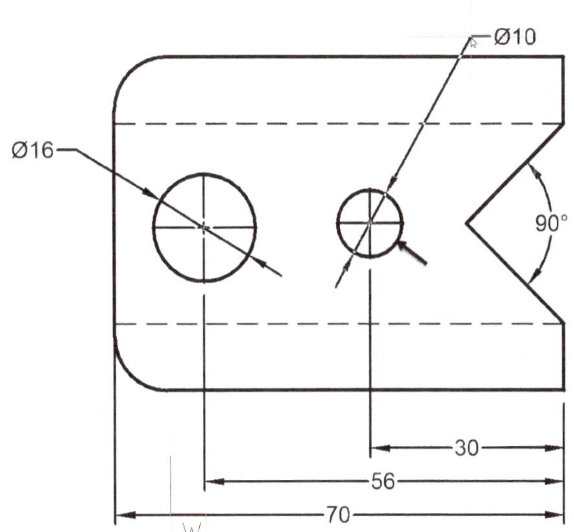

- On the ribbon, click **Annotate > Dimensions >**
  Radius.

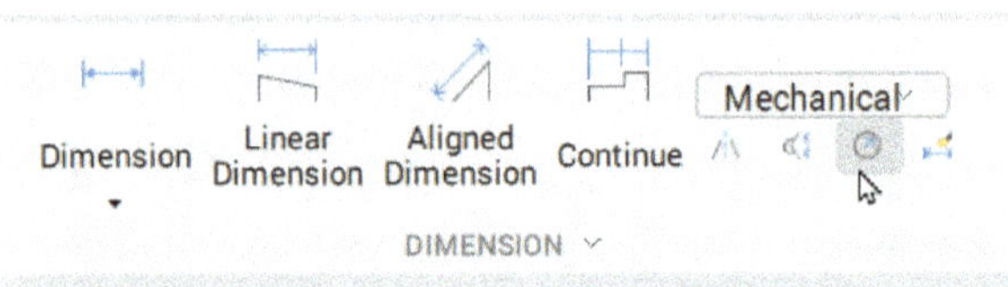

- Select the fillet located at the top left corner. Next,
  position the radial dimension approximately at 45
  degrees.

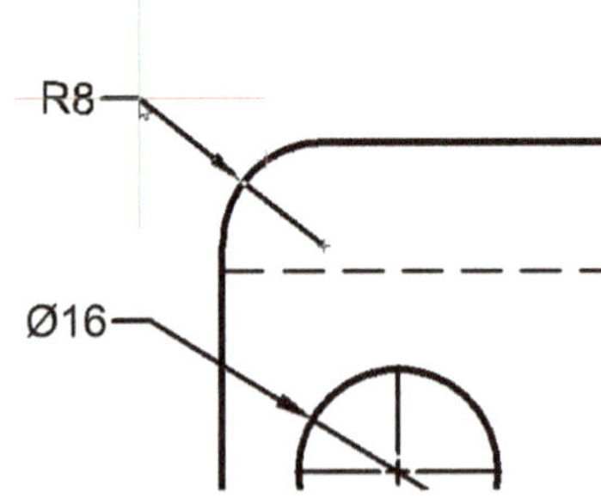

- Double-click on the radial dimension.
- Click before the dimension value. Next, type 2X and
  press the SPACEBAR.

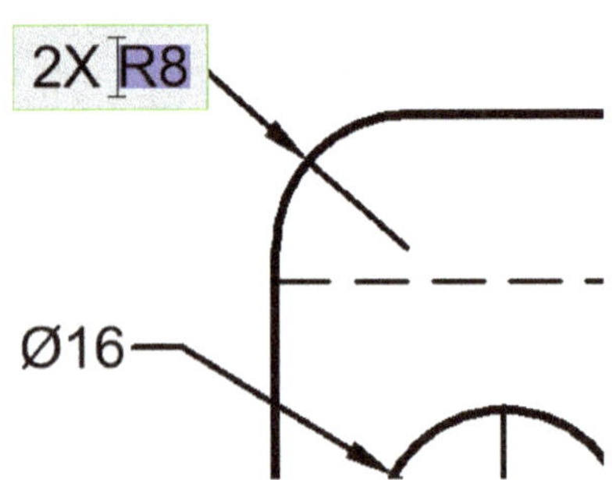

- Click in the graphics window to update the
  dimension text.
- Likewise, apply the other dimensions, as shown.
- Save and close the drawing.

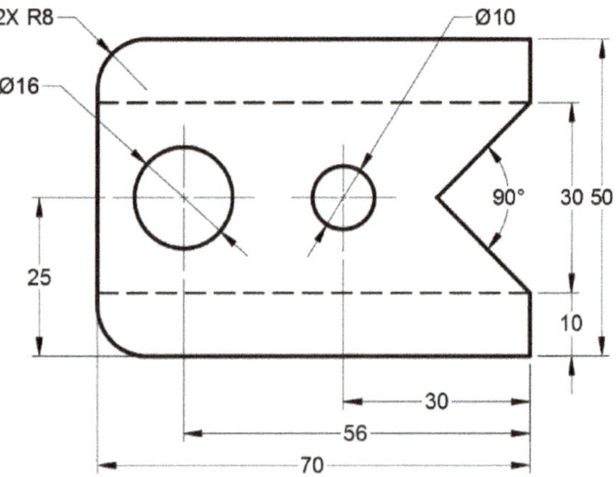

Tutorial 18 (Adding Dimensional Tolerances)

During the manufacturing process, the accuracy of a part
is an important factor. However, it is impossible to
manufacture a part with the exact dimensions. Therefore,
while applying dimensions to a drawing, we provide some
dimensional tolerances, which lie within acceptable
limits. The following example shows you to add
dimension tolerances in BricsCAD.

Example:

- Create the drawing, as shown below. Do not add
  dimensions to it.

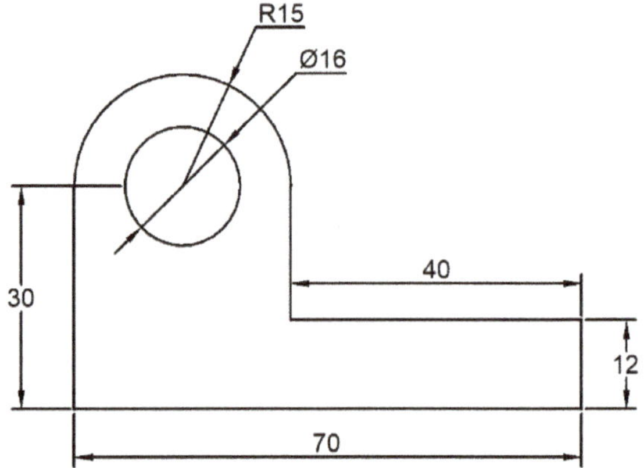

- Create a new dimension style with the name
  Tolerances.

Dimension Styles [Drawing1]

	C..	Dimension Style Name	Anno
1		<overrides on Tolerances>	
2		ISO-25	
3	○	Tolerances	

- In the **Drawing Explorer** dialog, in the **Tolerances** section, check the Display tolerance option.

- Set **Tolerance precision** to **0.00**.

- Set the **Tolerance limit lower** and **Tolerance limit upper** to **0.05**.

- Set the **Tolerance position vertical** to **Middle**.

Tolerances

Tolerance display	☑ Display tolerance
Limits display	☐ Generate dimension…
Tolerance precision	0.00
Tolerance limit lower	0.05
Tolerance limit upper	0.05
Tolerance text height	1
Tolerance position vertical	Middle
Tolerance suppress leading zeros	☐ Suppress leading ze…
Tolerance suppress trailing zeros	☑ Suppress trailing ze…
Tolerance suppress zero feet	☑ Tolerance suppress …
Tolerance suppress zero inches	☑ Tolerance suppress …
Alt tolerance precision	0.000
Alt tolerance suppress leading zeros	☐ Suppress leading ze…
Alt tolerance suppress trailing zeros	☐ Suppress trailing ze…
Alt tolerance suppress zero feet	☑ Alt tolerance suppr…
Alt tolerance suppress zero inches	☑ Alt tolerance suppr…

- Specify the following settings in the **Primary units**, **Lines and Arrows**, and **Text** sections:

The **Primary units** section:

Format: Decimal

Precision: 0.00

Decimal Separator: '.'Period

The **Text** section:

Text settings:

    Text height: 2.5

Text position vertical:Centered

Text position horizontal:Centered

Text inside align: Text inside align

Text outside align: Text outside align

The **Lines and Arrows** section:

Arrow Size: 2.5

Center mark: Line

Center mark size: 2.5

- Double-click on the Tolerances dimension style under the **Dimension styles** section.

- Close the **Drawing Explorer** dialog.

- Apply dimensions to the drawing.

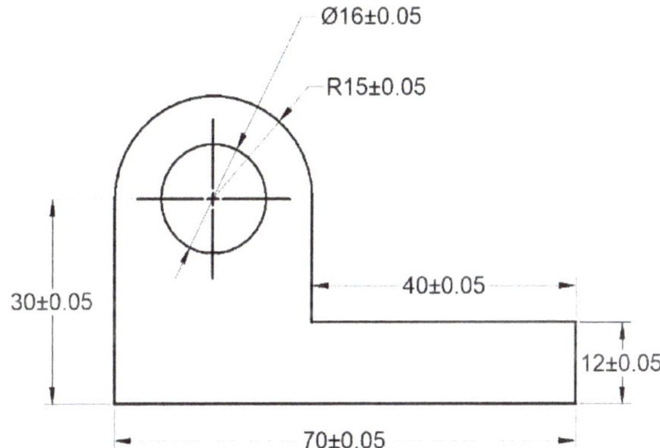

Tutorial 19 (Geometric Dimensioning and Tolerancing)

Earlier, you have learned how to apply tolerances to the size (dimensions) of a component. However, the dimensional tolerances are not sufficient for manufacturing a component. You must give tolerance values to its shape, orientation, and position as well. The following figure shows a note which is used to explain the tolerance value given to the shape of the object.

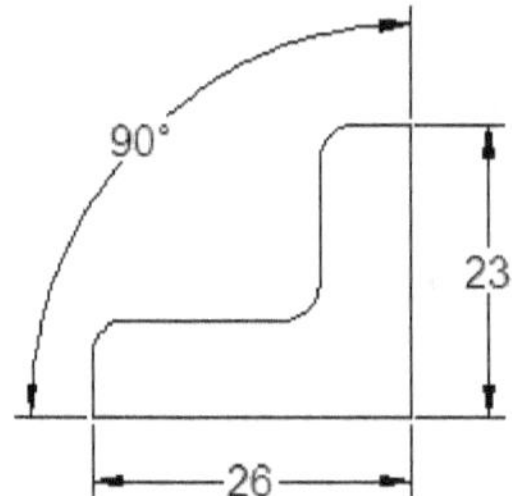

Providing a note in a drawing may be confusing. To avoid this, we use Geometric Dimensioning and Tolerancing (GD&T) symbols to specify the tolerance values to shape, orientation and position of acomponent. The following The Geometric Tolerancing symbols that can be used to interpret the geometric conditions are given in the table below.

figure shows the same example represented by using the GD&T symbols. In this figure, the vertical face to which the tolerance frame is connected must be within two parallel planes 0.08 apart and perpendicular to the datum reference (horizontal plane).

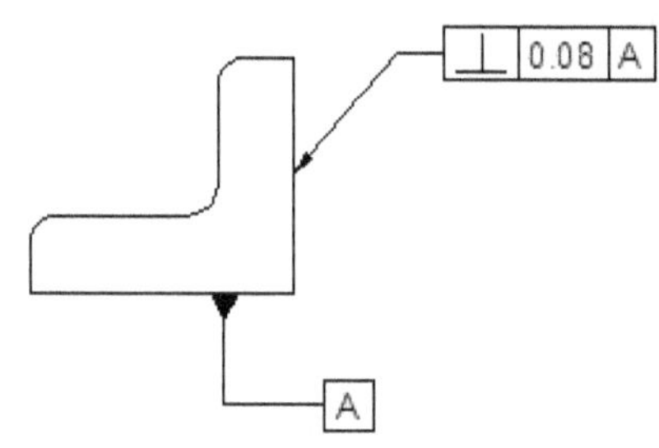

Purpose		Symbol
To represent the shape of a single feature.	Straightness	—
	Flatness	
	Cylindricity	
	Circularity	
	Profile of a surface	
	Profile of a line	
To represent the orientation	Parallelism	//
of a feature with respect to another feature.	Perpendicularity	⊥
	Angularity	∠
To represent the position of a feature with respect to another feature.	Position	⊕
	Concentricity and coaxiality	⊚
	Run-out	
	Total Run-out	
	Symmetry	

www.ingramcontent.com/pod-product-compliance
Lightning Source LLC
LaVergne TN
LVHW060504070726
842759LV00029BA/887